FOR REFERENCE

This book cannot
be checked out

11-91

Fantasy Literature
A Reader's Guide

Garland Reference Library of the Humanities
(Vol. 874)

Fantasy Literature

A Reader's Guide

EDITED BY Neil Barron

Garland Publishing, Inc.

NEW YORK & LONDON   1990

Library of Congress Cataloging-in-Publication Data

Fantasy literature : a reader's guide / edited by Neil Barron.
  p. cm. — (Garland reference library of the humanities : vol. 874)
  ISBN 0-8240-3148-2 (alk. paper)
  1. Fantastic literature—Bibliography. 2. Fantastic literature—History and criticism. I. Barron, Neil. 1934-   . II. Series.
Z5917.F3F36 1990 PN3435
016.8093'8766—dc20   8923693

Printed on acid-free, 250-year-life paper

MANUFACTURED IN THE UNITED STATES OF AMERICA

To Carolyn

On me your voice falls as they say
    love should
Like an enormous yes.

—PHILIP LARKIN

Contents

Preface

Neil Barron

Fantasy Literature: A Reader's Guide and its companion, *Horror Literature: A Reader's Guide*, provide the most comprehensive critical introductions to two literatures whose best works deserve far more critical attention than they have heretofore received. The popularity of fantasy's secondary worlds was stimulated by the publication of Tolkien's *Lord of the Rings* [F3-340], particularly the paperback reprints in the mid-1960s. Although individual works of horror fiction, such as *Dracula* [H3-386], have achieved widespread popularity, by far the most popular writer of horror fiction in history is Stephen King who, like Tolkien, has become somewhat of a cottage industry. They have spawned legions of imitators, but more importantly they have given greater legitimacy to two types of popular literature often scorned by literary critics who find anything popular automatically suspect.

These guides are companions to *Anatomy of Wonder: A Critical Guide to Science Fiction* (Bowker, 3rd ed., 1987), the standard in its field, and have a similar format. Like the science fiction guide, they are designed as collection development and evaluation and reader's advisory tools for librarians and as guides for any interested reader. Distinctions between popular literary genres are often artificial, and the distinctions between fantasy and horror are still more blurred, with some critics referring to horror as dark fantasy. One distinction suggested by some critics is in the type of emotion generated by the work: science fiction arouses interest, fantasy arouses wonder, horror fiction arouses fear, terror or revulsion. Many works blend elements: the film *Alien* is a good example. Because of the blurred distinctions between the two genres, there is some overlap in the coverage of these two guides. The chapters on the secondary literature ("Research Aids") are the same in both volumes except for those chapters devoted to history and criticism, to author studies and to films.

When it was judged necessary to split an author between the two guides, a generic cross-reference is used: [For other works of this author, see the companion guide to fantasy/horror.]. Approximately eighty authors appear in both volumes. Some authors could be placed equally well in either volume for reasons explained by Brian Stableford in his chapter 3 of the fantasy guide. The works of some authors are discussed in two chapters of the same guide. Consult the index or the adjacent chapter if you suspect this may be the case.

The scope of these guides is largely limited to prose works published in or translated into English. A small amount of poetry and some dramatic works were included. Readers interested in poetry may wish to consult the relatively comprehensive treatment in Steve Eng's "Supernatural Verse in English," a chapter in Tymn's *Horror Literature* [6-33].

The contributors were selected because of their expertise, briefly summarized in the notes on contributors. Outside readers also assisted in ensuring comprehensive coverage and balance in the selections. Preliminary lists of books to be annotated were circulated among contributors and later among the outside readers to ensure that no significant titles were overlooked. Although every attempt was made to limit choices to the best, better or historically or commercially important books, a strong element of personal judgment is unavoidable.

Each chapter provides a historical, analytical and critical introduction, followed by a critically annotated bibliography, in which many of the books mentioned briefly in the introduction are discussed more fully. The introductions collectively provide a relatively detailed history of fantasy and horror literature, although they are not meant as a substitute for the more comprehensive histories discussed in chapter 7. Coverage is through late 1988, with some editorial revisions added as late as summer 1989.

The bibliographies are usually arranged alphabetically by author of novel or collection, by author or editor of nonfiction works and by title of anthologies. In chapter 4, anthologies are listed separately, following novels and collections. Each annotation consists of these elements:

Entry number, assigned according to each chapter and used in the indexes and for cross-referencing within the text. Most cross-references refer to the same volume, but some refer to the companion volume. In the latter case the entry number is preceded by a letter: F3-340 refers to the fantasy volume, H3-340 to the horror volume.

Author. The most common form of an author's name is shown, with the less common portions in parentheses, e.g., James, M(ontague) R(hodes). In most cases the author's real name is used as the standard name. If the book was published under a pseudonym, this is indicated, e.g., King, Stephen (as by Richard Bachman), and cross-references are included in the author index.

Country of nationality of author or editor, if known and if other than the United States. Years of birth and death are shown when known.

Supplemental information. In order to make this guide as useful as possible to its various audiences, references to other sources of biocritical information on authors of novels and collections have been included. All sources except *Contemporary Authors* are annotated in chapter 6. The abbreviations in the list below follow the word "About:" on the line below the author's name. These supplemental sources include:

WW	Ashley, Mike. *Who's Who in Horror and Fantasy Fiction* [6-18]
GSF	Bleiler, E. F. *The Guide to Supernatural Fiction* [6-19]
SFW	Bleiler, E. F. *Supernatural Fiction Writers* [6-20]

F	Cawthorn, James, and Michael Moorcock. *Fantasy: The 100 Best Books* [6-21]
CA	*Contemporary Authors.* Gale Research [serial]
TCA	Cowart, David, and Thomas L. Wymer, eds. *Twentieth-Century American Science-Fiction Writers* [6-25]
FG	Frank, Frederick. *The First Gothics* [6-14]
NE	Gunn, James, ed. *The New Encyclopedia of Science Fiction* [6-26]
H	Jones, Stephen, and Kim Newman, eds. *Horror: 100 Best Books* [6-22]
SMFL	Magill, Frank N., ed. *Survey of Modern Fantasy Literature* [6-24]
SFE	Nicholls, Peter, gen. ed. *The Science Fiction Encyclopedia* [6-27]
MF	Pringle, David. *Modern Fantasy: The Hundred Best Novels* [6-23]
SFFL	Reginald, R. *Science Fiction and Fantasy Literature*, vol. 2 [6-3]
RG	Searles, Baird, et al. *A Reader's Guide to Fantasy* [6-29]
TCSF	Smith, Curtis C., ed. *Twentieth-Century Science-Fiction Writers* [6-30]
PE	Sullivan, Jack, ed. *The Penguin Encyclopedia of Horror and the Supernatural* [6-31]
ESF	Tuck, Donald H. *The Encyclopedia of Science Fiction and Fantasy through 1968* [6-4]
FL	Tymn, Marshall B., et al. *Fantasy Literature* [6-32]
HF	Waggoner, Diana. *The Hills of Faraway* [6-34]
FF	Winter, Douglas. *Faces of Fear* [H8-112]

Book-length works annotated in chapters 7 and 8 supplement these general reference sources, and they are indexed under the name of the subject. The reference works by Cowart, Gunn, Nicholls and Smith include many entries for writers of fantasy as well as science fiction. The entries emphasize the SF but do not usually exclude discussion of the fantasy fiction. *Contemporary Authors* is included because of its wide availability in all types of libraries, many of which will not own most of the more specialized reference works listed. A check of the cumulative index in the latest volume of CA will lead not only to entries in CA proper but also to other related Gale series, such as the *Dictionary of Literary Biography, Contemporary Literary Criticism*, etc.

Title. The title and subtitle, if any, are transcribed from the title page. Variant titles are common, especially for American and British editions, and these are usually listed, along with any note indicating significant differences in content.

Publisher. A shortened form of the publisher's name is used for most books, e.g., Knopf rather than Alfred A. Knopf. City of publication is included for books published in the nineteenth century and earlier and addresses are given for small specialty publishers for which such information is sometimes difficult to locate. See also the list of specialty publishers in chapter 5.

Translator. Every attempt was made to select the best books translated into English, and translators are credited when known. The original title and year of publication are also shown for translations.

Recommended editions. In most cases any complete edition of the text is satisfactory. Only the first edition is listed, relying on the bibliographies by Currey [6-2], Reginald [6-3], Bleiler [6-1] and Brown and Contento [6-6]. However, the collector should rely on detailed descriptive bibliographies such as Currey for the points necessary to identify true first editions. Specific editions are recommended when the text is more reliable, there is an introduction by the author or an editor or the text is annotated in some manner. Recommended editions are most common for books that have appeared in many editions, such as *Frankenstein* or *Dracula*.

Sequels; series. Many books, especially mass-market paperbacks of recent years, have been followed by sequels or been part of series. In most instances the first book in the series is used for the entry, with sequels or later books discussed in the body of the annotation. In other instances the individual books are annotated separately. Because readers are often interested in other books in a series, a relatively comprehensive list of series and sequels is included in chapter 13.

Collections. Short fiction is common in both fantasy and horror fiction, and some authors have distinguished themselves more at this length than in novels. The collections chosen contain the best or representative works of such authors, with other collections often discussed in the body of the annotations.

Annotations. The annotation in all cases is genuinely critical, assessing the book's merits and weaknesses. Although some plot summary is provided for novels and some collections to suggest what the book is "about," the emphasis throughout is on critical evaluation. Given the large number of books annotated and the need for terseness, we may occasionally somewhat alter or distort a book's central concept. We recognize that no work of art can be reduced to its paraphrasable content. Crucial plot elements or surprises are not revealed in the annotations. Significant awards are mentioned; see chapter 13 for a comprehensive list of awards. Many annotations conclude with a compare/contrast statement, in which the annotated book is linked to books having similar themes or structure.

First-purchase titles. Indicated by an asterisk preceding the entry number, these titles were selected on the basis of one or more of these characteristics: awards received (see chapter 13), influence of the work, outstanding or unique treatment of a theme, critical and/or popular acceptance, importance of the work in the author's total output, historical importance, especially for early works. Nonfiction works were judged by the usual criteria of scope, accuracy, currency, ease of use, critical acumen, balance and so on. Unstarred titles are those judged relatively less important, but include many works of distinction. Some books were selected as representative of their type; other, equally good works could have been selected. With few exceptions, all annotated books are recommended.

Young adult books. This is a marketing category for publishers and a useful category for librarians selecting books whose primary appeal is to teenage readers, although the precise age limits of YA books are hard to specify. Most YA books feature a teenage protagonist with whom the reader can identify, but in most other respects they are indistinguishable from nominally adult books. Many of the finest works of fantasy are nominally written for a younger audience, and any adult who overlooks such books will miss many riches. Horror fiction is much less common than fantasy for younger readers, perhaps because publishers or librarians feel that graphic horror is unsuitable for younger readers. As a matter of convenience, both fantasy and horror fiction are discussed in chapter 4B. The suggested age range in years is shown following all YA titles in chapter 4B. Contributors of other chapters were asked to identify those books they felt would have appeal to younger readers, and such books are cross-referenced in chapter 4B, which is included only in the fantasy guide.

In addition to the contributors who have shared their knowledge and enthusiasm, I wish to thank the following outside readers who have assisted in making this guide more reliable and useful: Sam Moskowitz, one of fantastic fiction's most prominent historians and a Pilgrim winner for 1981; Lloyd Currey, an antiquarian bookman specializing in fantastic literature (see chapter 5); Diana Waggoner, author of *The Hills of Faraway* [6-34]; David G. Hartwell, one of fantastic fiction's most knowledgeable editors and critics; R. Reginald, a catalog librarian and one of the field's principal bibliographers [6-3].

Thanks also to these people who assisted with specific topics: Milton Subotsky (film); Ruth N. Lynn (young adult fiction). Readers of these guides owe thanks to Garland's copy editor, Barbara Bergeron, whose careful checking and comments led to a much more accurate guide. I suspect she shares my goal: to strive for infallibility without pretending to it.

Special thanks are due the Atlanta Worldcon, Inc. committee, who generously provided a $5,000 grant from the surplus from the 1986 world SF convention. This grant was paid to the contributors to supplement the inadequate share of the royalties I could afford to distribute.

Although these guides are much better for my having edited three editions of *Anatomy of Wonder*, there are unavoidably errors and omissions, which will be corrected in future editions. I hope that conscientious readers will take the time to write me (see list of contributors) with suggestions for improving future editions.

Contributors

Neil Barron. A former academic librarian and sometime fan of fantastic literature, he has edited three editions of the standard critical guide to science fiction, *Anatomy of Wonder* (1976, 1981, 1987). The second and third editions were Hugo Award nominees. Address: 1149 Lime Place, Vista, CA 92083 (letters welcome).

Walter Albert. A professor of French and Italian literature at the University of Pittsburgh, a bibliographer of detective fiction and a longtime reader of horror fiction, with a particular interest in the vampire, his interest in the visual arts dates back to an early obsession with horror and fantasy films.

Mike Ashley. One of the leading bibliographers of fantastic literature, author/editor of more than twenty books and 250 articles and reviews, his *Science Fiction, Fantasy, and Weird Fiction Magazines* [11-54] is the standard study.

Michael Bishop. He has written fantasy and horror fiction, but is best known for his science fiction (*No Enemy but Time* won the 1982 Nebula Award). Each book he has written is significantly different from its predecessors, a praiseworthy practice which has led more to critical than to popular acclaim.

Maxim Jakubowski. Born in England, educated in France, he has extensive experience as a translator, writer, critic and book editor.

Michael Klossner. A librarian at the Arkansas State Library, Little Rock, he has an extensive knowledge of fantastic cinema and has reviewed film books for specialty journals.

Dennis M. Kratz. A specialist in medieval culture, he is a professor of Arts and Humanities at the University of Texas, Dallas, where he teaches graduate and undergraduate courses in fantasy.

Susan G. Miles. A reference librarian and coordinator of database services at Central Michigan University, she was formerly the Learning Resources librarian in the K-12 literature/curriculum library.

Francis J. Molson. A professor of English at Central Michigan University, he has long had an interest in juvenile fantasy and science fiction. His *Children's Fantasy* (1989) was recently published.

Randall W. Scott. A longtime reader of fantasy and horror, he is a cataloger for the Russel B. Nye Popular Culture Collection of Michigan State University Libraries [12-13]. He contributes a chapter, "Research Libraries of Interest to Fandom," to the annual *Fandom Directory*.

Brian Stableford. The author of many works of science fiction, he is also well known for his many critical and historical studies of fantastic literature. In 1987 he received the Distinguished Scholarship award of the International Association for the Fantastic in the Arts.

Richard C. West. With degrees in English and library science, he is associate director for public services at the University of Wisconsin's Wendt Library. He has written many articles on fantasy and SF authors and compiled *Tolkien Criticism* [F8-100].

Gary K. Wolfe. He has received the Eaton Award for *The Known and the Unknown* (1979) and the Pilgrim Award for his many contributions to the study of science fiction and fantasy (see chapter 13).

Children Who Survive:

AN AUTOBIOGRAPHICAL MEDITATION ON HORROR AND FANTASY

Michael Bishop

Many of my most vivid, and hence lasting, childhood memories are of terrifying or awe-inspiring scenes from storybooks, films, daydreams, nightmares.

By consensus definition, these genres all lack palpable reality. Oh, they exist, all right. Books we can find in bookstores and libraries; films we can see at movie theaters or on our state-of-the-art VCRs; daydreams are often real enough to lower our productivity at work; and nightmares have probably always sent us scurrying from the menace of their chaotic imagery to the real-life comfort of a loved one's arms.

No one disputes the *existence* of storybooks, films, daydreams, nightmares. What we doubt is their *seriousness*—their underlying redemptive significance. In fact, many of us seem to have been programmed by the imperatives of the workaday world to write off their images not only as unreal but also as totally irrelevant to the more crucial transactions of our waking lives:

"Don't worry about that, hon—it was only a dream." "For God's sake, Charlie, it was just a stupid story." "You're not letting an asinine old horror movie keep you awake, are you, Kit?"

But, such facile reassurances aside, our bravest longings and our deepest fears persist. We suspect—with Freud, with Jung, with Bettelheim, with the dream merchants themselves—that maybe these startling imaginings do have a deeper seriousness; that maybe they mean significantly *more* than, say, an everyday act like cashing in a certificate of deposit or trying to climb yet another rung on the corporate ladder.

And, of course, we suspect correctly. If we didn't, I wouldn't be writing these words.

Eisenhower is president. I am seven or eight years old. One Saturday afternoon I am walking with my mother and my stepdad-to-be along a busy street in Wichita, Kansas. We pass the open front of a movie theater. On the marquee above us, and also on the posters bookending the lobby, are garish invitations to come inside and see Vincent Price, Carolyn Jones and somebody named Charles Buchinsky (later Bronson) in a 3-D horror flick called *House of Wax.*

My mother's escort, Charles Edwin Willis, a captain in the Air Force, is the owner of a Distinguished Flying Cross. (During World War II, he nursed his B-17 back to England after it had taken some crippling anti-aircraft fire over Germany.) Today, Captain Willis has a keen peacetime fondness for pulp sci-fi and B-grade monster movies. He asks me if I'm game to see *House of Wax.*

"It's going to be spooky," he cautions, but there's an amiable dare in this warning. He also notes that it'll be expensive—not to mention disappointing to my mom and him—if the movie so badly scares me that I beg to be taken back out into the anxiety-allaying Kansas sunlight.

"I *want* to see it," I insist.

The two adults are skeptical. Says Mom, "Are you sure?"

Well, of course. *House of Wax* is something new, a 3-D movie. Every paying customer gets a pair of cardboard glasses with lenses of blue and red cellophane; these give the blurred images from the projector definition and impart an astonishing three-dimensionality to every actor and prop.

My stepdad-to-be buys us tickets. We go inside. We put on our glasses. The movie proves remarkably intense. The bearded fellow with the bolo paddle at the beginning isn't bad (in fact, snapping my head back to avoid getting bopped by the ball is sort of neat), but Price's tendency to hurl screaming, half-clad young women into vats of molten wax sabotages my equanimity. I melt into gibbering terror, utterly disgracing myself.

Even good old Wichita sunlight doesn't wholly restore my peace of mind, and for the next two weeks I go to bed with a night-light, irrationally persuaded that a berserk waxman is stalking Mulvane, Kansas, my hometown. Unless I'm vigilant, I'm doomed to awaken—*if* I awaken—sarcophagused from head to toe in paraffin. A worse fate I can't imagine, and the disappointed tut-tutting of my mother has no power to convince me that I can make it to adulthood without my "babyish" night-light.

Let her coax, let her chide, let her frown. Can't she see that my very life is at stake?

Later, or perhaps earlier, I find other unrealities—literary, filmic, psychological—to awe or terrify me. They bob in the sea of my memory like buoys, markers enabling me to strike out toward that ill-defined shore upon which, for better or worse, I must one day crawl and stagger to my feet.

A tableau from *The Odyssey* wavers on that shore. Polyphemus, the Cyclops, holds Odysseus and his men captive in his cave. In order to free themselves, the brave Greek traveler and his cohorts must blind this one-eyed giant with a flaming stake. Their escape, with the Cyclops raging at their backs, is such a dicey affair that I shudder to recall how close they come to *not* making it, to having to endure further imprisonment and the sanity-fragmenting threat of becoming, at any moment, Purina Cyclops Chow.

(A holdup on Main Street—especially if reported secondhand—could not have been more horripilating. I'd've faced a puny human villain over Polyphemus, any day.)

Every Easter on TV, long before I've read L. Frank Baum's book, *The Wizard of Oz* rolls out its yellow brick road in Motorola black-and-white. I tremble— hands clammy, eyes a-bulge, gut knotted—as the Wicked Witch of the West cackles like a crazy hen. Meanwhile, her herky-jerky flying monkeys afflict the opalescent MGM sky like a hideous simian plague. Dorothy and her companions are in mortal peril. The jig is almost up.

(A trip to Mulvane's dentist—in that boxy little office with a drill boom made in 1904—could not have bathed me in a funk-sweat any more copious or pungent.)

On *The Wonderful World of Disney*, an episode from the animated classic *Fantasia* plunges me into a similar kind of fretful dread. Mickey Mouse, as the sorcerer's apprentice, struggles mousefully to bail out of the troubles he has brought upon himself by commanding a broom to carry water. The broom won't desist, however, and when Mickey chops it to pieces in frustration, the splinters sprout arms and join the nightmarish bucket brigade.

(A pop spelling test for which I'm totally unprepared couldn't unsettle me more.)

One spring night, I dream. At my bedside, when I open my eyes, perches a solicitous skeleton—female. How do I know this upright assemblage of bones is female? Well, she's wearing a short-sleeved sweater, and although her arm bones and grinning skull emerge from its sleeves and neck as bald as ivory, my visitor has bosoms. This is the Lana Turner of skeletons, her inappropriate but well-shaped breasts caught within a sweaterly hammock of pink alpaca. I don't know whether to scuttle away from or to hug her—but, at her back, a male figure in cowboy garb hurtles through my bedroom window to safety.

(I couldn't've been more scared or confused if J. Edgar Hoover had strolled into my elementary school with a dozen federal agents and a warrant for my arrest.)

Lewis Carroll's Alice sidles into my ken, out of the pages of her *Adventures in Wonderland*. Beside her, huffing and puffing, the Queen of Hearts holds a flamingo under her flabby arm as a croquet mallet. She shouts, "Off with his head!" or "Off with her head!" and the playing-card soldiers doing double duty as wickets haul off her victims under unappealable sentence of execution. I'm appalled by the Queen's behavior—horror-struck, in fact—but I'm admiringly gape-mouthed at Alice's dauntlessness. Why can't I be as brave as this blonde little girl?

(Damn! An off-center look from one of my grandmother's friends *still* triggers in me a fluttery dyspepsia.)

At least I'm not as small—relatively speaking—as Gulliver in the kingdom of Brobdingnag, about which I read while recuperating from a groin injury sustained trying out, as a thirteen year old, for a football team in Tulsa, Oklahoma. (Scarcely over five feet tall and weighing maybe eighty-five pounds, I was an idiot to get involved. Most of the other boys towered over me like . . . well, teen-aged Brobdingnagians.) One day, a monkey seizes the minuscule Gulliver, climbs to the ridge of a building, feeds him by cramming disgorged food into his mouth, squeezes his sides and threatens to drop him to his death. And other incidents equally traumatic—to me as well as to Swift's hero—occur to Gulliver on his voyages to unmapped parts of the globe.

(Now, my own world seems less spooky—so long as I don't start diminishing to nothing like that joker in *The Incredible Shrinking Man*, another flick that scared the bejabbers out of me.)

And then I encounter Edgar Allan Poe. "The Fall of the House of Usher." "The Bells." "The Pit and the Pendulum." "Hop-Frog." "The Murders in the Rue Morgue." "Ligeia." "The Raven." "The Masque of the Red Death." "The Cask of Amontillado." "The Oval Portrait." Gloom, and dank, and November decay. Romantic loss and alliteration. Onomatopoeia and more lugubrious long vowels than a locomotive's dopplering wail.

Eventually, Poe mutates into Ray Bradbury, via the Brothers Grimm, Hans Christian Andersen, old Flash Gordon serials, Charles Dickens, H. G. Wells and a host of others; and, depending on your values, either I'm ruined forever or I'm willy-nilly rescued from the grinding humdrum of unadulterated reality. In the ninth grade, I compose a long, ambitious, very clumsy Poe-esque story—a *horror* story, you'd have to call it—portentously entitled "Of a Dying God," and my fate is sealed.

What is it, as children, that we most fear? Abandonment. The dark. Helplessness (as in being assigned a task that defeats our childish capabilities). Pain (particularly if, like violent abuse at the hands of adults, it's senseless). Betrayal. Mockery. And, yes, even death, the annihilation of our developing egos.

Monsters may figure vaguely in these fears—rampaging zombies, wrathful bears, hungry tyrannosaurs—but children's most elemental fears are of backassward relationships and the numbing indifference of those whose love they need. Monsters and impossible tasks are proxies for these fears; they structure a kid's fantasy life in the same way a wire armature supports a papier-mâché mask. By donning these fears, by wearing them in the thought-experiment realm of the imagination, children—hell, all of us—find a way to look through and to overcome them.

Grownups, then, are survivors.

In "Why Are Americans Afraid of Dragons?" [see 7-28]—an important essay on the necessity of fantasy and, by extension, of *honest* tales of horror—Ursula K. Le Guin writes, "I believe that maturity is not an outgrowing, but a growing up: that an adult is not a dead child, but a child who survived." Le Guin insists that the free but disciplined play of the imagination is a key to healthy survival. She argues that repressing such play as frivolous, or immoral, or false, is the surest

way of murdering the child in us—indeed, the surest way that the tyrants of mediocrity and the status quo could ever devise.

Why, however, would they want to murder that child? Because, fearing the chaotic powers of the imagination, they truly believe that sterility is better than fecundity; that a comforting cliché is preferable to an upsetting original truth; that a lived-with bias is better than an impromptu openness. They are dead children, who must sweep their own graves clean of the far-flying seeds of creativity. In Le Guin's estimation, they aren't real adults at all, for they've stifled a part of themselves that they should have nurtured.

Meanwhile, resourceful kids (or kids whose adult guardians *want* them to survive) fear the very same things that all other children fear, but they take (or they're given) the chance to confront their fears in wonderfully unthreatening guises. Namely, in celluloid or phosphor-dot fantasies; in fairy tales, horror stories and science fiction; in seemingly aimless woolgathering; and (least welcome of all but endurable if a sympathetic adult or sibling is nearby) even in grisly nightmares.

How much better to watch the Shrinking Man battle a spider than to go *mano a mano* with some living Goliath. To read about Rapunzel than to be locked in an honest-to-God tower. To daydream a journey down the Amazon than to get fanged by a real piranha. To nightview your own murder than to experience it in irreversible fact. Which is *one* of the reasons—along with our innate curiosity about every aspect of being human—that both children and adult survivors find fictive narratives so fascinating. Sometimes, it seems, we *do* like what is good for us.

Maybe the most insightful book ever written on the existential significance— the essential integrating function—of fairy tales is Bruno Bettelheim's *The Uses of Enchantment* (1976) [7-3]. I believe that Le Guin would second most of Bettelheim's conclusions; I believe, too, that his conclusions have legitimate application to the fields of fantasy writing and of adult horror fiction. Argues Bettelheim in his introduction:

> An understanding of the meaning of one's life is not suddenly acquired at a particular age, not even when one has reached chronological maturity. On the contrary, gaining a secure understanding of what the meaning of one's life may or ought to be—this is what constitutes having attained psychological maturity. And this achievement is the end result of a long development: at each age we seek, and must be able to find, some modicum of meaning congruent with how our minds and understanding have already developed.

And a little later:

> In child or adult, the unconscious is a powerful determinant of behavior. When the unconscious is repressed and its content denied entrance into awareness, then eventually the person's conscious mind will be partially overwhelmed by derivatives of these unconscious elements, or else he is forced to keep such rigid, compulsive control over them that his personality may become severely crippled. But when unconscious material *is* to

some degree permitted to come to awareness and worked through in imagination, its potential for causing harm—to ourselves or others—is much reduced; some of its forces can then be made to serve positive purposes.

Thus, I would contend that the contemporary horror novel—when well and truly done, as it is by such latter-day practitioners as Stephen King, Peter Straub, Anne Rice, Thomas Tessier, Robert R. McCammon and others—is the new adult equivalent of the folkloric stories of the Brothers Grimm and of the "literary" fairy tales of Hans Christian Andersen. Maybe, in fact, novel-length fantasies of ghosts, golems, vampires, werewolves, mad killers, hostile aliens and/or phantasmagoric after-Armageddon quests play the same sort of integrative psychological role for twentieth-century adults that "Hansel and Gretel," "The Ugly Duckling" and "Snow White" played for children a century ago and, of course, still play for children lucky enough to encounter them today.

Stephen King implies as much about modern horror writing when he declares, "[As] this mad century races toward its conclusion—a conclusion which seems ever more ominous and ever more absurd—it may be the most important and useful form of fiction which the moral writer may command."

Why, though, do we *like* stories that scare the living piss out of us? And what good does it do us to place ourselves, again and again, in situations—whether a theater seat at another sequel to *Halloween* or a wingback with the latest Clive Barker or K. W. Jeter opus—that produce these goosebump-lifting and/or bladder-draining sensations? Are all of us who enjoy this kind of "entertainment" already past hope of psychological reclamation? Have we bartered our twisted souls to Satan?

Absolutely not. Fear is not only a guilty pleasure—at least under circumstances where the threat is fictively distanced—it is also a psychological necessity. People who are literally fearless are people whom the rest of us regard as appallingly inhuman, and in *The Uses of Enchantment*, Bettelheim points out that many fairy tales dramatize the need to be able to experience fear. (Fear, after all, is an evolutionary adaptation. If you don't run from the hungry leopard, you get eaten.) The best example of this sort of story goes by such titles as "The Story of One Who Set Out to Study [or Learn] Fear" and "The Youth Who Could Not Shudder." It concerns a younger brother who wonders what he must do, in Lore Segal's amusing translation, "to make my flesh creep," for no task that his father assigns—even tiptoeing through a churchyard at midnight—has any power to make him tremble and he correctly feels that he's missing something.

The hero of this bizarre tale is a prodigy of courage. Better, a *monster* of courage. No "normal"—i.e., sane—human being could face the same daunting challenges with either the calmness or the confidence that our hero invariably summons. Seven hanged corpses don't in the least discomfit him; he cuts them down, places them around his fire to warm them and, when their rags ignite because he has put them too near the fire pit, disgustedly strings them up again. In a haunted castle, he lies down on a bed that begins to gallop him from room to room, but, rather than leap for safety, he commands the bed to go faster. One night later, he plays ninepins with a team of halved corpses that reassemble

themselves before him and challenge him to a bowling match. Altogether matter-of-factly, our Grimm hero uses a lathed skull for a bowling ball.

Strangely, none of these adventures has caused the young man to shudder; and even after he has married a beautiful princess—whose hand he has won by disenchanting the castle—his daily complaint is that he still doesn't know what it means for his "flesh to creep." At last, his new bride, fed up with this refrain, goes to a nearby brook, dips out a bucketful of icy water and squirmy minnows, pulls the blankets off her sleeping husband and dumps the cold water and its fishy contents all over him. Our hero, simultaneously shocked and delighted, cries, "Something is making my flesh creep! Dear wife, how my flesh is creeping! Ah, now I know what it's like when one's flesh creeps." Presumably, he and his ingenious bride live happily ever after.

Bettelheim identifies the young man's inability to shudder as the consequence of sexual repression, sexual anxiety. Readers out of sympathy with the Freudian approach may cry, "Bullshit!" After all, isn't it possible that the tale-teller who ended this narrative with a singularly unorthodox instance of the bedroom shivers just wanted to amuse us? And isn't a bed full of wriggling gudgeons as funny a climax as we are likely to imagine? Well, sure. Even so, Bettelheim *has* hit on something here.

"There is a subtlety in this story that is easy to overlook consciously," he points out, "although it does not fail to make an unconscious impression." He adds, "Whether or not the hearer of this story recognizes that it was sexual anxiety that led to the hero's inability to shudder, that which finally makes him shudder suggests the irrational nature of some of our most pervasive anxieties. Because it is a fear of which only his wife is able to cure him at night in bed, this is a sufficient hint of the underlying nature of the anxiety."

Bettelheim further explains that this story teaches the child that those who brag about their fearlessness may harbor immature fears that they are actively denying. It also hints that marital happiness requires both partners to acknowledge feelings that they have heretofore concealed. Another of the tale's messages is that "it is the female partner"—as in "The Beauty and the Beast"—"who finally brings out the humanity in the male. . . . [In] the last transition needed for achieving mature humanity, repressions must be undone."

That's a heavy lesson for a fairy tale to teach, but the point is that fairy tales—without sacrificing an iota of their cleverly disguised seriousness—teach such lessons lightly. They work on the unconscious, and they do this work through the attention-fixing enticements of narrative. "What's going to happen?" my children used to plead when I read to them from Grimm. "Daddy, what's going to happen?"

And horror novels like King's *The Shining* [H4-173], Straub's *Ghost Story* [H4-289], Rice's *Interview with the Vampire* [H4-250], Tessier's *The Nightwalker* [H4-297], McCammon's *Baal* (1978) and Thomas Harris's bloodcurdling study of the workings of a sociopathic killer's mind, *Red Dragon* [H4-135], are legitimate, sophisticated, set-your-flesh-to-creeping fairy tales for adults.

Wait a minute, I can hear a skeptic saying. Why must an adult, specifically a twentieth-century adult, go to such extremes to find something shudder-provoking? And aren't adults too far along in their psychological evolution to learn anything substantive from a mere horror novel? After all, we've got the H-bomb to worry about, and international terrorism, and Star Wars, and acid rain, and the greenhouse effect, and cancer, and heart disease, and, if we're of a religious turn of mind, even eternal damnation. Why flail around *inventing* stuff to fear, and why then claim that reading about our invented horrors—specters, zombies, bug-eyed aliens—is a viable means of achieving mental and emotional equilibrium?

In the introduction to his landmark anthology of contemporary horror tales, *The Dark Descent* [H4-345], editor David Hartwell writes, "A strong extra-literary appeal of such fiction"—he means here the stream of supernatural horror— ". . . is to jump-start the readers' deadened emotional sensitivities." Hartwell divides contemporary horror writing into three streams (the other two being metaphorical psychological horror and stories taking their peculiar frisson from a disturbing ambiguity about the reality of depicted events). "At the end of a horror story," he tells us, "the reader is left with a new perception of the nature of reality."

I agree with this last statement (about all three streams), and believe that both supernatural and psychological horror may serve "to jump-start . . . deadened emotional sensitivities"; that, in fact, doing so is not only an appeal of these types of horror, but also one of their primary goals.

Our sensitivities are deadened, of course, because the media—newspapers, TV, magazines—daily bombard us with horrific images. Moreover, we encounter these images in such brief, impersonal or clinical contexts (during the Vietnam War, for instance, as little more than jumpy frames of film on the six o'clock news) that it is difficult to *feel* about them. The threat of nuclear attack or the widening hole in the ozone layer, meanwhile, are such vast, complex problems that when we try to grapple with them, they self-destruct like taped *Mission: Impossible* assignments, again depriving us of a human-scale yardstick by which to measure them. Horror fiction and horror films, however, usually restore a tangible human context to the nightmares structuring them, enabling us, once again, to *care*—to cheer for those struggling to dispel the nightmare, to quake in terror when they seem to be failing, to hate the pernicious forces opposing them, and to find ourselves, because of this involvement, gratifyingly *alive*. And, of course, we undoubtedly take a certain guilty satisfaction in our awareness that the real danger is not to us, but to the imaginary characters battling the evil powers whose actions alternately thrill and repulse us.

King has written that horror is "the most important and useful form of fiction which the moral writer may command." Others have argued that because of its vivid provocativeness, it is dangerous; that it can corrupt. I would argue (on gut instinct rather than on statistics) that those adult readers most likely to be corrupted by horror fiction are precisely those who had no chance to internalize the tales of Grimm and Andersen as children. Those adults, in other words, who outgrew fantasy or who never discovered it at all. "Dead children," in Le Guin's canny formulation, rather than "children who survived"; children who've grown into adult monsters as a partial result of their deprivation.

The ideal reader of adult horror, then, is Le Guin's "child who survived." It is this reader who is most likely to appreciate it, most capable of recognizing the psychological validity of the grim archetypes at play in it, and most open to the healing catharsis of its violent images and apocalyptic resolutions. Which is not for a minute to deny with highfalutin' theory the simple fact that horror—a bang-up scare expertly administered—is great good fun, and all the more fun for our underlying awareness that the "danger" we are in is delectably hypothetical.

No, my point is that horror tales have a hidden, and important, function beyond entertaining us, and that the resurgence of their popularity in technological Western culture—a resurgence dating from the publication of Ira Levin's *Rosemary's Baby* [H4-206] in 1967 and building through the appearances of Thomas Tryon's *The Other* [H4-306] and William Peter Blatty's *The Exorcist* [H4-42], both in 1971—is a result of the ramifying anxieties attendant on the proliferating political, economic and ecological crises of the final quarter of our "mad" twentieth century.

It's reassuring to suffer a solid fright and to survive. It's also healthily edifying to our subconsciouses. For if we can find the psychological coin to get past a fictional slasher assault, or vampire invasion, or alien body-snatching expedition, or insidious satanic possession (pick one, and only one), then perhaps we also have the resourcefulness to deal with the real-world problems that seem, individually and collectively, so overwhelming and impervious to solution. We may or may not actually have this resourcefulness, of course, but I would argue that we need to believe we do and that horror fiction is finally, if paradoxically, a literature of hope, a literature of affirmation.

What did I learn as a well-loved but occasionally insecure kid from my most terrifying or awe-inspiring fantasy experiences? From the villain in *House of Wax*, from Polyphemus, from the Wicked Witch of the West and her ugly flying monkeys, from Mickey Mouse as the sorcerer's apprentice, from the skeletal pin-up girl leaning over my bed, from the Queen of Hearts, from the pint-sized Gulliver, and from the flamboyant writings of Poe and others?

Chiefly, I think, I learned not that horror fiction is at base affirmative (a conclusion that would have struck me as dumb, if not so abstruse as to be incomprehensible), but that, to rephrase David Hartwell's notion of horror's defining impact, reality isn't always what it appears to be. Wonder sometimes breaks in. Magic, black and white, can transform the two-dimensional outlines of life into dauntingly solid arabesques. Beneath the placid surfaces of habit, regimentation and order, fearful krakens lurk. The world is both more exciting and more terrible than we think, and fantasy—whether cinematic, literary or dream-triggered—is a surefire open-sesame to its secret awesomeness.

In October 1988, I was in Atlanta to do a reading at Georgia State University and to conduct a pair of seminars for advanced writing students. On the way to Georgia State's urban campus one morning, my host, Dr. Tom McHaney, took me to McGuire's Bookshop on Ponce de Leon Avenue, where the owner, Frank McGuire, told me of a recent horror novel called *Deliver Us from Evil* (1988) by a new Atlanta-based writer, Allen Lee Harris. "Bantam did it as an original paperback," Frank said, "and it sold pretty well for us. I don't have a copy in the store right now, but I'll send you one if you're interested." I was, and Frank did.

Deliver Us from Evil strikes me both as a strong, well-crafted representative of the contemporary horror novel and as a promising debut. Released in March 1988, it proves that the trend in horror writing inaugurated in the late 1960s/early

1970s, a trend given direction and impetus by the conspicuous successes of Stephen King, has by no means exhausted itself. Talented new writers can still find untilled territory within the field to stake out and claim as their own, and they can contour these parcels with as much élan and originality as their private visions allow. Meanwhile, they do this work within a tradition giving it additional resonance and simultaneously demanding structural and thematic innovations to keep it fresh.

Harris's *Deliver Us from Evil* is traditional horror, with many of the anticipated hackneyed trappings—from an evil-beset southern small town, to a Good Sheriff protagonist, to a ubiquitous Village Idiot, to a Mysterious Interloper, to an All-American Kid Who Saves the Entire Community—but the author, who began college at fourteen, got his degree at nineteen, attended Harvard Divinity School and later took a Masters in Philosophy at the University of Toronto, transfigures these weary plot elements with the power of his vision, the simple clarity of his writing, and the forcefulness of his intellection. As a result, his novel possesses exactly the sort of compassionate, existential dimension to qualify it as a mature adult fairy tale. Harris knows what a good horror story should demonstrate, and he also understands the sort of healthy psychological integration that this demonstration should work in us.

Jerry Robins, a character who describes himself as a "lapsed nihilist" (i.e., someone for whom the cynical belief in nothing has failed), relates for the novel's Good Sheriff, Charlie McAlister, why his grandfather used to like to tell, and subsequently gloss, the Old Testament story of Jacob's Ladder:

> "[What my grandfather] always dwelled upon was Jacob's terror at his vision. A terror that came out of the realization that the world around him, the everyday world he was so comfortable in, was not the only world. That there was another one, alien and awful, unyielding and incomprehensible. But even that wasn't the worst part of it. The worst part wasn't his vision of the other world but his vision of the ladder. Because, from then on, Jacob knew that this other world could erupt at any moment into his own world and that the two worlds were invisibly intertwined."

(Hartwell again: "At the end of a horror story, the reader is left with a new perception of reality.")

Although *Deliver Us from Evil* contains a lot of the requisite jeepery-creepery of the post-*Rosemary's Baby*, post-*The Other*, post-*The Exorcist* commercial horror novel (innocent characters groping about in the dark or facing bleak personifications of the forces of eternal night), several of its scenes actually managed to make my flesh crawl; they did so by brilliantly dramatizing the eruption of Robins's grandfather's "other world" into this one. And Harris, a fellow Georgian whom I have never met, corresponded with or talked to on the phone, redeems even his less sterling jeepery-creepery by visiting it upon unfailingly sympathetic characters and by giving his entire novel a hopeful, affirmative shape.

At the end of the book, Robins is lost in thought: "The wonder is not that there's so much darkness, his grandfather had told him. The wonder is there's any light at all."

I didn't understand that when I was yelling to get out of that theater in Wichita showing *House of Wax*, or when I edged away from the bony *femme fatale* at my bedside in Mulvane, Kansas, or when I eagerly imbibed the seemingly poisonous concoctions of Edgar Allan Poe's pen in Tulsa, Oklahoma—but, having made it to adulthood with my inner child intact, I do understand it now: *"The wonder is there's any light at all."*

Horror fiction teaches this essential lesson again and again, a lesson that bears repeating, preferably in new and more compelling guises, because the times are such that we can too easily surrender to the vitiating suspicion that the darkness is everywhere and the light is merely illusory. It may seem tautological to say so, but children who have survived are more likely than snuffed children—those stranded among us in the corpses of spiritually impoverished adults—to believe in, and work for, everyone's survival.

Thank you, *House of Wax*. Thank you, Polyphemus. Thank you, L. Frank Baum. Thank you, Mickey Mouse, Jonathan Swift, Edgar Allan Poe, Ray Bradbury, Stephen King, Peter Straub and, latterly, Allen Lee Harris. Thank you, thank you, one and all. . . .

Fantasy Literature
A Readers' Guide

1

Development of the Fantastic Tradition through 1811

Dennis M. Kratz

The fantastic plays such a prominent role in the early literature of virtually every culture that it is unrewarding if not foolish to discuss ancient narrative from any critical perspective that regards fantasy as in some way a departure from the higher art of realism. Relatively few narratives from antiquity depict fictional worlds that scrupulously imitate everyday reality. In some works marvels are incidental elements; but the fantastic permeates a large number of narratives, among them the most influential in their respective literary traditions. Indeed, fantasy forms the mainstream of Western literature until the Renaissance. The major narratives that form the basis of the Western literary tradition create fictional worlds where events considered impossible in the world of mundane experience can and do occur; in other words, they are fantasies. In the terms of one influential modern definition of fantasy, they are fictions "evoking wonder and containing a substantial and irreducible element of the supernatural with which the mortal characters in the story or readers become on at least partly familiar terms."[1]

Greek and Roman Traditions

The literary tradition of the Western world begins with the Greeks, and classical Greek literature, from Homeric epic on, is essentially fantastic. The fabulous nature of Greek literature derives primarily from the practice, initiated by the bards who created the epic tradition, of drawing their artistic subjects from the realm of mythology. A good deal of both Homer's *Iliad* and *Odyssey* [1-38] (and presumably their predecessors) is concerned with the gods, and the action hinges on their intervention. It is the *Odyssey*, however, that should be called the first self-conscious fantasy in the Western literary tradition, for marvels are central to its design. The origins, date and authorship of the *Odyssey* remain issues of scholarly debate, but the most widely accepted view holds that it was composed in the mid-eighth century BC by the same bard who a little earlier had composed the *Iliad*. The *Odyssey* is the first work of Western literature to assume acquaintance with another specific work, for in its opening scene Zeus discusses the implications of statements made by Achilles at the end of the *Iliad*. In addition, the *Odyssey* is the first narrative to concern itself with the nature of narrative. Among its subjects are art, deception and the reckless stupidity of those who cannot perceive the deeper meaning beneath the surface of beggars they see, gifts they receive or stories they hear. Odysseus prevails less by his strength than by his cleverness, by the ability to deceive and manipulate others through disguise and artful language. Significantly, the most marvelous events of the *Odyssey* occur within Odysseus's own account of his adventures—an account which he prefaces by calling attention to his reputation as a deceiver. Only then does he relate his victorious encounters with the likes of Circe (the witch with the power to transform men into animals) and the one-eyed giant Cyclops, his escape from the monsters Scylla and Charybdis and the alluring Sirens, as well as his visit with the souls of the dead. Odysseus's art rests not on reproducing events with literal accuracy, but on cloaking deeper truths beneath a "false" surface. Homer introduced into Western literature, then, three prominent elements of fantasy: the journey to strange lands, the theme of transformation and a warning against mistaking the apparent for the real.

The second author of Greek literature, and the first to identify himself, is Hesiod, a farmer from the rocky area of Boeotia. His *Theogonia* (*Theogony*, ca. 725 BC) [1-37] offers the first poetic attempt to select and arrange the available matter of mythology in such a way as to articulate a coherent vision of the universe, particularly its moral design. Combining traditional stories with tales of his own invention, he composed what is essentially a glorification of Zeus, who serves as a symbol of intelligent power as opposed to brute force. In his other poem, *Erga kai Hemerai* (*Works and Days*, ca. 690 BC), Hesiod continues his presentation of the moral cosmos. Less bold in its vision, this poem is an odd amalgam of mythic tales, ethical maxims, practical advice and what might best be called folk sayings, including the first beast fable in Western literature.

A long folktale tradition stands behind the beast fable, a form of fantastic fiction that was both popular and widespread among the Greeks. Such narratives, in which animals act and speak, served a wide variety of purposes, but the beast fable was especially suited to social criticism, allowing the storyteller to point out what is proper without giving offense to the powerful by expressing the point overtly. Almost certainly the beast fable reached the Greeks from the East, for such stories played an important role in the ancient cultures of both India and Mesopotamia. In India, animal fables seem to have been used as a medium for Buddhist instruction. The most important collection of Indian beast fables, the Sanskrit *Panchatantra* [1-59], has had an extraordinary influence on later world literature. Almost two hundred different versions are known in more than fifty languages. All the Western versions derive from a seventh-century Arabic version revolving around two jackals named Kalilah and Dimnah (a corruption of the Indian names Karataka and Damanaka) that is based on a Persian translation (*ca.* 550) of the Indian original.

The beast fable enters Greek literature, as I mentioned, through Hesiod's *Works and Days*. To illustrate the miseries of his world, in which justice is often defeated, Hesiod makes use of the story of a nightingale whose pleading cries are useless in the talons of a hawk. Animal fables next appear in the works of two seventh-century lyric poets, Archilochus and Semonides. In Greek literature, the panoply of satiric and didactic animal tales eventually became associated with the name of one supposed author, according to tradition a Phrygian slave who lived in the early sixth century BC. A wide range of folktales became associated with this Aesop, though the earliest extant collection of such stories was not assembled until centuries later.

Although Greek tragedy, because it drew on mythology for its themes and subjects, was often infused with fantastic elements, the Greek dramatic genre in which fantasy played the greatest role was comedy—specifically the form of comic drama known as Old Comedy that emerged in Athens in the early fifth century and whose greatest practitioner was Aristophanes. The primary mode of Aristophanic comedy, as Cedric Whitman first pointed out, is not social criticism but fantasy based on the disdain of limits.[2] Two related elements of the fantastic underlie most of Aristophanes' comedies: first, the fulfillment of a grandiose ambition by an apparently ordinary individual; second, this fulfillment occurs through supernatural means that overthrow many of the sequences of cause and effect that we associate with the "real" world. For example, in *Acharnes* (*The Acharnians*, 425 BC), Aristophanes' earliest extant comedy, a crusty Athenian farmer named Dikaiopolis declares and gains to great personal advantage a private peace between himself and Sparta. *Batrachoi* (*The Frogs*, 405 BC) [1-6] takes place in the Underworld; and in Aristophanes' most elaborate and imaginative fantasy, *Ornithes* (*The Birds*, 414 BC) [1-5], an Athenian citizen manages, with the help of birds, not only to build a city in the sky but also to supplant Zeus as the ruler of the universe.

In addition to the epic-mythic tradition and the beast fable, a third stream of Greek literature, similarly rooted in fantasy rather than mimetic storytelling and like the beast fable flowing for the most part beneath the cultural surface, is the novel. This term, though somewhat misleading, is used by many modern scholars to describe a form of long prose fiction that arose during the Hellenistic period (the conventional name for that period of Greek history ranging from the victories of Alexander the Great until the conquest of the last Greek state by Rome, *ca.* 330 to 30 BC) but reached its highest degree of popularity and artistic achievement in the second and third centuries after the birth of Christ. In one sense the Greek novel is the literary heir of the Homeric epic. From the beginning its authors borrowed epic plot elements, especially from the *Odyssey*, and included numerous allusions to characters and events in both the *Iliad* and *Odyssey*. Indeed, though the Homeric poems themselves were lost to Western literature for most of the Middle Ages, the imitation of motifs and themes from the *Odyssey* by authors of Greek novels helped preserve the influence of that essential work of fantastic narrative.

The most widely read form of the Greek novel was the romance. Love, adventure and travel are the essential elements on which the plots of the major Hellenistic romances are built. The emphasis is upon the tribulations and eventual happiness of young lovers. The oldest surviving romance, Chariton's *Chaereas and Callirhoe*, written in the middle of the second century, announces in its first sentence that it presents the story of a "love affair" (*pathos erotikon*). The elements of travel and adventure emerge from attempts to separate the lovers; in Chariton's romance, for example, Chaereas follows his beloved, who has been abducted by pirates, from Syracuse as far as Asia Minor. The action of Xenophon's *Ephesiaca* (*Ephesian Tale*, *ca.* 250) ranges over a large part of the Mediterranean world from Sicily to Egypt and Syria. Other tales are set in faraway lands, with distance and fantasy often directly related. Magic and ghosts figure prominently in the action of the *Babylonica* (*Babylonian Tale*, *ca.* 177) of Iamblichus, which is set in pre-Persian Mesopotamia. The longest extant Greek romance, the *Ethiopica* or *Ethiopian Romance* by Heliodorus of Emesa (*ca.* 350) was to play a significant role in the development of the romance in Renaissance English literature.

While the Hellenistic romance and its later manifestations often included elements of the fantastic, it was the concurrent rise of related genres of prose fiction that would prove most significant for the history of fantasy. The fantastic travel tale, or *Reisefabulistik*, emerged as a special genre during the Hellenistic era. These tales emphasize travel and adventure, while the theme of love, emphasized in the romances, is downplayed. Although no travel tale from the Hellenistic period survives, the historian Diodorus Siculus (first century) provides summaries of such stories written by Euhemerus (*ca.* 300 BC) and Iambulus (*ca.* 100 BC), the latter a tale about the narrator's adventures on an island on which much is strange and everything desirable. Antonius Diogenes' travel tale *Ta Huper Thoulen Apista* (*The Wonders beyond Thule, ca.* AD 100), which likewise survives only in a later summary, includes stories of a land in which the inhabitants can see at night but are blind in the daytime, and contains an episode in which a sorcerer causes the travelers in the tale, a brother and sister, to be dead in the daytime and alive only at night. Such travel tales are the butt of Lucian of Samosata's parody in his *Historia Aletheia* (*True Story, ca.* AD 175). Other forms of popular fiction from this period include the fictionalized biography of famous individuals and epistolary novels, or tales told through the exchange of letters between either historical or mythic characters.

One thread of this complex fabric deserves attention in some detail: the fictionalized treatment of the life and deeds of Alexander the Great known as the *Alexander Romance* [1-44]. No figure from classical antiquity has held so powerful or constant a grip on the world's literary imagination as has Alexander. The most influential source for Alexander's life, from late antiquity through the Renaissance, was a mixture of inaccurate fact and fantastic fiction composed in the third century by an unknown author (called Pseudo-Callisthenes since the work was once attributed erroneously to Alexander's court biographer). This work is an amalgam of various sources. Part is a romanticized biography of Alexander that made use of the rhetorical and thematic effects associated with the Hellenistic novel. To this fictionalized account of Alexander's life, other purely fictional elements were added. The most important of these was a series of fabricated letters between Alexander and the Persian king Darius. The author incorporated into his narrative in addition a separate series of longer letters, also invented, that were supposed to have been written by Alexander himself to his mother, Olympias, and to his teacher Aristotle. These letters, which are in fact examples of the popular genre of the *Reisefabulistik*, are filled with reports of Alexander's fabulous adventures in India and beyond. He encounters a dizzying variety of fantastic beasts (among them the basilisk) and strange human beings (dog-headed individuals, for example, as well as a race of nine-foot-tall people, called *fauni*, who are covered with hair and subsist on raw fish and water). As would happen often, particularly in medieval literature, the passage of time increased the role of the fantastic in accounts of historical events and individuals.

Roman literature, like Roman art and culture in general, was less sympathetic to fantasy than the Greek literature upon which it was largely based. Even so, partly as a result of the influence of Greek literature, the major works of Roman literature contain significant elements of the fantastic and the supernatural. Vergil's *Aeneid* (19 BC) [1-85], arguably the Roman work that has exerted the greatest influence on subsequent Western literature, is a transformation of the *Iliad* and *Odyssey*. It not only recreates the divine machinery of Homeric epic but also expands the motif of the trip into and through the Underworld. The other major Roman epic, Lucan's *De Bello Civili* (*Civil War*, also known as *Pharsalia*, AD 65), while pointedly eschewing the use of gods and goddesses, expands and elaborates the role of other supernatural elements.

The most evident and abiding contributions of Roman literature to the history of fantasy were made by three works of widely different nature. Two of these—Ovid's *Metamorphoses* and *The Golden Ass* by Lucius Apuleius—take as their starting point the concept of transformation. The third work is not a piece of fiction but a treatise on political philosophy. While the sober discussion of political theory and practice in Cicero's *De Republica* (*The Republic*, ca. 50 BC) may seem an odd place to look for a major example of Western fantasy, the final section of that work is a fiction that was to exert a powerful influence on the development of the "dream vision" as a motif of fantasy, especially in medieval literature. Cicero, imitating the "myth of Er" that concludes Plato's *Republic*, places a similar vision at the end of his philosophic discourse. Scipio Africanus Minor, a Roman general, relates a remarkable dream in which he sees "from an exalted place, bright and shining, filled with stars" (that is, from the highest celestial sphere, the *stellatum*) the physical and moral design of the universe. Cicero's *Somnium Scipionis* (*Dream of Scipio*) had an enormous impact on later literature. Lucan imitates it in his account of the flight of Pompey's soul in the *Civil War*, and it served as the prototype of numerous ascents to Heaven in medieval and Renaissance literature.

Without question the richest imagination of all Roman writers belonged to Ovid, whose epic poem *Metamorphoses* [1-58] has exerted an influence on later Western literature second only to that of Vergil's *Aeneid*. The *Metamorphoses* is an engaging and witty rather than a profound work. Around the unifying theme of transformation Ovid weaves a dizzying variety of stories in a wide range of moods. His skilled refashioning and presentation of so many familiar myths—of Daphne transformed into a laurel, Arachne into a spider, Actaeon into a stag—have lured readers even when they were appalled by Ovid's apparent lack of moral seriousness. The need of Christian readers, in particular, to "rescue" Ovid's fantasies would play no small role in the development of literary criticism in the Middle Ages and Renaissance.

The Roman transformation of Greek literary models extended to the romance, and produced two works of interest for the history of fantasy: the *Satyricon* of Petronius and *The Golden Ass* by Lucius Apuleius. The *Satyricon* (*ca.* AD 65) [1-62], whose author was in all likelihood the *arbiter elegantiae* ("judge of taste") for the Emperor Nero, survives only in fragments, the largest of which—the *Cena Trimalchionis* ("Trimalchio's Dinner")—is a biting satire of Rome's tasteless *nouveaux riches*. In many respects a cynical parody of the Greek ideal romance, the *Satyricon* presents the travels and adventures of the essentially amoral rogue Encolpius, whose name is derived from the Greek word for crotch. The *Satyricon* includes an elaborate werewolf story, one of the few in which the werewolf can transform himself at will into bestial form and back again.

The preeminent fantasy narrative of late antiquity is *Metamorphosis*, better known as *The Golden Ass* [1-2], composed in the mid-second century by Lucius Apuleius, a native of northern Africa who had traveled widely in the Roman Empire, studied Greek philosophy in Athens and practiced law in Rome. Apuleius probably took the central plot of his long prose novel—the adventures of a young man transformed into an ass—from a brief tale called *Loukios e Onos* (*Lucius, Or the Ass*), attributed to the Greek satirist Lucian. He expanded this basic tale with a variety of interpolated elements ranging from bawdy "Milesian tales" of adultery to the philosophic fairy tale of Cupid (Love) and Psyche (Soul). *The Golden Ass* is rich in fantastic events: the transformation of Lucius of course, but also a witch named Meroe who can turn men into animals, ghouls who devour a man's nose and ears when he falls asleep while guarding a corpse, various ghosts and the appearance to Lucius of the goddess Isis at the work's conclusion. Apuleius fashioned a work that employs the frame of a fantastic narrative as a means of exploring philosophic concepts. The influence of Plato pervades the narrative. Lucius's transformation is but a physical manifestation of his absorption in mundane, animal pleasures. Only when he is reduced to the form of a lowly, reviled beast of burden does he begin a slow learning process that enables him to recognize the animality of his existence and yearn for a deeper understanding by which to guide his life. The philosophic level of the narrative is expressed in the tale of Psyche's love for Cupid, their separation and her tortuous but successful reunion with him, resulting in the birth of their child, Joy. Apuleius's Greek model had ended with the ass regaining his human form by eating roses; but in *The Golden Ass* the transformation is occasioned by Lucius's acceptance of the worship of the goddess Isis.

The contribution of classical literature to the history and development of fantasy, then, is both substantial and complex. The Greek adaptation for secular use of matter drawn from myth has had a profound and continuous effect on all Western literature. Moreover, the *Odyssey* and its successors, particularly Greek romance and *Reisefabulistik*, provide models of fantastic fiction that play a prominent role throughout Western literary history. The popularity of another major form of fantastic narrative, the dream vision, can be traced to Cicero. Several forms of animal fantasy, rooted in folktale, are introduced into Western literature by the Greeks. Especially important are the fables, many based on Oriental sources, attributed to Aesop. A second strain of animal story, found in Greek literature but brought to greater artistic power by Latin authors such as Ovid and Apuleius, involves the transformation of human beings into animals; a variant of this theme is that of the transformed individual's retaining human intelligence and thereby the ability to recount the story of his adventures. Finally, the interaction of Platonism with the literary imagination established fantasy as a medium for the exploration of philosophic concepts. This wedding of entertainment and idea in fantastic narrative was among the most significant contributions of the classical world to the Western literary tradition.

Indian and Oriental Fantasy

For classical Western literature, the Orient served as both a setting for fantastic narratives and a source for fantastic themes. It has been argued that the origins of both the *Satyricon* and *The Golden Ass* are to be found in Oriental story traditions.[3] The Eastern sources of Aesopian animal fables are well established, as are the Eastern origins of many Greek and Roman myths. Eastern literature, then, has its own rich tradition of fantasy. No survey of fantastic narrative, for example, can fail to mention the extraordinary Mesopotamian *Epic of Gilgamesh* (*ca.* 2000 BC) [1-29], the outstanding literary achievement of the ancient Near East. The Egyptian *Book of the Dead* (established in its present form between 665 and 525 BC) is not, properly speaking, a work of literature; but within its collection of charms, formulae and funerary inscriptions are articulated many of the basic beliefs of Egyptian religion as well as a vivid picture of the other world awaiting the dead. The few examples of early Egyptian fiction that survive include several stories of wonder in which human beings encounter the supernatural, most notably *The Tale of the Shipwrecked Sailor* (*ca.* 2000 BC) and three tales found in the *Papyrus Westcar* (*ca.* 1600 BC).

The Indian literary tradition, like that of the Greeks, rests on two great epic poems, the *Mahabharata* and *Ramayana*. The *Mahabharata* [1-48] is an enormous narrative (roughly seven times the length of the *Iliad* and *Odyssey* combined); its text was composed, or better to say it evolved, between 400 BC and AD 400. Perhaps best understood as an encyclopedia of Brahmin-Indian civilization, the *Mahabharata* contains in its vastness numerous episodes of wonder and the supernatural. Unlike the *Mahabharata*, to which numerous authors from various eras contributed, the *Ramayana* [1-69] bears the name of a single author, Valmiki. A more unified, consciously literary work, it recounts the often fantastic adventures of the hero Rama. The world of the *Ramayana* is one of stark contrasts. The luxurious life of the city is opposed to the harsh environment of jungle and desert, inhabited by the supernatural demons against whom the hero must fight. In the twelfth century a poet living in South India refashioned Valmiki's *Ramayana* into a new work of art. While for the earlier poet Rama was a human hero, albeit of superhuman powers, the twelfth-century poet Kampan portrays Rama as fully aware of his divinity. His tale places particular emphasis on Rama's adventures in rescuing his kidnapped wife, Sita, from Ravana, the demon king. As Dante would summarize Western culture a century later, Kampan's retelling of the *Ramayana* summarizes the rich Hindu culture that was then flowering in South India.

In addition to the two great epics, Indian literature has a rich tradition of less artfully composed and more popular tales called *jatakas* ("birth stories"). The most influential collection of these stories is the *Panchatantra* ("Five Chapters"), already mentioned as a source for many of the animal fables that found their way into Western literature. The frame narrative for this collection of tales and fables is that a Brahmin uses them to teach the rules of right conduct to the sons of an Indian king. Two other extremely popular collections from the same period reflect the typically gnomic-fantastic nature of Indian narrative. In *Seventy Tales of the Parrot*, the parrot tells a sequence of stories that both enchant and keep a faithless wife from going out while her husband is away; a vampire, or *vetala*, recounts a similar series of extraordinary, pointed stories in *Twenty-Five Tales of the Vampire*.

Among the earliest examples of Chinese literature are accounts of strange occurrences (*chih-kuai*) and supernatural events (*ch'uan-ch'i*) from the period of the Six Dynasties (222–589). Ghosts, animal transformations, interaction of humans with fairies and gods, and magic are the frequent topics of these narratives. In the T'ang Dynasty (618–906) these popular tales were for the first time given careful literary form. The authors of these literary tales were for the most part educated men seeking both literary fame and political advancement through their art. A story from the early years of the T'ang Dynasty, *The Ancient Mirror* by Wang Tu, is typical of the emphasis on the supernatural. This long narrative recounts numerous miraculous events associated with the mirror. In one series of these episodes, a fox, snake, tortoise, rat and other animals assume human shape and participate in a number of bizarre adventures until the power of the mirror returns them to their proper existence. In *The White Monkey*, the wife of an army officer is kidnapped by a white monkey with extraordinary powers; when the woman is rescued, she is pregnant, and she later gives birth to a child who looks like a monkey but later becomes a famous poet.

During the Sung Dynasty (960–1279) the Chinese short story reaches its zenith. While many of the works from this period show a growing tendency toward greater realism in both plot and characterization, the supernatural remains a popular topic of these narratives. The tales of the master storyteller Wu Shu (947–1002), for example, are filled with accounts of marvels and supernatural events. The most important Sung short story collection, *Capital Version of Popular Stories*, survives only in fragmentary form; but of the eight tales that remain, two deal with ghosts. The bulk of later Chinese literature, particularly longer narrative, is similarly realistic in nature, but among the longer works generally regarded as the finest examples of Chinese fiction is one fantasy from the period of the Ming Dynasty (1368–1644): *Hsi-yu Chi* (*Journey to the West*, 1592; partially translated into English as *Monkey*) [1-94] by Wu Ch'eng-en. Deservedly praised for the vigor of its fantasy as well as the rich variety of its supernatural stories and characters, the narrative concerns the adventures of the priest Tripitaka and his three animal spirit companions, Monkey, Pig and Sandy (a fish spirit). Most of the tale deals with the various calamities suffered by

Tripitaka at the hands of demons, ghosts and monsters. He succeeds in reaching his destination only through the intelligence and magical powers of Monkey.

The fantastic plays a similar role in Japanese literature, which indeed was much influenced by that of China. Most early Japanese narratives deal with superior beings and fantastic events. Moreover, by the tenth century, many examples of both *chih-kuai* and *ch'uan-ch'i* had reached Japan; fascination with their marvelous elements is in part responsible for the rise of *monogatari* (stories), many of which dealt with fantastic themes. Among the finest examples of early Japanese fiction, *Taketori Monogatari* (*The Bamboo Cutter*) tells of a young maiden born miraculously from cut bamboo. Though written in the early tenth century, the story is clearly based on an earlier Chinese tale. As had happened in Chinese literature, later Japanese fiction also grew increasingly realistic in subject matter and tone, but in the eighteenth century Akinari Ueda gave new life to the tradition of the fantastic tale with his collection *Ugetsu Monogatari* (*Tales of Rain and Moon*) [1-84].

Medieval Fantasy

To return to the Occident, it is fair to say that the history of Western literature from late antiquity through the Middle Ages and Renaissance is essentially a history of Christian literature. Both the nature of Christianity itself and the influence upon it of Platonic philosophy led medieval literature to show minimal concern with mimetic depiction. Medieval literature and art tend to express underlying patterns of truth, to present narrative or pictorial exemplifications of abstract ideas rather than explore "character" or describe everyday physical reality. Elements of fantasy, therefore, occur in almost every genre and specific work of medieval literature. Among the other results of the Platonizing tendency of medieval literature is an affinity for allegory as a mode of both interpretation and artistic creation. Allegory had entered Western literature with the attempt of Greek philosophers to explain away the more marvelous and scandalous episodes of the Homeric epics by seeing in them a symbolic depiction of moral issues. It was a form of reading that proved useful to Christians confronted by the attractive yet dangerous literature of classical culture, enabling them to perceive beneath the surface narrative a deeper level of meaning—often unknown to the original author—consistent with Christian doctrine. Allegorizing in interpretation and creation is a consistent feature of not only medieval but also Renaissance literature. The prevalence of allegorical readings, by which Christian truths could be found even in pagan works like Ovid's *Metamorphoses*, played no small role in the survival of classical literature, and enabled visual artists to employ themes from classical mythology. Moreover, it is a feature of enormous importance for fantastic literature, since it enabled authors to employ fantastic scenes as a means of expressing deeper philosophic or religious truths.

As with the Greek and Indian literary traditions, each of the major Western European literatures places a great epic narrative at its generative center. The Old English *Beowulf* (*ca.* 725) [1-9], the French *Chanson de Roland* (*Song of Roland*, *ca.* 1100) [1-72] and the German *Nibelungenlied* (*ca.* 1200) [1-57]—each was composed by a single artist who, like Homer, refashioned inherited oral material to articulate a new vision of heroic excellence. They depict fantastic fictional worlds in which monsters roam, God's direct intervention aids the attempt of an emperor to avenge the death of his beloved vassal or magic cloaks confer invisibility upon those who wear them. The *Nibelungenlied* bears many resemblances to two late thirteenth-century Scandinavian works, the *Volsunga Saga* [1-86] and Snorri Sturluson's *Prose Edda* [1-80], at once a treatise on poetry and a vast compendium of Norse mythology to which modern fantasists have turned for inspiration and stories. To the same era belong many of the Finnish oral tales and ballads that were first compiled and given artistic shape in the nineteenth century by the philologist Elias Lonnrott, who entitled the whole work *Kalevala* [1-41], after the abode of Kaleva, the mythic hero whose exploits form the basis of many of the constituent narratives.

About the same time but a world away, driven perhaps by the same impulse to give artistic order to the cosmos that underlies books as disparate as Hesiod's *Theogony*, the *Prose Edda*, the *Kalevala* and the *Book of the Dead*, members of the Central American Mayan culture were inventing the tales of their gods and heroes that would first be written in hieroglyphs and transcribed in the Spanish alphabet in the sixteenth century. The *Popol Vuh* [1-63] centers on the exploits of two sets of twins, especially the pair known as the Hero Twins, who defeat the monstrous inhabitants of the Underworld and eventually reach apotheosis as the sun and the moon.

In Western Europe the beast epic enjoyed continuous popularity throughout the Middle Ages. In addition to the obvious oral transmission of the various fables attributed to Aesop, these stories were known in literary form through Latin versions produced first in poetry by Phaedrus in the first century and in prose by Avianus two centuries later. The existence of an oral tradition helps explain the appearance in the early ninth century of a Latin verse retelling by Paul the Deacon of a fable in which the fox cures the sick lion and then exacts vengeance on his rival the bear by prescribing the bear's skin as the lion's medicine. The first extended beast narrative in medieval literature was composed in Latin verse *ca.* 940 by a German monk. Known as the *Ecbasis Captivi* (*Escape of the Captive*), it tells of a calf that is captured by a wolf after running away from the farmyard, but is eventually rescued by the other animals. The story is certainly intended as an allegory (of the inexperienced monk who is captured by the devil, or perhaps a worldly monk, but saved through the intervention of other monks). The story of the curing of the lion, which appears again in the *Ecbasis Captivi*, stands at the thematic center of the next major medieval beast epic: the *Ysengrimus*, a long epic in more than 6,000 Latin hexameters composed in the twelfth century by Nivardus of Ghent. The *Ysengrimus*, which emphasizes the fall of Ysengrimus the wolf as a result of his unequal running conflict with the cleverness of Reynard the fox, is an elaborate satire that criticizes not only worldly monks but also all wolfish humans who use positions of power for selfish ends.

The beast epic has a long history in vernacular literature as well, although no text earlier than the twelfth century survives. In that century Marie de France adapted many animal fables in Franch verse. In the twelfth and thirteenth centuries numerous other collections of French translations, called *Isopets*, were made; and during the same period there appeared in French gatherings of the various narratives concerning the rivalry between Reynard and Ysengrim. The artistic innovation of these anonymous French narrators was to place the focus of the tales upon Reynard, and to alter his self-serving craftiness into a kind of comic heroism. Chaucer knew the French *Roman de Renart* [1-71] and used one of its stories—that of the fox and the chanticleer—as the basis for "The Nun's Priest's Tale" in his *Canterbury Tales* [1-15].

These French tales about Reynard proved extremely popular and were soon adapted in German by the Alsatian poet Heinrich der Glichezare. About 1250 a Flemish poet named Willem gathered these tales and organized them into an extended coherent narrative, which an anonymous author greatly expanded in the next century. A fourteenth-century prose rendition of Willem's expanded *Reinart de Vos* became the main source, either directly or through intermediaries, for most subsequent literary versions of the story of Reynard in English and German, from Caxton's *History of Reynard the Fox* (1481) to Goethe's *Reineke Fuchs* (1794). In France, interestingly enough, where the story first gained vernacular literary form, the story of Reynard was virtually ignored until the nineteenth century. Unfortunately for students of fantasy in general and animal fantasy in particular, neither the French *Roman de Renart* nor Willem's poem has been translated adequately into English.

In addition to the epic tradition emphasizing Reynard and Ysengrim, the humbler beast fable enjoys a long history in Western literature. The Arabic tales about the jackals Kalilah and Dimnah had been translated into numerous languages by the thirteenth century. One of these translations, in Hebrew, was the basis for the thirteenth-century Latin collection *Directorium Humanae Vitae* (*Guide for Human Life*) by John of Capua, the book primarily responsible for the reentrance of the Oriental animal fable into Western literature. The English poet Edmund Spenser's "Mother Hubberd's Tale" tells how an ape and a fox travel to court, only to discover that life there is not better than their life in the country. The high point of the shorter beast fable in Western literature, however, is certainly reached in the numerous volumes of satiric fables by the seventeenth-century French poet Jean de La Fontaine [1-42]. The first volume, containing 124 fables drawn mainly from Aesop and Phaedrus, appeared in 1668. Over the next twenty-five years La Fontaine produced 114 more fables; for these he used a much wider array of sources including not only works by classical Western writers such as Horace but also collections of Oriental tales.

Another form of animal fantasy that proved popular in medieval literature was the tale of the transformation of a human being into an animal, particularly a wolf. The Christian Middle Ages produced the finest literary treatments of the werewolf theme. The medieval interest in werewolves has a basis in theology as well as folklore and literary tradition; and the theological discussion of lycanthropy clearly establishes the werewolf as a figure of fantastic fiction. Because in medieval Christian doctrine sin must involve rational consent, no deed committed by a transformed human being could be sinful. And what would happen to the soul of a human being who dies in animal form? Among the Christian theologians to deal with the implications of werewolves and other werebeasts were St. Augustine and St. Thomas Aquinas, both of whom argue what became the orthodox Christian position that while God is of course capable of performing any metamorphosis, a human being cannot actually be transformed into an animal by either magic or the intervention of the devil. It became the official doctrine of the Church that werewolves do not exist, and that belief in them was a sin. Hence stories about werewolves are either fantasies themselves or depict an illusion of change that fools the reader. This theme of "illusory change" is used by Gerald of Wales, who includes in his *Topographia Hibernica* (*Topography of Ireland, ca.* 1215) a tale of a couple compelled to spend seven years as wolves. With his wife at the point of death, the husband goes to a startled priest to seek the last rites for her. When the priest balks at administering a sacrament to an animal, the husband peels back a portion of his wife's pelt, revealing her human form beneath.

An intriguing, innovative aspect of medieval werewolf fantasies is a tendency to take a sympathetic view of the transformed creature and place less emphasis upon depiction of animal savagery. Marie de France's *Lai de Bisclavret* (*Lai of Bisclavret, ca.* 1190) [1-51] concerns a gallant knight who must spend three days of every week as a werewolf as a result of a curse upon his family. When his faithless wife learns of his plight, she steals his clothes while he is a wolf, thus condemning him to live perpetually as a lycanthrope. In Marie's tale the knight retains his human intelligence despite the metamorphosis, and he manages to win back his human shape and rightful place in society by serving a just king by whom he is captured. Marie thus employs the werewolf theme to examine human morality. The werewolf is in fact less feral than his greedy wife, and he regains his humanity through the loving intervention of a king (perhaps a symbol of divine grace) who looks beneath his physical ugliness to see moral beauty in the wolf. A second articulate werewolf is portrayed sympathetically in the anonymous French narrative *Guillaume de Palerne* (*Guillaume of Palerne, ca.* 1195). Here the werewolf is in reality Alphonse, rightful heir to the Spanish throne, who has been transformed into a wolf through the evil magic of his stepmother. Even in his bestial form Alphonse, like the knight in the *Lai of Bisclavret*, retains his human reason, and he too regains his human form. A similar theme is explored in the Latin tale of *Arthur and Gorlagon* (*ca.* 1200), in which a king is transformed into a wolf by the trickery of his wife but restored to human form with the help of another king.

The werewolf theme is, by and large, ignored in literature from the end of the Middle Ages until the nineteenth century, its appearance generally incidental. Cervantes, for example, makes use of the folklore of lycanthropy in *Persiles and Sigismunda* (1617), and a werewolf appears as a character in John Webster's *The Duchess of Malfi* (1613). Most mentions of lycanthropy during the Renaissance and Reformation occur in legal and theological rather than literary texts. The Inquisition, during which numerous individuals were convicted of being werewolves, is responsible for many of these texts. Among the most influential such discussions of lycanthropy are Francesco Guazzo's *Manual of Witches* (1608) and Jean de Nynauld's *Lycanthropie* (1615).

From the *Odyssey* on, travel is a ubiquitous feature in Western narrative, particularly fantasy. In addition to those works in which journeys to wondrous places occur incidentally, medieval authors continued to compose narratives devoted primarily to the description of such fantastic journeys, a continuation of the ancient *Reisefabulistik*. These tales tend to fall into two general groupings: travel to faraway lands, including actual trips to a realm of enchantment that might best be called the Other World, and dream visions in which the narrator sees the Other World without traveling there in the flesh.

The best and most widely read medieval travel book was *The Buke of John Maundeville* (*The Travels of Sir John Mandeville*) [1-50]. Originally written in Norman French *ca.* 1360, this narrative was soon translated into virtually every major European language, including Latin. The first English translation was made *ca.* 1385, and the translator claimed to be the original author. Although the work is ostensibly a firsthand account of experiences and a pilgrim's guide to Jerusalem and the Holy Land, Mandeville's *Travels* is in reality a unified fantasy that its author has created from a wide range of literary sources. The various natural and unnatural wonders described in the work are drawn mostly but not exclusively from the encyclopedic *Speculum Maius* (*ca.* 1360) of Vincent of Beauvais, and the author made extensive use of two fourteenth-century travel narratives, by a German monk named William of Boldensele and by the Italian friar Odoric of Pordenone, for his description of the Near and Far East. Mandeville describes in lavish detail the imaginary kingdom of the so-called Prester John in India. Beyond this realm, according to Mandeville, lies a desert and a "derke regyoun" that extends to the Earthly Paradise. Here, the author admits, neither he nor any other mortal has ever been, though many have tried to reach it by the swift rivers that flow from it.

Trips to the Earthly Paradise should be regarded as a subgroup of the journey to the Other World, to which the largest number of fantastic journey narratives in medieval literature belong. Sometime in the twelfth century such a story was grafted onto the legends of Alexander the Great. In the brief twelfth-century narrative known as the *Iter ad Paradisum* (*Journey to the Earthly Paradise*) [see 1-44], Alexander reaches the walls of the Earthly Paradise, where he is given a wondrous (and clearly symbolic) jewel that outweighs everything placed opposite it on a scale until it is covered with dust, at which point it is lighter than even a feather. The hero of the thirteenth-century French romance *Huon of Bordeaux* [1-39] actually reaches Paradise in his travels.[4]

A large number of Christian accounts of voyages to the Other World are clearly derived from Celtic mythology, which has a long tradition of tales about men whose travels take them to exotic places or even to the abodes of the dead. Many of these tales were translated into Latin. Among the earliest to survive in literary form is the *Echtrae Brain* (*Voyage of Bran*), regarded by most scholars as a work of the eighth century. Told of a wondrous land far away, Bran travels to the Island of Merriment and the Land of Women, where he and his crew remain for many years. When they return to Ireland, the first crewman to step ashore turns immediately to ashes; Bran and his men leave, never to return. A ninth-century tale, the *Immram Curaig Maile Duin* (*Voyage of Maelduin's Boat*), recounts the adventures of the hero after he sets out on the sea in search of his father's murderers. The amazing adventures that he and his crew experience include encounters with magic trees, ants as large as ponies and a cat that guards a treasure by burning to death any who trespass. Celtic mythology and Christian hagiography are fused in the Latin *Navigatio Sancti Brendani* (*Voyage of St. Brendan*) [1-91], which transforms what had been an expedition to a pagan

Elysium into a journey to the Christian Promised Land in which the fantastic elements are suffused with religious meaning.

The dream vision forms a separate genre of medieval fantasies that depict imagined travels to exotic or enchanted lands. This form of narrative is too vast in number and scope to deal with here. Dreams of course figure in the literatures of every culture. (A character in the *Epic of Gilgamesh* has a vision in sleep of the Afterworld.) Visions reach an unprecedented state of literary importance, however, in the medieval literature of Western Europe. The sources of these dream narratives include not only classical literature but also Judeo-Christian tradition.[5] Irish Christianity was a particularly rich source of such visions. Many, composed originally in the vernacular, were later translated into Latin. The two best known of these are the *Vision of Tundale* and the *Purgatory of St. Patrick*.

The most famous medieval dream visions trace their literary heritage back to Cicero's *Dream of Scipio*. This philosophic fable was known to the Christian Middle Ages through a commentary by Macrobius (*ca.* 400). Of no little importance is Macrobius's detailed discussion of the "truth" of dreams and other fictions (*figmenta*); Macrobius argues that some fictions lead the reader to perceive a deeper truth by stimulating the reader's mind to perceive some appearance of virtues (*quandam virtutum speciem*). Macrobius's treatment is but one of many justifications, based on Platonic principles, of allegory as both a form of literary creation and a tool of interpretation.

The thirteenth-century allegory *Roman de la Rose* (*Romance of the Rose*, 1230/1275) [1-73] begins with a mention of both the *Dream of Scipio* and Macrobius's commentary, and Chaucer begins *The Parliament of Fowls* (*ca.* 1382) with a lengthy discussion of the dream of Scipio as recorded by Cicero. Chaucer composed three other dream poems: *The Book of the Duchess* (1369), *The House of Fame* (1379) and his prologue to *The Legend of Good Women* (1386). English literature produced both a goodly number of dream vision narratives and some of the finest. Two of the most famous are by contemporaries of Chaucer. *The Pearl* (*ca.* 1400), almost certainly by the same poet who wrote *Sir Gawain and the Green Knight*, is both a vision and an allegory; in it, the poet laments his loss of a precious pearl, which as he sleeps appears to him in the form of a girl clad in white. During the same period (1365-85) that Chaucer and the *Pearl*-poet were writing, William Langland composed the three versions of his long poem *The Vision of William concerning Piers the Plowman* (*ca.* 1362-87), a complex work that combines allegory with social commentary in the frame of a dreamer's vision. Chaucer's work influenced a large number of imitations by both English and Scottish writers in the fifteenth and sixteenth centuries: for example, John Lydgate's *The Temple of Glass*; *The Kingis Quair* (*The King's Book*, a Scottish poem written *ca.* 1424 and widely attributed to King James I of Scotland); John Skelton's earliest surviving work, a dream vision called *The Bowge of Court*, as well as his later poem *The Garland of Laurel*.

The divergent strands of travel narrative and dream vision are but two of the many threads woven together by Dante in his *La Divina Commedia* (*The Divine Comedy*, 1360) [1-19]. Dante tells of his physical and spiritual sleep as a prelude to his entry into the forest, which begins his narrative. Dante's journey through the fantastic and symbolic landscapes of Hell, Purgatory and Heaven is also a narrative of spiritual pilgrimage that must be read—as Dante himself advises in a famous letter about his poem—concurrently on four levels of meaning. On another literary level, Dante's inclusive vision of a Christian universe is an extension of the genre of romance.

It is within the genre of the romance that the most profound and enduring contribution of the Middle Ages to the literature of fantasy occurs. The rise of the romance as a distinct literary genre in the twelfth century is associated with a complex series of cultural changes in Western Europe. The most important of these changes emerged from a momentous shift in theology that emphasized the humanness of Christ and the divine love expressed in his willingness to assume human form; now both theologians and secular writers began to explore human love as a manifestation of divine love. Concurrently, the human search for salvation began to be expressed as an active quest that was linked with and ennobled intellectual striving, an attitude first expressed in the late eleventh century by St. Anselm of Bec in the phrase *fides quaerens intellectum* ("faith seeking understanding"). The new genre of the romance is both a reflection and a development of this new vision of humanness that placed love and questing at the center of the Christian life.

Medieval romance is a genre that is easier to describe than define. As with the older Greek romances, love and adventure are inextricable elements, but while the medieval romances, particularly of the twelfth and early thirteenth centuries, are good stories, the story itself is not the point. As epics tend to be about action, romances are about meaning within action. Like Dante's journey to salvation through the love of Beatrice, those of the Arthurian knights-errant (Lancelot, Yvain, Galahad, Tristan) to win the love of an idealized lady or to find the Grail (Parsifal, Galahad) are outward manifestations of a deeper quest for understanding in a symbolically meaningful universe. The predilection of romances for the marvelous and the supernatural must be understood in this light. Such elements serve not only to evoke a sense of wonder but also to announce and direct the reader to deeper levels of meaning embedded in the text.

The earliest attempts to forge a new form of literature to express the new emphasis on love and intellectual questing took the form of retellings of material inherited from classical antiquity. That classical literature provided the material for the earliest authors of romance is not surprising, for in the eleventh and especially the twelfth centuries the authors of romance were clerks, that is, professional writers, usually attached to a court, who had been trained in grammar (the study of the Latin language and the interpretation of Latin literature) in the cathedral schools. The earliest extant romance of antiquity, the French *Roman de Thèbes* (*Romance of Thebes*) was composed in the mid-eleventh century. The poem was an immediate success, and its methods were soon imitated, as for example in the *Roman de Troie* (*Romance of Troy*) by Benoît de Ste.-Maure, whose version of the Trojan war, based not on Homer but on a late classical prose account, stressed the love affairs rather than the martial prowess of Achilles. Not long after, Vergil's *Aeneid* was recast as a romance. In the anonymous *Roman d'Enée* (*Romance of Aeneas*, 1185) the politically inspired marriage of Aeneas and Lavinia now takes center stage as a tale of passionate love.

In like manner, numerous romances based on the life of Alexander the Great were composed. These works combined depiction of Alexander's martial exploits and his travels to exotic lands with explorations of love and the emerging chivalric values of twelfth-century Europe. The best romances about Alexander, like those of Arthurian romance, explore the tension arising from the conflicting obligations of secular and spiritual excellence. The ultimate source for most of these fictional accounts was the Greek life of Alexander by Pseudo-Callisthenes. Much of the credit for the emergence of Alexander as the focus of a major series of fantastic narratives belongs to a certain Archpriest Leo of Naples, who in 952 translated the Greek *Alexander Romance* [1-44] into very mediocre Latin. Leo's Latin text was subsequently rewritten (to improve the Latin) and expanded (to include a wide range of moral lessons, legendary material and fantastic episodes) three times; these three expanded versions served as a source of numerous narratives composed in every major Western European language.

The French *Roman d'Alexandre* (*Romance of Alexander*), based on one of these expanded versions of Leo's translation, was begun in the early years of the twelfth century by Alberic de Briançon and continued by other poets. Alberic and his followers emphasized the fantastic nature of Alexander's adventures, including such episodes as his journey to the bottom of the sea, his journey through the air in a chariot pulled by griffins as well as his encounters with dog-headed men, flower-maidens growing in a forest, talking trees and other marvels. Other major Alexander romances in which marvels figure prominently include Alexander of Bernay's *Roman d'Alexandre* (1177), the Middle English *Kyng Alisaunder*, the Spanish *Libro de Alexandre* (*ca.* 1250) and the Swedish *Konung Alexander* (*ca.* 1280).

The Arthurian Tradition

Subjects taken from classical antiquity were soon augmented by tales about the "matter of Britain," stories about King Arthur and his court. The origins of the matter of Britain remain hidden in the obscurity of early Celtic myth and folklore. The first known mention of Arthur occurs in a Welsh poem (*Gododdin, ca.* 600), whose hero is praised as second only to Arthur. Although Arthur appears in other early sources, the work that brought him to the literary consciousness of Western Europe was Geoffrey of Monmouth's largely fictitious *Historia Regum Britanniae* (*History of the Kings of Britain*, 1130). Geoffrey, who may have been trying to create a British king to rival and even replace Charlemagne, offers his book not as fiction but as his translation of a "very old book" originally written in English. He introduces many of the basic elements of the Arthurian legend. He describes Arthur as a great king, defending his land against both the Romans and the barbarians, whose downfall is accomplished through the treachery of his nephew Mordred. Soon afterward, an Anglo-Norman poet named Robert Wace composed *Brut d'Angleterre* (*Brut*, 1155), a verse paraphrase and expansion of Geoffrey's pseudo-history that introduced the Round Table into the legend. Wace's poem was later translated into English by a priest named Layamon (*ca.* 1205).

Though Arthur was introduced into literature by British writers, the site of the literary development of the matter of Britain shifted almost immediately to France. The most profoundly influential as well as the earliest Arthurian romances that we know are those by the French poet Chrétien de Troyes. In addition to other works, Chrétien composed five romances drawn from the matter of Britain, the most significant of which are *Lancelot* (*ca.* 1180), *Yvain: Le Chevalier au Lion* (*Yvain: The Knight of the Lion, ca.* 1180) [1-16], and *Perceval: Li Contes del Graal* (*Perceval: The Story of the Grail, ca.* 1190) [1-17]. The role of fantasy in Chrétien's romances is inextricably linked not only with the mythic and folkloric origins of the tales themselves but also with the Platonic nature of his narratives, which exist simultaneously on two levels: the mutable world of experience and the unchanging world of transcendent truth. In Chrétien's romances, the knight's quest to attain the ideal of courtly excellence reflects a greater quest: that of the human being for spiritual perfection. By making the adventures of the knight an analogy for this spiritual quest, Chrétien was able to incorporate miraculous elements and events into his narratives. These marvels serve to direct the reader to meaning at a deeper level. In *Yvain*, for example, a knight marries the woman he desires before he has reached the maturity to behave as a true lover. Rejected by his wife through his own fault, Yvain descends into madness, recovering only through the help of a lion. Since Yvain first encounters this lion locked in combat with a serpent, the potential for a symbolic reading is immediately evident; but that symbolism has numerous interpretive possibilities (as years of scholarly disagreement prove) instead of one directed right reading.

In addition to the tales concerning the court of King Arthur, numerous medieval romances took for their subject the adventures of Charlemagne and his vassals. Among the most popular of these cycles were those concerning the exploits of Ogier the Dane, who was celebrated in the twelfth-century French epic *Chevalerie Ogier de Danemarcke* (*The Chivalry of Ogier the Dane*) and later in a fifteenth-century German epic. The most artful of the romances concerning Ogier is the *Enfances Ogier* (*Ogier's Childhood*), composed in the thirteenth century by Adenet le Roi, also the author of the romance *Cléomadès*, a wildly imaginative fantasy in which a wooden horse with the power of flight carries knights to a series of extraordinary adventures. The evolution of the fictional Ogier, like that of Alexander, reflects the tendency of medieval story cycles, even those grounded in historical characters or events, to grow increasingly fantastic. By the fifteenth century the legend even has Morgan Le Fay sending Ogier, one hundred years old but magically rejuvenated, to the court of King Arthur.

Whatever their matter, medieval romances took place in an imaginary world. The world of Arthurian romance derives much of its strangeness from its Celtic origins, a mythology based on the belief in an Other World that humans can enter, whose inhabitants they can challenge and where they can enjoy the love of fairy women. Other romances were set in faraway lands or, like the *Reisefabulistik*, transported characters there either unwillingly or of their own volition. The same predilection for the exotic can be found even in romances supposedly set in recognizable historic locales. The French romance *Huon de Bordeaux* (*Huon of Bordeaux, ca.* 1220) [1-39] and its companion the *Roman d'Auberon* (*Romance of Oberon, ca.* 1310) can be considered examples of the "parallel world" theme, for they embody a wholly imaginary Roman history where Cesarius, emperor of Rome, has married the fairy daughter of Judas Maccabeus. His son, Julius Caesar, is made ruler of Hungary after rescuing that country from a giant. Even different legendary traditions can be mingled: Oberon, king of the fairies, is the son of Caesar and Morgan Le Fay, whom Caesar had met when he visited the court of King Arthur.

Among the most fantastic and marvel-filled of the medieval romances, *Huon of Bordeaux* enjoys a long history in Western literature. It belongs to the body of legends concerning Charlemagne and his vassals, taking its origin from an event during the reign of Charlemagne's son, Charles the Bald, whose son was mortally wounded in a duel. The romance, which appears in literary form for the first time in the thirteenth century, has Huon of Bordeaux provoked to murder by Charlemagne's son, named Charlot. Charlemagne requires Huon to travel to Baghdad, kiss the emir's daughter three times, bring back a hair of the emir's beard along with four of his teeth and kill the most prominent Saracen at the court. Huon succeeds in each of the tasks, and the emir's daughter, Esclarmonde, even falls in love with him. With the help of the Fairy King Auberon, Huon and Esclarmonde escape together and return to France after a series of fabulous adventures. Huon's adventures proved extremely popular. After its translation by Lord Berners (1525–33), the *Romance of Huon*, and more specifically the character of the Fairy King Oberon, exerted a strong influence on later English literature. Elizabethan writers seemed especially fond of him; Oberon plays a major role in Edmund Spenser's great romance *The Faerie Queene* (1590–96) [1-79], Shakespeare's *A Midsummer Night's Dream* (1591–96) [1-76] and the masque *Oberon, the Fairy Prince* (1611) by Ben Jonson. A compelling portrait of the Fairy Court appears in *Nymphidia* (1627) [1-21] by Michael Drayton, a contemporary of Spenser and Shakespeare and a prolific creator of a wide range of otherwise forgettable works. The most influential treatment of Oberon in later literature is the romantic epic *Oberon* (1780) by the German author Christoph Wieland.

Romance, especially romance based on Arthurian themes, was the dominant narrative genre in the thirteenth century, but during this period it took on new forms. The great changes in thirteenth-century romance are by and large a product of a shift in authorship from clerks to churchmen. The Arthurian narratives of this period are characterized by two new goals: first, the attempt to elucidate from the matter of Britain a meaning that was more obviously related to Christian doctrine; second, a desire to combine the fictional histories of the Holy Grail and the reign of King Arthur into a coherent whole. Both these tendencies can be observed for the first time in two late twelfth-century French verse romances, *Joseph of Arimathea* and *Merlin* (*ca.* 1190), by Robert of Boron. By far the most popular and influential of these comprehensive romances was the so-called Vulgate Cycle (1215–30). The three prose narratives in French that comprise this cycle are *Lancelot* [1-43], *Queste del Saint Graal* (*Quest of the Holy Grail*) [1-66] and *Li Mort Artu* (*The Death of Arthur*). Each was composed by a separate author, but the entire project may have been guided by a supervising "architect," for the three are artfully linked together by a complex network of analogous events and direct references.

The tendency of medieval romance to use story as a means of expressing deeper meaning persisted. In these narratives, however, the ambiguous symbolism of the marvels in Chrétien's romance is replaced by a precise allegorical interpretation. At the same time, the Vulgate Cycle not only seeks to weave all the disparate threads of Arthurian legend into one whole fabric, but also differs from twelfth-century romance by stressing the historicity rather than the otherworldliness of Arthur's court. The *Queste*, for example, concludes with a declaration of its historical authenticity, with the supposed author Walter Map claiming to have taken his tale from records based on an eyewitness account of one of the Arthurian knights (Bors) that was preserved in the library at Salisbury; and the *Mort Artu* concludes with a similar claim to have recorded everything "according to the way it happened."

The thirteenth-century prose Arthurian romances, then, were based on the combining of two incompatible elements: claiming historical veracity on the one hand while on the other justifying themselves as expressing an allegory whose surface narrative is a shell beneath which lies a kernel of religious rather than historical truth. Only in Scripture, however, could allegorical and historical truth coexist without contradiction. The authors of romances had somehow to reconcile the two elements. In the *Mort Artu,* the author avoids this contradiction by largely eschewing marvels. In the *Lancelot* and *Queste* portions of the Vulgate Cycle, however, there is a heightening of the role of fantasy. Sacred vessels become airborne, stones float in the air, cloud-wrapped knights are magically transported over long distances. This facet is complemented by a greater emphasis on providing a clear symbolic meaning for marvelous events. Marvels, especially in the *Queste,* are now doubly presented in the narrative, as actual occurrences and allegorical lessons.

Romance retained its popularity and vitality throughout the later Middle Ages and Renaissance. Two general tendencies can be observed in these later romances: an increased role of the fantastic and the continued popularity of encyclopedic narratives. Most fail to maintain the creative balance between idea and event that characterizes the best twelfth- and thirteenth-century romances. Marvels, divorced from their symbolic value, are multiplied in an effort to keep the reader in a state of wonder. Typical is the massive French romance *Perceforest* (*ca.* 1330). Filled with wonderful events but lacking in enchantment, it seeks to unite the Arthurian story of the Grail with the legendary history of Alexander. Four romances tower over all others from this era: in English literature, Malory's *Morte d'Arthur* and *The Faerie Queene* by Edmund Spenser; in Italian, Ariosto's *Orlando Furioso*; in Spanish, *Amadis de Gaule.*

Sir Thomas Malory's *Morte d'Arthur* [1-49] both begins and ends a literary tradition. On the one hand, it represents the culmination of the matter of Britain in medieval English literature. On the other hand, no book has had a greater influence on the subsequent treatment in English of Arthurian narrative in general and fantasy in particular. The critical role of British authors in the early development of Arthurian legend has been mentioned. In the thirteenth and fourteenth centuries most of the major characters and tales of Arthurian legend already appear in English works, but with one exception, the works are both derived from and inferior to French works. Among these English romances are *Arthour and Merlin* (1250), *Yvain and Gawain* (1350) and the *Alliterative Morte d'Arthure* (1360).

The exception to the general drabness of medieval English romances is *Sir Gawain and the Green Knight* (*ca.* 1370) [1-25]. The poet's more restricted narrative focus, upon a few characters and the ramifications of one critical event, aligns his work more with the earlier romances of Chrétien de Troyes than with the encyclopedic tendencies of most fourteenth-century romances. *Sir Gawain and the Green Knight* is also among the most clearly fantastic of all Arthurian narratives. Recent literary theory has emphasized the aspect of fantasy as a literary game, and from beginning to end, both games and the fantastic play a prominent, indeed central, role in this romance. It begins with the sudden appearance at Arthur's court of a strange green knight, who challenges anyone there to a game: to strike a blow at him, if he can return the blow a year later. When Sir Gawain accepts the challenge and decapitates the green knight, the knight picks up his severed head and leaves. A year later Gawain travels to meet the knight, but pauses at a castle where he is involved in another game. With the agreement that the two men will share at the end of the day whatever he has won, the host goes hunting on three consecutive days, while leaving his guest within the castle, where the host's wife tries to seduce him. This game, like the first, is revealed at the end of the narrative to be a plot by Morgan Le Fay to embarrass Arthur and his court. The poet, presumably the same artist who composed *The Pearl*, has drawn on a wide variety of sources, including Celtic mythology, to create a narrative that invites a number of interpretations. The poet even dwells on the "game" of symbolic reading in a meditation on the multiple levels of meaning suggested by the pentangle (five-pointed star) that decorates Gawain's shield. In this regard too *Sir Gawain and the Green Knight* is closer in spirit to the ambiguous symbolism of Chrétien than to the more narrowly Christological allegory of later medieval romance.

Without question the most important contribution to the development of Arthurian narrative in English literature is the encyclopedic retelling of the matter of Britain by Malory that was published by William Caxton in 1485 under the title *Le Morte d'Arthur*. Malory took numerous earlier romances, mostly the thirteenth-century French Vulgate Cycle but also at least one English work, the *Alliterative Morte d'Arthure*, which he translated, altered, occasionally abridged and wove into a unified narrative of extraordinary power. It is now generally accepted that he changed his sources in accord with his own controlling artistic vision. One example may serve as representative. In his French source, the *Queste*, a monk warns Lancelot to avoid Guinevere when he returns to Arthur's court; once Lancelot renews their affair, the implied judgment on his culpability is clear. Malory, however, in a passage that otherwise follows his model rather closely, adds the slight but significant phrase "as best you can" to the monk's warning, and in so doing gives a new level of interpretive possibility to the later events. Occasionally disparaged but continuously read since its publication, Malory's version of the Arthurian world has exercised by far the greatest influence on later English writers. Although Malory tends to suppress the role of the supernatural in his retellings, nonetheless the presence in his narrative of such characters as Merlin and Morgan Le Fay as well as a wide range of marvels canonized the presence of the fantastic in later English Arthurian fiction.

Renaissance Fantasy

Arthurian romances retained their popularity on the Continent, especially in Italy and Spain, where elements of fantasy and the supernatural played an increasing role with the passage of time. In Italy the more serious themes of the quest for the Grail and the death of Arthur were usually ignored. Rather, the matter of Britain was often fused with material drawn from epics concerning

Charlemagne and his knights to create *romans d'aventure* stressing love affairs and extraordinary adventures. The two most famous Italian romances, Matteo Boiardo's *Orlando Innamorato* (*Roland in Love*, 1483) and Ludovico Ariosto's *Orlando Furioso* (*Roland Insane*, 1532), are both based on such a fusion of Carolingian and Arthurian material, and in both fantasy plays a major role.

The Italian romance tradition is primarily concerned with the career of Roland, the hero of the aforementioned French *chanson de geste* known as *The Song of Roland*. There is evidence from as early as the fourteenth century of Italian writers adapting and translating French narratives about Roland and the other peers of Charlemagne. The first major literary treatment of Roland in Italian, Luigi Pulci's *Morgante* (1484), introduces the emphasis on fantasy that will reach its apex in Ariosto's great romances. Pulci retells the story of Roland at Roncevaux, but only after describing a series of fabulous adventures in the Levant that include Roland's capturing Babylon. Among Pulci's innovations are his introduction into the story of the theme of Roland's passionate love for his wife, Alda ("la belle Aude" of *The Song of Roland*), and an early example of the madness that would become central to Ariosto's version. Pulci's work abounds in fantastic elements—sorcerers, monsters and giants; indeed, his most compelling achievements as an artist are his portrayals of the evil Astarotte and the giant Morgante (from whom the romance received its title).

It was Boiardo, with his *Orlando Innamorato*, who, in his retelling of Roland's life, first displayed the rich artistic possibilities of combining the exotic adventure tale with the theme of love. The passion inspired by Angelica, daughter of the Great Khan, is the unifying theme of Boiardo's tale. Roland's pursuit of her involves him inevitably in the fantastic adventures common to Arthurian romance. Indeed, Boiardo's narrative is a phantasmagoria of enchanted gardens, magicians and knights who battle monsters and are able to rout entire armies. But the fantastic elements in Boiardo's romance are interwoven, at least in part, with its central theme and also, at least occasionally, invite reading at a symbolic level. Its many enchanted gardens (among them those of Morgana, Dragontina and Falerina), which first attract because of the lushness with which they are depicted, appeal also to the intellect as symbolic Hells that reflect the internal lost state of their enchanted victims.

The finest of Italian romances, and arguably the pinnacle of Renaissance literature, is Ariosto's *Orlando Furioso* [1-4]. Like so many romances, Ariosto's is a continuation and transformation of another work, in this instance Boiardo's *Orlando Innamorato*. As a fantasy, *Orlando Furioso* is a triumph of extravagance spiced by ironic amusement and refined by elegance of language. Ariosto's light-hearted and generally unrestrained use of the marvelous and magical stands in sharp contrast to the thematic, symbolic tradition of early medieval romance. As the *Iliad* begins with the anger of Achilles, so Ariosto takes as the starting point of his narrative Roland's madness, a jealous frenzy that arises from his love for Angelica. The *Reisefabulistik* plays a large part in the narrative. Among the marvelous journeys is that of Astolfo to the moon to recover his friend Orlando's lost wits. The characters also wander this world from France to Cathay, sometimes on a flying hippogriff (half-horse, half-griffin). The episodes take the reader through the history of romance fiction: prodigious feats of arms, enchanted gardens, incredibly convenient wishing rings, enchanted palaces that arise and disappear as the plot requires. Ariosto populates his imagined world with a wide variety of monsters and giants. Yet the power of the narrative emerges only partially from Ariosto's imagination; his wit leads often to a mesh of the fantastic with the mundane. One example must suffice: the king Ruggiero, riding on the hippogriff, saves Angelica from a sea monster; but when, maddened by desire, he attempts to possess her, he is thwarted by his inability to take his armor off.

Even Ariosto's unrestrained imagination and exuberant wit are outdone by François Rabelais, author of *Gargantua and Pantagruel* (1532–64) [1-67], the English title by which his five-part comic fantasy is known. Like that of Aristophanes, Rabelais's comedy is anchored not in satire but in fantasy. It protests— no, it disregards—all limits. As Mikhail Bakhtin has shown, *Gargantua and Pantagruel* aims at the defeat, through laughter, "of authoritarian commandments and prohibitions."[6] In Rabelais's fabulous world, "every constraint may be suspended at will in the limitless good cheer of a new Saturnian age."[7]

For different but related reasons, the immediate success of both *Orlando Furioso* and *Gargantua and Pantagruel* gave rise to aesthetic controversies that were intensified toward the end of the sixteenth century largely as a result of two developments: the publication of Francesco Robortello's commentary on Aristotle's *Poetics* (1548) and the climate of moral seriousness in literature fostered by the Council of Trent (1545–63). The literary theory of the late sixteenth century eventually contributed to the decline of romance as a major literary genre and to fantasy as the preeminent mode of European narrative. Basing much of their thinking on narrow and in some cases distorted interpretations of Aristotle, particularly his concept of *mimesis* (imitation), the Renaissance theorists emphasized a series of dichotomies that continue to affect Western criticism. Among these were the separation of high art from popular art and verisimilitude from fantasy. In an era of growing scientific awareness and disputes over the nature of religious truth, marvelous fictions lost their place of honor. Ariosto's fantasy was not to engender any progeny of note in Italy.

A similar line of literary history occurs in Spain. In the fifteenth and early sixteenth centuries, the romance of chivalry proved even more popular and influential in Spain. The most important contribution of late medieval Spanish literature to the tradition of romance and to fantasy was the publication of the prose romance known as *Amadis de Gaule* (*Amadis of Gaul*) [1-54]. The origin and authorship of *Amadis* are matters of conjecture and argument. The first known literary version was published in 1508, but its author, Garcia Ordonez de Montalvo, was in fact retelling and transforming a late thirteenth-century Portuguese romance. *Amadis*, though influenced by Arthurian romance, differs from Arthurian (and Carolingian) romances in that it is wholly fictitious. The romance is placed vaguely in both time ("not many years after" the crucifixion of Christ) and place. Its scenes are set in a mythical Britain and an imaginary Firm Island. In Montalvo's version, Amadis is a thoroughly idealized knight, and stories of his incredible military triumphs (the hero never suffers defeat) are intertwined with the story of his love for Oriana, daughter of the king of England. Marvels abound. Amadis fights against monsters and magicians, especially Arcelaus the Enchanter, from whom he rescues his beloved Oriana. The Arthurian inspiration for characters and events is not difficult to discern. Arcelaus is derived from Merlin, and the good fairy Urganda the Unknown is descended, at least in part, from Morgan Le Fay. *Amadis of Gaul* was both popular and praised. Ariosto and Tasso both lauded its excellence, and Cervantes held it in high esteem, calling it the finest example of chivalric romance.

It would be difficult to overestimate either the popularity of Montalvo's romance or its impact on the literature and culture of sixteenth-century Spain. *Amadis* defined for subsequent writers of chivalric romance that genre's nature and constituent elements: a wandering prince, constant battles and tournaments, the service of a beloved maiden and, of course, ubiquitous marvels. The popularity of *Amadis of Gaul* led to its becoming the most "continued" work in the history of Western literature. The entire series eventually reached twelve volumes, presenting the adventures of various relatives of Amadis. Montalvo initiated this history by adding to the four books of his model a fifth, entitled *Sergas de Esplándian* (*The Exploits of Esplandian*), which recounts the adventures of Amadis's son. This book, far inferior to the preceding four, places even greater emphasis on marvels and fantastic adventures, and the supernatural becomes an even more prominent element in the subsequent works based on *Amadis*. In the typical sixteenth-century romance of chivalry, the knight is in conflict with one enchanter, aided by another. He confronts monsters, overcomes obstacles created by magic, travels vast distances in conveyances propelled by magic and may be held captive by enchantment in a castle for a protracted length of time until he escapes, again usually through supernatural help.

With one exception, these continuations are but poor exaggerations of their original model. They are characterized by larger casts of characters and even more complex plots that increased the frequency but not the imaginative quality of fantastic elements. Many adopted a pseudoarchaic and highly mannered form of expression in imitation of Montalvo's style. The exception to this general mediocrity is the ninth book in the series, *Amadis de Grecia* (*Amadis of Greece*, 1535), by Feliciano de Silva, which recounts the adventures of Amadis's grandson and his love for the queen of Babylon. Silva's narrative revived interest in the *Amadis* series after unfavorable public reaction to the eighth book, *Lisuarte de Grecia* (*Lisuarte of Greece*). Silva both imitated and altered the conventional elements of the series. As in *Orlando Furioso*, Silva's exaggerations of typical supernatural motifs reflect a kind of ironic criticism. Moreover, though Silva retains the narrative importance of love in his story, the love he describes is less idealized and more sensual.

In addition to the many continuations that it spawned, *Amadis* also inspired numerous new romances. Chief among these is the series based on the exploits of the hero Palmerin. The first work in this series, which at times rivalled *Amadis* in popularity, is *Palmerin de Oliva* (*Palmerin of Oliva*, 1511). The final volume, regarded by many as the best, is *Palmerin de Inglaterra* (*Palmerin of England*, 1547), known to many modern readers as one of the romances spared by the barber and priest who examine Don Quixote's library. Robert Southey published an English translation of *Palmerin of England* in 1807.

The power of *Amadis* and its successors to fascinate readers was not limited to Spain. The romances were widely read in England in the sixteenth and seventeenth centuries in translations made by Anthony Munday.[8] *Amadis* and the romance tradition it inspired form one thread of the complex fabric woven by Sir

Philip Sidney to form his pastoral romance *Arcadia* (1590) [1-78]. Of *Amadis* Sidney noted that while it may move men to exercise "courtesy, liberality and especially courage," it "wanteth much of a perfect poesy."[9] Sidney combined the newly popular Italian pastoral with the chivalric romance and the ancient Greek romance (specifically the *Ethiopica* of Heliodorus) to create a new form of fiction. Virtually every cultured Elizabethan was familiar with Sidney's romance, which proved a major source of inspiration and established the genre of pastoral romance in English for the next century.[10]

The influence of *Amadis* can even be observed, though faintly, in the other great romance of Renaissance English literature, Sir Edmund Spenser's *The Faerie Queene* (Books I–III, 1590; Books IV–VI, 1596; *Cantos of Mutabilitie*, 1609) [1-79]. In contrast to the ironic tone of *Orlando Furioso*, which Spenser avowedly was trying to eclipse, *The Faerie Queene* returned to the tradition of systematic allegorical fantasy; his romance is "medieval" in the best sense of the term. The characters, monsters and events of his complex narrative all exist on multiple levels of meaning. The supernatural elements have "an important spiritual significance . . . and [are] integrated with Christian allegorical and symbolic meanings."[11]

In drama as well as fiction the literature of Renaissance England displayed a strong interest in the fantastic and supernatural. Apparitions, especially ghosts urging vengeance, are stock dramatic devices of both Elizabethan and Jacobean theater. The ghost in *Hamlet* (*ca.* 1601) [1-74] is merely the most famous of a long line. Revenge-seeking spirits include the ghost of Don Andrea in Thomas Kyd's *The Spanish Tragedy* (*ca.* 1587); the ghost of Gorlois, in Thomas Hughes's *The Misfortunes of Arthur* (1588), who seeks to "glut on revenge"; and the spirits who appear to urge vengeance in George Chapman's *Revenge of Bussy D'Ambois* (1612) and in *The Changeling* (1622) by Thomas Middleton and William Rowley. An exception to the revenge-ghost character is the ghost of the murdered king in Cyril Tourneur's *The Atheist's Tragedy* (1611), who urges his son "to leave revenge to the King of Kings."

Sorcery also appealed to the imagination and art of dramatists. The witches who appear at the beginning of Shakespeare's *Macbeth* (*ca.* 1606) [1-75] have many counterparts. Hecate, chief of witches, presides over the preparation of a similar brew in Thomas Middleton's *The Witch* (1609), and Maudlin, the Witch of Papplewick, is a major character in Ben Jonson's *The Sad Shepherd* (1637). Though witches are almost always malevolent figures, *The Witch of Edmonton* (1621), written by John Ford, Thomas Dekker and Samuel Rowley, presents a sympathetic portrait of a woman driven into a pact with the devil by the cruelty of her neighbors. Dramas about male conjurors include Robert Greene's comedy *Friar Bacon and Friar Bungay* (1589), Greene and Henry Chettle's tragedy *John of Bordeaux* (1590) and of course Shakespeare's *The Tempest* (*ca.* 1611) [1-77].

The most famous conjuror of Elizabethan drama is without question the title character of Christopher Marlowe's *The Tragical History of Dr. Faustus* (1604) [1-52]. The main source for Marlowe's drama was a German chapbook (*Das Volksbuch von Doktor Faust*, 1587) that had been translated into English in 1592. This German account, based on the life of a real sixteenth-century individual, a strange mixture of scholar and charlatan, who had made a pact with the devil that cost him his soul, strongly condemns Faust. The English translation, on the other hand, while it condemns Faust's dealings with Satan, is more sympathetic to the thirst for learning that impelled him. Marlowe's version is still more complex; he makes Faust a symbol of the Renaissance spirit of inquiry, a man driven to transgress human limitations for the sake of knowledge. Marlowe was not the only Renaissance dramatist to deal with the Faustian theme. Pedro Calderón de la Barca's *El magico prodigioso* (*The Wonderful Magician*, 1637) deals with a pact made by Cyprian with the devil. Other playwrights on the Continent imitated or transformed Marlowe's *Dr. Faustus*. In an odd twist, the Faust theme became extremely popular on the puppet stage, though in this manifestation comedy rather than tragedy prevailed. There the legend languished until its rediscovery and recovery as a theme of serious literature in the late eighteenth century.

Neither the importance of the fantastic in Shakespearean drama nor the importance of Shakespeare in the history of fantasy should be underestimated. I have already made cursory mention of the role of the fantastic in several of Shakespeare's dramas. In addition to *Hamlet*, he makes use of ghosts in *Richard III* (1594) and *Julius Caesar* (1599). The supernatural is most prominent in *Macbeth*, with Banquo's ghost and the three oracular apparitions that come to warn Macbeth, in addition to the "weird sisters," the three witches. Among the comedies, peripheral fantastic elements can be found in the idealized setting of *As You Like It* (1599), and a statue miraculously comes to life in *The Winter's Tale* (1610). In two comedies, however, fantasy is central, and in them Shakespeare's fantastic art reaches its zenith. *A Midsummer Night's Dream* (1595-6) [1-76] takes its characters to an enchanted wood where Oberon and Titania, king and queen of the fairies, rule; where magic love potions work; and where Puck, Oberon's mischievous lieutenant, turns Bottom's head into that of an ass. *The Tempest* (*ca.* 1611) [1-77], with its enchanted island and magic, is not only a fantasy but also a play about the role of the imagination in life and art. Shakespeare's prominent use of fantastic elements has particular importance for the history of English literature, for the revival of fantasy by the English Romantics in the nineteenth century owes much to their view of Shakespeare as a fantasist. The confidence of writers like Samuel Taylor Coleridge and John Keats that in writing fantasy they were recovering a major feature of their finest literary tradition rests in large part on their admiration for Shakespeare and their belief that by engaging in the writing of fantasy they were following his lead.

By the beginning of the seventeenth century, prose had become the primary medium for fiction both in England and throughout Europe. Despite the growing popularity of more realistic fiction, fantastic narratives continued to be written and, just as important, read. Modern critical studies, which tend to approach the fiction of the seventeenth century primarily as an embryonic stage in the development of the realistic novel, have overlooked or undervalued a number of intriguing fantasies produced during this period. I have mentioned above the continuing popularity of the *Amadis* series, which prompted the creation of a large number of late sixteenth- and early seventeenth-century chivalric romances. Among the most popular of these was Richard Johnson's *The Seven Champions of Christendome* (Part I, 1596; Part II, 1597), a work brimming with astounding and frequently supernatural events. In one chapter, for example, Saint Dennis, who had "liued seuen yeares in the shape of a Hart," manages, with the magical aid of his horse, to recover his own true shape as well as to restore that of a princess who had been transformed into a mulberry tree. The opposite extreme of the popular romance, which was almost devoid of intellectual content, was surely the allegorical fable, which tended toward obvious if not always enjoyable moralizing. And yet the most famous, most read and most influential fantasist of the seventeenth century was surely John Bunyan, author of three allegorical narratives, *The Pilgrim's Progress* (Part I, 1678; Part II, 1684) [1-12], *Mr. Badman* (1680) and *The Holy War* (1682). Often imitated during the next century, Bunyan, though occasionally tiresome, continued the long tradition of embedding a philosophic or religious discourse within an entertaining fantastic tale.

Other traditional forms of fantasy persisted. Tales of imaginary voyages retained their popularity, but with a significant new direction. The steady development of the scientific approach to traveling that began in the Renaissance changed the nature of travel literature for all time. Most, and certainly the best, seventeenth-century travel narratives should be regarded less as fantasy than as precursors of science fiction, that is, tales whose fantastic events are made plausible by the use of a rhetoric of science. Works like Francis Godwin's *The Man in the Moone* (1638) and Cyrano de Bergerac's *Histoire comique des états et empires de la lune* (*The Comical History of the States and Empires of the Moon and Sun,* 1659; English 1687) take pains to establish the scientific possibility of the journeys and worlds they depict. Of the voyages that are unquestionably fantasy, one often but unfairly neglected work of the seventeenth century deserves special mention. In the preface to her alluring romance *The Blazing World* (1666) [1-13], Margaret Cavendish unabashedly admits that she has "made a world of my own," since Fortune gave her no real one to conquer. In a provocative innovation, Cavendish's imaginary traveler is a woman. The Aristophanic urge to transcend limits through fantasy persisted as well.

In the eighteenth century the literature of the imaginary voyage grew increasingly satiric, as in Jonathan Swift's fantasy *Gulliver's Travels* (1726) [1-81], or was made more scientifically plausible, as in Robert Paltock's *The Life and Adventures of Peter Wilkins* (1751). On the other hand, the eighteenth century would also produce the most unabashedly mendacious teller of travel tales since Homer's Odysseus in the person of Baron Münchhausen. Strange to say, Rudolph Erich Raspe's *Baron Münchhausen's Narrative of His Marvellous Travels and Campaigns in Russia* (1795) [1-70] was intended in part as a parody of the true but incredible reports by the English explorer James Bruce of his exploration of the Nile, which had mistakenly been labeled lies by such skeptical readers as Samuel Johnson and Horace Walpole.

In summary, the growing rationalist emphasis of seventeenth- and eighteenth-century European thought led to a diminished role of the fantastic in art and literature. Cervantes had signaled the end of the chivalric romance with *Don Quixote* (1605, 1615), and the intellectual climate of the eighteenth century, which was dominated by scientific empiricism, fostered the growth of realism in literature and the visual arts. The marvelous and the supernatural came to be regarded as manifestations of regressive superstition and not of the imaginative power of human intelligence. The major development in the fiction of the seventeenth and eighteenth centuries was the ascendance of the novel and its emphasis on the depiction of observable reality. Most accounts of the history of fiction chronicle this development almost exclusively. The resulting imbalance in literary history has led to the neglect of a number of first-rate fantasies. Alain René Laesage, for example, is praised for *Gil Blas* (1747), often called the first novel of manners, while his fantasy masterpiece *Le Diable Boîteux (The Devil on Two Sticks* 1707) [1-45] is rarely mentioned. At the center of Jacques Cazotte's ingenious *Le Diable amoureux (The Devil in Love,* 1772) [1-14] is a female demon summoned by a young soldier. Of lesser art and value are François-Augustin Moncrif's *Adventures de Zeloîde et d'Amanzarifdine* (1714), an adventure tale set in India; *Le Sopha (The Sofa,* 1745) by Claude-Prosper Crébillon *Fils* and the verse narratives of Stanislas-Jean Boufflers; but their existence and apparent popularity attest to a continuing interest in nonrealistic fiction.

The rise of realistic fiction created for critics and writers an alternative form of fiction, measured against which fantasy seemed somehow lacking. Indeed, by the end of the seventeenth century William Congreve could devote the preface to his *Incognita: or, Love and Duty Reconciled. A Novel* (1692) to drawing a clear distinction between the romance and the novel: "Romances give more of Wonder, Novels more Delight," with romances "composed of . . . miraculous Contingencies and impossible Performances." By the end of the eighteenth century the distinction is even clearer. The "eminent characteristic of each," the critic George Canning writes in the periodical *The Microcosm* (1787), may be "fiction." But there the resemblance ends, for the fiction of romance "is restricted by no fetters of reason, or of truth; but gives a loose to lawless imagination." In sum, it is fantastic. The novel, on the other hand, "is shackled with a thousand restraints . . . by the barriers of reason."[12] The long tradition in Western literature of transcending limits through the exercise of the creative imagination had been replaced, temporarily, by an aesthetic position that willingly assumed shackles and barriers.

Fairy and Folk Tales

Nonetheless, in addition to the isolated works cited above, the late seventeenth and eighteenth centuries witnessed two developments of great importance for the history of fantasy. The first of these was the invention of the literary fairy tale. Fairy tales and other forms of oral folk narrative had often been incorporated into fantastic literature—Apuleius's retelling of the tale of "Cupid and Psyche," for example—and as early as the mid-sixteenth century the Italian writer Gianfrancesco Straparola had included more artful versions of traditional tales in his collection of stories entitled *Le tredici piacevoli notti (Thirty Pleasant Nights,* 1550). Another Italian writer, Giambattista Basile, included in his collection *Pentamerone* (1634-36) literary retellings of such folktales as "Snow White" and "Sleeping Beauty."

The most significant figure in the creation of the literary fairy tale was the Frenchman Charles Perrault. An accomplished poet (he was elected to the Académie Française in 1671) and champion of modern literature, Perrault's most enduring literary achievements are his fairy tales. Throughout the eighteenth century, particularly in France, collections of fairy tales were published. Evidence of the passion of eighteenth-century French readers for fairy tales can be seen in the forty-one volumes of the series *Cabinet de Fées*, or Library of Fairy Tales (1785–89). Most of these fairy tales, however, were composed for a sophisticated adult readership. The fairy tales (1698) of Comtesse d'Aulnoy [1-7], for example, are long and intricate, clearly not designed for children. Perrault's influence can be traced to both his talent as a storyteller and his decision to write his fairy tales for children. He is widely and justly regarded as the author of the first children's book, the collection of tales—drawn from oral sources as well as earlier literary collections such as those of Straparola and Basile—that was published in Paris in 1697 as *Histoires et contes du temps passé, avec des moralités*, though with the subtitle *Contes de ma Mère l'Oye* (*Tales of Mother Goose*) [1-60]. Perrault's collection, which was translated into English in 1729, proved enormously influential, and became the source for the best-known versions of such stories as "Cinderella" and "Little Red Riding Hood."

Included in the *Cabinet de Fées* was another traditional collection of stories that was to exert enormous influence on Western literature, Antoine Galland's translation *Les Mille et une nuit* (*The Thousand and One Nights*) [1-23], the first volume of which appeared in 1704. The stories that comprise *The Thousand and One Nights* were drawn from various sources. The frame story, of the princess who postpones her execution by telling a story each night, is probably Indian; the tales themselves, including the fabulous voyages of Sinbad, are situated in a wide range of places. Many of the stories are of Indian origin, but were recast by Islamic storytellers. Galland's translation, completed in 1717, remained standard well into the nineteenth century, and parts of it were even retranslated into Arabic. Galland's version was translated into English, as *Arabian Nights Entertainments*, for the first time in 1706.

Galland's translations unleashed a torrent of interest in Arabian and other Oriental literature. This interest took three main creative forms. First, others translated original manuscripts. The most prominent of these translators was Pétis de la Croix, who translated a collection of Persian tales into French as *Histoire de la sultane de Perse et des visirs, contes turcs* (1707, published in English as *Persian Tales* 1710–12) and *Les mille et un jour, contes persanes* (1710–12) [1-61]. Actual translations, however, were far outnumbered by pseudotranslations, that is, original fictions that claimed to be translations. The most popular French pseudotranslator, Thomas-Simon Gueulette, produced collections of pretended Chinese, Mogul and Tartarian tales [see 1-36]. In England, James Ridley published under the pseudonym of Charles Morell *Tales of the Genii* [1-55], an uninspired but widely read collection of invented stories masquerading as translations. Such pretense, of course, has a long and honorable tradition in Western fantasy. Geoffrey of Monmouth, remember, had presented his history of King Arthur as the translation into Latin of an earlier work, and numerous later romances continued this conceit.

Finally, the popularity of the *Arabian Nights* inspired a large number of original fantasies set in the exotic Orient.[13] Voltaire makes specific reference to the *Arabian Nights* in the introduction to his philosophic fantasy *Zadig* (1747) [1-90]. Among his prodigious output as an author, Voltaire composed three other major *contes philosophiques*: *Micromégas* (1752), the eponymous hero of which is a giant inhabitant of the star Sirius; *Le Taureau blanc* (*The White Bull*, 1774)

[1-89] and of course his best-known narrative, *Candide* (1759). In the Age of Reason, even fantasy was employed to further the primacy of rational thought. Published within a few weeks of *Candide* was another fantasy of the Orient, the philosophic romance *Rasselas* (1759) [1-40] by Samuel Johnson. Also set in the Orient is *Manuscrit trouvé à Saragosse* (*The Saragossa Manuscript*, 1804) [1-65] by the Polish Count Potocki. Perhaps the most famous of the eighteenth-century Oriental fantasies is *Vathek* [1-8], written in French by William Beckford, but first published in 1786 in Samuel Henley's English translation. Beckford, interestingly enough, presents his romance as a translation. These narratives all present an imagined Orient, a fairyland somewhere in the remote East, rather than attempting to recreate historical or cultural reality.

A second form of fairy tale emerged during the florescence of German Romanticism, some of whose most influential authors cultivated the form of short narrative called *Märchen*. This term includes but has a broader range than the English term "fairy tale." The *Märchen* can in fact refer to the *Volksmärchen*, that is, the traditional popular tale such as those collected by the Brothers Grimm, or to the more artful tales (i.e., those by Perrault) written in imitation of the folktale. On the other hand, the term was also used to refer to the *Kunstmärchen*, in practice less the "artful folktale" suggested by the label than a form of sophisticated philosophic allegory. The *Kunstmärchen* is an uncomfortable amalgam that attempts to evoke both the wonder of folk literature and intellectual speculation. Among the first German authors to compose or refashion fairy tales was Johann Musaeus [see 1-56], who earlier had fashioned a reputation with two satiric novels. Novalis, who composed numerous *Märchen*, claimed to see in the fairy tale a reflection of the original union of the human mind with nature. Ludwig Tieck, who later turned to more realistic fiction, also wrote numerous *Kunstmärchen*. He eventually collected his fairy tales and other writings into one volume and welded them together by a frame story (young men and women debating the merits of fairy tales and other forms of fiction). This collection, *Tales from the Phantasus* [1-83], is a major document of German fantasy, and includes his play *Der Gestiefelte Kater*, a satiric treatment of the Puss 'n Boots story. Among the most famous *Kunstmärchen*, Friedrich de la Motte Fouqué's *Undine* (1811) [1-22] tells the story of a water sprite who marries a human but is then rejected by her husband and returns to her watery element. Towering above every other German attempt to create a modern philosophic fairy tale is Johann Wolfgang von Goethe's cryptic but compelling narrative *Das Märchen* (1795) [1-32].

The European Romantics' interest in fantasy was a reflection of their rebellion against the rationalism that had dominated eighteenth-century thought and had all but banished fantasy from the domain of high art. The *Märchen* is but one expression of this larger characteristic of Romantic literature both on the Continent and in England. The German Romantics especially favored supernatural motifs as a means of conveying irrational experience. An example of this technique is to be found in Tieck's strange, imaginative *Märchen* "Der Blonde Eckbert." Similarly, Coleridge writes in his *Biographia Literaria* (1817) that the intent of *The Rime of the Ancient Mariner* [1-18], the finest fantastic narrative of early English Romanticism, was to express the experiences of irrational dread by employing "incidents and agents [that were], in part at least, supernatural."

The Gothic Tradition

The second of the developments of importance for fantasy is, of course, the emergence of the Gothic romance. In a sense, the Gothic belongs less to the history of fantasy than to that of the horror novel, since its supernatural elements are often given naturalistic explanations[14]; but the Gothic too represented an attempt to return the irrational to literature. Horace Walpole, in his preface to the second edition of *The Castle of Otranto* [1-92], widely and rightly regarded as the first Gothic, declares that his goal was "to blend the two kinds of romance," by which he clearly means blending the older romance, in which "all was imagination and improbability," and the newer novel, in which "the great resources of fancy have been dammed up by a strict adherence to common life."[15] Influenced by the success of Walpole's romance, a host of English and German writers responded to a growing popular taste for sensationalism. *The Castle of Otranto* provided a basic fable that was repeated and embellished hundreds of times during the next three decades: the escape of a fair heroine, threatened with sexual violation, from imprisonment in an isolated castle.

At its best, the Gothic, like the *Märchen* and some other Romantic literature, used physical phenomena symbolically to explore inner spiritual decay.[16] Such is the case with Matthew Lewis's ill-written but powerful exploration of sexual desire in *The Monk* (1796) [1-46]; its horrors, though supernatural, are also psychologically symbolic. Lewis acknowledged a debt to another Gothic novel, Ann Radcliffe's *The Mysteries of Udolpho* (1794) [1-68], whose psychological concerns are clear and place the work among the few minor masterpieces that the genre produced. The first American novel to employ the trappings of Gothic romance was Charles Brockden Brown's *Wieland; or, The Transformation* (1798) [1-11]. Brown greatly admired the writings of William Godwin, whose *St. Leon. A Tale of the Sixteenth Century* (1799) [1-30] must be reckoned among the finest Gothic romances.

The popularity of Gothic romance stands as a constant reminder of the interest of reader and artist in the dark side of the irrational. Confrontation with the supernatural is likely to yield tragic results, as in "Der Freischütz," or "The Enchanted Marksman" [1-1], from Johann August Apel's collection of ghost stories (*Gespensterbuch*, 1810–17), which recounts the dire results of a pact made with a supernatural being known as the "black hunter." Apel's story later became the basis of an opera by Weber (1821). The plot of "Der Freischütz" is a variant of the Faust legend, which the eighteenth century rediscovered as a major subject for literary treatment. Much of the credit for the revival of German interest in Faust belongs to the dramatist G. E. Lessing, who both praised the story and began but failed to complete a drama based on it. The first important version of the legend was written by Paul Weidmann. His *Johann Faust* (1775), though not a comedy, borrows the comic ending of Faust's salvation and the expiration of his pact with the devil. Subsequent treatments of Faust grew increasingly sympathetic. In Friedrich Maximilian von Klinger's novel *Fausts Leben, Thäten, und Höllenfahrt* (*Faust's Life, Deeds and Journey to Hell*, 1791), Faust is portrayed as a moral idealist moved by rebellion against tyranny. The greatest version of the theme is unquestionably Goethe's *Faust* [1-31], first published in the form of a drama in

1808. Goethe's great work reflects the best of the fantastic tradition of which it partakes. Faust's encounter with the supernatural resulted from his dissatisfaction with the limits of human knowledge, and Goethe's telling fused narrative with philosophic speculation.

Until recently the bias of critics and philosophers who, discomfited by fantasy, postulated and favored a "great tradition" of mimetic fiction, has obscured the rich history and central position of fantasy in world and especially Western literature.[17] But even this cursory and superficial examination of fantastic fiction up to the beginning of the nineteenth century suggests that fantasy forms the mainstream, and realism a younger, shallower tributary of literary expression. A major theme of this tradition has been the rejection and transcendence of limits. As befits an approach to art that refuses to be constrained, fantastic fiction has assumed delightfully diverse forms; they include epic, romance, dream vision, *Reisefabulistik*, beast fable, fairy tale, *Märchen* and Gothic novel. Moreover, freed from the restraints of realism, fantasists as diverse as Apuleius, Chrétien de Troyes and Goethe have combined the pleasures of story and philosophic speculation. A second major theme has been that of metamorphosis or transformation. From the fabricated tales of Odysseus to Baron Münchhausen the other, primary great tradition reminds us of the power of the imagination to transform the everyday into something wondrous. The great works of art that form the basis of the Western literary tradition invent alternative realities rather than imitate or duplicate the mundane. They are fantasies: imaginative fictions designed to evoke both wonder and thought.

Notes

1. Colin Manlove, *Modern Fantasy* (Cambridge: Cambridge Univ. Press, 1975), p. 1.

2. Cedric Whitman, *Aristophanes and the Comic Hero* (Cambridge, Mass.: Harvard Univ. Press, 1964), pp. 22–23.

3. Graham Anderson, *Ancient Fiction: The Novel in the Graeco-Roman World* (London: Croom Helm, 1984), pp. 198–210.

4. See Howard R. Patch, *The Other World* (1950; repr. New York: Octagon Books, 1970), pp. 134–174.

5. Discussed by A. C. Spearing in *Medieval Dream-Poetry* (Cambridge: Cambridge Univ. Press, 1976), pp. 1–23; see also Patch, *op. cit.*, pp. 80–133.

6. Mikhail Bakhtin, *Rabelais and His World*, tr. Helene Iswolsky (Cambridge, Mass.: MIT Press, 1968), pp. 90–91.

7. Robert M. Torrance, *The Comic Hero* (Cambridge, Mass.: Harvard Univ. Press, 1978), p. 147.

8. See John J. O'Connor, *Amadis de Gaule and Its Influence on Elizabethan Literature* (New Brunswick, N.J.: Rutgers Univ. Press, 1970).

9. *Miscellaneous Prose of Sir Philip Sidney*, ed. K. Duncan-Jones and J. Van Dorsten (Oxford: Oxford Univ. Press, 1933), p. 92.

10. See A. C. Hamilton, "Sidney's *Arcadia* as Prose Fiction: Its Relation to Its Sources," *English Literary Renaissance* 2 (1972): 30–33.

11. Rosemond Tuve, *Allegorical Imagery: Some Medieval Books and Their Posterity* (Princeton, N.J.: Princeton Univ. Press, 1966), p. 339.

12. George Canning, *The Microcosm* (1787); cited in Geoffrey Day, *From Fiction to the Novel* (London: Routledge and Kegan Paul, 1987), p. 3.

13. See James Beattie, "On Fable and Romance," in *Dissertations Moral and Critical* (London, 1783), pp. 505–518.

14. See W. R. Irwin, *The Game of the Impossible: A Rhetoric of Fantasy* (Urbana: Univ. of Illinois Press, 1976), pp. 94–96.

15. Horace Walpole, *The Castle of Otranto*, ed. W. S. Lewis (Oxford: Oxford Univ. Press, 1982), p. 7.

16. See R. D. Hume, "Gothic versus Romantic: A revaluation of the Gothic Novel," *PMLA* 84 (1969): 283.

17. The classic statement of this position is made by R. D. Leavis in his influential *The Great Tradition* (1948); see also Ian Watt, *The Rise of the Novel* (1957; repr. London: Pelican Books, 1972), p. 35: "Formal realism [is] implicit in the novel form in general." For a discussion of mimetic criticism and the long shadow cast by Plato and Aristotle on Western literary theory, see Kathryn Hume, *Fantasy and Mimesis* (New York: Methuen, 1984), esp. pp. 5–51.

Bibliography

Many of the works cited in this chapter are classics of world literature, readily available in numerous editions and/or translations. I have listed specific editions for works of English literature only if one edition is clearly preferable by virtue of a more authoritative text or a particularly valuable introduction. I have recommended translations for all works of foreign literature. My thanks to Mike Ashley for supplying annotations of several anthologies, which are designated (MA).

Alexander Romance. See Leo of Naples [1-44].

Amadis of Gaul. See Montalvo, Garcia Ordonez de [1-54].

Apel, Johann August (Germany), 1771–1816.
ABOUT: GSF

1-1. "Der Freischütz." From *Gespensterbuch* [*Ghost Stories*], 1810–17.
Apel's short story "Der Freischütz" ("The Enchanted Marksman," also translated as "The Magic Balls") presents an interesting variant on the theme of a pact with the devil. A young gamekeeper, desperate to win a shooting competition, obtains from a supernatural being known as the "black hunter" magic bullets that invariably hit their mark. The story was adapted to form the libretto of Carl

Maria von Weber's opera *Der Freischütz*, although the operatic version replaces the tragic conclusion of Apel's story with a happy ending.

Apuleius, Lucius (North Africa), *ca.* 120–180.
ABOUT: SFW

*1-2. The Golden Ass. Second century. Recommended translation by Robert Graves. Farrar, Straus and Giroux, 1951.
Fascinated by black magic, a young man travels to Thessaly, where instead of being transformed into a bird (as he hoped) he drinks a potion that turns him into an ass. In this form he then wanders the land, becoming involved in a series of adventures that enable him to observe the glaring faults of humanity and the foolishness of his own absorption in transitory pleasures. Apuleius succeeded in fashioning a narrative that is simultaneously a ribald amusement and a philosophic fable recounting Lucius's growth toward recognition of the true good. At one point in the story, someone asks, "Are we to let an ass lecture us in philosophy?" The answer is yes. The preeminent fantasy of classical literature.

***
ABOUT: SFW

*1-3. The Arabian Nights' Entertainments. (Arabia), assembled *ca.* 1450. Recommended translation by Powys Mathers. 4 vols. Routledge and Kegan Paul, 1964; repr. 1986 (originally published 1923).
The most famous story collection ever assembled, *Alf Layla wa-Layla* (*The Thousand and One Nights*, more commonly known in English as *The Arabian Nights*) was first brought to the attention of the Western world by the translation of Antoine Galland [see 1-23]. Edward Lane provided a partial English translation in 1838-1842; the first complete English translation is that by Sir Richard Burton (1885-86). The supernatural is an integral part of the stories; the chief sources for magic are the beings known as jinni, who possess fantastic strength and are able to transform themselves or humans into various alien forms. The frame story, in which Scheherazade postpones her death by telling a story each night, is of Persian origin, but the tales themselves are primarily from Arab sources. Such tales as "Aladdin's Lamp," "Ali Baba and the Forty Thieves" and "Sinbad the Sailor" have become part of the common heritage of Western and world literature. This work rivals Arthurian legend for impact on modern fantasy. Tales from the collection have inspired not only a wide range of literary endeavors but also operas and innumerable works of visual art.

Ariosto, Ludovico (Italy), 1474–1533.
ABOUT: HF

1-4. Orlando Furioso. 1532. Recommended translation by Barbara Reynolds. 2 vols. Penguin, 1975.
It is impossible to recount briefly the profusion of events, characters and wonders woven together to form Ariosto's romantic epic. Orlando—Roland from the *Song*

of Roland—searches for his beloved Angelica, but the narrative concerns equally Ruggiero, progenitor of the Este family, Ariosto's patrons. *Orlando Furioso* may be considered a compendium of the romance, as Ariosto makes use of almost every motif of that tradition—travel to exotic places, encounters with monsters, enchantments and more. This is one of the literary worlds visited in *The Incomplete Enchanter* [3-106].

Aristophanes (Greece), *ca.* 445–380 BC.

1-5. The Birds. 414 BC. Recommended translation by William Arrowsmith. Univ. of Michigan, 1969.
When Peisetairos, an Athenian citizen, convinces the birds to build a fortified city between the gods and mankind, the gods are forced to capitulate. Peisetairos receives the sovereign power of Zeus, marries the divine housekeeper who is in charge of the thunderbolts and by the end of the play has become the ruler of the entire universe. *The Birds* is surely Aristophanes' most daringly imaginative comedy, presenting one of literature's earliest and most elaborate "wish fulfillment" fantasies.

1-6. The Frogs. 405 BC. Recommended translation by William Arrowsmith. Univ. of Michigan, 1969.
The god Dionysos (ineptly disguised as Herakles) and his slave are in the Underworld looking for the recently deceased Euripides, whom Dionysos misses and wants to bring back to Athens. The action of the comedy centers on a contest to determine who is more worthy to be resurrected, Euripides or Aeschylus. Witty and irreverent, *The Frogs* is an early example of a fantastic premise used to explore the nature of art.

Aulnoy, Marie Catherine, Comtesse d' (France), *ca.* 1650–1705.
About: GSF

1-7. Tales of the Fairies in Three Parts, Compleat. 1715. Repr. Garland, 1977 (facsimile of 1715 edition).
The other great French writer of fairy tales, Madame d'Aulnoy, differed from Perrault by creating more intricate plots and writing in ornate language suited for sophisticated adults rather than children; nor do her characters always live "happily ever after." In "The Yellow Dwarf" [see 1-82], for example, the King of the Gold Mines is slain, and his beloved dies of a broken heart. Both are then transformed (in fantasy a favorite balm for loss) into trees with intertwining branches. More lavish, less influential but occasionally more arresting as art than Perrault's fairy tales. See [1-60].

Beckford, William (U.K.), 1760–1844.
About: WW, GSF, SFW, CA, F, FG, SMFL, PE, ESF

*1-8. Vathek. First published as *An Arabian Tale, from an Unpublished Manuscript, with Notes Critical and Explanatory.* J. Johnson, 1786. Recommended edition: ed. E. F. Bleiler. Dover, 1966.
The self-indulgent Caliph Vathek, tempted by a demonic stranger and encour-

aged by his sorceress mother, abjures the worship of Mahomet and sets off to discover the Palace of Subterranean Fire. After committing various heinous crimes (including sacrificing the fifty most beautiful boys in his kingdom) and reveling in various sensual delights (particularly with the beautiful Nouronihar, daughter of a man who offers shelter to the traveler), he reaches the palace of Eblis; but he is there trapped forever, his heart tortured by an unquenchable fire. This strange tale, a notable contribution to both fantasy and horror, presents a stunning depiction of moral disintegration. The telling reflects both Beckford's admiration for *The Arabian Nights* and his own eccentric imagination. Clark Ashton Smith wrote a "continuation" of Beckford's novel, "The Third Episode of Vathek," in *The Abominations of Yondo* [H3-182]. Also annotated as [H1-6].

***

*1-9. **Beowulf**. (U.K.), *ca*. 725. Recommended edition: ed. and tr. by Howell D. Chickering. Doubleday/Anchor, 1977.
The earliest extant narrative of length in English. The story is told in two complementary parts. In the first, the hero Beowulf travels across the sea to rescue the aged King Hrothgar from the monster Grendel and his mother. In the second, Beowulf, now himself an aged king, dies in battle with a dragon that is ravaging his own land. Both a stirring tale of heroism and a profound Christian assessment of the tragic flaws of the heroic code. Retold from the monster's point of view in John Gardner's *Grendel* [4A-112]. Tolkien transformed aspects of the poem in his fiction, and his brilliant essay "The Monster and the Critics" (1936) transformed scholarly opinion by emphasizing the artfulness of the narrative.

Bibiena, Jean Galli de (France), 1710–1780.
ABOUT: GSF

1-10. **The Fairy Doll**. French title: *La Poupée*. 1747. Recommended edition: *Amorous Philandre*. Avon, 1948 (retitled reprint of 1925 translation).
A young abbé purchases a doll that turns out to be a living creature known as a sylphid. She in turn reveals to him secrets of success with women. Popular eighteenth-century plot device [see 1-45], inspired by story of Aladdin. A pleasant tale that uses faery as a means of presenting erotic information and scenes.

Brown, Charles Brockden, 1771–1810.
ABOUT: WW, GSF, SFW, F, CA, FG, SMFL, PE, ESF

1-11. **Wieland, or The Transformation**. H. Caritat, 1798. Recommended edition: Hafner, 1960.
The first American Gothic. Set in Pennsylvania, the novel explores the sinister influence of a ventriloquist named Carwin on the Wieland family. As fantasy, it falls midway between the overtly supernatural *Castle of Otranto* [1-92] and the rationalizing *Mysteries of Udolpho* [1-68]. While the reader perceives rational explanations for the seemingly fantastic events of the narrative, Clara Wieland (the narrator and protagonist) wavers between rational and supernatural explana-

tions for the uncanny events in her life. An awkward tale, important historically rather than as a gripping work of literature. Also annotated as [H1-9].

Bunyan, John (U.K.), 1628–1688.
ABOUT: CA

1-12. The Pilgrim's Progress. 1678–84. Recommended edition: ed. by Roger Sharrock. Oxford, 1960.
The full title explains the subject and the theme: *The Pilgrim's Progress from This World to That Which Is to Come*. One of the most popular books of its time. Bunyan's skill at characterization, vivid description and natural conversation enabled him to create that rarity of rarities: an allegory that is readable. Neither the bad advice of Mr. Worldly-Wiseman, the allure of Vanity (the town where a year-round fair sells the empty delights of this world) nor the monster of the Doubting Castle can defeat the pilgrim. A book too often condemned by those who know only that it is an allegory, and that allegories are supposed to be dull.

Cavendish, Margaret (U.K.), 1624–1674.

1-13. A Description of a New World Called the Blazing World. 1666.
The Blazing World is an unusual, compelling but not altogether successful blend of imaginary voyage, utopia, autobiography and philosophic discourse. It takes place in a parallel world that adjoins our own at the North Pole. The young woman who is its heroine reaches this world alone (all her companions having been killed by a storm and the arctic cold) where she becomes Empress over a fascinating array of inhabitants: among them bird-men, ant-men, ape-men and even worm-men. Much of the novel concerns the new Empress's attempt to develop a philosophy for her land; to aid her she hires Margaret Cavendish (whom she admires for her wit and learning), and so the author becomes a part of her own fiction.

Cazotte, Jacques (France), 1719–1792.
ABOUT: GSF, SFW, FG

1-14. The Devil in Love. 1772. Recommended translation: Anonymous. Heinemann, 1925.
Using a magic spell, a young soldier conjures up a beautiful woman who declares her love for him. He agrees to marry her, and they set off to gain his mother's permission; but on the way he learns that his mother has died, and that his brother, blaming him for her death, is seeking revenge. Both catastrophes, however, turn out to be illusions created by the woman, a demon in disguise. *The Devil in Love* was among the most popular and highly regarded novels of its day. Entertaining but hardly profound.

Chaucer, Geoffrey (U.K.), *ca.* 1343–1400.

1-15. The Canterbury Tales. *ca.* 1387–1400. Recommended modern English edition: ed. by Nevill Coghill. Penguin, 1952.
The greatest medieval English poet and storyteller, Chaucer made significant

contributions to numerous forms of fantastic narrative. *The Canterbury Tales* is a collection of stories woven into an extended narrative by the frame of pilgrims entertaining one another on their way to Canterbury. Of particular interest: "The Nun's Priest's Tale" is an animal fable. In "The Friar's Tale" the Devil is a major character, and drags a reprobate Summoner off to Hell. "The Wife of Bath's Tale" is an Arthurian fantasy that gives the answer to the riddle of what women want. (The answer, of course, is "their own way.") The incomplete "Squire's Tale" is an Oriental fantasy including such elements as a brass horse with the power to fly its rider anywhere and a magic ring that enables its bearer to understand the language of birds. Spenser wrote a continuation of this romance in *The Faerie Queene* [1-79].

Chrétien de Troyes (France), *fl.* 1160–90.
ABOUT: SFW

1-16. Yvain: The Knight of the Lion. *ca.* 1180. Recommended translation by Burton Raffel. Yale, 1987.
The apex of twelfth-century romance. Yvain marries before he understands love. Divorced by his wife when he fails to return home after gaining her leave for a designated period of time, he descends into madness. With the aid of a lion, whom he saves from a serpent, Yvain learns the qualities of fidelity and love that enable him to win back his wife. A profound and entertaining writer, Chrétien was the first to explore the new subject matter of love with subtlety and intellectual depth.

1-17. Perceval: The Story of the Grail. *ca.* 1190. Recommended translation by Ruth H. Cline. Univ. of Georgia, 1985.
The romance that introduced the Grail into Arthurian literature, it is the story of an innocent young man setting out into the unfamiliar, sophisticated world. Chrétien died before completing it, but it was transformed and continued in Wolfram von Eschenbach's *Parzifal* [1-93].

Coleridge, Samuel Taylor (U.K.), 1772–1834.
ABOUT: SMFL, PE

1-18. The Rime of the Ancient Mariner. 1798.
Coleridge ranks among the greatest English poets and literary critics. *The Rime of the Ancient Mariner* is a compelling ballad of only 625 lines that uses the supernatural as a vehicle for articulating the experience of the abnormal mind. An old sailor tells his story to a wedding guest. Having killed a bird of good omen (the albatross), he suffers terrible misfortunes; guided back to land by angelic spirits, he must wander forever teaching by his example love and reverence for the creatures of the world. A work of enduring fascination about the power of the imagination.

Dante Alighieri (Italy), 1265–1321.

*1-19. The Divine Comedy. Composition completed about 1320. Numerous translations available; for the modern reader the best poetic translation is by Allen Mandelbaum. Univ. of California, 1980.

The most encompassing and profound Christian fantasy, that is, an attempt to depict within the frame of an imaginative story the essential spiritual design, from a Christian perspective, of the universe. Dante travels through Hell, Purgatory and Paradise. His guides include the poet Vergil (who represents in part the highest attainment of human intelligence) and his beloved Beatrice (a symbol of divine revelation); but no character or event in this most complex and subtle of all symbolic narratives is limited in significance. Dante's comedy (a tale that begins in confusion and ends in joy) combines symbolic explorations of the journey of the soul toward God, humankind toward peace and the human mind toward understanding.

***

*1-20. Dragons, Elves and Heroes. Ed. by Lin Carter. Ballantine, 1969.

Contains selections from *Beowulf*, the *Volsunga Saga, Mabinogion, Grettir's Saga*, Malory's *Morte d'Arthur, Kalevala, Gesta Romanorum* and Voltaire's *The Princess of Babylon*, to mention only titles annotated in this chapter. Includes a brief fragment from *Palmerin of England*. See also *Golden Cities, Far* [1-33]. (MA)

Drayton, Michael (U.K.), 1563–1631.

1-21. Nymphidia. 1627.

A mock epic in the style of Spenser's *The Faerie Queene* [1-79]. Nymphidia, the narrator, is an attendant of Queen Mab, in Drayton's fairy lore the wife of King Oberon. The tale revolves around the marital problems of the royal couple. *Nymphidia*, a charming if trifling work, reflects the delight taken by early sixteenth-century audiences in the depiction of "miniaturized" universes. Compare the treatment of fairyland in Sylvia Townsend Warner's *Kingdoms of Elfin* [4A-263].

Fouqué, Baron Friedrich de la Motte (Germany), 1777–1843.
ABOUT: WW, GSF, SFW, SMFL, PE, FL, HF

1-22. Undine. 1811. Recommended translation: George Soane, tr.,Simpkin, Marshall, 1818.

This tale of the tragic love of the water sprite Undine has become a classic of German Romantic literature. The knight Huldbrand penetrates the magic forest in which Undine lives and marries her. But when they travel to the civilized world, Huldbrand soon loses interest in his bride, and rebukes her to marry another. Undine, however, returns on his wedding night, and kills Huldbrand with her kiss. Fouqué combines an unusually successful evocation of an enchanted landscape with a thoughtful exploration of the gulf separating civilization from nature. He wrote many other fictional works, including numerous fantasies, but they are by and large forgotten today. Nonetheless, Fouqué was an extremely popular and influential writer, and he, rather than William Morris, is considered by some to be the founder of the medievalizing romance. Also annotated as [2-59].

Galland, Antoine (France), 1646–1715.
Aʙᴏᴜᴛ: WW

1-23. Les Mille et une nuit [*The Thousand and One Nights*]. 12 vols. 1704–17.
Galland was a student of Oriental languages who became interested in Arabic manuscripts while serving the French government in Constantinople. His twelve-volume translation into French of the collection known as *Alf Layla wa-Layla* is responsible for the introduction to Europe of *The Arabian Nights* [1-3]. It inspired not only other translations but also a flood of narratives set in the Orient, some claiming (falsely) to be themselves translations of other texts. See [1-36] and [1-61].

***

*1-24. The Garden of Romance. Ed. by Ernest Rhys. Kegan Paul Trench Trübner, 1897.
Rhys worked as a book editor and anthologist for over fifty years. In this early volume he assembled a selection of early Romantic tales including examples from the *Arabian Nights*, *Decameron*, *Morte d'Arthur*, *Don Quixote* and *Tristram Shandy* as well as more recent examples by Irving, Scott, Hawthorne, Poe and Hans Christian Andersen. Though several of the stories are only marginally (if at all) fantasy, this volume is useful for its portrayal of the lineage of the Romantic tale. (MA)

***

Aʙᴏᴜᴛ: SFW

*1-25. Sir Gawain and the Green Knight. (U.K.), *ca.* 1370. Recommended translation by Marie Borroff. Norton, 1967.
An important narrative in which the fantastic story provides a frame for the exploration of the deeper issues of valor, fidelity and the proper interpretation of fantastic events. At the center of the romance are games. A green knight allows Gawain to cut off his head, but requires Gawain to travel to his castle for a reciprocal blow. On the way, Gawain stays at a strange castle where he participates (unwittingly) in a series of games with the host and his wife. Like *The Odyssey* [1-38], the medieval work intertwines entertaining fiction with a lesson about the importance of looking beneath appearances for a deeper level of meaning.

***

1-26. The German Novelists. Ed. by Thomas Roscoe. 4 vols. Colburn, 1826.
One of the many works produced in the wake of the popular appreciation of German literature, this collection consists chiefly of folklore but also makes

selections from the works of Fouqué, Tieck and Musaeus and includes an interesting early example of the Faust legend. (MA)

***

1-27. German Romance. Ed. by Thomas Carlyle. 4 vols. Tait, 1827.
Another bumper volume of early German folklore and literature, this collection repeats several items from [1-26] and [1-64], with selections from the works of Hoffmann, Musaeus and Tieck. Also included are several interesting essays by Carlyle on German literature. Carlyle's translations of the stories are idiosyncratic and dialectal but carry a spirit of fascination missing from some other versions. (MA)

***

1-28. Gesta Romanorum. [*Deeds of the Romans*]. Assembled *ca*. 1475. Recommended translation by Charles Swann, revised by Wynnard Hooper. AMS, 1970; reprint of 1894 edition.
Compiled over several centuries, the *Gesta Romanorum* is a treasury of moral tales useful for preachers. The stories are supposedly based on Roman history, but are in fact legends drawn from a wide range of sources from classical literature to Oriental folktales. The collection provided basic tales later amplified by such artists as Boccaccio, Chaucer and Schiller.

***

1-29. Gilgamesh Epic. (Babylonia), *ca*. 2000 BC. Recommended translation by John Gardner and John Maier. Knopf, 1985.
This mighty Babylonian narrative intertwines stories about the legendary King Gilgamesh, the wild man Enkidu and Utnapishtim, a Mesopotamian analogue of Noah. Enkidu and Gilgamesh become friends, then engage in a series of marvelous adventures, defeating even the fire-breathing monster Humbaba and the storm bull sent against them by the goddess Ishtar. When Enkidu dies, Gilgamesh sets out to discover the secret of immortality. Utnapishtim tells him of a magic herb growing on the bottom of the sea, but a snake steals it from Gilgamesh as he rests by a spring. He returns home and dies. The *Gilgamesh Epic* contains numerous subjects and themes that later appear in Greek epic: the wandering hero, the conquest of monsters and, above all, the futility of seeking immortality.

Godwin, William (U.K.), 1756–1836.
ABOUT: CA, FG, SMFL

1-30. St. Leon. A Tale of the Sixteenth Century. 4 vols. G. G. and J. Robinson, 1799; repr. Arno, 1972.
The father of Mary Shelley, Godwin was a leading radical intellectual of the eighteenth century. *St. Leon* seems partly autobiographical. Godwin felt himself to possess great and useful philosophic insights that had been rejected. The hero of *St. Leon* similarly gains the secrets of the "philosopher's stone" and the *elixir*

vitae, only to be frustrated in his attempts to use his supernatural powers for the good of mankind. Instead he is forced into exile, denied the social usefulness he desires, an outcast from both society and family. The Gothic form here serves as a shell to cover a philosophic fable; this uneasy alliance produces an intellectually absorbing result. Also annotated as [H1-33].

Goethe, Johann Wolfgang von (Germany), 1749–1832.
ABOUT: FG, SMFL

1-31. Faust, Part One. 1808. Recommended translation by F. D. Luke. Oxford, 1987.
Goethe's monumental verse tragedy was published in two parts, the first in 1808. The story of Faust occupied Goethe's mind during almost all of his adult life, and his several versions have generated an extraordinary range of interpretations. The work stands at the center of modern European literature. Above all, Goethe's *Faust* insists upon endeavor, intellectual dissatisfaction and unceasing activity as three aspects of essential human excellence. Compare the treatment of the same theme by Marlowe [1-52].

1-32. Das Märchen. 1795. Recommended translation by Thomas Carlyle. Osgood, 1877.
Goethe's *Märchen* stands apart from all other Romantic attempts at sophisticated fairy tales. It is less a narrative than a cryptic sequence of symbolic scenes and situations, all revolving around the intertwined themes of doom and regeneration. See also [1-64].

***

*1-33. Golden Cities, Far. Ed. by Lin Carter. Ballantine, 1970.
A companion to *Dragons, Elves and Heroes* [1-20]. The second volume plunders more ancient texts, among them the Egyptian *Book of Thoth* and the Sumerian *Angalta Kigalshe*, and includes extracts from *The Arabian Nights*, *Huon of Bordeaux*, *Amadis of Gaul* and *Orlando Furioso*. Enhanced by Carter's usual exuberant introductions, the two books are fine collections of ancient and modern myths and tales. (MA)

Gottfried von Strassburg (Germany), *fl. ca.* 1210.
ABOUT: SFW

1-34. Tristan. *ca.* 1210. Recommended translation by Arthur T. Hatto. Penguin, 1960.
The most profound, subtle and engrossing narrative written in the Middle Ages, or perhaps ever, about passionate love. Gottfried explores the mutual love of Tristan, King Mark's vassal, and Isolde, Mark's wife. Though he based his narrative on earlier sources, Gottfried invests his version with deeper meaning; he declares that he is writing for a special audience, those with *edele herzen* (noble hearts) who can respond both intellectually and empathically. While he retained such supernatural elements as the love potion that inflames Tristan and Isolde, Gottfried used them to describe symbolically the complexity of love, which

mingles joy with sorrow, the sensual with the spiritual. For example, whereas his models depicted the lovers as despondent, even though together, when banished from court, Gottfried transforms this episode into a sojourn in a kind of Earthly Paradise. The grotto in which they live for a time is described allegorically as if it were a church, only for Gottfried to reveal that it is in fact a symbol of the human heart. In *Tristan* the medieval romance reaches its apex as a vehicle for the presentation of ideas. Unfortunately, it is available only in prose translations. The Wagner opera is probably the best known adaptation of the many versions of the Tristan and Isolde story.

***

1-35. Grettir's Saga. (Iceland), *ca*. 1375. Recommended translation by Denton Fox and Hermann Palsson. Univ. of Toronto, 1974.
Most Icelandic sagas are brutally realistic, but the story of Grettir centers on his struggle with a ghost who, when defeated by Grettir, compels him to a life of wandering and a fear of sleep. The fantastic aspects of the story are brilliantly blended into a study of a man made an outcast by the changing values of the society in which he lives.

Gueulette, Thomas-Simon (France), 1683–1766.
ABOUT: SFW

1-36. Tartarian Tales: or a Thousand and One Quarters of Hours. J. and R. Tonson, 1759. Original French publication, 1730.
A collection of tales claiming to be direct translations from original manuscripts, but in fact the invention of the author. The frame story involves the blinded king of Astrakhan, who listens to various tales while awaiting the return of his court physician from a quest for a potion to cure him. A profusion of marvelous and supernatural events fails to rescue the tales from Gueulette's general dullness as an author. He wrote numerous collections of such fakelore, including *Chinese Tales* (1725) and *Mogul Tales* (1736), that were translated into English. Their popularity attests to the vogue for Orientalizing fiction.

Hesiod (Greece), eighth century BC.

1-37. Theogony. *ca*. 725 BC. Recommended translation by Apostolus Athanassa-kis. Johns Hopkins, 1983.
Hesiod describes the history of the universe from its origin until Zeus's ascendance to sovereign power. Violence and bloody father-son strife predominate: the first lord of the gods, Ouranos (Sky), is overthrown by his son Kronos, whom Zeus in turn defeats. Much of the poem is devoted to showing that Zeus has replaced brute force with power guided by reason.

Homer (Greece), eighth century BC.

*1-38. The Odyssey. *ca*. 750 BC. Recommended translations by Richmond Latti-more. Harper and Row, 1968; and by Robert FitzGerald. Anchor/Doubleday, 1963.
Odysseus (Ulysses) Wends his way home after the Trojan War. First he must

extricate himself from the dangerous affections of women, mortal and divine (Calypso, Circe, Nausikaa), and outwit numerous monsters (Cyclops, the Sirens). Once home, he must defeat the nobles who have been trying to persuade his faithful and extremely clever wife, Penelope, to marry one of them. The theme of artful invention (manifested by Odysseus in his talent for disguise, deception and storytelling) stands at the center of this most famous and imitated of all Western epics. Homer introduces three major themes that resonate through Western fantasy: travel in strange and wondrous lands, transformation and the foolishness of mistaking the apparent for the real.

***

1-39. Huon of Bordeaux. (France), *ca.* 1220. No adequate translation exists, but available in Lord Berners's euphuistic sixteenth-century translation revised by Robert Steele. G. Allen, 1895; reprinted R. West, 1979.
This marvel-filled romance has two centers of interest: the adventures of the protagonist, Huon, and the support given him by Oberon, the fairy king, described as a dwarf with a child's body but an old man's face. Huon travels to the court of Babylon, where he meets and wins the emir's daughter. Their escape back to France is filled with fantastic dangers and battles. Oberon not only provides the young knight with the magical implements necessary for his many successes but also remains loyal when Huon disregards his good advice. Medieval fantasy in its most entertaining but least intellectual guise. The romance was retold by Andre Norton in her *Huon of the Horn* (1951).

Johnson, Samuel (U.K.), 1709–1784.
ABOUT: CA

1-40. Rasselas. 1759.
Johnson's contribution to a popular eighteenth-century genre: the philosophic fable set in the Orient. Prince Rasselas of Abyssinia is to be confined to a "happy valley" until he ascends the throne, but he escapes with his sister and the poet Imlac in order to explore the world outside and discover what condition or profession makes men truly happy. In the end he discovers that happiness is an illusion, and returns home. Like Voltaire's *Candide* and *Zadig* [1-90], *Rasselas* is an attack on naive optimism, but Johnson's sober moralizing lacks the imaginative allure and the wit that give Voltaire's fables their enduring power.

***

1-41. Kalevala. (Finland). Recommended translation by W. F. Kirby. Humanities, 1985.
The *Kalevala* is the child of various bards' imaginative genius and the painstaking efforts of one scholar, Elias Lonnrott. The stories go back to antiquity; the first publication, by Lonnrott, occurred in 1835. The *Kalevala*—as he compiled, arranged and named it—begins with an account of the origin of the world, then records the adventures of the three sons of the hero Kaleva as they battle against

the evil witch Louhi. Its depiction of the dismal arctic wasteland Pohjola is an unparalleled achievement. An absorbing fantasy masterpiece too little known. de Camp and Pratt's "The Wall of Serpents" [see 3-106] is set in the world of the *Kalevala*. Tolkien drew on the *Kalevala* for his tale of Túrin in *The Silmarillion* [4A-251].

La Fontaine, Jean de (France), 1621–1695.

1-42. Fables. 1668. Recommended translation by Norman Shapiro. Univ. of Illinois, 1988.
A prolific writer in an impressive range of genres, La Fontaine is chiefly remembered today for his elegant poetic versions of animal fables. There exists no more pleasurable or sophisticated introduction to stories adapted from sources including Aesop and the Indian *Panchatantra* [1-59]. La Fontaine differs from other animal fantasists in one important respect. Although he draws the obligatory maxims from the trials and triumphs of mice, ants, crows and the like, his fables are only minimally moralistic; their primary purpose seems to be entertainment.

***

1-43. Lancelot of the Lake. (France), thirteenth century. Recommended translation by Corin Corley. Oxford, 1989.
The first of the three works that constitute the influential French Vulgate Cycle. The first volume tells of Lancelot's childhood, his arrival at King Arthur's court and the development of his love affair with Queen Guinevere. A major work of Western literature, important in its own right and as a basic source for Malory's *Morte d'Arthur* [1-49].

Leo of Naples (Italy), tenth century.

1-44. Alexander Romance. 952. Recommended translation by Dennis M. Kratz: *Romances of Alexander*. Garland, 1990.
An extremely influential book. Leo translated the Greek *Alexander Romance* into unadorned Latin. His version, expanded by several later editors, became the basic source for most Western European narratives on the life and exploits of Alexander the Great. These fictional versions incorporate numerous fantastic themes, most notably the strange journey and encounters with sundry extraordinary beasts and odd humanoids. Collection includes *Journey to the Earthly Paradise*.

Lesage, Alain-René (France), 1668–1747.
ABOUT: GSF

1-45. The Devil on Two Sticks [alternate English title: *Asmodeus*]. 1707. Recommended translation: Anonymous. Nimmo and Bain, 1891.
Cleofas, to avoid an unappealing marriage, takes refuge in a magician's laboratory, where he discovers a lame devil (hence the title) whom he frees from imprisonment in a bottle. In return, the devil, Asmodeus, teaches him about life

by magically transporting him around the city. As the tale ends, Asmodeus even arranges for Cleofas to marry a wealthy young woman. Less a novel than a sequence of highly entertaining satirical episodes, *Asmodeus* became the model for numerous narratives in which a demon gives a human being a magical tour of contemporary life and vice.

Lewis, Matthew Gregory (U.K.), 1775–1818.
ABOUT: WW, GSF, SFW, F, CA, FG, H, SMFL, PE, ESF

*1-46. Ambrosio, or The Monk. A Romance. J. Bell, 1796. Recommended edition: Grove Press, 1952. Authoritative text with excellent introduction by John Berryman.
A novel that lurches to excellence in spite of itself. The monk Ambrosio falls prey to temptation through a triad of flaws: lust, pride and inexperience. The devil leads him to depravity and destruction in the guise of a beautiful woman, Matilda, who first seduces him, then encourages his desire for the innocent Antonia, whom Ambrosio eventually rapes and murders. Some recent criticism finds in *The Monk* an examination of moral decay, but such readings must never lose sight of the lurid sensationalism that made it popular and remains its most alluring trait. The quintessential Gothic. Also annotated as [H1-58].

***

1-47. Mabinogion. (Wales), *ca.* 1400. Recommended translation by Patrick Ford, *The Mabinogi*, Univ. of California, 1977.
A compilation of medieval Welsh prose tales first translated into English (1838–49) by Lady Charlotte Guest. There are eleven tales in all, including *Kulhwch and Olwen*, one of the earliest known Arthurian stories. The most important portion of the collection consists of four stories, known as *Four Branches of the Mabinogi*, that recount the fabulous adventures of Pwyll, his son Pryderi, and his family and descendents. These tales have inspired several modern works of fantasy, among them a retelling by Evangeline Walton [3-356, 4A-261], Lloyd Alexander's "Prydain" series [4B-8] and Garner's *The Owl Service* [4B-51]. Although first committed to writing sometime in the late fourteenth century, the tales originated as early as the eleventh.

***

1-48. Mahabharata. (India), 400 BC–AD 400. Recommended translation by J. A. Van Buitenen. 3 vols. Univ. of Chicago, 1974–78.
In Indian tradition, the *Mahabharata* is called an encyclopedia (*jnanakosa*) as distinguished from a literary construct such as the *Ramayana* [1-69]. As a vast reservoir of tales and information, it defies synopsis. Generations of poets and thinkers added to the core story (a great battle fought by descendants of King Bharata) a wide range of religious and narrative material. A Western analogy might be a single work encompassing both Homeric epics, Plato and the Christian Gospels somehow formed into one frame. So much is contained in the

Mahabharata that of it Indians say, "What is not here is not found anywhere else."

Malory, Sir Thomas (U.K.), *ca.* 1408–1471.
ABOUT: SFW, CA

*1-49. Le Morte d'Arthur. 1485.
The one work most responsible for the continuing fascination of English literature with the romance of Arthur. Drawing primarily but not exclusively upon the so-called French Vulgate Cycle [see 1-43 and 1-66], Malory refashioned the disparate medieval stories about Arthur into a continuous, coherent narrative. Malory tends to minimize the role of the marvelous and the supernatural. His own work has many times since been the source of the same kind of revision and transformation to which he subjected his sources. To attempt a list of modern fantasies based on or influenced by *Le Morte d'Arthur* would be a task at once Herculean and Quixotic. A considerable academic industry has emerged devoted to that very undertaking.

Mandeville, John (also spelled Maundeville) (U.K.), died 1372.

*1-50. The Travels of Sir John Mandeville. *ca.* 1385. Recommended translation by Charles W. Moseley. Penguin, 1984.
The book that Mandeville claimed to have written himself was actually a translation of a French text; moreover, he never took the travels he described. This most famous and enticing of all imaginary travel narratives first appeared in English around 1385. It can be said to have prepared the way for the Western reception of the *Arabian Nights* by firing the Western curiosity for the Orient with its vivid and fanciful accounts of the Fountain of Youth, the Valley Perilous, the courts of Prester John and the Great Khan of Cathay. Mandeville helped make the East a concept as much as a place, a screen on which Western writers and artists could project their wishes and fears.

Marie de France (France), *fl.* 1160–90.

1-51. Bisclavret. *ca.* 1190. Recommended translation by Robert Hanning and Joan Ferrante: *The Lais of Marie de France.* Dutton, 1978.
Marie is thought to have been the half sister of King Henry II of England. She spent most of her life at the English court, though she wrote in French. She was the greatest master of the *lai*, generally speaking a short romance in rhyme that fuses a theme based on chivalric love with supernatural elements and a fairy-tale setting. Her masterpiece, *Bisclavret*, has a werewolf hero; the transformation does not rob him of his intelligence. Service to a great king ends with the transformed man's regaining his rightful form. Like all good medieval tales, this one hides beneath the entertainment an idea: here, the role of divine grace in the struggle for virtue. Compare the very different treatment of the werewolf in such modern tales as Guy Endore's *The Werewolf of Paris* [H3-67] or the melodramatic *Wagner: The Wehr-Wolf* by George W. M. Reynolds [H2-82].

Marlowe, Christopher (U.K.), 1564–1593.
ABOUT: CA

1-52. The Tragical History of Dr. Faustus. 1604.
Marlowe was the greatest figure in Elizabethan drama before Shakespeare. Marlowe's finest tragedies are dominated by individuals gripped by an unrelenting passion for power or knowledge. His Faustus seeks power through knowledge, and though the play ends with a moralistic warning based on his tragic end, the play throughout portrays sympathetically Faustus's hatred of limits. In the play's most memorable scene, two angels, manifestations of the hero's deep inner conflict, fight for possession of his soul. Second only to Goethe's *Faust* [1-31] as a treatment of the theme.

Milton, John (U.K.), 1608–1674.

1-53. Paradise Lost. 1667.
An epic much indebted to the *Aeneid, Paradise Lost* ranks with Dante's *Divine Comedy* as one of the two greatest Christian fantasies. It tells the story of Adam and Eve and of the loss of Paradise and the entrance of Sin and Death into the world through Satan's wiles. For generations Milton fixed in the Western imagination its vision of Lucifer, Pandemonium and Gabriel. Mary Shelley placed Adam's complaint ("Did I request thee . . . ") on the title page of *Frankenstein* [H1-97], thus giving that most influential of all modern mythic narratives an inescapable religious dimension.

Montalvo, Garcia Ordonez de (Spain), died *ca.* 1530.

*1-54. **Amadis of Gaul.** 1508. Recommended translation by Edwin B. Place and Herbert C. Behm. 2 vols. Univ. Press of Kentucky, 1974.
Perhaps the most popular chivalric romance ever written. Amadis exemplifies the ideals of courage, purity and fidelity. Amadis is the illegitimate son of the king of Gaul. His cradle is cast to sea by his mother, but Amadis is rescued and reared by the king of Scotland. He performs a series of incredible exploits (defeating giants and monsters as well as other knights), all for the love of Oriana, daughter of the king of England, whom he eventually weds. The adventures are secondary to the settings of *Amadis*; the beauty and dangers of the imagined world are described in lush and exaggerated detail. Numerous continuations of *Amadis* were written. Indeed, this work might justly be called the originator of the whole genre of sword-and-sorcery fantasy. Among the best of the continuations was *Palmerin of England* [see 1-20], first translated into English in 1596 by Anthony Munday, but *Amadis* surpassed both its predecessors and its imitative, usually dull progeny by lending to its outrageous events a sense of mystery and moral importance.

Morell, Charles (pseud. of James Ridley) (U.K.), 1736–1765.
ABOUT: SFW

1-55. Tales of the Genii: or, The Delightful Lessons of Horam. 2 vols. G. Wilkie, 1764.
An idiosyncratic manifestation of the eighteenth-century mania for Oriental tales

inspired by Galland's translation of *The Arabian Nights* [1-23]. The author was allegedly "formerly ambassador in India to the Great Mogul," but was in fact a British clergyman who had never traveled abroad. The stories imitate the style of *The Arabian Nights.* The "exotic" names of characters are often anagrams of English names. Morell's one substantive innovation is his conclusion, in which an evil magician flies off to wreak havoc in England—an interesting if accidental foreshadowing of the menace from the East so effectively employed by Bram Stoker in *Dracula* [H3-186].

Musaeus, Johann Karl August (Germany), 1735–1787.
ABOUT: GSF, SFW, FG

1-56. "Dumb Love." From *Volksmärchen der Deutschen* [*German Fairy Tales*]. 5 vols. 1782–87. See [1-27].
Musaeus composed a large number of optimistic, often comic *Märchen*, a term used by him to signify a traditional fantastic tale that appealed to a wide audience. "Dumb Love" (also translated as "The Spectre Barber"), his best-known and most widely anthologized story, concerns a ghost-barber destined to a Sisyphean existence of shaving until someone offers to shave him in return. As usual with Musaeus, the encounter with the supernatural in this story is reassuring rather than frightening. Other stories of note, both in [1-27], are "Melechsala" and "Libussa." Musaeus may be said to reflect the bright side of the Romantic fascination with the fantastic. As Everett Bleiler has said, he uses the supernatural as a "metaphor to explore an idyllic bourgeois world."

***

1-57. Nibelungenlied (Germany), *ca.* 1200. Recommended translation by Frank G. Ryder. Wayne State, 1962.
The hero Siegfried possesses the treasure of the Nibelungs and their magic cape, which makes its wearer invisible. He comes to Worms to court the famous beauty Kriemhild. While there, he helps King Gunther win Brunhild, and a double wedding is celebrated. The retainer Hagen, aided by Kriemhild's own brothers, treacherously assassinates Siegfried, seizes the treasure from Kriemhild, to whom Siegfried had given it, and sinks it in the Rhine. The widow then plots revenge. She marries Etzel (Attila the Hun), and at the wedding feast murders her brothers and Hagen before she herself is killed. A dark tale of revenge and honor, the *Nibelungenlied* is drawn from the same body of legends that produced the *Volsunga Saga* [1-86].

Ovid: Publius Ovidius Naso (Italy), 43 BC–AD 17.

*1-58. Metamorphoses. AD 17. Recommended translation by Horace Gregory. Viking, 1958.
Although it has a vaguely historical structure, the *Metamorphoses* is an epic without a plot. It presents a series of episodes all illustrating the theme of transformation. It has been a treasure trove of episodes for later writers and artists.

The desire of Christian readers in the Middle Ages and Renaissance to make Ovid less morally objectionable was among the impulses encouraging the allegorical reading of classical literature.

***

1-59. Panchatantra. (India), *ca.* 500. Recommended translation by Arthur G. Ryder. Univ. of Chicago, 1964.

A Sanskrit collection of fables and tales, of uncertain date, supposedly compiled at the behest of King Amarasakti for the education of his sons. The title means "book of the five chapters," and each chapter emphasizes a different area of proper conduct. Many of the animal fables within the collection stress the cleverness of two shrewd jackals, Karakata and Damanaka. The *Panchatantra* is among the most frequently translated works of Indian literature and has had a pervasive influence on world literature, particularly the animal fable.

Perrault, Charles (France), 1628-1703.
ABOUT: CA

*1-60. Histoire et contes du temps passé, avec des moralités. Contes de ma mère l'Oye. 1697. Recommended translation by A. E. Johnson: *Perrault's Fairy Tales*. Dover, 1969. (YA)

Both scholar and artist, Perrault is chiefly remembered for two reasons: his championship of the "moderns" in the "quarrel between the ancients and the moderns" and because he is usually given credit for having written the first children's book. The two achievements are related, for part of the program of the "moderns" was to elevate the folktale to a literary form, with a new band of immortals replacing the old classical gods. Although others had collected fairy and folktales before him, Perrault clearly designed them to be read to children. "Cinderella" and "Little Red Riding Hood" are but two of the stories, known to everyone, that owe their initial fame to inclusion in *Mother Goose Tales*.

Pétis de la Croix (France), 1653-1713.
ABOUT: SFW

1-61. The Persian and the Turkish Tales. Mears and Browne, 1714.

After Galland, the most important translator of Oriental tales into French was Pétis de la Croix. *Persian Tales* proved extremely popular in English translation. Contained in the collection is the story of the Princess Tourandoct and Prince Calaf. The Italian playwright Carlo Gozzi adapted this story for the stage; his version became the basis for Puccini's opera *Turandot*.

Petronius, Gaius (Italy), died AD 66.

1-62. The Satyricon. *ca.* 65. Recommended translation by John P. Sullivan. Penguin, 1969.

A cynical combination of the *Odyssey*, *Aeneid* and love romance. Encolpius, hounded by the angry fertility god Priapus, travels the Mediterranean seeking to regain his virility. His encounters are more freakish than fantastic. Embedded in the narrative is an elaborate tale of a werewolf who can change his shape at will.

***

1-63. Popol Vuh. *ca.* 1554-58. Recommended translation by Dennis Tedlock. Simon and Schuster, 1985.

The greatest surviving work of the early Meso-American imagination, the *Popol Vuh* presents the Mayan vision of the universe from the time of its creation by the gods Tepeu and Gucumatz to the founding of the first Mayan kingdom. Only fragments remain, but much of the extant text describes the horrors of the Underworld and the conquest of the gods of that Underworld by the great Hero Twins. The Mayan equivalent of the Egyptian *Book of the Dead*, Hesiod's *Theogony* [1-37] and perhaps the Finnish *Kalevala* [1-41].

***

1-64. Popular Tales and Romances of the Northern Nations. Anonymous translations. 3 vols. Simpkin, Marshall, 1823.

A rich selection of German fantasy issued to take advantage of the success of *German Popular Tales*. Selections from the works of Fouqué ("The Bottle-Imp"), Musaeus ("Dumb Love"), Tieck ("Blond Eckbert") and Apel ("Der Freischütz"), plus other works of dubious origin, and a rare English translation of Goethe's *Das Märchen* [1-32]. A landmark volume in the popularization of German legends in English. (MA)

Potocki, Count Jan Hrabia (Poland), 1761–1815.
   ABOUT: WW, GSF, FG, SMFL, PE, ESF

*1-65. The Saragossa Manuscript. 1804. Recommended edition: ed. by Roger Caillois, tr. by Elisabeth Abbott. Orion, 1960. Excellent introduction, most accurate translation available.

A series of linked tales. Although Potocki was Polish, he wrote in French. The central narrative concerns the adventures of a traveler, Alphonso van Worden, who becomes involved with two sisters who may be vampires. The episodes abound in supernatural elements. Especially interesting is the history of the bandit Zoto. As the "manuscript" progresses, the stories tend to become less fantastic and more erotic. Much admired by the Russian writer Pushkin, *The Saragossa Manuscript* is a marvel of elegant storytelling that uses exotic settings to lure the reader into accepting impossible events. One of the true masterpieces of fantasy.

***

1-66. Quest of the Holy Grail. Thirteenth century. Recommended translation by P. M. Matarasso. Penguin, 1969.

The second of the three volumes that constitute the French Vulgate Cycle (see also *Lancelot of the Lake* [1-43]) is of particular interest to readers of fantasy. Written by a Cistercian monk, the *Quest* abounds in marvels that are immediately and in great detail explained as allegories of Christian truth. Galahad alone sees the mystery inside the Grail vessel and dies in ecstasy; the failure of the other knights signals both the spiritual inadequacy and the eventual fall of Arthur's kingdom.

Rabelais, François (France), 1494?–1553.

1-67. Gargantua and Pantagruel. 1532–64. Recommended translation by John M. Cohen. Penguin, 1955.
The English title for Rabelais's five-part compendium of humor, fantasy and philosophy. His work celebrates freedom, excess and life. A work so passionately devoted to breaking limits cannot be easily captured in a description or synopsis. One of its plots, involving a voyage by Pantagruel and his friend Panurge to the Oracle of the Holy Bottle, somewhere in India, enables Rabelais both to imitate and parody the motif of the fantastic voyage.

Radcliffe, Mrs. Ann (U.K.), 1764–1823.
ABOUT: WW, SFW, CA, FG, SMFL, PE, ESF

1-68. The Mysteries of Udolpho. 1794. Recommended edition: ed. by Bonamy Dobrée. Oxford, 1966.
Radcliffe did not, properly speaking, write fantasy. Only her final novel, *Gaston de Blondeville* (published 1826), contains elements of the supernatural; in all the rest, seemingly occult events are explained with relentless logic. In *The Mysteries of Udolpho*, Emily de St. Aubert encounters but escapes from evil in the person of the malevolent Montini. Also annotated as [H1-83].

***

1-69. Ramayana of Valmiki. (India), *ca.* 500 BC. Recommended translation by Hari P. Shastri. Routledge Chapman and Hall, 1985.
Attributed to the poet Valmiki, the *Ramayana* consists of approximately 25,000 couplets divided into seven books. The first and last were probably added by religious writers, for they glorify Rama as God, while the middle books celebrate him as a human hero. The heart of the narrative concerns the adventures of an exiled prince questing for his abducted princess. The story is full of the fantastic. Rama's search for Sita takes him into wild jungles and deserts, abodes of all manner of monsters and demons, especially the demon-king Ravana. On the level of religious symbolism that permeates Valmiki's epic, Rama can be said to represent order, duty and controlled power (*dharma*). Within Indian tradition, the *Ramayana* occupies a place analogous to that of the Homeric poems in Greek tradition; it is the first literary artifact (*adikavya*) and has had an incalculable influence on later literature. See *Mahabharata* [1-48].

Raspe, Rudolf Erich (Germany), 1737–1794.
ABOUT: SMFL

1-70. Baron Münchhausen's Narrative of His Marvellous Travels and Campaigns in Russia. 1785. Recommended editions: Pantheon, 1969, Cresset, 1948.
Written in English, the story of Baron Münchhausen's travels belongs jointly

with the many narratives of *Reisefabulistik* (the incredible journey) and with the *Odyssey* as a masterpiece of fictional self-aggrandizing. Raspe, a German satirist who had been forced to flee to England, was identified as the author only later. The original edition presented fourteen outlandish tales linked together as the reminiscences of an old soldier. Unfortunately, the popularity of this edition prompted numerous "continuations" not unlike those inspired by *Amadis of Gaul* [1-54]. These later stories lack the originality and droll style of Raspe's originals. Münchhausen's name has become synonymous with exaggeration.

***

1-71. Reynard, Romance of. (France), twelfth century. Recommended translations by Patricia Terry (selections from the French *Roman de Renart*). Northeastern Univ. Press, 1983; and by Adriaan Barnouw in E. Colledge, ed., *Reynard the Fox and Other Medieval Netherlands Secular Literature* (the Flemish *Reinart de Vos*). Sijthoff, 1967.
In the twelfth century stories about Reynard the Fox were given sophisticated literary expression. They offer comic tribute to the desire to be free of traditional morality. Unfortunately, the medieval French *Roman de Renart* has not been translated in its entirety. The story is not really a romance or an epic, but is rather a loose collection of tales with the comic hero Reynard at their center. The English reader is directed to Adriaan Barnouw's translation of the Flemish *Reinart de Vos*. This adaptation of various French tales became the main source, directly or indirectly, for most of the subsequent versions of the Reynard story in English. Compare the similar treatment of the animal hero Monkey in the Chinese *Journey to the West* [1-94].

***

1-72. Roland, Song of. (France), *ca.* 1100. Recommended translation by Frederick Goldin. Norton, 1978.
The epic falls into two parts. In the first, Charlemagne's vassal Roland, betrayed by Ganelon, is ambushed by a force of Saracens. His pride stops him from calling for help (by sounding his ivory horn) until it is too late to save himself or any of his companions. In the second part, Charlemagne avenges Roland's death; he defeats the army of the Saracens and puts Ganelon to death. The supernatural elements of the poem emphasize the rightness of Charlemagne's cause. God makes the sun stand still as he pursues the Saracens, and later the angel Gabriel intervenes to assure his victory in single combat against the Saracen leader Baligant. Roland became known in Italy as Orlando, and his exploits were reshaped and retold by, among others, Ariosto in *Orlando Furioso* [1-4].

***

1-73. Rose, Romance of the. (France), 1230/1275. Recommended translations by Harry W. Robbins. Dutton, 1962; and by Charles Dahlberg. Princeton, 1971.
In some respects the one work most representative of medieval fantasy, for it

combines the popular genre of the dream vision, the medieval passion for allegorizing, with the period's equally strong fascination with encyclopedic system-building. The romance was written in two distinct parts: the first by Guillaume de Lorris, the second by Jean de Meung. The romance relates a dream in which Idleness admits the author to a garden, where he falls in love with a Rose but cannot pluck it until he has gone through a long series of symbolic encounters. The final section, in which the lover finds his rose, is a marvel of sexual symbolism. Compare the concept of the dream vision in George MacDonald's *Phantastes* [2-116].

Shakespeare, William (U.K.), 1564–1616.
ABOUT: CA, H, PE

1-74. Hamlet, Prince of Denmark. *ca.* 1601.
His father's ghost appears to Prince Hamlet, demanding vengeance for his murder at the hands of his brother, Claudius. Though ostensibly a drama of revenge, the greatness of *Hamlet* lies in its exploration of human nature, particularly the character of the philosophic and contemplative prince. The complexity and thematic richness of *Hamlet* have led to hundreds of interpretations, and no definitive reading is possible. The elusiveness of meaning, one of the play's major concerns, is illustrated by Shakespeare's presentation of the ghost: perhaps real, perhaps an illusion, perhaps telling the truth, perhaps a trick of the devil.

1-75. Macbeth. *ca.* 1606.
The most marvel-filled of Shakespeare's tragedies. Three mysterious witches prophesy that Macbeth will become king and Banquo will "beget" kings. Urged on by his wife, Macbeth acquires the throne of Scotland by murdering Duncan, the king; but he in turn is overthrown and killed by the Scottish thane Macduff and Malcolm, Duncan's son. Macbeth is a devastating study of a man who forfeits his humanity to ambition. The many supernatural trappings of the play—especially the prophetic witches and the visits to Macbeth by the ghost of Banquo, whom he murdered—intensify that theme.

1-76. A Midsummer Night's Dream. *ca.* 1595–6.
The interwoven loves of three couples, all of whom are wed at play's end. Most of the action occurs in an enchanted wood, where the lovers encounter the fairy king Oberon, his wife, Titania, and Oberon's irrepressible lieutenant, Puck. Much of the comedy ensues from Puck's rather indiscriminate use of a magic love potion and his transformation of the head of the young weaver Bottom into that of an ass. Among the sources for this comedy of fairyland are Apuleius's *The Golden Ass* [1-2], for Bottom's transformation, and Ovid's *Metamorphoses* [1-58]. Compare the allusions to the play and the inventive treatment of fairyland in John Crowley's *Little, Big* [4A-79].

*1-77. The Tempest. *ca.* 1611.
Shakespeare's final play. The magician Prospero reigns over an enchanted island with his daughter, Miranda. Among the creatures in his power are the ethereal Ariel and the brutish Caliban. He raises a tempest that brings to the island a

group of those (including his own brother and Alonso, king of Naples) who had wronged him. Alonso's son, Ferdinand, separated from the others, meets and falls in love with Miranda. All ends well. Alonso blesses the union of Ferdinand and Miranda; he restores Prospero to his throne; and Prospero abjures magic, freeing Ariel. *The Tempest* is, in part, a play about plays. Prospero's farewell may be Shakespeare's veiled farewell to the theater. Such a reading suggests that the fantastic is central to Shakespeare's dramatic art. Freely adapted as the 1956 science fiction film *Forbidden Planet.*

Sidney, Sir Philip (U.K.), 1554-1586.

1-78. Arcadia. 1590.
Written originally for the Countess of Pembroke, Sidney's sister, *Arcadia* is a prose romance with eclogues at the conclusion of each book. The narrative emphasizes the adventures of two pairs of young lovers: Pyrocles and Philoclea, and Musidorus and Pamela. In part, Sidney refashioned and modernized the Greek romance; in part, he was imitating *Amadis of Gaul* [1-54] and its scenes of chivalric valor. The plot is confusing and, at any rate, secondary. *Arcadia* is a fantasy not through supernatural events, but because of its idealized setting; it is Sidney's evocation of pastoral landscape that is the book's crowning achievement.

Spenser, Edmund (U.K.), 1552?-1599

1-79. The Faerie Queene. Books I-III, 1590; Books IV-VI, 1596.
Spenser states that the didactic purpose of *The Faerie Queene* is to "fashion a gentleman or noble person in vertuous and gentle discipline." Using the frame of Arthurian romance, he created a multi-level allegory. Indeed, the work most comparable to it is Dante's *Divine Comedy* [1-19], for Spenser seems to have aimed at nothing less than a comprehensive depiction of sixteenth-century England, physically, intellectually, morally. His primary literary model was the chivalric romance. Arthur has a dream vision of the Fairy Queen Gloriana (who signifies Glory on one level and Queen Elizabeth on another), and determines to "seek her out in Faeryland." The subsequent adventures of Arthur and his knights can be said to represent an allegory of the quest for spiritual salvation, with each of the knights signifying a particular virtue. The modern dislike of allegory leads many readers to avoid or underestimate this monumental poem. Part of *The Incomplete Enchanter* [3-106] is set in Spenser's world.

Sturluson, Snorri (Iceland), 1178-1241.

1-80. Prose Edda. Thirteenth century. Recommended translation by Jean I. Young. Univ. of California, 1964.
Snorri Sturluson, who may also have composed *Grettir's Saga* [1-35], intended the *Prose Edda* as a manual of instruction for professional poets. In addition to advice on meter and diction, he included a section on mythology. Few single works have had a greater impact on modern fantasy, for the *Prose Edda* is the ultimate written source of almost all the stories that we associate with the Norse gods: the stories of Baldur, of Odin, of the death of the gods. Distinct from

Sturlusson's textbook for poets is the *Poetic* or *Elder Edda*, a collection of 38 anonymous poems composed in the eleventh and twelth centuries. The poems fall into two groups: heroic lays about figures such as Sigurd and Helgi and mythological lays chronicling the Norse gods from the creation to apocalypse. Modern works ranging from Poul Anderson's *The Broken Sword* [3-2] to Tolkien's *Lord of the Rings* [3-340] have made use of the *Eddas*.

Swift, Jonathan (U.K.), 1667–1745.
ABOUT: F, CA, SFE, ESF

*1-81. Travels into Several Remote Nations of the World, by Lemuel Gulliver. 1726. (YA)
Swift's satire makes use of two elements of fantastic fiction: the genre of *Reisefabulistik* (the incredible journey) and the theme of transformation. Although Gulliver himself is not transformed, the varying sizes and natures of those he visits create a metamorphosis of the human through their perception. Gulliver makes four voyages: to Lilliput, whose inhabitants are six inches tall; to Brobdingnag, inhabited by giants; to the flying island of Laputa; and to Houyhnhnmland, home of the Houyhnhnms and Yahoos. The imaginative fantasy of Swift's narrative is alluring in itself, but also serves as a vehicle for his bitter criticism of human society.

***

1-82. Tales of the Wild and Wonderful. Hurst, Robinson, 1825.
This collection of stories has been attributed to George Borrow, but its authorship remains unsettled. It includes a selection of stories from various national folklores, including "The Prediction" from Welsh legend, "The Yellow Dwarf" from Madame d'Aulnoy's fairy tales [1-7] and Apel's "Der Freischütz" [1-1]. An interesting early volume. (MA)

Thousand and One Nights. See *Arabian Nights' Entertainments, The* [1-3].

Tieck, Ludwig (Germany), 1773–1853.
ABOUT: GSF, SFW, FG, SMFL, PE

1-83. Tales from the Phantasus. Tr. by Julius C. Hare *et al.* J. Burns, 1845.
Tieck wrote the first and the best German Romantic *Kunstmärchen*, or polished literary fairy tales. *Phantasus* is a three-volume collection of works, including *Märchen* and other supernatural stories, composed between 1796 and 1811, and published in Berlin, 1812–1816. The diverse contents are linked by a frame story in which a group of young men and women discuss the merits of the fairy tale and other forms of literature. In some tales, an encounter with the supernatural brings about ruin: "Blond Eckbert" ("Der Blonde Eckbert"), Tieck's refashioning of the Oedipus myth, recounts Eckbert's discovery of his marriage to his own sister. In "The Goblet" ("Der Pokal"), on the other hand, Tieck employs the supernatural

to tell a positive tale of abiding love that transforms the commonplace into the marvelous. More than any other German writer of the early nineteenth century, Tieck demonstrated that a self-consciously literary fairy tale need not be devoid of wonder or delight. See also [1-27].

Ueda, Akinari (Japan), 1734–1809.

1-84. Tales of Rain and Moon. 1789. Recommended translation by Leon M. Zolbrod. Allen and Unwin, 1974.
Ueda is widely considered the finest Japanese writer of fantastic fiction. His two most famous tales are "The Dream Carp," which combines the motifs of dream vision and transformation to tell of a poet-painter who dreams that he becomes a carp; and "A Tryst at Chrysanthemum Time," a tale of honor. In the latter, a young man, wrongly imprisoned, commits suicide so that he—or at least his spirit—can keep a solemnly promised appointment with his dearest friend. The friend then avenges his death. Akinari's stories are characterized by their emphasis on elegant language, the creation of an uncanny atmosphere and philosophic suggestiveness. Many of his tales were refashioned by the fantasist Lafcadio Hearn [3-168]. Two of Akinari's stories provided the basis for the fantasy film *Ugetsu Monogatari* (1953).

Vergil: Publius Vergilius Maro (Italy), 70–19 BC.

1-85. Aeneid. 19 BC. Recommended translation by Allen Mandelbaum. Bantam, 1971.
Vergil transformed the Homeric epic into a vehicle for the expression of Roman values. Odysseus's quest for glory is replaced by Aeneas's laborious ascent to a value system based on duty and the subordination of self to the public good. The elements of fantasy are, by and large, imitative of Greek models. A modern fantasy closely modeled on the *Aeneid* is Richard Adams's *Watership Down* [4B-1].

***

1-86. Volsunga Saga. (Scandinavia), thirteenth century. Recommended translation by George K. Anderson. Associated Univ. Presses, 1982.
A Scandinavian cycle of legends, the same body of material that produced the German epic *Nibelungenlied* [1-57]. It is a dark tale of revenge centering on the characters Sigurd, Brunhilde and Gudrun. The Norse *Eddas* deal with much the same material. William Morris retold the saga in his *Sigurd the Volsung* (1877).

Voltaire (pseud. of François-Marie Arouet) (France), 1694–1778.
ABOUT: F, NE, SFE

1-87. Micromégas: A Comic Romance. 1753. Recommended translation by Donald Frame: in *Candide, Zadig and Selected Stories*. Indiana Univ. Press, 1961.
A philosophical fantasy indebted to Swift's *Gulliver's Travels* [1-81]. Voltaire described *Micromégas* as "a severe satire upon the philosophy, ignorance and self-conceit of mankind." As a vehicle for his satire, he introduced into Western

literature the concept of the alien observer of human mores. Micromégas, a giant from the star Sirius, visits Earth with a friend from Saturn. Conversations with a group of scientists (observed through a microscope fashioned from a diamond) impress the giants with the Earthlings' scientific knowledge; but the stupidity of our religious dogmas and wars horrifies them. On their leaving Earth, Micromégas gives the scientists a book of "correct answers" to philosophic questions. It contains blank pages. The central argument of the romance is to be found in Micromégas's assumption that intelligent beings spend their lives in love and thought, since these constitute the true life of the spirit and the only genuine sources of happiness.

1-88. The Princess of Babylon. 1768.
Formosanta, the only daughter of Belus, king of Babylon, is eighteen and beautiful beyond description. Separated from her lover, Amazan, she travels the world to find him. Accompanied by a sage phoenix, she visits such distant lands as China and Scythia (providing Voltaire ample opportunity for satiric comment along the way). In the end the lovers are united and marry. One of Voltaire's finest romances. Selections are in [1-20].

1-89. The White Bull. 1774. Recommended translation: in *Voltaire*, ed. by Edmund Fuller. Dell, 1959.
Another Oriental tale that reflects Voltaire's interest in *The Arabian Nights* [1-3]. The narrative concerns the adventures of Amasis, the daughter of the king of Egypt, and her lover, King Nebuchadnezzar, who has been transformed into a white bull. Voltaire's mockery is directed at the Old Testament. Among the other characters are Balaam's ass, the whale that swallowed Jonah and the serpent that tempted Eve. Voltaire's fantasy is rarely enchanting, since he employs it almost exclusively to subject what he regards as foolish superstition to rational attack.

*1-90. Zadig. 1748. See [1-87] for recommended translation.
Voltaire's longest and most intricately plotted Oriental romance, first published in 1747 as *Mémnon, histoire orientale*. The fantastic elements of the tale include an articulate parrot and an angel disguised as a hermit; but Voltaire, as usual, subordinates both fantasy and narrative to the presentation of a philosophic message, in this instance the related problems of determinism and freedom. The surface narrative concerns the adventures of a noble young man, Zadig (the name means "just" in Arabic), who after a series of adventures and near catastrophes becomes king when he marries the queen of Babylon. More important, Zadig learns that there is no such thing as chance; that the events he attributed to its power are part of a moral design of the universe in which evil and good are always balanced. Divine wisdom, like the blank pages of the book described in *Micromégas* [1-87], must remain a mystery.

***

1-91. Voyage of St. Brendan. *ca.* 850. Recommended translation: in *Lives of the Saints*, tr. by J. F. Webb. Penguin, 1965.
The Latin account of St. Brendan's voyage enjoyed enormous popularity during the Middle Ages; it was translated or refashioned in French, English, Welsh and

other languages. The Latin version is itself a transformation of earlier Irish journey narratives, especially the voyage of Maelduin. Brendan travels to a series of marvelous islands, eventually reaching the Island of Promise, a form of the Earthly Paradise. The narrative provides an opportunity to observe the medieval imagination reworking inherited motifs of fantastic literature in order to give them Christian meaning.

Walpole, Horace (U.K.), 1717–1797.
ABOUT: WW, GSF, SFW, F, CA, FG, SMFL, PE

*1-92. The Castle of Otranto: A Gothic Story. Tho. Lownds, 1765. Recommended edition: in *Three Gothic Novels*, ed. by Mario Praz. Penguin, 1968.
The themes of transgression, revenge and justice generate the action of the novel that began the trend for Gothic horror fiction. Manfred, having usurped the throne of Otranto, inhabits its castle unlawfully. When his only son is killed (crushed by a giant helmet that falls from the sky) on the eve of his wedding to the beautiful Isabella, Manfred is driven by lust and family ambition to divorce his almost unbearably virtuous wife and marry Isabella; but she hides in the subterranean vaults of the castle, where she meets a handsome youth (Theodore) who turns out to be the rightful heir to the throne. A complex sequence of adventures and supernatural events ends with Theodore both restored to his throne and married to Isabella, the repentant Manfred in a monastery and the castle destroyed by the ghost of its founder. Strikingly original in conception but flawed in its execution, *The Castle of Otranto* owes its importance to what it inspired as much as to what it is. Also annotated as [H1-108].

Wolfram von Eschenbach (Germany), *fl. ca.* 1210.

1-93. Parzifal. Recommended translation by Arthur T. Hatto. Penguin, 1980.
Wolfram continued and radically altered Chrétien de Troyes's incomplete story [1-17] of the innocent young knight who becomes the Grail King. Wolfram presents the story as a search for an ideal that is more spiritually elevating than knighthood. The most fantastic elements of Wolfram's tale concern not Parzifal but Gawain, whose adventures in the Castle of Wonders of the magician Klingsor would be imitated in countless later romances from *Amadis of Gaul* to *Orlando Furioso*. The quest for the Grail receives a particularly powerful modern retelling in Charles Williams's *War in Heaven* [3-379].

Wu Ch'eng-en (China), 1500–1582.

1-94. Journey to the West. 1592. Partial English translation by Arthur Waley published as *Monkey*. Allen and Unwin, 1942.
Although the framework of this wonderful novel is the pilgrimage of the Buddhist monk Tripitaka, the real hero is Monkey. Tripitaka, a passive figure, is terrified by the slightest danger, while Monkey overcomes every obstacle with his ingenuity. Monkey is a Chinese equivalent of the Western comic hero, similar to Reynard in Western animal fantasy. He is curious, energetic and bursting with ideas and chafes against any restrictions on his creative energy. The narrative

emphasizes moral values as well as adventure. In the first half of the tale, a spirit of rebellion against limits and authority emerges most clearly in the character of Monkey; the second half, however, stresses an ideal of perseverance. A great and enduring work of imaginative literature, unfortunately available only in part to English readers.

2

The Nineteenth Century, 1812–99

Brian Stableford

—

Bright lights cast dark shadows, and the illumination which visited the great minds of the Western world in the so-called Age of Enlightenment proved, after all, to be only partial. The philosophic and scientific revolution of the seventeenth and eighteenth centuries was a triumph of wisdom over superstition, of tolerant skepticism over mean-spirited dogma, which brought about a new confidence in the power of the human mind. That power was reflected in understanding and control—a new science feeding a nascent industrial and technological revolution—but the increase in power fell far short of omnipotence, and was accompanied by a certain residual sense of frustration. Anxiety was not obliterated, but merely sent into exile, concentrated in those areas of experience which illumination did not reach.

In terms of this metaphor, therefore, the Enlightenment had the effect of lighting a lantern in the twilight; besides adding to the sum of illumination, it also separated out light and darkness, throwing that which was not bright-lit into a deeper and more threatening gloom. It created opposition where before there had been permeation. This situation is clearly reflected in the literary products of the Enlightenment, where we find the gradual emergence of a new Realism in dialectical opposition to a new Romanticism.

The most obvious species of Romantic anxiety was exhibited in the Gothic literature of terror which thrived in the late eighteenth and early nineteenth centuries, and which is dealt with in the companion volume on horror literature, but there were other aspects of that anxiety which also found expression in terms of supernatural fictions of various kinds. It is the task of the chapters in the present volume to track the development of these other aspects of the Romantic opposition to Realism, most importantly the comic, the sentimental and the mystical.

Because these aspects are several, "fantasy" as a genre is rather less distinct in its character and its boundaries than the two genres of imaginative fiction from which it is usually distinguished: horror fiction on the one hand and speculative fiction (or science fiction) on the other. Horror fiction can be characterized by its relation to anxiety; speculative fiction by its attempt (or at least its pretense) to remain within the bounds of hypothetical possibility. Fantasy is easier to characterize, at least in the first instance, by means of a series of negatives: it is that fiction which is not mundane, yet does not belong to either of the two other genres of supramundane fiction.

To characterize fantasy as a kind of residual category, however—simply containing that which is left when all the other genres have been taken away—is undoubtedly misleading. There *is* a meaningful sense in which we can speak of a fantasy genre emerging in the nineteenth century, possessed of some degree of coherency in spite of its hybrid nature. What we see when we look at the work of the period is not an amorphous mass but an assembly of texts grouped around certain key themes, which evolves certain characteristic methods in the course of its progress.

Like any other genre, fantasy derived its instruments largely from preexisting forms. It borrowed from the folkloristic material which had been adapted into fiction and molded to the cause of *bourgeois* moralizing for the purpose of "civilizing" young minds by the likes of Perrault and the Grimms. It borrowed from the chivalric romance of the late Middle Ages, which had recently begun to escape (albeit rather halfheartedly) from the straitjacket of moralistic and pietistic allegory into which it had earlier been crammed by the monks who controlled the distribution of literacy in medieval Europe. It borrowed from the Oriental fantasies which (aided by a less rigorous style of moralizing) had become popular in the wake of translations of the *Arabian Nights* [1-3, 1-23]. It borrowed too from the ancient religious systems of Europe, especially the Greek and Roman mythology which was so richly interwoven into the texture of classical literature, and thus into the ideological heritage of Western Europe. Despite this debt to and dependence on preexistent materials, though, an examination of its history reveals that as the new genre evolved in the course of the nineteenth century, it gradually acquired a character of its own.

When "fantasy" is used as a label for a modern publishing category, it is often used in a narrow sense to refer to what J. R. R. Tolkien, in his classic essay "On Fairy-Stories" [7-62], describes as Secondary World fantasies: stories set in imaginary worlds whose spatial and temporal connection with the real world are frankly mysterious, but whose nature and contents are intelligibly related to it. This basic characterization was taken up by Lin Carter, whose Ballantine Adult Fantasy series (1969–75) was the first to colonize the market space in which the contemporary publishing category now exists, in his book *Imaginary Worlds* [7-10].

The purest fantasy, for both Tolkien and Carter, consists of stories set entirely within a Secondary World. In many stories of a closely related kind, however, the characters must move from our mundane world into the Secondary World, and may move repeatedly back and forth across the boundary between the two. Any reasonable definition of fantasy must obviously accommodate these works. A broader definition, though, must also take in stories in which a part of the mundane world is briefly infected or transformed by the characteristics of a Secondary World, even if no such Secondary World is formally allotted a space of its own. Such transformations are frequently likened to (or "explained" as) dreams and hallucinations. Within the actual historical tradition of fantastic fictions there are many brief and limited transformations associated with the displacement from a hypothetical Secondary World of a single magical character or object. If the effect of this temporary transformation is (at least partly) enlivening or life-enhancing, then the work properly qualifies as a fantasy—the qualification being necessary, of course, because works in which supramundane intrusions are exclusively threatening or life-denying belong to the horror genre.

Lin Carter alleges in *Imaginary Worlds* that what differentiates Secondary Worlds from the mundane one can be summed up in a single word: magic. As one-word summings-up go, this serves quite well, and it makes a convenient point of entry to the most interesting questions about the nature of the fantasy *genre*—which are, of course, questions about the rewards to be obtained from reading it. The genre has required a rhetoric of apology ever since its earliest days because of an apparent paradox in its nature. It has always seemed puzzling to some critics that anyone should be interested in reading stories about a magical world in an era when mature and reasonable adults have ceased to believe in magic. Some nineteenth-century educators were, in fact, sternly opposed to fairy stories and other tales traditionally told to children on the grounds that such fictions could only mislead and confuse, and would handicap intellectual development.

This apparent paradox sometimes invites a simplistically uncharitable interpretation, which makes a taste for fantasy symptomatic of a failure to cope with the rigors of real life. This line of argument suggests that our remote and ignorant ancestors believed in the efficacy of magic because they were simple-minded, and that we might therefore grant a tacit license to children, which permits them to believe in magic until they are old enough to "know better," but that modern adults ought to have "grown out of" such silly fancies, and can sustain an interest in supramundane fiction only if they too are simpleminded.

This is, of course, a ridiculous allegation: it is a grotesque misunderstanding to assume that reading fantastic fiction requires an acceptance of the reality of magic. Most commentators refer to what is actually required as a temporary and limited "willing suspension of disbelief," but Tolkien goes further, characterizing the contact between writer and reader in more positive terms, as a demand for a distinct species of "Secondary Belief." With this observation as a prelude to explanation, he opens the way to a more sensible discussion of the psychological utility of this cognitive move.

Tolkien's essay refers to three functions of fantasy, which he discusses under the rubrics of Recovery, Escape and Consolation. It is part of his thesis that fantasy is the natural partner of reason, neither "insulting" nor undermining it, and that our sense of what *is* necessarily has as its logical counterpart a sense of that which *is not*. The ability to take up a fantastic viewpoint can therefore aid us in putting things in a better perspective; what we "recover" in fantasy is actually a clearer sight than we normally employ in viewing the world, because it is a less narrow sight—a sight which does not take for granted the limitations of mundanity.

To argue thus is to assert that we cannot see reality clearly enough if we are trapped within it, and that only when we can perform the imaginative trick of moving outside the actual can we properly appreciate its bounds. This is the fundamental task of the literature of fantasy, and in the nineteenth-century evolution of the genre we can see the principal contributors of the genre coming to this realization, and developing a series of literary devices adapted to this purpose.

Once we accept this argument we can see that giving children fantasies to amuse them and to work upon is not at all a matter of granting them temporary license to believe absurdities. It is instead an entirely appropriate means of helping them to arrive at a sensible distinction of the real and the unreal. At the beginning of the period under consideration in this chapter, this was not widely understood, and one of the motive forces which we see at work in the evolution of nineteenth-century children's fantasy is a campaign to rehabilitate and revitalize those fictions essential to the education of the developing mind.

The function of Escape is seen by Tolkien in much the same light as the function of Recovery. He asserts unhesitatingly that the escapism of fantasy is to be evaluated as if it were the escape of a prisoner rather than the desertion of a soldier; it is a liberation, not a moral failure. This statement is not entirely without qualification, though, because if it is to be genuinely rewarding, the escapism of fantasy cannot be content simply with drawing the reader away from oppression; it must also lead to some kind of goal. This is where the third function of fantasy—that of Consolation—emerges. The consolatory goal which fantasy should have Tolkien calls "eucatastrophe," by which he means a climactic affirmation of both joy and right: pleasure alloyed with moral confidence. This does not mean that fantasy cannot be tragic; it often is. But it *does* mean that fantasy should not be despairing (as speculative fiction and horror fiction sometimes are); in this view, the work of fantasy is essentially committed to the cause of moral rearmament.

It is in the nature of magic not only to permit but to define the kind of moral rearmament of which fantasy is capable. In preliterate societies, where belief in magic is sustained, there is an intimate connection between magic and morality. Magical explanations and magical practices are invoked at precisely those points at which the real world fails to measure up to the ideal. The hunter in search of meat makes magic against the possibility of failure, but he may fail if he has broken a taboo. The crop grower makes magic to bring the rain which he needs, and magic to fertilize the soil, but if the tribal ancestors have been offended by the wickedness of their children, the rain will not come and the soil will not bear fruit. The medicine man makes magic not only to fight illness but also to oppose the evil intent of witches who would bring all manner of misfortunes upon the tribe. Magic is an expression of desire—the attempt to create in the imagination a world where the human will is the master of fate—but desire without moral responsibility is itself an evil, and magic of that kind is *black magic*. Licit magic is intimately bound up with the question of whether men truly *deserve* to succeed in their endeavors.

The utility of magic lies not in the practical arena of human endeavor but in the theater of the psyche. Licit magic builds confidence and *morale*; it opposes defeatism and despair. Magic—or some psychological substitute—is vital to all human endeavor at a causal level, because confidence may be a necessary condition of success, and despair a guarantee of failure. In societies where belief in magic is sustained (including ours, which has by no means been purged of such beliefs), forms of magical practice and species of magical conviction are largely defined by moral priorities, dependent upon notions of reward and punishment.

The characterization of magic as an expression of desire is neatly and ironically inverted in Jean-Paul Sartre's theory of the emotions, which attempts to characterize emotion as a "magical" form of sensation. How we feel about an object, Sartre suggests, reflects the relationship we would have with that object if the world were indeed magical, and the emotions fill a spectrum which extends from a conviction of our own omnipotence to a sensation of utter helplessness—from megalomania to paranoia. The emotions, of course, have a moral gravity of their own: whenever passion moves us, there is moral danger.

If we look at supernatural fiction from this perspective, we will recognize that horror fiction exemplifies the negative end of the emotional spectrum, while fantasy exemplifies the positive. Horror fiction characteristically deals with the frustration of desire, or with temptation leading to destruction; fantasy characteristically deals with the measured victory of desire, or with constructive temptation. Horror stories frequently build to a climax which involves the escape of the characters from whatever has threatened them, but such an ending is a matter of relief rather than achievement. By the same token, fantasy stories often contain a partial negation of their own logic, which shows not only in occasional tragic resolutions, but also—and more often—in a bittersweet undercurrent of irony.

The lovely sadness of knowing that fantasy is, after all, fantasy supplies a characteristic savor to the masterpieces of the genre. In every case, though, matters of morality are at stake. Good and evil are in the balance, and the question at issue is whether and how the characters will be delivered from evil. Horror fiction tends to emphasize the threat, and to build suspense upon the question of whether deliverance is possible; a happy ending, in a horror story, is a restoration of normality. Fantasy, though it is often comic or calculatedly quaint, conceals beneath its relative lightness of tone a greater ambition; in fantasy, normality is never enough, and though the preferable ideal may in the end turn out to be unattainable—or attainable only at a terrible price—fantasy nevertheless moves in search of eucatastrophe, in the hope of improving the quality of life. The horror genre contains the fiction of fear; the fantasy genre contains the fiction of hope.

When we examine the syncretic historical process by means of which the fantasy genre was consolidated in the nineteenth century, one of the most striking things we observe is how differently imaginative fiction evolved in different nations. Although these national differences can be seen to some extent in the other genres of supramundane fiction, they are not nearly so important there: science fiction and terror have a common vocabulary of ideas which transcends cultural boundaries with relative ease, but because of its dependence on folkloristic motifs on the one hand, and its particular relationship to moral order on the other, fantasy is much more likely to retain the idiosyncratic characteristics of its cultural and historical context.

We can see these national differences quite clearly in the extent to which the different supramundane genres gained popularity. Gothic horror was enormously successful in Germany, and was taken up with hardly less enthusiasm in England, yet its appeal in France and the United States was much more muted. This is not unconnected with the fact that France and the United States both had political revolutions while England and Germany both contrived to stifle and contain the spirit of revolution in such a way that its unrelieved tensions helped to nurture an anxious sense of threat. There is, however, more to the matter than the superficialities of political history.

The earliest exercises in the sociology of literature, including the writings of Madame de Staël, observed that the literature of northern Europe seemed significantly different in character from that of the Mediterranean countries, and had tried to link this to landscape and climate. However eccentric such theories may seem in application to mundane fiction, there is an undeniable link between the perceived character of the natural world and the inventions of myth and folklore, which are manifest in the differences between the mythology of the Greeks and Romans on the one hand, and the mythology of the Norsemen and Teutons on the other. The supramundane world imagined by northern Europeans tends to be a bleak and wintry one, while that imagined by southern Europeans is a warm and summery one; it is the difference between Asgard and Olympus.

Something of this difference is reproduced in the contrasting fantasies of Germany and France, while the ambiguous situations of Britain (warmed by the gulf stream) and America (geographically vast and various) are to some extent reflected in certain paradoxical qualities of British and American fantasy. One can find similar factors at work in the kinds of aesthetic theory favored in the different nations. Germany and Britain played host to idealistic theories which exhorted the use of the imagination to capture the "sublime": a sense of awe in the face of the wildness of nature and the dark immensity of the cosmos. Such theories assisted in the glamorization of the Gothic imagination. In France, on the other hand, the Romantics were much more concerned with the worship of beauty (strongly contrasted with the sublime in Burke's famous essay) and with a sensibility far more Epicurean in character. Although the maverick Edgar Allan Poe was sufficiently in tune with French aestheticism to be considered more highly there than in his homeland, the general tenor of American work owed more to the Transcendentalism of Emerson and his circle, which had less room for awe and astonishment as well as less regard for Epicurean niceties.

Of the major nations to be considered. France was the first to develop an elaborate supramundane literature which had relatively little horror in it. Long before the revolutionary period, France had been the principal home of chivalric romance, and in the eighteenth century French writers—aided in their inspiration by the examples of Perrault and the Galland translation of the *Arabian Nights* [1-23]—produced dozens of exotic romances which combined the whimsicality of fairy tales or the lushness of Arabian mythology with the *politesse* of French courtly manners.

In the early nineteenth century, therefore, we find the French Romantic writers still fascinated by "the Orient" (which for them included North Africa as well as Persia and more mysterious points eastward), and with the interface between classical antiquity and mythology. The extension of this Orientalism and its associated sensibilities into prose fiction is associated first and foremost with Gautier [2-64–2-65], but it can also be seen very conspicuously in the work of Anatole France [2-60–2-62; 3-143–3-145] and Pierre Louÿs [2-111–2-112; 3-224]. Its most impressive productions constitute a series of novels set in the world of antiquity, which are fantasized not so much by explicit supramundane intrusions as by an acute sense of moral separation: Flaubert's *Salammbô* [2-55], France's *Thaïs* [2-61] and Louÿs's *Aphrodite* [2-111]. In all the works of this tradition there is an explicit challenge to the oppressive "official" morality of Christianity—to the extent that many of them were considered too indecent for early translation into English. Fantasy in France thus became an extravagantly eloquent champion of a warm and humane liberalism, frequently celebrating the power of erotic attraction.

As might be expected, this contrasts with the development of fantasy in nineteenth-century Britain, where Victorian morality eventually came to exercise a powerful dominion over the written word. Early in the century one can find Shelley attempting to claim for the poets the privilege of being the world's true legislators, and Keats proclaiming the equivalence of truth and beauty (while his poems exhibit a fascination with antiquity very similar to that which the French were to retain). In the same period one can find a certain passionate Orientalism in the earlier work of John Sterling [2-145–2-146], and a determined irreverence in the early work of Edward Bulwer-Lytton [2-113] and the self-styled "Modern Pythagorean" Robert MacNish [2-119]. Later prose work by these and other writers was, however, conspicuously chilled by the icy winds of moral oppression. By the time Victoria came to the throne British fantasy was already becoming more primly and conservatively moralistic—a primness which is striking even in the comic vein of Dalton's *Invisible Gentlemen* [2-40] and Dickens's Christmas Books [2-42–2-44], and which becomes exaggerated almost to the point of grotesquerie in the work of such ardent disciples of Victorianism as Mrs. Craik [2-35] and Christina Rossetti [2-140].

Victorian painters were able to use fantasy motifs as a means of sidestepping moral restraint—the mid-century fashionability of fairy painting reflects, in part, the irony that one way to present images of female nudity while insulating the artist from accusations of indecency was to add a pair of gossamer wings to the figure in question (a similar exception was made for female figures in paintings illustrating scenes from classical myth). Writers found no such parallel move available; verbal indecencies and indelicacies could not be excused by context. Thus, the most obvious response to Victorianism in supramundane fiction was the development of a highly stylized and carefully chastened school of fantasy best exemplified by George MacDonald's *Phantastes* [2-116] and the medieval romances of William Morris [2-124–2-128].

The anarchic spirit in Victorian fantasy tended to sidestep confrontation with official morality by displacing its energies into a more radical confrontation with logic and reason, best exemplified by the nonsense poetry of Edward Lear [2-104] and Lewis Carroll's Alice books [2-23]. It was not until the 1880s that this kind of deliberate trafficking with absurdity began to confront issues of behavioral morality in a less elliptical fashion—very cautiously in the works of Charles Wentworth Lisle [2-109] and F. Anstey [2-5–2-8], more calculatedly in the deceptively light fantasies of H. G. Wells [2-154-2-155] and Oscar Wilde [2-157-2-158]. Even then the forces of repression remained sufficiently powerful to destroy Wilde for his temerity. Beneath the surface of the classic Victorian fantasies, though—usually hidden by a veil of grotesquerie or humor—bitter responses to the pressure of Victorian moral extremism can be discovered; a sensitive decoding of the allegories of Dickens, Sterling, MacDonald, Carroll and Morris reveals a full measure of confusion and pain.

American supramundane fiction was rather more heterogeneous than that of France or Britain, and it is significant that this heterogeneity is to be found within the work of each of the major writers. In the works of Washington Irving [2-92], Nathaniel Hawthorne [2-79] and Fitz-James O'Brien [2-134] (and also in the remarkably varied output of Edgar Allan Poe [H2-77]) we find the comic rubbing shoulders with the horrific and the sentimental, and though the authors pull in different directions—Irving toward the grotesque, Hawthorne the moralistic, Poe the paranoid—their canons each present the appearance of a mélange with less internal consistency than is exhibited by any European author.

To some extent this variety reflects the fact that America had only the most meager resources to draw upon in terms of a native folklore, and its writers tended to take their pick from a wide spectrum of European sources. One could argue with reasonable conviction that American fantasy stood in an imaginative relationship with Europe very similar to the relationship which existed between French fantasy and "the Orient." Europe was, from the American viewpoint, a kind of antiquity, and when American fantasists came to mine its resources they tended to adopt the same open door philosophy which was subsequently to be formally articulated as an item of immigration policy.

The distanced haphazardness of American borrowings from folkloristic sources, coupled with a marked irreverence in the invention of "new" folklore by writers like Irving and Austin [2-11] (which seemed entirely appropriate to authors working in the thoroughly disenchanted milieu of the newborn nation), gave American fantasy a conspicuously ironic flavor. It was inevitable that in America it would be the humorists who would eventually gain ascendancy within the genre in the latter part of the century: Mark Twain [2-152], Frank R. Stockton [2-147-2-148] and John Kendrick Bangs [2-12-2-13] in the United States, Max Adeler [2-1] in Canada. No greater contrast can be imagined than that which separates the clownish disrespect of the fiction produced by these writers from the awesomely respectful drama of the French historical fantasists.

German fantasy began to crystallize at a relatively early stage in the theoretically supported *Kunstmärchen* ("art fairy tales") of Goethe [1-32], Novalis and Fouqué [2-57-2-59]—a tradition which was carried forward by such writers as Wilhelm Hauff [2-76] and Paul Heyse—but German Romanticism always leaned so far toward the anxious pole of the magical spectrum that the greater part of its prose fiction belongs to the horror genre. Surprisingly little mid- or late nineteeth-century fantasy has been translated from the German, though other nations of northern Europe produced such notable writers as Gogol [2-69], Hans Christian Andersen [2-4] and Jonas Lie [2-108]. It seems to be the case that writers in Germany did not take the opportunity of constructing moralistic fantasies either to support (as in Britain) or oppose (as in France) the dominant morality of the day; nor (unsurprisingly, in view of the temper of German literary culture) were they drawn to the kind of humorously skeptical fantasy which came to be produced in some quantity in America.

Despite these sharp differences between the emergent traditions of fantasy in various nations there was one important influence which came to affect them all in fairly similar fashion, and that is the resurgence of credulity with respect to the occult which swept through the Western world in the latter part of the nineteenth century. Its manifestations were many and various, but the most important ones included Baron von Reichenbach's championship of the healing powers of magnetism and the subsequent clinical uses of hypnotism; the cult of Spiritualism associated with those dishonest conjurors who set up in business as mediators between the human and spirit worlds; the Theosophy of Madame Blavatsky and Annie Besant; and the neo-Rosicrucianism of such would-be ceremonial magicians as "Eliphas Levi" and the founders of the Order of the Golden Dawn.

The scholarly fantasies inspired by these overlapping cults attracted the interest and involvement of a good many notable persons, including both scientists and novelists. A number of writers began to import the ideative flotsam and jetsam of these cults into superstitious didactic fantasies which took their place within nascent traditions of moralistic fantasy, and though a substantial part of what they produced is more conveniently discussed as a species of horror fiction, they did produce a good deal of generic fantasy, including many mawkishly optimistic literary accounts of the afterlife, which helped to open up imaginative space in Britain for the later development of a more philosophically inclined subgenre of posthumous fantasy. Most of this fiction is awful, the missionary zeal of its authors setting mere questions of literary competence firmly aside, but there were some good writers among the credulous and there were other writers who were prepared to borrow the vocabulary of ideas popularized by the credulous, without necessarily committing their own faith.

There is little point in quibbling over such questions of definition as whether a credulous occult romance ought to qualify as mundane fiction because its author believes religiously in the possibility of all that he (or, more often, she) has set forth. It is certainly true, though, that the literary interest of such works tends to stand in inverse proportion to the degree of conviction which the author has. This is not to say that credulous occult romance was never popular; the author who outsold all others in Britain during the last few years of the century was Marie Corelli [2-31-2-34], who was by far the most fervent and most earnest of such writers. But the likes of Marie Corelli and Elizabeth Stuart Phelps (her American counterpart) occupy a very curious position in literary history. We can try to account for their popularity only in psychological terms; any estimation of their literary merits is bound to be confused and compromised by the knowledge that what they were writing is, after all, utter rubbish in terms of its sincerest assertions.

Credulity is certainly not incompatible with the ability to tell a convincing horror story, but it does not lend itself effectively to the construction of a story whose ultimate intention is to be consolatory or uplifting. We know only too well that we are being paid in false coin when an author asks us not only to recognize the moral propriety of what he or she is saying, but also to believe that the world really is like that. Life in Heaven is a eucatastrophe in which many people try to preserve real belief, but such real belief is actually threatened and undermined by attempts at literary description—which inevitably raise more questions than they answer. For some of their readers Mrs. Oliphant's tales of the Little Pilgrim [2-135] presumably did fulfill a consolatory function, but if one approaches them as moral parables rather than divine revelations, they lead to confusion and doubt, not to certainty.

The most effective moral allegories are produced by skeptics who need not be confused or weighed down by matters of dogma, and it is significantly noticeable that when readers do find such stories as Mrs. Oliphant's, George Eliot's "The Lifted Veil" [2-53] or Bourdillon's *Nephelé* [2-20] effective they may well be quite unsure whether the stories are credulous or not. Nowhere is the difficulty of writing fantasies based in credulity more obvious than in the "new legends" produced by devout Christians, who are attempting to elaborate a mythos which is still, for them, sacred. The most successful nineteenth-century writings in that vein are to be found in the work of Laurence Housman, and his collections *All Fellows* and *The Cloak of Friendship* [2-84], together with MacDonald's *Lilith* [2-115], offer clear evidence that serious and efficient literary investigation of the moral tenets of a sincerely held faith cannot leave that faith unaltered, and when the believer resists the loss of his belief he is inevitably led toward an uncomfortable heterodoxy—and may, if he is entirely scrupulous in his self-examination, arrive at the fearfully heretical conclusion which Anatole France reached in *The Human Tragedy* [2-62].

Nineteenth-century fantasy is sufficiently various that it is not easy to isolate key themes or point to coherent undercurrents guiding its evolution. However, Tolkien's identification of three key features of Secondary World fantasy—Recovery, Escape and Consolation—does offer a set of analytic instruments which can be applied on a broader front than the one on which he mounts his own campaign, and which may help to make such unifying themes and methods as the fantasy genre has a little clearer.

Tolkien is certainly right to argue that recovery of a clear view of the world is something which requires imaginative effort. That effort is required to make us look beyond and through the triteness of the taken-for-granted, and to discover new perspectives from which the familiar looks odd. Tolkien calls the latter effect "Mooreeffoc," quoting an argument by G. K. Chesterton based in an odd thrill experienced by Dickens upon observing from the wrong side the phrase "Coffee Room" inscribed on a glass door. We have all experienced similar things; it is not only words spelled backwards which have this mysterious aesthetic appeal but most other kinds of wordplay, whether they consist of sophisticated exercises in rhyming and punning or the malapropisms and naive misunderstandings of children. Language, as a map of the world, is mutable in all sorts of ways which introduce happy absurdities and discontinuities into its work of reference. So it is with fiction, which maps human experience in a fashion analogous to the way in which language maps reality, and which generates many of its happy absurdities and discontinuities in the form of fantasy.

A large number of nineteenth-century fantasies work in this fashion, creating new viewpoints which administer a series of shocks to our conventional assumptions about the way our world works. The characters whom Alice meets in her odysseys underground and through the looking glass [2-23] use the instruments of wordplay to do this, but there are other ways in which the trick can be worked. There are, for instance, the wonderful visits paid to our world by the ambassadors of other ways of thought: more-or-less amiable demons like Dalton's *Gentleman in Black* [2-39] or Lytton's Asmodeus [2-113]; or angels like Wells's [2-155]; or the characters borrowed from pagan religions by F. Anstey [2-6, 2-7]. Then again, fantasy provides the opportunity for personalities to be displaced by trading places, as in Besant's *Doubts of Dives* [2-16], Donnelly's *Doctor Huguet* [2-47], Gautier's "Avatar" [2-65], MacNish's "The Metempsychosis" [2-119] or Sterling's *The Onyx Ring* [2-146], so that one character's assumptions can be brought face-to-face with another's constraints and frustrations. All these stories serve the function of showing their characters and their readers the world's stage lit from an unconventional angle.

The fantasies which we make up for ourselves in order to escape temporarily from everyday life are often described as "idle fancies," mainly because they come to us in moments of idleness and may be used to distract us from burdensome matters of duty. But our everyday fantasies are often idle in another way too: they fall readily into stereotyped patterns, and we rarely elaborate them beyond the point of enjoying their vicarious satisfactions. For the most part, we obtain gratification from our fantasies quite easily; we usually do not put a great deal of effort into their formation. We may, of course, enter into collaboration with writers in the construction of our own fantasies, appropriating their efforts to make our daydreams more detailed and more lively, but the best writers inevitably do this kind of job more thoroughly and more artfully than the vast majority of their readers and if we draw too heavily on their resources, we may find our daydreams reduced in value because they are not specifically tailored to link up with our particular feelings and frustrations.

There are some kinds of fiction which apparently exist largely to fulfill this kind of daydream-fueling purpose; pornography is the most obvious example. Those who despise fantasy as a genre often speak of it as if it belonged entirely to this category, and had no further functions, but that is a very mistaken view. Fantasy writers may indeed elaborate a wish fulfillment scheme, but any survey of the genre's history will quickly reveal that they normally and characteristically do so in order to interrupt, interrogate and subvert that scheme. This subversion can most easily be seen in parables which warn against the futility of wish fulfillment itself, informing us that the wishes which are granted (such wishes traditionally, but not necessarily, come in sets of three) will always lead us to disaster. Nineteenth-century fantasy contains many examples of such stories, which show us ill-advised wishes going absurdly or tragically wrong; the bibliography includes excellent examples by Chamisso [2-27], Dalton [2-40], Dickens [2-44], Gilbert [2-66] and Jerrold [2-95], among others. Nineteenth-century fantasy is also rich in accounts of dream worlds where characters are educated in the folly of their fancies; we find interesting—and very varied—instances in the work of Adeler [2-1], Mrs. Craik [2-35], Dostoyevsky [2-48], du Maurier [2-51], Nicholson [2-131] and Twain [2-152]. Where writers are more generous in their treatment of daydreaming—as they often are in children's stories, such as those by Jean Ingelow [2-91] and Mrs. Molesworth [2-123]—they remain very conscious of the temporary nature of such fantasies and of the fact that they must not take over the child's whole life.

When nineteenth-century fantasy writers lead us into Secondary Worlds they are certainly facilitating an escape from our imprisonment by mundanity, and we may often feel ourselves to be tourists out for enjoyment rather than earnest seekers after knowledge avid for instruction. Nevertheless, the authors invariably have some didactic purpose in escorting us upon such odysseys. Even when they boldly declare that they are peddling pure nonsense, they are guiding us toward an entirely proper irreverence for the sordid habit of taking things for granted. In the great majority of instances there is far more going on than the simple instructive process of the knowledgeable dictating wisdom to the initiate. The most significant of the nineteenth-century journeys into the Land of Faerie and its many analogues were authentic voyages of exploration and discovery, undertaken by writers who were concerned to learn as much as to teach. The authors too are trying to escape, and though they are usually uncertain of their destination, they are nevertheless eager to make progress in their journey toward it. That destination is, of course, the ideal which, even if it proves ultimately unattainable, will bring moral confidence and psychological harmony to life by lighting the preferable path of thought and behavior.

Reading works of this kind, one is all too sharply aware that the writing of the greatest fantasies must have been an act of catharsis: an attempt to purge confusion. Inevitably, the purgation was in all cases only half-effective. Allegory, though it can be a valuable instrument of thought, can produce no real solutions to the moral problems which it brings into sharper focus. Nevertheless, we must not underestimate the value of that half-effect simply because it is, in functional terms, entirely magical.

The magical worlds devised by nineteenth-century fantasy writers, whether they lie in a hypothetical past or in some parallel dimension, often seem to lie closer to the world of Platonic archetypes than to the real world of the nineteenth century. They are dramatically purified worlds, where good and evil are more clearly polarized and whose characters very often embody single virtues and vices. They are worlds where rewards and punishments are more extreme, where social roles are generally very distinct. But for the heroes who move through them they remain problematic, and no matter what success the heroes attain in material and spiritual terms, those problematic features can never be resolved. Often, the conclusion of the story is a mere dissolution of the dream, which can only leave the protagonist with mixed feelings—richer in experience and understanding, but no more certain than before how the question of how men and women should live is to be answered. Obvious failures of character may be easily redeemed, as Dickens demonstrated in *A Christmas Carol* [2-43], but his later Christmas fantasies [2-42, 2-44] bear ready testimony to his acceptance that more subtle failures are not easily overcome.

For this reason, even the most positive and constructive of nineteenth-century fantasies have their darker, more anxious side. The quest for eucatastrophe is haunted by the awareness that success rests on compromise. Fantasy is by no means as simpleminded or ritualistic as its opponents sometimes claim, and those works which might be assembled retrospectively into a tradition of nineteenth-century Secondary World fantasies—extending from Fouqué [2-57] through MacDonald [2-116] to Morris [2-128]—bear adequate testimony to the moral doubts as well as the moral determination of the authors.

These doubts extend into the antiquarian interest in folkloristic themes and motifs which was taken by so many nineteenth-century fantasists. Their anthropological attitudes—even when the authors are clearly unconscious of any implied theoretical context in their work—are founded in uneasy contemplation of the moral and practical dimensions of the beliefs and motifs which they are recapitulating. Though this is particularly obvious in the German tradition of the Grimms [2-71] and Hauff [2-76], it is also noticeable in other northern European traditions, such as the Scandinavian (exemplified here in the works of Andersen [2-4] and Lie [2-108]).

A conservationist regard for the value of folklore is frequently to be found in cultures which have come to fear their own erosion, as can be seen in those parts of the British Isles whose language and folkways were becoming increasingly marginal because of the economic and political dominion of the English. Scottish writers like James Hogg [2-81] and "Fiona Macleod" [2-118]—and to a lesser extent Andrew Lang [2-102] and Mrs. Craik (in *Alice Learmont*) [2-35]—used fantastic fiction to capture something of the spirit of the eroded mythos. Though Yeats [2-160] did something similar for Ireland and the Welsh mythology of the *Mabinogion* was redeployed by Peacock [2-136], it was the Scots who retained a thriving print culture of their own in Edinburgh and Glasgow, and had the invaluable *Blackwood's Magazine* to assist in their cause, so it was they who made the most conspicuous impact on nineteenth-century fantasy.

Nostalgia generated by the erosion of mythos and mystery is correlated in much nineteenth-century fantasy with the notion of the banishment of superstition by the march of reason and the corollary feeling that there is something to be regretted in this banishment. There is a depth of tragic consciousness in parables which describe the exile of the fairy folk from England, including Sterling's "Chronicle of England" [2-146], or the sad fate of outdated objects of worship in Garnett's "Twilight of the Gods" [2-63]. This regret can also be seen, in vulgarized form, in the curious subgenre of stories featuring revivified Egyptian mummies which had its origins in such works as Lee's *Pharaoh's Daughter* [2-105] and Holland's *Egyptian Coquette* [2-82]. It is also a key component of one of the more popular subgenres of nineteenth-century fantasy: the lost race story. Lost race stories rarely give a prominent role to the supernatural, but their internal dynamic takes them beyond the map into those exotic regions of the Earth where men may seek a romantic destiny outside the possibilities of actual society. Like the more admirable Secondary World fantasies, the best lost race fantasies offer no easy solutions by this route, and the eccentric masterpiece of the subgenre— Haggard's *She* [2-74]—is paradoxically determined in its uneasy ambivalence.

We can also see in the uneasy undercurrents of nineteenth-century fantasy the effects of a trend which was to be much more influential in horror fiction: the burgeoning of interest in the altered states of consciousness associated with hallucination and delusion. We can see the more clinical side of this fascination in the "medicated novels" of Oliver Wendell Holmes [2-83], which have their European counterparts in William Gilbert's fictitious accounts of the forms of "monomania" [H2-31], but more interesting exhibitions are to be found in hallucinatory grotesques moving in the direction of surrealism and absurdism, such as can be found in the work of writers as various as Gogol [2-69], Nicholson [2-131] and Gérard de Nerval [2-130]. Such themes are historically linked to ideas associated with mesmerism, animal magnetism and hypnotism, which are staples of credulous occult romance, but are by no means subject to the constraints of scholarly fantasy. Earnest fantasies like Julian Hawthorne's *The Professor's Sister* [2-78] and du Maurier's *Trilby* [2-52] have an intrinsic interest which transcends mere questions of plausibility.

Given all this, there can be no doubt that the Tolkienian function of Consolation, as served by nineteenth-century fantasy, is by no means to be dismissed as a mere literary equivalent of the compensatory consolations of private daydreams. The Escape which it offers is by no means a cushioned refuge which simply insulates its readers from the stresses of confrontation with the real and the weariness of social conformity. Both these functions remain associated with (and perhaps subservient to) the function of Recovery, in which we are allowed to regain a proper reverence for the strangeness of our own world by confrontation and intercourse with imaginary ones which, because they are magical, are less strange to the emotional aspects of perception.

With very few exceptions, nineteenth-century fantasy existed on the periphery of the literary world. If we leave aside children's books, which compete in a specialized marketplace, the best-selling novels of nineteenth-century fantasy are few in number: *She* [2-74]; the romances of Marie Corelli [2-31–2-34]; Anstey's *Vice Versa* [2-8]; Twain's *Connecticut Yankee* [2-152]. On the other hand, some nineteenth-century fantasies were spectacularly successful because they created—or at least colonized—their own market niches. Dickens's Christmas Books helped to create a norm by which the Christmas annuals issued by British publishers in association with their periodicals were licensed to indulge in supernatural whimsy and other fanciful tales. This license was shared by many of the annual volumes issued to take advantage of the Christmas present-buying season: *The Keepsake, The Continental Annual and Romantic Cabinet, Friendship's Offering* and many others.

Periodicals were vital to the promulgation of all kinds of imaginative fiction in the nineteenth century, because so much imaginative fiction works best in short forms. Although literacy spread more slowly in Britain than in France or America, the relatively large population of Britain—and especially of London—meant that British writers were at least as well supplied with outlets as their French and American counterparts. An enormous influence in the development of British supramundane fiction was *Blackwood's Magazine*, which played host to John Sterling [2-146], James Hogg [2-81] and Robert MacNish [2-119] as well as publishing important works such as Eliot's "Lifted Veil" [2-53]. In England, *Bentley's Miscellany* was an outlet of some importance, featuring Barham's *Ingoldsby Legends* [2-14] and work by James Dalton as well as reprinting material from America and Europe.

American periodicals were no less important to American fantasy writers like O'Brien [2-134], but the publishing of Christmas annuals was not such an industry there, and a writer like Kip [2-99] was very much an exception. Other differences in the British and American traditions are linked to the fact that many American periodicals using fiction were newspapers rather than magazines, physically ephemeral. Upmarket periodicals like *Harper's, The Atlantic Monthly* and *Lippincott's Magazine* carried a certain amount of fantasy, but as with the more prestigious British journals such as the *Cornhill*, they gave a very considerable priority to realistic material, and the American market remained relatively restricted until the spectacular rise of the pulps after the turn of the century.

It is probably true that the more downmarket a mid-nineteenth-century journal was, the more space it was likely to give to imaginative fiction—both fantasy and horror. Popular British magazines like *The Olio; or Museum of Entertainment* (founded 1828) and Vickers's *London Journal* (founded 1845) are replete with stories of the supernatural, though almost all of them are either reprinted from familiar sources or of negligible quality. Penny fiction periodicals were usually well spiced with "Tales" and "Legends," the latter often masquerading as "true stories" or as items of authentic folklore (neither pretense being particularly convincing). The same was probably true of American and continental European nations, though the ephemeral nature of the periodicals concerned makes it far more difficult for researchers to test the proposition, and we must remember in examining the cross-section of nineteenth-century fantasy presented in the following bibliography that it is a very selective account of what was published and read in that period. We must take it on trust that the vast majority of works deserving preservation have actually survived, and there are certainly some writers who have been undeservedly forgotten. John Sterling [2-145–2-146] and James Dalton [2-39–2-40] are among those who have so far received little attention in other reference books and whose works have been out of print for more than a century. A scrupulous examination of obscure periodicals would almost certainly turn up others.

In selecting the following works for annotation I have tried to illustrate, so far as I can, the breadth of nineteenth-century fantasy as well as exhibit its finest examples. I have been fairly ruthless in excluding all but a handful of the posthumous fantasies inspired by the boom in supposed communication with the spirit world (most of which are worthless in literary terms) and I have been rather economical in my coverage of such marginal categories as lost race stories. I have made no attempt to consider routine fantasies written for children, restricting my coverage to works of classic status. On the other hand, I have tried to give appropriate coverage to the nonsupernatural historical fantasies produced by French writers, and have tried to find at least one example of notable fantasy fiction from each of the major nations of Europe.

In planning this chapter and the parallel chapter in the companion volume on horror fiction, I was inevitably forced to make difficult decisions about the appropriate place to annotate works close to the borderline between the two genres. For the most part I have allocated ghost stories to the horror genre except where they are outrightly comic; this means that certain consolatory fantasies, like Lanoë Falconer's *Cecilia de Noël* [H2-26], are in the other volume although a logical case could certainly be made for including them here instead. The division of work by short story writers like Nathaniel Hawthorne [2-79; H2-39] into the two genres was inevitably made problematic by the fact that different kinds of work are mingled in the same collections. In order to avoid too much careful slicing of this kind, I have confined coverage of several writers, including Edgar Allan Poe [H2-76-2-77] and Robert Louis Stevenson [H2-92-2-93], to the bibliography of nineteenth-century horror, even though a perfectly good case could be made for some of their output being of interest as fantasy. Similar fairly arbitrary exercises of judgment have been applied in a few other cases, and other critics might easily have made different decisions about where to place annotations of novels and story collections by writers like William Gilbert [2-66; H2-31-2-32] and Julian Hawthorne [2-77-2-78; H2-37].

By far the best source for information about works not covered here is Everett Bleiler's invaluable *Guide to Supernatural Fiction* [6-19], which is unparalleled in its scope and in its accounts of the content and readability of texts. Intelligent commentaries on the work of many authors here discussed, which present much more detailed consideration of their import and significance than space permits in a bibliography of this kind, can be found in *Supernatural Fiction Writers* [6-20], edited by Bleiler, and in *Fairy Tales and the Art of Subversion* by Jack Zipes [7-67].

Bibliography

Adeler, Max (pseud. of **Charles Heber Clark**) (Canada), 1847–1915.
ABOUT: GSF, CA

2-1. An Old Fogey and Other Stories. London: Ward, Lock, 1881. U.S. title: *The Fortunate Island and Other Stories.*
Collection including two dream stories. In the title story, an elderly man slips back in time so that he can learn the error of his nostalgic ways. In "Professor Baffin's Adventures" (retitled "The Fortunate Island" in the U.S. edition of 1882), castaways find an island where Arthurian knighthood is still in flower, and startle its inhabitants with modern inventions; the story is considered by some to have inspired Twain's *Connecticut Yankee* [2-152]. Adeler's earlier collection, *Random Shots* (1878), includes "Mr. Skinner's Night in the Underworld," featuring a similar comic confrontation between the values of contemporary America and those of pagan antiquity.

Alarcón, Pedro Antonio de (Spain), 1833–1891.
ABOUT: GSF

2-2. The Strange Friend of Tito Gil. London: Lovell, 1890. Tr. by Mrs. Francis J. A. Darr of *El amigo de la muerte*, 1852.
Posthumous fantasy in which a suicide believes that he has been befriended by Death, aided by him to become a successful physician and make a good marriage; the experience tests his true mettle. Striking imagery enlivens the folkloristic theme; reprinted in *Ghostly by Gaslight* (1971), ed. by Sam Moskowitz and Alden H. Norton.

Allen, F. M. (pseud. of **Edmund Downey**) (Ireland), 1856–1937.

2-3. The Little Green Man. London: Downey, 1895.
At the time of the great famine a poor Irish farmer is befriended by a leprechaun, who is subsequently taken by the farmer's son to California, where he finds a fairy bride and starts the Gold Rush. A sentimental and anti-materialistic fantasy, not without charm.

Andersen, Hans Christian (Denmark), 1805–1875.
ABOUT: CA, RG, HF

2-4. Stories for the Household. London: Routledge, 1872. Tr. by H. W. Dulcken.
Collection of 137 tales (Andersen wrote 156 in all). Though sometimes mistaken for folkloristic tales, all but a handful are original compositions; the most popular are "The Tinderbox," "The Princess and the Pea," "The Little Mermaid," "The Ugly Duckling" and "The Snow Queen." A constant theme is humility rewarded by magic; that such stories reflect deep personal feelings is revealed by the remarkably sharp edge possessed by the best works. Andersen's later stories became more obviously allegorical, requiring a more sophisticated reading, but they remain less convoluted than the equivalent works of George MacDonald [2-114; 2-117] and Oscar Wilde [2-157]. *The Complete Fairy Tales and Stories* (Doubleday, 1974) is a recent translation by Erik Christian Haugaard of all the tales, based on the 1874 Danish edition which Andersen himself edited. With 1,100 pages and no illustrations, it is more suitable for the serious adult reader than the child.

Anstey, F. (pseud. of **Thomas Anstey Guthrie**) (U.K.), 1856–1934.
ABOUT: WW, GSF, SFW, CA, NE, SMFL, SFE, ESF, HF

2-5. The Black Poodle and Other Tales. London: Longmans, 1884.
Comic tales including two parodies of Victorian ghost stories: "The Wraith of Barnjum" and "The Curse of the Catafalques." In much the same vein is the title story of *The Talking Horse and Other Tales* (1892), but Anstey's later stories tend more to the grotesque; the best are "The Lights of Spencer Primmett's Eyes" in *Salted Almonds* (1906), about a man made monstrous by an odd pair of spectacles, and "Ferdie" in *The Last Load* (1925), in which a man dreams that he is being persecuted by a mandrake-child. *Salted Almonds* and "The Talking Horse" are reprinted with [2-6], [2-7], [2-8] and [3-5] in the omnibus *Humor and Fantasy* (1931).

*2-6. A Fallen Idol. London: Smith, Elder, 1886.
A young painter acquires a Jain idol infused by a spirit elevated to godly status by mistake; its malevolent miracles threaten to blight his life and he has great difficulty getting rid of it. Some genuinely horrific moments set off the comedy nicely to make this Anstey's best novel.

2-7. The Tinted Venus; a Farcical Romance. Bristol: Arrowsmith, 1885.
A statue of Aphrodite comes to life when a confused hairdresser puts an engagement ring on its finger. The police inquiry into the statue's disappearance and his fiancée's jealousy compound the difficulties which the hero has in coping with his erotically inclined guest. Unfortunately truncated to fit Arrowsmith's standard format.

*2-8. Vice Versa; or, a Lesson to Fathers. London: Smith, Elder, 1882.
The first and most popular of Anstey's fantasies featuring the disruption of Victorian bourgeois society by anarchic magic. Here the Garuda stone switches the personalities of a smug businessman and his scamp of a son. Anstey gleefully puts the father through merry hell before acknowledging that order must, after all, be restored. Very funny, making clever use of the author's own experiences at a minor prep school.

Arnold, Edwin Lester (U.K.), 1857–1935.
ABOUT: WW, GSF, CA, SMFL, SFE, TCSF, ESF, HF

2-9. The Wonderful Adventures of Phra the Phoenician. London: Chatto & Windus, 1891.
The eponymous hero has a British witch-wife whose magic allows him to survive being sacrificed in a Druid ceremony to awaken in several key periods of British history, always pitching in on the side of right and always finding new incarnations of his true love. A lighthearted, all-action version of the theme of Lee's *Pharaoh's Daughter* [2-105].

Aubrey, Frank (pseud. of Francis H. Atkins) (U.K.), 1840–1927.
ABOUT: GSF, SFE, TCSF

2-10. The Devil Tree of El Dorado. London: Hutchinson, 1896.
The heroes discover the lost city of El Dorado and encounter the eponymous carnivorous plant, to which humans are sacrificed. One of several lost race fantasies by Atkins; others signed Aubrey are *A Queen of Atlantis* (1899) and *King of the Dead* (1903), while *By Airship to Ophir* (1910) and *The Black Opal* (1915) are signed Fenton Ash. All are in the standard vein of jingoistic boys' book fiction.

Austin, William, 1788–1841.
ABOUT: GSF

2-11. Literary Papers of William Austin. Boston: Little, Brown, 1890.
Includes the celebrated novelette "Peter Rugg, the Missing Man" (1824), about a man condemned to wander the roads, unable to reach his destination (Boston); when he finally makes it, there is no longer a place for him and he must join the world's company of accursed wanderers. "The Man with the Cloaks" (1836) features a man cursed by an eternal chill—but he has the chance to expiate his sin through good works. Interesting period pieces, the first having strong affinities with Washington Irving's items of quasi-folkloristic Americana [2-92].

Bangs, John Kendrick, 1862–1922.
ABOUT: WW, GSF, SFW, CA, SMFL, SFE, ESF

2-12. A Houseboat on the Styx. New York: Harper, 1895.
Hell's élite use the eponymous vessel as a men's club where a jolly time is had by all until their womenfolk demand admission; Captain Kidd takes advantage of the confusion to steal the boat. *The Pursuit of the Houseboat* (1897) continues the

story, bringing it to a belated resolution. Amiable slapstick, utterly superficial. *The Enchanted Typewriter* (1899) is a follow-up whose Earthly narrator establishes a source of infernal gossip.

2-13. The Water Ghost and Others. New York: Harper, 1894.
"The Water Ghost of Harrowby Hall" is a nuisance until frozen solid; other stories in the same vein feature in this collection and in *Ghosts I Have Met and Some Others* (1898); Bangs's tall stories boldly explore extremes of silliness to which no other writer deigned to go.

Barham, Richard Harris (U.K.), 1788–1845.
Авоuт: WW, GSF

2-14. The Ingoldsby Legends, or Mirth and Marvels, by Thomas Ingoldsby, esq.
3 vols. London: Bentley, 1840, 1842, 1847.
Collection of prose parodies and humorous rhymes published in *Bentley's Miscellany* between 1837 and the author's death. The best prose items are "The Spectre of Tappington," about a trouser-stealing ghost; "The Leech of Folkestone," about an abortive attempt at murder by sympathetic magic; and "Jerry Jarvis's Wig," about the curious effects of wearing said object. The verses include, among other grotesque treatments of medieval legend, the tale of the Jackdaw of Rheims, cursed for stealing an archbishop's ring. The prose tales are minor, but the verses, which have much in common with the comic verses of Thomas Hood, are striking.

Barr, Robert (U.K.), 1850–1912.
Авоuт: WW, GSF, SFE, PE, ESF

2-15. From Whose Bourne. London: Chatto & Windus, 1893.
Short novel in which a spirit enlists the aid of a ghost detective to solve his murder, with which his wife has been wrongly charged. "The Man Who Was Not on the Passenger List" in *In a Steamer Chair and Other Shipboard Stories* similarly features a spirit's concern for the widow left behind, while "The Vengeance of the Dead" in *Revenge!* (1896) also mixes spirits and murder.

Besant, Walter (U.K.), 1836–1901.
Авоuт: WW, GSF, SMFL, SFE, ESF

2-16. The Doubts of Dives. Bristol: Arrowsmith, 1889.
A wealthy socialite is inspired by his ennui to exchange bodies with a friend who feels that his talents are frustrated by poverty. Each finds the change rewarding, but it causes romantic complications. Besant's interest in such oppositions is also displayed in his multiple-personality novel *The Ivory Gate* (1892). The present novel makes an interesting comparison with Newte's *The Ealing Miracle* [3-271]; it is reprinted in the collection *Verbena Camellia Stephanotis* (1892), along with *The Demoniac* (1890), a short novel presenting a lurid account of the horrid afflictions of alcoholism.

in collaboration with **James Rice** (U.K.), 1843–1882.

2-17. The Case of Mr. Lucraft and Other Tales. London: Sampson Low, 1876 (published anonymously).
In the highly original and very striking title story, a young man leases his healthy appetite to an old sybarite, taking upon himself the unpleasant side effects of the other's overindulgence. The collection also includes four light ghost stories and the novella *Titania's Farewell*, a didactic tale in which the fairies leave England in protest against modern social trends.

Black, William (U.K.), 1841–1898.
ABOUT: GSF, ESF

2-18. The Magic Ink and Other Stories. London: Sampson Low, 1892.
Collection including two fantasies. In the title novella a young man in trouble is saved by the magic ink which reveals his true plight to those whose feelings he tries to spare; "A Hallowe'en Wraith" is a sentimental story in which a man is summoned to his loved one's sickbed by an apparition.

Boothby, Guy (Australia), 1867–1905.
ABOUT: WW, GSF, PE

2-19. Pharos the Egyptian. London: Ward, Lock, 1899.
An artist falls in love with the ward of the eponymous occultist (who employs her as a medium); thinking that he is helping to return a mummy to its tomb, he travels with the two in Egypt, but he is actually being used in an altogether more cynical fashion. The most luridly inventive of Boothby's melodramas; the author's fascination with charismatically sinister adversaries is further exhibited in his popular series featuring the hypnotically talented Dr. Nikola, begun with *A Bid for Fortune* (1895).

Bourdillon, Francis William (U.K.), 1852–1921.
ABOUT: SMFL

2-20. Nephelé. London: Redway, 1896.
A music student falls in love with a female spirit raised by his playing; he later discovers that she is a living woman engaged to his best friend. Their relationship reaches a climax when they play his composition as a duet, the emotional crescendo proving more than flesh and blood can stand. More earnest and intense than Gautier's similar romances [2-64, 2-65], though less polished.

Bradshaw, William R(ichard), 1851–1927.
ABOUT: GSF, SFE, HF

2-21. The Goddess of Atvatabar. New York: Douthitt, 1892.
Symmesian hollow world romance featuring a society which has harnessed psychic energy somewhat after the fashion of Lytton's *The Coming Race* (1871). A literary curiosity, sometimes unwittingly funny.

Butler, Samuel (U.K.), 1835–1902.
    ABOUT: CA, SFE, ESF

*2-22. Erewhon; or, Over the Range. London: Trübner, 1872.
Utopian satire whose targets include Darwinian evolution and the Church (here replaced by Musical Banks); the roles of criminals and the sick are reversed. The hero's escape by balloon initiates a new religion whose later forms and reaction to its messiah's return are featured in *Erewhon Revisited* (1901). Also of interest as a scientific romance; its scathing treatment of religion was unparalleled in Victorian times.

Carroll, Lewis. (pseud. of **Charles Lutwidge Dodgson**) (U.K.), 1832–
    1898.
    ABOUT: SFW, CA, NE, SMFL, SFE, RG, ESF, FL

*2-23. Alice's Adventures in Wonderland. London: Macmillan, 1865.
Classic fantasy in which Alice follows a White Rabbit into a world where the stability of things is very much in doubt. She drops in at the mad tea party, plays croquet with the Queen of Hearts and attends the trial of the Knave of Hearts, which so offends her sensibilities that she reduces the grotesques to their ordinary status as a pack of cards. In the sequel, *Through the Looking Glass and What Alice Found There* (1872), she visits a world where all is topsy turvy and all commonplace logic subverted. The characters are mostly chesspieces and the plot is orchestrated by the moves in their game; she also meets Tweedledum and Tweedledee and encounters the celebrated poems "Jabberwocky" and "The Walrus and the Carpenter." Carroll, as a logician, was perfectly placed to use the trickery of words and ideas to undermine the pompous rigidity of the Victorian worldview, producing a phantasmagoric negative image of its follies which is unsurpassed. Martin Gardner's *The Annotated Alice: Alice's Adventures in Wonderland & Through the Looking Glass* (Clarkson Potter, 1960) provides thorough notes and all the Tenniel illustrations in their proper places.

2-24. The Hunting of the Snark: An Agony in Eight Fits. London: Macmillan, 1876.
A comic narrative in verse in which ten would-be heroes go in quest of the legendary Snark, the difficulties of finding it compounded by the possibility that it might turn out to be a Boojum. The apparently amiable nonsense conceals, as usual, sharply barbed wit.

2-25. Sylvie and Bruno. London: Macmillan, 1889.
The first part of a long and heavily moralistic fairy romance; its sequel is *Sylvie and Bruno Concluded* (1893). Most readers have been horrified that a man of such evident genius should have produced such a dull and awkward book, but it does serve to demonstrate what an anarchic spirit Carroll had; here he attempts to be constructive, offering a reconstituted version of the stern worldview undermined in his earlier works, using the same fabular materials in an allegorical fashion. The abysmal magnitude of his failure is, in its way, revealing.

Chambers, Robert W(illiam), 1865–1933.
ABOUT: WW, GSF, SFW, H, SMFL, SFE, RG, PE, ESF, HF

2-26. The Maker of Moons. New York: Putnam, 1896.
Collection of linked stories, some of which combine various aspects of Chambers's work: his penchant for light, frothy romance and his fascination with the exotic and the occult. The oft-reprinted title story features a sinister Oriental sorcerer whose creations include monsters and a beautiful girl (who is rescued from his clutches by the hero and the Secret Service). "A Pleasant Evening" is an earnest occult romance similar in tone to the novel *Athalie* (1915); "The Man at the Next Table" is a joke involving sortilege and metempsychosis. Its popularity notwithstanding, the title story is an uneasy combination of incompatible elements.

[For other works of this author, see the companion guide to horror.]

Chamisso, Adalbert von (Germany), 1781–1838.
ABOUT: GSF, SFW, SMFL

***2-27. Peter Schlemihl.** London: Whittaker, 1823. Tr. by Sir John Bowring of *Peter Schlemihl's Wundersame Geschichte*, 1814; this edition is misattributed to Fouqué.
Schlemihl makes a bargain with a Man in Gray, trading his shadow for a bottomless purse, but his wealth proves valueless when he is shunned and despised for his lack of a shadow. The Man in Gray offers to return the shadow in exchange for his soul, but Schlemihl prefers to become a lonely wanderer, aided by seven-league boots. A bizarre Faustian classic, avowedly written as a mere distraction, which has seemed to the majority of its readers to harbor a sinister symbolism.

Coleridge, Sara (U.K.), 1802–1852.
ABOUT: GSF, SMFL

2-28. Phantasmion, Prince of Palmland. London: Pickering, 1837 (published anonymously).
Fairy romance by Coleridge's daughter in which the hero, aided by the flower fairy Potentilla, undertakes a quest that is in part a microcosmic romance. Though somewhat ungainly, it contains elements anticipating George MacDonald's fairy romances [2-116, 2-117], William Morris's heroic fantasies [2-124-2-128] and Kingsley's *Water-Babies* [2-98]. Some of its dramatic moments are quite effective—notably the chapter in which the tiny hero is menaced by a stag beetle.

Collodi, Carlo (pseud. of Carlo Lorenzini) (Italy), 1826–1890.
ABOUT: CA, HF

2-29. The Story of a Puppet; or, The Adventures of Pinocchio. London: Unwin, 1892. Tr. by M. A. Murray of *Pinocchio*, 1882.
A wooden puppet is brought to life but behaves very badly until harsh experience teaches him the error of his ways. Today known primarily through the Disney film version. A key work of admonitory children's fantasy.

Cooper, James Fenimore, 1789–1851.
ABOUT: CA

2-30. The Monikins. London: Bentley, 1835 (published anonymously).
Ponderous pseudo-Swiftian satire whose hero, John Goldencalf, meets an intelligent and philosophically inclined monkey, Dr. Reasono, and then sets forth to discover the homeland of his kind. The aphoristic account of what he learns there fills three pages. Silly wordplay fails to redeem the dull didacticism.

Corelli, Marie (pseud. of Minnie Mackay) (U.K.), 1855–1924.
ABOUT: WW, GSF, SFW, CA, SMFL, SFE, ESF

2-31. Ardath; the Story of a Dead Self. London: Bentley, 1889.
The hero falls in love with an angel in the ruins of Babylon, then journeys five thousand years into the past to the city of Al-Kyris, where he meets himself in a former incarnation and becomes sufficiently enlightened to be worthy of his supernatural inamorata. Highly regarded by its author on both artistic and philosophical grounds.

2-32. A Romance of Two Worlds. London: Bentley, 1886.
Credulous and pious occult romance in which an enfeebled young woman is revitalized by a self-styled Chaldean master of "human electricity"; after taking a tour of the universe with an angel, she sees God (a "Great Circle of Electric Fire"). A consummately silly story which became a runaway best-seller, riding on the coattails of the vogue for religious pseudoscience as exemplified by Spiritualism and Theosophy. No other author managed to inject such deep feeling and obvious sincerity into works of this stripe.

2-33. The Sorrows of Satan. London: Methuen, 1895.
An author makes a Faustian pact with Satan in order to become rich. Satan remains nearby to watch the slow victory of corruption, though it makes him ineffably sad to see humans repeating his own fatal error. When the protagonist becomes infatuated with the saintly Mavis Clare, Satan falls in love with her too, and is overjoyed when he fails to tempt her from the path of righteousness, seeing in her a glimmer of hope for his own eventual salvation. Marie Corelli modestly denied that Mavis Clare was a self-portrait, but no one believed her.

2-34. The Soul of Lilith. London: Bentley, 1892.
An occultist imprisons the soul of a girl in her body after her death, hoping that he may use it as an instrument of enlightenment, perhaps ultimately learning enough to resurrect her. He is taught the error of his God-defying ways.

Craik, Mrs. (Dinah Maria Mulock) (U.K.), 1826–1887.
ABOUT: CA, HF

2-35. Avillion and Other Tales. London: Smith, Elder, 1853 (published anonymously).
Collection of stories including several fantasies (which were reprinted along with other items in *Romantic Tales*, 1859). The title novella is a visionary fantasy about the Isles of the Blest, featuring Ulysses and King Arthur in cameo roles;

"The Self-Seer" is a more interesting novella in which two friends learn more about themselves by adopting the viewpoints of their spirit *Doppelgängers*. "Erotion" is a romance of antiquity about a priestess of Diana; "Kong Tolv" is a fantasy based in Danish folklore, of the magical bridegroom variety; "The Rosicrucian" is a Faustian romance. The tales have a certain charm, although they are bogged down by the author's pietistic affectations. Her fairy romances for children are also of interest, the most notable being *Alice Learmont* (1852), based in Scottish folklore.

Crawford, F(rancis) Marion, 1854–1909.
ABOUT: WW, GSF, SFW, CA, SMFL, PE, ESF, HF

2-36. Khaled; a Tale of Arabia. London: Macmillan, 1891.
Oriental fantasy modeled on the *Arabian Nights*. The eponymous hero is a genie made mortal, who must win the love of a princess in order to receive the redeeming gift of an immortal soul. It proves easy enough to marry her but much more difficult to win her sincere regard, despite his good looks and heroic exploits.

2-37. The Witch of Prague. London: Macmillan, 1891.
Occult romance; the protagonist awakens the interest of a sorceress, who uses magic to woo him away from the search for his true love but cannot in the end prevail. Like *Khaled* [2-36] this seems to be mere dabbling with genre materials, ill-planned and padded, though not without effective moments. Crawford's interest in the occult is also reflected in *Mr. Isaacs* (1882) and *Cecilia* (1902), but his fiction in this vein lacks the punch of his horror stories.

[For other works of this author, see the companion guide to horror.]

Croly, George (U.K.), 1780–1860.

2-38. Salathiel: A Story of the Past, the Present, and the Future. London: Colburn, 1828 (published anonymously). Also known as *Tarry Thou Till I Come*.
Religious fantasy by a clergyman, about the Wandering Jew. Despite the title, the story is set entirely in the distant past, leading up to the destruction of Jerusalem by Titus; it belongs to the same subgenre as *Ben Hur* (1880), whose author, Lew Wallace, called it "one of the six great English novels."

Dalton, James (U.K.).
ABOUT: GSF

2-39. The Gentleman in Black. London: William Kidd, 1831 (published anonymously).
The eponymous gentleman is the devil, who contracts with an Englishman and a Frenchman to give them unlimited wealth if they will promise to double their quota of sins every year, beginning with one second of sin per year. The geometric series eventually lands them in deep trouble, but the ingenious lawyer Bagsby is enlisted to find loopholes in the contracts. Amusing, despite typical Victorian coyness in compiling the accounts of sin.

*2-40. The Invisible Gentleman. 3 vols. London: Edward Bull, 1833 (published anonymously).
The hero—a man who has everything—recklessly wishes for the power to make himself invisible. He gets it, but his use of it leads him into a tangled web of deceit; his attempts to extricate himself bring misfortune to himself and others, and it is only with the utmost difficulty that he redeems himself and manages to get rid of his awful gift. A very striking moral tale, rather contrived but very pointed and quite witty. An undeservedly neglected forerunner of Jerrold's *Man Made of Money* [2-95]. Dalton's short story "The Beauty Draught" (*Blackwood's*, 1840) is in the same vein.

de Mille, James (Canada), 1837–1880.
ABOUT: SFE

2-41. A Strange Manuscript Found in a Copper Cylinder. New York: Harper, 1888 (published anonymously).
An account of a lost race living in a temperate enclave near the South Pole, which has developed a remarkable darkness-loving worldview, embodied in a pessimistic but humane religion. A very striking exercise in imaginary anthropology, it is the outstanding example of the lost race subgenre.

Dickens, Charles (U.K.), 1812–1870.
ABOUT: WW, GSF, SFW, CA, SMFL, PE, ESF, HF

*2-42. The Chimes. London: Chapman & Hall, 1844 (dated 1845).
The innocent hero has been persuaded by hypocritical cant that the poor deserve their misery, but he is shown what his pessimistic resignation might lead to by a vision into which he is summoned by haunted bells; he returns rearmed for the war of spiritual survival. Dickens hoped that the story would "strike a great blow for the poor," but the deep feeling embodied in it made his readers uneasy, and they much preferred the cozy sentimentality of *A Cricket on the Hearth* (1845; dated 1846).

*2-43. A Christmas Carol. London: Chapman & Hall, 1843.
The first and best-remembered of Dickens's Christmas books, in which Ebenezer Scrooge is taken on a trip through time and space so that he may learn the error of his miserly ways. Dickens was the great prophet and popularizer of the Christmas spirit (Christmas was not at the time a particularly important holiday); it is largely to him and to this story that we owe the mythology that subsequent generations were to convert into crass commercial cant, far more hypocritical than anything Dickens could have imagined. No other work better demonstrates the power of fantasy to affect the real world, and the history of its effect might be seen as a striking demonstration of the moral enshrined in so much Victorian fantasy: that the consequences of fantastic interventions always fail, ironically and/or tragically, to live up to optimistic expectations.

*2-44. The Haunted Man and the Ghost's Bargain. London: Bradbury & Evans, 1848.
The miserable and self-pitying hero is visited by a *Doppelgänger* which volunteers to take away the burden of his sorrows if he will agree to infect others with

the same immunity. He makes the bargain, but sees that wherever sorrow is banished, pity and empathy disappear—and without the power of those emotions, the lives of the poor people who surround him are blighted. He revokes the bargain, and the saintly wife of his servant then becomes the center of infection with a renewed spirit of fellowship. The most unusual and ambitious of all the Victorian moralistic fantasies, awkward because it does not quite fit its format: a flawed masterpiece.

[For other works of this author, see the companion guide to horror.]

Dilke, Lady (Emilia Frances) (U.K.), 1840–1904.
ABOUT: GSF

2-45. The Shrine of Death and Other Stories. London: Routledge, 1886.
Nine prose poems in a tragic vein, most with allegorical pretensions. The title story concerns a girl whose ambition is to marry Death in order to know the secrets of life. "A Vision of Learning" draws a boy into a similarly hopeless quest. *The Shrine of Love and Other Stories* (1891) offers seven more, equally downbeat but with fewer supernatural intrusions.

Disraeli, Benjamin (U.K.), 1804–1881.
ABOUT: GSF, CA, SMFL, ESF

2-46. The Voyage of Captain Popanilla. London: Colburn, 1828.
Popanilla lives in happy innocence on the Isle of Fantaisie until he discovers various productions of the Society for the Diffusion of Useful Knowledge and is banished lest he corrupt the populace. He ends up in Vraibleusia, a parody of Tory England, whose politics, economics and imperial ambitions he cannot quite understand. A neat satire, frequently reprinted with three other fantasies: the novel *Alroy* (1833) is a romance of Jewish history with supernatural embellishments; the novella "The Infernal Marriage" (1832) is a classical fantasia sarcastically retelling the story of Proserpine; "Ixion in Heaven" (1847) is similar in kind, more sharply satirical in its portrait of an upstart reformer among the gods. Disraeli fared much better among the real Tory Olympians of England than Ixion or Popanilla among the imaginary ones, proving that reality can—albeit very rarely—be more rewarding than fantasy.

Donnelly, Ignatius, 1831–1901.
ABOUT: GSF, CA, NE, SFE, ESF

2-47. Doctor Huguet. Chicago: Schulte, 1891.
A liberal physician fights against the oppression of American blacks but weakens under the threat of political defeat; his personality is then exchanged with that of a black ne'er-do-well. He eventually accepts this fate as a judgment of God, while the personality now inhabiting his former body embarks upon the road to self-destruction. Racist in spite of its purpose; possibly more revealing than the author intended. Makes an interesting comparison with Newte's *Ealing Miracle* [3-271].

Dostoyevsky, Fyodor Mikhailovitch (Russia), 1821–1881.
ABOUT: SFE

2-48. The Dream of a Ridiculous Man; Another Man's Wife; A Meek Young Girl. London: Drummond, 1945. Tr. by Beatrice Scott of *Son smeshnogo cheloveka,* etc. Collection of three tales; the first is a fantasy also known as "A Funny Man's Dream" and "The Comic Man's Dream." The solipsistically inclined protagonist has a vision of a sinless world, which is corrupted by his observations; when he tries to redeem our own world by importing a new innocence, he fails. The story was originally presented as part of the serial *Diary of a Writer* (1873–74; first full translation, 1949), which also includes the macabre fantasy "Bobok," involving a conversation between two recently buried corpses.

Doughty, Francis W(orcester).

2-49. Mirrikh; or, a Woman from Mars. New York: Burleigh & Johnston, 1892. Travelers in the East discover that communication between Earth and Mars is possible via astral projection, the waystation being in darkest Tibet; disaster at the station causes difficulties for the disembodied characters. Possibly inspired by Flammarion's *Urania* [2-54].

Dryasdust (unattributed pseud.).
ABOUT: WW, GSF, SFE, ESF

2-50. Tales of the Wonder Club. London: Harrison, 1899, 1900.
Collection of stories related in a haunted inn; there are three volumes in all, but only the first two contain supernatural material. They were reprinted in the same format under another pseudonym, "M. Y. Halidom," and some stories were subsequently recombined under other titles. The collections feature tall stories, mostly in the flippant vein of Barham's *Ingoldsby Legends* [2-14], but of markedly inferior quality. The Dryasdust name appears on one novel, *The Wizard's Mantle* (1902; rev. 1903 as by Halidom), a historical fantasy featuring a cloak of invisibility; later Halidom novels were horror stories.

[For other works of this author, writing as Halidom, see the companion guide to horror.]

du Maurier, George (U.K.), 1834–1896.
ABOUT: GSF, SMFL, SFE, HF

*2-51. Peter Ibbetson. 2 vols. London: Osgood & McIlvaine, 1891.
The eponymous hero is able to share his dreams with a woman, and in those dreams the two can recreate the idyllic times they shared in childhood. The woman, who is married and has a child, refuses further intercourse of this kind when she realizes what is happening, but when Peter is imprisoned for the murder of his vile uncle, the relationship resumes. The most striking of Victorian sentimental fantasies, taking the iconography of childhood innocence to its extreme.

2-52. Trilby. 3 vols. London: Osgood & McIlvaine, 1894.
An art student falls in love with the eponymous heroine, but the affair is frustrated. Later, he discovers that she has married a sinister music teacher, Svengali,

by means of whose hypnotic power her originally awkward voice has been refined into a unique instrument; he sets in motion a chain of events that leads to her ironic liberation from this dominion. The central motif, taken somewhat out of context, has become a modern myth, and Svengali a household name. Like the preceding item, though, the story is really a curious allegory of the ambiguous corruptions which attend maturation and adaptation to the demands of society.

Eliot, George (pseud. of Mary Ann Evans) (U.K.), 1819–1880.
ABOUT: CA

2-53. "The Lifted Veil." *Blackwood's Magazine*, July 1859.
The narrator explains how his ability to foresee the future and read minds has isolated him from his fellows; he married the only person whose mind is opaque to him, but this attempt to find normal companionship went tragically wrong. A sophisticated moral fantasy.

Flammarion (Nicholas) Camille (France), 1842–1925.
ABOUT: GSF, SFE

2-54. Urania. Boston: Estes & Lauriat, 1890. Tr. by A. R. Stenson of *Urania*, 1889.
A curious best-seller in which a sense of wonder based in astronomical discoveries is combined with ardent spiritualist faith to produce a narrative in which immortal souls may be reincarnated in other worlds. This "revelation" apparently came to Flammarion (the leading French astronomer in his day) early in life, and is elaborately described in the dialogues assembled as *Lumen* (1872; first translated in *Stories of Infinity*, 1873; revised for separate publication, 1887; translated and further revised, 1897). A unique and intriguing combination of scientific and religious imagination.

Flaubert, Gustave (France), 1821–1880.
ABOUT: SMFL

2-55. Salammbô. London: Saxon, 1886. Tr. by M. French Sheldon of *Salammbô*, 1863.
An extravagant romance of antiquity endeavoring, as the author claimed, to "perpetuate a mirage by applying to antiquity the methods of the modern novel." The eponymous heroine is a priestess of Tanit in Carthage who must sacrifice herself in order to save the sacred veil of Tanit when it is stolen by Mathô, whose mercenaries lay siege to the city. Though there is nothing formally supernatural in the story, it is essentially an account of the working out of a curse, and it belongs to the same species of mythologized historical novels as Louÿs's *Aphrodite* [2-111] and France's *Thaïs* [2-61].

2-56. The Temptation of St. Anthony. London: Nichols, 1895. Tr. by D. F. Hannigan of *La Tentation de Saint-Antoine*, 1874.
Fantasy of Christian mythology inspired by the Breughel painting in which the saint is surrounded by grotesque demons. The phantasmagoric prose poem has elements of the medieval allegory and mystery play in its dramatic dialogues. The

standard version was written in 1874, but some critics consider it inferior to the more extravagant and exotic version written in 1856, translated as *The First Temptation of St. Anthony* (1908; tr. 1910). The collection *Three Tales* (1877; tr. 1903) includes a briefer fantasy of the same species, "The Legend of St. Julian Hospitator."

Fouqué, Baron Friedrich de la Motte (Germany), 1777–1843.
ABOUT: WW, GSF, SFW, SMFL, PE, FL, HF

2-57. The Magic Ring. Edinburgh: Oliver and Boyd, 1825. 3 vols. Tr. of *Der Zauberring*, 1813.
A long and involved chivalric romance with allegorical undertones. The hero is one of various knights who have tried to recover a magic ring for the heroine; he must subsequently undertake other quests on behalf of members of his family and in the cause of Christianity. It may be regarded as the prototype of the kind of heroic fantasy which William Morris was later to develop [2-124–2-128]; its central motif recurs in more famous works, though the probability of direct influence is slight.

2-58. Sintram and His Companions. London: Ollier, 1820. Tr. by Julius C. Hare.
Novella inspired by Dürer's engraving "The Knight, Death and the Devil," sharing the background and some of the characters of the preceding item; as might be expected, its theme is similarly pietistic.

*2-59. Undine. London: Simpkin, Marshall, 1818. Tr. by George Soane of *Undine*, 1811.
A classic *kunstmärchen* in which a changeling water sprite marries a young knight whose inability to be faithful to her has tragic results. The work, which marks the beginning of this period in the history of fantasy fiction, is of great importance as an exemplar and a fine story in its own right. Also annotated as [1-22].

France, Anatole (pseud. of Jacques-Anatole-François Thibault) (France), 1844–1924.
ABOUT: GSF, SFW, CA, SMFL, SFE, ESF

2-60. Honey-Bee. London: John Lane, 1911. Tr. by Mrs. John Lane.
A long fairy tale, also known as *Bee* and "The Kingdom of the Dwarfs." The heroine is abducted by dwarfs, while her childhood sweetheart is imprisoned by nixies. The king of the dwarfs loves her, but altruistically lends himself to the cause of reuniting her with her loved one in order to secure her happiness. An elegant and sentimental moral fable.

*2-61. Thaïs. London: John Lane, 1909. Tr. by R. B. Douglas of *Thaïs*, 1890.
A lush romance of antiquity in which the anchorite Paphnutius sets out to reclaim the soul of a famous Alexandrine actress; he succeeds in making her a drab nun, but the subsequent attentions of the Devil and a sorceress reveal to him that his desire to save her was merely a perversion of his sexual passion. Though closely allied to Flaubert's *Temptation of St. Anthony* [2-56], the story is deeply

critical of Christianity, laying the groundwork for *The Human Tragedy* [2-62] and *The Revolt of the Angels* [3-144].

*2-62. The Well of St. Clare. London: John Lane, 1909. Tr. by Alfred R. Allison of *Le Puits de Sainte Clare*, 1895.
Collection of stories set in Renaissance Europe that includes several fantasies. In "San Satiro" a monk is led into a heretical regard for pagan values by visions associated with the tomb of a canonized satyr, and suffers the consequences. In "Lucifer" a handsome and dark-skinned Satan takes an artist to account for misrepresentation. These stories continue a whimsical vein established in the earlier *Mother of Pearl* (1892; tr. 1908), which includes stories in which Christian saints meet up with a faun and a unicorn. The present volume concludes with the brilliant novella *The Human Tragedy* (published separately in 1917), in which a monk who attempts to apply the principles of Jesus's teaching too literally for luxury-loving clergymen is cast into prison, where he is befriended and aided by Satan. This is a moving and effective moral fantasy, more radical than any other work of the period in its questioning of orthodoxy.

Garnett, Richard (U.K.), 1835–1906.
ABOUT: GSF, SFW, SMFL, ESF, FL

*2-63. The Twilight of the Gods. London: Fisher Unwin, 1888.
Collection of sixteen stories, enlarged in later editions to twenty-eight. Most are romances of antiquity or historical fantasies; all are related with an unparalleled deftness of style and a magnificent sense of irony. The title story follows the career of Prometheus, freed from his gruesome punishment when the gods of Olympus give way to the spread of Christianity. In "Ananda the Miracle Worker" pride is the downfall of the most-favored disciple of Buddha. In "The City of the Philosophers" Greek Utopians are given the chance to make their ideal republic a reality, but find practical difficulties they had not anticipated. In "The Demon Pope" Satan finds the college of cardinals fertile ground for his temptations; and in "Alexander the Ratcatcher" the Borgia pope returns to tempt one of his successors, in a role inspired by the pied piper. The anti-clerical satires outdo Anatole France's (see [2-62]) in wit; the romances of antiquity are in a lighter vein than John Sterling's (see [2-146]), but have hints of the same affectionate exoticism.

Gautier, Théophile (France), 1811–1872.
ABOUT: WW, GSF, SFW, SMFL, PE, ESF

*2-64. One of Cleopatra's Nights. New York: Worthington, 1882. Tr. by Lafcadio Hearn of *Une Nuit de Cléopâtre*, 1883, etc.
Collection of six stories. The title novella is a lush historical *conte cruel* and "King Candaules" (1844) is a nonsupernatural fable in the same vein. "Arria Marcella" (1852) is the best of several Gautier fantasies in which young men experience visions in which they encounter fabulous phantom women who are infinitely more desirable than mundane women could ever be; here the dream is more extended than usual and more tragic in its effect. "Clarimonde" (1836) is a feverish and phantasmagoric exercise in the same vein, featuring a more demand-

ing lamia; "Omphale" (1834) and "The Mummy's Foot" (1840) represent the lighthearted end of the spectrum.

2-65. The Works of Théophile Gautier. 24 vols. New York: Sproul, 1900–1903. Tr. by F. C. de Sumichrast.

The definitive edition of Gautier's works, including new translations of the items in [2-64]. Other fantasies of note include the novella "Avatar" (1856), in which a young man persuades an occultist to transfer his intelligence to the body of a man whose wife he covets, but then cannot accomplish the desired seduction, and the novel *Spirite* (1865; tr. 1877), a sentimental version of his most frequent theme, featuring a love affair between a young cavalier and a ghost, successfully consummated in the afterlife. Less typical are "Onuphrius" (1832), whose hero is driven mad by his inability to capture the substance of his dreams; and "The Divided Knight" (1840), a *Doppelgänger* story in which the good and evil parts of a man's personality must settle their dispute in combat.

[**For other works of this author, see the companion guide to horror.**]

Gilbert, William (U.K.), 1804–1890.
ABOUT: GSF, CA

2-66. The Magic Mirror. London: Alexander Strahan, 1866.

Collection of linked stories set in the fifteenth century, featuring a mirror which grants the wishes of those who look into it. As usual, no good comes of them. The stories range from the comic tale of a sacristan who wishes to be tempted as St. Anthony was in order to demonstrate his piety to the macabre story of a physician who unwisely wishes that the corpse of his beloved wife might be reanimated for a single day.

[**For other works of this author, see the companion guide to horror.**]

Gilbert, W(illiam) S(chwenck) (U.K.), 1836–1911.
ABOUT: CA, ESF

2-67. Foggerty's Fairy and Other Tales. London: Routledge, 1890.

Collection including several fantasies, all exercises in sarcastic absurdity. In the title story a feckless confectioner is allowed to sample alternative fates which would have befallen him had he made key decisions differently. In "An Elixir of Love" an infatuated swain tries to share his ecstasy with everyone else by wholesale distribution of an aphrodisiac. "The Triumph of Vice," "Creatures of Impulse" and "The Wicked World" are sardonic variants of fairy tale motifs. The satirical edge is blunted by extravagant silliness.

Godfrey, Hal (pseud. of Charlotte O. Eccles) (U.K.), died 1911.

2-68. The Rejuvenation of Miss Semaphore. London: Jarrolds, 1897.

Ansteyan fantasy in which a mean old lady overdoses on the elixir of youth, reverting to infancy and suffering many indignities before accelerated growth brings her back to maturity. Aptly subtitled "a farcical novel."

Gogol, Nikolai Vasilievich (Russia), 1809–1852.
ABOUT: WW, SMFL, PE

2-69. The Collected Tales and Plays of Nikolai Gogol, ed. by L. J. Lent, tr. by Constance Garnett. Pantheon, 1964.
Many of Gogol's short stories involve elements of the bizarre and the supernatural, ranging from the mock-folkloristic aspects of *Evenings on a Farm Near Dikanka* (1831–32) through the vividly horrible story of supernatural destruction, "Viy" (1835) and the uniquely surreal story of a wayward organ, "The Nose" (1835) to "The Overcoat" (1842), in which a man's obsession with a winter coat kills him with remorse after it is stolen, but then brings him back to life to gain his revenge. The graphic grotesquerie of these stories presumably reflects Gogol's own neuroses.

Griffith, George (pseud. of **George Griffith-Jones**) (U.K.), 1857–1906.
ABOUT: GSF, CA, NE, SFE, TCSF, ESF

2-70. Valdar the Oft-Born. London: Pearson, 1895.
The protagonist, a demigod, pursues his violent vocation in various periods of history, continually meeting new incarnations of his beloved Ilma. Highly derivative of Arnold's *Phra the Phoenician* [2-9], and perhaps also of Lee's *Pharaoh's Daughter* [2-105], which is also echoed in the first of Griffith's revivified mummy stories, *The Romance of Golder Star* (1897; the other is *The Mummy and Miss Nitocris*, 1906). Griffith's fantasies never duplicated the verve of his early future war novels, which played an important role in the development of British scientific romance.

Grimm, Jakob Ludwig (Germany), 1785–1863, and **Wilhelm Karl Grimm,** (Germany), 1786–1859.
ABOUT: CA

2-71. German Popular Stories. 2 vols. London: Baldwin, 1824–26. Tr. by Edgar Taylor of *Kinder- und Hausmärchen*, 1812–13.
The Grimms' collection of European folktales overlaps to some extent with earlier ones, and it is interesting to compare their versions of the most famous stories with Perrault's [1-60]. The Grimms retain the crueller aspects of the tales, often featuring graphic revenges inflicted upon the evil characters. This (with the aid of Jakob's reputation as a scrupulous scholar) gave them the appearance of being closer to the texture of authentic folklore, though the tales were in fact extensively adapted and rewritten by the brothers as they passed through various manuscript versions. The collection remains a vital storehouse of European folkloristic motifs, which have been borrowed and further transfigured by dozens of subsequent writers and remain perennially available for further mutation. *The Complete Tales of the Brothers Grimm* (Bantam, 1987), thirty-two of them previously unpublished in English, were translated by Jack Zipes.

Haggard, H(enry) Rider (U.K.), 1856–1925.
ABOUT: WW, GSF, SFW, F, CA, NE, H, SMFL, SFE, RG, TCSF, ESF, FL, HF

2-72. Eric Brighteyes. London: Longmans, 1891.
A pastiche Icelandic saga. The eponymous hero's love match is blighted by the machinations of a witch; he becomes involved in a series of bloody conflicts. More forthright in style than William Morris's similar exercises in pastiche.

2-73. King Solomon's Mines. London: Cassell, 1885.
The first of the Allan Quatermain series; a robust adventure story celebrating the imposition of British values and imperial power upon the mysterious wildness of Africa. Quatermain is the archetypal Victorian hero, whose Herculean labors attempt to bring moral order to the heart of darkness, represented initially by a series of imaginary realms and in later books by eras of the remote past recalled in ancestral memories. Quatermain actually died in *Allan Quatermain* (1887), but his career and Haggard's were inextricably linked and his adventures continued to appear until 1927 when the posthumous *Allan and the Ice-Gods* found his indomitable spirit struggling for the cause of moral evolution in prehistoric times. The title novella of *Allan's Wife and Other Tales* (1889) presents a theme which preoccupied Haggard (and other Victorian fantasists) and which has been carried forward as one of the standard clichés of fantasy fiction: an eternal triangle which contrasts a woman embodying the virtues of wifeliness with a wild, amoral female whose rapacity spoils the domestic idyll. The later works in the series, especially *The Ancient Allan* (1920), *Heu-Heu; or, the Monster* (1924) and *The Treasure of the Lake* (1926), reflect Haggard's growing interest in the occult and in James Frazer's writings on magic and religion.

***2-74. She.** New York: Harper, 1886.
A handsome young man, descendant and reincarnation of an ancient priest of Isis, searches the heart of Africa for the immortal white queen who killed his earlier self. Ayesha—"She-Who-Must-Be-Obeyed"—welcomes him, determined that this time he will not refuse to share her destiny. Her meek rival for the hero's love is casually dispatched, but the hero has too little of the Sacher-Masoch in him to succumb to the temptations of such powerful sexuality, and she pays the awful price of her failure to defeat his moral fortitute. In *Ayesha* (1905) she is reincarnated in Asia, old and hideous, awaiting the hero's blessing before she can recover her former beauty; the end of the Victorian era is unwittingly symbolized by Ayesha's transfiguration into a lost soul, unable to set aside her evil sexuality but acceptable to the hero anyhow. Haggard brought his archetypal hero and his archetypal anti-heroine together in *She and Allan* (1920) and offered an account of Ayesha's early history in *Wisdom's Daughter* (1923), but the passage of time had stripped away her symbolic significance, and she had become but a pale shadow of her more fabulous self.

2-75. The World's Desire. London: Longmans, 1890. In collaboration with **Andrew Lang** (U.K.), 1844–1912.
Romance of antiquity in which Odysseus finds Ithaca in ruins and is sent by Aphrodite to seek out Helen of Troy. His quest is subverted by the lustful queen

of Egypt, who seduces him with the aid of magic. Another version of Haggard's favorite story, somewhat enlivened by Lang's input.

Hauff, Wilhelm (Germany), 1802-1827.
ABOUT: WW, GSF, SFW, ESF

2-76. Tales by Wilhelm Hauff. London: Bell, 1890. Tr. by J. Mendel.
Collected edition of Hauff's three fairy tale cycles, which combine the influences of the Brothers Grimm and the *Arabian Nights*. There is a strong comic element, which combines satire and sheer grotesquerie. The best known of the tales is "The Cold Heart," in which a charcoal burner disposes of three wishes with customary foolhardiness, and goes on, with tragic consequences, to sell his heart for wealth—a theme which anticipates T. F. Powys's bleak masterpiece *The Two Thieves* [3-303].

Hawthorne, Julian, 1846-1934.
ABOUT: WW, GSF, CA, PE, ESF

2-77. Archibald Malmaison. London: Bentley, 1879.
The eponymous hero has two very different personalities, each having no knowledge of the other, which take over his being at intervals of several years. One such exchange sets up a highly contrived but nevertheless effective tragedy. An intriguing variation on the theme of multiple personality.

2-78. The Professor's Sister. New York: Belford Clarke, 1888. U.K. title: *The Spectre of the Camera*.
Occult novel based in idiosyncratic metaphysical theory. A scientist's sister falls victim to her stepmother when the two become rivals for the affections of a man; he preserves her from death by placing her in suspended animation, and ultimately revives her to enjoy for a brief span the legitimate fruits of her passion. An interesting attempt by Hawthorne *fils* to interweave morality and metaphysics in an extended fable, which understandably fails to reach the high standard set by his father's similar experiments.

    [For other works of this author, see the companion guide to horror.]

Hawthorne, Nathaniel, 1804-1864.
ABOUT: WW, GSF, SFW, CA, SMFL, SFE, PE, ESF

***2-79. Twice-Told Tales**. Boston: American Stationers, 1837.
The first of two classic collections that include many moralistic fantasies. "The Great Carbuncle" (1837) is an allegory of greed; "The Prophetic Pictures" (1837) raises questions of fate and causation; in "Dr. Heidegger's Experiment" (1837) the elixir of life briefly reignites the ignoble qualities of four friends. The edition of 1851 added several more stories, including "The White Old Maid" (1835), featuring a fateful meeting between two women who once loved and lost the same man. *Mosses from an Old Manse* (1846) includes "The Birthmark" (1835), in which a quest for perfection leads to destruction; the Bunyanesque posthumous fantasy

"The Celestial Railroad" (1843); a pessimistic account of "The New Adam and Eve" (1843); and "Feathertop" (1852), about the career of an animate and englamored scarecrow. Also significant are three stories from *The Snow-Image and Other Twice-Told Tales* (1852): the title story (1851) contrasts the enchantment of a childish worldview with the narrowness of adult perception; "Ethan Brand" is an allegorical account of a man's search for the unpardonable sin; in "The Man of Adamant" (1837) an eremite is unsuccessfully wooed by a loving ghost. At his death Hawthorne left three drafts of a fantasy about the elixir of life, variously known as *Septimius* or *Septimius Felton* (1872) and *The Dolliver Romance* (1876), but never brought it to a satisfactory state. The above tales represent the cream of American moralistic fantasy: bitter and sometimes misanthropic, but very deeply felt and executed with great precision.

[For other works of this author, see the companion guide to horror.]

Hinton, C(harles) H(oward) (U.K.), 1853-1907.
ABOUT: SFE, ESF

2-80. Scientific Romances. London: Swan Sonnenschein, 1886.
Collection of essays on metaphysics which includes the curious theological fantasy "The Persian King," which imagines a world in which pain functions as a transferrable fluid, offering strange possibilities regarding the functioning of a redeemer. Hinton later published the two novellas *Stella & An Unfinished Communication* (1895; reprinted in *Scientific Romances: Second Series*, 1902), the second of which is a remarkable posthumous fantasy in which characters seek redemption by operating in the fourth dimension (time) to amend the errors they made in life.

Hogg, James (U.K.), 1770-1835.
ABOUT: WW, GSF, SMFL, PE, ESF

2-81. The Brownie of Bodsbeck and Other Tales. 2 vols. Edinburgh: Blackwood, 1818.
Three short novels. The title story is a historical novel supernaturalized by the enigmatic presence of the brownie. "The Hunt of Eildon" owes more to Scottish folklore, with good spirits in canine form battling evil wherever the devil's agents show their hand. Hogg was a prolific contributor to Victorian periodicals, signing himself "The Ettrick Shepherd"; he collected and counterfeited traditional tales in prodigious fashion, recklessly mixing folklore, allegory, the comic and the grotesque with episodes from history. Material from his regular columns for *Blackwood's* crops up in various collections, notably *The Shepherd's Calendar: Tales Illustrative of Pastoral Occupations, Country Life and Superstitions* (2 vols., 1828) and *Tales and Sketches of the Ettrick Shepherd* (6 vols., 1837). Hogg's work is not to be taken seriously as genuine folklore, but has a distinctive favor which captures something of the authentic Scottish *volksgeist*.

[For other works of this author, see the companion guide to horror.]

Holland, Clive (pseud. of **Charles James Hankinson**) (U.K.), 1866–1959.

2-82. An Egyptian Coquette. London: Pearson, 1898.
Credulous occult romance in which a hypnotized girl stabs a man and falls into suspended animation; the key to the mystery must be sought among the tombs of the Valley of Kings, where her alter ego is interred. A heavily revised edition was issued in 1923 as *The Spell of Isis*. An interesting variant on the revivified mummy theme, better than George Griffith's imitation *The Mummy and Miss Nitocris* (see [2-70]).

Holmes, Oliver Wendell, 1809–1894.
ABOUT: CA, SMFL

2-83. Elsie Venner. Boston: Ticknor & Fields, 1861.
The tragic story of a young girl who inherits certain ophidian characteristics because her mother was bitten by a rattlesnake while pregnant; this becomes a parable relating to the question of how much moral responsibility people must bear for their actions. By far the most interesting of Holmes's "medicated novels"; the other two are more straightforward psychological case studies: *The Guardian Angel* (1867) involves multiple personality; *A Mortal Antipathy* (1885) features an unusual phobia.

Housman, Laurence (U.K.), 1865–1959.
ABOUT: WW, GSF, CA, SFE, ESF, HF

2-84. All-Fellows: Seven Legends of Lower Redemption. London: Kegan Paul, 1896.
Collection of reverent Christian fantasies—affectively powerful tales of dutiful suffering. In "The King's Evil" Satan blights a good king with leprosy, but the king is compensated with healing gifts; "The Merciful Drought" offers an ingenious apology for natural disaster, and an account of the saving of a saintly man. Seven more stories in the same vein are collected in *The Cloak of Friendship* (1905), which contains some truly heartrending tales of virtue uncrushable by evil circumstance. A strong sense of tragedy in contemplating the sufferings of the good and meek drags Housman toward heretical unorthodoxy in much the same way that Anatole France (see [2-62]) and T. F. Powys (see [3-301]) were drawn, though Housman is more reluctant to abandon his trust in the Church and the saints. "Damien, the Worshipper" retains conventional piety in its account of a young man torn between his visions of St. Agnes and the guiles of a temptress, but "When Pan Was Dead" has more than a little sympathy for the wood nymph who tempts a company of nuns to indecency, and "The Troubling of the Waters" is a fine moral fantasy which bleakly accepts that miracles may have evil as well as good consequences. The two collections were combined with one new story as *All-Fellows and the Cloak of Friendship* (1923); they are among the finest works of their kind.

2-85. A Farm in Fairyland. London: Kegan Paul, 1894.
The first in a series of fairy tale books, followed by *The House of Joy* (1895), *The Field of Clover* (1898) and *The Blue Moon* (1904). The contents of the four

collections were reprinted in two volumes as *Moonshine and Clover* and *A Doorway in Fairyland* (both 1922). Though some stories have aspirations to moral seriousness, in a more veiled fashion than [2-84], the collections are most notable for their whimsical idiosyncrasy and the occasional reversal of traditional sex roles, as in "The Prince with the Nine Sorrows" and "Japonel."

2-86. Gods and Their Makers and Other Stories. London: Allen & Unwin, 1897. The young protagonist of the title short novel belongs to a tribe where every person must manufacture a personal deity. Tragic folly leads to his banishment to the isle where these gods come to life following the deaths of their makers; they are so hungry for worship that he becomes their precarious emperor in this unusual and fascinating story. The collection also contains two fine allegories, "Let Us Make Gods" and "The Blind God," and two ironic fantasies.

Hudson, W(illiam) H(enry) (U.K.), 1841–1922.
ABOUT: CA, SMFL, SFE, ESF, HF

*2-87. A Crystal Age. London: Fisher Unwin, 1887 (published anonymously).
A brash young man timeslips into a future where people live in supernatural harmony with nature in small communities governed by the power of mother love; he fails to adapt to this idyllic existence. A pioneering and affectively powerful work of ecological mysticism, also of interest as a utopian vision. Its reverence for an idealized maternal figure is recapitulated in Hudson's children's fantasy *A Little Boy Lost* (1905).

Hume, Fergus (U.K.), 1859–1932.
ABOUT: WW, GSF, CA, ESF

2-88. Aladdin in London. London: Black, 1892.
The protagonist acquires Aladdin's ring; it puts a vast fortune at his disposal so long as he is not tricked into letting go of the talisman. Hume, alas, could think of no better way for him to use this opportunity than to let him involve himself in a sordid Ruritanian romance. Unusual in being an earnest treatment of an Ansteyan theme.

Hyne, C(harles) J(ohn) Cutcliffe (U.K.), 1866–1944.
ABOUT: WW, GSF, CA, SMFL, SFE, TCSF, ESF, HF

2-89. Beneath Your Very Boots. London: Digby & Long, 1889.
A cheerful and playful account of an eccentric and tradition-bound race living in deep caves beneath England. A thin satirical veneer enlivens a self-indulgently silly romance.

Ibsen, Henrik (Norway), 1828–1906.
ABOUT: CA, SMFL

2-90. Peer Gynt. London: Walter Scott, 1892. Tr. by William and Charles Archer of *Peer Gynt*, 1867.

Classic play borrowing heavily from Norwegian folklore. The hero is seduced by a troll-maiden, visits the Hall of the Mountain King, battles the Great Boyg and hears Memnon's statue sing. Then the Button Moulder comes to collect his soul, challenging him to prove that he has been true to himself. A fine phantasmagoric allegory.

Ingelow, Jean (U.K.), 1820–1897.
ABOUT: FL, HF

2-91. Mopsa the Fairy. London: Longmans, Green, 1869.
Episodic fairy romance for children, of historical interest because the customary sentimentality is underlaid by a vaguely anarchic spirit, linking it tenuously to the reaction against moralizing to be found in Carroll and Lear.

Irving, Washington, 1783–1859.
ABOUT: WW, GSF, SFW, CA, SMFL, PE, ESF

*2-92. The Sketch-Book of Geoffrey Crayon. New York: Van Winkle, 1819–20.
A mélange of oddities including two classic items of mock-folkloristic Americana, "Rip van Winkle" and "The Legend of Sleepy Hollow," plus the more straightforwardly eerie "The Spectre Bridegroom" (also annotated as [H1-46]). It was followed by *Tales of a Traveller by Geoffrey Crayon, Gentleman* (1824), which has a greater quantity of fantastic items, including "The Devil and Tom Walker" and the oft-reprinted weird tale "The Adventure of the German Student" (also annotated as [H1-47]). A more reverent approach to supernatural themes is found in Irving's collection of items about Moorish Spain, *The Alhambra* (1832); this includes "The Legend of the Arabian Astrologer" and "The Legend of the Enchanted Soldier" among other folkloristic items, some of them based on authentic materials.

James, G(eorge) P(ayne) R(ainsford) (U.K.), 1799–1860.
ABOUT: WW, GSF

2-93. The String of Pearls. London: Bentley, 1832 (published anonymously).
Juvenilia imitating the *Arabian Nights*. The six stories employ familiar motifs and exemplify conventional moral conclusions, but have a certain precocious liveliness.

[For other works of this author, see the companion guide to horror.]

Jerome, Jerome K(lapka) (U.K.), 1859–1927.
ABOUT: CA, PE, ESF

2-94 Told After Supper. London: Leadenhall Press, 1891.
Collection parodying Christmas ghost stories. Similar in spirit to Bangs's tales of absurd hauntings [2-13]. A more elaborate and rather striking fantasy story is "The Soul of Nicholas Snyders, or the Miser of Zandam," a moral fable reprinted in the collection *The Passing of the Third Floor Back* (1907), whose title story— made famous as a play in 1908—is a fantasy of moral rearmament set in a

boarding house where an enigmatic character (perhaps an angel) takes up temporary residence.

Jerrold, Douglas (U.K.), 1803–1857.
ABOUT: GSF

*2-95. A Man Made of Money. London: Punch, 1848–49.
The protagonist, besieged by demands from his wife and stepdaughters, wishes that he were "made of money"; he then finds himself able to peel banknotes from his breast. As his fortune increases, his substance dwindles, while his temper and reputation go steadily to the bad. The acidic wit is assisted by a remarkably extravagant style, giving the story more savage bite than Dalton's *Invisible Gentleman* [2-40]. In Jerrold's *Collected Works* it is coupled with the odd mock-utopian romance *The Chronicles of Clovernook* (1846), into which are inserted a few tall tales, the best of which offers an account of a haunted cash register.

Jókai, Mór (Hungary), 1825–1904.
ABOUT: SFE, ESF

2-96. Tales from Jókai. London: Jarrold, 1904. Tr. by R. Nisbet Bain.
Varied collection including the novella "City of the Beast" (1856), a gaudy and highly dramatic account of the end of Atlantis (assured by the refusal of its citizens to heed the words of a prophet of Jehovah). Also included are three graphic *contes cruels*: "The Justice of Soliman" (1858), "The Sheriff of Caschau" (1858) and the bizarre tale of "The Hostile Skulls" (1879).

Keats, John (U.K.), 1795–1821.
ABOUT: PE

2-97. Lamia, Isabella, The Eve of St. Agnes & Other Poems. London: Taylor & Hessey, 1820.
"Lamia" is a narrative poem which borrows a story from Philostratus via *The Anatomy of Melancholy*. The hero falls in love with Lamia, but at their wedding feast his old mentor reveals that she is a serpent in disguise; in this version Lamia is innocent of any evil intent and her fate is tragic. The poem is one of several allegorizing the conflict between the artistic imagination and the demands of the reality principle. Compare Gautier's "Clarimonde" (see [2-64]) and Lee's "Prince Alberic and the Snake Lady" (see [H2-48]), which offer more ironic allegorical versions of the same story. Keats uses supernatural themes in many other classic poems first issued here, including a more callous variation of the female vampire in "La Belle Dame Sans Merci."

Kingsley, Charles (U.K.), 1819–1875.
ABOUT: CA, SMFL, HF

2-98. The Water-Babies. London: Macmillan, 1863.
Classic posthumous fantasy in which a chimney sweep's boy, who never had a chance to learn morality in his human incarnation, finally succeeds in achieving

virtue as a water-baby. Embodies the author's conscious preoccupations with evolutionary theory and evangelism, and is said to reveal less conscious obsessions to the Freudian eye. Fascinating and excruciating in more-or-less equal proportions.

Kip, Leonard, 1826–1906.
ABOUT: GSF, ESF

2-99. Hannibal's Man and Other Tales. Albany, NY: Argus, 1878.
Collection of stories mostly reprinted from Christmas numbers of the Albany *Argus*. The title story features the revival of a deep frozen Carthaginian soldier, while "The Secret of Apollonius Septrio" is a marvelous visionary fantasy spanning the centuries to witness the future evolution of mankind. The remainder are lively but fairly conventional Christmas ghost stories.

Kipling, Rudyard (U.K.), 1865–1936.
ABOUT: WW, GSF, SFW, CA, NE, SMFL, SFE, RG, TCSF, PE, ESF, HF

2-100. The Jungle Book. London: Macmillan, 1894.
The first of two volumes, followed by *The Second Jungle Book* (1895). They include eight stories featuring the feral child Mowgli, raised by wolves in an environment which includes various partly anthropomorphized animals: Baloo the bear, Bagheera the panther, Shere Khan the tiger and Kaa the python most significant among them. These curious fables offer the Law of the Jungle—an idiosyncratic but essentially Rousseauesque social contract—in place of conventional morality, and there is a good deal of bitter misanthropy beneath the surface of the narratives; these stories were reprinted as *All the Mowgli Stories* (1933). They outshine by far the other stories—of which the best known is "Rikki-Tikki-Tavi"—and stand at the head of the rich twentieth-century tradition of adventure stories featuring feral children; later examples attempt (in vain) to be more realistic in narrative form while retaining moral pretensions, but none has the wit or the polish of these originals.

[For other works of this author, see the companion guide to horror.]

Laforgue, Jules (France), 1860–1887.
ABOUT: ESF

2-101. Moral Tales. New Directions, 1985, Tr. by William Jay Smith of *Moralités légendaires*, 1887.
Heavily ironic prose poems presenting reinterpretations of ancient tales, including "Perseus and Andromeda; or, the Happiest of the Three" and "Pan and the Syrinx; or, the Invention of the Reed Pipe." Heroes like Perseus, Lohengrin and Hamlet are mercilessly deflated; the heroines fare little better. Closer in spirit to Jarry (see [3-193]) than to Louÿs (see [2-112]); a possible source of inspiration for John Erskine [3-129–3-131].

Lang, Andrew (U.K.), 1844–1912.
ABOUT: WW, GSF, CA, SMFL, SFE, ESF, HF

2-102. The Gold of Fairnilee. Bristol: Arrowsmith, 1888.
The best of Lang's fairy romances, with a plot recalling Andersen's "The Snow Queen" (see [2-4]), drawing heavily upon Scottish folklore; it presents an image of a bleak and dour fairy kingdom, similar to that in Mrs. Craik's *Alice Learmont* (see [2-35]). The later *Prince Prigio* (1889) and its sequel, *Prince Ricardo* (1893), are much lighter in tone and more colorful, and were more popular. Lang edited an important series of anthologies begun with *The Blue Fairy Book* (1889), which offered versions of traditional folktales and literary pastiches eclectically drawn from many sources (occasionally rewritten by Lang). The series eventually exhausted the colors of the spectrum; the last was entitled *The Lilac Fairy Book* (1910).

2-103. In the Wrong Paradise and Other Stories. London: Kegan Paul, 1886.
Collection of ironic stories including several fantasies. The title story is a posthumous fantasy whose protagonist visits several versions of the afterlife. Lang's anthropological interests are also exhibited in the romance of antiquity "The End of Phaeacia"; in the prehistoric parody "The Romance of the First Radical"; and in the classic satirical essay "The Great Gladstone Myth," which uses a then standard mode of anthropological argument to demonstrate that Gladstone never existed, but was simply a symbolic representation of the sun.

Lear, Edward (U.K.), 1812–1888.
ABOUT: CA

2-104. The Book of Nonsense. London: Warne, 1846 (early editions by-lined Derry Down Derry).
The first of Lear's volumes of humorous verses, which helped popularize the limerick and pioneered the tradition of nonsense poetry later taken up by Carroll. Lear sided with children who were tired of moral instruction and wanted pure fun. Expanded editions of this first book were issued in 1861 and 1863; it was followed by *Nonsense Songs, Stories, Botany and Alphabets* (1871), which included "The Owl and the Pussycat" and "The Jumblies"; and *Laughable Lyrics* (1877), including "The Dong with the Luminous Nose" and "The Pobble Who Has No Toes." All were collected in *Edward Lear's Nonsense Omnibus* (1943).

Lee, Edgar (U.K.).

2-105. Pharaoh's Daughter. Bristol: Arrowsmith, 1889.
Timeskipping romance. The hero wakes periodically in order to discover whether the world is yet fit for the revival of his beloved, who was placed in suspended animation in the fifteenth century BC; it never is. Inspired by Rider Haggard's *She* [2-74], it may in turn have inspired Arnold's *Phra the Phoenician* [2-9] and Griffith's *Valdar the Oft-Born* [2-70].

Lefebvre-Laboulaye, Edouard René (France), 1811–1883.

2-106. Abdallah; or, The Four-Leaved Shamrock. London: Sampson, Low, 1895. Tr. by Mary Booth of *Abdallah; ou le trèfle à quatre feuilles*, 1859.
Oriental fantasy in which a rich merchant obtains three wishes for his newborn son, donating health, wealth and freedom from the claims of affection; he thus guarantees that it will be the boy's poor "brother" who will enjoy the favor of heaven and the privilege of reassembling the four leaves of the plant which Eve smuggled out of Eden. Piously sentimental, but interesting in its embellishment of the superstition regarding four-leaf clovers.

Le Queux, William (U.K.), 1864–1927.
    ABOUT: CA, SFE, TCSF

2-107. The Great White Queen. London: F. V. White, 1896.
Lost race story set in Africa, the first of two novels which Le Queux wrote in imitation of Rider Haggard's *She* [2-74]; the second was *The Eye of Istar* (1897). Both run out of inspiration toward the end, but the second is unusual in having an Arab hero and draws upon the same resources as the author's exotic thriller *Zoraida* (1895), provocatively subtitled "A Romance of the Harem and the Great Sahara."

Lie, Jonas (Norway), 1833–1908.
    ABOUT: WW, GSF, CA, PE, ESF

2-108. Weird Tales from the Northern Seas. London: Kegan Paul, 1893. Tr. by R. Nisbet Bain of *Trold I & II*, 1891–92.
Tales in a folkloristic vein which explore the inexplicable aspects of human nature—the "trolls," often here represented by sea demons called draugs. Women are frequently portrayed as semi-supernatural creatures, and Lie adds an intriguing surreal dimension to otherwise conventional accounts of magical brides.

Lisle, Charles Wentworth (U.K.)

2-109. The Ring of Gyges. London: Bentley, 1886.
The author poses as editor to introduce the diaries of a man who acquires the power to render himself invisible and uses the gift to penetrate the polite appearances of the world, thereby discovering various deceptions and plots against himself. His salvation from said plots is bought at the price of increasing cynicism and paranoia which ultimately destroy him. An earnest moral fantasy with considerable bite; makes a most interesting comparison with Dalton's *Invisible Gentleman* [2-40].

Lloyd, John Uri, 1849–1936.
    ABOUT: GSF, SMFL, SFE

2-110. Etidorhpa; or, The End of Earth. Cincinnati: Lloyd, 1895.
Long and bizarre romance in which the mysterious I-Am-The-Man gives the

narrator an account of his quest for occult and spiritual enlightenment, which took him into very strange realms beneath the Earth's surface. Its references to hallucinogenic mushrooms and to a pseudo-Rosicrucian occult secret society have attracted a certain amount of academic interest, but it remains a classic among bad books, its fantastic imagery bogged down by clotted style and rambling discourses in daft metaphysics.

Louÿs, Pierre (France), 1870–1925.
　ABOUT: CA, SMFL

*2-111. Aphrodite. Paris: Borel, 1900. Tr. by Stanley Reynolds of *Aphrodite*, 1896. Erotic fantasy set in a fantasized version of ancient Alexandria. Queen Berenike's lover becomes infatuated with the courtesan Chrysis, and proves his ardor by stealing—at her command—three objects. The crime involves him in murder and blasphemy; as soon as it is complete his passion dies, and he forces her to take the blame upon herself, condemning herself to death. The text is sufficiently explicit that no edition was published in Britain or America until the 1920s, when small private presses issued limited editions. It is the most gorgeous and extraordinary of the fabulously exotic historical novels in the tradition of Anatole France's *Thaïs* [2-61] and Flaubert's *Salammbô* [2-55].

2-112. The Twilight of the Nymphs. London: Fortune Press, 1928. Tr. by Phyllis Duveen of *Le Crépuscule des nymphs*, 1925.
Six prose poems, originally published as separate booklets between 1893 and 1896. The motifs are mostly drawn from Greek mythology, including the stories of "Leda; or, The Glory of Blessed Darkness" and "Danaë; or, Sorrow." Louÿs's other short stories, included in his *Collected Works* (1932) as *Sanguines*, include more ironic fantasies—"A New Sensation" is a cynical version of Gautier's oft-repeated dream-woman plot; "The In-Plano" is an anti-clerical jest recalling Anatole France's subversive versions of saintly intervention.

Lytton, Lord (Edward George Bulwer) (U.K.), 1803–1873.
　ABOUT: WW, GSF, SFW, CA, SMFL, SFE, PE, ESF

2-113. Asmodeus at Large. London: Carey, Lea & Blanchard, 1833.
First separate publication of a serial from *The New Monthly Magazine* (1832–33); it is appended to later British editions of *The Student* (first published 1835), reabsorbing the Faustian fable "The Tale of Kosem Kesamim," which had earlier appeared there as a separate item. A curious satire, featuring an Asmodeus rather different from Lesage's (see [1-45]), allegedly an allegorical representation of Excitement, whose wit and wisdom keep the narrator's ennui at bay until he is driven out by ill-fated passion. A quirky and intriguing period piece. Other eccentric allegories from this early phase of Bulwer's career can be found in *The Student* and *The Pilgrims of the Rhine* (1834).

　　[For other works of this author, see the companion guide to horror.]

MacDonald, George (U.K.), 1824–1905.
ABOUT: WW, GSF, SFW, CA, SMFL, SFE, RG, ESF, FL, HF

2-114. At the Back of the North Wind. London: Strahan, 1871.
The life of a poor but saintly child is illuminated by his adventures with the quasi-maternal North Wind—who is, on another level, the delirium brought by the sickness which is gradually destroying him. The most famous example of the Victorian suspicion that the best fate for a child is to die young, before the corruptions of adulthood set in—though this must have had a more personal meaning for MacDonald. An equally odd mother figure appears in *The Princess and the Goblin* (1872); her lofty position is opposed to the sinister tunneling goblins in an allegory of the psyche. The latter has a sequel, *The Princess and Curdie* (1883).

*2-115. Lilith. London: Chatto & Windus, 1895.
The narrator, Vane, follows the mysterious Raven into a mirror world, through which he later undertakes an allegorical odyssey, becoming involved in a conflict which opposes the wicked Lilith and her shadowy consort to Adam (Raven's true identity) and Eve. This odyssey is ultimately frustrating (and seems to have frustrated MacDonald in his attempt to bring it to a satisfactory state); its confusions—including the problematic characterization of the bitter and lamenting mother figure, Mara—presumably reflect confusions in MacDonald's self-analysis. It has parallels with *Phantastes* [2-116] and shows the slight influence of Carroll (see [2-23]), but it is easily the strangest product of Victorian fantasy. It is the obvious parent of Lindsay's *Voyage to Arcturus* [3-221] and fascinated C. S. Lewis (see [3-213-3-216]); as an allegory of heterodox Christianity it bears an interesting relation to the works of T. F. Powys [3-300-3-304].

*2-116. Phantastes: A Faerie Romance for Men and Women. London: Smith, Elder, 1858.
The most significant English *Kunstmärchen*; it describes the allegorical quest of Anodos, whose ideals are continually frustrated as he attempts to discover an appropriate spiritual orientation in a world populated by symbolic characters. The temptations of the flesh (decorously disguised) are far more evident here than in the author's later adventure in self-exploration, *Lilith* [2-115]; the story is relatively clear-cut, but at the level of meaning it remains confused and full of doubt. An interpolated tale which is separately reprinted as "The Woman in the Mirror" (among other titles) describes a young man's infatuation with a woman imprisoned in a magic mirror; it compares interestingly with Gautier's tales of dream brides [2-64, 2-65], especially in terms of its very different conclusion.

*2-117. Works of Fancy and Imagination. 10 vols. London: Strahan, 1871.
Collection including [2-116] and *The Portent* [H2-57] as well as shorter fairy tales written before 1871. Most had appeared earlier in *Adela Cathcart* (1864) and *Dealings with the Fairies* (1867). Some, like "The Light Princess," are fine children's stories, but the best have understated allegorical themes underlying some marvelous phantasmagoric imagery. "The Golden Key" and "The Carasoyn" are perhaps the finest Victorian fairy tales; both are reprinted in the collection *Evenor* (1972), which also includes the novella *The Wise Woman*

(1875); the latter is a simpler moral tale, which loses something in its simplicity. The most significant work in this vein which MacDonald published after this collection was the *Kunstmärchen* "The History of Photogen and Nycteris" (1879).

[For other works of this author, see the companion guide to horror.]

Macleod, Fiona (pseud. of William Sharp) (U.K.), 1855–1905.
ABOUT: GSF, SFW, SMFL, ESF

2-118. The Writings of Fiona Macleod. 7 vols. London: Heinemann, 1909–10.
Omnibus collection of novels, short stories, poems and other items constituting a broad tapestry of Celtic myth and folklore. The novels *Pharais* (1894) and *Green Fire* (1896; here reduced to the novella "The Herdsman" and a few fragments) are contemporary romances with modest supernatural embellishments, while *The Divine Adventure* (1900) is a curious parable in which a man is divided into three personalities: Body, Will and Soul. Better work is to be found in the shorter pieces derived from *The Sin-Eater and Other Tales* (1895), *The Washer of the Ford and Other Legendary Moralities* (1896) and *The Dominion of Dreams* (1899), which include some contemporary tales of the supernatural and many tales of ancient Britain. "The Sin-Eater" is perhaps the best of the former, while "The Honey of the Bees" and "The Harping of Cravetheen" stand out among the latter. Obviously influenced by James Macpherson's impostures in connection with Ossian, and perhaps also by James Hogg (see [2-81]).

MacNish, Robert (U.K.), 1802–1837.
ABOUT: GSF

2-119. The Modern Pythagorean. 2 vols. Edinburgh: Blackwood, 1838.
"A Modern Pythagorean" was the pseudonym which MacNish attached to his regular contributions to *Blackwood's*, here collected in volume II of this posthumous collection; volume I is a biography by D. M. Moir. "The Metempsychosis" (1826) is an early identity exchange story whose protagonist is the hapless victim of a deal made with the devil by another. It remains an eminently readable grotesque. Many of the other stories are extremely grotesque in their imagery, some featuring deranged states of consciousness and strange obsessions, perhaps inspired by the author's doctoral dissertation on "The Anatomy of Drunkenness." There are also three neatly retold folktales: "Terence O'Flaherty," "Death and the Fisherman" and "A Vision of Robert the Bruce." An intriguing curiosity.

Markwick, Edward (U.K.).

2-120. The City of Gold. London: Tower, 1896.
Lost race story set in Africa, slightly more exotic than most. Borderline scientific romance, but very closely akin to William Le Queux's imitations of *She* [2-107].

Marsh, Richard (U.K.), 1857–1915.
    ABOUT: WW, GSF, PE, ESF

2-121. The Devil's Diamond. London: Henry, 1893.
A miserly businessman inherits the eponymous jewel, whose reputation for bringing ill-luck is entirely justified, and whose angry resistance to being sold is demonstrated to spectacular effect. The tale is hasty and overextravagant hackwork, obviously made up as the author went along, but has a certain fascination because of the sadistic quality of the magical slapstick. *The Mahatma's Pupil* (1893) is a more moderate but equally casual Ansteyan fantasy of respectable middle-class life disrupted by anarchic magic; the magician is only trying to help, but it all goes wrong. Marsh's third work in this vein was *The Magnetic Girl* (1903), an elaborate reprise of Dalton's "The Beauty Draught" (see [2-40]) featuring a plain girl who recklessly wishes to be irresistible to men.

   [For other works of this author, see the companion guide to horror.]

Meredith, George (U.K.), 1828–1909.
    ABOUT: GSF, CA, SMFL, HF

2-122. The Shaving of Shagpat: An Arabian Entertainment. London: Chapman & Hall, 1856.
Baroque Oriental fantasy in the tradition of the *Arabian Nights,* in which a barber must try to redeem himself from the ill-repute attached to his profession by discovering the magical Sword of Events which alone can remove a particularly exotic hair from the head of the clothier Shagpat. A bizarre and rather unclear allegory, full of grotesque humor. Meredith followed it with the novella *Farina* (1857), a boisterous historical romance set in the Rhineland and embellished by supernatural intrusions: a water sprite who helps the heroes overcome apparently insuperable odds and (in a cameo role) the Devil.

Molesworth, Mrs. (**Mary Louisa Stewart**) (U.K.), 1839–1921.
    ABOUT: WW, GSF, PE, ESF, HF

2-123. The Cuckoo Clock. London: Macmillan, 1877 (first edition as by Ennis Graham).
The cuckoo in a clock becomes the mentor of the alienated young heroine until she no longer needs the solace of the adventures he creates for her. An exemplary Victorian version of one of the classic themes in children's fantasy.

   [For other works of this author, see the companion guide to horror.]

Morris, William (U.K.), 1834–1896.
    ABOUT: WW, GSF, SFW, CA, SMFL, SFE, RG, TCSF, FL, HF

2-124. The Early Romances of William Morris. London: Dent, 1907.
Collection including verse and prose, mostly reprinted from the short-lived *Oxford and Cambridge Magazine* of 1856. The most notable are the novelette

"The Hollow Land," which has much in common with George MacDonald's allegories [2-115–22-117], "Gertha's Lovers" and "Golden Wings" (the story, not the poem of the same title); the latter two anticipate the manner and style of Morris's long chivalric romances.

*2-125. The Story of the Glittering Plain. Hammersmith: Kelmscott, 1891.
The hero's search for his betrothed takes him ultimately to the land of the undying—the Glittering Plain—whose king he offends; unlike Orpheus, he recovers his beloved after returning to the world of mortals. More carefully composed than the later, more prolix romances (which were often dictated rather than written).

*2-126. The Water of the Wondrous Isles. Hammersmith: Kelmscott, 1897.
The heroine is kidnapped by a witch and grows up in her charge, but with supernatural aid she contrives to escape and tour the eponymous isles in search of her mother and her true love. A rather ponderous allegory, unusual in featuring a female protagonist and enlivened by some grotesque imagery. Posthumously published; followed by *The Sundering Flood* (1897)—a similar allegory of maturation with a male hero—which Morris left incomplete at his death.

2-127. The Well at the World's End. Hammersmith: Kelmscott, 1896.
Long and elaborate story of a young man's quest for the mysterious well, which takes him through a quasi-Arthurian landscape and involves him in many adventures. Unusual in that the well's attainment is not the climax of the story but is merely a turning point from which the hero and his beloved must progress (or regress?) to a mature acceptance of ordinary responsibility.

2-128. The Wood Beyond the World. Hammersmith: Kelmscott, 1894.
The unhappy hero is lured into the magic wood by a vision; he rescues a girl held captive there, though it is her magic which ultimately delivers them from her enemies and finds them a place in the world. Perhaps the most personal of Morris's allegories, somewhat lacking in narrative drive; it was followed by *Child Christopher and Goldilind the Fair* (1895), which offers a rather stilted retelling of the legend of Havelok the Dane.

Murray, G(eorge) G(ilbert) A(imé) (U.K.), 1866–1957.
ABOUT: CA

2-129. Gobi or Shamo: A Story of Three Songs. London: Longmans, Green, 1889.
Adventure story about the search for a lost colony of Hellenes in Asia; they have thrived, but their presence has had odd effects on the beliefs and customs of their barbaric neighbors, as the Europeans who find them discover to their cost. A classy example of the lost race subgenre.

Nerval, Gérard de (France), 1808–1855.
ABOUT: CA

2-130. Selected Writings. Univ. of Michigan, 1957. Tr. by Geoffrey Wagner.
Collection of poetry and prose. Includes the dreamlike story "Sylvie" (1854) and the remarkable surreal novella *Aurélia* (1855), which describes the hallucinations attendant upon the hero's descent into madness, which are here construed as a

visionary revelation. The latter is a unique work, perhaps the most curious product of French Romanticism.

Nicholson, Joseph Shield (U.K.), 1850–1927.

2-131. A Dreamer of Dreams. Edinburgh: Blackwood, 1889 (published anonymously).
Moralistic fantasy. The hero cultivates the art of dreaming with the aid of drugs; after becoming convinced that he has murdered his cousin in order to inherit a fortune, he embarks upon a hallucinatory odyssey, in which he is blackmailed by Mr. Smith (the devil) into using his money to seduce two friends into moral ruin; he eventually learns the error of his ways.

2-132. Toxar. London: Longmans, 1890 (published anonymously).
Conte philosophique and romance of antiquity in which the philosopher Xenophilos tells the tale of the eponymous scholar-slave, whose talent for telling his masters how to gain their ends leads them all to destruction. Lust and the corruptions of power overcome nobility of spirit, and the power to see into the hearts of men is exterminated by those who fear its revelations. Nicholson's scientific romance *Thoth* (1888) has a similar moral, but is not as good.

Nisbet, Hume (U.K.), 1849–1921.
ABOUT: WW, GSF, PE

2-133. Valdmer the Viking. London: Hutchinson, 1893.
A romance set in the eleventh century which presents a curious mélange of themes; the hero visits the north pole en route to a rendezvous with the wife of a previous incarnation, who is in suspended animation. An equally eccentric mix is to be found in *The Great Secret* (1895), which similarly borrows themes from George Griffith (see [2-70]) and adds a generous seasoning of the occult. Nisbet's short fiction includes some conventional fantasies.

O'Brien, Fitz-James, 1828–1862.
ABOUT: WW, GSF, SFW, NE, SMFL, SFE, PE, ESF

*2-134. The Poems and Stories of Fitz-James O'Brien. Boston: Osgood, 1881.
Collection including several classic fantasies: "The Diamond Lens" (1858), whose hero falls in love with a sylphide glimpsed in the microcosm revealed by a magical microscope; "The Wondersmith" (1859), featuring murderous homunculi armed with poisoned poniards; and "What Was It?" (1859), about an invisible creature. A definitive modern collection is *The Supernatural Tales of Fitz-James O'Brien*, edited by Jessica Amanda Salmonson (1988).

Oliphant, Mrs. (Margaret Oliphant Wilson Oliphant) (U.K.), 1828–1897.
ABOUT: WW, GSF, SFW, CA, SMFL, SFE, PE, ESF

2-135. A Little Pilgrim in the Unseen. London: Macmillan, 1883 [1882].
Fix-up combining two tales of the posthumous adventures of a saintly woman. The adventures are further continued in two of the three stories in *The Land of*

Darkness (1888). Typical of the pious sentimentality of Victorian posthumous fantasies, which mostly answer a powerful hunger for good news from Heaven. The title story of the second collection, which offers a tour of the parallel Hell, is (inevitably) more interesting. A third volume, *"Dies Irae"; the Story of a Spirit in Prison* (1895), adds to the otherworldly guide by displaying Purgatory, while "The Land of Suspense" (1897) examines the predicament of a soul that cannot gain entry to Heaven and seems to be lost in Limbo. Of interest mainly as period pieces, though the later ones are nourished by the anguish of the author's own spiritual crises.

[For other works of this author, see the companion guide to horror.]

Peacock, Thomas Love (U.K.), 1785–1866.

2-136. The Misfortunes of Elphin. London: Hookham, 1829 (published anonymously).
Arthurian fantasy based on the *Mabinogion* [1-47] about the career of the bard Taliesin, who is raised from boyhood in Elphin's Ceredigion and must go to Avallon in search of Arthur when Elphin is imprisoned by a powerful enemy. Peacock had earlier written *Maid Marian* (1822), from which much of the modern mythology of Robin Hood is drawn.

Pearce, J(oseph) H(enry) (U.K.), born 1854.
    ABOUT: GSF

2-137. Drolls from Shadowland. London: Lawrence & Bullen, 1893.
Collection of fables, allegories and prose poems; the most interesting are "The Man Who Coined His Blood into Gold" and "The Unchristened Child," items of Cornish folklore embodying some Cornish dialect terms. *Tales of the Masques* (1894) is a companion volume, in which the most interesting items are the sardonic tale "A Droll Result" and the prose poem "The Sorcery of the Forest."

Phillpotts, Eden (U.K.), 1862–1960.
    ABOUT: WW, GSF, SFW, CA, SMFL, SFE, PE, ESF

2-138. A Deal with the Devil. London: Bliss, Sands & Foster, 1895.
Boisterous fantasy in which an old man bargains with the devil for ten more years, becoming younger all the while at an accelerated rate. A lively version of an oft-used theme.

Pyle, Howard, 1853–1911.
    ABOUT: CA, ESF, HF

2-139. Twilight-Land. New York: Harper, 1894.
Sixteen stories imitating traditional tales, ostensibly related by characters who were themselves made famous by folkloristic accounts of their adventures, including Dr. Faustus and Sindbad (sic). Intended for young readers, but not written in

the glutinously patronizing style of *The Garden Behind the Moon* (1895); the stories have a nice sense of irony and a certain charm.

Rossetti, Christina (Georgina) (U.K.), 1830–1894.
ABOUT: CA, PE

*2-140. Goblin Market and Other Poems. London: Macmillan, 1862.
The title poem is a remarkable erotic allegory in which goblins tempt two sisters with "forbidden fruit"; one falls prey to temptation and nearly dies, but is redeemed by her resilient sister; the author practiced the self-sacrificing asceticism which she here preached.

Ruskin, John (U.K.), 1819–1900.
ABOUT: CA, SMFL, FL, HF

2-141. The King of the Golden River; or, The Black Brothers. London: Smith, Elder, 1851 (first edition anonymous).
Kunstmärchen in which three brothers live in an Edenic valley until the greed of the elder two leads to its desolation; the youngest, with the aid of the eponymous fairy king, restores it to its paradisal state. A conventional moral tale, gracefully told.

Russell, W(illiam) Clark (U.K.), 1844–1911.
ABOUT: WW, GSF, SFE, PE, ESF

2-142. The Frozen Pirate. 2 vols. London: Sampson Low, 1887.
The only survivor of a storm at sea finds a vessel trapped in the Antarctic ice; when he builds a fire he thaws out a pirate, who cannot believe that half a century has passed, though he begins to age with unnatural rapidity. Marginal, but interesting in its pioneering use of two common fantasy motifs.

[**For other works of this author, see the companion guide to horror.**]

Southesk, Earl of (James Carnegie) (U.K.), 1827–1905.

2-143. Suomiria: A Fantasy. London: Author, 1899.
The eponymous heroine is a sphinx girl from the Earth's interior who surrenders her supernatural powers for human form and a human soul so that she may wed the hero. He tires of her and marries another, but must eventually call upon her aid. An odd version of the theme whose classic versions are *Undine* [2-57] and "The Little Mermaid" (see [2-4]).

Stables, Gordon (U.K.), 1840–1910.
ABOUT: SFE

2-144. The Cruise of the Crystal Boat. London: Hutchinson, 1891.
An Arab prince broadens his mental horizons while seeing the world with the aid of a magical airship. A curious hybrid of the Oriental tale and the Vernian romance of imaginary tourism, with slight allegorical pretensions.

Sterling, John (U.K.), 1806–1844.
ABOUT: GSF

2-145. Arthur Coningsby. 3 vols. London: Effingham Wilson, 1833 (published anonymously).
Novel about the disillusionment of a British political radical caught up in the French Revolution. Though the story itself is not fantastic, it contains eight embedded tales which are, including a ghost story and two religious fantasies as well as as the ones reprinted in [2-146].

*2-146. Essays and Tales. 2 vols. London: John Parker, 1848.
Posthumous collection. Volume II includes fourteen short stories and a novel, *The Onyx Ring* (1838–39). The latter is a deeply felt fantasy in which an unhappy man is enabled to share the experiences of various others in order to search out the key to happiness. Though many of its characterizations are bitter, it refuses cynicism and despair. More earnest than most contemporary moralizing fantasies, and more intense than Anatole France's parable *The Shirt* (see [3-145]), it is in its way a minor masterpiece. The earlier tales were written for the *Athenaeum*, of which Sterling was co-proprietor for a while; these are classical fantasies with allegorical overtones, not so ironic as Richard Garnett's [2-63]. "Zamor" (1828), about a vision experienced by Alexander the Great, and "Cydon" (1829), about a youth driven by a spirit to search for the cave of Prometheus, are especially fine. There are also two allegories and an antiquarian romance reprinted from [2-145]. The remainder formed, with *The Onyx Ring*, a series in *Blackwood's* entitled "Legendary Lore." This began with the delicate prose poem "The Palace of Morgana" (1837) and also included "Land and Sea" (1838), a fine weird tale about a sea sprite, and "A Chronicle of England" (1840), a beautiful allegorical fairy tale. Ill health and premature death prevented Sterling from becoming one of the major writers of his generation, but the neglect into which his excellent fantasies have been allowed to fall is dreadfully unjust.

Stockton, Frank R(ichard), 1834–1902.
ABOUT: GSF, SFW, CA, NE, SFE, TCSF, ESF, FL, HF

*2-147. The Bee-Man of Orn and Other Fanciful Tales. New York: Scribner, 1887.
Collection of nine ironic fables, strongly seasoned with absurdity, and with a subtle underlying moralism. In the title story the bee-man, informed that he has been transformed from his natural shape, goes in search of his true self. "The Griffin and the Minor Canon" become firm friends but suffer from the vicious tongues of others and the conflicts of their own natures. These are excellent stories, the closest thing America produced to the profound nonsense of Carroll [2-23, 2-24] and Lear [2-104]. *A Story-Teller's Pack* (1897) includes several fantasy stories, among them "The Magic Egg," a moral fable about a hypnotist, and occasional fantasies appear in Stockton's other collections; the most notable are the title story of *Amos Kilbright: His Adscititious Experiences* (1888), about the problems of adaptation suffered by a reincarnated spirit, and "The Philosophy of Relative Existences" (in *The Watchmaker's Wife*, 1893), in which an empty town is haunted by ghosts from the future.

2-148. The Vizier of the Two-Horned Alexander. London: Cassell, 1899.
Light fantasy in which an immortal recalls some of his adventures in famous
locales of the ancient world. An amiable assembly of tall stories, very similar in
theme and tone to Cutcliffe Hyne's *Abbs* (1929).

Stoker, Bram (Ireland), 1847–1912.
ABOUT: WW, GSF, SFW, CA, NE, H, SMFL, SFE, PE, ESF

2-149. Under the Sunset. London: Sampson, Low, 1881.
Collection of downbeat allegorical fairy tales, perhaps reflecting Stoker's own
psychological crises. The best is "The Invisible Giant," which translates a plague
into supernatural symbology after the fashion of Gotthelf's *Black Spider* [H2-35].
Though cruder than the similar tales of George MacDonald [2-117] and Oscar
Wilde [2-157], the stories have a certain fascination.

[For other works of this author, see the companion guide to horror.]

Sue, Eugène (France), 1804–1857.
ABOUT: WW, GSF, H, SMFL, PE

2-150. The Wandering Jew. 3 vols. London: Chapman & Hall, 1844–45.
Long and amazingly intricate melodrama originally published as a newspaper
serial. The descendants of a man who once gave succor to the cursed wanderer are
commanded to assemble in Paris on a certain day to become the heirs to his
fortune, but the evil Jesuits plan to get the fortune for themselves, to hold back
the cause of progress. The story was too popular to be concluded at the first
climax, so the entire theme repeats. The supernatural elements are symbolic, the
novel being a parable of radical politics which unfortunately loses its narrative
drive toward the end. The Modern Library Giant edition (1940) is one of the few
unabridged translations.

Thackeray, William Makepeace (U.K.), 1811–1863.
ABOUT: CA, SMFL, ESF, HF

2-151. The Rose and the Ring. London: Smith, Elder, 1855 (published as by M. A.
Titmarsh).
Christmas fantasy presented as a "fireside pantomime," as wild and silly as
pantomimes usually are, parodying many fairy tale motifs. The slapstick effect is
enhanced by the author's Tennielesque illustrations.

Twain, Mark (pseud. of **Samuel Langhorne Clemens**), 1835–1910.
ABOUT: GSF, SFW, CA, NE, SMFL, SFE, TCSF, ESF, HF

*2-152. A Connecticut Yankee in King Arthur's Court. New York: Webster, 1889.
Classic novel in which a timeslipped engineer tries to modernize the world of
Arthurian legend by means of his knowledge of technology and political econ-
omy. He enjoys moderate success before the forces of reaction strike back, with a

ferocity which brings the dream to an apocalyptic end. Very funny in parts, the comedy ultimately turns to highly effective tragedy in bleakly sardonic fashion. A masterpiece of fantasy.

Watson, H(enry) B(rereton) Marriott (U.K.), 1863–1921.
ABOUT: GSF

2-153. Marahuna. London: Longmans, 1888.
The eponymous heroine is the last survivor of a separate Creation; she is supernaturally attractive but has no moral sensibility, and cannot adapt to the world of men. The parable is unsubtle, but it features one of nineteenth-century fantasy's more intriguing *femmes fatales*.

Wells, H(erbert) G(eorge) (U.K.), 1866–1946.
ABOUT: WW, GSF, SFW, CA, NE, H, SMFL, SFE, RG, TCSF, PE, ESF

2-154. The Plattner Story and Others. London: Methuen, 1897.
Collection including several fantasies, the best being the title story (1896), in which an explosion sends the protagonist into a curious dimension populated by ghostly beings, and "The Apple" (1896), a fable whose protagonist misses out on the opportunity to taste the fruit of the Tree of Knowledge. Other early fantasies by Wells include the classic "The Man Who Could Work Miracles" (1898, see [3-361]) and the ironic apocalyptic fantasy "A Vision of Judgment" (1899).

*2-155. The Wonderful Visit. London: Dent, 1895.
Satirical fantasy based on a remark by Ruskin to the effect that if an angel were to visit Earth, some sportsman would be sure to shoot him. The wounded angel from the Land of Dreams finds Victorian England an ugly place where hypocrisy and injustice reign supreme; it has no place for such as he. Slightly awkward, but effective in its sentimentality and moral indignation.

Whiting, Sydney (U.K.), ?–1875.

2-156. Heliondé; or, Adventures in the Sun. London: Chapman & Hall, 1855.
Visionary romance whose hero finds the sun inhabited by beautiful ethereal people; he falls in love there but ultimately must return to Earth. A slightly sickly dream of paradise.

Wilde, Oscar (Ireland), 1854–1900.
ABOUT: WW, GSF, SFW, CA, SMFL, RG, PE, ESF, HF

*2-157. The Happy Prince and Other Tales. London: Nutt, 1888.
Collection of five moralistic children's stories, the best being the bleak tale "The Nightingale and the Rose," in which human fickleness and insincerity make the bird's noble self-sacrifice futile. Followed by the brilliant collection *A House of Pomegranates* (1891), which represents the peak achievement of the Victorian tradition of allegorical fairy tales. It contains "The Young King," "The Birthday

of the Infanta," "The Fisherman and His Soul" and "The Star-Child," all bitter parables describing the ways in which human infidelity and vanity make virtue and charity almost impossible to achieve.

2-158. Lord Arthur Savile's Crime. London: Osgood McIlvaine, 1891.
Collection containing two classic comic fantasies: the neatly ironic title story, whose hero is told by a palmist that he is destined to commit murder and who submits to the dictates of fate; and "The Canterville Ghost," in which the boorish cynicism of new American owners threatens to drive the haunter of a stately home to despair. The second story is very fine, its broad comedy deepened and redeemed by a delicate touch of sentimentality.

[For other works of this author, see the companion guide to horror.]

Winter, John Strange (pseud. of Henrietta Stannard) (U.K.), 1856–1911.

2-159. A Seventh Child. London: F. V. White, 1894.
The story of a girl whose clairvoyance enables her to avert some of the tragedies which threaten other members of her family, but cannot avert the one which ultimately spoils her own love life. An exercise in sentimental melodrama with a peculiarly bleak ending.

Yeats, William Butler (Ireland), 1865–1939.
ABOUT: CA, PE

2-160. Early Poems and Stories. London: Macmillan, 1925.
Collection reprinting Yeats's early prose pieces, which reflect his interest in Irish folklore and his fascination with contemporary occultism (he was at one time a disciple of Madame Blavatsky, at another a member of the Order of the Golden Dawn). The items from *The Celtic Twilight* (1893) are mostly slight; those initially published in *The Secret Rose* (1897) include more substantial folkloristic materials in the six "Stories of Red Hanrahan." The most interesting of the occult sketches are the two subtitled "Rosa Alchemica." Yeats left incomplete an allegorical novel dramatizing his adventures in the occult, *The Speckled Bird* (written 1896–1902; published 1976).

3

From Baum to Tolkien, 1900–56

Brian Stableford

I n 1900 Sigmund Freud published *The Interpretation of Dreams*, a book which was to bring about a dramatic change in attitudes to the substance of fantasy and the activity (whether private or literary) of fantasizing. Whether Freud's account of the logic of dreams was true, or how widely it was believed, was a matter of little significance in bringing about this change. The point was that a set of ideas had been produced which could not be entirely ignored, and whose attempt to penetrate the symbolism of fantasy—even if it was to be deemed entirely fatuous—could not help making writers and readers more self-conscious in their fantasizing. It was the first of a series of highly influential works in which Freud worked out his theory of the unconscious and his ideas regarding the process of repression. It argued strongly that dreaming—and, by implication, other kinds of fantasizing—operate as a means of vicarious wish fulfillment, in which the wishes and the means of their fulfillment are often disguised even from the fantasist by their encryption in a pattern of symbols. It went on to link the fountainhead of fantasy, and its internal symbolism, to the libido. Once fantasists had heard of this theory, even if they heard of it only in its popular extensions as rumor and jest, it was unforgettable. Its central theses might be rejected, but they could not be disregarded.

There were, of course, to be other theories of the unconscious and other interpretations of fantastic symbolism; Freud's renegade disciple Jung was later to produce a much more elaborate account of what the "collective unconscious" shared by all mankind might contain, and how those contents might be indirectly expressed in various kinds of archetypal imagery, but substitution of one theory for another could not blot out the original; it could only add a further dimension to the new self-consciousness of fantasists and readers in confronting fantasy.

It was, of course, well known to many literary fantasists of the nineteenth century that their creative work might involve symbolization, and that symbols could be used to convey sexual meanings whose direct expression was taboo. When Christina Rossetti wrote in "Goblin Market" [2-140] about "forbidden fruit," she used the euphemism quite deliberately, and it may have been in her mind when she wrote of the goblins trying to force their fruit past Lizzie's resistant lips that the word "lips" was susceptible of more than one meaning (though it is doubtful that she had more than one meaning in mind—or suspected that there might be another possible—when she later made Lizzie say to her less resilient sister, Laura, "Hug me, kiss me, suck my juices . . ."). But in making such symbolic wordplay, Christina Rossetti was not referring her practice to any theoretical context which spoke of the intrinsic nature of fantasy; she was simply making a fantasy of one particular kind. The way that twentieth-century writers came to handle sexual symbolism in their fiction could not help being different: when James Branch Cabell piles innuendo upon innuendo in *The Cream of the Jest* [3-63] or *Jurgen* [3-67], he is not simply writing a fantasy—he is writing a fantasy *about the utility of fantasy*; the self-consciousness of the author is reflected in the self-reference of the work.

There are several possible ways in which self-consciousness may affect literary fantasizing. All are prefigured to some extent in nineteenth-century work, but it is in twentieth-century fantasy that they reach their most exaggerated expression. The principal responses are closely linked to the most common ways in which we publicly confront sexual matters, with the aid of polite masks of humor and sentimentality.

Comic fantasy, which derives mainly from the dialectical interaction of the real and the fantastic, had been brought to its most sophisticated pitch in the concluding years of the nineteenth century by F. Anstey [2-5-2-8; 3-5-3-6]. His most successful twentieth-century counterpart was the American humorist Thorne Smith [3-323-3-329], who employed the same basic formulas but focused much more intently on the sexual components of the fantasies involved. Both writers could be ruthless in undercutting pretensions of "respectability," but for Anstey the poses of respectability were connected first and foremost with matters of social class, and he rarely went beyond exposure of snobbery and affectation; he was reasonably reverent in his treatment of love, courtship and marriage. For Smith, on the other hand, the poses of respectability were much more intimately connected with matters of sexual morality, and with the hypocritical concealment of sexual desire; his treatment of love, courtship and marriage was not entirely cynical, but he was very conscious of the misrepresentations of popular mythology and convention.

To some extent the difference between these two writers is a difference of cultural context, but one can also compare Smith with earlier American humorists like John Kendrick Bangs [2-12-2-13], and one can see a similar drift in later British Ansteyan fantasies—notably the ones written by women like Susan Alice Kerby [3-200-3-201] and "R. A. Dick" [3-112], which have an obviously conscious—though carefully restrained—sexual subtext.

It was the sentimental fantasies of the nineteenth century that came closest to a self-conscious acceptance of the erotic motive in fantasization, though it was unrestrained only in French writers—Gautier [2-64-2-65] provided the most striking example, while the work of Pierre Louÿs [2-111-2-112; 3-224] straddled the turn of the century. The 1920s, however, were to produce a remarkable series of fantasies in post-Victorian Britain in which the erotic component of fantasy, though not necessarily unveiled, became the center of attention and the true object of consideration; key examples include Gerald Bullett's *Mr. Godly Beside Himself* [3-55]; Margaret Irwin's *These Mortals* [3-189]; Hope Mirrlees's *Lud-in-the-Mist* [3-250] and Ronald Fraser's *Flower Phantoms* [3-147]. In America the issue was made most explicit in the same decade by George Viereck and Paul Eldridge, in their trilogy featuring the Wandering Jew [3-350], but the writer who constructed the most elaborate rhetoric—James Branch Cabell [3-63-3-72]—was extravagant in sentimental construction only to withhold his final assent in regard to its propriety. The American tradition remained cynical to an extraordinary extent, evidenced not only by Cabell's skepticism but by the works of John Erskine [3-129-3-131], Faulkner's *Mayday* [3-134] and Viereck's *Gloria* [3-349], but America also produced Robert Nathan [3-262-3-266], the writer who might be reckoned the most sentimental of all sentimental fantasists.

The Freudian allegation that the libido is the motor of fantasy has an ironic reflection in the common sentimental fantasy motif which dissolves the barriers of space and time in response to a protagonist's exaggerated state of frustration. Although the appearance of a doorway into a Secondary World is often represented as a mere relief from tedium (as in Edwin Arnold's *Lieut. Gullivar Jones; His Vacation* [3-111]) or generalized spiritual enervation (as in Stella Benson's *Living Alone* [3-29], closer inspection suggests that in these, as in many more explicit examples, the opportunity comes in answer to specifically libidinous tensions. *Femmes fatales* are very frequently involved, as they are when the traffic moves in the opposite direction and apertures open which allow our world to be invaded by magical persons; mermaids are, of course, a popular favorite, as in [3-194], [3-354] and [3-362], but sirens of many other kinds may fill similar roles.

The extension of bridges in time usually has the same emotional impetus—indeed, the breaching of time is so often connected with matters of romantic crisis (even in the most carefully metaphysical studies) that there is a quite distinct subgenre of "timeslip romances," in which an ideal sexual contact becomes possible—albeit very fleetingly in some cases—only by transcending the barrier of time. The origin of the timeslip romance is certainly to be found in the nineteenth century; Gautier's "Arria Marcella" (see [2-64]) is the prototype, while Vernon Lee's "Amour Dure" [H2-48] and Robert Chambers's "The Demoiselle d'Ys" [H2-12] are two of the most intense. The twentieth century has, however, produced much more elaborate versions of it: it is a favorite formula of Robert Nathan (see especially [3-265]); other classic versions include Margaret Irwin's *Still She Wished for Company* [3-188] and Edith Pargeter's *By Firelight* [3-283]. Reference to these stories as "timeslip *romances*" should not, of course, be taken to imply that consummation is routinely achieved, as it is in the love story genre which has hijacked the label "romance"; in many of the examples cited, consummation of the transtemporal love affair is impossible or undesirable, and in at least one example of the subgenre—Christopher Morley's *Thunder on the Left* [3-254]—the preservation of innocence against the possibility of corruption is the point at issue.

It is obvious to the twentieth-century eye that many nineteenth-century fantasies mask erotic themes with humor and sentimentality in much the same way that these twentieth-century examples do, but those which did not do so innocently did so reverently. Thanks to Freud, all twentieth-century innocence has come to seem mere pretense, and reverence a stylistic affectation. Just as dirty jokes came to be accompanied by a ritual nudge and wink, and sentimental displays with a mime of mournful violins, fantasies began to be packaged with token acknowledgments of their own particular artificiality; naïve literary dreaming was very largely replaced by a form of "lucid dreaming" whose lucidity was supplied by theories of natural symbolism.

It may be as well to say at this point, quite unequivocally, that Freud's *Interpretation of Dreams* is not true in any strong sense; as a whole and coherent scientific theory, it is quite exploded, though some of its shards can still be taken seriously and its bare bones might yet be fleshed out into a theory which, though falling short of a general explanation of the phenomenon of dreaming, could still have some relevance to the business of thinking seriously about the psychological utility of fantasy.

Freudian theory is itself, therefore, no more than a fantasy about fantasies, exactly on a par with many of the literary works whose composition and substance it overshadows. Freudian theory cannot *explain* literary fantasies any more than it can really explain dreams, but it is still significant that we can see similar ideas at work in the invention of psychoanalysis and in the creation of a new wave of literary fantasies whose purpose is to explore the utility (and perhaps the necessity) of fantasy.

Despite their rapid trickling down to the level of popular wisdom, Freudian ideas did not quite obliterate naïve fantasization from the literary map. They did, however, make naïveté into a rare commodity—arguably rare enough to make those writers who could still capture it rather precious. Some children's fantasy remained calculatedly naïve, but this is not quite the same thing as spontaneous naïveté, and many twentieth-century children's classics do have a certain submerged self-awareness which surfaces as an ironic gloss that only adult readers can properly appreciate. In adult fantasy, naked unself-consciousness can be found only in writers who first found their niche in the pulp magazines, the cardinal example being Edgar Rice Burroughs [3-59-3-62]—though even Burroughs had acute problems in handling the issue of Tarzan's sexuality and could not resist the temptation to theorize about psychosexual matters in his eccentric timeslip romance *The Eternal Lover* [3-60]. Burroughs's main successor as a popular pulp fantasist, A. Merritt [3-242-3-246], was a prolific manufacturer of *femmes fatales*, and there is no mistaking the libidinous motive in his work, but he was far more interested in luxuriating in the substance of his dreams than in worrying about their priority, and the same can be said of Robert E. Howard [3-181-3-182], who was not quite so successful in his own day but achieved posthumous celebrity as a writer of wholehearted romances of swords and sorcery.

Outside the realms of children's fantasy and the pulp magazines, however, writers of fantasy were unable to avoid the new awkwardness which had crept into questions of why they were doing what they did; while consciously formulating their own systems of symbols and meanings, they could not avoid being simultaneously preoccupied with what their creative processes might themselves symbolize and mean. Freudian theory provided not only a theoretical perspective but also a threat, especially to those writers who wished to conserve the possibility of constructing allegories and metaphysical fantasies which either had nothing much to do with sexual matters, or wished to deal with sexual matters only in a much broader context. Serious allegorists and metaphysical fantasists like the brothers Powys [3-295–3-299] and [3-300–3-304], David Lindsay [3-218–3-221], Algernon Blackwood [3-33–3-37], C. S. Lewis [3-213–3-216] and Charles Williams [3-373–3-379] are all very intently concerned with matters of psychology as well as matters metaphorical and metaphysical, and this puts a remarkable distance between their efforts and the works of William Morris and George MacDonald.

Although it is of cardinal importance, Freud's is not the only scholarly fantasy which needs to be considered in its relation to the history of fantasy literature, for wherever turn-of-the-century scholarship tried to come to terms with the phenomenon of fantasy, it did so (as the cold light of skeptical hindsight informs us) by fantasizing. James Frazer, attempting to draw up an anthropological theory to account for belief in magic and magical practices, produced three editions of *The Golden Bough* between 1890 and 1915, knitting multifarious items of anecdotal evidence into a rich tapestry of groundless speculation, and inspired many others to follow his example—Robert Graves's speculations about the Earth Mother and the myth-encoded victory of patriarchy over matriarchy cast a more impressionistic eye over the evidence; and Margaret Murray's work in proposing that the Christian persecution of imaginary witches was really a disguised persecution of a hypothetical pagan religion set new standards in making theoretical bricks without empirical straw. Like Freud's scholarly fantasy, though, these theses did not lack for believers, and they had a considerable influence on literary fantasists. In a slightly different vein, there was J. W. Dunne, who set out to "explain" why dreams were (sometimes!) prophetic, and was not content until he had redesigned the universe to accommodate such phenomena. The real universe remained stubbornly unaffected by his efforts, but the constructed worlds of dozens of timeslip romances were by no means so disobliging.

The scholarly fantasies of the nineteenth century, which had (rather furtively) undertaken to rescue magic from the murderous hand of skepticism, went gradually out of fashion as the twentieth century progressed and the allure of newer fantasies made them seem passé, but they left behind a residue, not merely of believers, but of life-style fantasists who had embraced them even more wholeheartedly than those whose interest was merely academic. The wave of fashionability left the ideas of the neo-Rosicrucians and Theosophists far behind, but their most fervent exponents had already discovered the joy and prestige of belonging to a misunderstood and persecuted minority too noble in mind and spirit for the common herd to comprehend.

The greatest of the twentieth century's life-style fantasists was Aleister Crowley (see [3-94]), who hijacked the Hermetic Order of the Golden Dawn from its meeker founders soon after joining it in 1898; tired of the magical rituals which they had "received" from their imaginary masters, he soon began to receive his own and to make his own organization in the image of the one he had outgrown:

the Argentinum Astrum. His one-time disciple Violet Firth (see [3-140-3-141]) did likewise, to become the centerpiece of the Fraternity of the Inner Light. As with so many life-style fantasists of a milder stripe, they both also became literary fantasists, and took no less inspiration from other people's literary fantasies than they took from other people's scholarly fantasies in formulating the fantasies in which they lived; thus they not only did their bit to help the circulation of magical ideas, but further confused and stimulated contemplation of the utility of such ideas. The debt that writers as various as Charles Williams [3-373-3-379] and Dennis Wheatley [3-366] owe to the example of Crowley and his ilk should not be underestimated.

It is surely fitting that the confusion between scholarly, literary and life-style fantasy should most obviously have transcended the threat of incipient silliness in the person and work of the man whose masterpiece marks the end of this period in the history of fantasy fiction: J. R. R. Tolkien (see [3-339-3-340]). He was far too good a scholar to present his fantasies as authentic scholarship, and far too sensible a man to imagine himself a magician, but he became extraordinarily earnest in the scholarly study of his own fantasy world, and made no apology for the part of his life which he gave entirely to its development. He was not the first man to invent a hypothetical universe in which he became obsessively interested (Cabell and Eddison [3-126-3-127] anticipated him in that, and also in applying their scholarly talents to the extrapolation of their imaginary realms), but he was the first to create a sensible theory to explain and justify what he was doing.

Readers and critics are fully entitled to groan when they contemplate the number of slavish imitations *The Lord of the Rings* [3-340] has spawned, but if they are to take seriously Tolkien's own explanation of the what and why of his work, they should not be surprised by it; nor should they be surprised by the parallel phenomenal growth that has taken place in fantasy role-playing games— a remarkable domestication of life-style fantasy, which renders it at worst harmless and at best rewarding. The truth of which writers like Bullett, Mirrlees and Lord Dunsany [3-116-3-124] set out so hesitantly to persuade us—that the Secondary World of Faerie really is necessary to the health and wealth of that life we live in our private thoughts—Tolkien has helped to demonstrate with all due authority.

The ideas which Freud began to elaborate in *The Interpretation of Dreams* were extended in other works to become the latest in a long series of images which represent the human psyche in terms of a crucial division and opposition. In one of Freud's terminologies, the *ego* must somehow negotiate between, and if possible reconcile, two sets of contradictory pressures: the anarchic and amoral bundle of appetites which is the *id*; and the censorious and orderly *superego*. In the conflict between these forces we can see one more version of the battle between passion and reason which has been recognized since the birth of philosophy.

Plato, one of the first great champions of reason, imagined the human soul to be purely rational, but when embedded in its material shell it had perforce to be associated with irrational impulses. Even in Plato's view this was not entirely unfortunate, for there were some impulses which were noble ones—ambition; the desire for power; righteous wrath—but the rest of these passionate forces were "lower" in kind, to be feared, despised and disciplined. Their temptations ought, in Plato's view, to be subject to a ruthless tyranny of the intellect. From the ideal society he outlined in the *Republic*, poets were to be cast out, because they "nourished the well of the emotions" while the true aim of civilized society should be to dry it up.

Few of Plato's successors were quite as ruthless as he in their opposition to the emotions, but their more moderate views were usually aligned on the same side. Aristotle felt that emotions could enrich experience—but he too drew a distinction between nobler emotions and the vulgar passions connected with basic bodily processes, which constituted the "animal part" of man. Among later Greek philosophers, the Stoics shared Plato's suspicions to the full, regarding the passions as perturbations of the mind, almost as a kind of mental disease. Their rivals the Epicureans took a different view, insisting on the naturalness of plea-sure and preaching a kind of hedonism, but there was no vulgarity in their pleasure seeking; their search was for a purified, rather cerebral species of joy, fit for connoisseurs, and one of their mottoes was "Nothing to Excess."

For Christian philosophers of a later period, the passions were temptations of the devil, and giving way to them was the very essence of sin. True godliness was based in asceticism, and those emotions suited to life in Heaven would be very stringently purified, consisting mainly of love of God and a joyful knowledge of that Divine Love which would be returned. When rationalist philosophers set to work again within the Christian tradition, they tended to do little more than secularize this view. Descartes considered the passions as excitations of the soul caused by the movement of "animal spirits"; Spinoza, in laying down the founda-tion of his quasi-Euclidean system of Ethics, accepted it as axiomatic that human freedom was based in the rational power of the intellect, while the opposing power of the emotions must be reckoned a burdensome kind of servitude.

Writers of the nineteenth century proposed new terminologies which were ostensibly more scientific, but the dualistic story which most of them told was little different. The Victorian biologist Darwin, meditating upon *The Expression of the Emotions in Man and Animals* (1872), considered our appetites and passions to be part of our evolutionary heritage, operating independently of the will, as an "undirected flow of nerve-force." The psychologist Havelock Ellis, in *Studies in the Psychology of Sex* (1897), identified two "great fundamental impulses" supplying the "dynamic energy" of all behavior: hunger and sexual desire; like Freud he was to become preoccupied with the idea that the latter might easily be transformed by "sublimation" into other kinds of creative en-deavor, including literary work.

Some other nineteenth-century writers tried to make fundamental connec-tions between the divided nature of man and the exercise of artistic creativity. Notable among them was Nietzsche, whose account of *The Birth of Tragedy* (1872) contrasted the "Apollonian" and "Dionysian" elements which, in fusion, formulated the worldview of tragedy (whose subsequent death was procured by the victory of rationalism). Later writers were to borrow this dialectical pair to describe phases through which whole cultures might pass, in the one striving for the rule of calm reason, in the other for the wild abandonment of ecstasy.

Throughout the history of these dualistic accounts of human beings there emerged only a handful of true champions of the passions. The most prominent was probably the eighteenth-century French philosopher Rousseau, who firmly believed in the nobility of savagery, and who became the father figure of the cult of *sensibilité*. In his later writings, though, Nietzsche remade his image of Dionysus, making him a symbol of a healthy reconciliation of the Apollonian and the Dionysian: passion sublimated into creative endeavor. In this view, reason was a counterpart to rather than an enemy of the passions, and the real contrast to be made was between the harshly repressive dominion of asceticism, which was perverted and life-denying, and a benevolent quasi-Epicurean acceptance of passionate purpose and rational method. He condemned the excesses of Christianity on this account.

The principal process of ideological evolution which is visible in the fantasy genre is perhaps best summed up (though any summing up is bound to be an oversimplification) as the discovery and championship of an essentially Nietzschean position. In the lushness of nineteenth-century French fantasy we can find the earliest evidence of this evolution—aided, no doubt, by the residual influence of Rousseauesque sensibility—and it reached its climax in the work of Anatole France, especially *The Revolt of the Angels* [3-144]. The process was slower in other nations, but in the post-Freudian era of reasoned contemplation of the libido and all its works, its progress was steady. This is the real achievement of the new self-awareness whose effects were discussed above.

Twentieth-century fantasy writers, in building their apologia for the work of the imagination, often replaced Nietzsche's Dionysus with Pan, or with Satan, both of whom could stand as warm figures opposed to the tyrannous threat of Christian asceticism; key examples are to be found in Eden Phillpotts's *Pan and the Twins* [3-294]; Lord Dunsany's *Blessing of Pan* [3-116]; William Gerhardi and Brian Lunn's *Memoirs of Satan* [3-154] and David H. Keller's *The Devil and the Doctor* [3-197]. Pan is not always regarded favorably, and Satan frequently remains the arch-adversary of mankind, but even the Pan of Stephen McKenna's *The Oldest God* [3-230] or the Satans of Robert Nathan's *The Innocent Eve* [3-263], and Mikhail Bulgakov's *The Master and Margarita* [3-54] have a benevolent aspect reflecting the fact that in them, reason and passion have worked out a better accommodation than mere humans have yet achieved. It was possible even for devoutly religious writers, like Alfred Noyes in *The Devil Takes a Holiday* [3-273], to show Satan playing a constructive role allied to this line of argument.

The essay introducing the previous chapter pointed out that intimate connections between magic and morality arise because magic has always been associated with the passions. The notion of the magician-as-ascetic (exemplified, for example, in the Eastern "adept" of Theosophical mythology) is a very recent one, born of the Victorian compulsion to sanitize, and there was never any real possibility of its displacing more traditional images of witches and sorcerers driven by lust and unconstrained by moral law. What has happened instead in twentieth-century fantasy is that writers began assiduously to search for the better uses of passion-driven magic.

In the Sartrean theory of emotion quoted in that earlier essay—which is, like modern fantasy fiction, an unmistakable product of twentieth-century thought, and might well be reckoned yet another of its scholarly fantasies—passion ceases to be defined in quasi-mechanical terms. The ideas of "animal spirits" and "nerve-force" are consigned to the same dustbin. Sartre urges us instead to view emotional experience as a kind of perception, characterized by a "magical" worldview which contrasts with, but also complements, the "instrumental" worldview which underlies our rational/scientific understanding. In this view we see the world in two ways, which overlap but never quite come into perfect focus; we see a world of objects to be manipulated, and a world of objects of desire; these two worlds are differently conceptualized and differently evaluated, and though we live simultaneously in both we can no more force our experience into a repressive existential straitjacket which recognizes only one form of perception than we can separate ourselves into two distinct individuals. Our task instead— and this is what twentieth-century fantasy also asserts, in its most interersting fictions and in its theory as articulated by Tolkien—is to reach the most life-enhancing compromise we can. The Nietzschean image of the reformulated Dionysus is as apt a symbol as any for that goal.

This is the *zeitgeist* of modern fantasy literature, within which many and very various writers seem to be trying to find their moral bearings. The writers of the twentieth century inherited the task along with the tradition from their nineteenth-century forebears, and there is little among their materials that is authentically new. All the subgenres of fantasy, major and minor—Secondary World fantasies, posthumous fantasies, timeslip romances, Ansteyan comic fantasies, tales of feral children, etc.—were recovered from ancient oral tradition and redeployed in popular fiction during the nineteenth century. But the twentieth-century use of these subgenres is always distinctive, and the distinctiveness of each subgenre fits into an overall pattern, whose key element is an attempt to reconcile more intimately and more cleverly the two modes of our experience: the emotional and the rational; the magical and the instrumental; the fantastic and the mundane. If we take several exemplary subgenres in turn, we can easily see the parallel lines of their development.

The Secondary Worlds of nineteenth-century fantasy are various enough, including numerous imaginary pasts and parallel worlds, but whatever literary device is used to separate the Secondary World from the mundane world, or to achieve transition in those instances where a character must move between the worlds, the key metaphor is that of the dream from which the character will ultimately awaken. Literal use of this device is very common, but even in those romances where it has no place within the narrative—as, for instance, in those stories set entirely within a Secondary World—some such separation is generally explicit. What happens within the Secondary World, in these cases, is an allegory of sorts (whether it consists of pietistic homilies, of metaphysical explorations or simply of demystifying nonsense) whose significance lies in its relevance to the mundane world.

Twentieth-century Secondary World fantasy, however, gradually dissolves this separation; its "dreamed worlds" not only do not have to be banished into an oblivion of discarded illusion, but also *should not* be banished in such a way. What readers and/or characters can carry back from them is decidedly *not* limited to matters of moral instruction (though those too may be important); the Secondary World itself is something of value to be kept, retained and used again.

It is, therefore, particularly apt that the period covered in this chapter begins with Baum's *Wonderful Wizard of Oz* [3-20], which was to be the first of many fantasies whose basic materials were subsequently to be elaborated into a vast series. Edgar Rice Burroughs's Mars [3-61]; Cabell's Poictesme [3-65 etc.]; Dunsany's Pegana [3-118]; Eddison's Zimiamvia [3-126]; Howard's Hyborian Age [3-182]; Phillpotts's ancient Greece [3-290 etc.]; T. F. Powys's Dorset [3-302 etc.]; Tolkien's Middle-earth [3-339]; and T. H. White's Arthurian Period [3-370] are extraordinarily various in detail, but each one was something with which the author—and, at second hand, the reader—kept in touch for long periods of time. Not one dissolved with the dream which first spawned it, and several contrived to survive the deaths of their creators, to be further extended by other hands.

Even those twentieth-century fantasy writers who have, as a matter of habit, continually moved on from one dreamed world to another—examples include L. Sprague de Camp [3-101–3-104], David Lindsay [3-218–3-221], A. Merritt [3-242–3-246] and John Cowper Powys [3-295–3-299]—have tended nevertheless to reiterate certain key aspects of their ritual, cultivating a certain constancy of relationship in spite of changes of scenery. When the character or the reader "awakens" from these dreams, they leave behind an echo which is far more substantial than any mere emphasis of moral conviction. The Secondary Worlds of twentieth-century fantasy are robust; they have lost the essential fragility of mere dreams.

The posthumous fantasies of the nineteenth century did not treat the Christian mythos as a straitjacket; they were inventive, after their own fashion, in providing Purgatory and Hell with landscapes and the dead with a variety of phantom forms. Nevertheless, the basic conditions of the afterlife are treated as a kind of received wisdom; they are true to doctrine if not to dogma. Twentieth-century writers of posthumous fantasies, by contrast, characteristically adopt a different approach, which—even when traditional notions of Heaven and Hell are retained—binds the afterlife very much more closely to the business of life. Characters in twentieth-century posthumous fantasy often have difficulty recognizing or accepting that they are, in fact, dead. Their life after death is very often taken up with an intensive re-examination or even recapitulation of the social relationships which they formed (ineptly) during life. The afterlife (from which it is often, paradoxically, possible to return) provides an opportunity not merely for the reappraisal of values and decisions, but for the practical investigation of alternatives, and Hell is very rarely a Dantean phantasmagoria of fiery torments, being far more likely to assume the appearance of a slum or a city, or to be a mere state of mind.

We find that the moral crises of twentieth-century Britain are engraved as deeply in the surreal *bizarrerie* of British posthumous fantasies as they are in the most earnest of mundane fictions, mapped out in a long series of works both comic and intense: Arnold Bennett's *The Glimpse* [3-26]; Wyndham Lewis's *Childermass* [3-217]; Sutton Vane's *Outward Bound* [3-347]; Rebecca West's *Harriet Hume* [3-365]; Lady Saltoun's *After* [3-317]; Michael Maurice's *Marooned* [3-238]; Claude Houghton's *Julian Grant Loses His Way* [3-179]; Marmaduke

Dixey's *Hell's Bells* [3-113]; John Cowper Powys's *Morwyn* [3-298]; Neil Gunn's *Green Isle of the Great Deep* [3-161]; Charles Williams's *All Hallows' Eve* [3-373]; C. S. Lewis's *The Great Divorce* [3-213]; and Harry Blamires's trilogy begun with *The Devil's Hunting-Grounds* [3-38]. All these works feature an intimate inter-penetration of the business of divine judgment and moral evaluation with the motives and means of everyday social intercourse. None demands that a good life should be self-denying to the point of saintliness; but each requires some produc-tive and creative harnessing of passion.

The nineteenth-century timeslip romance was rarely a fulfilling affair, and even in such nearly idyllic versions as Gautier's "Arria Marcella" (see [2-64]) the ecstasy was impossible to sustain. Passion could produce an erotic dream, but the dream must inevitably be dispelled, and those characters who dared to ask for more (as did, for instance, the heroine of Gautier's *Spirite* [2-65]) must pin their hope to arcane metaphysics and the (unelaborated) notion of a hospitable after-life.

In twentieth-century fantasy, however, the power of passion to transcend the limitations of time and space is much increased, and even when the dream must in the end dissolve, its effect on the dreamer is more powerful and more profound than the extended postcoital *tristesse* which spoiled mundane existence for Gau-tier's characters. The meeting of lovers from different eras rarely leads to a stable relationship in this early part of the century, but its failure to do so is frequently and typically seen as an agonizing tragedy—as it is, for instance, in Knittel's *Nile Gold* [3-205], Nathan's *Portrait of Jennie* [3-265] or Pargeter's *By Firelight* [3-283]. Even when the disruption of time is seen as a version of death, as in Machen's *Hill of Dreams* [3-229], there is a perverse triumph in the achievement of transcendence which is much more assertive than the saccharine climax of *Spirite*.

It is noticeable too that in twentieth-century fantasy the effects of timeslip-ping are subject to much more careful analysis—in which the metaphysical mirrors the psychological—in a series of works which extends from Arnold's *Lepidus the Centurion* [3-10] and Cromartie's *Out of the Dark* [3-93] through Lindsay's *The Haunted Woman* [3-219], Irwin's *Still She Wished for Company* [3-188] and Sitwell's *The Man Who Lost Himself* [3-322] to Marlow's *The Devil in Crystal* [3-232], Harding's *The Twinkling of an Eye* [3-165] and Finn's *Time Marches Sideways* [3-136]. There are tragedies here too, but there are also victo-ries, and the fact that the victories are mainly partial, ironic or perverse does not detract from the power of the fantasy to disrupt and transform reality in a way that mere dreams never could.

Ansteyan comedy in its original nineteenth-century form deals with disrup-tions of normality which must eventually be set right. Reckless wishers and exchangers of personality inevitably learn from their experiences, and one of the most important things they learn is to be content with the world as it is. In its twentieth-century variants, however, the educational process is by no means so simple. Indeed, what is essentially to be learned by the people whose lives are disrupted in the fantasies of Thorne Smith [3-323-3-329] or Susan Alice Kerby [3-200-3-201] is that they should *not* be content with the world as it is, but must break out of the straitjacket of conformity to change themselves, even if they cannot change the world by whose dullness they are all but damned.

The nineteenth-century characters in novels by Anstey and such imitators as Marsh [2-121] learned when their lives were briefly transformed by magic to be more tolerant of others and more contented with their lot, but they were always encouraged by their experiences to keep their wilder desires under more careful control. Twentieth-century characters, even in relatively pessimistic or cynical works such as Baker's *Sweet Chariot* [3-14], Darlington's *Wishes Limited* [3-97], Dunsany's *Strange Journeys of Colonel Polders* [3-122], Alan Griffiths's *Spirits under Proof* [3-160] and John Van Druten's *Bell, Book and Candle* [3-346], often learned exactly the opposite—to give their imagination freer rein, to relax their inhibitions and to break through the barriers of repression. Wishes may still be reckoned to be reckless, and granting them may still lead to all kinds of trouble, but recklessness itself gets a much better press in twentieth-century fantasy than it ever did in the nineteenth century, and the trouble which arises from fantastic visitations is at worst no worse than the sad drudgery of an unillumined life.

Although stories of feral children can hardly be reckoned a major subgenre of twentieth-century fantasy (and I have made no attempt to give an extended list of them in the bibliography), it is certainly worth adding a comment on them to this section of the discussion, because it is in stories of this kind that we see one of the clearest and most startling instances of twentieth-century fantasy's attempts to strike a new attitude to the notion of man's "animal spirits." Even at the very end of the nineteenth century, fantasies of feral children either offered a dramatically transfigured version of the wild life, as Kipling did [2-100]—for what Mowgli has to learn as he grows up with his animal "parents" and "teachers" is essentially a higher form of civilized behavior than so-called civilization offers—or a very anxious image of feral man, such as can be found in Ronald Ross's *Child of Ocean* (1889; see [H2-85]). The twentieth-century examples are very different; Burroughs's Tarzan stories [3-62] offer us an entirely new character, whose wildness (as lord of the jungle) is certainly to be contrasted with his nobility (as Lord Greystoke), but is also, in a marvelous sense, its natural counterpart.

The fact that Tarzan has been so widely imitated—Otis Adelbert Kline, C. T. Stoneham, William L. Chester and F. A. M. Webster wrote similar fantasies about boys raised by tigers, lions, bears and leopards, respectively—reflects not simply the commercial success of Tarzan, but also the inherent fascination of the character. It is interesting to see the dialectical play of wildness and civility in all these novels, and perhaps most interesting of all to see it in one of the very few accounts of a female feral child, in H. M. E. Clamp's *Wild Cat* (1935). The literary merits of these works are usually negligible, and there is not one which could be reckoned anything other than absurd in terms of logic and plausibility, but it is because rather than in spite of this that they exhibit their central thesis in such sharp and striking fashion.

There are a good many twentieth-century writers—including some fantasy writers—who have found the passions every bit as fearful as Plato did. This is to be expected; Freud had little enough sympathy for the id, and certainly did not suggest that we should give it freer rein or hold it in greater affection. What Freud did try to do, however, was to make it clear that the id (and the argument holds no matter what other name we might choose to use instead) is, after all, a part of us which cannot simply be cut out and thrown away. Nor, he suggested, can it be reduced to ineffectuality without considerable difficulty and danger of psychological unease. He came to the conclusion, in the end, that the repressive force of civilization, though necessary, had its costs as well as its benefits.

Twentieth-century fantasy, by and large, arrives at the same conclusion; while never denying the necessity of civilization and measured repression, and accepting wholeheartedly the propriety of the benevolent dictatorship of morality over appetite and desire, the overwhelming majority of twentieth-century fantasies have sided with the Epicureans against the Stoics, and with Nietzsche against the ascetics. They advocate an essentially *liberal* rule of reason, which not only concedes a necessary degree of freedom to the passions (and to the magical worldview which they entail) but asserts uncompromisingly that they can enhance life as well as threaten its stability.

The first half of the twentieth century saw the emergence of considerable differences between the market situation of British and American fantasy writers. These differences paralleled those which can be seen in the history of other genres, especially the closely related genre of speculative fiction.

In Britain, speculative fiction (which, when it was identified at all, tended to be called "scientific romance") remained an eccentric offshoot of middlebrow fiction; though peripheral to the literary "mainstream," it was a genre available to reputable writers, and was used for the most part in a relatively cerebral—and correspondingly cautious—fashion to explore and dramatize anxieties regarding the future. In America, by contrast, speculative fiction was extensively developed as a species of pulp magazine fiction, which was separated out when the pulps proliferated in number and began to specialize in a genre which came to be called "science fiction." Although it had an obvious middlebrow sector (represented primarily by *Astounding Science Fiction*), the genre as a whole was tainted by the lowbrow image of the pulp marketplace, which meant that reputable writers mostly steered clear of it. This lowbrow image did, however, have advantages as well as disadvantages, because it not only permitted but positively encouraged a lack of inhibition which ebulliently swept aside the boundaries of caution and common sense, and avoided the conservatism which tied the greater part of scientific romance to anxious contemplation of near-future possibility.

The history of the fantasy genre reproduces most aspects of this pattern. The bulk of British fantasy from this period is offbeat middlebrow fiction, sometimes produced in the early part of their careers by writers who subsequently concentrated on more mundane and orthodox work; examples include Stella Benson [3-29], Gerald Bullett [3-55], Margaret Irwin [3-188–3-189], Edith Pargeter [3-283] and Sylvia Townsend Warner [3-357]. It was produced more prolifically by writers who were determinedly eccentric or socially isolated, or both; examples include Frank Baker [3-12 etc.], Algernon Blackwood [3-33 etc.], Lord Dunsany [3-116 etc.], David Lindsay [3-218 etc.], Eden Phillpotts [3-288 etc.], the brothers Powys [3-295 etc.] and [3-300 etc.], T. H. White [3-368 etc.] and Charles Williams [3-373 etc.]. The work of such writers as these is relatively cerebral even when playful, and rarely lacks a degree of stylistic inhibition and inventive caution, even when steadfastly defending the exercise of the imagination.

Interestingly, there was a brief period between the end of the Great War and the onset of the Depression when British fantasy produced a group of exceptionally fine works—Benson's *Living Alone* [3-29], Eddison's *The Worm Ouroboros* [3-127], Garnett's *Lady into Fox* [3-152], Bullett's *Mr. Godly Beside Himself* [3-55], Irwin's *These Mortals* [3-189], Mirrlees's *Lud-in-the-Mist* [3-250] and Fraser's *Flower Phantoms* [3-147]—whose duration corresponds with a noticeable hiatus in the history of British scientific romance; this may serve to remind us that although the worldviews of scientific romance and fantasy stand in apparent contradiction, the genres also have a certain complementarity.

American fantasy was not relegated to the pulp magazines as completely as speculative fiction. Writers like James Branch Cabell [3-63 etc.] and John Erskine [3-129 etc.] managed to retain a certain respectability for their work, while Thorne Smith [3-323 etc.], if he never quite qualified for respectability, at least showed that there was serious money in fantastic comedy. Nor, by comparison with science fiction, was fantasy a successful genre in terms of demarcating a particular audience whose appetite could be served by specialist magazines. There were only three specialist pulp magazines which used a good deal of original fantasy: *Weird Tales* [11-20]; *Unknown*, later *Unknown Worlds* [11-18]; and *Fantastic Adventures* [11-6] (though there were two notable reprint fantasy pulps, *Famous Fantastic Mysteries* [11-4] and *Fantastic Novels*). Of these three, *Unknown* was relatively short-lived, producing only thirty-nine issues between 1939 and 1943, while *Weird Tales* and *Fantastic Adventures* gave first preference to other kinds of fiction—*Weird Tales* was primarily a horror fiction magazine; *Fantastic Adventures* was primarily a science fiction pulp.

Despite this lack of a distinct and separate genre identity, though, fantasy did well in the pulp market by courtesy of the example set by a handful of prominent and popular authors—notably Edgar Rice Burroughs [3-59 etc.] and A. Merritt [3-242 etc.]. The success of the subgenres popularized by these writers ensured that the pulps did play an important role in the development of American fantasy, which had close parallels with the role they played in the evolution of American SF. The advantage of the pulps was that they allowed imaginative inhibition to be set aside, and thus played host to the exuberant daydream fantasies which were Burroughs's stock-in-trade, and to the lush odysseys in exotica which were Merritt's. It is difficult to imagine that those writers' careers would have taken the directions they did in any other market context.

Burroughs and Merritt influenced SF writers too, and their example helped to retain within American SF a kind of exoticism which never got into British scientific romance; the lowbrow SF pulps which were unashamedly publishing colorful adventure fiction thus became home to a peculiar hybrid form of SF/fantasy adventure, sometimes nowadays called "science fantasy," early examples of which crop up frequently in the work of Henry Kuttner and his wife, C. L. Moore, and in the work of such writers as Leigh Brackett. *Startling Stories* was an SF pulp which played host to a good deal of lightly disguised fantasy, including Bok's "The Blue Flamingo" (see [3-40]) and Kuttner and Moore's *The Dark World* [3-208]. It was, however, the three specialist pulps cited above which allowed experimentation within the fantasy genre proper. *Weird Tales* was the vehicle for the development of "sword and sorcery" fiction—which was pioneered by Robert E. Howard [3-181–3-182]—and *Unknown* [11-18], a companion to the most sophisticated of the SF magazines, *Astounding*, benefited in a parallel fashion from editor John W. Campbell, Jr.'s insistence that stories should be worked out by enterprising and reasonably rigorous extrapolation from their premises.

It is probable that Howard's invention of sword and sorcery fiction was an accident of compromise. Howard was a prolific writer who sold fiction in considerable volume to a number of pulp magazines. His earliest contributions to *Weird Tales* were indeed relatively brief weird tales suited to the magazine's horror fiction priorities, but his real forte as a writer was the production of longer stories of a violent action-adventure stripe. He experimented with a longer story in the *Weird Tales* vein when he produced the novella *Skull-Face* (see [H3-95])—a pastiche of Sax Rohmer—but that was one of his worst failures as a writer. He found a much better way of fitting action-adventure to the priorities of *Weird Tales* when he began to write stories of remote historical eras, to which monsters and magic could be added quite comfortably. After pausing briefly in Roman Britain to write about the travails of the last surviving enclaves of Picts, he quickly retreated to an imaginary phase of civilization before the last Ice Age, where he first set stories of the aristocratic King Kull and then (discovering his true métier) switched to the side of the barbarians in cultivating the career of Conan [3-182].

Chimerical hybrid or not, this new fantasy milieu quickly proved attractive to many other writers, offering far greater scope for the development of imaginary histories and eccentric theologies than Merrittesque parallel world fantasy. C. L. Moore [3-252] and Fritz Leiber [3-211] were the most important early recruits to the cause; Fletcher Pratt [3-305–3-306] joined in later, and his one-time collaborator L. Sprague de Camp was eventually to become one of the chief promoters of the subgenre [3-105]. Sword and sorcery fiction took a long time to break out of the pulp ghetto but, like several other kinds of initially esoteric pulp fiction (SF, Lovecraftian horror fiction and hard-boiled detective fiction), it was ultimately to thrive in a destratified marketplace (by which time Robert E. Howard was unfortunately no longer around to enjoy the belated flood of royalties).

The fantasy which became characteristic of *Unknown* was, dispassionately considered, an even odder accident of combination. It was written mainly by SF writers who were in the process of being trained by John Campbell's editorial insistence to be both rigorously rational and determinedly adventurous in the business of extrapolation. The application of this bold hard-headedness to calculatedly zany premises borrowed from the motifs of folklore and mythology resulted in a remarkable kind of playfulness. The best *Unknown* fantasy had a distinctive wit which emerged from happily absurd bisociations of logic and illogic, but it also had a robust problematic component which took seriously the predicaments of clued-up Americans rudely thrust into dangerously exotic contexts. Although much *Unknown* material slid into ordinary categories of adventure-inclined fantasy fiction, the magazine produced in its four short years of life a series of classic works the like of which had never been seen before: de Camp and

Pratt's early Harold Shea stories [3-106] and *Land of Unreason* [3-107]; de Camp's *Undesired Princess* [3-104]; Robert Heinlein's "The Devil Makes the Law" (see [3-171]); L. Ron Hubbard's "Typewriter in the Sky" [3-185]; and numerous shorter stories [3-28]. The more horrific stories which *Unknown* produced were, thanks to the same imaginative processes, of an equally original kind, best exemplified by Leiber's *Conjure Wife* [H3-125] and Jack Williamson's *Darker Than You Think* [H3-214].

American pulp fantasy in the first half of the century was mostly lightweight, but it was not necessarily unsophisticated; much of it was written in a breezy and fairly careless fashion, but the best of the sword and sorcery extravaganzas lack nothing in intensity and the best of the *Unknown* comedies are clever and deft in deploying their wit. Each of these subgenres made a considerable contribution, in its own way, to a process by which the Secondary World milieux of fantasy (both imaginary pasts and parallel worlds), whether they were populated by elves, knights in armor, mysterious allegorical figures, exotic alien cultures, classical deities or jinni, were gradually brought together into a shared context where they could touch, overflow, and be used as resources for the syncretic construction of all-purpose private universes.

The foundations were laid in this period for the kind of reckless plundering which nowadays goes into the construction of hypothetical realms for fantasy role-playing games, where anything and everything is up for grabs and available for use. At the beginning of the period the Land of Faërie was still Balkanized, its individual states marginalized within the complex politics of the imagination; by the end of the period wars of unification had created a vast empire whose political power was adequate (though the time was not yet quite ripe) to make a claim on the private and intimate moments of millions of people; Middle-earth is only one of the names by which that empire has come to be known.

In selecting works for inclusion in the following bibliography, I have tried to follow the same priorities as were used in the previous chapter; the process of selection has inevitably been dogged by the same difficulties. There are many writers whose works straddle the boundary between the fantasy and horror genres, and it has not always been easy to separate their books into exemplary groups for separate consideration in this volume and its companion. Thus, for instance, the work of Clark Ashton Smith is annotated in the other volume [H3-182], though some commentators might argue that the contribution made by his remarkably ornate and grotesque stories to the evolution of the fantasy genre is as great as or greater than their contribution to horror fiction. On the other hand, I have included the metaphysical fantasies of writers like Charles Williams, David Lindsay and Algernon Blackwood here, when others might have displaced at least some of them to the other volume.

There emerged in early twentieth-century supramundane fiction a number of new subgenres which have a particularly confusing effect on the boundaries between fantasy, science fiction and horror fiction. One of these is the above-mentioned subgenre of "science fantasy," which I have accommodated here only in a few exemplary annotations; for the most part, the veneer of science fiction jargon which such stories have can be considered adequate to justify application of the SF label. Rather more difficulties arise as a result of a kind of horror fiction whose aim one of its promulgators—H. P. Lovecraft—described as the attempt to instill a sensation of "cosmic horror." This subgenre fits uneasily into the gray area where all three of the major genres overlap, and though Lovecraft's own work is not too difficult to divide up in terms of separating the horror from the fantasy (see [3-225] and [H3-132]), it is not so easy to separate out these elements in the work of the other major *Weird Tales* writers who dabbled in it. It is equally difficult to make judgments regarding other writers of a similar stripe—one could plausibly file a work like William Hope Hodgson's *The Night Land* [3-178] under any one of the three headings. Most of the fiction in this "cosmic horror" subgenre has been annotated in the companion volume, but many of the sword and sorcery stories annotated here do also have a substantial horror component.

Because of the arbitrariness of some of these judgments, I will undoubtedly have committed what connoisseur readers consider to be sins of omission and commission. Even when dealing with less knotty problems, such as how broadly the fantasy genre should be defined and how prolifically the more marginal of its subgenres (lost race stories, stories of feral children, talking animal stories, etc.) ought to be represented, I am bound to have given cause for annoyance to some. I am content to remain as apologetically unrepentant about this as anyone else would in the same circumstances.

Readers in search of more detailed commentaries on this period in the history of the fantasy genre should refer first of all to Bleiler's *Guide to Supernatural Fiction* [6-19] and to *Supernatural Fiction Writers* [6-20], which he edited. Lin Carter's *Imaginary Worlds* [7-10] and the Salem Press *Survey of Modern Fantasy Literature* [6-24] also include some useful commentary on the work of the major authors, together with some reasonably thought-provoking arguments about the nature of the genre.

Bibliography

Abdullah, Achmed (formerly **Alexander Romanowski**), 1881–1945.
  About: WW, GSF, CA, ESF

3-1. The Thief of Bagdad. H. K. Fly, 1924.
Book of the famous silent movie starring Douglas Fairbanks and lots of special effects. The thief falls in love with the caliph's daughter and must embark on an exotic quest to win her hand, competing against three princes to discover the most amazing gift.

Anderson, Poul, 1926– .
  About: WW, GSF, SFW, F, CA, TCA, NE, SMFL, MF, SFFL, RG, TCSF, ESF, FL, HF

***3-2. The Broken Sword.** Abelard-Schuman, 1954.
Complex heroic fantasy novel set in Britain, which overlaps the land of Faerie and is subject to the Norse gods—though both the old gods and the fairy folk are

under threat. The hero, having received as an enigmatic birth gift a broken sword, must learn its secret in order to play a crucial role in the war between the elves and the trolls. Like the Icelandic sagas on which it is modeled, the story is grim and violent, told with considerable style and conviction. The Ballantine edition of 1971 is somewhat revised.

3-3. Three Hearts and Three Lions. Doubleday, 1961.
Expanded version of a serial from *The Magazine of Fantasy & Science Fiction* (1953). A magical world parallel to ours suffers its own crisis during the years of World War II; an American in occupied Denmark is displaced thereto, and his attempts to find a way back involve him in many adventures before he learns that his destiny is already mapped out. The Secondary World is eclectically populated in the *Unknown* style but the adventure element is taken entirely seriously. Also annotated as [4A-7].

Andom, R. (pseud. of **Alfred W. Barrett**) (U.K.), born 1869.
    ABOUT: GSF

3-4. The Magic Bowl and the Bluestone Ring. Jarrolds, 1909.
Two Ansteyan fantasies run together. Both feature wish-granting jinn whose methods cause trouble; both are slapdash, having more in common with the hackwork of Richard Marsh [2-121] than with Anstey's own works [2-6-2-8 and 3-5]. The title novella of *The Strange Adventure of Roger Wilkins* (1895; also known as *The Identity Exchange*) is a personality-exchange story of similar stripe.

Anstey, F. (pseud. of **Thomas Anstey Guthrie**) (U.K.), 1856–1934.
    ABOUT: WW, GSF, SFW, CA, NE, SMFL, SFE, ESF, HF

*3-5. The Brass Bottle. Smith, Elder, 1900.
A young architect releases an imprisoned jinni but finds the fruits of its boundless gratitude a great embarrassment, utterly blighting his image of middle-class respectability. The jinni becomes resentful when its grandiose plans are brought to naught, and the young man's powers of diplomacy are stretched to the limit. An excellent comedy, with threatening undercurrents to sharpen the narrative.

*3-6. In Brief Authority. Smith, Elder, 1915.
Anstey here reverses his standard formula. After a middle-class matriarch is mistakenly proclaimed queen of the fairies, her whole family moves into the Märchenland of the Brothers Grimm, where their attempts to import Victorian respectability cause chaos—and where insidious enemies plot their downfall. Poorly received (probably because the satire was out of date) but much better than it is generally given credit for; Anstey's wit is here at its most biting.

Apollinaire, Guillaume (**Wilhelm de Kostrowitzky**) (France), 1880–1918.
    ABOUT: CA, SMFL, ESF

3-7. The Heresiarch and Co. Doubleday, 1965. Tr. by Rémy Inglis Hall of *L'Heresiarch et cie*, 1910. U.K. title: *The Wandering Jew and Other Stories*.

Collection of stories by an important avant-garde poet and dramatist which carry forward in aggressively decadent fashion the tradition of anti-clerical fantasy begun by Anatole France; here we find a series of impish Antichrists ranging from an ebullient Wandering Jew who can rejoice in his corruption to the mercurial confidence trickster Baron d'Ormesan. The U.K. edition has wonderfully appropriate Beardsleyesque illustrations by Anthony Little.

Armstrong, Anthony (pseud. of Anthony A. Willis) (U.K.), 1897–1976.
ABOUT: GSF, CA, SFE, ESF

3-8. The Pack of Pieces. Michael Joseph, 1942. U.S. title: *The Naughty Princess.* Collection of mock-fairy tales which selectively import items of modern slang and contemporary folkways into traditional tales. "The Story of Sindrelia" explains how an incompetent fairy godmother sent the hapless heroine to a godawful ball she would have given anything to miss; "The Princess and the Frog" offers one of many cynical variations on that vulnerable theme. Follows an earlier collection, *The Prince Who Hiccupped and Other Tales* (1932).

Armstrong, Martin (U.K.), 1882–1974.
ABOUT: WW, GSF, ESF

3-9. The Bazaar and Other Stories. Cape, 1924.
Collection including three ironic fantasies; the most notable is "Mrs. Barber's Christmas," about a vision of Heaven. *General Buntop's Miracle and Other Stories* (1934) has two others, including the very funny "Presence of Mind," in which a lie invented as an excuse comes true, and must then be extended, becoming more preposterous (and more threatening) all the while. "Saint Hercules" in *The Fiery Dive* (1929) is an earnest religious fantasy which has more in common with the works of Laurence Housman (see [2-84]).

Arnold, Edwin Lester (U.K.), 1857–1935.
ABOUT: WW, GSF, CA, SMFL, SFE, TCSF, ESF, HF

3-10. Lepidus the Centurion. Cassell, 1901.
The eponymous hero arises from the tomb in late Victorian times to set an example to an ineffectual young Englishman, who is eventually driven to fight him for the hand of the woman he loves. By defeating his idealized *Doppelgänger* the Englishman acquires self-confidence and flair. An interesting psychological parable.

*3-11. Lieut. Gullivar Jones; His Vacation. Langham, 1905.
A naval officer travels to Mars on a magic carpet and finds it a marvelously exotic world where his swashbuckling daydreams are realized in no uncertain terms. An attempt to update *Arabian Nights*-style fantasy—Jones has much more in common with Sinbad than with his near-namesake—which anticipates Edgar Rice Burroughs [3-61] closely enough for some to suspect direct copying. Colorful and highly enjoyable for those who can share in the casting aside of inhibition. Reprinted in paperback as *Gulliver of Mars*.

Baker, Frank, 1908–1982.
ABOUT: WW, GSF, SFW, CA, ESF

3-12. Before I Go Hence. Andrew Dakers, 1946.
The third and most intense of Baker's earnest moralistic fantasies, following *The Birds* (1936) and *Mr. Allenby Loses His Way* (1945). It draws heavily upon Dunne's time theories in recounting the story of an author who builds a psychic link with a former inhabitant of his home—a quest for enlightenment which estranges him from his wife. Might be seen as a skeptical version of Irwin's *Still She Wished for Company* [3-188], and as such thematically close to Harding's *The Twinkling of an Eye* [3-165], but becomes very preoccupied with the metaphysical questions at issue—which were then carried forward into the intricate metaphysical fantasy *The Downs So Free* (1948).

*3-13. Miss Hargreaves. Eyre & Spottiswoode, 1940.
Two friends invent an acquaintance with the imaginary Miss Hargreaves to impress an innocent, and then find their fantasy embarrassingly fleshed out; attempts to persuade her of her nonexistence inevitably prove inadequate, and the business of procuring her banishment from the world becomes vexatious. A comic tour de force.

3-14. Sweet Chariot. Eyre & Spottiswoode, 1942.
An ineffectual schoolmaster trades places with his guardian angel, but the angel's innocent naïveté proves as ill-fitted to life on Earth as the man's unleashed spiritual pride is to life in Heaven. A skeptical reprise of Bullett's *Mr. Godly Beside Himself* [3-55], dolefully suggesting that it may take more than a touch of magic to resuscitate a life embalmed by dullness and inhibition.

Baring, Maurice (U.K.), 1874–1945.
ABOUT: WW, GSF, CA, PE, ESF

3-15. Orpheus in Mayfair and Other Stories and Sketches. Mills & Boon, 1909.
Collection including several fantasies. "The Flute-Player's Story" is a fine tragedy in which Marsyas's curse falls upon those inspired by Apollo; in "The Island" two tourists find Circe's elusive abode; "Venus" is an interesting interplanetary fantasy; "A Luncheon Party" is a comedy in which a hostess sells her soul for the perfect dinner guest (Shakespeare), who can hardly get a word in edgewise in competition with modern bores; Shakespeare also crops up in the fairy romance "The Conqueror." A few of the fantasies from this collection were reprinted in *Half a Minute's Silence and Other Stories* (1925).

Barrie, J(ames) M(atthew) (U.K.), 1860–1937.
ABOUT: GSF, SFW, CA, PE, ESF

3-16. Dear Brutus. Hodder & Stoughton, 1922.
Play in which assorted characters who believe that their lives would be better if only they had made key decisions more wisely are allowed into a magic wood where things are as they might have been; they find their revised lives equally blighted by the faults and follies ingrained in their personalities.

3-17. Mary Rose. Hodder & Stoughton, 1924.
Play featuring an island which steals people out of time. The young bride who returns unchanged after many years cannot come to terms with what has happened, and her confrontations with the grown son she last saw as a baby are harrowing to watch, carrying the same emotional impact that Barrie—who felt, because of his small size and sexual impotence, that he had never been able properly to "grow up"—imported into his tales of the time-dislocated Peter Pan [3-18].

*3-18. Peter Pan. Scribner, 1904.
Classic fantasy play which borrows its central character from the sentimental novel *The Little White Bird* (1902), where he figured in a tale-within-the-tale subsequently published separately as *Peter Pan in Kensington Gardens* (1906). In the original story, Peter Pan lives on an island where little boys begin their existence as birds before being born; he is a "Betwixt-and-Between" who flew back there after being born and now can never grow older. In the play he lives in Never Land, enjoying wild adventures with Indians and forever dodging Captain Hook's pirates; there he takes the children of the Darling family, most importantly Wendy, to whom he looks for a special relationship. The fantasy is deeply felt, symbolically reflecting what Barrie felt to be paradoxical qualities in his own nature, and it carries a unique emotional charge. The story was retold in the novel *Peter and Wendy* (1911), which adds an epilogue further elaborating the personal allegory. The play demonstrates the remarkable fact that audiences everywhere can be brought to the brink of tears by the plight of a character played by a spotlight.

Barringer, Leslie (U.K.), 1895–1968.
ABOUT: SMFL, HF

3-19. Gerfalcon. Heinemann, 1927.
The first in a trilogy of novels, followed by *Joris of the Rock* (1928) and *Shy Leopardess* (1948). The stories are chivalric romances set in an imaginary French province; the supernatural plays a very muted role, being explicit only in the second volume, but the stories qualify marginally as Secondary World heroic fantasies and are exceptionally well written. Though each volume has a different central character, the three in combination contain the whole history of Raoul of Ger as he grows from boyhood to claim and secure his noble heritage.

Baum, L(yman) Frank, 1856–1919.
ABOUT: CA, SMFL, SFE, RG, ESF, FL, HF

*3-20. The Wonderful Wizard of Oz. G. M. Hill, 1900.
Classic moralistic fantasy in which a young girl joins forces with the Scarecrow, the Tin Woodman and the Cowardly Lion to solicit help from the eponymous wizard, and must battle the Wicked Witch of the West. The basis of one of Hollywood's most famous films. Baum wrote thirteen sequels; more were added by other authors. A valuable edition for the serious reader interested in Baum's creation is *The Wizard of Oz*, ed. by Michael Patrick Hearn (Schocken, 1983),

which contains the complete text, the Denslow illustrations and a number of valuable essays.

Beauclerk, Helen (U.K.), 1892–1969.
ABOUT: GSF, CA

3-21. The Love of the Foolish Angel. Collins, 1929.
Sentimental romance of antiquity in which a good angel, fallen through mistaken loyalty to Lucifer, loves and protects a human girl of the third century, and eventually becomes human. Less mannered than the author's Secondary World fantasy *The Green Lacquer Pavilion* (1926), which appropriates the French fascination with the Orient but is hampered in its exoticism by British reserve.

Beck, L(ily) Adams, died 1931.
ABOUT: WW, GSF, ESF

3-22. The Ninth Vibration and Other Stories. Dodd, Mead, 1922.
Collection of stories including some credulous occult romances. In the title story a young man has a vision in which he meets the young woman who is to be his inspiration on the path of enlightenment; the theme was subsequently expanded in the related novel *The House of Fulfillment* (1927). Another novel in the same vein, with a more pronounced action-adventure element, is *The Way of Stars* (1925), while more short stories are collected in *The Openers of the Gate* (1930). Having long lived in the East, Beck was better acquainted with Oriental mysticism than most writers of this stripe, and was more assured in providing local color.

Beerbohm, Max (U.K.), 1872–1956.
ABOUT: GSF, F, CA, SMFL, ESF

3-23. Seven Men. Heinemann, 1919.
Collection of stories including the classic "Enoch Soames," in which a poet makes a diabolical bargain allowing him to travel forward in time to research his own works in the British Museum Reading Room. The other six men (and the "two others" added to the 1950 edition) are less interesting.

3-24. Zuleika Dobson. Heinemann, 1911.
The eponymous heroine is so beguiling that all the young men in Oxford fall recklessly in love with her; their infatuation forces them to romantic demonstrations more extreme than anyone could consider reasonable. A charmingly absurd satire.

Benét, Stephen Vincent, 1898–1943.
ABOUT: CA, RG

*3-25. Thirteen O'Clock: Stories of Several Worlds. Farrar & Rinehart, 1937.
Collection of stories including a classic item of Americana, "The Devil and Daniel Webster" (1936), in which a lawyer must plead for his client to be excused from the consequences of a diabolical bargain before a jury comprised of the worst felons American history can provide. "Daniel Webster and the Sea Ser-

pent," which tells the story of a strange infatuation, is even taller but much less pointed. Also included is a story based in translocated European folklore, "The King of the Cats" (1932). *Tales Before Midnight* (1939) contains a moral fantasy about personified Death, "Johnny Pye and the Fool-Killer" (1937), plus the leprechaun story "O'Halloran's Luck" and the ironic posthumous fantasy "Doc Mellhorn and the Pearly Gates" (1938); some minor fantasies were included in the posthumous collection *The Last Circle* (1946). The first two collections were combined as *Twenty-Five Short Stories* (1943); all but one of the stories named are in volume 2 of *The Selected Works of Stephen Vincent Benét* (1942).

Bennett, Arnold (U.K.), 1867–1931.
ABOUT: GSF, CA, PE

3-26. The Glimpse; An Adventure of the Soul. Chapman & Hall, 1909.
Elaborate posthumous fantasy in which an egotist's soul passes through various phases of wish fulfillment (each leading to eventual frustration) on the way to an enlightenment which paves the way for his return to the real world. An interesting early contribution to the rich twentieth-century British tradition of inventive posthumous fantasies.

[For other works of this author, see the companion guide to horror.]

Benoît, Pierre (France), 1886–1962.
ABOUT: CA, SMFL, HF

3-27. Atlantida. Duffield, 1920. Tr. by Mary C. Tongue and Mary Ross of *L'Atlantide*, 1919. U.K. title: *The Queen of Atlantis*.
Two Spahi officers on a mission in the Ahaggar mountains are abducted to the last remnant of Atlantis, where they fall under the spell of the magnificent Antinea, who pursues a feminist vendetta by condemning all her lovers to death. Intriguingly masochistic homage to the *femme fatale*.

Bensen, Donald R., editor.

3-28. The Unknown. Pyramid, 1963.
First of two anthologies drawn from the pages of the famous pulp magazine, followed by *The Unknown Five* (1964). The second is better, presenting Asimov's "Author! Author!," which missed publication when the magazine was suspended in 1943, and Alfred Bester's wonderfully melodramatic novella "Hell Is Forever" (1942), in which members of a house party each get a chance to create their own heaven. A further selection is *Unknown* (1988), edited by Stanley Schmidt.

Benson, Stella (U.K.), 1892–1933.
ABOUT: GSF, CA

***3-29. Living Alone.** Macmillan, 1919.
An unhappy social worker in wartime London finds her life illuminated and transformed by her meeting with an amiable witch, who offers her temporary

refuge in the magical House of Living Alone. A mad, merry and marvelous fantasy which is without parallel, though it has affinities with other near-contemporary works which celebrate the liberating power of enchantment, notably Bullett's *Mr. Godly Beside Himself* [3-55]. Benson's *Collected Short Stories* (1936) contains a few fantasies, including "The Awakening," in which an ancient and decrepit god looks back over his career of underachievement; the nightmarishly surreal "The Man Who Missed the 'Bus"; and the satirical "Christmas Formula."

Beresford, J(ohn) D(avys) (U.K.), 1873–1947.
ABOUT: WW, GSF, SFW, CA, SFE, TCSF, PE, ESF

3-30. Nineteen Impressions. Sidgwick & Jackson, 1919.
Collection of stories including several timeslip stories and some remarkable studies in abnormal psychology, plus two fine metaphysical fantasies: "The Little Town" (1912) and "The Empty Theatre" (1914). *Signs and Wonders* (1921) includes several visionary fantasies inspired by reflections on the Great War, often involving timeslips; they exhibit the author's growing interest in paranormal phenomena. Beresford's later visionary fantasies, inspired by World War II, are also of interest as scientific romances: *"What Dreams May Come . . ."* (1941) and *The Riddle of the Tower* (1944; written in collaboration with Esmé Wynne-Tyson); the former exhibits a fascination with messianic figures also seen in *All or Nothing* (1928) and *The Gift* (1947; with Wynne-Tyson).

Bessand-Massenet, Pierre (France), born 1899.
ABOUT: GSF, ESF

3-31. Amorous Ghost. Elek, 1957. Tr. by Hugh Shelley of *Magie Rose*, 1956.
A young student in Paris finds that his lodgings are haunted by a phantom courtesan; his fiancée does not approve, but how can her merely human attractions measure up to the allure of supernatural romance? A sentimental updating of Gautier's "Omphale" (see [2-64]).

Black, Ladbroke (U.K.), 1877–1940.
ABOUT: GSF, SFE

3-32. The Gorgon's Head. Sampson Low, Marston, 1932.
Ansteyan fantasy in which the eponymous relic runs riot in England, turning people into statues—much to the embarrassment of the head's unwilling custodians. Better than most such exercises in pastiche, but essentially trivial.

Blackwood, Algernon (U.K.), 1869–1951.
ABOUT: WW, GSF, SFW, CA, H, SMFL, RG, PE, ESF, FL, HF

***3-33. The Centaur.** Macmillan, 1911.
Metaphysical fantasy in which two men on a cruise become involved with an enigmatic Russian *Urmensch*, through whom they are put in touch with the World-Soul—an experience which only one of them can savor to the full. The

supernaturalization of nature evident in so many of Blackwood's weird tales [H3-26] is here theoretically extrapolated in earnest manner. A very stylish exercise in mysticism.

3-34. The Fruit-Stoners. Grayson & Grayson, 1934.
A female child enters a sinister Secondary World where she must search for a treasure while avoiding the Man Who Wound the Clocks; she is aided by the elemental Fruit-Stoners. Not really a juvenile—if that was Blackwood's initial intention, he was soon sidetracked by the allure of his own allegory into deeper philosophical discourse. The author's fascination with childhood innocence was earlier displayed in *The Education of Uncle Paul* (1909) and its eccentric sequel, *A Prisoner in Fairyland* (1913), which develop more tedious allegories of the same stripe.

*3-35. The Human Chord. Macmillan, 1910.
Occult fantasy. The hero becomes involved with an adept who has harnessed the magical powers of sound but still needs a particular chord to perfect his powers—but is such power meant to be attained by man? A very unusual and original work which binds its allegory neatly into its narrative; it has affinities with the metaphysical fantasies of David Lindsay [3-218-3-221].

3-36. Julius Levallon. Cassell, 1916.
Occult fantasy structurally similar to [3-35] but more complicated; the protagonist here takes a more active role and the eponymous would-be magician is less of an adept; as in the earlier book, their ultimate experiment goes awry but has some good consequences. Preferred to the earlier work by some readers, though it is less coherent and less original. *The Bright Messenger* (1921) continues the story but is more a fictional essay than a story and demonstrates the ease with which credulity can undermine literary interest.

3-37. The Promise of Air. Macmillan, 1918.
Metaphysical allegory; the protagonist and his soul-mate are infected with an airy spirit which makes them kin to the birds; motherhood dulls the spirit in the woman but it is inherited to the full by her daughter. Fails to recapture the magic of [3-35], again because the author is too earnestly committed to the theory which underlies the narrative.

[For other works of this author, see the companion guide to horror.]

Blamires, Harry (U.K.), 1916–
ABOUT: CA, ESF

3-36. The Devil's Hunting-Grounds. Longmans, 1954.
The first of a trilogy of posthumous fantasies, followed by *Cold War in Hell* (1955) and *Blessing Unbounded* (1955). The three volumes present an account of contemporary conditions in Purgatory, in Hell and on the road to Heaven, showing how the inhabitants of these regions have adopted many ideas from the politics and social institutions of the modern world. A satirical Divine

Comedy which makes some sharp moral points, though it avoids the difficulties of showing us a plausible Paradise. Compare Hales's *Chariot of Fire* [4A-127].

Bloch, Robert, 1917– .
ABOUT: WW, GSF, SFW, CA, NE, H, SMFL, SFE, SFFL, RG, TCSF, PE, ESF

3-39. Dragons and Nightmares. Mirage Press, 1969.
Exercises in literary pastiche. "A Good Knight's Work" (1940) and its sequel, "The Eager Dragon" (1943), confront mobsters with Arthurian magic in boisterous adventures narrated in the style of Damon Runyon; "Nursemaid to Nightmares"—which absorbs the sequel, "Black Barter" (1943), to the original story of that name (1942)—is a freewheeling comedy in the manner of Thorne Smith. The latter combination had earlier been reprinted in the magazine *Imaginative Tales* in 1955; several other early issues of the magazine featured similar adventures in Smithian slapstick by Bloch, including the novellas "Mr. Margate's Mermaid" (March 1955); "The Miracle of Ronald Weems" (May 1955); and "The Big Binge" (July 1955).

[For other works of this author, see the companion guide to horror.]

Bok, Hannes, 1914–1964.
ABOUT: WW, GSF, NE, SMFL, SFE, RG, PE, ESF, HF

3-40. Beyond the Golden Stair. Ballantine, 1970.
The complete text of a novel first published in heavily abridged form as "The Blue Flamingo" (1948). A group of jailbreakers find a gateway to a strange Secondary World in the Everglades, where they are severely tested as to their moral worth and potential for redemption. An intriguing moralistic fantasy, heavily influenced by A. Merritt [3-242–3-246].

3-41. The Sorcerer's Ship. Ballantine, 1969.
Merrittesque Secondary World fantasy first published in *Unknown* (1942). The displaced hero becomes involved in a conflict between warring nations; he and a princess seek the aid of an obliging god to make the underdogs into winners. An unabashed adventure story, not nearly as interesting as [3-40].

Bond, Nelson S(lade), 1908– .
ABOUT: GSF, CA, SFE, SFFL, ESF

3-42. Mr. Mergenthwirker's Lobblies and Other Fantastic Tales. Coward-McCann, 1946.
Collection mixing SF and ironic fantasy; the title story (1937) involves invisible companions; it was later adapted into a play and a radio series, but its several sequels are not included here. "The Fountain" (1941) features the fountain of youth; "The Bookshop" is a place where unwritten books end up. *The Thirty-First of February* (1949) offers a similar mix, including the Runyonesque "The

Gripes of Wraith" and an irreverent tale of an unappreciated halo, "Saint Mulligan" (1943).

Borges, Jorge Luis (Argentina), 1899–1986.
ABOUT: CA, NE, SMFL, SFE, RG, TCSF, PE, ESF

*3-43. Ficciones. Grove Press, 1962. Tr. by Anthony Kerrigan *et al.* of *Ficciones, 1935–1944*, 1944. U.K. title: *Fictions*.
Classic collection of *contes philosophiques*. Includes "Tlön, Uqbar, Orbis Tertius," in which a curious Secondary World is described by entries in an enigmatic variant edition of an encyclopedia; "Pierre Menard, Author of Don Quixote," in which a modern scholar recreates Cervantes's work without having read the original; "The Circular Ruins," a curious dream story; "The Babylon Lottery," a metaphysical fantasy; "The Library of Babel," which describes the ultimate library; "Funes the Memorious," about the existential predicament of a man with a phenomenal memory; and "Death and the Compass," a metaphysical fantasy cast in the mold of a detective story. All these stories and others are included in *Labyrinths* (1964). A few are further reprinted, with others, in *The Aleph and Other Stories 1933–1969* (1970), whose title story was the title story of Borges's second major collection, *El Aleph* (1949); it tells of a magical point in space which contains all others, and in which the whole infinite universe can be glimpsed. Borges has no equal as a modern writer of *contes philosophiques* and these early works, a crucial contribution to that neglected genre, are a landmark in twentieth-century literature. *Labyrinths* is also annotated as [4A-41].

Boucher, Anthony (pseud. of William Anthony Parker White), 1911–1968.
ABOUT: GSF, CA, TCA, NE, H, SMFL, SFE, SFFL, TCSF, PE, ESF, HF

3-44. The Compleat Werewolf and Other Tales of Fantasy and Science Fiction.
Simon & Schuster, 1969.
Collection whose title novella (1942) is a humorous account of an unwilling werewolf's endeavors in support of the war effort. Also included is the excellent novella "We Print the Truth" (1943), in which Wayland the Smith grants his temporary employer the wish that his small-town newspaper will print only the truth—but the power this confers is localized, and its beneficiaries feel morally bound to rejoin the warring world.

As editor, in collaboration with **J(esse) Francis McComas**, 1911–1978.

3-45. The Best from Fantasy and Science Fiction. Little, Brown, 1952.
First of a long-running series of annual anthologies reprinting stories from *The Magazine of Fantasy & Science Fiction* [11-13], the digest magazine which carried forward a tradition of quirky but slickly written fantasy short stories, alongside intelligent SF. It attracted contributors of the caliber of C. S. Lewis [3-213–3-216] and Gerald Heard [H3-83]) as well as genre writers, and used well-chosen reprints; the early selections are appropriately eclectic.

Bowen, Marjorie (pseud. of **Gabrielle Long**) (U.K.), 1886–1952.
ABOUT: WW, GSF, F, CA, H, PE, ESF

3-46. The Haunted Vintage. Odhams, 1921.
Historical fantasy set in the Rhineland. The hero is intrigued by a strange girl
locked up in an asylum; she really belongs to a company of ancient gods who
periodically return to the region in order to supervise the making of a special
wine. An unusual variant on the theme of a young man torn between real and
supernatural lovers; intriguing and well written.

[For other works of this author, see the companion guide to horror.]

Brahms, Caryl (U.K.), 1901(?)–1982(?), and **Simon, S. J.** (U.K.).
ABOUT: CA

3-47. No Nightingales. Michael Joseph, 1944.
The ghosts of two military men must haunt a house in Berkeley Square until a
member of the royal family crosses the threshold; they have a long wait. A
whimsical comic fantasy, followed by *Titania Has a Mother* (1944), in which
characters from nursery rhymes and fairy tales figure in a quirky satire on
contemporary mores.

Bramah, Ernest (pseud. of **Ernest B. Smith**) (U.K.), 1869?–1942.
ABOUT: WW, GSF, SMFL, ESF, HF

3-48. The Wallet of Kai Lung. Grant Richards, 1900.
The first of several collections of Oriental tales featuring the itinerant storyteller
Kai Lung. The others are: *Kai Lung's Golden Hours* (1922); *Kai Lung Unrolls
His Mat* (1928); *The Moon of Much Gladness* (1932); and *Kai Lung Beneath the
Mulberry Tree* (1940). The first three were reprinted in a *Kai Lung Omnibus*
(1932), and a selection of stories appeared as *The Celestial Omnibus* (1963). The
supernatural plays little or no part in most of these stories of crime and conspiracy, but the China in which they are set is a fantastic creation, less exotic than the
imaginary Orient of French literature but no less artificial. The stories are
mannered and playful, less moralistic than they pretend to be, and constitute a
unique series of literary confections.

Brodie-Innes, J(ohn) W(illiam) (U.K.), 1848–1923.
ABOUT: GSF, PE

3-49. Morag the Seal: A West Highland Romance. Rebman, 1908.
A young lawyer travels to the highlands to help an enigmatic laird prove his title,
but as the search for missing documents proceeds he begins to suspect foul play; the
mystery is complicated by the magical appearances of the eponymous heroine. The
hero and his confidant, a doctor, search for a "rational" explanation of Morag's
manifestations, producing a theory of the occult which reflects the author's interest
in such—he was a one-time member of the Order of the Golden Dawn.

[For other works of this author, see the companion guide to horror.]

Bromfield, Louis, 1897–1956.
> ABOUT: CA, ESF

3-50. The Strange Case of Miss Annie Spragg. Cape, 1928.
Religious fantasy set in Italy; the writer of a book debunking miracles investigates the case of Annie Spragg, daughter of a self-proclaimed prophet. He concludes that despite her stigmata she was no saint—but was she a witch? A subtle championship of pagan rebellion against oppressive Christian moralism.

Brown, Fredric, 1906–1972.
> ABOUT: GSF, CA, TCA, NE, SFE, SFFL, RG, TCSF, PE, ESF

3-51. Angels and Spaceships. Dutton, 1954.
The first of several collections mixing fantasy and SF stories, this one has several comical items from *Unknown*, including "Etaoin Shrdlu" (1942), about an animate linotype machine; and "The Angelic Angleworm" (1943), a preposterous story of reality put out of joint by typographical errors. *Honeymoon in Hell* (1958) includes a few trivial fantasies from later in the period.

Bruce, Kennedy (U.K.).

3-52. The Fakir's Curse. Jenkins, 1931.
An unusual story set in India, in which a fakir bewitches an Englishman's camera so that its photographs will reveal hidden truths of motivation; the revelations of the camera are far from comfortable, though their penetration of lying appearances allows the thwarting of a native rebellion.

Buchan, John (later **Baron Tweedsmuir**) (U.K.), 1875–1940.
> ABOUT: WW, GSF, F, CA, SMFL, PE, ESF, FL

3-53. The Magic Walking-Stick. Hodder & Stoughton, 1932.
The eponymous object will carry its owner wherever he wishes; it sometimes lands him in difficulties, but it also gives him a priceless advantage in tight corners. An upmarket boys' book.

> [For other works of this author, see the companion guide to horror.]

Bulgakov, Mikhail (Russia), 1891–1940.
> ABOUT: CA, SMFL, SFE, TCSF, ESF

*3-54. The Master and Margarita. Collins, 1967. Tr. by Michael Glenny of *Master i Margarita*, written 1938; first published 1967.
A magnificent fantasy reflecting the author's bitter frustration at the stifling of his career. A poet becomes briefly involved with the enigmatic Professor Woland; he is incarcerated in an asylum where he meets the self-styled Master, who has written a philosophical novel about Pontius Pilate, and who recognizes that Woland is Satan, come to wreak havoc in the world of men. While the novel-within-the-novel tells the "true" story of the Crucifixion, the devil, having

granted Moscow a well-deserved taste of Hell, offers consolation (salvation being beyond his scope) to the despairing Master and his innocent inamorata. A masterpiece of tragedy and grotesquerie; one of the finest fantastic novels of the period. Bulgakov's satirical allegory *The Heart of a Dog* (1925; 1968), though it uses the jargon of SF, is also of interest in this context.

Bullett, Gerald (U.K.), 1893–1958.
ABOUT: WW, GSF, PE, ESF

*3-55. Mr. Godly Beside Himself. John Lane, 1924.
The eponymous hero, whose work and marriage have become utterly colorless, is fascinated by his new secretary, who turns out to be a visitor from Fairyland; he ultimately changes place with his elfin *Doppelgänger* Godelik, only to discover that the other world is facing revolutionary change thanks to the forces of reason—the imagination must discover an appropriate balance. A fine book, exploring the same moral territory as Mirrlees's *Lud-in-the-Mist* [3-250] and Irwin's *These Mortals* [3-189], but in a more ironic vein. A preparatory sketch of the theme appears in the short story "The Enchanted Moment" in *The Street of the Eye* [H3-40].

3-56. Helen's Lovers and Other Tales. Heinemann, 1932.
Collection including three fantasies and two horror stories (see [H3-40]). The title story is a curious timeslip romance anticipating the theme of Nathan's *Portrait of Jennie* [3-265]; "Fiddler's Luck" and "Tangent in Trouble" provide an ironic gloss upon a common folkloristic motif involving ordinary men with supernatural females.

[For other works of this author, see the companion guide to horror.]

Burdekin, Katharine (U.K.), 1896–1963.
ABOUT: GSF, SFE

3-57. The Rebel Passion. Thornton Butterworth, 1929.
Historical fantasy in which a medieval scholar monk is enabled by supernatural means to oversee the entire history of England and the sufferings of its people—including a glimpse of a utopian future. The "rebel passion" is pity. Burdekin had earlier written a more moderate timeslipping fantasy, "The Burning Ring" (1927), in which a wishing ring takes the hero a little further along the road to enlightenment than he might have preferred. Less adventurous than her "Murray Constantine" novels (see [3-86]), but just as deeply felt; she is an underrated writer.

Burnett, Frances Hodgson (U.K.), 1849–1924.
ABOUT: GSF, CA

3-58. The White People. Harper, 1911.
Consolatory fantasy whose heroine's second sight allows her to perceive the

White People (ghosts) and thus to know that our loved ones remain with us in spirit once they are dead. Spinoff from the Spiritualist movement.

Burroughs, Edgar Rice, 1875–1950.
ABOUT: WW, GSF, F, CA, TCA, NE, SMFL, SFE, TCSF, ESF, HF

3-59. The Cave Girl. McClurg, 1925.
An effete young man must learn to get tough when he is cast away on an island replete with menacing survivors from prehistory; he is assisted in the educative process by a girl who has already adapted to circumstance, and they become quite a team. A somewhat tongue-in-cheek recapitulation of the themes commonplace in Burroughs's work.

3-60. The Eternal Lover. McClurg, 1925.
Fix-up of two novellas from *All-Story* (1924–25). Nu of the Niocene is liberated from suspended animation by an earthquake and sets out to find his destined mate. Can she possibly be reincarnated in the heroine?—or is she still unconscious (thanks to the earthquake) and dreaming of her ideal man? An eccentric study in female psychology, not recommended to feminists.

*3-61. A Princess of Mars. McClurg, 1917.
Burroughs's first novel, serialized in *All-Story* as "Under the Moons of Mars" (1912). A soldier of fortune dreams his way to Mars, which is the perfect place for exotic derring-do, liberally supplied as it is with nasty monsters, peculiar humanoids (some friendly, some not) and a lovely princess whose egg-laying habits have not interfered with her mammary endowment. Uninhibited daydream fantasy, subsequently extended in ten more volumes, the last few of which show distinct signs of imaginative exhaustion. Not really SF, despite the interplanetary setting and occasional borrowings from SF writers; possibly inspired by Arnold's *Lieut. Gullivar Jones, His Vacation* [3-11] and certainly in the same spirit.

*3-62. Tarzan of the Apes. McClurg, 1914.
Classic fantasy adventure story which became the foundation of a modern hero-myth. The nobly born John Clayton is orphaned in infancy when his shipwrecked parents die on the shore of Africa; raised by apes, he becomes a perfect combination of morally superior aristocrat and powerful product of the struggle for existence, both sets of characteristics exaggerated by hybrid vigor. Later castaways include Jane Porter, who opens up a vision of new horizons which draws him, by degrees, back to civilization. In a supremely happy ending he triumphs over romantic convention by handing Jane to a rival, thereby retaining his heroic self-sufficiency. *The Return of Tarzan* (1915) brought a fatal compromise which trapped him in marriage. A subsequent attempt by the author to kill off this disastrous encumbrance was deemed too cruel, but in most of the later volumes of the series (which descended by degrees into self-plagiarism and occasional self-parody), Burroughs settled for ignoring her, so that Tarzan could get on with his adventures. The ultimate in boys' fiction: a perfect embodiment of prepubescent masculine power fantasy alloyed with primitive moral idealism. Fabulously and uninhibitedly silly; a landmark in popular fiction.

Cabell, James Branch, 1879–1958.
ABOUT: WW, GSF, H, CA, SMFL, SFE, ESF, FL, HF

*3-63. The Cream of the Jest; a Comedy of Evasions. McBride, 1917.
An author finds a supposedly magical charm which shapes his dreams into a quest for Ettarre, the personified ideal of sexual desire; the colorful adventures he undergoes in the person of his alter ego Horvendile are always interrupted when he actually makes contact with this essentially unpossessable ideal. He ultimately draws upon this dream life to enrich his real experience, discovering in his own wife an avatar of Ettarre, but from the viewpoint of a more critical observer the magic charm is only a piece of packaging and the dreams mere folly. This argument about the moral and aesthetic worth of romantic ideals and illusions is carried forward from earlier works like *Chivalry* (1909; rev. 1921) and *The Soul of Melicent* (1913; rev. as *Domnei; a Comedy of Woman-Worship*, 1920) which, as it were, take a slightly more sentimental and sympathetic view of the Quixotic philosophy than Cervantes did; later works continue the discourse, moving steadfastly toward the cynical end of the spectrum.

3-64. The Devil's Own Dear Son; a Comedy of the Fatted Calf. Farrar, Straus, 1949.
A hotel proprietor discovers that he is the son of a lecherous demon and sets off to find his father in Hell, but eventually learns that he is not cut out for a more grandiose existence than the one he previously enjoyed. A sarcastic comedy; one more trip along a well-trodden path.

*3-65. Figures of Earth; a Comedy of Appearances. McBride, 1921.
The story of Dom Manuel of Poictesme, ostensibly the central character of an eccentric assembly of twenty-one assorted texts, *The Biography of the Life of Manuel* (including [3-63, 3-66, 3-67, 3-68, 3-70 and 3-72]). On the surface level the texts are linked by their interest in the genealogy of Manuel's descendants, but the underlying theme of the assembly is the relationships among genealogists, biographers, novelists and their subjects—which represent more general relationships between men and ideals (especially ideals symbolically enshrined in heroic and sexual fantasies). In this central text Manuel, an ambitious swineherd aided by a magician, pursues various ideal women but has great difficulty in finding the true path to happiness. Meanwhile, he poses as a hero and deliverer, and ends by being hailed by his people as a great redeemer, though it is by no means obvious that he deserves much moral credit. The cynical Cervantean view of appearances is clearly dominant here, but the story is not without a compensating undercurrent of sentimentality.

*3-66. The High Place; a Comedy of Disenchantment. McBride, 1923.
An eighteenth-century French youth, imagining himself to be cast in the mold of a hero of chivalric romance, sets out to find his own Holy Grail, a fairytale princess; but this is the Age of Enlightenment, when the illusions of the past are to be set aside brutally, and he learns the extent of his self-delusion. Satire developing the Cervantean worldview in an uncompromisingly sarcastic manner.

*3-67. Jurgen; a Comedy of Justice. McBride, 1919.
Jurgen is a Poictesmian pawnbroker caught between romantic and cynical worldviews: a would-be poet who cannot be entirely taken in by his own patter. After

gaining his reckless wish to be rid of a nagging wife, he finds himself the poorer for it, and sets out to make good his loss. His quest ranges through various scenarios borrowed from history, myth and fiction, involving many allegorical figures, but he fails to discover any better way of being than the one which discomfort had urged him to cast off. Libidinous impulses lie at the very heart of his quest, and certain manifestations thereof led critics (unjustly and unwisely) to condemn the book on moral grounds, thus assuring its commercial success despite the complexity which renders it virtually opaque to unsophisticated readers.

*3-68. The Silver Stallion; a Comedy of Redemption. McBride, 1926.
Episodic novel, direct sequel to [3-65]. After Manuel's death his associated company of knights and wizards disintegrates and each individual member must find his own destiny. In a summary conclusion Jurgen assesses the glittering legacy of the great Redeemer; though his verdict is basically Cervantean, he finds that the sham had some good consequences.

3-69. Smirt; an Urbane Nightmare. McBride, 1934.
First of a trilogy signed "Branch Cabell" to signal that the works belonged to a different realm of discourse than the *Biography of the Life of Manuel*; the remaining volumes are *Smith; a Sylvan Interlude* (1935) and *Smire; an Acceptance in the Third Person* (1937). The central character, in three different "states of being," undertakes an odyssey through the worlds of dream, myth and history in search of a fulfillment which (unsurprisingly) he never finds. Quirkier and more self-indulgent than the books of the *Biography*; the lack of discipline succeeds only in producing a muddle.

*3-70. Something About Eve; a Comedy of Fig-Leaves. McBride, 1927.
A partial recapitulation of [3-63]; a repressed author goes questing in the land of dreams and is forced to penetrate the veil of mystery which had hitherto concealed from him the crucial role of libido in human affairs and creative endeavor—but he fails to derive much benefit from his enlightenment. More relaxed and mischievous than earlier books in the series, with many of the allegorical figures deliberately made less obscure by the use of crude anagrams in naming them.

3-71. There Were Two Pirates; a Comedy of Division. Farrar, Straus, 1946.
A pirate who harbors a few Quixotic illusions is given the opportunity to be divided from his shadow, which will continue to carry forward his career while he relives his innocent youth. A lightweight reprise of familiar themes.

3-72. The Witch-Woman: A Trilogy about Her. Farrar, Straus, 1948.
Collection of three stories, the only ones completed from a projected series of ten. The witch-woman is Ettarre, the epitome of female seductiveness, who is here pursued by three very different protagonists. "The Way of Ecben" (1929) is a poignant tragedy of disillusionment; "The Music from Behind the Moon" (1926) is a more delicate and romantic fantasy, which makes more concessions to Quixotry than Cabell usually did; "The White Robe" (1928) is a story of medieval lycanthropy which features the Lord of the Forest, an embodiment of seductive romanticism who also plays a part in Cabell's fine mock-Jacobean romance *The King Was in His Counting-House; a Comedy of Common Sense* (1939).

Calthrop, Dion Clayton (U.K.), 1878–1937.

3-73. Hyacinth: An Excursion. Williams & Norgate, 1927.
Sentimental fantasy in which the eponymous immortal visits London to spread a little happiness and gather stories to amuse the Muses. A less subtle version of "The Passing of the Third Floor Back" (see [2-94]).

Calvino, Italo (Italy), 1923–1985.
ABOUT: CA, NE, SMFL, SFE, TCSF, ESF

3-74. The Non-Existent Knight and The Cloven Viscount. Collins, 1962. Tr. by Archibald Colquhoun of *Il cavaliere inesistente*, 1959, and *Il visconte dimezzato*, 1952.
The Cloven Viscount is cut in two by a cannonball but both halves survive, embodying the good and evil parts of his personality. The evil half initially takes control of his estate, but his cruel reign is ameliorated by the return of the good half; both fall in love with the same woman and must fight a duel to determine who will have her. An excellent modern version of an old theme in moralistic fantasy. Also annotated as [4A-57].

Ĉapek, Karel (Czechoslovakia), 1890–1938, and Josef Ĉapek (Czechoslovakia), 1887–1945.
ABOUT: GSF, CA, SMFL, SFE, TCSF, ESF

3-75. "And so *ad infinitum*"; the Life of the Insects. Oxford Univ. Press, 1923. Tr. by Paul Selver of *Ze zivota hmyzu*, 1921. Also known as *The World We Live In* and *The Insect Play*.
Play in which a drunken tramp sees a series of visions in which the follies of human life are dramatized in the behavior of man-sized insects. The hypocrisies of love are exposed in the careless flirting of butterflies; materialism is made grotesque by a study of the life-styles of dung beetles and parasites; nationalism and its propensity to produce wars are phantasmagorically represented in the ant hive. In a bitter conclusion the tramp is offered a commentary on his own mortality by moths rushing to extinguish themselves in a naked flame. The authors denied that the worldview of the play was utterly pessimistic, but had clearly mistaken their own argument.

Chambers, Robert W(illiam), 1865–1933.
ABOUT: WW, GSF, SFW, H, SMFL, SFE, RG, PE, ESF, HF

3-76. The Slayer of Souls. Doran, 1920.
Thriller in which a girl whose soul has been destroyed by a powerful Oriental magician joins forces with a Secret Service agent to thwart a Yezidee plot to take over the world. A hyped-up pastiche of Rohmer's Fu Manchu novels, more glamorous than its model but no less silly.

[For other works of this author, see the companion guide to horror.]

Chesterton, G(ilbert) K(eith) (U.K.), 1874–1936.
ABOUT: GSF, SFW, F, CA, H, SMFL, SFE, ESF, HF

3-77. The Ball and the Cross. Wells Gardner, 1909.
A young Catholic, enraged by attacks made by a rationalist on the veneration of the Virgin Mary, tries to engage him in a duel; the rationalist is keen to cross swords but the world seems bent on preventing the fight. Their attempts to find a battlefield draw them closer together, and when they are separately tempted by the devil they see the error of their ways and join forces against him. A boisterous allegory, made seductively persuasive by the author's zestful rhetoric.

3-78. The Flying Inn. Methuen, 1914.
A new social movement inspired by a Mohammedan preacher introduces prohibition to Britain, but a charismatic rebel will have none of this enforced sobriety and sets out to spread intoxication and merriment wherever he can. In the decoded allegory, of course, his mission is to make men drunk with the holy spirit, in defiance of the demystifications of rational skepticism—which may or may not qualify Chesterton as Catholic apologetics' answer to Al Capone.

*3-79. The Man Who Was Thursday: A Nightmare. Arrowsmith, 1908.
Parody thriller in which the hero infiltrates a seven-man cell within a supposed organization of Anarchists, and discovers that all the other members (save perhaps the leader, code-named Sunday) are also infiltrators on the side of law and order. They all set out in mad pursuit of Sunday, who leads them a merry dance before revealing himself, in the climactic masked ball, to be God. An utterly preposterous and ill-defined allegory redeemed from incipient imbecility by the author's wit, verbal cleverness and sheer panache; one of the great bad books of the twentieth century.

Clouston, J. Storer (U.K.), 1870–1944.
ABOUT: SFE, ESF

3-80. Two's Two. Blackwood, 1916.
A baronet finds himself divided into two persons: his pious but ineffective "better half" and his energetically roguish "baser self." An Ansteyan fantasy of confusions and embarrassments rather than a moralistic fantasy in the vein of [3-74], related with amiable gusto.

Coblentz, Stanton A(rthur), 1896–1982.
ABOUT: CA, NE, SMFL, SFE, TCSF, ESF

3-81. When the Birds Fly South. Wings, 1945.
A young American lost in Afghanistan is found and adopted by a tribe whose members mysteriously disappear each winter; he persuades his native wife to stay with him rather than follow her own people, with tragic consequences. An interesting allegory which has affinities with Hudson's *Green Mansions* [3-186] and Phelps's *The Winter People* [4A-204].

Coles, Manning (pseud. of **Cyril H. Coles**, 1898–1965, and **Adelaide Manning**, 1891–1959).
ABOUT: GSF, CA, ESF, HF

3-82. Brief Candles. Doubleday, 1945 (U.K. ed. as by Francis Gaite).
Two tourists in France awaken the ghosts of a pair of their ancestors, who wreak havoc in the manner of Thorne Smith's mischievous spirits (see [3-328]). A sequel is *Happy Returns* (1955).

Collier, John (U.K.), 1901–1980.
ABOUT: WW, GSF, SFW, CA, SMFL, SFE, PE, ESF, HF

*3-83. Fancies and Goodnights. Doubleday, 1951.
Massive collection of fifty short stories which reprints all the items from the earlier *Presenting Moonshine* (1941) and adds many new items. The fantasies include three classics: "Green Thoughts" (1932), about a predatory orchid which absorbs its owner; "Evening Primrose," in which a poor young man who takes up clandestine residence in a department store finds ghosts in charge of it; and "Thus I Refute Beelzy," in which a little boy's friendship with a demon saves him from paternal abuse. Several slapstick posthumous fantasies which were originally issued in the collection *The Devil and All* (1934) are also reprinted: "The Right Side," "Half Way to Hell," "The Devil, George and Rosie," "After the Ball" and the excellent "Hell Hath No Fury," in which an angel and a demon take rooms together on Earth because the supernatural realms are too crowded. *The Touch of Nutmeg and Other Unlikely Stories* (1943) also reprinted many of the best fantasies from the two earlier collections. Collier tended to revise his older stories when they were reprinted (sometimes more than once), making them more similar in style to his later works, which are subtler in tone and content; some readers prefer the more exuberant early versions. Many of the stories were reprinted yet again in *The John Collier Reader* (1972), which also includes a few previously uncollected short stories and [3-84]. Collier's brilliant wit and verbal cleverness make his best short fantasies incomparable.

3-84. His Monkey Wife; or, Married to a Chimp. Peter Davies, 1930.
A young Englishman returns to England with a young female chimpanzee, whose true love for him saves him from the unhappy fate of marriage to a New Woman; he is initially overwrought but ultimately sees what a pearl he has found. Elegant and witty satire, parodying Bloomsbury affectations and the clichés of popular romantic fiction with scrupulous evenhandedness.

Connelly, Marc, 1890–1980.
ABOUT: CA

3-85. The Green Pastures. Farrar & Rinehart, 1929.
Play based on the vernacular versions of biblical mythology popular among the slave-descended blacks of the American South, first given literary expression in Roark Bradford's *Ol' Man Adam an' His Chillun* (1928). This sentimental post-

humous fantasy describes the Heaven implied by these beliefs, and suggests in its final act that God Himself might be able to learn a thing or two from these good-hearted believers.

Constantine, Murray (pseud. of Katharine Burdekin) (U.K.), 1896–1963.
ABOUT: GSF, SFE

3-86. The Devil, Poor Devil! Boriswood, 1934.
Lucifer returns to Earth to find that his hegemony over the souls of men has almost disappeared, along with God's. His spiritual opponent is now the Independent, who represents a secular moral sensibility. Possessing the body of a wayward young man, Lucifer sets out to further the cause of evil, but is frustrated. An unusual and interesting allegory by the author of the feminist scientific romances *Proud Man* (1934) and *Swastika Night* (1937).

Coppard, A(lfred) E(dgar) (U.K.), 1878–1957.
ABOUT: WW, GSF, SFW, CA, SMFL, PE, ESF

3-87. Adam and Eve and Pinch Me. Golden Cockerel Press, 1921.
The first of Coppard's works to be issued by this private press; it was followed by a second collection, *Clorinda Walks in Heaven* (1922), and by the novelette *Crotty Shrinkwin* (1932). The best of these, together with fantasies taken from Coppard's later collections, are reprinted in the Arkham House collection *Fearful Pleasures* (1946). "Clorinda Walks in Heaven" is a fine posthumous fantasy whose heroine must reappraise her career as a wife; "The Elixir of Youth" is one of several excellent cautionary tales which draw on Irish folklore; "Polly Morgan" is a haunting tale of love which endures after death. Coppard's fantasies are highly idosyncratic, light on the surface but usually carrying a grim allegorical message or a wry twist.

Corley, Donald, 1886–1955.
ABOUT: GSF

3-88. The House of Lost Identity. McBride, 1927.
Collection of stories whose style presents an odd mixture of the ornamental and the calculatedly naïve. The title story is a parable of maturation, as are several of the others; most are cast in a mock-folkloristic mold though they often involve no supernatural apparatus. A second collection in the same vein is *The Haunted Jester* (1931). The novel *The Fifth Son of the Shoemaker* (1930) is a more elaborate story of maturation, framed as a kind of nonsupernatural fairy tale, which has affinities with the work of Robert Nathan [3-262–3-266].

Coulton, G. G. (U.K.), 1858–1947.
3-89. Friar's Lantern. Clarke, 1906.
Timeslip novel by a noted medievalist which makes fun of nostalgia for the

medieval church as promoted by the likes of G. K. Chesterton and Hilaire Belloc. Two modern churchmen discover to their cost the truth of clerical corruption, perverse persecutions, the trade in relics and the methods of the inquisition. Witty and well told; the author offered to print at his own expense any convincing refutation, but none was forthcoming.

Cox, Erle (Australia), 1873-1950.
ABOUT: GSF, CA, SFE, TCSF, ESF

3-90. The Missing Angel. Robertson & Mullen, 1947.
A downtrodden man makes a diabolical bargain in order to get some fun from life, then decides to make use of an escape clause in his contract which promises him freedom if he can set the devil an impossible task. Amiable nonsense, related with a certain style.

Cozzens, James Gould, 1903-1978.
ABOUT: CA, ESF

3-91. Castaway. Random House, 1934.
Baroque posthumous fantasy in which a man finds himself at large in a huge empty department store and sets out to make what use he can of its resources. A symbolic assessment of the contribution made by commodity fetishism to the alienation of modern man.

Crawshay-Williams, Eliot (U.K.), 1879-1962.
ABOUT: WW, GSF

3-92. Night in No Time. John Long, 1946.
The brash protagonist argues with his father about changing mores in 1920; he is then enabled by the mysterious Mr. Cloxeter to witness his father in a similar predicament in 1894, and to see how well he relates to his own son in 1943. Has strong affinities with Priestley's *Three Time Plays* [3-308], though clearly stamped from the same template as Dickens's *Christmas Carol* [2-43]. A similar timeslip theme is neatly deployed in the title story of the collection *The Man Who Met Himself* (1947), which also includes "Nofrit," about the revivification of an ancient Egyptian princess, and two visionary fantasies.

Cromartie, Countess of (Sibell Lilian Blunt, later Mackenzie) (U.K.), 1878-1962.

3-93. Out of the Dark. Elkin Mathews, 1910.
Unusual erotic fantasy in which a young Scottish girl becomes besotted with Arâs, a one-time king among the Celtic invaders who came to ancient Scotland from Tyre, who returns to Earth when his grave is disturbed. A counterpart to the many stories of revived Egyptian princesses.

Crowley, Aleister (U.K.), 1875–1947.
    ABOUT: WW, GSF, CA, SMFL, RG, PE, ESF

3-94. Moonchild. Mandrake Press, 1929.
White magicians led by two idealized projections of the author plan to produce a special child, but their attempts are hampered by the interference of a rival group, which mounts magical attacks on the mother-to-be. The plot eventually dwindles away as the last chapters digress into matters connected with World War I. Fiction as wish fulfillment, testifying to the unsteadiness of Crowley's life-style fantasies.

[**For other works of this author, see the companion guide to horror.**]

Cullum, Ridgwell (U.K.), born 1867.

3-95. The Vampire of N'Gobi. Chapman & Hall, 1935.
Lost race story set in Africa; the (metaphorical) vampire is yet another copy of She-Who-Must-Be-Obeyed. Not aimed at the juvenile market, but a blood-and-thunder boys' book in spirit.

Darlington, W(illiam) A(ubrey) (U.K.), 1890–1979.
    ABOUT: GSF, CA

3-96. Alf's Button. Herbert Jenkins, 1919.
Ansteyan fantasy adapted for working-class readers; the cockney hero is a private in World War I who obtains some release from the rigors of trench warfare when he finds that rubbing one of his buttons evokes a genie. His efforts to exploit the situation are, to save the least, naïve. Two sequels are *Alf's Carpet* (1928) and *Alf's New Button* (1940); Alf's attempts to alter the course of World War II in the latter are just as feeble-minded and ill-fated as his earlier plot to kidnap the Kaiser.

3-97. Wishes Limited. Herbert Jenkins, 1922.
The best of Darlington's Ansteyan pastiches, deploying the formula in its more usual middle-class setting. The hero is a struggling novelist whose fairy god-mother appoints her staff to produce a best-seller for him; he then suffers hideous embarrassment because of its risqué nature. An incident in which a minor character is unhappily transformed into a black beetle presumably inspired Darlington to produce his next work in the same vein, *Egbert* (1924), whose hero is transformed into a rhinoceros after offending a magician.

Dawson, Coningsby (U.K.).

3-98. The Road to Avalon. Hutchinson, 1911.
After the battle of Camlan, a charcoal burner's son embarks upon a quest to find Avalon, so that Arthur may return. Though he is frequently led from his true path by the enchantress Lilith and her allies, he eventually reaches his goal. Allegory crossing Arthurian mythology with *The Pilgrim's Progress*; the hybrid is awkward but not without interest.

Day, Langston (U.K.).
ABOUT: ESF

3-99. Magic Casements. Rider, 1951.
Collection of variously set mythological fantasies, including "The Three Boun-
ties of Bacchus," in which a beggar ambitious to be emperor of Rome falls victim
to his own vainglory; and the political allegory "Bel-Suzubb Comes to Babylon."
There are echoes of Kipling's *Just-So Stories* [3-202] as well as an obvious debt to
Richard Garnett (see [2-63]), but the author labors under the handicap of an
unfortunate prolixity.

Dearmer, Geoffrey (U.K.), born 1893.
ABOUT: GSF, CA

3-100. They Chose to Be Birds. Heinemann, 1935.
A philosophical biologist offended by a priggish preacher slips him a hallucinogenic drug; he dreams that he is put on trial by enigmatic angels who condemn
him to live as a parrot—while his rival masquerades as a parson—until he has
learned a more appropriate creed. A strange moralistic comedy, appealing in its
eccentricity.

de Camp, L(yon) Sprague, 1907– .
ABOUT: WW, GSF, SFW, F, CA, TCA, NE, SMFL, SFE, MF, SFFL,
RG, TCSF, ESF, HF

3-101. Divide and Rule. Fantasy Press, 1948.
Two short novels; in the title story, from *Unknown* (1939), aliens who look like
kangaroos have brought back the age of chivalry. A bizarre comedy on the
borderline between fantasy and SF.

3-102. Solomon's Stone. Avalon, 1957.
Novel from *Unknown* (1942). An accidentally invoked demon takes over the
hero's body and displaces him to an astral plane populated by the fantasy selves of
people on Earth, where he is a swashbuckling bravo. He must recruit help to
recover the eponymous object, which will set matters straight. The uninhibited
invention gets sufficiently out of hand to become slightly silly.

3-103. The Tritonian Ring and Other Pusadian Tales. Twayne, 1953.
In the title novel (1951) a threat to the hero's homeland sends him forth in search
of a talisman which the gods themselves fear; it is an antidote to magic which
might ultimately dis-enchant the whole world. This edition includes three short
stories set in the same world; these stories are not included in the Owlswick
edition of 1977.

3-104. The Undesired Princess. Fantasy Publishing Co., 1951.
Comic fantasy from *Unknown* (1942). A puzzle fan is shifted into a Secondary
World rigorously made in the image of logic and language, where everything is
rigidly defined and all categories are distinct; there he must out-riddle the andro-

sphinx to save a princess, and confront the philosopher-god who has ordered the world. The best of de Camp's solo works in this vein, though it suffers somewhat from lax organization. The book also contains the short story "Mr. Arson."

as editor.

3-105. Swords and Sorcery. Pyramid, 1963.
First of a series of showcase anthologies of heroic fantasy, featuring (among others) Lord Dunsany [3-116–3-124], Robert E. Howard [3-181–3-182], Clark Ashton Smith [H3-182], C. L. Moore [3-252], Fritz Leiber [3-211] and Poul Anderson [3-2–3-3]. It was followed by *The Spell of Seven* (1965), *The Fantastic Swordsmen* (1967), and *Warlocks and Warriors* (1970).

with **Fletcher Pratt**, 1897–1956.

*3-106. The Incomplete Enchanter. Holt, 1941.
Fix-up of two short novels from *Unknown: The Roaring Trumpet* and *The Mathematics of Magic* (both 1940). When a scientist friend persuades him that all possible worlds exist, and that any one of them can be reached by a trick of the mind, psychologist Harold Shea sets off in search of the world of Irish legend; instead he finds himself first in the world of Norse mythology as *Ragnarok* approaches, then in the world of Spenser's *Faerie Queene* [1-79]. His exploits there are a perfect admixture of comedy and adventure, delightful to read. The series continued with *The Castle of Iron* (*Unknown*, 1941; expanded for book publication, 1950), set in the world of Ariosto's *Orlando Furioso* [1-4]. The collaborators returned to the series much later, adding *Wall of Serpents* (1953), set in the world of the *Kalevala* [1-41], and *The Green Magician* (1954), where Shea finally gets to the world he originally wanted to visit; these two novellas were reprinted in *Wall of Serpents* (1960). The omnibus *The Compleat Enchanter* (1975) reprints only the first three stories; *The Intrepid Enchanter* (1988) and *The Complete Compleat Enchanter* (1989) include all five.

3-107. Land of Unreason. Holt, 1942.
Comic fantasy from *Unknown* (1941). An American in Britain is carried off as a changeling by the little people, becoming involved in a quest to save their Secondary World from magical corruption; he ultimately takes up his allotted role as its savior. Less successful than the Harold Shea novellas [3-106], but much better than *The Carnelian Cube* (1948), the most strained and least amusing of de Camp and Pratt's collaborative endeavors.

De Comeau, Alexander (U.K.).
ABOUT: GSF, SMFL

3-108. Monk's Magic. Methuen, 1931.
A lay brother appointed by his abbot to search for the elixir of life is driven by the failure of his experiments to seek out those immortals who have already perfected it; he travels with a physician and a youth who turns out to be a girl in disguise. After many fantastic adventures the best he can offer his superior is the chance to make a deal with the devil, and even that goes awry. An eminently readable adventure story which has affinities with Mervyn Wall's Fursey novels [3-355].

Deeping, Warwick (U.K.), 1877–1950.
ABOUT: CA, ESF

3-109. I Live Again. Cassell, 1942.
Romance of serial reincarnation, in which the relative social positions of two unhappy lovers are gradually altered until they can break the self-destructive pattern of their attraction, redeeming their moral debts in the London blitz. A melodramatic follow-up to Deeping's morale-boosting timeslip fantasy *The Man Who Went Back* (1940).

de la Mare, Walter (U.K.), 1873–1956.
ABOUT: WW, GSF, SFW, CA, SMFL, PE, ESF, FL, HF

3-110. Broomsticks and Other Tales. Constable, 1925.
Collection of sophisticated fairy tale fantasies. The title story is a nice fantasy about the secret life of a spinster's cat; also included are two fine cautionary tales of temptation which must be resisted, "Miss Jemima" and "Alice's Godmother." More stories in the same vein are in *The Lord Fish* (1933), which includes an ironic sequel to the story of Jack and the Beanstalk, "Dick and the Beanstalk." All these stories and others are in *Collected Stories for Children* (1947). The stories are sufficiently sophisticated to be read by adults as well as children.

3-111. The Three Mulla-Mulgars. Duckworth, 1910. U.S. title: *The Three Royal Monkeys.*
Animal fable in which three monkey siblings must travel to the land of their father's birth in order to claim their royal heritage; they encounter many adventures en route. An unusual children's book narrated in an ornamented and curiously musical style.

[For other works of this author, see the companion guide to horror.]

Dick, R. A. (pseud. of Josephine Leslie) (U.K.), 1898–1979.
ABOUT: GSF, CA

3-112. The Ghost and Mrs. Muir. Harrap, 1947.
The ghost of a sea captain tries to scare off the widow who buys the house which was once his, but is eventually reconciled to her presence and becomes a true friend to her and her children. A pleasant romantic fantasy akin to Susan Alice Kerby's novels [3-200–3-201].

Dixey, Marmaduke (U.K.).

3-113. Hell's Bells. Faber & Faber, 1936.
Ex-solicitor Majorian Pilgrim is at first resigned to his condemnation to a modern and not altogether uncomfortable Hell, but later becomes determined to escape. He makes it to Heaven before being re-drafted into the Eternal Conflict. Amusing; this novel neatly bridges the gap between the slapstick infernal comedies of Bangs [2-12] and Kummer [3-207] and the satirical moral fables of Blamires [3-38] and Hales [4A-127].

Douglas, Norman (U.K.), 1868–1952.
ABOUT: GSF, CA, SFE

3-114. In the Beginning. Douglas, 1927.
Quasi-classical fantasy; the hero is sired by a god upon a mortal woman, but when he in his turn gets a goddess pregnant, the event is unprecedented. After being revived from the dead, he eventually becomes the consort of his daughter and, aided by the advice of friendly satyrs, puts mankind on the road to civilization. An elegant flight of fancy, mischievously championing the values of liberal paganism.

3-115. They Went. Chapman & Hall, 1920.
Story based on the legend of Lyonesse, a realm destroyed by inundation. The urbane Theophilus, champion of beauty and enemy of moral tyranny (in the tradition of the Romantic Satan), tempts the daughter of the king with exotic utopian visions, but her schemes are subverted by the heavy hand of divine providence. Allied in spirit to France's *Revolt of the Angels* [3-144] and other works in the French tradition, but rather more subtle in its championship of aestheticism.

Dunsany, Lord (Edward J. M. D. Plunkett) (Ireland), 1878–1957.
ABOUT: WW, GSF, SFW, F, CA, SMFL, SFE, RG, TCSF, PE, ESF, FL, HF

3-116. The Blessing of Pan. Putnam, 1927.
A village boy who has learned to play the music of Pan leads a revival of paganism in a rural parish; the ineffectual vicar cannot stem the tide of apostasy and ultimately must learn to swim with it. An ironic confection which has affinities with the classical fantasies of Eden Phillpotts [3-288–3-294].

*3-117. The Charwoman's Shadow. Putnam, 1926.
A young man must pledge his shadow before being apprenticed to a magician; the magician's charwoman once made a similar pledge but now regrets it bitterly, and they plot to recover the lost parts of their souls. An excellent fantasy in the tradition of George MacDonald (see [2-117]).

*3-118. The Gods of Pegana. Elkin Mathews, 1905.
Collection of prose poems describing the evolution of a pantheon and its relationship with the human-inhabited material world which the gods subsequently create. A fascinating literary entity whose nearest analogue is Patrick Woodroffe's *Pentateuch of the Cosmogony* (1979)—a series of paintings with associated texts (*The Gods of Pegana* is considerably enhanced by the illustrations accompanying the text, which are by Sidney Sime). The mythology of this imaginary world is further elaborated in *Time and the Gods* (1906), a varied assembly of allegories and legends.

3-119. The King of Elfland's Daughter. Putnam, 1924.
The prince of a kingdom which borders Elfland sets out to claim its princess as his bride; he succeeds, but she is unhappy in the human world and he has a much harder time when he once again sets out to fetch her from her father's realm. The

marriage of worlds once made, however, cannot entirely be broken, and the eventual reunion of the two lovers sets in motion the decline and fall of Enchantment. The allegory, which is close in spirit to Irwin's *These Mortals* [3-189] and in its choice of materials to Mirrlees's *Lud-in-the-Mist* [3-250], is unfortunately let down by the story, which is uncharacteristically prolix and overburdened with detail.

3-120. The Last Revolution. Jarrolds, 1951.
Mankind's machines turn on their makers, having acquired a life of their own and an ambition to be rulers of creation. A nostalgic fantasy expressing regret for the loss of a simpler way of life.

3-121. The Man Who Ate the Phoenix. Jarrolds, 1949.
The title novella is the story of an Irish poacher who shoots a golden pheasant, believing it to be a phoenix, and finds himself in touch with the phantasmagoric world of the supernatural, to which Ireland is still close. The fables and vignettes which accompany it are weak exercises in self-pastiche.

3-122. The Strange Journeys of Colonel Polders. Jarrolds, 1950.
A jingoistic military man offends an Eastern adept and is given a salutary lesson in metempsychosis, experiencing the world in many different animal forms ranging from insects to mammals. An expansion of the theme of Dunsany's earlier fantasy about a man who remembers a former incarnation as a dog, *My Talks with Dean Spanley* (1937).

*3-123. The Sword of Welleran and Other Stories. Allen, 1908.
Collection of stories and sketches; these can be seen as a further elaboration of the exercise begun in [3-118], progressing formally from legend to romance, but the background to the stories is by now far removed from that laid out in *The Gods of Pegana*. The title story is a very stylish heroic fantasy, as is the marvelous "The Fortress Unvanquishable Save for Sacnoth"; "The Kith of the Elf-Folk" is Dunsany's variant on the classic theme in which a supernatural creature (a "Wild Thing" here) obtains a soul in order to live among humans, but is disappointed by the experience. *A Dreamer's Tales* (1910) is more languorously self-indulgent in mood, and includes the excellent "Idle Days on the Yann." *The Book of Wonder* (1912) and *Tales of Wonder* (1916; U.S. title: *The Last Book of Wonder*) contain ironic exercises in fabulation which are brilliantly deft and delicate. *Fifty-One Tales* (1915) offers slighter vignettes in the same vein. *Tales of Three Hemispheres* (1919) is a less striking collection which reprints "Idle Days on the Yann" in order to add two lackluster sequels; by this time the vein of inspiration had finally worn thin, but the earlier works are incomparable. An eclectic selection by E. F. Bleiler from these and the other collections described in [3-118] and [3-124] is *Gods, Men and Ghosts* (Dover, 1972); a more extensive selection is presented in three volumes edited by Lin Carter: *At the Edge of the World* (1970), *Beyond the Fields We Know* (1972) and *Over the Hills and Far Away* (1974).

3-124. The Travel Tales of Mr. Joseph Jorkens. Putnam, 1931.
The first of several collections of anecdotal tall tales, many of which use folkloristic themes in a playfully absurd manner. Followed by: *Mr. Jorkens Remembers Africa* (1934), *Jorkens Has a Large Whiskey* (1940), *The Fourth Book of Jorkens*

(1948) and *Jorkens Borrows Another Whiskey* (1954). Dunsany is not quite as impressive in this irreverent Wodehousian vein as when he is at his most self-indulgently romantic, but all the tales are amusing and some are very funny.

Dutourd, Jean (France), 1920–
ABOUT: CA, ESF

3-125. A Dog's Head. Lehmann, 1951. Tr. by Robin Chancellor of *Une Tête de chien*, 1950.
The unfortunate hero, born with the head of a spaniel, is made miserable by negative reactions to his condition until he is redeemed by the love of a good woman. A stylish satire.

Eddison, E(ric) R(ucker) (U.K.), 1882–1945.
ABOUT: WW, GSF, SFW, F, CA, SMFL, SFE, RG, TCSF, ESF, FL, HF

3-126. Mistress of Mistresses: A Vision of Zimiamvia. Faber & Faber, 1935.
The first published (but chronologically last) volume of a trilogy loosely connected with [3-127]. Zimiamvia is a highly personal dream world: Renaissance Europe transfigured by arbitrary cultural embellishments, metaphysical theories and allegorical characters. Eddison's alter ego Lessingham is projected after his death in our world into Zimiamvia's symbolic political intrigues, in which he plays an ambivalent part. Glossy but too self-indulgently esoteric to interest most readers. In the "prequel" *A Fish Dinner in Memison* (1941), episodes in Lessingham's Earthly life run parallel to events in Zimiamvia before his arrival there; the interweaving of mundane and supernatural and the greater clarity of the metaphysical speculations make this a more coherent and satisfying work. The posthumously published *The Mezentian Gate* (1958) was left unfinished and has little to recommend it as a novel, but its attempt to fill in the background and make the world of Zimiamvia more coherent has a certain fascination, in exactly the same way that Tolkien's obsessive concern with the history and ontogeny of Middle earth (see [4A-251]) warrants attention. The whole exercise is, like Tolkien's, a testament to the extent to which intellectuals can become intensely involved with the shaping of hypothetical worlds.

*3-127. The Worm Ouroboros. Cape, 1922.
Baroque heroic fantasy, reckoned by many to be the archetype of the literary species. The frame narrative, in which the author's alter ego is conducted to Mercury, is soon forgotten, overwhelmed by the tale of the great war between the honorable Demons and the "naughty" Witches, which must ultimately be settled by the valiant endeavors of the champions of Demonland and the wayward sentiments of the traitorous Lord Gro. Allegorical overtones and moralistic undercurrents are eventually cast aside, overshadowed by the sheer magnificence of the conflict, so that in the end the climax most devoutly to be wished is that time can be turned back on itself to let the whole glorious adventure echo through eternity. A masterpiece, altogether without parallel in its grandiosity and eccentricity.

Eliade, Mircea (Rumania), 1907–1986.
ABOUT: CA, SMFL

3-128. Two Tales of the Occult. Herder & Herder, 1970. Tr. by William Ames Coates of *Nopte la Serampore* and *Secretul Doctorului Honigberger*, 1939–40.
Two novellas based in yogic folklore, both involving timeslips which reveal that all is illusion. In "Nights at Serampore" three Europeans become lost in the Indian jungle and play a minor part in events which happened long before; in "The Secret of Dr. Honigberger," a young student is mysteriously enabled to examine the journal of a scholar who sought the way to a parallel dimension. Interesting modern examples of credulous occult romance.

Erskine, John, 1879–1951.
ABOUT: CA, SMFL, ESF

3-129. Adam and Eve. Bobbs-Merrill, 1927.
An account of the very first instance of the Eternal Triangle. The vain but none-too-bright Adam is beguiled by the exciting Lilith, but is intimidated by her cleverness and energy; he is less beguiled by the wheedling and hypocritical Eve, inventor of the fig leaf and doyenne of dutiful domesticity. He never can work out a way to have his cake and eat it too, thus setting the pattern for the countless stupid tragedies in which future men will be torn between wives and mistresses.

3-130. Penelope's Man. Bobbs-Merrill, 1927.
Subtitled "The Homing Instinct"; offers an ironically subversive alternative account of the fall of Troy and Odysseus's subsequent wanderings, making the hero into an archetype of the faithless modern man, ever duplicitous in his dealings with women. Pointed satire, more subtle than Viereck's similarly motivated *Gloria* [3-349]. The female of the species had received equally cynical treatment in *The Private Life of Helen of Troy* (1925).

3-131. Venus, the Lonely Goddess. Morrow, 1949.
The story of the sentimental education of the goddess of love, who thinks that she has a lot to teach mankind but in fact has a lot to learn; her involvement with Achilles and his son Pyrrhus in the climactic phase of the Trojan War leaves her a little wiser. More sadly sentimental than Erskine's earlier Trojan novels [3-130].

Farjeon, Eleanor (U.K.), 1881–1965.
ABOUT: GSF, CA, SFFL, HF

3-132. Martin Pippin in the Apple-Orchard. Collins, 1921.
First of two collections of stories linked by the framing motif of the Puckish puzzle solver Martin Pippin; the second is *Martin Pippin in the Daisy Field* (1937). Inventive children's fantasy in an idiosyncratic vein, old-fashioned in the best sense.

3-133. The Soul of Kol Nikon. Collins, 1923.
Folkloristic fantasy describing the career of a child shunned by his fellow humans because they perceive (or perhaps only believe) him to be a soulless changeling;

the ultimate consequences of this treatment are tragic, as they were bound to be whether the suspicions were warranted or not.

Faulkner, William, 1897–1962.
ABOUT: CA, PE

3-134. Mayday. Univ. of Notre Dame Press, 1977.
Novelette; an allegorical medieval romance written in 1926 and presented in holograph to a girl Faulkner wished to marry. The hero, traveling in the company of Hunger and Pain, makes love to three women of legendary beauty (including Tristan's Yseult), but comes away dissatisfied and finds his ideal only in oblivion. Heavily influenced by Cabell (see [3-63–3-72]), but desperately downbeat; as a courtship ploy the presentation can only have been a dreadful mistake, a gesture whose naked romanticism contrasts sharply with the pessimism of the story.

Fessier, Michael, 1907–1988.
ABOUT: GSF, ESF

3-135. Fully Dressed and in His Right Mind. Knopf, 1935.
A little man with a dreadfully intimidating stare can drive his victims to insanity and death, but the hero resists him with the aid of an enigmatic female who loves him, and manages to evade his spell despite being framed for murder. An odd allegory, which might be regarded as an eccentric meditation upon the message given to Depression-era America by Franklin D. Roosevelt in his 1933 inaugural address: "the only thing we have to fear is fear itself."

Finn, Ralph L(eslie) (U.K.), 1912–
ABOUT: CA, SFE, ESF

3-136. Time Marches Sideways. Hutchinson, 1950.
Timeslip story; one of three novels by Finn that develop ideas borrowed from Dunne's *Experiment with Time*—the others are *The Lunatic, the Lover, and the Poet* (1948) and *Twenty-Seven Stairs* (1949). The protagonist is convinced that he could have made a success of his unhappy love life if only he had met his inamorata five years earlier, but when he gets the chance, events inevitably take an unexpected turn. Well executed; compare J. B. Priestley's "time plays" (see [3-308]) and Louis Marlow's *The Devil in Crystal* [3-232].

Finney, Charles G(randison), 1905–1984.
ABOUT: WW, GSF, SFW, F, CA, SMFL, SFE, SFFL, RG, PE, ESF, HF

*3-137. The Circus of Dr. Lao. Viking, 1935.
Classic novella in which a Chinese magician brings his circus to the archetypal American small town of Abalone so that the inhabitants may briefly confront the true nature of their most secret fantasies and desires—which are, of course, mainly libidinous in nature. The opportunity for a glorious liberation of the human

spirit is momentarily presented, but the prospect of giving free rein to the impulses conventionally repressed as Satanic is incipiently chaotic and the moment is quickly put away, leaving a lingering sensation of disappointment. A marvelous fabulation, far more erotic than the more controversial *Jurgen* [3-67], whose message it echoes and reinforces in uncompromising fashion. This edition is strikingly illustrated by Boris Artzybasheff; the U.K. edition (Grey Walls Press, 1948) has equally striking illustrations by Gordon Noel Fish.

3-138. The Unholy City. Vanguard, 1937.
Short novel whose crash-landed hero is guided through the city of Heilar-Wey by an enigmatic character who promises to show him a really good time but never quite manages to deliver—as one might expect, given that we first meet him optimistically trying to improve a lily with paint. Never did the reality principle exert itself in such a mad and surreal way as it does herein—a paradox which may help to explain why the book is underappreciated (though it is certainly not in the same league as [3-137]).

Forster, E(dward) M(organ) (U.K.), 1879–1970.
   ABOUT: GSF, SFW, CA, SFE, RG

3-139. The Celestial Omnibus and Other Stories. Sidgwick & Jackson, 1911.
Collection of idiosyncratic fantasy stories. The title story features an omnibus driven by Thomas Browne which conducts those blessed with a true aesthetic sensibility to the Heaven which great writers share with their creations; the other stories confront ordinary mortals with glimpses of alternative, often ecstatic, existences which they must shut out if they are to continue with the business of everyday life. More of the same species can be found in *The Eternal Moment and Other Stories* (1928), which includes two fine posthumous fantasies: the enigmatic "The Point of It" and the ironic "Mr. Andrews." The two collections are combined in *Collected Short Stories* (1948; U.S. title: *Collected Tales*).

Fortune, Dion (pseud. of **Violet M. Firth**) (U.K.), 1890–1946.
   ABOUT: WW, GSF, SFW, SMFL, PE, ESF

3-140. The Demon Lover. Noel Douglas, 1927.
Credulous occult romance in which the Crowleyesque secretary of an occult society goes to the bad and is executed, becoming a vampiric spirit until his growing love for the woman he abused (an obvious alter ego of the author) allows him to set things posthumously to rights and redeem himself. One wonders what confused feelings Violet Firth took with her when she left the Order of the Golden Dawn in order to take control of the shaping of her future career as a life-style fantasist.

3-141. The Sea Priestess. [The Author], 1938.
Occult romance carrying forward themes from *The Winged Bull* (1935) and *The Goat-Foot God* (1936); the male protagonist is recruited by a reincarnated Morgan Le Fay to help her celebrate the erotic magical rites of lost Atlantis and become more than human. In the posthumously published sequel, *Moon Magic* (1956),

which is much more obviously an exercise in wish fulfillment, the female adept is the viewpoint character, who once again seduces a desirable male to act as her acolyte. One can, of course, only speculate about the relative levels of seductive success which Crowley and Firth were able to attain by means of their preposterous poses once they were fat and over forty.

[For other works of this author, see the companion guide to horror.]

Foster, George C(ecil) (U.K.), born 1893.
ABOUT: SFE

3-142. The Lost Garden. Chapman & Hall, 1930.
A group of immortals survive the sinking of Atlantis and live until the present day, witnessing many significant events in world history. The moral, nicely exemplified by the priest who continually changes his faith (but never becomes Vicar of Bray), is *plus ça change, plus c'est la même chose.* Compare Arnold's *Phra the Phoenician* [2-9] and Cutcliffe Hyne's *Abbs* (1929).

France, Anatole (pseud. of Jacques-Anatole-François Thibault) (France), 1844–1924.
ABOUT: GSF, SFW, CA, SMFL, SFE, ESF

3-143. Penguin Island. John Lane, 1909. Tr. by A. W. Evans of *L'Ile des pingouins,* 1908.
Celebrated satire in which a population of penguins mistakenly baptized by a nearsighted saint are given human form by God and recapitulate the course of human history. The early chapters remain amusing, but the long parody of the Dreyfus affair, which caused a sensation in its day, is no longer of much interest.

*3-144. The Revolt of the Angels. John Lane, 1914. Tr. by Mrs. Wilfrid Jackson of *La Révolte des anges,* 1914.
A satirical masterpiece which embraces the Romantic view of Satan as a champion of liberal humanist values against the oppressive moral tyranny of the "demiurge" Jehovah. A guardian angel neglects his duties in order to seek wisdom in books and, having become enlightened, is seized with revolutionary fervor. He tries to unite the many fallen angels who live quietly among men, and searches for Satan in order to beg him to be their general in a new crusade, but Satan, when found, explains to him where the proper battleground is. Brilliantly witty and rhetorically powerful; one of the great fantastic novels.

3-145. The Seven Wives of Bluebeard and Other Marvellous Tales. John Lane, 1920. Tr. by D. B. Stewart of *Les Sept Femmes de la Barbe-Bleu et autres contes merveilleux,* 1909.
Collection of fables including three ironic tales purporting to reveal the "truth" behind well-known folktales, plus the excellent novella "The Shirt," in which a king sends forth emissaries to bring him the shirt of a happy man, having been assured that it will cure him of all his ills when he puts it on—but where on Earth can one find a truly happy man?

Frankau, Gilbert (U.K.), 1884–1952.
ABOUT: SFE, ESF

3-146. The Seeds of Enchantment. Hutchinson, 1921.
Political allegory employing the conventions and clichés of the lost race story. Three men brave dire hardship to travel into the heart of Indo-China in search of a white tribe which cultivates a marvelous euphoric plant. They find contrasting images of utopia in the lotus-eater society and the State Socialist mini-empire which threatens its survival, and reject both in favor of the individualistic ideal. The fervor of the author's convictions enlivens the violent climax. Makes an interesting contrast with Hilton's *Lost Horizon* [3-175].

Fraser, Ronald (U.K.), 1888–1974.
ABOUT: GSF, CA, SFE, ESF

*3-147. Flower Phantoms. Cape, 1926.
A female student at Kew Gardens faces a crisis in her love life, dramatized by her growing awareness of the life of the plants which surround her. An orchid finally initiates her into the mysteries of sex and gives her the experiential grounding which she needs in order successfully to carry forward her career. A marvelous idiosyncratic story, told with delicacy and amazing conviction. A baroque footnote to Erasmus Darwin's magnificently absurd *Loves of the Plants* (1789).

3-148. The Flying Draper. Unwin, 1924.
A Wellsian self-made man is sufficiently superior to the common herd to rise above them in a perfectly literal fashion, but must eventually pursue his quest beyond the life which men lead. A satirical parable which compares interestingly with other stories using the same motif: Neil Bell's fantasy of a failed messiah, "The Facts about Benjamin Crede" (1935), and Michael Harrison's *Higher Things* [3-166].

Frazer, Shamus (James I. A. Frazer) (U.K.), 1912– .

3-149. Blow, Blow Your Trumpets. Chapman & Hall, 1945.
Antediluvian fantasy which reveals, in satirical fashion, why God was sufficiently distressed with the state of the world to flood it; cunning men have wheedled magical secrets out of their guardian angels while Satan's legions are plotting to send barbaric hordes against civilization. The author's delight in the comic and adventure elements of his eccentrically designed story keeps the plot afloat (along with Noah's Ark) in spite of its inherent silliness.

Fryers, Austin (U.K.).

3-150. The Devil and the Inventor. Pearson, 1900.
An inventor frustrated by lack of capital makes a deal with the devil whereby he is given the facilities to perfect his inventions but must surrender his life if he cannot make them pay. He finds it harder than he expected to be a benefactor of

mankind, but narrowly escapes his sad fate by ironic means. Lightweight fantasy in the tradition of Dalton's *Gentleman in Black* [2-39].

Gallon, Tom (U.K.), 1866–1914.

3-151. The Man Who Knew Better: A Christmas Dream. Constable, 1902.
A cynic's worldview is challenged by a "ghost" which emerges from a picture of himself as a child. He experiences visions which allow him to recover the spontaneous feelings of charity and hope which he had long lost. One of a group of pastiches of Dickens's *Christmas Carol* [2-43]; rather better than Marie Corelli's self-righteous *Strange Visitation of Josiah McNason* (1904). Gallon had earlier produced *The Charity Ghost: A Tale of Christmas* (1902) and went on to write *Christmas at Poverty Castle* (1907).

Garnett, David (U.K.), 1892–1981.
ABOUT: WW, GSF, SFW, F, CA, SMFL, SFE, ESF, HF

*3-152. Lady into Fox. Chatto & Windus, 1922.
Classic novella about a man whose loyalty and devotion to his wife survive her metamorphosis into a fox, though she ultimately deserts him to play her new existential role to the full, until it reaches a predictable end. The tale evoked a number of parodies, most notably Christopher Ward's *Gentleman into Goose* (1924), while Vercors's *Sylva* [4A-259] is a deliberate inversion of its theme. It can also be seen as a sentimental counterpart in Kafka's *Metamorphosis* [H3-110]. In later editions it is usually paired with the equally stylish parable *A Man in the Zoo* (1922), in which a young man disappointed in love offers himself to a zoo as a specimen of *Homo sapiens* and forms fruitful relationships with some of the other animals.

Garrett, Garet, 1878–1954.
ABOUT: CA

3-153. The Blue Wound. Putnam's, 1921.
Allegorical fantasy of history whose protagonist learns why civilization seems bent on destroying itself in war. Compare Burdekin's *The Rebel Passion* [3-57].

Gerhardi, William (U.K.), 1895–1977, and Lunn, Brian (U.K.).
ABOUT: CA, SFE

3-154. The Memoirs of Satan. Cassell, 1932.
Satan explains and excuses himself, claiming that he—as champion of Mind against Body, skepticism against faith, curiosity against self-satisfaction and ambition against humility—has been a far better friend to man than the All-Highest, though he is now in much reduced circumstances. Clever and witty; apparently inspired by Viereck and Eldridge's *My First Two Thousand Years* [3-350].

Gilman, Charlotte Perkins (formerly **Charlotte P. Stetson**), 1860–1935.
ABOUT: GSF, F, CA, PE

*3-155. Herland. Pantheon, 1979.
Feminist utopian lost race story; one of three which were serialized in Gilman's periodical *The Forerunner: Herland* appeared in 1915; *Moving the Mountain* in 1911; *With Her in Ourland* in 1916. Three males discover an all-female society whose organization and morality call into question all their preconceptions about human nature and social order. Written with elegance, wit and conviction; a classic of its kind.

Gould, Arthur Lee (pseud. of **Arthur S. G. Lee**) (U.K.), 1894–1975.
ABOUT: GSF, SFE

3-156. An Airplane in the Arabian Nights. Werner Laurie, 1947.
A light aircraft timeslips to Harun-al-Rashid's Bagdad, where its passengers, including an American businessman and his beautiful daughter, undergo various discomfiting adventures, including a meeting with Sinbad. Less ingenious and less lively than similar material in *Unknown*, with magic mostly proving superior to twentieth-century technology and know-how.

Grahame, Kenneth (U.K.), 1859–1932.
ABOUT: CA, SMFL, RG, ESF, HF

*3-157. The Wind in the Willows. Methuen, 1908.
Classic animal fantasy in which the irrepressible Toad creates havoc wherever he goes, proving a sore trial to the Mole, the Badger and the Water Rat, though they still pitch in to help when the Weasels and their rotten kin take over Toad Hall. The perfect expression of English rural nostalgia, which laughs at itself in order to emphasize how utterly seriously it must be taken. Tolkien's work, especially in its less earnest manifestations, shares something of the same sensibility.

Grant, Joan (née **Marshall**; later **Joan Kelsey**) (U.K.), 1907–   .
ABOUT: WW, CA, ESF

3-158. Winged Pharaoh. Arthur Barker, 1937.
The first of several lush fantasies of ancient history ostensibly based on Mrs. Grant's memories of previous incarnations; the inevitable controversy helped to boost it to best-seller status. The more fantastic novels in the series include *Life as Carola* (1939) and *Return to Elysium* (1947). Better written and more carefully constructed than most credulous occult romances.

Green, Roger Lancelyn (U.K.), 1918–1987.
ABOUT: CA, SFE, ESF

3-159. From the World's End. Edmund Ward, 1948.
Visionary fantasy; a novella with much interpolated verse. Two young people stranded while motoring in Wales must spend the night in a strange house, where

they dream of a phoenix, a maze and a Singing Rose, and learn to celebrate the magic of life. A mannered allegory in the tradition of George MacDonald (see [2-116]). Reprinted in *Double Phoenix* (1971), edited by Lin Carter.

Griffiths, Alan (U.K.).
ABOUT: GSF, CA

3-160. Spirits Under Proof. Werner Laurie, 1935. U.S. title: *Authors in Paradise.* An uneducated medium receives the sequel to *Gulliver's Travels* from Swift, and passes it off as his own; he finds it more difficult than he anticipated to pose as a literary man, and gets into deeper water by plagiarizing Shakespeare's greatest posthumous play. An amiable comedy. In much the same vein as *The Passionate Astrologer* (1936), in which a reckless young angel allows a few pages of the book of destiny to fall into Earthly hands; can the power of free will subvert the prophecies there once they are made known?

Gunn, Neil M(iller), 1891–1973.
ABOUT: WW, GSF, CA, SMFL, ESF

3-161. The Green Isle of the Great Deep. Faber & Faber, 1944.
An old man and a boy are translocated into the land of the dead, which has been comprehensively reorganized by its administrators. The fruits of ecstasy are forbidden and the inhabitants have settled for a more orderly existence—but the spirit of rebellion in the boy cannot be quelled, and his example inspires the old man to demand to see God, who is dismayed to discover what the tyranny of "reason" has done to the world which he made for his loved ones. It was all too easy to believe in 1944 that God must have forgotten His Creation, and that the political machines of the day were a poor substitute.

Haggard, H(enry) Rider (U.K.), 1856–1925.
ABOUT: WW, GSF, SFW, F, CA, NE, H, SMFL, SFE, RG, TCSF, ESF, FL, HF

3-162. The Ghost Kings. Cassell, 1908. U.S. title: *The Lady of the Heavens.*
The daughter of a missionary is hailed by African tribesmen as an incarnation of the Zulu sky goddess, and is summoned to the king's court; the rigors of the journey weaken her body and mind and she must be dispatched to the land of the enigmatic Ghost People, who may or may not save her. The Ghost People are fascinating, but so atypical of Haggard's work that he really had no idea what to do with them.

3-163. The Mahatma and the Hare: A Dream Story. Longmans, Green, 1911.
Haggard's involvement late in life with spiritualism and other occult ideas led to a conversion from his earlier love of blood sports; here a hare on the Great White Road, along which the souls of the dead must pass, explains to the dreaming narrator what sufferings are caused by the cruelty of men. Earnest conviction produces a more powerful narrative here than in such ponderous psychic romances as *Love Eternal* (1918).

3-164. The Wanderer's Necklace. Cassell, 1914.
Romance of reincarnation; the narrator recalls his life as an eighth-century Danish mercenary in the Byzantine court, where he attracted the attention of the cruel empress Irene—who overreacted when he cast her aside in favor of his predestined One True Love. Well, she would, wouldn't she? Yet another version of Haggard's favorite plot (see [2-73-2-75]).

Harding, D(olores) C(harlotte) F(rederica) (U.K.).

3-165. The Twinkling of an Eye. Hutchinson, 1945.
A curious timeslip romance, made odder by anachronisms which arise because it was written in 1943 but is set in 1950. A young man, despite his apparently happy marriage, gradually loses his grip on the present in pursuit of a doomed affair with a young woman living in the eighteenth century, with whom he first made contact in childhood. Unusually bleak and more complex than other examples of the species; compare Irwin's *Still She Wished for Company* [3-188].

Harrison, Michael (U.K.), 1907– .
ABOUT: SFE, ESF

3-166. Higher Things. Macdonald, 1945.
A disenchanted bank clerk discovers that he has the ability to levitate; he comes to see his fellow men from a new angle, as it were, and after an unsuccessful attempt to sort out the world's problems in conference with "the Dictator," he determines that he will leave them all to stew in the horrid muddle they have made. A fine sarcastic fantasy in the Wellsian vein.

Hauptmann, Gerhart (Germany), 1862–1946.
ABOUT: CA

3-167. The Island of the Great Mother. Secker, 1925. Tr. by W. and E. Muir of *Die Insel der grossen Mutter*, 1924.
Robinsonade tracking the evolution of society, religion and myth on an island where one hundred women are cast away with a single male juvenile. The author was most famous as a playwright, and wrote several fantasy plays, the best known being *The Sunken Bell* (1896; tr. 1900). His interest in religious mysticism is also evident in *The Heretic of Soana* (1918; tr. 1960).

Hearn, Lafcadio, 1850–1904.
ABOUT: WW, GSF, CA, SMFL, PE, ESF

3-168. Kwaidan. Houghton Mifflin, 1904.
Collection of stories, vignettes and prose poems based on Japanese folklore.The style is deft, the stories designed to be savored for their poignancy and calm fatalism. Reprinted in full, with some other items in the same vein, in *The Selected Writings of Lafcadio Hearn* (Citadel, 1949).

Hecht, Ben, 1893–1964.
ABOUT: GSF, CA, SFE, ESF

3-169. A Book of Miracles. Viking, 1939.
Collection of stories; most are religious fantasies, including two remarkable novellas: "Death of Eleazer," in which an American Nazi who might be a demon incarnate is brought to book by the ghost of a rabbi; and "Remember Thy Creator," in which the archangel Michael is incarnated in order to lead men back to God, but comes to a different understanding of human interests. The latter was presumably inspired by France's *Revolt of the Angels* [3-144]. There are also two satires: "The Adventure of Professor Emmett," in which a disillusioned entomologist is reincarnated as a termite; and "The Heavenly Choir," in which the dead are given a voice by radio. All the named stories are reprinted in *Collected Stories* (1945).

*3-170. Fantazius Mallare. Pascal Covici, 1922.
A brilliant novella describing an artist's scrupulous observation of his own descent into madness—a study handicapped by the fact that he loses his ability to separate delusion and reality. An angry book which rejoices in its own decadence and is openly exultant about the shock which it is supposed to produce in the reader; it sports the most aggressively sarcastic dedication ever penned and wonderfully morbid Beardsleyesque illustrations by Wallace Smith. The sequel, *The Kingdom of Evil* (1924), is set in a phantasmagoric private universe in which fragments of Mallare's shattered psyche appear as characters awaiting the arrival of the god Synthemus, whose advent proves to be not quite what they had anticipated. Deeply felt exercises in sarcastic fantasy, which contrast very markedly with Hecht's carefully commercial and saccharine romance *Miracle in the Rain* (1943).

Heinlein, Robert A(nson), 1907–1988.
ABOUT: GSF, CA, TCA, NE, SMFL, SFE, MF, SFFL, RG, TCSF, ESF, HF

3-171. Waldo and Magic, Inc. Doubleday, 1950.
"Magic, Inc."—first published in *Unknown* as "The Devil Makes the Law" (1942)—is a hard-boiled crime story set in an alternative America where magic works; the hero discovers that the racketeers he is fighting plan a political takeover which must be subverted. Although "Waldo" originally appeared in *Astounding* (1942) and features much futuristic technology, it too is really fantasy, and features as its *deus ex machina* the restoration of magical power to a world which sorely needs it.

[For other works of this author, see the companion guide to horror.]

Hering, Henry A(ugustus) (U.K.), born 1864.
ABOUT: GSF, ESF

3-172. Adventures and Fantasy. Wright & Brown, 1930.
Collection of lightweight tall tales from turn-of-the-century periodicals, including four stories of Psyche & Co. (from *Cassell's Magazine*, 1900–9), whose stock-

in-trade is varied and very remarkable. The humor is laid back by comparison with the hackwork of Ansteyan imitators like Marsh (see [2-121]) and "Andom" (see [3-4]).

Hesse, Herman (Germany), 1877–1962.
ABOUT: CA, SMFL, SFE

3-173. Siddhartha. Peter Owen, 1954. Tr. by Hilda Rosner of *Siddhartha*, 1924.
Philosophical novel which examines the pretensions of Eastern mysticism by telling the story of the eponymous hero's journey to enlightenment. A pastiche religious fantasy, incorporating ideas borrowed from Jung and other modern sources.

*3-174. Steppenwolf. Secker, 1929. Tr. by Basil Creighton of *Der Steppenwolf*, 1927.
Classic study of alienation whose protagonist represents his situation as that of a "wolf of the steppes," essentially incapable of integration into civilized society—but is there hope for him within the "Magic Theatre" of the imagination, where the emotions have a power which transcends vulgar materialistic values?

Hilton, James (U.K.), 1900–1954.
ABOUT: GSF, F, CA, SMFL, SFE, ESF, HF

*3-175. Lost Horizon. Macmillan, 1933.
An ill-assorted group of Westerners are hijacked to a remote region of the Kuen-Lun mountains, where they are brought to the utopian valley of the Blue Moon and the monastery of Shangri-La. It is suggested to the hero that world civilization is sick almost to death, and that he would do better to sit out its self-destruction in this haven of tranquility, where everyone enjoys supernatural longevity—but he unwisely listens to other counsel, and is persuaded to leave. Made into a classic film by Frank Capra. A novel which testifies to the extent of contemporary disillusionment, with hope for a better world having become a fragile, futile dream of seclusion. Contrast Frankau's *Seeds of Enchantment* [3-146].

Hinton, C(harles) H(oward) (U.K.), 1853–1907.
ABOUT: SFE, ESF

3-176. An Episode of Flatland; or How the Plane Folk Discovered the Third Dimension. Swan Sonnenschein, 1907.
An account of life and mores in the two-dimensional world of Unæa, including a description of the world at war. A combination of thought-experiment and social satire rather different from Abbott's classic *Flatland* (1884), featuring a differently shaped world and much more homely characters—which makes the action all the more bizarre.

Hobson, Harold (U.K.), 1891–1973.
3-177. The Devil in Woodford Wells. Longmans, 1946.
The hero is led by his fascination with early cricket matches to investigate the

puzzling circumstances surrounding a match played in 1808, when a young man's promising career was nipped in the bud. Did the devil himself play an inning in that match? And what has Enoch Soames to do with it? A witty and lively fantasy with calculated echoes of Beerbohm.

Hodgson, William Hope (U.K.), 1877–1918.
ABOUT: WW, GSF, SFW, F, CA, NE, H, SMFL, SFE, RG, TCSF, PE, ESF, FL, HF

*3-178. The Night Land. Eveleigh Nash, 1912.
The narrator, heartbroken by the loss of his beloved, dreams of the very far future, when he and she can be reunited—but not without extreme difficulty, because the sun is extinct and the pyramid-citadels in which people live are besieged by a great array of monstrous forces of destruction. The hero's future self must cross this nightmarish landscape in order to rescue his inamorata when disaster strikes the pyramid where she lives. The peculiar mock-archaic style which the author uses as a distancing device irritates many readers, but even its detractors concede that as a visionary phantasmagoria it is without parallel. The edition of 1921 is abridged, and a very drastic abridgment (reducing a very long novel to a novelette) was issued in the U.S. to protect American copyright, in *Poems and The Dream of X* (1912). This version was reprinted as *The Dream of X* (Grant, 1977).

[For other works of this author, see the companion guide to horror.]

Houghton, Claude (pseud. of Claude Houghton Oldfield) (U.K.), 1889–1961.
ABOUT: GSF, SFE

3-179. Julian Grant Loses His Way. Heinemann, 1933.
Posthumous fantasy in which a man must re-examine his life in order to find out how a promising and able youth was gradually transformed into a callous and predatory creature; a suitably decadent Hell is ready for him, which he might avoid if he can take advice from an artistic guardian angel. A subtle work which uses the plight of an exemplary individual to offer a ruthlessly scathing analysis of the condition of England between the wars; its desperate pessimism was to reach a more frenetic level in Houghton's scientific romance *This Was Ivor Trent* (1935).

Housman, Laurence (U.K.), 1865–1959.
ABOUT: WW, GSF, CA, SFE, ESF, HF

3-180. Ironical Tales. Cape, 1926.
Mixed collection including allegories, fabular *contes philosophiques* and parodies. Notable items include the religious fantasy "The Real Temptation of St. Anthony," which carries on arguments begun in [2-84]; and "Lady into George Fox," a parody of [3-152]. Housman subsequently published two more similarly mixed collections, *What Next?* (1938) and *Strange Ends and Discoveries* (1948), but never recovered the intensity of his earlier work.

Howard, Robert E(rvin), 1906–1936.
ABOUT: WW, GSF, SFW, F, CA, SMFL, SFE, MF, RG, PE, ESF, HF

3-181. Bran Mak Morn. Dell, 1969.
Collection of stories set in a remote area of British history when the neolithic
Picts, driven to near extinction by more sophisticated Celtic invaders, survive in
isolated pockets until Roman times; Howard, inevitably (see [3-182]), is on the
side of the Picts, whose last king is Bran Mak Morn. Includes the violent and
angry revenge-fantasy "Worms of the Earth" (1932), which became the title story
of a slightly abridged reprint (Grant, 1974).

*3-182. Conan the Conqueror. Gnome Press, 1950.
The first of several volumes reprinting from *Weird Tales* the adventures of the
mighty warrior Conan in the prehistoric "Hyborian Age," whose budding civilization was obliterated by the last ice age. This novel-length story, originally "The
Hour of the Dragon" (1935–36), is one of the last in terms of the internal chronology of the series, which features Conan as king of Aquilonia threatened by rebels,
invaders and an evil revenant wizard. *The Sword of Conan* (1952) consists of four
stories, including the novellas "The People of the Black Circle" (1934) and "Red
Nails" (1936); *The Coming of Conan* (1953) has two stories about an earlier phase
of the imaginary history starring King Kull—"The Shadow Kingdom" (1929) and
"The Mirrors of Tuzun Thune" (1929)—plus several Conan stories, including
"Queen of the Black Coast" (1934) and two which had been edited from Howard
manuscripts by L. Sprague de Camp. *King Conan* (1953), which included the first
published Conan story, "The Phoenix on the Sword" (1932); and *Conan the
Barbarian* (1954), including the marvelously extravagant "A Witch Shall Be Born"
(1934), completed the job of reprinting the stories which had appeared in *Weird
Tales*. The publisher later added to the series *The Return of Conan* (1957), a
pastiche written by Björn Nyberg and edited by de Camp.

A revival of interest in Howard (and Conan in particular) in the 1960s
resulted in the series being re-edited and expanded by numerous new exercises in
pastiche by de Camp and Lin Carter (most of the new stories were based on
fragments left by Howard). Lancer published eleven volumes of a projected
twelve-volume series, which was subsequently completed and reprinted by Ace.
The twelve volumes, in order of their internal chronology, are: *Conan* (1967);
Conan of Cimmeria (1969); *Conan the Freebooter* (1968); *Conan the Wanderer*
(1968); *Conan the Adventurer* (1966); *Conan the Buccaneer* (1971); *Conan the
Warrior* (1967); *Conan the Usurper* (1967); *Conan the Conqueror* (1967); *Conan
the Avenger* (1968); *Conan of Aquilonia* (1977); and *Conan of the Isles* (1968).
Also associated with this series is *King Kull* (1967), featuring tales mostly written
by Lin Carter around Howard fragments. In the great tradition of modern literary
hero-myths, Conan's career has been further extended in a series of pastiches by
other hands.

Conan has become established as an archetypal hero of the "sword-and-
sorcery" subgenre. Unsophisticated even by the standards of his own hypothetical
time, he must pit his inexhaustible strength and courage against the wiles of more
cultured men and the magical armory of ill-wishing wizards; his resources—in
defiance of all logic—are always adequate. Like all superhero fantasies, this one

appeals to readers (especially adolescent males) who feel that they are objects of scarcely veiled contempt in a world with whose complications they cannot cope. Howard, like all great writers of this stripe, proves that nothing succeeds like excess, and is never in the least inhibited about going way over the top. The writers of the many pastiches usually suffer the handicap of their own relative literary sophistication, and cannot capture the quasi-paranoid fervor which Howard built up in projecting himself into his work, the best examples of which were presumably written in a white heat of imaginative intensity.

[For other works of this author, see the companion guide to horror.]

Hubbard, L(afayette) Ron, 1911–1986.
ABOUT: WW, GSF, F, CA, NE, SMFL, SFE, TCSF, ESF

3-183. Death's Deputy. Fantasy Publishing Co., 1948.
Short novel from *Unknown* (1940) whose hero is posthumously recruited to the cause of personified Destruction, and returned to Earth so that he can precipitate minor disasters wherever he goes—a job which he does not relish and from which he eventually resigns. There is no truth to the rumor that Hubbard died in 1948 but was sent back to Earth in order to invent Scientology.

3-184. Slaves of Sleep. Shasta, 1948.
Swashbuckling adventure from *Unknown* (1939), in which the world of the *Arabian Nights* is the one our minds visit while we sleep; ordinarily we forget all about it when we wake, but the hero of the story is cursed with "eternal wakefulness," so his two selves come into contact with one another—ultimately to their mutual benefit. An intriguing premise, somewhat let down by slapdash development; a sequel, "Masters of Sleep," appeared in *Fantastic Adventures* in 1950, but its plot is dominated and ultimately stifled by Hubbard's fulminations against "orthodox" (i.e., non-Dianetic) psychiatry. Other slapdash *Arabian Nights*-inspired fantasies by Hubbard are "The Ultimate Adventure" (*Unknown*, 1939; in *Fear and The Ultimate Adventure*, 1970) and "The Case of the Friendly Corpse" (*Unknown*, 1941).

*3-185. Typewriter in the Sky; Fear. Gnome Press, 1951.
In "Typewriter in the Sky" (*Unknown*, 1940) a hack writer models the villain of a pirate potboiler on a friend, who finds himself trapped within the world of the novel, struggling to avoid the fate which is inevitably reserved for villains in routinized adventure stories. Colorful and very funny, with a sharp punchline; one of the classic *Unknown* fantasies.

[For other works of this author, see the companion guide to horror.]

Hudson, W(illiam) H(enry) (U.K.), 1841–1922.
ABOUT: CA, SMFL, SFE, ESF, HF

*3-186. Green Mansions. Duckworth, 1904.
A young Venezuelan travels into the interior and is adopted by Indian tribesmen

who hope that he will kill a "demon" who interferes with their hunting—but the "demon" is a girl who has a magical rapport with nature, and he eventually joins forces with her in trying to find the mysterious homeland where her people live. Alas, the land is lost—and so, ultimately, is she. A powerful tragedy which turns a Gautieresque account of the impossibility of ideal love into an allegory of man's supposed alienation from the natural world.

Hyne, C(harles) J(ohn) Cutcliffe (U.K.), 1866–1944.
ABOUT: WW, GSF, CA, SMFL, SFE, TCSF, ESF, HF

3-187. The Lost Continent. Hutchinson, 1900.
Haggardesque adventure story about the destruction of Atlantis. The hero (Deucalion, as in the Greek version of the Deluge myth) is recalled from Yucatán by a new empress who has set herself up as a goddess; he resists her attempts to seduce him and then must fight to save his true love from her vengeance. Hyne borrows the version of the Atlantis myth recently poplarized by Ignatius Donnelly, but is uninterested in pursuing its pseudohistorical aspects; he just wants to tell an exciting story, and succeeds.

Irwin, Margaret (U.K.), 1889–1967.
ABOUT: WW, GSF, CA, SMFL, PE, ESF

*3-188. Still She Wished for Company. Heinemann, 1924. U.S. title: *Who Will Remember.*
A breach in time permits the experiences of two young women living in the 1770s and 1920s to become entangled and interwoven; both are romantically fixated upon the brother of the eighteenth-century girl, whose experiments in occultism are partly responsible for the temporal breakdown. Their fixation is, in its way, as much a defiance of nature as the temporal link and must somehow be "healed." A subtle but deeply felt story; the most intriguing example of the "timeslip romance" subgenre.

*3-189. These Mortals. Heinemann, 1925.
The sorcerer Aldebaran has withdrawn from intercourse with mortal men, but his daughter Melusine is very curious about them; in an inversion of the theme of *The Tempest*, she leaves her island to find their "brave new world": a fairy tale kingdom where she becomes involved in the social and emotional intrigues of the court and falls in love with a prisoner in a dungeon. But her generosity to the vain and hypocritical humans eventually leaves her impoverished and miserable, and she must fight fiercely for her own redemption. A brilliant story developing in fabular form a harsh view of the human existential predicament; it draws upon the same emotional currents as Stella Benson's much more sentimental *Living Alone* [3-29] and anticipates Angela Carter's allegories of female sexuality hampered in its development by a male-dominated social context [4A-63–4A-66]. A neglected classic.

[For other works of this author, see the companion guide to horror.]

Jacks, L(awrence) P(earsall) (U.K.), 1860–1955.
ABOUT: GSF, CA, ESF

3-190. All Men Are Ghosts. Williams & Norgate, 1913.
Collection of six curious *contes philosophiques* in which unoriginal themes (including posthumous fantasy, animal reincarnation, parallel worlds each of whose inhabitants has paranormal experience of the other) are set out in a prolix manner which hovers uneasily between the jokily playful and the earnestly didactic. It follows the earlier *Among the Idolmakers* (1912), which is equally eccentric but mostly avoids fantasy motifs. The contents of both collections were reprinted in the six-volume *Writings by L. P. Jacks* (1916–17) along with other collections of stories and one of essays, all highly idiosyncratic, but the reprint volume entitled *All Men Are Ghosts* contains only four stories, one of the others being displaced into the volume called *Among the Idolmakers*, which similarly has only four of the eight stories contained in the original collection of that title, the remaining items being displaced into earlier volumes. Several stories are recombined yet again in *The Magic Formula and Other Stories* (1927).

Jaeger, C(yril) K(arel) (U.K.), 1912–   .
ABOUT: CA, ESF

3-191. The Man in the Top Hat. Grey Walls, 1949.
Phantasmagoric comic fantasy in which an author is dragged into a wild adventure by the Golden Opportunity Man—the devil operating as a recruiter of door-to-door salesmen. Utterly bizarre and replete with sardonic literary allusions.

James, M(ontague) R(hodes) (U.K.), 1862–1936.
ABOUT: WW, GSF, SFW, CA, H, SMFL, PE, ESF

3-192. The Five Jars. Edward Arnold, 1922.
Epistolary story whose narrator uses magical means to liberate five extra senses which allow him to perceive the supernatural world surrounding the one which our ordinary senses reveal; he becomes vulnerable to the forces of evil but resists them with the aid of the fairies. A pleasant allegory of the power of imagination, composed—after the fashion of Carroll's *Alice* books [2-23]—to amuse a young friend.

    [For other works of this author, see the companion guide to horror.]

Jarry, Alfred (France), 1873–1907.
ABOUT: CA, SMFL

***3-193. The Supermale.** Cape, 1968. Tr. by Barbara Wright of *Le Sûrmale, roman moderne*, 1902.
Surreal novella whose hero (a clandestine superman) demonstrates his prowess by intruding upon a race between an express train and a team of bicyclists fed on a new Perpetual Motion Food, and by breaking the legendary world lovemaking record; but these exploits break his cover and lead, ironically, to his destruction in

the grip of an impassioned machine. A Rabelaisian black comedy; a key work of absurdist fantasy.

Jones, Guy and Constance.
ABOUT: GSF, ESF

3-194. Peabody's Mermaid. Random House, 1946.
During World War II the convalescent hero catches a mermaid and becomes fascinated by her; his wife suspects him of having an affair, the police wonder whether he is harboring an illegal alien, and the whole thing might be a delusion. A sentimental comedy closely comparable with Walker's *Loona* [3-354].

Joyce, Michael (U.K.).
ABOUT: GSF

3-195. Peregrine Pieram. John Murray, 1936.
Novella about an author whose stories persist in coming true—a talent which he uses opportunistically to control reality until he becomes disenchanted with the self-corruption to which this power has led him. Delicately ironic, with an appropriately sentimental conclusion.

Karinthy, Frigyes (Hungary), 1888–1938.
ABOUT: SMFL, SFE, ESF

3-196. Voyage to Faremido and Capillaria. Corvina, 1965. Tr. by Paul Tabori of *Utazás Faremidóba*, 1916, and *Capillaria*, 1922.
Two satirical novellas featuring Lemuel Gulliver. In the first he encounters a machine society whose language consists of musical notes and whose inhabitants find the idea of organic life rather disgusting; in the second he studies the life of a submarine civilization whose sexual politics are based in a biology radically different from ours. Brilliant exercises in Swiftian misanthropy on the border of fantasy and SF.

Keller, David H(enry), 1880–1966.
ABOUT: WW, GSF, SMFL, SFE, TCSF, PE, ESF

3-197. The Devil and the Doctor. Simon & Schuster, 1940.
Fix-up of two sentimental novellas in which a retired M.D., who suspects that Christian mythology offers a very biased account of Jehovah's war with Lucifer, yearns to build a stone fence around his property; he is privileged to hear the devil's side of the story and benefits from that worthy's kindly patronage. An amiable American counterpart to such works as France's *Revolt of the Angels* [3-144] and Gerhardi and Lunn's *Memoirs of Satan* [3-154].

3-198. The Homunculus. Prime Press, 1949.
A male chauvinist doctor attempts to demonstrate the redundancy of the human female by following Paracelsus's recipe for producing a homunculus. Various enemies try to interfere, but he comes under the protection of Pan and Lilith, here

represented as twins, who join his household and help bring the project to fruition. A highly eccentric exercise in revisionist mythology, in the same charmingly self-indulgent vein as [3-197].

[For other works of this author, see the companion guide to horror.]

Kellett, E(rnest) E(dward) (U.K.), 1864–1950.
ABOUT: GSF

3-199. A Corner in Sleep and Other Impossibilities. Jarrolds, 1900.
Collection of absurd fantasies featuring some comic ghost stories and some very odd magic potions, as well as a diabolically inspired machine for converting prose into poetry. Similar in spirit to the works of John Kendrick Bangs (see [2-13]) but executed with greater dexterity and defter wit.

Kerby, Susan Alice (pseud. of Alice Elizabeth Burton) (U.K.), 1908– .
ABOUT: GSF, CA

3-200. Miss Carter and the Ifrit. Hutchinson, 1945.
Ansteyan fantasy in which an overenthusiastic ifrit becomes the slave of an English spinster during the hard years of World War II; he helps to rebuild her flagging morale and to rekindle an old love affair. He learns a little too. Obviously inspired by *The Brass Bottle* [3-5], but more restrained and sentimental; compare also Dick's *The Ghost and Mrs. Muir* [3-112].

3-201. Mr. Kronion. Werner Laurie, 1949.
Life in an Oxfordshire village is much enlivened by an enigmatic visitor who turns out to be a classical deity. Retirement from active service as an object of worship has mellowed him, and the sexual appetites which once dominated his visits to the world of men are now constrained by urbane sophistication. A pleasant mixture of comedy and sentimentality with a little more depth than [3-200].

Kipling, Rudyard (U.K.), 1865–1936.
ABOUT: WW, GSF, SFW, CA, NE, SMFL, SFE, RG, TCSF, PE, ESF, HF

3-202. Just So Stories. Macmillan, 1902.
Classic collection of children's stories and verses offering fanciful fabular explanations of such puzzles as "How the Leopard Got His Spots" and "How the Camel Got His Hump," as well as an unlikely account of "How the Alphabet Was Made" and the moral tales of "The Elephant's Child" and "The Cat That Walked by Himself." A worthy contribution to the "nonsense" tradition of Carroll (see [2-23–2-24]) and Lear (see [2-104]), despite being full of good sense.

3-203. Puck of Pook's Hill. Macmillan, 1906.
First of two episodic works in which the eponymous sprite befriends two children and introduces them by way of stories told by spirits to the fascinations of English

folklore and history; the second is *Rewards and Fairies* (1910). Some of the stories draw subtle links between the resilience of the indigenous peasantry under Roman occupation and the recalcitrance of Indian natives under British rule.

Knight, Eric (U.K.), 1897–1943.
ABOUT: GSF, CA, ESF

3-204. Sam Small Flies Again. Harper, 1942. U.S. title: *The Flying Yorkshireman.*
Collection of tall stories featuring the archetypally pugnacious comic Yorkshireman Sam Small. The novella "The Flying Yorkshireman" (1938; used the same year as the title story of an anthology) tells of his discovery, while visiting America, that he can fly. The stories have something in common with Darlington's fantasies about cockney Alf [3-96], but are written with a more satirical eye and a surer grasp of regional idiosyncrasies.

Knittel, John (Switzerland), 1891–1970.
ABOUT: CA

3-205. Nile Gold. Hutchinson, 1929.
An archaeologist obsessed with Queen Nitocris discovers her tomb. There follows a long hallucinatory sequence in which he believes himself to be harboring the spirit of her husband, Mernere; Nitocris is restored to life and they flee, pursued by an enigmatic villain in whom resides the spirit of Menna, murderer of Mernere. Intense and phantasmagoric; the outstanding work of the Egyptian revenant subgenre.

Knowles, Vernon (Australia), 1899–1968.
ABOUT: WW, GSF, SMFL, ESF

3-206. The Street of Queer Houses and Other Tales. Wells Gardner, Darton, 1925. The U.S. collection *The Street of Queer Houses and Other Stories*, 1924, has different but overlapping contents.
The first of three collections of quaint stories, which are mostly quirky fables with weak allegorical pretensions; the title novella features an oddly designed street which attracts eccentrics. It was followed by *Here and Otherwhere* (1926), which includes "The Shop in the Off-Street" and the novella "A Set of Chinese Boxes"; and *Silver Nutmegs* (1927), which has the novella "The Ladder" (published separately, 1929), in which the population of a village is gradually seduced into performing the Indian rope trick by climbing a rope ladder, and "The Gong of Transportation." Stories selected from the latter two collections were combined with some new material in *Two and Two Make Five* (1935). Knowles's work is in the tradition of Richard Garnett (see [2-63]), and has affinities with the work of Lord Dunsany (see [3-123]) and Donald Corley (see [3-88]), but he affects a more naïve and relaxed style than any of these. His best stories are amusing literary confections.

Kummer, Frederic Arnold, 1873–1943.
ABOUT: GSF

3-207. Ladies in Hades; A Story of Hell's Smart Set. Sears, 1928.
Eve sets up a women's club in Hell and its members (Hell's Belles!) reflect upon their tactics in the war of the sexes; when the club's minutes are stolen, Satan fears that their publication on Earth might prove a setback to his cause. Followed by *Gentlemen in Hades; the Story of a Damned Debutante* (1930), in which a new arrival in Hell demonstrates the indomitability of modern sex appeal by vamping her way to the very top. A slick updating of Bangs's infernal fantasies [2-12]; compare the first volume also to Viereck's *Gloria* [3-349].

Kuttner, Henry, 1915–1958.
ABOUT: WW, GSF, SFW, F, CA, TCA, NE, H, SMFL, SFE, SFFL, RG, TCSF, PE, ESF, FL, HF

3-208. The Dark World. Ace, 1965.
Novel first published in *Startling Stories* in 1946; one of a series of Merrittesque stories written for that magazine by Kuttner in collaboration with his wife, C. L. Moore (who probably wrote the greater part of this one). Basically a pastiche of *Dwellers in the Mirage* [3-242] it tells the story of a man suddenly displaced into the parallel Secondary World where he really belongs and in the determination of whose fate he must play the crucial role. "Lands of the Earthquake" (1947); *The Mask of Circe* (1948; in book form 1975); "The Portal in the Picture" (1949; in book form as *Beyond Earth's Gates* by Lewis Padgett); and *The Well of the Worlds* (1952; reprinted as a Galaxy Novel in 1953 under the Padgett pseudonym) are other exercises in the same vein, science fictionalized to varying degrees. *The Dark World* inspired a pastiche of its own in Marion Zimmer Bradley's *Falcons of Narabedla* (1957; in book form 1964) and also prefigures in its basic pattern the Amber novels of Roger Zelazny [4A-276]; it might be reckoned a key example of the colorful pulp hybrid sometimes called "science fantasy," which borrows a gloss of SF jargon to enhance the plausibility of emotionally attractive fantasy themes.

Lambourne, John (U.K.), born 1893.
ABOUT: CA

3-209. The Kingdom That Was. Murray, 1931.
A hunter takes a nap in the African bush and wakes in a strange prehistoric realm where the animals talk. The true ruler of this land, the Elephant, has unwisely entrusted its administration to the vicious leopard; the hero seems certain to become a victim of this reign of terror unless the friends he has made can save him. *The Second Leopard* (1932) is a sequel. A parable which "explains"—but refuses to excuse—man's cruelty to animals. Has links with Kipling's Mowgli stories [2-100], and with his *Just So Stories* [3-202]; compare also Gunn's *Green Isle of the Great Deep* [3-161].

Lawrence, D(avid) H(erbert) (U.K.), 1885–1930.
ABOUT: CA, SMFL, ESF

3-210. The Woman Who Rode Away and Other Stories. Secker, 1928.
Collection of stories; the title novelette is a curious fantasy whose female protagonist encounters mysterious Amerindians who are in touch with ancient powers of
darkness, and can therefore resist the oppressions of white civilization; the sexual
symbolism of the story's climax is grotesque.

Leiber, Fritz, 1910– .
ABOUT: WW, GSF, SFW, F, CA, TCA, NE, H, SMFL, SFE, MF,
SFFL, RG, TCSF, PE, ESF, FL, HF

*3-211. Two Sought Adventure. Gnome Press, 1957.
Collection of early tales in the extensive series featuring Fafhrd and the Grey
Mouser (see [4A-165]), including all those initially published in *Unknown* but
not the earliest written, the brilliant novella *Adept's Gambit*, which first appeared in *Night's Black Agents* [H3-126]. The features which were ultimately to
make this the finest of all sword-and-sorcery series are evident in embryo here:
exuberance, cleverness and wit, plus an ability to shift seamlessly into a quasi-
allegorical mode, here shown to best effect in "The Bleak Shore" (1940). In the
definitive set of the series stories these items are reprinted in volume 2, *Swords
against Death* (1970).

[For other works of this author, see the companion guide to horror.]

Lernet-Holenia, Alexander (Austria), 1898?–1976.
ABOUT: CA, SMFL, ESF

3-212. Count Luna: Two Tales of the Real and Unreal. Criterion, 1956. Tr. by
Jane B. Greene of *Baron Bagge*, 1936, and by Richard and Clara Winston of *Graf
Luna*, 1955.
Two novellas. "Count Luna" is a phantasmagoric tale of a man haunted by
another whom he had failed to save from a concentration camp; "Baron Bagge" is
the story of a cavalry officer involved in a suicidal attack in World War I who
loses contact with the reality of his situation and is lost in a dream built upon
foundations which he laid in his reckless love life. The latter has significant
connections with the subgenre of posthumous fantasies.

Lewis, C(live) S(taples) (U.K.), 1898–1963.
ABOUT: GSF, SFW, CA, NE, SMFL, SFE, RG, TCSF, ESF, FL, HF

3-213. The Great Divorce. Geoffrey Bles, 1945.
Novella; an exercise in Christian apologetics which boldly attempts to describe
Heaven as well as providing moral advice on how to get there. A busload of visiting
tourists, who have come from the slums of Hell, mostly prove to be incapable of
adapting. Closer in spirit to the apologetic fantasies of Chesterton [3-77] than such
posthumous fantasies as Mrs. Oliphant's [2-135], but less energetic.

3-214. Out of the Silent Planet. John Lane, 1938.
Famous novel in which Lewis uses science fiction (as he was later to use children's fantasy in the Narnia books [4B-101]) as a vehicle for constructing a mythology which would embody the same moral insights as the Christian mythos. An academic, Ransom, is kidnapped and taken to Mars by two adventurers, one of whom is the philosophical biologist Weston (a parodic amalgam of H. G. Wells and J. B. S. Haldane). Mars is a utopia, its people obedient to benevolent ruling spirits—unlike Earth, which (as in Marie Corelli's work [2-32]) is a horrid freak where evil reigns. In *Perelandra* (1943) Ransom must oppose Weston again, this time on Venus, where the story of Adam and Eve is being replayed; that the book was written during World War II is obvious in Ransom's acceptance of his moral duty to destroy the evil enemy. *That Hideous Strength* (1945) completes the trilogy—rather inaptly, in that it is all too obviously (and inexpertly) modeled on the fantasies of Charles Williams [3-373–3-379]. Ransom is here transformed into a magus figure and Merlin is drafted into the holy war in which Good (myth) must make a crucial stand against Evil (science).

3-215. The Screwtape Letters. Geoffrey Bles, 1942.
An ingenious exercise in Christian apologetics which takes the form of letters of advice written by the wily old devil Screwtape to his inexperienced nephew Wormwood, whose command of the tactics of temptation leaves much to be desired. Lewis cleverly manages to give his central character all the wit and charm of John Collier's urbanely malevolent devils (see [3-83]) without actually making the reader too sympathetic to his cause.

*3-216. Till We Have Faces. Geoffrey Bles, 1956.
Classical fantasy written around the myth of Cupid and Psyche; Psyche's ugly sister Orual, now queen of Glome, tells the story of her life. She is bitterly resentful of the way that she has been mistreated by the gods, but when she actually confronts a god (whose face is hidden, as Cupid's was from Psyche until she tragically sought to see it), conscience forces her to reappraise her indictment and to see herself more clearly. A brilliant and subtle moral fantasy, less clumsy in construction and implication than Lewis's other allegories, yet retaining the same sincerity and depth of feeling.

Lewis, Wyndham (U.K.), 1884–1957.
ABOUT: CA, SMFL, ESF

3-217. The Childermass. Chatto & Windus, 1928.
The first part of a bizarre modern (and conspicuously modernist) *Divine Comedy* collectively entitled *The Human Age*; the other two published parts are *Monstre Gai* and *Malign Fiesta* (both 1955). In a wasteland outside the gates of the Magnetic City, the "emigrant mass" of humankind awaits examination by the Bailiff, whom they presume to be the guardian of paradise; Pullman and the appalling Sattersthwaite (who was once his servant underclassman) occupy themselves in interminable and linguistically pyrotechnic debates about the state of contemporary civilization and its true legislators. In the second volume they find, once inside, that the Magnetic City is certainly not Heaven, and are further

involved with the enigmatic Bailiff—but there is even worse to come in the third, where they become embroiled in the ongoing war between God's armies and the fallen angels. A fourth section, paralleling the *Paradiso* and called *The Trial of Man*, was planned but never written; some fragments outlining its intended contents are appended to part three.

Lindsay, David (U.K.), 1876–1945.
ABOUT: WW, GSF, SFW, F, CA, NE, H, SMFL, SFE, RG, TCSF, ESF, FL, HF

*3-218. Devil's Tor. Putnam, 1932.
The heroine's male cousin returns to Dartmoor from Tibet with a magical object which is half of a powerful talisman. The other half turns out to be nearby, contained in the tomb of the being who was worshipped in the ancient past as the Earth Mother; bringing the two together will precipitate an apocalyptic return of the goddess. Other men arrive in search of the talisman and the heroine must play the crucial role in determining whether the two halves of the talisman will be reunited—and, ultimately, in what will follow. Marvelously atmospheric and admirably conscientious in its design of a hypothetical mythology and the metaphysics to go with it.

*3-219. The Haunted Woman. Methuen, 1922.
A timeslipped stairway materializes occasionally in a haunted house, giving access to rooms in the Saxon edifice which once stood there. Here people may be briefly liberated from the burden of repressions and constraints to which centuries of civilization have subjected human consciousness. The owner of the house and the niece of a woman who might buy it discover there that they love one another, but can they bring this love back with them into the modern world, adapting it to the degraded and derelict species of experience which ordinary life permits? An extraordinary metaphysical fantasy, whose great intensity of feeling is not lessened by its painstaking attention to matters of theory.

3-220. The Violet Apple and The Witch. Chicago Review Press, 1975.
A complete novel and a fragment of another which Lindsay left unfinished. *The Violet Apple* is an underappreciated work which tells the story of two engaged couples, and the destruction of their relationships when the male half of one couple and the female half of the other eat the fruit of a tiny tree grown from a seed reportedly carried from the Garden of Eden; like the timeslip in [3-219], this allows them a dramatic expansion of consciousness and a brief enjoyment of authentic experience. Afterward, there is no way that they can return to the life which had been shaped for them by their repressed and narrowed minds—but what possible place is there for them in the scheme of things? "The Witch" was apparently to have been a visionary novel in the vein of [3-221], incorporating some of the metaphysical theories which Lindsay had developed in his intervening works; the fragment is sufficiently intriguing to sharpen one's regret that it was never completed.

*3-221. A Voyage to Arcturus. Methuen, 1920.
Maskull is taken by Krag and Nightspore to Tormance, supposedly a planet of

Arcturus. There he undergoes a series of educative experiences, involving him in many encounters with strange beings, transformations of his own person and much suffering. He is perpetually under threat as he tries to understand the metaphysics of this world and the creative force of Shaping, whose relationship with the key figures of Crystalman and Surtur is a riddle to be solved. Some of the imagery is borrowed from Norse mythology (Surtur and Muspel) but the metaphysics which is gradually elaborated is basically a transformed evolutionary theory which applies a harsh metaphorical Darwinism to the business of personal intellectual development. A masterpiece, unparalleled in its graphic imagery and in its ambition.

Linklater, Eric (U.K.), 1899–1974.
ABOUT: GSF, CA, ESF, FL

3-222. God Likes Them Plain. Cape, 1935.
Collection of stories including several light and slightly risqué fantasies. The title story features a partial personality exchange between a queen and a storyteller; in "The Abominable Imprecation" an enterprising dragonslayer wins his princess, but must face the problem of a sex-changing curse. More confections in the same vein can be found in *Sealskin Trousers* (1947). Linklater wrote several fantasy plays, mostly fantasies of the afterlife which engage characters from various phases of history in satirical conversations much more serious in their import than those in the infernal comedies of Bangs [2-12] and Kummer [3-207]; the most notable examples are *The Cornerstones* (1942) and *Crisis in Heaven* (1944).

London, Jack, 1876–1916.
ABOUT: WW, GSF, CA, TCA, NE, SFE, TCSF, ESF

3-223. The Star Rover. Macmillan, 1915. U.K. title: *The Jacket.*
A prisoner in an American jail is tortured by confinement in a painful straitjacket, and learns to endure this by dissociating his personality from his body and experiencing previous incarnations. An attempted overview of the human condition which has affinities with Henri Barbusse's *Chains* (1925), though it is rather crudely executed by comparison.

Louÿs, Pierre (France), 1870–1925.
ABOUT: CA, SMFL

3-224. The Adventures of King Pausole. Pierre Louÿs Society, 1926. Tr. by Mitchell S. Buck of *Les Aventures du roi Pausole,* 1901.
Rabelaisian fantasy in which the monarch of the Cokaygnian land of Tryphême and his irreverent servant Giguelillot set out in pursuit of the king's daughter, who has eloped with an actor (who is, in fact, a girl in disguise); meanwhile, the attempts of the steward Taxis to keep order in the king's harem are thrown into confusion. Very stylish and very funny, with a neatly satirical moral at the end.

Lovecraft, H(oward) P(hillips), 1890–1937.
ABOUT: WW, GSF, SFW, F, CA, NE, H, SMFL, SFE, RG, TCSF, PE, ESF, FL, HF

3-225. The Dream-Quest of Unknown Kadath. Shroud, 1955.
Visionary fantasy written in 1926 and first published in 1943. Randolph Carter (used as protagonist in several Lovecraft stories) tours a fantasy world whose landscapes bring him into contact with other Lovecraftian places and persons, including a few borrowed from the Cthulhu Mythos. Not a horror story and not a Dunsanian fantasy either, it is perhaps better regarded as an extended exercise in whimsical self-examination. As a story it is flaccid, but its imagery is not without charm. Among the fantasies whose locations are borrowed are "The Cats of Ulthar" (1920) and "Celephais" (1922). Other dream fantasies featuring Carter are "The Silver Key" (1929) and "Through the Gates of the Silver Key" (1934; written in collaboration with E. Hoffman Price), but the most notable of Lovecraft's non-horrific fantasies is "The Quest of Iranon" (1935).

[For other works of this author, see the companion guide to horror.]

Lovelace, Delos W(heeler), 1894–1967.
ABOUT: CA

3-226. King Kong. Grosset & Dunlap, 1932.
Novelization of the famous film, "conceived by Edgar Wallace and Merian C. Cooper." The ultimate macho male beats up various saurians to save his tiny inamorata, rebels against his subsequent exhibition as a freak and is shot down while signaling his incomprehension of civilized ways from the top of the Empire State Building. It might have been Edgar Wallace's most interesting book, if only he had lived to write it.

McCarthy, Justin Huntly (U.K.), 1860–1936.
ABOUT: GSF

3-227. The Dryad. Methuen, 1905.
Medieval romance set at the end of the thirteenth century, when Greece is under French rule. The magical daughter of a dryad, given immortality by Zeus, still lives in the Eleusinian wood; she falls in love with a young prince, but has to pose as a man and defeat him in a tournament in order to reclaim him from the sinister domination of a rival enchantress. Less mannered than William Morris's fantasies [2-124–2-128]; the heroine provides a virtuous counterpart to the masquerader in Bowen's *Black Magic* [H3-32].

Machen, Arthur (U.K.), 1863–1947.
ABOUT: WW, GSF, SFW, CA, H, SMFL, SFE, RG, PE, ESF, HF

3-228. The Bowmen and Other Legends of the War. Simpkin, Marshall, Hamilton, Kent, 1915.
Pamphlet reprinting "The Bowmen" (1914) and explaining how the Angels of Mons became a piece of "instant folklore" following newspaper publication of

Machen's brief story about how the longbowmen of ancient England provided cover for the retreating British forces at Mons. The war news was so appalling (despite the sanitizing efforts of the censors) that morale at home was at an all-time low, and the avidity with which people seized upon the rumor of a miracle was astonishing. Also included are three other vignettes in the same vein. Pastiches of "The Bowmen" by other hands include the title story of E. B. Osborn's *The Maid with Wings* (1917).

*3-229. The Hill of Dreams. Grant Richards, 1907.
An unsuccessful author is plagued by a supernatural sensitivity which makes modern life unbearable to him. Occult training expands this consciousness, transforming the world into an image of the glorious past when Britain was part of the Roman Empire, but such a dramatic withdrawal from the actual world can have only one end. The ultimate novel of escapism, obviously deeply felt and written with considerable artistry. Its themes are partially recapitulated in *The Secret Glory* (1922), which offers an account of the inspirational escapist imagination domesticated and controlled—and which is in consequence a lackluster work, vitiated by the injection of common sense. *The Hill of Dreams* celebrates, by contrast, the ultimate triumph of sensibility over sense and the suicidal splendor of overdosing on fantasy.

[For other works of this author, see the companion guide to horror.]

McKenna, Stephen (U.K.), 1888–1967.
ABOUT: GSF, CA

3-230. The Oldest God. Thornton Butterworth, 1926.
A Christmas country house party is dominated by a discussion of the problem of evil and the efforts of the Christian religion to combat it; in the meantime the characters face moral dilemmas of their own. All is dreadfully complicated by the interventions of Pan, who is present incognito. Cleverly ironic.

Mann, Thomas (Germany), 1875–1955.
ABOUT: CA, SMFL

3-231. The Transposed Heads: A Legend of India. Knopf, 1941. Tr. by H. T. Lowe-Porter of *Die vertauschten Köpfe*, 1940.
Two friends beloved by the same woman are driven by their plight to behead themselves, but the goddess Kali resurrects them; unfortunately, the woman replaces the heads on the wrong bodies, setting off a chain of circumstances which leads inexorably to a repetition of the sacrifice. An ironic *conte philosophique* in which human folly stubbornly resists the generosity of divine intervention.

Marlow, Louis (pseud. of Louis Umfreville Wilkinson) (U.K.), 1881–1966.
ABOUT: CA, SMFL, SFE

3-232. The Devil in Crystal. Faber & Faber, 1944.
The narrator's mature consciousness timeslips from 1943 to 1922 into his younger

self. He believes at first that he might alert the world to the dangers facing it and thus prevent World War II, but soon finds that his ability to interfere with the course of events is negligible, and that he is a virtual prisoner within the pattern of history. In the end he manages to win one small victory against the relentless pressure of determinism, and comes to realize the relative impotence of free will. Better than Ouspensky's very similar *Strange Life of Ivan Osokin* [3-277] and Priestley's *I Have Been Here Before* (see [3-308]).

Marshall, Archibald (U.K.), 1866–1934.
ABOUT: SMFL

3-233. Upsidonia. Stanley Paul, 1915.
Utopian satire about a world in which the profit motive works in reverse—poverty is the social ideal; luxury and conspicuous consumption are scorned. The displaced hero imagines himself in paradise for a while, but soon realizes that the goodwill of one's fellow men (and women) matters more than wealth. Very funny and quite effective.

Marshall, Edison, 1894–1967.
ABOUT: WW, CA, SFE, SFFL, ESF

3-234. Ogden's Strange Story. Kinsey, 1934.
Novel first serialized in the *Popular Magazine* in 1928; the narrator is injured in an accident and becomes the victim of atavistic memories which produce in him a primitive state of consciousness. The theme—borrowed from Jack London's "When the World Was Young" (1910)—continues to crop up occasionally in American fiction, perhaps most effectively in Paddy Chayevsky's SF novel *Altered States* (1978).

Marshall, Robert (U.K.), 1863–1910.
ABOUT: GSF, ESF

3-235. The Haunted Major. Leicester Square Library, 1902.
A military sportsman is rash enough to challenge his rival in love to a game of golf (which he has never played), with the loser to withdraw his suit; he is on the brink of defeat when he acquires a set of magical clubs and the aid of a vengeful ghost. There are no stories taller than those told by sportsmen, and this is a very amusing send-up of the species.

Martyn, Wyndham (U.K.).
ABOUT: SFE

3-236. Stones of Enchantment. Jenkins, 1948.
One of the Anthony Trent series which departs from the detective genre in order to send Trent into the heart of Africa in search of a magic mountain where the secret of longevity is to be found. A readable Haggardesque adventure story with fantastic embellishments.

Masefield, John (U.K.), 1878–1967.
  About: GSF, CA, HF

3-237. The Midnight Folk. Heinemann, 1927.
An extravagant fantasy for young readers in which the young hero receives abundant magical aid in order to find a treasure and restore it to its rightful owners before the witches can get it. The sequel, *The Box of Delights* (1935), is even better, with marvelously nasty villains and the wonderful magical box.

Maurice, Michael (pseud. of **Conrad Arthur Skinner**) (U.K.), born 1889.
  About: GSF

3-238. Marooned. Sampson Low, 1932.
Posthumous fantasy whose protagonist first imagines himself to be alone on an island and then travels in spirit back to England. There, his experiences as a ghost force him to reappraise his career, in preparation for his passing on to another phase of existence. An earnest and painstaking moralistic fantasy, better than most attempts by clergyman-authors to describe the afterlife. Compare Houghton's *Julian Grant Loses His Way* [3-179] and Lady Saltoun's *After* [3-317].

3-239. Not in Our Stars. Fisher Unwin, 1923.
Strange fantasy in which a disruption of time associated with a meteor strike forces the protagonist to live his future days in reverse order, beginning with the day of his execution for murder. An eccentric study of determinism, in some ways akin to Marlow's *Devil in Crystal* [3-232]; the ending is subtle (and was apparently misread by Bleiler, who gives a mistaken account of it in his *Guide*).

Maurois, André (pseud. of **Emile Herzog**) (France), 1885–1967.
  About: WW, GSF, CA, SMFL, SFE, SFFL, TCSF, ESF

3-240. A Voyage to the Island of the Articoles. Cape, 1928. Tr. by David Garnett of *Voyage au pays des Articoles*, 1928.
Satirical novella about a utopian island where the artistic Articoles are elevated above the mass of materialistic Beos; the intrusion of visitors eventually puts too much of a strain on the delicate sensibilities of their Articole hosts. A lightweight exercise in sarcasm at the expense of aesthetes.

3-241. The Weigher of Souls. Cassell, 1931. Tr. by Hamish Miles of *Le Peseur d'âmes*, 1931.
A doctor has apparently discovered how to trap the energy of the soul as it leaves the body after death, and that the fusing of compatible souls makes them more radiant. When he dies, his friend must make the attempt to conjoin his soul with that of his wife. An exercise in sentimental metaphysics, obviously indebted to Gautier's *Spirite* (see [2-65]).

Merritt, A(braham), 1884–1943.
  About: WW, GSF, SFW, F, CA, NE, SMFL, SFE, RG, TCSF, ESF, FL, HF

*3-242. Dwellers in the Mirage. Liveright, 1932.
An American explorer who, while in Asia, was initiated into the cult of a Uighur

monster-god discovers a warm Alaskan valley where the cult still thrives, along-side a race of Amerindian pygmies. The protagonist, his own personality partly submerged by ancient race memories, is hailed as a redeemer and becomes the lover of the queen—though, in classic Haggard fashion, the queen has a less glamorous but more virtuous rival for his affections. Merritt's ending was rewrit-ten by the original publisher but has been restored in some later reprintings, and the authentic version is much to be preferred. Merritt was much more whole-hearted in grasping the nettle with input to basic theme of *She* [2-74] than Haggard could ever bring himself to be, and the story is told with great intensity.

*3-243. The Face in the Abyss. Liveright, 1931.
Fix-up of the title novella (*Argosy*, 1923) and its sequel "The Snake Mother" (*Argosy*, 1930). Explorers in the Andes find a mysterious girl; some abuse her in the hope that she might lead them to Inca treasure, but she has a powerful protector in the Snake Mother, the last of a race which flourished in prehistoric times. The hero, who helps the girl, is spared, and eventually returns to her realm to take a hand in a battle to decide its destiny between opposed godlike forces. The fantastic devices are shored up with science fictional jargon, but it is the phantas-magoric imagery which is important and effective.

3-244. The Fox Woman and Other Stories. Avon, 1949.
Posthumous collection of short stories; the title piece is a fragment about an American woman whose unborn child becomes host to a benevolent fox spirit. "The Women of the Wood" (1926) is an effective tale in which a tourist is recruited by tree spirits to save them from loggers. "Three Lines of Old French" (1919) is a sentimental timeslip romance; "Through the Dragon Glass" (1917) features a mirror which is a portal to a fantasy world. Colorful work infused with a telling sincerity.

3-245. The Moon Pool. Putnam, 1919.
Fix-up of the title short story (*All-Story*, 1918) and its novel-length sequel *The Conquest of the Moon Pool* (1919). An explorer sees a strange radiant entity which eventually pursues and engulfs him; several of his friends follow him through a dimensional doorway into a land where many exotic races with various superscientific powers coexist uneasily. A queenly *femme fatale* and a hand-maiden compete for the affections of the handsome hero, who is forced to play a crucial role in the battle to decide the destiny of the Secondary World. Merritt followed Edgar Rice Burroughs [3-59–3-62] in winning great popularity as a pulp magazine purveyor of exotic odysseys—escapist fantasies whose protagonists enjoy themselves in gorgeously decorated dream worlds. Although his penchant for purple prose annoys some critics, Merritt provided much more vivid descrip-tions of his dream worlds than Burroughs ever could, and was much more intense in his involvement with his Secondary Worlds, though his plots tend to be weak ritualistic affairs following the favorite formula of Rider Haggard [2-72–2-74]. This first novel was his weakest, but it remains interesting.

*3-246. The Ship of Ishtar. Putnam, 1926.
The hero is periodically precipitated into a Secondary World where he finds himself in the middle of a conflict between the evil god Nergal and the goddess

Ishtar. He seizes the opportunity to play a swashbuckling role and win the hand of a beautiful priestess. Honestly self-indulgent romantic fantasy. This edition is abridged; the full text is in the Borden "Memorial Edition" of 1949.

in collaboration with **Hannes Bok,** 1914–1964.

3-247. The Fox Woman and the Blue Pagoda. New Collectors Group, 1946.
Bok's completion of "The Fox Woman" (see [3-244]) examines the later career of the young woman inhabited by the fox spirit, who becomes the vehicle of a complex revenge exacted against the uncle who murdered her father. The apparatus is appropriate, but Bok could not match Merritt's intensity of feeling. Bok also extended a novel, *The Black Wheel* (1947), from another Merritt fragment, with a similarly disappointing result, but he contributed excellent illustrations to both volumes.

[For other works of this author, see the companion guide to horror.]

Middleton, Richard (U.K.), 1882–1911.
ABOUT: WW, GSF, PE, ESF

3-248. The Ghost Ship and Other Stories. Fisher Unwin, 1912.
Posthumously assembled collection of stories. The title story is a classic light fantasy in which the ghosts of a seaside village run away to sea aboard a ghostly pirate ship which is briefly blown to its shore; among the other items are the posthumous fantasy "The Brighton Road" and a quirky story of a ghostly "Shepherd's Boy."

Milne, A(lan) A(lexander) (U.K.), 1882–1956.
ABOUT: CA, ESF, HF

3-249. Winnie-the-Pooh. Methuen, 1926.
First of two classic fantasies starring animated versions of the toy animals possessed by Christopher Robin Milne (born 1920); followed by *The House at Pooh Corner* (1928). Witty and idiosyncratic episodes are described with much relish, little didacticism and deft wit—fantasy for fun, of a kind which can be constructed only with a child's attention as inspiration and collaborator.

Mirrlees, Hope (U.K.), 1890?–1978.
ABOUT: GSF, SFW, SMFL, FL, HF

*****3-250. Lud-in-the-Mist.** Collins, 1926.
The inhabitants of a town down river from Fairyland have carefully and thoroughly disenchanted their lives, but the forbidden fruit of Faerie occasionally drifts by and is surreptitiously seized and consumed by delinquents. The mayor's son becomes implicated and runs away; he must undertake a journey into Fairyland, as a result of which he becomes converted to the cause of imaginative liberation, which is what the fruit brings. A beautifully written allegory unashamedly celebrating the necessity of enchantment, after the fashion of Bullett's *Mr. Godly Beside Himself* [3-55].

Mitchell, J(ames) Leslie (U.K.), 1901–1935.
ABOUT: GSF, CA, SFE, ESF

3-251. The Lost Trumpet. Jarrolds, 1932.
Novel-length addition to the story series "Polychromata" (*Cornhill*, 1929–30; in book form as *The Calends of Cairo*, 1931). The extremely disenchanted hero joins archaeologists attempting to recover the trumpet with which Joshua demolished the walls of Jericho—which is, symbolically, "the lost trumpet of human sanity." But who among the cynical company is sufficiently uncorrupted to sound it, and what response to its clarion call is possible? Compare Mitchell's *angst* with that of Claude Houghton (see [3-179]).

Moore, C(atherine) L(ucille), 1911–1988.
ABOUT: WW, GSF, SFW, F, CA, NE, SMFL, SFE, SFFL, RG, TCSF, ESF, FL

*3-252. Black God's Shadow. Grant, 1977.
Collection of five *Weird Tales* stories starring Jirel of Joiry, which had earlier featured in the paperback *Jirel of Joiry* (1969), and first saw book publication in the collections *Shambleau and Others* (1953) and *Northwest of Earth* (1954). Jirel was the first Amazonian heroine of pulp sword-and-sorcery fiction. "Black God's Kiss" (1934) is a remarkably fevered story in which she visits a demonic Underworld in search of magic to destroy the conqueror of her tiny realm; in "Black God's Shadow" (1934) she must go back again to save his soul; "Jirel Meets Magic" (1935), "The Dark Land" (1936) and "Hellsgarde" (1939) match her against a series of intriguingly sinister opponents. Unlike Conan, who broke magic spells with sheer *machismo*, Jirel is impelled by feverish torrents of emotion (described in Merrittesque purple prose). Moore's later work, written in collaboration with her husband, Henry Kuttner (see [3-208]), is often more carefully plotted and better organized, but these early solo works, like her marvelously exotic science fantasy stories starring Northwest Smith, have a gorgeously melodramatic and utterly uninhibited fervor.

Moore, E. Hamilton (U.K.).

3-253. The Story of Etain and Otinel. David Nutt, 1905.
Heroic fantasy in the style of William Morris [2-124–2-128]. Otinel, King of Farlands, is given a fateful sword by the immortal shield-may Arlette, who knows that his desire to marry the lovely Etain will lead to war with her other suitors and to the ruin of all the land. More downbeat than Morris, perhaps owing some inspiration to Maurice Maeterlinck's tragedy *Alladine and Palomides* (1894; tr. 1899).

Morley, Christopher, 1890–1957.
ABOUT: GSF, CA, SMFL, ESF

*3-254. Thunder on the Left. Doubleday, Page, 1925.
A group of children contemplating the mysteries of adulthood decide to send a "spy" to discover its secrets; the protagonist's persona timeslips into the future,

where he finds his friends grown up. He is in an adult body, but one of them eventually recognizes him for what he is; she decides that his innocence must at all costs be preserved, and that he must not be allowed to realize the full horror of the tawdry hypocrisies of adult life. A deeply felt novel of disenchantment, all the more powerful by virtue of its obliquity.

Morris, Kenneth (U.K.), 1879–1937.
ABOUT: GSF, CA, SMFL, ESF, FL

*3-255. The Secret Mountain and Other Tales. Faber & Gwyer, 1926.
Collection of ten stories—fabular poems in prose in a vein similar to the work of John Sterling [2-146] and Lord Dunsany [3-123]. They range from a sentimental account of "The Last Adventure of Don Quixote," to a wonderful Oriental fantasy, "The Rose and the Cup," to the marvelous syncretic myth-fantasy "The Divina Commedia of Evan Leyshon," and the stories are without exception brilliant. Morris also produced literary renderings of material from the *Mabinogion* [1-47] in *The Fates of the Princes of Dyfed* (1914) and *The Book of the Three Dragons* (1930).

Mottram, R(alph) H(ale) (U.K.), 1883–1971.
ABOUT: ESF

3-256. The Gentleman of Leisure. Hutchinson, 1948.
Nostalgic and sentimental story of a tolerant and warm-hearted man who receives just reward in the afterlife for his good works, despite never having held down a job or gone in for art. An interesting example of fantasy as a form of special pleading. Mottram later added an infernal counterpart, *To Hell, with Crabb Robinson* (1962).

Muddock, Joyce E. Preston (U.K.), 1842–1934.
ABOUT: WW, GSF, PE, ESF

3-257. The Sunless City. F. V. White, 1905.
Curious hollow world fantasy which begins as a Vernian novel of exploration and continues as a rather flaccid utopian satire. Possibly inspired by Hyne's *Beneath Your Very Boots* [2-89].

Mundy, Talbot (pseud. of William L. Gribbon) (U.K.), 1879–1940.
ABOUT: WW, GSF, SFW, NE, SMFL, SFE, ESF

3-258. All Four Winds. Hutchinson, 1932.
Omnibus edition of four of Mundy's offbeat adventure stories set in India: *King of the Khyber Rifles* (1916), *Jimgrim* (1931), *Om: The Secret of Ahbor Valley* (1924) and *Black Light* (1930). Characters from these books crop up in many others, mostly nonfantastic, the ones of most fantasy interest being *Caves of Terror* (1924; also known as *The Grey Mahatma*), *The Nine Unknown* (1924) and *The Devil's Guard* (1926; also known as *Ramsden*). Mundy had lived in the East and was very interested in pseudo-Eastern mysticism of a Theosophist stripe; he drew on these

resources to enliven his exotic adventure stories, which often feature Rohmer-esque plots. His skill in handling robust and fast-paced narrative sustains his readability even in extreme circumstances, but it is unfortunately the case that the supernatural intrusions usually weaken his stories when they are not merely peripheral. The extravagant and pseudo-science fictional *Jimgrim* fails to avoid absurdity; only *Om* rally manages to fuse its occult materials with the other elements of its plot in a seamless and interesting fashion.

Munn, H(arold) Warner, 1903–1982.
ABOUT: WW, GSF, CA, SMFL, SFE, SFFL, RG, PE, ESF, HF

3-259. King of the World's Edge. Ace, 1966.
Heroic fantasy first serialized in *Weird Tales* (1939) whose Roman-descended hero leaves Britain with Myrdhinn (Merlin) after Arthur has supposedly gone to Avalon; they cross the Atlantic to the American shore, where they hew out an empire among the Aztecs long before the coming of Cortez. Book publication led Munn to add sequels: *The Ship from Atlantis* (1967; combined with *King of the World's Edge* as *Merlin's Godson*) and *Merlin's Ring* (1974). This series is also annotated as [4A-191].

[For other works of this author, see the companion guide to horror.]

Murray, Violet T(orlesse) (U.K.), born 1874.
ABOUT: GSF, ESF

3-260. The Rule of the Beasts. Stanley Paul, 1925.
After civilization is all but wiped out by war, God appoints the beasts to teach the survivors how to live better lives, by making use of the life-enhancing technology which was discovered on the eve of the war. An ironically sentimental fable.

Myers, John Myers, 1906–1988.
ABOUT: GSF, CA, SMFL, MF, ESF, SFFL, HF

3-261. Silverlock. Dutton, 1949.
Gulliverian fantasy in which a castaway is washed up on the shore of the Commonwealth, where all the great characters of literature are to be found; the hapless hero wanders around, repeatedly getting himself into difficulties and finding famous rescuers, eventually cultivating a kind of heroism. An amusing if slightly overextended exercise in literary game playing. A semi-sequel is *The Moon's Fire-Eating Daughter* [4A-193].

Nathan, Robert, 1894–1985.
ABOUT: GSF, SFW, CA, SMFL, SFE, SFFL, RG, ESF, HF

3-262. The Bishop's Wife. Bobbs-Merrill, 1928.
The archangel Michael comes to Earth in answer to a bishop's prayer for help in raising money to build a new cathedral, but he also fills a gap for the bishop's wife, whose life has lost its color and romance. Earnest sentimentality and

understated pathos, in a vein which Nathan was to mine productively for half a century, and which remains uniquely his.

3-263. The Innocent Eve. Knopf, 1951.
Lucifer and a female demon crash a high society party, offering the fulfillment of wishes in exchange for his taking control of the atom bomb, but he finds his schemes confounded by the naïve moral honesty of a Hollywood starlet. The central motif is handled with infinitely greater delicacy than it was in Marie Corelli's *Sorrows of Satan* [2-33]; its whimsical proposal that the problem of modern weapon technology transcends traditional moral boundaries was soon to be earnestly echoed by Noyes's *The Devil Takes a Holiday* [3-273], and was developed more extravagantly by Nathan in *Heaven and Hell and the Megas Factor* (see [4A-194]).

3-264. Jonah. McBride, 1925.
Biblical fantasy about the career of the unfortunate prophet. Begins in an ironic and rather cynical vein reminiscent of John Erskine (see [3-129]) but becomes a much more earnest meditation on Jewish psychology and culture; compare Bernard Malamud's *God's Grace* (1982).

*3-265. Portrait of Jennie. Knopf, 1940.
An enervated artist makes sketches of a little girl which reignite his creativity and further his career; she timeslips from the past on several occasions, each time becoming older, but as sexuality dawns and she falls in love, she resolves not to come again until she is able to meet him on equal terms—but she reaches him only briefly, in the moment of her death. An excellent tragic romance, beautifully written and unashamedly heartrending.

3-266. The River Journey. Knopf, 1949.
A party of four embark on a river cruise. The two women each have medical conditions which will soon prove fatal; they are accompanied by the husband of one of them and by Mr. Mortimer (personified Death). Nathan's Death, like his archangels and devils, is a gentle and sentimental fellow, and his presence helps to soothe all anxieties and foolish ambitions. Compare T. F. Powys's *Unclay* [3-304].

Nesbit, Edith (U.K.), 1858–1924.
ABOUT: WW, GSF, CA, SMFL, RG, PE, ESF, HF

3-267. Dormant. Methuen, 1911.
Romantic fantasy, one of whose characters has a strong interest in the alchemical quest for the elixir of life. In his ancestral home he discovers the body of a young woman who has lain there in suspended animation for half a century; he revives her and falls in love, but no good can possibly come of it all. Nesbit in a wistful mood, which contrasts intriguingly with the indignant melodrama of *Salome and the Head* [H3-152].

3-268. The Enchanted Castle. Fisher Unwin, 1907.
Four children discover a magic ring which first gives them the power to become invisible and later grants their wishes, including bringing to life their scarecrow

constructions the Ugly-Wuglies. As is usual with Nesbit, the children quickly learn from experience to use their opportunities cleverly and benevolently. The most colorful and ingenious of Nesbit's fantasies.

3-269. Five Children and It. Fisher Unwin, 1902.
The first volume of a trilogy about the Bastable children; here they find the Psammead, an eccentric and rather bad-tempered creature which grants their wishes; they quickly learn the essential folly of idle fancy. *The Phoenix and the Carpet* (1904) is a more exuberant fantasy in the Ansteyan vein. *The Story of the Amulet* (1906) brings back the Psammead and a firmer didactic intention; much stronger than the first volume, it embraces many of Nesbit's reformist ideas (radical for their time) and is an intriguing moralistic fantasy even at the adult level.

[For other works of this author, see the companion guide to horror.]

Newbolt, Henry (U.K.), 1862–1938.
ABOUT: CA, SMFL

3-270. Aladore. Blackwood, 1914.
Long allegorical medieval romance in the manner of William Morris. Ennui drives Ywain from his homeland to roam the world, not knowing what it is that he seeks. He allies himself with the Lady Aithne and shares several different ways of life with her in various exotic environments, but ultimately finds fulfillment only in self-sacrifice for a noble cause. Interesting in comparison with Morris (see especially [2-127]), given the very different values and political philosophies of the two men.

Newte, Horace W. C. (U.K.), 1870–1949.
ABOUT: GSF

3-271. The Ealing Miracle. Mills & Boon, 1911.
A pious paragon of middle-class rectitude exchanges bodies (apparently at the command of Christ) with a young nurse down on her luck after bearing (and losing) an illegitimate child. She learns that her moral assumptions are ill-fitted to the world in which she now must live. The tedious sermonizing about the plight of working girls in London is offset by the development of the woman's relationship with the girl's lover (which is put aside when the author nearly gets carried away). The ending is surprisingly ambivalent, and though the book is rather patchy, it is one of the best of its kind. Compare Besant's *The Doubts of Dives* [2-16].

Nichols, Robert (U.K.), 1893–1944.
ABOUT: SMFL

3-272. Fantastica. Chatto & Windus, 1923.
Collection of three *contes philosophiques*, billed as "Romances of Idea: Volume One" (no others were ever published). "The Smile of the Sphinx" is a rather enervated Oriental tale in the Voltairean style; "Sir Perseus and the Fair Andro-

meda" is a fine ironic novella crossing Arthurian fantasy with Greek mythology; "Golgotha & Co." is a prolix futuristic novel in which the Antichrist argues with a boatload of businesmen about the ideal way to run the world. A mixed bag, showing sufficient enterprise to make one regret the abandonment of the larger project.

Noyes, Alfred (U.K.), 1880–1958.
ABOUT: WW, GSF, CA, SFE, ESF

3-273. The Devil Takes a Holiday. Murray, 1955.
The devil visits California, deeply concerned that man's adventures in nuclear weaponry will produce an end more dreadful than even he would desire. Noyes had earlier featured a "doomsday weapon" in his scientific romance *The Last Man* (1940); that he was a convert to Catholicism makes his (heretical) portrayal of Satan all the more interesting, though the book is by no means up to the standard of Bulgakov's *The Master and Margarita* [3-54]. Compare Nathan's *The Innocent Eve* [3-263] and *Heaven and Hell and the Megas Factor* (see [4A-194]).

O'Brien, Flann (pseud. of **Brian O'Nolan**) (Ireland), 1911–1966.
ABOUT: CA, SMFL, SFE, MF, SFFL, ESF

3-274. At Swim-Two-Birds. Longmans, 1939.
A complex novel which offers a multidimensional account of Dublin life and culture, incorporating much folkloristic material in a comic context as well as a story-within-the-story which an author is writing about the legendary hero Finn MacCool. Heavily influenced by James Joyce, whose *Finnegans Wake*, published in the same year, also plays surreally with the Finn legend.

O'Duffy, Eimar (Ireland), 1893–1935.
ABOUT: GSF, SFE

3-275. King Goshawk and the Birds. Macmillan, 1926.
A philosopher (borrowed from James Stephens [3-332]) fetches Cuchulain from Tir nan Og to oppose the American plutocrat Goshawk, who has bought up nature and is running it as a commercial operation—but this enemy is too powerful for the hero or his son Cuandine. The story continues in *Asses in Clover* (1933), when America and Ireland go to war over a songbird; Cuandine covers himself with glory but fails to halt the capitalist juggernaut. Written with great verve and scalding wit, though it lacks the ambition of O'Duffy's science fictional satire *The Spacious Adventures of the Man in the Street* (1928), which blazes away more freely at sexual mores and religion.

Orwell, George (pseud. of **Eric Blair**) (U.K.), 1903–1950.
ABOUT: SMFL, CA, NE, SFE, ESF

***3-276. Animal Farm.** Secker & Warburg, 1945.
Classic satirical allegory mirroring the failure of the Russian Revolution to live up to its own ideals; the animals turn out the farmer who exploits them and lay

down a set of egalitarian principles to live by, but the pigs (once the opportunist Napoleon has disposed of the idealist Snowball) prove to be the animals who are more equal than the others, and in the end they have become indistinguishable from the farmers.

Ouspensky, P(eter) D(emianovich) (Russia), 1878–1947.
ABOUT: GSF, SMFL

3-277. The Strange Life of Ivan Osokin. Stourton Press, 1947.
Novel developing the author's Gurdjieff-derived theory of eternal recurrence, dramatizing the supposed difficulty of exerting the influence of the will to subvert the pressure of universal determinism. The hero gets to live his life over again, but finds it infinitely harder than he had supposed to avoid the mistakes which he regrets. Compare Marlow's *The Devil in Crystal* [3-232].

Owen, Frank (pseud. of Roswell Williams), 1893–1968.
ABOUT: WW, GSF, CA, SFE, ESF

3-278. The Wind That Tramps the World. Lantern Press, 1929.
The first of several collections of Oriental tales, some from *Weird Tales*. Followed by *The Purple Sea* (1930), *Della Wu, Chinese Courtesan* (1931) and *A Husband for Kutani* (1938). *The Porcelain Magician* (1949) is an eclectic selection which adds a few new stories. Like the Kai Lung stories of Ernest Bramah [3-48] these are essentially items of fake Chinoiserie, but they have a delightful delicacy which links them stylistically to the stories of Donald Corley [3-88]. Outstanding among them are the title story of the first book (1920; also in the fifth-named), in which a flower grower is waiting for the return of the wind which stole his masterpiece; "The Tinkle of the Camel's Bell" (1928; in the second-named), about a beautiful vampiric spirit; and "Doctor Shen Fu" (in the third- and fifth-named books), which features a sinister alchemist who possesses the elixir of life.

Pain, Barry (U.K.), 1865–1928.
ABOUT: WW, GSF, CA, SMFL, PE, ESF, FL

3-279. An Exchange of Souls. Eveleigh Nash, 1911.
A scientist experimenting with anesthetics in the hope of isolating and analyzing the human soul is killed by a malfunction in his equipment, but his personality is displaced into the body of his young assistant and fiancée, which begins a slow transmogrification. The narrator is impotent to help and matters progress to their inevitable conclusion. An intriguing Frankensteinian fantasy.

3-280. The New Gulliver and Other Stories. Werner Laurie, 1913.
The title novella is a fascinating example of neo-Gulliveriana whose hero finds himself in a grotesquely overdeveloped scientific utopia—Laputa writ large. "Zero" is a novelette about a loyal dog which has premonitions; "In a London Garden" is one of Pain's whimsical meditations, after the fashion of his earlier *In a Canadian Canoe* (1891), and includes some supernatural material.

3-281. Going Home. Werner Laurie, 1921.
The author's swan song. Subtitled "The Fantastic Romance of the Girl with Angel Eyes and the Man Who Had Wings," which sums up the plot very neatly. Two rank outsiders in the human race seem to have a chance of redeeming one another from the desolation which passes for everyday life. Sentimental in the extreme, seemingly animated by the same combination of postwar *tristesse* and desperate optimism as Benson's *Living Alone* [3-29].

3-282. The One Before. Grant Richards, 1902.
Ansteyan fantasy about a ring which causes each of its owners to take on the personality traits of the previous one. The central motif is more interesting than the ones tiredly exhibited by the common run of Ansteyan pastiches.

[For other works of this author, see the companion guide to horror.]

Pargeter, Edith (U.K.), 1913– .
ABOUT: GSF, CA, ESF

*3-283. By Firelight. Heinemann, 1948. U.S. title: *By This Strange Fire.*
A widow whose emotions have all but atrophied moves into a neglected house in a rural backwater; while she patiently endures the rival attentions of a farmer and his nephew, who are bound together by mutual hatred, she begins to record the story of a former owner of the house who was executed as a witch in the 1620s. This contact makes her wish devoutly that the house might become haunted and that the man might return as a demon lover, but her invocation of his spirit is interrupted by the culmination of her earthly suitors' rivalry. The interpolated story is easily the best literary recreation of an English witch trial and the story is by far the most harrowing timeslip romance (if it can be classified as such); indeed, there is no work in the entire canon of fantastic literature quite as pain-racked and bleak as this one—the intensity of feeling is presumably a hangover from the war years, when the author served in the W.R.N.S. Pargeter's earlier novel, *The City Lies Four-Square* (1939), is an overtly supernatural timeslip romance in which an Earth-bound ghost seeks solace in friendship with the living because he is barred from heaven. The same depth of feeling is there, but it lacks the refinement of the later novel.

Peake, Mervyn (U.K.), 1911–1968.
ABOUT: WW, F, CA, NE, SMFL, SFE, MF, SFFL, RG, TCSF, ESF, HF

3-284. Mr. Pye. Heinemann, 1953.
The hero comes to Sark determined to preach his gospel of love and kindness to the islanders; the Great Pal sees fit to reward (or punish) him with angelic wings, an embarrassment which causes him to embark upon a compensating career of petty sins. Alas, this wins him only a pair of horns. A frothy burlesque of morals and moralists.

*3-285. Titus Groan. Eyre and Spottiswoode, 1946.
In the marvelous Gothic edifice of Gormenghast the eponymous heir is born, son

of the melancholy Lord Sepulchrave and brother to the weak-spirited Lady Fuschia, who is a key element in the plans which the opportunistic Steerpike makes in the hope of rising from despised servant to master of the realm. Among the magnificent cast of fabulous grotesques, Steerpike stands out as the perfect anti-hero, and the story of his quest for power is utterly fascinating, but there are many other brilliant set-pieces, none better than the fight between the manservant Flay and the loathsomely obese cook Swelter. The story continues in *Gormenghast* (1950), in which Titus grows to adolescence and Steerpike's Machiavellian career runs its full and gripping course to an appropriately horrid conclusion. Titus must leave his home for the greater world, whose exploration is begun in *Titus Alone* (1959 in heavily edited form; an edition closer to Peake's text was edited from his manuscripts by Langdon Jones in 1970), a novel whose grotesquerie becomes increasingly exaggerated, eventually running completely out of control as the writer's brain was progressively disturbed by a degenerative disease. An offshoot of the series, the brilliant phantasmagoric novella *Boy in Darkness* (in the anthology *Sometime, Never*, 1956) involves the young (and here unnamed) Titus in an allegorical encounter with several persons characterized as animals. The series is incomplete, but what exists constitutes one of the masterpieces of fantasy—a breathtakingly vivid and incomparably stylish tour de force of the imagination.

Perutz, Leo (Austria), 1884-1957.
ABOUT: GSF, SMFL, ESF

3-286. The Marquis de Bolibar. John Lane, 1926. Tr. by Graham Rawson of *Der Marques de Bolibar*, 1920.
The eponymous hero is fighting with the guerrillas in the Peninsular War, and has devised a plan to defeat the French and their nasty German allies. He is killed by the Germans (though they do not realize who he is), but his indomitable spirit finds a way to save the situation. The Wandering Jew is also around, vainly attempting to put an end to his unwelcome immortality. An intriguing tale.

Phillips, Alexander M(oore), 1907- .
ABOUT: GSF, ESF

3-287. The Mislaid Charm. Prime Press, 1947.
Comic fantasy after the manner of Thorne Smith. An imp gets a writer drunk and plants a stolen charm on him, which runs riot until its rightful owners turn up to reclaim it. Amiable nonsense from *Unknown* (1941); compare Robert Bloch's similar pastiches [3-39].

Phillpotts, Eden (U.K.), 1862-1960.
ABOUT: WW, GSF, SFW, CA, SMFL, SFE, PE, ESF

3-288. Arachne. Faber & Gwyer, 1927.
Allegorical retelling of the myth of Arachne, the weaver who challenged Athene to a contest. The humanist Phillpotts naturally takes her side against the goddess, whose superior technique cannot compensate for a lack of human warmth.

Arachne is here allowed to escape with one of her two suitors, the other having become an ardent devotee of Athene. Slightly pompous but charmingly persuasive.

*3-289. Circé's Island. Grant Richards, 1925.
Two novellas. In the title story a boy goes to the isle of the celebrated enchantress in search of his father—who has been turned, like all her lovers, into an animal. Circé likes the boy, and so does Odysseus, whose visit coincides with his, but before they can secure his father's release they must first figure out which animal he is. *The Girl and the Faun* (first published 1916) is a beautiful story of the love affair of an immortal faun and a mortal girl. These are the most sentimental of Phillpotts's classical fantasies; the moral of each story is made more powerful by poignancy and delicacy.

3-290. Evander. Grant Richards, 1919.
The first of Phillpotts's extended *contes philosophiques* based in classical mythology. The wife of a worshipper of Bacchus is seduced to the worship of Apollo by the handsome Evander, but she is not really cut out for the noble Apollonian cause and eventually reverts to a Dionysian view of the quality of life. The fundamental contrast between Apollonian and Dionysian worldviews is, of course, borrowed from Nietzsche. It was followed by *The Treasures of Typhon* (1924), a painstaking allegorical account of a young man's education in an essentially Epicurean philosophy of life.

3-291. The Lavender Dragon. Grant Richards, 1923.
Ironic mock-medieval romance in which a benevolent dragon steals lonely humans to populate his utopian community, in spite of the attempts by knights errant to keep them in a world ruled by intolerance and injustice. A delightful exercise in inverted perspective; reprinted in Lin Carter's *Great Short Novels of Adult Fantasy Volume II* (1973).

3-292. The Miniature. Watts, 1926.
Extended *conte philosophique* which tells the story of the philosophical evolution of mankind from the viewpoint of the classical gods, who take a particular interest in the psychological utility of religion. In an unusually bleak conclusion, mankind is annihilated in a nuclear holocaust. Reprinted in Lin Carter's anthology *Discoveries in Fantasy* (1972). *The Apes* (1929) is a similar allegory of evolution which makes its point more subtly.

3-293. The Owl of Athene. Hutchinson, 1936.
A council of classical gods decides to test the mettle of mankind by arranging an invasion of the land by giant crabs; this work signaled a significant change of direction in Phillpotts's imaginative fiction, which subsequently took him into the field of scientific romance.

*3-294. Pan and the Twins. Grant Richards, 1922.
The story of two brothers separated at birth; one preserves the dying cult of Pan while the other embraces Christianity. Phillpotts considers the two faiths evenhandedly, and finds the possibility of virtue in both, but he stands alongside Anatole France (see [2-61]) in favoring an Epicurean humanism against the

unadmirable excesses of Christian piety, and his championship of Pan (here portrayed as warm and gentle) is steadfast.

Powys, John Cowper (U.K.), 1872–1963.
ABOUT: WW, GSF, SFW, CA, SMFL, SFE, ESF

3-295. Atlantis. Macdonald, 1954.
Slow-moving and highly decorated classical romance in which the aging widower Odysseus travels beyond the Pillars of Herakles to visit sunken Atlantis and the American shore. The gods are still around but are almost entirely preoccupied with their own troubles; various animals and inanimate objects are personalized after the fashion of brother Theodore's *Fables* [3-300] or Powys's own bizarre novelette *The Owl, the Duck, and—Miss Rowe! Miss Rowe!* (1930). The sexual symbolism common in Powys's later works is also very prominent. Idiosyncratic and esoteric.

3-296. The Brazen Head. Macdonald, 1956.
Historical fantasy based on the legend of the bronze head alchemically given an oracular voice by Roger Bacon (or, in another version, Albertus Magnus). Here Bacon and Albert are working together with St. Bonaventura, while opposed to their cause is the self-styled Antichrist Peter Peregrinus; there is also the first of the many giants which were to populate Powys's later work. More accessible than [3-295] or [3-299], but its philosophical implications remain rather opaque.

*3-297. A Glastonbury Romance. Simon & Schuster, 1932.
A vast novel of ideas whose sprawling mundane narrative is continually linked to its theological context, and in which apparitions and visions occasionally trouble the characters. Powys confronts the perplexities and perversities of his own character through the medium of John Crow's unorthodox love for his wife, Mary; the crisis of faith which alienates Sam Dekker from his clergyman father; the crusading mission of John Geard; and Owen Evans's attempts to exorcise his sadistic impulses. The invented theology is basically Manichaean but involves many lesser godlings, including the Earth-Mother Cybele. An elaborated Grail myth underlies the plot. A highly idiosyncratic tour de force whose method might appeal to students of "Magic Realism," though its closest analogue in English literature is probably David Lindsay's *Devil's Tor* [3-218].

3-298. Morwyn; or, The Vengeance of God. Cassell, 1937.
Anti-vivisectionist novel in which the narrator is cast down with his dog, a scientist and Morwyn (the scientist's daughter) into a Hell made by sadists, where the scientist joins forces with Torquemada; the narrator and Morwyn must flee from them, guided by the Marquis de Sade and Taliesin to the navel of the universe, where Merlin sleeps with Cronos and other forgotten deities. Powys's rejection of the supposed sadism of scientists is, of course, complicated by his own acknowledged fascination with sadistic imagery, for which he provides an apologetic case, but that serves to make him all the more fervent in his cause.

*3-299. Porius. Macdonald, 1951.
Historical fantasy subtitled "A Romance of the Dark Ages." The book is named for a soldier involved in the battles which the Welsh warlord Arthur fights against

the Saxons, but the real central character is Myrddin Wyllt (Merlin), worshipper of the Earth-Mother, symbol of and spokesman for Natural Man. He works very few magical tricks, but is the very embodiment of the magical worldview which—like the legacy of the Roman occupation—will soon be swept away by the barbarous invaders. Perhaps Powys's best book, though as difficult as any; this text was reduced and rewritten at the insistence of the publisher, and the text which the author initially prepared has never been published.

Powys, T(heodore) F(rancis) (U.K.), 1875–1953.
ABOUT: WW, GSF, SFW, CA, SMFL

3-300. Fables. Chatto & Windus, 1929. Also known as *No Painted Plumage*.
Collection of quirkily surreal stories, mostly dialogues. Some, like "John Pardy and the Waves" and "Darkness and Nathaniel," confront human characters with forces of nature; others, like "The Seaweed and the Cuckoo Clock" and "The Corpse and the Flea," involve only nonhuman creatures and inanimate objects. Their commentary on the world is bleak but not entirely pessimistic.

3-301. The Key of the Field. William Jackson, 1930.
Allegorical novelette in which Jar (Yahweh) appears in his lordly role, proprietor of the Heaven to which a poor man is belatedly welcomed. Another pamphlet, *Christ in the Cupboard* (1930), offers a parable in which a prosperous family put Christ in the cupboard when his message is too uncomfortable to hear; when they need him, they find that the devil has replaced him. *The Only Penitent* (1931) is the story of a vicar who opens a confessional which no one will attend, until Jar comes to confess *His* sins. The first and third were reprinted in *Bottle's Path* (1946); the second in *The White Paternoster* (1930); all three (plus "The Left Leg"—see [3-303]) are in the inaptly titled omnibus *God's Eyes A-Twinkle* (1947). Oddly enough,the most hopeful and upbeat of these allegorical novelettes, "Come and Dine"—in which Mr. Weston (see [3-302]) appears in a bountiful role—remained unpublished during Powys's lifetime; it is in *Two Stories: Come and Dine and Tadnol* (1967).

*3-302. Mr. Weston's Good Wine. Chatto & Windus, 1927.
An earnest and sentimental allegory. The village of Folly Down is visited by God in the guise of traveling salesman Mr. Weston, with Michael acting as book-keeper/recording angel. The devil, in the form of a lion, is locked in the back of his car ready for release if required. The villagers must each decide whether they are ready for his wares—a light wine which illuminates life with a hint of divine intoxication, or a dark one which is merciful oblivion. A masterpiece, carefully balancing Powys's natural pessimism with a scrupulous counting of blessings.

*3-303. The Two Thieves. Chatto & Windus, 1932.
Collection of three novellas; the title story is the last of Powys's brilliant allegories. The protagonist steals Greed, Pride, Anger and Cruelty from the devil's luggage—but the delighted fiend warns him to beware of another thief, Tinker Jar (here in his Christly role), who might rob him in his turn, and leave him nakedly to bear the burden of the sins which will make him rich. An unparalleled

study of evil, much more powerful than the similarly inspired novella which began Powys's career, the title story of *The Left Leg* (1923).

*3-304. Unclay. Chatto & Windus, 1931.
Death, having mislaid the warrant which entitles him to gather certain souls, must bide awhile in the village of Dodder, where the local miser is conniving the sale of his innocent daughter to a sadistic farmer; the monstrous rape to which this plotting leads makes it all the more urgent that Death gather her soul—and that of the boy who loves her—before their sufferings are further extended. The most affectively powerful of Powys's novels, much bleaker than [3-302] (and much less popular in consequence) but at least equal to it in literary worth.

Pratt, Fletcher, 1897–1956.
ABOUT: WW, GSF, F, CA, NE, SFW, SMFL, SFE, MF, SFFL, RG, TCSF, ESF, FL, HF

*3-305. The Blue Star. Ballantine, 1969.
Novel first published in the anthology *Witches Three* (Twayne, 1952). Secondary World fantasy in which magic is the privilege of female witches, but can be transferred to their chosen lovers along with talismanic Blue Stars. The hero, a conspirator against the political order, seduces a witch in order to gain this advantage, but must then flee into exile. He meets the girl again in a land ruled by a quasi-Albigensian theocracy, and must combine forces in order to make a further bid for freedom. A rather dour novel, written with a rare sophistication and attention to detail; it cultivates a degree of realism almost unknown in its romantic subgenre. Also annotated as [4A-211].

3-306. The Well of the Unicorn. William Sloane, 1948 (this edition under the pseud. George U. Fletcher).
Heroic fantasy set in an imaginary realm borrowed from a play by Dunsany. The son of a dispossessed landowner joins guerrilla fighters involved in a revolution against the conquerors of his homeland; he must use his talents for magic and military strategy to the full while undergoing a difficult sentimental education. The mythical well, a fountain of peace rather than youth, plays a symbolic role. An admirable attempt to import realism into heroic fantasy, which does not quite attain the high standard to which it aspires.

Priestley, J(ohn) B(oynton) (U.K.), 1894–1984.
ABOUT: GSF, CA, NE, SFE, SFFL, TCSF, ESF

3-307. The Other Place and Other Stories of the Same Sort. Heinemann, 1953.
Collection of fantasies. "The Other Place" is a pleasant parallel world visited all too briefly by the protagonist; the unlucky "Guest of Honour" is given an equally brief taste of an altogether less pleasant place. The other stories are whimsical tales of illusion and strange experience, saved from triviality by Priestley's sincere fascination with the moral opportunities afforded by timeslips and similar excursions.

3-308. Three Time Plays. Pan, 1947.
Priestley was fascinated by Dunne's time theories, and was drawn thereby into much other reading—ultimately culminating in his nonfiction study *Man and Time* (1968). This omnibus combines the time-loop melodrama *Dangerous Corner* (1932); a Dunneian fantasy of precognition at the periphery of the serial universe, *Time and the Conways* (1937); and the Ouspenskian drama of not-quite-eternal recurrence *I Have Been Here Before* (1938). *An Inspector Calls* (1945) is also a time-play of sorts, as is the remarkable posthumous fantasy *Johnson over Jordan* (1939).

Quinn, Seabury, 1889–1969.
ABOUT: WW, GSF, F, CA, SMFL, SFE, RG, PE, ESF

3-309. Roads. Ruppert, 1938.
Pamphlet edition of a *Weird Tales* novelette, subsequently revised for an Arkham House edition of 1948. Religious fantasy in which King Herod's star gladiator saves the child Christ; he later becomes the soldier who administers the *coup de grace* to the crucified Jesus and is rewarded with immortality, ultimately adopting another famous role related to the celebration of the Nativity. An odd combination of piety and pulp romance.

[For other works of this author, see the companion guide to horror.]

Read, Herbert (U.K.), 1893–1968.
ABOUT: GSF, CA, SMFL, SFE, ESF

*3-310. The Green Child. Heinemann, 1935.
A philosophical novel whose hero, having grown disenchanted with the imperfections of the quasi-utopian state which he has established in South America, returns to England where (following an item of English medieval folklore) he discovers a mysterious green child. He goes with her into a subterranean realm whose people have established a truly utopian mode of existence. Obviously inspired by Hudson's *Green Mansions* [3-186], but rather more daring in its ambitions; its philosophy of the good life is closely connected with Read's aesthetic theories as outlined in *The Meaning of Art* (1931).

Rice, Elmer, 1892–1967.
ABOUT: CA, SFFL, ESF

3-311. A Voyage to Purilia. Cosmopolitan, 1930.
An exuberant satirical romance which mercilessly sends up the clichés and coy conventions of Hollywood by imagining a world where all the tricks of cinematography and follies of scriptwriting are reflected in reality; the plot proceeds at a fast pace to the inevitable fadeout. Also of note is Rice's expressionist play *The Adding Machine* (1923), in which Mr. Zero, made redundant by advancing technology, is driven figuratively and literally beyond the limits that flesh and blood can endure.

Rolfe, Frederick W(illiam), 1860–1913.
ABOUT: WW, GSF, CA, SMFL

3-312. Hadrian VII. Chatto & Windus, 1904 (most editions as by "Baron Corvo").
Wish fulfillment fantasy in which an unappreciated theologian is summoned to become pope, and performs that role better than anyone has ever done before. Not without a certain wry wit, often displayed in self-indulgent sniping at actual and imagined enemies, but essentially a work which cries out for analysis as a case study in Freudian psychology.

Romains, Jules (pseud. of **Louis Farigoule**) (France), 1885–1972.
ABOUT: CA, ESF

3-313. Tussles with Time. Sidgwick & Jackson, 1952. Tr. by Gerard Hopkins of *Violation de frontières,* 1951.
A short novel, "A Struggle with Time and Death," and a novella, "Breaching the Frontiers." Both stories confront analytically minded narrators with metaphysical puzzles in the form of paranormal phenomena. In the first story a dead man makes brief reappearances, perhaps momentarily displaced within a Dunneian serial universe; the second involves experiments to make contact with a spiritual domain.

Ross, Malcolm, 1895–1965.
ABOUT: CA, SFE, ESF

3-314. The Man Who Lived Backward. Farrar, Straus, 1950.
Novel whose core is a diary kept by the central character. After two excerpts from 1865, just after Lincoln's assassination (in which the writer bitterly regrets that he will not live long enough to prevent it), we get a more extended life history extending backward from 1901 (when the narrator, having been born in 1940, is approaching middle age). The author does not really succeed in overcoming the logical difficulties which arise in treating seriously what is usually a comic theme; compare Maurice's *Not in Our Stars* [3-239].

Russell, Bertrand (U.K.), 1872–1970.
ABOUT: GSF, CA, SFE, SFFL, ESF

3-315. Satan in the Suburbs. Bodley Head, 1953.
Collection whose title novella is subtitled "Horrors Manufactured Here," that being the advertisement of the sinister practice which Dr. Mallako sets up in a suburban street in order to play a subtly diabolical role. Also included are the mock-science fictional farce "The Infra-Redioscope" and an equally farcical mock-Gothic account of "The Corsican Ordeal of Miss X." *Nightmares of Eminent Persons* (1954) opens with a sequence of visionary fantasies mocking various forms of narrow-mindedness; the remaining stories are satirical SF.

Saint-Exupéry, Antoine de (France), 1900–1944.
ABOUT: CA, SMFL, ESF, HF

3-316. The Little Prince. Harcourt, 1945. Tr. by Katherine Woods of *Le Petit Prince*, 1944.
A little boy comes to Earth from a distant world to discover the meaning of love and happiness; he finds various animal friends to aid him in his quest. A children's book, but it retains its affiliation with the Voltairean tradition of Anatole France's fable *The Shirt* (see [3-145]).

Saltoun, M(ary) (**Lady Saltoun**) (U.K.), died 1940.
ABOUT: GSF

3-317. After. Duckworth, 1930.
Posthumous fantasy whose mean-spirited protagonist finds himself in a kind of hedonistic "heaven" where attendants are only too willing to gratify his every sensual whim. But nearby is the abysmal Pit, and he gradually comes to realize that he is in a kind of inverted Purgatory, where the process of degradation which his soul began on Earth must be completed before he is fit for eternal damnation. But is there a way out? One of the best and most original novels of its subgenre.

Sewell, Elizabeth (U.K.), born 1919.
ABOUT: CA, ESF

3-318. The Dividing of Time. Chatto & Windus, 1951.
Striking surreal fantasy in which a female civil servant intermittently experiences a curious dream world populated by assorted guides and *Doppelgängers*, which ultimately lure her away from her unrewarding work, back to the literary labors she had forsaken. Compare Ruthven Todd's allegorical landscapes [3-338].

Shaw, George Bernard (Ireland), 1856–1950.
ABOUT: CA, SMFL, SFE

3-319. The Adventures of the Black Girl in Her Search for God. Constable, 1932.
Allegory in which a new convert to Christianity interviews various sages (concluding with a cantankerous Irishman) about their various images of the deity. The story inspired several ironic ripostes and replies in kind, including *Adventures of the White Girl in Her Search for God* (1933) by Charles Herbert Maxwell; *The Adventures of Gabriel in His Search for Mr. Shaw* (1933) by W. R. Matthews; *The Adventures of the Young Soldier in His Search for the Better World* (1943) by C. E. M. Joad; and *The Adventures of God in His Search for the Black Girl* (1973) by Brigid Brophy. It was reprinted in *The Black Girl in Search of God and Some Lesser Tales* (1946); the lesser tales, reprinted from *Short Stories, Scraps and Shavings* (1934), include "The Miraculous Revenge" (1885), a neat ironic tale of a subverted miracle; "Aerial Football: The New Game" (1907), a posthumous fantasy suggesting that the gate of Heaven is open to all callers; and "Don Giovanni Explains" (1934), in which the ghost of the famous lover explains how history has misrepresented him.

Shiel, M(atthew) P(hipps) (U.K.), 1865–1947.
ABOUT: WW, GSF, SFW, CA, NE, SMFL, SFE, TCSF, PE, ESF

3-320. This Above All. Vanguard, 1933. U.K. title: *Above All Else.*
Various persons miraculously raised from the dead by Jesus are still living in the early twentieth century; the girl Rachel Jeshurah is physically a child despite being old in experience, while Lazarus now poses as Prince Surazal—these two would like to be united but Fate, aided by a third immortal (and perhaps by Jesus too), is determined to keep them apart. A philosophical novel murkier in its implication than is usual with Shiel, who never quite succeeded in working out a coherent attitude to Jesus and biblical mythology.

[For other works of this author, see the companion guide to horror.]

Sinclair, Upton, 1878–1968.
ABOUT: CA, SFE, SFFL, TCSF, ESF

3-321. What Didymus Did. Wingate, 1954.
A jobbing gardener is commissioned by an angel to put an end to war, and given supernatural power to assist him. He performs miracles for the press and founds a new religion, but the modern world is too intractable to be saved by such old-fashioned methods. An amiable and sentimental satire, though it was apparently considered too controversial for publication in the author's native land.

Sitwell, Osbert (U.K.), 1892–1969.
ABOUT: CA, SFE

3-322. The Man Who Lost Himself. Duckworth, 1929.
Novel, set partly in the future, describing the career of a brilliant but oversensitive poet whose life and writings are dramatically changed by a visionary meeting with his future self—an event which he subsequently manages to forget until he approaches it once again from the other viewpoint. Written in a remarkably dense style with much elaborate digression, presumably intended to exemplify and evaluate the cultural changes brought about by World War I.

[For other works of this author, see the companion guide to horror.]

Smith, Thorne, 1893–1934.
ABOUT: WW, GSF, SFW, F, SMFL, RG, ESF, HF

3-323. The Glorious Pool. Doubleday, Doran, 1934.
A garden pool is magically transformed into the fountain of youth; the aging hero, his wife and his mistress all make use of it, and are rejuvenated in outlook as well as physique, with the usual farcical results.

3-324. The Night Life of the Gods. Doubleday, Doran, 1931.
An inventor whose magic ray can petrify flesh is seduced by a girl whose magic can bring statues to life; his inhibitions are thrown overboard and they set about creating mayhem, bringing to life the statues of several Greek deities, who

respond to reincarnation by going on an Olympian binge. All good not-so-very-clean fun.

3-325. Rain in the Doorway. Doubleday, Doran, 1933.
The department store doorway in which the hero takes shelter proves to be a portal to another world, where all his heart's desires can be gratified—which breaks the dominion of his defeatist moral obedience. Confronts questions of sexual morality more directly than earlier books, but the abandonment of sly obliquity does not work entirely to the text's literary advantage.

3-326. Skin and Bones. Doubleday, Doran, 1933.
The hero is sporadically and unpredictably transmogrified into an animated skeleton, with the usual absurd and chaotic consequences. Pure slapstick without the serious undercurrents which enliven Smith's best works.

*3-327. The Stray Lamb. Cosmopolitan, 1929.
The middle-aged hero is liberated from his suburban rut by the combined efforts of his daughter's seductive best friend and an elf who keeps changing him into different animals. The curse of respectability is lifted, but not without a certain amount of suffering—indeed, the hero must undergo the biblical penalty of stoning in order to obtain his deliverance; this thorny underside to the risqué comic adventures gives the book a certain pointedness.

3-328. Topper. McBride, 1926. U.K. title: *The Jovial Ghosts.*
The novel in which Smith first began to set the pattern of his fantasies, which brought Ansteyan formulas into a new phase, in which the anarchic magical intrusions work against pre-Depression/post-Volstead Act American suburban conventions instead of Victorian ones. The matters of propriety involved are typically (and fundamentally) sexual, and they are handled in a sly, rather flirtatious way which has links with James Branch Cabell's more sophisticated and more sentimental comedies [3-63–3-72]. Here a boring commuter is taken up by a pair of freewheeling ghosts and taught to loosen up; the sequel, *Topper Takes a Trip* (1932), is a poor reprise of its theme.

*3-329. Turnabout. Doubleday, Doran, 1931.
Mr. and Mrs. Modern American Everyman spend much of their time bickering, each claiming to be trapped and charging the other with having it made. The family idol swaps their personalities around so that each see how the other half lives. Sophisticated comedy with much metaphorical nudging, winking and outright leering, but the calculated naughtiness overlays a cutting satirical examination of the "problem" of middle-class ennui.

in collaboration with **Norman Matson**, 1893–1965.

3-330. The Passionate Witch. Doubleday, Doran, 1941.
Novel developed by Matson from a work left incomplete by Smith. A businessman is seduced into marriage with a sexy but nasty witch; her death does not end his problems because he remains afflicted by her curse. It is difficult to believe that Smith intended the witch to be a villain; it is entirely appropriate that the film *I Married a Witch* and the subsequent TV series *Bewitched* redressed the

balance in her favor. Matson's solo sequel, *Bats in the Belfry* (1943), is likewise more sympathetic in its treatment of her, but is still by no means true to the spirit of Smith's work.

Speight, T. W. (U.K.), 1830-1915.

3-331. The Strange Experiences of Mr. Verschoyle. Chatto & Windus, 1901.
The protagonist, having been turned down by the woman to whom he has proposed marriage, is badly injured in a fall, but his spirit is allowed to take possession of another body. In his new guise he renews his suit, but finds matters complicated by the fact that his new body is that of a known felon. Led to follow a life of crime, he can escape the gallows only by taking over the body of an aging Jew, in which guise he begins to make atonement for his follies. Melodrama with an unusual edge of bitterness.

Stephens, James (Ireland), 1882-1950.
ABOUT: GSF, SFW, CA, RG, ESF, HF

*3-332. The Crock of Gold. Macmillan, 1912.
Complex fantasy based in Irish folklore but with an eye on many aspects of the modern world. The central character is a philosopher, a master of science and reason, whose wife belongs to the fairy-folk, here called the Shee (i.e., Sidhe). When he helps a peasant get revenge on the leprechauns for a petty prank by stealing their gold, the little people exact their own revenge by framing him for murder—from which predicament it needs no less than a god to extract him. Pan is also around. A classic, richly embroidered both thematically and stylistically; quite incomparable. Stephens's versions of ancient Irish stories, including *Deirdre* (1923), sometimes have propagandist overtones, but the tales in *In the Land of Youth* (1924) are simply beautiful. His short stories—some of which are in *Etched in Moonlight* (1928)—frequently include visionary episodes and allegorical undertones.

Sterling, George, 1869-1926.
ABOUT: CA, PE

3-333. A Wine of Wizardry and Other Poems. A. M. Robertson, 1907.
The title poem, published at the behest of Ambrose Bierce in *Cosmopolitan*, is an extraordinarily lush narrative describing the odyssey of personified Fancy through the most exotic realms which the imagination can distribute in hypothetical space and time. It builds upon, though it has important contrasts with, Sterling's earlier fantastic poetry, which has strong affinities with the morbidly philosophical "graveyard poetry" of Edward Young and Thomas Parnell. Some readers were appalled by what they considered its excesses, but others—including Clark Ashton Smith, who adopted it as a paradigm for the whole of his literary and artistic endeavour (see [H3-182])—found it inspiring. It is reprinted in Sterling's *Selected Poems* (1923) and in Lin Carter's anthology *New Worlds for Old* (1971).

Stevens, Francis (pseud. of **Gertrude Bennett**), 1884–1939?
ABOUT: GSF, SMFL, SFE, TCSF, ESF, HF

3-334. The Citadel of Fear. Paperback Library, 1970.
Novel first serialized in *Argosy* in 1918. It begins as a lost race fantasy, with two explorers getting into difficulties among descendants of the Aztecs, but then skips to modern America; one of the explorers is now the agent of the evil god Nacoc-Yaotl, performing experiments whose success might enable him to conquer the world. It is up to his erstwhile companion and friends to put a stop to it all. Conventional pulp adventure, better written than most, bringing a touch of Merrittesque exoticism to a Rohmeresque plot.

Thurber, James, 1894–1961.
ABOUT: SFW, CA, SMFL, RG, ESF, FL, HF

3-335. Fables for Our Time and Famous Poems Illustrated. Harper, 1940.
The fables are brief and very witty tales with aphoristic morals entirely appropriate to modern life. Many more are in *Further Fables for Our Time* (1956). Some champion the life-enhancing labor of the imagination against the sterile outlook of crude materialism, as does Thurber's most famous story, "The Secret Life of Walter Mitty" (in *My World—and Welcome to It*, 1942).

*3-336. The Thirteen Clocks. Simon & Schuster, 1950.
An evil duke, so cold and callous that time has frozen around him, has imprisoned a beautiful princess; a prince disguised as a minstrel, aided by the enigmatic Golux, must try to rescue her by restoring the dominion of time. A marvelously stylish and witty fantasy, full of polished wordplay; accessible to children but by no means a juvenile work.

*3-337. The White Deer. Harcourt, Brace, 1945.
The youngest of three princely brothers is the only one not devoted to hunting and fighting, but when a white deer hunted by his elders turns into a beautiful girl, he is as ardent as they to win her hand. Each of the princes is given a task to fulfill, but in the end only love can prove the worthiness of the one who may claim her. An excellent sentimental fantasy, beautifully written.

Todd, Ruthven (U.K.), 1914–   .
ABOUT: GSF, CA, SMFL, SFE, ESF

3-338. The Lost Traveller. Grey Walls Press, 1943.
Surreal political satire, probably a posthumous fantasy. The hero crosses a jewel-strewn wilderness to an overregulated city whose citizens are mostly faceless and which is ruled by the unseen and possibly nonexistent *Him*. After rebelling against its restrictions he is tried, convicted and exiled on an impossible quest to bring back two great auks; this ends with his apparent transmogrification into a great auk as he is being beaten to death. Has obvious affinities with Kafka's *Trial* [H3-11], Kubin's *The Other Side* [H3-118] and Rex Warner's surreal anti-fascist satire *The Wild Goose Chase* (1937); also anticipates Orwell's *Nineteen Eighty-*

Four (1949) in certain important respects. A response to the rise of Fascism and the apparently imminent extinction of liberal values, written before *Over the Mountain* (1939), which is a less enigmatic work in the same vein.

Tolkien, J(ohn) R(onald) R(euel) (U.K.), 1892-1973.
ABOUT: WW, GSF, SFW, F, CA, SMFL, SFE, MF, SFFL, RG, TCSF, ESF, FL, HF

*3-339. The Hobbit. Allen & Unwin, 1937.
Bilbo Baggins, a hobbit, is encouraged by the wizard Gandalf to join forces with dwarves who wish to recover their wealth from the hoard of a dragon; with his help they succeed. In a minor incident Bilbo meets the awful Gollum, whose lost ring—which makes its wearer invisible—Bilbo has found; this ring is, of course, the object around which the plot of [3-340] revolves. A fine, robustly plotted adventure story, richly detailed by virtue of the fact that Tolkien already knew very much more about the Secondary World setting ("Middle-earth") than he was yet ready to publish.

*3-340. The Lord of the Rings. Allen & Unwin, 1954-55. 3 vols.: *The Fellowship of the Ring* (1954); *The Two Towers* (1954); *The Return of the King* (1955). The 1987 Houghton Mifflin hardcover edition incorporates all the textual corrections made piecemeal in earlier British reprints.
Paradigmatic work of modern heroic fantasy; sequel to [3-339] but very much more ambitious in scope. Gandalf realizes that the ring which Bilbo acquired from Gollum is a magical object of awesome power, which can corrupt its owners in proportion to their use of it. The diabolical Sauron is most anxious to have it, so that he can bring the entire world under the dominion of evil; the rival wizard Saruman is also keen to appropriate it if he can, as is the obsessive Gollum. An assorted band of companions is formed with the aim of destroying the ring in the only possible way—which involves taking it into Sauron's own land of Mordor, to the Crack of Doom. The group is soon scattered, but its surviving members find assorted allies in pursuing their quest to its bitter end, including Tom Bombadil and the treelike Ents; the forces arrayed against them include the warrior Orcs, the giant spider Shelob and the dreadful Lord of the Nazgûl. In the process Gandalf is lost, only to be magnificently reborn and later to migrate with the Elves and other characters to the Undying Lands; the outcast human Strider comes into his true inheritance as Aragorn, under whose kingship a new era of history will begin; and the humblest of the questing hobbits attains exactly that measure of heroic status which can yet be set aside when he returns to his own hearth and home. The story proper is augmented by a series of appendices which fill in much "nonfictional" background about the history and metaphysics of Middle-earth, which Tolkien had been engaged in elaborating as a private universe for many years, drawing upon the whole of his scholarly expertise as a philologist, medievalist and folklorist.
    No one else ever developed such a rich and detailed Secondary World, though a few other authors—Cabell and Eddison prominent among them—certainly put sufficient effort, intelligence, and depth of feeling into their own imaginary worlds to be reckoned obsessive in their inventiveness. Tolkien's Secondary World proved

unique, however, in its capacity to capture the imagination of readers—and that in spite of all its idiosyncrasies and a certain amount of carefully cultivated esotericism. Its success was not immediate, but its publication in U.S. paperback was an event sufficiently momentous to transform completely the market situation of heroic fantasy, and hence bring about a new era in its history. *The Lord of the Rings* made fantasy a significant publishing category and inspired a deluge of new works, ranging from literally hundreds of crude imitations to at least a handful of works of comparable achievement; if it had not been published, at least a thousand other books would never have come into being (including this one). The astonishing reception and influence of the novel qualify it as one of the most remarkable literary phenomena of the twentieth century.

Travers, P(amela) L. (U.K.), 1906– .
ABOUT: CA, RG, HF

3-341. Mary Poppins. G. Howe, 1934.
First of a series of books starring the perfect nanny, who is everything nannies are supposed to be and so much more, opening the way to all kinds of fantastic adventures. Followed by *Mary Poppins Comes Back* (1935), *Mary Poppins Opens the Door* (1943) and *Mary Poppins in the Park* (1952). Nice books, shame about the film.

Trevor, Elleston (U.K.), 1920– .
ABOUT: CA, ESF

3-342. The Immortal Error. Swan, 1946.
A man made ill by his fear of spiders is cured of his phobia in the hospital, but while he is being driven home by a friend the two are injured in an accident. The friend seems to recover—but which soul is now inhabiting his body? A careful and earnest treatment of a familiar theme.

Twain, Mark (pseud. of Samuel Langhorne Clemens), 1835–1910.
ABOUT: GSF, SFW, CA, NE, SMFL, SFE, TCSF, ESF, HF

3-343. Extracts from Captain Stormfield's Visit to Heaven. Harper, 1909.
Satirical fantasy of the afterlife which mocks the follies of religious fundamentalism and the absurdities which figure in popular images of paradise. Other cynical reflections upon Christian mythology can be found in *Extracts from Adam's Diary* (1904), *Eve's Diary* (1905) and in various posthumously published items, most interestingly the title piece of the collection *Letters from the Earth* (1962) and the miscellaneous "Papers of the Adam Family" which are also to be found there.

3-344. The Mysterious Stranger. Harper, 1916.
Short novel cobbled together by Twain's executor, Albert Bigelow Paine, from various fragments left by Twain; the patchwork certainly does not reflect Twain's intentions and might be reckoned fraudulent. In sixteenth-century Austria a young man poses as Satan's nephew, working petty miracles to the detriment of those who seek to benefit from them; intruded into the story is much moral philosophical

discussion. The plundered manuscripts are reprinted in full in *The Mysterious Stranger Manuscripts* (Univ. of California Press, 1969), edited by William M. Gibson. Twain produced many other eccentric *contes philosophiques*, most of which remained incomplete and unpublished during his lifetime. Several, including "The Great Dark" and the bizarre "Three Thousand Years among the Microbes," can be found in *The Devil's Race-Track: Mark Twain's Great Dark Writings* (Univ. of California Press, 1980), edited by John S. Tuckey.

Vance, Jack, 1916– .
ABOUT: WW, GSF, SFW, F, CA, TCA, NE, SMFL, SFE, MF, SFFL, RG, TCSF, ESF, FL

*3-345. The Dying Earth. Hillman, 1950.
Cycle of stories set in a decadent far future when civilization has virtually disappeared and magic has reclaimed the world. Some, like "Liane the Wayfarer," are virtual pastiches of Clark Ashton Smith (the scenario is presumably modeled on his Zothique; see [H3-182]), but longer stories such as the novella "Guyal of Sfere" find a more distinctive narrative voice. In the tradition of pulp adventure fiction but exceptionally well written with a fine appreciation of grotesquerie and a light seasoning of allegory. Compare the much later work set in the same world, *The Eyes of the Overworld* [4A-256].

Van Druten, John, 1901–1957.
ABOUT: CA

3-346. Bell, Book and Candle. Random House, 1951.
Play in which witchcraft still flourishes in New York, practiced by witches whose power depends on their alienation from emotional involvement. A lovely young witch suffering from terminal ennui uses magic to seduce her amiable neighbor away from his materialistic fiancée; by the time he contrives to get disenchanted, she has fallen in love with him and lost her power. A pleasant romantic comedy.

Vane, Sutton (U.K.), 1888–1963.
ABOUT: CA

3-347. Outward Bound. Chatto & Windus, 1929.
Novelization of a play (1924); a noted posthumous fantasy in which various passengers on an enigmatic cruise ship gradually realize that they are on their way to the Seat of Judgment; two participants in a suicide pact realize that they are in for a tough time, but there may yet be the possibility of a second chance to make good. Sentimental propaganda for moral rearmament.

van Vogt, A(lfred) E(lton), 1912– .
ABOUT: GSF, F, CA, NE, SMFL, SFE, MF, SFFL, TCSF, ESF

3-348. The Book of Ptath. Fantasy Press, 1947. Also known as *Two Hundred Million A.D.*
Novel of the very far future first published in *Unknown* (1943). Having reincar-

nated himself in the twentieth century to get a taste of the human perspective, the god Ptath returns home to discover that one of his two goddess/wives has brought off an Olympian *cout d'état*, and he faces an uphill struggle to restore his supremacy. Most of van Vogt's SF features men who have or acquire godlike power; it is entirely appropriate that his one overt foray into fantasy should feature gods striving for manlike power.

Viereck, George Sylvester, 1884–1962.
ABOUT: WW, GSF, CA, SMFL, SFE, PE, ESF

3-349. Gloria. Duckworth, 1952.
An American psychologist meets the mysterious Gloria de la Mar on a cruise. She is the Goddess of Love, and takes advantage of their brief encounter to tell him the unflattering truth about the so-called great lovers of history. Firmly in the tradition of John Erskine's cynical fantasies; compare especially *Venus, the Lonely Goddess* [3-131].

in collaboration with **Paul Eldridge**, born 1888.

*3-350. My First Two Thousand Years. Macaulay, 1928.
Two scientists who take shelter in a monastery encounter the Wandering Jew, Cartaphilus, who tells them the story of his life and his three great projects: a quest for wisdom which has taken him to consult the world's great sages, a quest for the ultimate erotic experience (the secret of "unendurable pleasure indefinitely prolonged") and a series of attempts to smash the Empire of Faith which commemorates the one-time acquaintance who gave him his immortality. Two sequels tell the stories of the other immortals whose fates have been interwoven with his: *Salome; The Wandering Jewess* (1930) is the story of Herod's famous niece, cursed with eternal life by Jokanaan, and her feminist determination to advance the cause of womankind (perennially frustrated because her mortal instruments ultimately fall victim to the enervating effects of their "bloody sacrifice to the moon"); *The Invincible Adam* (1932) is the story of the proto-human Kotikokura, who lacks the cultural sophistication of Cartaphilus, as whose servant he poses, but still has the Adam's rib of biblical legend, a penile bone. A sweeping pseudo-allegorical fantasy, lavishly decorated with irony, presenting psychosexual theories which are only slightly tongue-in-cheek. The authors' breezily casual treatment of history is amusing, and their determination to challenge (and if possible offend) conventional moral sensibility has a certain debonair panache.

[For other works of this author, see the companion guide to horror.]

Vines, Sherard (U.K.), born 1890.
ABOUT: GSF

3-351. Return, Belphegor! Wishart, 1932.
Widespread apostasy on Earth threatens Satan with extinction by unbelief, so he sends Belphegor to England in the person of a clergyman's nasty son, to bring about a religious revival with all the finery and fervor of persecutions and the

burning of heretics. Exuberant and very sharp satire poking fun at various contemporary literary vogues as well as trends in morality and matters of faith; pulls no punches, and manifests a rather suspect relish in describing the burnings. Compare Constantine's *The Devil, Poor Devil!* [3-86].

Visiak, E. H. (pseud. of **Edward Harold Physick**) (U.K.), 1878–1972.
 ABOUT: WW, GSF, H, SMFL, SFE, PE, ESF

3-352. Medusa. Gollancz, 1929.
Long sea adventure story in which the young protagonist sails with a ship owner who must rendezvous with pirates in order to ransom his captured son; their own ship nearly follows the pirate ship to a mysterious doom in the grip of a very strange sea monster. The veiled and not easily penetrable allegory makes the novel seem closer in spirit to *Moby Dick* than to William Hope Hodgson's marine horror stories [H3-88; H3-90], warranting its annotation here rather than in the companion volume.

Vivian, E(velyn) Charles (U.K.), 1882–1947.
 ABOUT: WW, GSF, SMFL, SFE, ESF

3-353. City of Wonder. Heinemann, 1922.
Lost race story with more supernatural apparatus than usual; explorers hunting the legendary city of Kir-Asa in Southeast Asia must brave many hazards, including sinister ghostly guardians left over from the Theosophists' version of Lemuria. Vivian wrote several other lost race stories, including *Fields of Sleep* (1923), featuring the last remnant of the Babylonian empire; its sequel, *People of the Darkness* (1924); and *The Lady of the Terraces* (1925), set in South America. *Woman Dominant* (1929) is also a romance of exploration, featuring a South American tribe whose men are rendered docile by a drug. *A King There Was—* (1926) is an interesting pseudo-historical fantasy set in a hypothetical ancient civilization of South America.

Walker, Norman (U.K.).

3-354. Loona: A Strange Tail. Longmans, 1931.
A man trapped by the dreariness of village life and conventional marriage is seduced by a possibly illusory mermaid. Likable, though it obviously owes much to Wells's *The Sea Lady* [3-362], and perhaps a little to Bullett's *Mr. Godly Beside Himself* [3-55].

Wall, Mervyn (Ireland), 1908–   .
 ABOUT: GSF, SFW, ESF

*3-355. The Unfortunate Fursey. Pilot Press, 1946.
Various haunters plaguing an Irish monastery attach themselves to a luckless lay brother, who is consequently thrown out into the wicked world; he has magic powers foisted upon him by a witch and seems doomed, but for the fact that Satan has found a soft spot for him. A beautifully polished comedy with a healthy dose

of sentimentality and some very pointed satirical comment on Irish Catholicism. A work of art, almost on a par with France's *Revolt of the Angels* [3-144]. In the sequel, *The Return of Fursey* (1948), Fursey falls prey to Machiavellian exploitation by an English king and is sufficiently disenchanted to sell his soul to the only real friend he has ever had—but Satan too is in reduced circumstances, and Fursey's loyalty to the cause of evil is sorely tested when he falls in with Vikings bent on sacking his old monastery. Slightly more maudlin than its predecessor, but still a fine exercise in bittersweet philosophical romance. The two novels were reissued in *The Complete Fursey* (Wolfhound, 1985).

Walton, Evangeline, 1907– .
ABOUT: WW, GSF, CA, SMFL, RG, PE, ESF, FL, HF

3-356. The Virgin and the Swine. Willett Clark, 1936.
Novel based on the fourth branch of the *Mabinogion* [1-47], extensively developing the story of Gwydion, his sister Arianrhod and their son Llew Llaw Gyffes. As is usual with works in this subgenre, Walton draws upon other folkloristic materials, and also deploys the Gravesian anthropological theory which suggests that many ancient myths tell the encoded story of the replacement of matrilineality by patrilineality, but she is quite happy to leave the magic in place rather than attempting (after the fashion of Henry Treece and others) to produce a speculative account of the history which may actually underlie the myth. An impressive work, considerably better than the sequels which the author produced when this book was reprinted in the Ballantine Adult Fantasy series as *The Island of the Mighty* (1970) (see [4A-261]).

[For other works of this author, see the companion guide to horror.]

Warner, Sylvia Townsend (U.K.), 1893–1978.
ABOUT: GSF, CA, SMFL, SFFL, RG, ESF, FL

*3-357. Lolly Willowes; or, The Loving Huntsman. Chatto & Windus, 1926.
A confirmed spinster is casually exploited as a babysitter by her family until she moves into a country cottage, where she is wooed for the first time by that "loving huntsman," the devil. She gladly joins the ranks of his harem of witches, but ultimately finds the society of the coven as stifling as its greater counterpart. A touching and highly original exercise in quasi-feminist cynicism.

Wells, H(erbert) G(eorge) (U.K.), 1866–1946.
ABOUT: WW, GSF, SFW, CA, NE, H, SMFL, SFE, RG, TCSF, PE, ESF

3-358. All Aboard for Ararat. Secker & Warburg, 1940.
God, again disappointed with the ways of man, decides on a second deluge, and suggests to Noah Lammock that a new Ark is in order. Noah is not as meek as his prototype, and wants to make conditions. Somewhat clipped in the final stages, suggesting that the aged author ran out of steam, but has some sharp and bitter dialogue.

3-359. The Country of the Blind and Other Stories. Nelson, 1911.
Collection of stories mostly reprinted from earlier collections, but also featuring two classic parables: the title story (1904), about the sighted man who cannot after all make himself king among the blind; and "The Door in the Wall" (1906), about a man who keeps passing up the opportunity to go through a door connected with a treasured childhood memory. The reprints include "The Magic Shop" (1903). *The Short Stories of H. G. Wells* (1927) includes all these plus a few other fantasies from this period, most notably "The Truth about Pyecraft" (1903), about a fat man who seeks magical aid in losing weight; "The Inexperienced Ghost" (1902), about a haunter who cannot remember the passes that will return him to the land of the dead; and "The Story of the Last Trump" (1915), in which the instrument designed to signal the Day of Judgment is accidentally mislaid.

3-360. The Croquet Player. Chatto & Windus, 1936.
Novella—a curious amalgam of fantasy and scientific romance. The narrator is told the allegorical story of the village of Cainsmarsh, where the ghosts of man's brutal ancestors are not yet laid to rest and continue to cause much violence and misery. The narrator fails to grasp the point. One of several "sarcastic fantasies" featuring satirically meaningful delusions which Wells wrote in the latter part of his career; others are *Mr. Blettsworthy on Rampole Island* (1928) and *The Autocracy of Mr. Parham* (1930).

3-361. The Man Who Could Work Miracles. Cresset Press, 1936.
The script of the excellent film developed from Wells's classic short story, in which a playful immortal gives the luckless Mr. Fotheringay the power to gratify his wishes—a power whose intemperate use inevitably leads him to disaster. An ancient folkloristic theme developed into a first-rate modern parable.

3-362. The Sea Lady. Methuen, 1902.
Subtitled "A Tissue of Moonshine." A mermaid accidentally hooked off the British coast seduces a young politician away from his worthy but unmagical fiancée; he chooses romance over realism, and meets his inevitable fate. Ruthlessly desentimentalizes its Gautieresque theme, yet cannot help testifying to the powerful allure of the *femme fatale* (of which Wells probably believed he could speak from experience).

3-363. The Undying Fire. Macmillan, 1919.
Allegory retelling the story of Job in a contemporary setting. A headmaster is sorely tested by circumstance and pestered by comforters but preserves his reconstructed faith in the God of Progress. A product of Wells's brief flirtation with Faith, pioneered in *God the Invisible King* (1917) and *The Soul of a Bishop* (1917). Fervent enough, but clumsy by comparison with the great fantasies based in the Christian mythos.

Werfel, Franz (Austria), 1890–1945.
ABOUT: CA, SMFL, SFE, TCSF

3-364. Star of the Unborn. Viking, 1946. Tr. by Gustave O. Arlt of *Stern der Ungerborenen*, 1946.
Philosophical novel which confronts various theological issues, cast in the form

of a fantasy of the far future. The narrator is reincarnated in the future as a party trick to amuse the guests at a wedding, and is given the grand tour of the "Astromental" civilization, including interviews with the High Floater and the Animator. Parallels are drawn with the *Divine Comedy* but there is much comedy of a less divine kind, in some ways reminiscent of the calculated silliness of John Cowper Powys's last works.

West, Rebecca (U.K.), 1892–1983.
ABOUT: CA

3-365. Harriet Hume: A London Fantasy. Hutchinson, 1929.
Posthumous fantasy; the eponymous heroine finds it impossible to live with her inamorato because her preternatural sensitivity penetrates all his delusions and false representations, but once death has stripped away pretense they can begin to explore the great city they loved and the new opportunities which the afterlife affords. One of the best novels of the subgenre, achieving far more than Houghton's *Julian Grant Loses His Way* [3-179], which it may have inspired.

Wheatley, Dennis (U.K.), 1897–1977.
ABOUT: WW, GSF, SFW, CA, SMFL, SFE, SFFL, TCSF, PE, ESF

3-366. They Found Atlantis. Hutchinson, 1936.
An expedition to find Atlantis is used as cover for a jewel theft, but the dispossessed duchess and her companions, cast into the sea, really do end up in the sunken continent after battling their way past subhuman marauders. The Atlanteans, though few in number, are masters of the occult who live in Olympian splendor. Can mere humans be worthy of a place in such a society?

[For other works of this author, see the companion guide to horror.]

White, Frank L. (U.K.).
ABOUT: ESF

3-367. The Dryads and Other Tales. Warne, 1936.
Three novellas; the title story purports to present a series of fifteenth-century documents in which four observers offer accounts of the events which gave rise to the fairy tale "Sleeping Beauty," followed by a contemporary story of her awakening. The other two—"Ramshackle Keep" and "The Djinn"—purport to supply the real stories of Cinderella and Aladdin. Very eccentric; the first story is quite striking.

White, T(erence) H(anbury) (U.K.), 1906–1964.
ABOUT: WW, GSF, SFW, F, CA, SMFL, SFE, MF, RG, ESF, FL, HF

3-368. The Elephant and the Kangaroo. Putnam, 1947.
An English atheist visiting Ireland is witness to a visitation of the Archangel Michael bringing news of a new deluge; with the characteristic exaggerated zeal

of the convert, he sets out to build an ark in spite of the procrastinations of his hosts. Amusing; one cannot help admiring the temerity of an Englishman who sets out to make fun of the Irish, given that the Irish do the job so very well themselves.

3-369. Mistress Masham's Repose. Putnam, 1946.
On the eponymous islet a young girl discovers a colony of Lilliputians brought to England after their discovery by Gulliver; her guardians want to sell them to Hollywood, but with a little help from her friends she stoutly defends their (and her own) interests. A satire in which the bitterness characteristic of White's later work is nicely offset by the charm of the heroine.

*3-370. The Sword in the Stone. Collins, 1938.
Classic fantasy about the boyhood of Arthur, in which the lowborn Wart comes under the tutelage of Merlyn and enjoys an education without parallel in fact or fiction. The characterizations are exceptionally fine and the story has a perfect blend of humor and sentimentality—a balance maintained in none of its sequels. *The Witch in the Wood* (1939) is a broader comedy whose action revolves around Morgause, wife of King Lot of Lothian and sister of Morgan Le Fay, who tries ineffectually to win the love of comic knights while her four children—the eldest of whom is Gawain—grow up confused. *The Ill-Made Knight* (1940) is earnest and sentimental, moving toward tragedy in telling (very sympathetically) the story of unlucky Lancelot. The Holy Grail is introduced into the scheme here, diverting the series in the direction of moralistic fantasy—a cause which was enthusiastically (indeed, almost obsessively) pursued when the three books were knitted together as parts of *The Once and Future King* (1958) [4A-266], whose version of *The Sword in the Stone* is abridged and somewhat rewritten, and whose version of the second novel is extensively revised as *The Queen of Air and Darkness.*

Whiteing, Richard (U.K.), 1840–1928.

3-371. All Moonshine. Hurst & Blackett, 1907.
The protagonist, anxious about the dangers of overpopulation, has a vision in which the spirits of all the people in the world are assembled on the Isle of Wight. He also meets his soul mate. Pleasantly silly.

Wilkins, Vaughan (U.K.), 1890–1959.
ABOUT: SFE, ESF, HF

3-372. Valley Beyond Time. Cape, 1955.
Three people cross the threshold which occasionally connects the British Isles to another dimension, where descendants of earlier emigrants coexist with the superhuman inhabitants of the timeless Valley of the Ever-Young. One returns, bringing a girl from the Valley, but neither can readapt to a world ruled by time. A heavily nostalgic and engagingly old-fashioned swansong. Wilkins's swashbuckling lost race story *The City of Frozen Fire* (1950) is also of interest.

Williams, Charles (U.K.), 1886–1945.
ABOUT: WW, GSF, SFW, F, CA, SMFL, SFE, RG, ESF, FL, HF

*3-373. All Hallows' Eve. Faber & Faber, 1945.
Posthumous fantasy in which two women adrift in the City of the Dead restore contact with the world of the living so that one of them may oppose the grandiose plans of the master occultist Simon the Clerk. A fine moralistic fantasy, very earnest is its treatment of the phenomenon of evil and its speculations about the ways in which evil may and must be defeated; the best of Williams's metaphysical thrillers.

*3-374. Descent into Hell. Faber & Faber, 1937.
Metaphysical fantasy in which the worlds of the dead and the living overlap as in [3-373]; it develops a similar theme but in a more intimate and mundane setting. Here it is a male poet who must follow the Doctrine of Substituted Love in order to help secure the redemption of a disturbed woman, while a Lilith-figure operates in the cause of evil. Remarkable for its intensity, derived from strong convictions at which the author, by courtesy of the philosophical explorations conducted in his earlier novels, had at last arrived.

3-375. The Greater Trumps. Gollancz, 1932.
Metaphysical thriller based in the symbolic scheme of the Tarot, here represented as a game board as well as a pack of cards. The board (the world) and the pack (the means of manipulating it magically) are in separate hands, but an occultist plans to bring them together, using his grandson's fiancée (whose father has the pack) as an unwitting instrument; like all Williams's magi, however, he cannot quite cope with the forces of good arrayed against him. The allegory is remarkably cryptic but intriguing nevertheless.

3-376. Many Dimensions. Gollancz, 1931.
A would-be magus gains illicit possession of the stone of Solomon, which has the power of being infinitely divisible and gives its users marvelous powers. The forces of law and order become sufficient to defeat him only when augmented by the innocent honesty of a young woman, who can surrender herself to the Absolute without reservation. The robust narrative is adequate to the task of carrying the burden of mysticism.

3-377. The Place of the Lion. Gollancz, 1931.
A Neoplatonist magician brings into the mundane world the Ideal *eidola* of various human qualities—strength, wisdom, etc.—but they are too potent a force, without the control of Reason, to do aught but harm; they must be put away again, if the hero and heroine can figure out how to do it. A fascinating idea, somewhat let down by unclear development and a rather inept plot.

3-378. Shadows of Ecstasy. Gollancz, 1933.
A magus bent on world domination has already won the hearts of black men, his new ecstatic creed having given them the unity of purpose necessary to carry forward a new *jihad* against white oppression; can the forces of reason and traditional religion possibly stem the tide? This very talky novel was the first

metaphysical romance which Williams wrote, and its initial failure presumably made him resolve to import much more action into [3-379].

3-379. War in Heaven. Gollancz, 1930.
Murder mystery whose plot revolves around a conspiracy to obtain and employ the Holy Grail for evil purposes; an Archdeacon and a worthy aristocrat must join forces in an attempt to stop them. The fast-moving but rather disorganized plot is not well integrated with the metaphysical themes, but this was probably a necessary first step in preparing the reading public for the pattern of development which was ultimately to produce [3-374] and [3-373].

Wodehouse, P(elham) G(renville) (U.K.), 1881–1975.
ABOUT: CA, SFE, ESF

3-380. Laughing Gas. Herbert Jenkins, 1936.
Wodehouse's only venture into Ansteyan fantasy, presumably inspired by *Vice Versa* [2-8]. Anesthetics carelessly deployed in dental treatment result in a personality exchange between an earl and a spoiled child star. Stylish slapstick in the customary Wodehousian vein.

Woolf, Virginia (U.K.), 1882–1941.
ABOUT: CA, SMFL, SFE, ESF, HF

3-381. Orlando: A Biography. Hogarth Press, 1928.
The hero, born an Elizabethan gentleman, undergoes a considerable evolution (including a sex change) in the course of a life which extends into the twentieth century. The author refers to the work in her diary as a farce written purely for fun, but it is also an ironic reflection of Vita Sackville-West and her family, embodying a satirical study of English aristocratic nostalgia for the past.

Wright, Austin Tappan, 1883–1931.
ABOUT: SMFL, SFE, RG, TCSF, ESF, HF

3-382. Islandia. Rinehart, 1942.
Utopian fantasy, relevant here mainly because of the way that Islandia became for its author a private universe in which he was as obsessively interested as Eddison in Zimiamvia (see [3-126]), Cabell in Poictesme (see [3-65]) or Tolkien in Middle-earth (see [3-340]); one can see in the narrative the same wish fulfillment element which enlivens more fanciful exercises in rigorous escapism. Mark Saxton, Wright's editor, has continued the story of Islandia in *The Islar* (1969), *The Two Kingdoms* (1979) and *Havoc in Islandia* (1982).

Wright, S(ydney) Fowler (U.K.), 1874–1965.
ABOUT: NE, SMFL, SFE, TCSF, ESF

3-383. Beyond the Rim. Jarrolds, 1932.
Lost race story set in the Antarctic. A group of explorers testing the heretical

proposition that the world might after all be flat follow a subterranean river to a valley warmed by an active volcano, where descendants of Elizabethan puritans still pursue their simple life, haunted by a desperate fear of heresy which places the visitors in dire peril. A striking and fascinating story, one of the outstanding examples of its subgenre.

Wylie, Elinor, 1885–1928.
ABOUT: GSF, SMFL, HF

*3-384. The Venetian Glass Nephew. Doran, 1925.
An eighteenth-century cardinal becomes innocently jealous of his fellows, who mostly have "nephews" to provide them with solace and affection, and commissions a magician to make him a nephew in spun glass. This marvelous youth falls in love, but lives in terror lest the rough-and-tumble of lovemaking shatter his delicate frame—until his inamorata finds a way to bring about parity. The stylistically sophisticated and ornamental surface overlays an acidly sarcastic satire, which holds up sexual ideologies to merciless parody; one of the masterpieces of antisentimental fantasy.

Wylie, Philip, 1902–1971.
ABOUT: GSF, CA, NE, SFE, SFFL, TCSF, ESF

*3-385. The Disappearance. Rinehart, 1951.
Wylie's angry excoriation of the mores and customs of contemporary America, *Generation of Vipers* (1942), inspired charges of misogyny, so Wylie produced this careful thought experiment, dividing the world in two so that men must get by without women and vice versa; in tracking, with clinical precision, the progress of the sundered halves, he develops his theories regarding the psychology of sex and the social philosophy best attuned to human needs and desires. A well-written and admirably thought-provoking book.

[For other works of this author, see the companion guide to horror.]

Yates, Dornford (pseud. of Cecil William Mercer) (U.K.), 1885–1960.
ABOUT: CA

3-386. The Stolen March. Ward Lock, 1926.
The protagonists are fortunate to find the long-lost way into Etchechuria, the country whose history is outlined in many popular nursery rhymes, where they become embroiled in its politics. In the same vein as Anstey's *In Brief Authority* [3-6], but told in Yates's inimitable style (which some find excruciating).

4A

Modern Fantasy for Adults, 1957–88

Maxim Jakubowski

With the British publication in October 1955 of *The Return of the King* (1956 in the U.S.), completing the *Lord of the Rings* trilogy [3-340], fantasy underwent a profound change. Although the impact and influence of Tolkien's famed chronicle was initially a muted, underground one, its paperback appearance in 1965 from Ballantine in the U.S. (compounded by an earlier semi-pirated edition released by Ace, which took advantage of a lapse in the copyright registration of the trilogy) was to make it in effect one of the twentieth century's major "cult" books and transformed the fortunes of the genre for better and for worse.

Post-Tolkien fantasy has become a commercial rather than a literary genre, and its future is now inseparable from the fortunes of the publishing industry and media complex. One might even speciously argue that from the mid-1970s onward, fantasy lost its status as a literary genre and became a commodity, a category in the media marketplace, where books to a large extent lose their individual identity and become a simple product, much like soap. A better analogy might be romance yarns, which offer similar placebos of harmless escapist fare, which connect with the reality of sex and human interaction no more than most modern fantasy can be said to relate to the social, moral or political problems of the late twentieth century.

There is much irony in the way that fantasy writing since (and because of) Tolkien has thus become a sad prisoner to market forces, an increasingly formulaic landscape of worn clichés, dueling swords and warring dragons, a vast kingdom of unending wish fulfillment for a generally passive, often subliterate audience. The other side of the coin, however, is that throughout the three decades since the adoption and consequent bastardization of Tolkien, quest fantasy tropes have increasingly dominated the field, but much distinguished fantasy has also been published. Adopting Theodore Sturgeon's "law" that 90% of all writing is rubbish, one can only applaud the mindless proliferation of bad fantasy writing, insofar as its overall quantity has increased to such a large extent that the remaining 10% share of gold is itself larger. The increasing commercialization of fantasy has stimulated the advent of major talents, who have possibly found a perverse and rewarding pleasure in exploring, subverting and expanding the other neglected realms of fantasy writing relegated to the sidelines by the sheer bulk of Tolkien's heritage. Not that these other strands had ever been invisible. Before the coming of Tolkien, many of them, like the Gothic tradition, the lightweight comedy of manners exemplified by *Unknown* or Thorne Smith, the germs of magical realism, had in fact constituted the mainstream of what was then considered fantasy (see chapter 3). So, if blame is ironically to be laid at Tolkien's feet, it is because the overwhelming success of *Lord of the Rings* equated fantasy in the public consciousness as exclusively the domain of quest-based trilogies, with a lesser smattering of Conan-like sword-and-sorcery shenanigans.

Lest this appear as a terminal denunciation of the publishing process and economics that brought about the explosion of fantasy as a major category from the mid-1960s, one must also apportion much of the blame to the herd mentality of those readers and fans who created the element of cult. This is also the generation who in affluent middle-age are adopting wholesale the worst elements of so-called New Age consumerism (crystals, astrology and other major irrational quirks). It is interesting to ponder for one moment the similar phenomenon which occurred when George Lucas's *Star Wars* movie grossed its many millions. Science fiction pundits were then divided on the impact it would have on the field, but it soon became evident that the many new-found fans of the genre (possibly attracted to *Star Wars* by the many fantasy connotations the galactic epic plundered?) quickly reverted to the lowest common denominator and moved on to both comics and game-playing rather than the works of Asimov, Dick or Silverberg. Indeed, in 1988, the most profitable area of fantasy publishing remains the undemanding books inspired by gaming.

Thirty or so years after the completion of Tolkien's epic, we are now confronted by a massive field, with much dross but also a surprising quantity of nuggets in all shapes and sizes. And in spite of the despairing effect and parallel success of bad fantasy—and when fantasy writing is bad, it is indeed doubly so—we are nonetheless in the midst of what I would consider another golden age of fantasy. Ursula K. Le Guin, Jonathan Carroll, Robert Holdstock, Gene Wolfe, John Crowley, Pat Murphy, Tim Powers, James Blaylock, Avram Davidson, Thomas M. Disch, Michael Moorcock, Angela Carter, D. M. Thomas—the list could be much longer, an honor roll that any literary genre or category could rightfully be proud of.

Looking at recent and current publications and awards in the field, one can recognize only a healthy state of affairs, as horror fiction makes a temporary surge in the paperback market and, one hopes, reduces the number of mid-list outlets for formulaic fantasy trilogies and sagas. The best fantasy writing is being assimilated into the mainstream of world literature, from which it had always come, lest the ignorant forget (see introduction to chapter 1).

Heroic fantasy, as we now perceive it, did not, however, spring fully grown and primed for the voracious paperback market from the hobbit loins of Tolkien's busy kingdoms. Long before *Lord of the Rings*, or indeed *The Hobbit* [3-339], high fantasy, fed by parallel streams of mythology, fairy tales and legend, had already shown itself adept at creating imaginary worlds where the power of magic, nature and the irrational held sway. Earlier chapters have already examined the innovative strengths of authors like Lord Dunsany, Kenneth Morris, Abraham Merritt, David Lindsay and others, but I feel one must journey back to the past to find the other major influence on the commercial boom of fantasy in the 1960s onward: Robert E. Howard's creation of Conan [3-182].

In effect a pulp retread of high fantasy tropes, the ever-battling and traveling swordsman of fortune, whether noble barbarian or prince in exile or hiding, was to become a potent factor in heroic fantasy's future attraction. Representing the power of the sword and the will at a time when right-wing political movements were expressing similar tendentious notions badly assimilated from Nietzsche's philosophy, the triumphant hero of destiny continues to this day to fascinate the popular psyche, supplying ever-mutating power fantasies to young audiences. Writers like Fritz Leiber with his Fafhrd and the Grey Mouser stories were to inject the heroic fantasy canon with wit and imagination, by creating characters as fallible as you and I, while still retaining the power of alien settings and strange customs through which they move. But despite the success of his saga from 1939 to 1988 (with further adventures still to come), Leiber was to prove very much an exception. The brutal barbarian, however, was to be a lasting feature on the fantasy scene, whether as Conan by various pens (L. Sprague de Camp, Poul Anderson, Karl Edward Wagner, Robert Jordan and others) or under other guises (Wagner's Kane, and characters created by Lin Carter, John Jakes and countless others).

Although a highly derivative writer of sword-and-sorcery and Arabian fantasies in his own right, Lin Carter (1930–1988) is a major figure in any survey of fantasy post-Tolkien. Responding to the surprising success of *Lord of the Rings*, Ballantine Books, in an attempt to consolidate its share of the fantasy market, accepted Carter's suggestion to launch in paperback format a series of reprints of classic fantasy texts. Carter's choices were initially exemplary, and it is very much thanks to his pioneering efforts that major books by authors like Lord Dunsany, William Morris, E. R. Eddison, James Branch Cabell, Francis Stevens, David Lindsay, William Hope Hodgson, William Morris, George MacDonald, Robert W. Chambers and many others were resurrected. The field owes much to Lin Carter for unveiling for a new, young audience fantasy's forgotten past, and there is little doubt that his rediscovery program was to have an important influence on authors trying their hand at fantasy after the Tolkien boom.

To accompany his reprint list of novels from the past, Lin Carter was also active in compiling many anthologies: *Dragons, Elves and Heroes* (1969) [1-20], *The Young Magicians* (1969), *Golden Cities, Far* (1970) [1-33], *New Worlds for*

Old (1971), *Discoveries in Fantasy* (1972), *Great Short Novels of Adult Fantasy*, 2 vols. (1972, 1973), and others. While these volumes also served to unearth many wonderful gems from the past, they unfortunately also helped to codify high fantasy as the dominant strand of fantasy writing, badly neglecting the Gothic influence, the whimsy of a Thorne Smith, the "logical" fantasy in a magazine like *Unknown*, and other manifestations in different literary modes.

Carter's influence on the field must therefore attract both praise and criticism. When he later edited a series of annual "best of the year" reprint volumes [4A-305], his personal taste for heroic fantasy was to become even more pronounced and manifested itself in a further series of anthologies (*Flashing Swords* [4A-292], *Realms of Wizardry, Kingdoms of Sorcery*, etc.) in which sword-and-sorcery yarns dominated to the exclusion of all other forms of fantasy writing.

This is not to say that heroic fantasy can at its best not be an exhilarating experience in the hands of its more thoughtful and elegant practitioners like L. Sprague de Camp, Jack Vance, Poul Anderson, Tanith Lee or C. J. Cherryh. Even John Crowley's first novel, *The Deep* [4A-78], fits comfortably into this fascinating subgenre, although he also added to the mix a heady brew of subversion.

But for me the best of the heroic fantasy bunch and also its head spoilsport must be Michael Moorcock. In addition to impeccable pulp credentials as the teenage editor for the British edition of *Tarzan Adventures* and comics scripter, and much love and affection for the planetary romances of Leigh Brackett and the rakish sword-and-sorcery picaresques of Fritz Leiber, Moorcock brought an intelligent and iconoclastic approach to heroic fantasy and its previous standards of bludgeon and thunder and paper-thin characterization. In his closely cross-linked tales of Elric of Melniboné, the Eternal Champion, Corum and Dorian Hawkmoon [4A-181–4A-183], Moorcock not only "directed" with much aplomb a multiverse full of metaphysical conflicts on an epic scale, where Order and Chaos ceaselessly fight through a welter of confusion toward an all-too-spectacular global Armageddon, he also introduced human characters, anti-heroes with strong existential traits and recognizable frailties. Whether readers identified or not with his tortured heroes, Moorcock forever muddied the clean waters of fantasy, turning his gaudy, imaginary worlds into subtle reflections of our own, full of pain and contradictions. In a way, Moorcock brought reality to fantasy. Seldom again would it prove possible to accept passively and seriously simplistic tales of derring-do with ever-triumphant lily-white heroes.

Although many of Moorcock's sword-and-sorcery series were in fact rapidly written for purely monetary reasons, and although the links between his fast-moving sagas often appear to have been injected at a late stage as an afterthought, they also introduced a new maturity into the genre. Not that this kept his books from being thoroughly misunderstood by a meekly admiring audience as just "more of the same" with added blood and guts. A prolific writer, Moorcock was later to synthesize his subversion of the heroic fantasy genre in the Conan tradition with his earlier, purer literary influences, principally Mervyn Peake and Spenser, in the bleak Gothic panoramas of *Gloriana* [4A-184] and the melancholy *War Hound and the World's Pain* [4A-186].

Also full of doomed characters at odds with the inevitable forces of entropy are the works of two other British writers, encouraged by Moorcook, who cleared the way for their modernistic approach to the genre: M. John Harrison, with the ever-evolving tales of twilight city Viriconium [4A-133], and the younger Colin Greenland (see [4A-123]).

Later books by Moorcock include the autumnal *Dancers at the End of Time* series [4A-182], a sophisticated, witty extravaganza with a nod toward Ronald Firbank, another of Moorcock's major influences, a bittersweet collection of extended vignettes about the loves of gods and mortals in a distant far future. Many of Michael Moorcock's preoccupations are similarly reflected in his science fiction and mainstream work, and he is also noted as an idiosyncratic, sometimes bitchy observer of fantasy literature in his short critical book on the field, *Wizardry and Wild Romance* [7-40].

While Moorcock in England was gleefully subverting the simplistic plots and characterization of heroic fantasy, the legions of Tolkien imitators were blithely ignoring his example and marching on to the triumphant sound of cash registers.

One of the earliest of the blatant Tolkien imitators to achieve massive commercial success was the American Terry Brooks, with the opening volume of what was to become an obligatory trilogy: *The Sword of Shannara* [4A-51]. In addition to the general questing theme, the Tolkien connotations dominate the slick, well-paced adventures of an eponymous hero in a far future, possibly post-nuclear Earth, on a journey to find his ancestor's magic sword and use it to defeat the evil which threatens his world. Dark inhuman creatures reminiscent of Middle-earth's Black Riders, greedy gnomes, a disappearing magician who returns as *deus ex machina* for the grand finale, even the names of places and characters are evocative of Tolkien. But Brooks's novels were to find a large audience who, seemingly, were content with just more of the same. This is a far from uncommon publishing phenomenon (aided by astute marketing by Ballantine, the publishers of Tolkien) and a sad reflection of public taste, immortalized elsewhere by the countless sequels which invariably follow any successful movie, or, in a different field, the unending stream of hard-boiled private eyes who fearlessly tread in the footsteps of Chandler's Philip Marlowe.

In fairness, Terry Brooks's later series *Magic for Sale* (1986–) is an enjoyable romp in the *Unknown* tradition about a man who buys a magic kingdom and is installed as its ruler only to discover the downside of the deal, but Brooks's place in contemporary fantasy will always be compromised by the slavish manner in which he carried the Tolkien baton through an unnecessary series of new incarnations.

Thereafter, the quest trilogy floodgates opened wide, with every new book contributing a Hollywood-style high concept twist to the classic Tolkien formula—*Lord of the Rings* with animals, with feminist overtones, with child protagonists—until Donaldson's ultimate existential concept of leper as hobbit.

Also published in 1977 were the four volumes of Niel Hancock's Atalantan Earth series *Circle of Light* [4A-131] (another quartet of novels, *The Wilderness of Four*, was to appear in 1982). Although its public impact was less visible than Brooks's formulaic exercise in genre, Hancock's work proved more innovative, blending elements of animal fable into the quest melting pot, with an otter and a bear joining the regulation dwarf in his travails. This crossover with the animal fable stream of fantasy would culminate some years later with William Horwood's *Duncton Wood* (1980) [4A-141], itself following in the trail of Richard Adams's *Watership Down* (1972) [4B-1], a hybrid of quest, talking animals and Christian fantasy of redemption (see also Wangerin's *Book of the Dun Cow* [4A-262]), as codified by Tolkien's contemporary and friend C. S. Lewis in his Narnia stories [4B-101].

The year 1977 can in fact be seen as a turning point for that area of fantasy charted by Tolkien. Not only was this the year when both Brooks and Hancock broke into print, it was also a year that saw the publication of the first trilogy of the Chronicles of Thomas Covenant [4A-90] by Stephen Donaldson. This young American author deliberately set out to write an adult fantasy within the standard quest framework. Thomas Covenant is a writer suffering from leprosy, who is transported to the Land where he becomes an important pawn in a particularly well-drawn battle between good and evil. Donaldson's innovative concept was to make his hero a man of many doubts, a complex, questioning, at times even cowardly person at odds with the customary bouts of heroism so prevalent in the average fantasy fare. So Covenant's progress through the Land also becomes a metaphor for his reconciliation with humanity. Donaldson's initial trilogy, despite its gargantuan length and a style that is often verbose and tiresome, is nonetheless a major achievement. Seldom before had characterization in the quest fantasy genre been so acute, and readers evidently responded and identified with the complex and often contradictory Covenant.

Although post-1977 quest fantasies still multiplied like rabbits at the printing presses, the link with Tolkien gradually became more strained as other influences were brought to bear on the genre: folklore, various mythologies, feminism, the heroic strain of post-Conan sword and sorcery, science fiction, etc.

A final, almost definitive trilogy in the Tolkien tradition was to begin appearing in 1984 with *The Summer Tree*, Book One of The Fionavar Tapestry [4A-147] by Guy Gavriel Kay, a Canadian author with undeniable links to Tolkien; in 1974–75, he had spent a year in Oxford assisting Christopher Tolkien in his editorial construction of the posthumously published *The Silmarillion* [4A-251]. The Fionavar Tapestry is a rich blend of suspense and sorcery inveigling five twentieth-century students into a shadow world where the conjured elements of power and magic are inextricably wedded to the all-too-human figures who must wield them or confront them. Synthesizing the human frailties introduced to the genre by Donaldson with the exemplary myth creation of Tolkien's tradition, Kay has possibly put the ghost of *Lord of the Rings* to rest and taken this particular branch of fantasy as far as it can be taken.

Sadly, the dilution of the wonderful heritage of Tolkien continues unabated. The gaming, role-playing phenomenon which sprouted in the 1970s as a curious, derivative by-product of fantasy literature has since grown at a tremendous pace and initiated a whole body of imitative sagas (Enchanted Realms, Dragonlance Chronicles) dominated by authors like Rose Estes, Margaret Weiss and Tracy Hickman. The overwhelming commercial success of the myriad fantasy novels inspired by gaming has been one of the dominant manifestations of fantasy in the late 1980s and truly represents a cynical exploitation of the genre by market forces preaching and appealing to the lowest common teenage denominator. One can only hope that this proves only a fad, not a lasting trend. Much preferable and certainly more honest with their acknowledgment of sources and influences are the prolific and commercial writers of the fantasy mainstream like David Eddings, David Duncan and Barbara Hambly or those with a foot in the healthy young adult market like Patricia McKillip, Cherry Wilder, Nancy Bond, Nancy Springer and others.

Naturally, while the Tolkien imitators manufactured their yard goods, other strands in fantasy writing were far from inactive. One of the most interesting areas has, in fact, occurred where fantasy writing has strongly interfaced with SF. The connection between the two genres has always been a very close one, to the extent that the Nicholls *Science Fiction Encyclopedia* [6-27] postulates that SF is a part of the fantasy realm and remains as indivisible from it as fish from fowl.

World building in the SF mode has provided us with some of fantasy's most entertaining moments, whether we are confronted with other planets or worlds where physical laws are different and magic works, or with the fascinating cosmologies exemplified by authors like Roger Zelazny or Philip José Farmer.

One of the more potent attractions of this particular area of fantasy writing has always been its sheer exoticism. In this respect the Hyperborean lands of Conan are as alien as Bradbury's poetic visions of the planet Mars. One can even go back for direct inspiration to the many lost world stories of the early part of the century and note a direct connection between the barbaric *terrae incognitae* of Rider Haggard's Africa and, say, the highly colored wild lands of Atlantis in the novels of Jane Gaskell. In much the same way, it could be argued that the exotic Martian marvels of Leigh Brackett, Burroughs or C. L. Moore belong as much to fantasy as they do to SF.

Where the borderline between the genres lies uneasy, and claimants on both sides seek to take the credit, is with the classic category of adventures on another planet which owe little to science and rationality and more to magic or fantastic exoticism. Prime examples are Andre Norton's Witch World series [4A-200], Anne McCaffrey's Dragon novels [4A-179] or Marion Zimmer Bradley's adventures on the alien if familiar world of Darkover [4A-47]. Many of these books are worthy achievements in whichever genre you choose to allocate them to, and demonstrate how fantasy and science fiction coexist with imaginative storytelling to create a genuine feel of the fantastic. Authors like Piers Anthony, Fred Saberhagen, Samuel R. Delany, Larry Niven and Glen Cook navigate this rewarding interface, as does even a writer like John Norman with his tendentious but popular Gor series, itself in the tradition of Burroughs.

Another interface common in post-1957 fantasy has been with the historical novel, and nowhere has this been more apparent and rewarding to the genre than in the many treatments of the myth of Arthur, Guinevere and their Round Table acolytes. From Malory and Tennyson onward, the figure of Arthur Pendragon has inspired so many historical and fantasy writers that their tales have constituted almost a small genre in its own right. Indeed, the fascination of this particular myth lies in its uncommon blend of Celtic elements, romance and Christian allegory. Somehow, most writers since 1957 have succeeded in providing the myth with new twists, perspectives and moralities. Chronologically, highlights remain T. H. White's *The Once and Future King* (1958) [4A-266], Mary Stewart's trilogy (1970 and after) [4A-240], Laubenthal's *Excalibur* (1973) [4A-158], Vera Chapman's novels (1975 and after) [4A-67], Robert Nye's *Merlin* (1978) [4A-201] and Marion Zimmer Bradley's *Mists of Avalon* (1983) [4A-48]. While the historical field also tackles the Arthurian myth from a necessarily limited angle, fantasy has enabled modern storytellers to radically renew the myth's relevance to contemporary readers. Merlin, that paragon of the eternal mage, who appears in the books of authors as varied as Zelazny, John Cowper Powys and H. Warner Munn, has proved a popular character even in SF books. Such is the power of the Arthurian legend which has perforce become a fantasy trope as frequently used as the quest epic form pioneered, or at least modernized, by Tolkien.

The transmutation of legend into and through fantasy thus encouraged, the modern period saw a literal explosion in the adaptation of myths, fairy tales and folklore of all ilk. Where purely historical novelists like Rosemary Sutcliff, Henry Treece, Cecelia Holland and Naomi Mitchison serve up a broadly colored landscape but essentially stick to the facts, fantasy writers have broken free and set loose their imaginations on the embroidering of all types of mythologies: Greek and Roman (Thomas Burnett Swann), Norse (Poul Anderson), Chinese (Barry Hughart), Oriental (Piers Anthony), Central European (Lisa Goldstein).

Through fantasy devices, Jane Yolen and Italo Calvino reactualize traditional fairy tales, Sylvia Townsend Warner revisits the world of faerie, Holdstock externalizes atavistic emotions and man's relationship with the forces of nature, Le Guin confronts the image and concept of death. All these are major aspects of the modern fantasy literature that feeds on past forms, and impressively demonstrate the phoenix-like power of fantasy writing as it repeatedly cannibalizes its past and sources to elaborate an increasingly more complex and mature genre in constant evolution, as it moves steadily from early myths to new mythologies.

While an amorphous school of fantasy writers innovate on traditional grounds like myth, faerie and legend, we have also witnessed the triumphant emergence of yet another strand in the magic tapestry of the field: the adoption of fantastic "attitudes" by the literary mainstream not only in the United States and Canada, but also overseas. Here, devoid of any obedience to pulp traditions, major writers like Günter Grass, Borges, Cortázar, Mark Helprin, John Barth, John Updike and Anthony Burgess have been adept at taking on the imaginative mantle and giving the genre respectable *lettres de noblesse*. The forms adopted by these distinguished authors vary from the picaresque to the ghost story, the magical realism of some of the South American authors to the intellectual rigor of the fables of Jorge Luis Borges, but the influence of these isolated works is already a major one. A particularly unique modern master like John Crowley has drunk in these waters, and his esoteric, deceptive sagas belong as much to the literary mainstream as to the fantasy field, as does much of Gene Wolfe's fantasy.

What attracts these writers to fantasy is the power that it holds to focus on the soul and reality through fantastic devices that magnify everyday occurrences. The magical realism of a García Márquez often consists of a minute attention to detail and the prosaic acceptance of the unreal as part of ordinary life. In fantasy, nothing can surprise, everything is possible; this certainly gives credence to the widely accepted theory that all literature is in essence fantastic.

* * *

While the mainstay of American fantasy writing from 1960 onward thus owes allegiance to Tolkien, Howard and traditional sources in myth, magic and folklore, with a later leavening of mainstream influences, British authors less restricted by a burdensome pulp heritage proved far more individualistic in their literary approach to fantasy. Curiously enough, few authors in Britain followed in the footsteps of Tolkien unless they were working in the children's or young adult areas.

While the prolific Moorcock quietly subverted the heroic fantasy heritage, his contemporary J. G. Ballard, also much active in the SF field, also crossed the blurred genre borderline to convey uneasy fantastic visions of worlds, sometimes futuristic and at other times uncomfortably close to our own, askew (the Vermilion Sands stories, *High-Rise* [H4-18], *The Unlimited Dream Company* [4A-16]). Other grand British individualists must also include Angela Carter, for her often erotic reconstructions of traditional fairy tales and her baroque visions of America and Victorian England, which borrow successfully from what is Britain's major influence in the realm of fantasy: the Gothic tradition. This strand, honed to literary perfection in the Titus novels of Peake [3-285], can be seen reflected to a large extent in the modern novels of many British writers: Anthony Burgess, prolific in the mainstream, in *The Eve of Saint Venus* [4A-56] and the gentle ghost story *Beard's Roman Women* [4A-55]; Kingsley Amis and his son Martin Amis (*Dead Babies*); and others.

Also in evidence among British authors to a degree much less visible with their American counterparts is an acute sense of the romantic. Combined with the gaudy exoticism of science fantasy, this expresses itself best in the colorful sagas of Jane Gaskell and, later, Tanith Lee; tempered with literary influences, it also surfaces in the works of Christopher Priest, Keith Roberts and Joy Chant, while the feel of nature of Robert Holdstock blends both U.S. and British traditions in a delicate mix of contemporary fantasy reinterpretation of classic tropes. In isolated novels other writers like Brian Aldiss, the poet D. M. Thomas and Ian Watson have also provided new twists and reinterpretations that owe little to Tolkien or Conan, and give the map of fantasy new allure. Colonial influences and foreign mythologies take an important part in Salman Rushdie's home-brewed version of South America's magic realism, while Robert Nye's often gleeful retellings of history and legend are noted for their wicked humor. In all, British authors have been less restricted by genre straitjackets, and even if their works do not exhibit the all-encompassing breadth of American contemporary fantasy, they often appear to be important breakers of new ground and an essential component in the constant renewal of fantasy.

One type of modern fantasy writing that began as an essentially British prerogative is the animal fable. Richard Adams with *Watership Down* [4B-1] added much new perspective to what had been until then essentially an area of children's writing, and his successors soon combined this new tradition with other subgenres to mixed effect: the Christian redemption of Wangerin's *Book of the Dun Cow* [4A-262], the quest motif in Hancock's Atalantan Earth series [4A-131], etc. Notable achievements in this area comprise Bach's *Jonathan Livingston Seagull* [4A-14], despite its American New Age pseudo-philosophical, humanist message; Horwood's moles in *Duncton Wood* [4A-141], Aeron Clement's *Cold*

Moons (1987) and Garry Kilworth's *Hunter's Moon*. Mary Stanton's *Heavenly Horse from the Outermost West* [4A-238] cleverly annexes horse mythology through an American perspective in what promises to be an important series.

But the truly outstanding modern practitioners remain those authors who have resolutely not allowed themselves to be pigeonholed and whose work combines originality, feeling and a new sense of the fantastic as a prolongation of everyday life.

Peter S. Beagle, from his first novel, *A Fine and Private Place* (1960) [4A-22], onward, displayed an originality decidedly at odds with current fashions. Moving from subtle ghost stories to a nostalgic tale of unicorns (*The Last Unicorn*, 1968 [4A-24]), or delving into the dark side of game-playing activities and their magic counterparts (*The Folk of the Air*, 1986 [4A-23]), his spare style combines humor with serious fantasy and shifts easily through allegory and symbolism when required.

Californian James Blaylock emerged on the scene only in the 1980s but has quickly established as his own a quirky patch of highly distinct dimensions, a blend of historical whimsy with romance and bittersweet humor. His light touch and idiosyncratic subjects already mark him clearly as a successor to Charles G. Finney and Ray Bradbury as one of contemporary American fantasy's finest exponents; he has in a short time carved for himself a unique and lasting niche.

Being based in Europe has possibly contributed a necessary touch of levity and Old World weariness to the subtle novels of dislocation of American writer Jonathan Carroll. With *The Land of Laughs* [4A-61], *Bones of the Moon* [4A-60] and *Sleeping in Flame* [4A-62], he has produced oddly affecting novels, always walking an uneasy tightrope between literary affectation and all-out horror. The tension between the said and the unsaid, the moving characterization and quirky portrayals of animals (particularly in the World Fantasy Award–winning "A Dog's Best Friend") are quite unlike anything in the work of his contemporaries, in the U.S. or elsewhere.

John Crowley is potentially the greatest talent at present involved in the fantasy field. His evocative and poetic writing seems to inhabit a parallel world of its own, a mirror of our own. In novels like *Little, Big* [4A-79] and *Aegypt* [4A-77], Crowley has created awesome parallel realms, in essence capitalizing on the alienness of the close and familiar. Crowley's ability to hint at a thousand hidden truths under the surface of reality is unique, and indeed, he stands like a rock between past and present fantasy trends, unaffected by the current, moving in some yet unknown direction.

For over thirty years Avram Davidson has been a rewarding joker in the pack, erudite, witty and often mischievous. He has resolutely refused to fit into any single category. His Vergil Magus sequence [4A-81], Peregrine novels [4A-80] and short stories reveal a flamboyant series of imaginary worlds, drawn with scholastic minutiae. Davidson's knowledgeable treatment of science fantasy is both a dazzling display of bookish scholarship and pure entertainment.

Although he has written only short stories in the fantasy field, Harlan Ellison is the genre's undoubted gadfly and shining star. His stories seldom fit into comfortable slots and often hang uneasily in the reaches of science fiction, but his sheer inventiveness when he is at his best makes him one of today's unique storytellers of the fantastic. His voice is loud and disturbing even though he has also shown that he can function with the most delicate of touches ("Jeffty Is Five," 1977, see [4A-96]). A controversial writer full of impassioned energy, Ellison is also the most dramatic and adept in involving the reader, but his manipulation of the senses comes from the heart.

R. A. Lafferty came to writing only in his mid-forties, but for the last thirty years his voice has been another highly distinctive feature of the fantasy scene. A baroque, humorous and benevolent wisdom emerges from his hundreds of short stories. An iconoclastic narrator of tall tales impregnated with strongly Catholic and Irish influences, Lafferty is yet another oddball writer with few ties to traditional fantasy tropes, and possibly also one of the field's most underrated.

In contrast, Ursula K. Le Guin needs no further plaudits. Equally accomplished in fantasy as she is in SF, and accepted by the literary Establishment, Le Guin initially made her mark on the genre with her Earthsea trilogy [4B-98], ostensibly written for children. A crystal-clear tale of apprenticeship, maturity and the death quest of a magician, the Earthsea books have codified the trilogy format as strongly as Tolkien's *Lord of the Rings*. Later books by Le Guin (*Orsinian Tales* [4A-163], *The Beginning Place*) and her stories, including the award winner, "Buffalo Gals? Won't You Come Out Tonight," have confirmed her status as America's leading fantasy writer. Le Guin has also proved one of the genre's most elegant commentators and analysts in her critical work [7-28].

Tim Powers, like Blaylock a younger, California-based writer, has quickly made a mark for himself in the genre. His early novel *The Drawing of the Dark* [4A-208] is a clever historical fantasy presenting Renaissance Europe as an alien culture, but it was *The Anubis Gates* [4A-207], winner of the Philip K. Dick Award, which established his reputation. A memorable novel whose historical setting in nineteenth-century London transcends fantasy, *The Anubis Gates* starts as SF, moves through horror, blends genres with alacrity and includes time travel and magic. Despite knowingly pulpish elements (resurrected Egyptian gods, bodysnatching), Powers somehow captures the sheer essence of the fantastic in this accomplished novel. His talent for adventure writing was confirmed in *On Stranger Tides* [4A-209], an innovative blend, seldom attempted before, of pirates, romance and voodoo.

The last modern master worth highlighting is also one of the most important. Gene Wolfe is another writer who came into his own only in his forties but quickly proved himself a rewarding author for the thinking reader, through his combination of pulp, science fantasy and a deep understanding of human nature. Following *Peace* [4A-272] and *The Devil in the Forest*, two low-key novels in a minor mode, Wolfe proved with a series of short stories of note that he was an author who, like wine, improves with age. He demonstrated this with the wondrous reach of Book of the New Sun (1980–87) [4A-270], which blurs all distinctions between fantasy and SF, and the historical alien feel of his recreation of ancient Greece in *Soldier of the Mist* [4A-273]. Wolfe affirmed himself a master of the sense of wonder, an author whose intelligence is always on display but who somehow never attracts attention to it until after the fact.

Synthesizing as they do the many strands that make up fantasy and creating private universes of their own to which most readers can readily relate, these ten leading contemporary authors are also perfect examples of modern fantasy at its best: an unlimited exercise of the imagination, based in the solid foundations of fantasy's historical traditions in myth, folklore and the supernatural.

While the writers briefly discussed above now represent the cutting edge of fantasy's mainstream, many other authors have naturally prospered in other, sometimes more marginal areas of fantasy. The European tradition of the absurd pioneered by people like Eugene Ionesco or the protean French writer Boris Vian has also proved a rewarding one whose influence should not be ignored. Vian's tender combination of whimsy, surrealism and romance, although little known in the English language, positions him at the forefront of the absurdist stream of fantasy. The more rigorous intellectual exercises of Argentinian Jorge Luis Borges also had an undeniable effect on his later peers, who strive to recapture existential angst and dilemmas through recourse to a new architecture of the imaginary. Such self-referential forms of surrealism were reflected strongly in European writing in some of the books of Günter Grass and Patrick Suskind and in Michael Ende's *Momo* [4A-97] in Germany, while in France traces of this influence appear in the rare works of Michel Bernanos and, with a powerful added Germanic Gothic influence, in the dark short stories of Daniel Walther. Italo Calvino tempered this surrealist streak in Italy with a touch of metaphysics and is often considered one of the more remarkable essayists of the philosophical tale, bridging the gap with some of the fantastic utopias of previous centuries.

A number of major mainstream American writers also belong or pay allegiance to this fruitful surrealist stream: Philip Roth with *The Breast* [4A-219], the picaresque tales of John Barth, Donald Barthelme, and the fascinating puzzles of Thomas Pynchon. A more recent American writer with a possible Ballardian influence is Steve Ericsson. In Australia, Peter Carey also belongs to the great tradition of surreal fabulists.

Of course a major ingredient in this fabulist stream is humor. Never an important component in formulaic fantasy, humor has nonetheless tempered some of the genre's darker excesses and was highlighted in pre-1957 days in the works of James Branch Cabell, John Collier and Anthony Boucher, among others. Today, the principal writers offering a well-balanced cocktail of humor and fantasy are both British: Terry Pratchett and Tom Holt. Manifestations of humor in modern American fantasy are usually broader in intent and appear more as a parody of the heroic fantasy genre in series by Piers Anthony, Alan Dean Foster or Craig Shaw Gardner. The one highly individualistic writer who blends both the absurd and humor is Rudy Rucker, although with his strict obedience to mathematical laws and improvisation, he is more generally categorized as a science fiction writer.

Alongside the absurdist stream, it is also possible to identify two further accomplished, if minor, strands, which have both been responsible for fairly important books. The highly romantic, and specifically American theme of time travel romances as exemplified by the many touching fantasies of Jack Finney and Richard Matheson stands out, as does the eternal theme of life after death, with its often conflicting visions of heaven, hell and elsewhere (Rucker, E. E. Y. Hales, Niven and Pournelle, Stanley Elkin).

Of necessity, the circumscribed frontier of fantasy writing is as elusive as it is limitless. So many books, stories and authors juggle precariously over sundry interfaces, sometimes opting for the specificity of one genre or another, but more often than not standing at unstable crossroads where they can be claimed by proselytizers of the various genres. Particularly adept at riding the never never land of the interface with horror are writers like Stephen King, Peter Straub, Manly Wade Wellman, Scott Baker, Lisa Tuttle, Chelsea Quinn Yarbro, Charles L. Grant, Robert McCammon, Raymond Feist and many others. In fact, as is pointed out in the companion volume to this guide, exponents of horror literature often describe their field as one of dark fantasy.

An even more crowded interface is that with science fiction, where the borderline between adventure-led science fantasy and SF is increasingly blurred as in the works of a variety of authors fluent in both genres, among them Jack Vance, C. J. Cherryh, Orson Scott Card (Tales of Alvin Maker [4A-58]), L. Sprague de Camp and Tanith Lee.

A recent phenomenon which appears to have taken deep root in fantasy, in particular heroic fantasy, is that of shared worlds. Although, thanks to the increasingly social aspects of the field (conventions, writers' workshops), authors have been known on occasion to share locales and even minor characters, this was not properly codified until the appearance of the first Thieve's World anthology [4A-301] in 1979. Created and edited by Robert Lynn Asprin, the series took the collaborative idea one step further and hatched a series of tightly woven short stories wherein various authors continue a basic storyline and set of characters within a preset structure. In Thieve's World and many of the similar follow-ups (Bull and Shetterly's Liavek, Janet Morris's "Hell," C. J. Cherryh's Merovingen Nights), the setting is customarily a semi-barbarian sword-and-sorcery background with magic a determining factor; this allows for easy plot development. The commercial success of these series (which have also bred some solo novels) has been quite surprising, as the anthologies mix both "name" authors and relative unknowns. The concept has now been adopted by writers with already established fictional worlds, which they have subsequently opened up to others (Marion Zimmer Bradley's Darkover, Andre Norton's Witch World). Although some interesting stories have come about this way (in particular Robert Silverberg's contributions to the "Hell" series), this trend represents a creative dead end, denying authors a full imaginative canvas.

From the romance of the nineteenth century, the commercial sea change of pulp between the two world wars, the coming of age of heroic fantasy in its abbreviated and more violent sword-and-sorcery incarnation, the exemplary harnessing of myth by Tolkien that became an obtrusive landmark, to the complex multi-stream that fantasy is today, the field has traveled a long and exciting way. Despite the natural pressures of publishing's commercial environment, there can be no denying that a literary form that can accommodate Jonathan Carroll, John Crowley, Ursula K. Le Guin and Gene Wolfe; straightforward entertainers like Jack Vance, C. J. Cherryh, Robert Silverberg and Michael Moorcock; appealing oddballs like Lafferty or Powers; and mainstream refugees like Anthony Burgess or Mark Helprin, as well as the myriad diluted and derivative sagas like the Dragonlance Chronicles and Gor series, shows signs of great health.

The main hope for the future is that all these complementary streams and subgenres that make up fantasy writing continue to prosper and to cross-fertilize one another, for in diversity also lies the potential for innovation and quality. From high fantasy to dark fantasy and surrealism, there is a place for all aspects of the genre. There will always be a fascination with the dark, the unreal and the imaginary, and there can be little doubt that there will always be writers, old and new, to provide the necessary skills and thrills, the parts that unleash the mysteries of the imagination.

Bibliography

A number of annotations, signed (BS), have been contributed for this chapter by Brian Stableford.

Ackroyd, Peter (U.K.), 1949– .
ABOUT: F, CA, H, MF

4A-1. Hawksmoor. Hamish Hamilton, 1985.
An effective ghost story of sorts from the acclaimed biographer of T. S. Eliot. The devilish eighteenth-century architect Nicholas Dyer has secretly dedicated to evil all the churches he is building, and arranges for a series of ritual murders on their foundations. These are investigated by Inspector Hawksmoor of Scotland Yard, when the deaths are echoed in the twentieth century. As the two parallel plots converge, Ackroyd intelligently conveys uncomfortable analogies between the barbarism of the past and the modern worlds. A literary and sometimes gruesome essay on the nature of evil and creativity. Also annotated as [H4-1].

Adams, Richard (U.K.), 1920– .
ABOUT: CA, SMFL, MF, SFFL, RG, PE, FL, HF

4A-2. Shardik. Allen Lane, 1974; **Maia.** Viking, 1984.
Although both are set in the Rider Haggard-like fantasy setting of the Beklan Empire, these two novels by the creator of *Watership Down* [4B-1] differ sharply in mood and theme. In the first book, the appearance of Shardik, a giant bear with supernatural powers, brings war and upheaval to the Empire. A heavy-handed allegory of the coming of Christ, *Shardik* is laden with symbolism and replete with hardship and suffering. *Maia*, on the other hand, strikes a lighter note with the colorful romance of a young slave girl's rise to power in a pica-resque world in strife, often reminiscent of Jane Gaskell's Atlan series [4A-115].

[For other works of this author, see the companion guide to horror.]

Aldiss, Brian W(ilson) (U.K.), 1925– .
ABOUT: CA, NE, SMFL, SFE, MF, SFFL, TCSF, ESF

4A-3. The Malacia Tapestry. Cape, 1976.
A delightful anachronistic fantasy full of color and pathos by one of Britain's leading imaginative writers. In the medieval and slightly Levantine city of Malacia, tame dinosaurs roam the streets and mechanical innovation and new ideas are strictly banned. A dashing young actor courting the beautiful Armida becomes involved in the development of a curious form of cinematography which stirs up the status quo. Quietly picaresque and reflective, a novel of great charm. Compare Le Guin's *Orsinian Tales* [4A-163].

Anderson, Poul, 1926– .
ABOUT: WW, GSF, SFW, F, CA, TCA, NE, SMFL, SFE, MF, SFFL, RG, TCSF, ESF, FL, HF

4A-4. The Merman's Children. Putnam, 1979.
Anderson's chronicle of fourteenth-century medieval Europe evokes the end of the magical realm of faerie as Christianity becomes dominant. An emotional tale of conflict and adventure unfolds as a family of mer-folk are cast adrift in a world that has no more need of them. An immensely satisfying epic fantasy, with pronounced dark overtones.

4A-5. A Midsummer Tempest. Doubleday, 1974.
A rare but effective example of Shakespearean fantasy. Opposing magic and technology, Anderson's romantic tale of conflict between Puritans and the realm of Oberon is a naïve paean to the forces of nature in a world where Shakespeare is considered a great historian. Although flirting at times with science fiction, *A Midsummer Tempest* also interfaces with Anderson's other major fantasy, *Three Hearts and Three Lions*.

4A-6. Three Hearts and Three Lions. Doubleday, 1961.
A young Danish engineer is transported back to a magical, medieval world. Here he struggles to assist the forces of Christianity and Order to triumph over magic and Chaos. A boisterous romantic fantasy (initially serialized in *The Magazine of Fantasy and Science Fiction* in 1953) of the clash between magic and religion, steeped in Scandinavian myths. Also annotated as [3-3].

in collaboration with **Karen Anderson.**

4A-7. King of Ys series (*Roma Mater*, Baen, 1987; *Gallicenae*, Baen, 1987; *Dahut*, Baen, 1988; *The Dog and the Wolf*, Baen, 1988).
Historical fantasy set in the days of the Roman Empire, in the mythical kingdom of Ys, which was engulfed in water. The series follows an assortment of sharply drawn characters—centurions, kings, priests, queens and princesses—through Roman civil wars, Irish invasion and other blights, mapping, through meticulous research and a strong, ever-darkening mood, a complex saga of a world that might never have been.

Anthony, Piers, 1934– .
ABOUT: SFW, CA, TCA, NE, SMFL, SFE, SFFL, RG, TCSF, ESF, FL

4A-8. Apprentice Adept series (*Split Infinity*, Ballantine, 1980; *Blue Adept*, Ballantine, 1981; *Juxtaposition*, Ballantine, 1982; *Out of Phaze*, Ace, 1987; *Robot Adept*, Ace, 1988; *Unicorn Point*, Ace, 1989).
Effective blend of fantasy and SF in a light mood. Two parallel worlds are respectively governed by magic and science. An ecological fable, this clever series involves robots, struggle and magic in intriguing proportion in opposition to an all-reigning computer force. Minor but enjoyable tales, with a gentle sting in the tail. Notable for its SF setting.

4A-9. Hasan. Borgo Press, 1977.
Initially published in 1969 in *Fantastic Stories*, *Hasan* is one of modern fantasy's first successful attempts to break out of the restrictive traditional Celtic/Norse/Arthurian mold. This entertaining *Arabian Nights* fantasy follows the loves and adventures of a young Persian youth in his quest for wealth in mysterious lands. Anthony's light touch prefigures his later Xanth books.

4A-10. Incarnations of Immortality series (*On a Pale Horse*, Ballantine, 1983; *Bearing an Hourglass*, Ballantine, 1984; *With a Tangled Skein*, Ballantine, 1985; *Wielding a Red Sword*, Ballantine, 1986; *Being a Green Mother*, Ballantine, 1987; *For Love of Evil*, Morrow, 1988).
Although initially planned in five volumes, this series is still ongoing. Highly symbolic novels in which all facets of humanity are examined as individuals who are forced to bear the mantle of, respectively, death, time, nature, war and fate. A struggle and a personal/global quest usually ensue. Fast-moving and ambitious, if not always coherent, these are challenging novels in which Anthony appears to have invested much emotional energy.

4A-11. Xanth novels series (*A Spell for Chameleon*, Ballantine, 1977; *The Source of Magic*, Ballantine, 1979; *Castle Roogna*, Ballantine, 1979; *Centaur Aisle*, Ballantine, 1981; *Ogre, Ogre*, Ballantine, 1982; *Night Mare*, Ballantine, 1982; *Dragon on a Pedestal*, Ballantine, 1983; *Crewel Lye*, Ballantine, 1985; *Golem in Gears*, Ballantine, 1986; *Vale of the Vole*, Avon, 1987; *Heaven Cent*, Avon, 1988).
A highly popular commercial series of decidedly light-hearted fantasy adventures in the magical world of Xanth. Much word play and boisterous humor permeate the continuing adventures of a group of sympathetic but fallible characters whose humanity grows from volume to volume. Escapist but entertaining fare of great skill.

Arnason, Eleanor.
ABOUT: FL

4A-12. The Sword Smith. Condor, 1978.
First novel in a high fantasy mold by an author whose early promise has sadly remained unfulfilled. A young blacksmith reared by dragons roams a sparse fantasy world on a voyage of exploration, and discovers that his craft gives his life

meaning. Well-developed characterization and a lean style mark an unusual, rather unheroic tale.

Asprin, Robert Lynn, 1946– .
ABOUT: CA, NE, RG, TCSF

4A-13. Myth series (*Another Fine Myth*, 1978; *Myth Conceptions*, 1980; *Myth Directions*, 1982; *Hit or Myth*, 1983; *Myth-ing Persons*, 1984; *M.Y.T.H. Inc. Link*, 1986; *Little Myth Marker*, 1985; *Myth-Nomers and Impervections*, 1987; *M.Y.T.H. Inc. in Action*, 1989; all Donning).
A popular series of slapstick-like novels set in a world not unlike a comic strip version of *Arabian Nights*, peopled with djinn, homunculi, dragons, spells galore and a bevy of seductive women. Inspired by the Bob Hope–Bing Crosby "Road" movies, this is pure entertainment, and a clever (and pun-full) use of fantasy as backdrop to comedy.

Bach, Richard, 1936– .
ABOUT: CA, SMFL, SFFL

4A-14. Jonathan Livingston Seagull. Macmillan, 1970.
One of the great cult books of the 1970s and a dubious precursor of much of the next decade's "New Age" brand of pseudo-philosophy. The eponymous Jonathan is a bird with a vision, which sets him apart from his fellow birds. Rejected by the Flock, he dies and is reborn, Christ-like, to bring a message of a better life to all. A maudlin classic.

Baker, Scott, 1947– .
ABOUT: CA

4A-15. Nightchild. Putnam, 1979.
An odd rite-of-passage novel, in which the hero, reared in a church-run orphanage, joins the priesthood of a mysterious cult which involves vampirism. Soon the young man realizes the nature of supernatural powers. Borderline fantasy and horror quest for transcendence.

Ballard, J(ames) G(raham) (U.K.), 1930– .
ABOUT: CA, NE, SMFL, SFE, MF, SFFL, TCSF, ESF

4A-16. The Unlimited Dream Company. Cape, 1979.
Although most of Ballard's science fiction and mainstream novels swim in an ambiguous sea of undeclared irreality, *The Unlimited Dream Company* is his only true venture into the realm of the fantastic. The hero crashes his stolen plane into the river Thames, deep in British suburbia, dies and is reborn into a new world of the British provinces revised by the naïve allegorical painterly visions of a Douanier Rousseau. Full of wonderful, ironic imagery of luxuriant greenery and birds, Ballard's book is a curious life-affirming, Dionysiac vision of modern times.

[For other works of this author, see the companion guide to horror.]

Banks, Iain (U.K.), 1954– .
ABOUT: CA, MF

4A-17. The Bridge. Macmillan, 1986.
A man, comatose following a bad automobile accident, dreams what his life was or might be. A giant bridge dominates his consciousness, and he must puzzle out its significance. A terse, imaginative novel by the young Scottish author of *The Wasp Factory* [H4-19], which combines black humor, sword-and-sorcery parody and keen psychological insights.

[For other works of this author, see the companion guide to horror.]

Barker, Clive, 1952– .
ABOUT: CA, PE

4A-18. Weaveworld. Collins, 1987.
A massive mixture of classic quest interlaced with true examples of visceral horror and sexual evocation from one of the contemporary stars of dark fantasy. Beginning in Barker's native Liverpool, the novel follows a young couple's struggle to preserve the integrity of the weaveworld, a magic realm hidden within a carpet, from the well-evoked forces of evil. Although overlong, the novel never ceases to excite, and demonstrates how the blending of horror into the clichéd quest motif can invigorate it no end. Possibly a new direction in fantasy. Also annotated as [H4-23].

[For other works of this author, see the companion guide to horror.]

Barth, John, 1930– .
ABOUT: CA, SMFL, SFE, SFFL, ESF

4A-19. Chimera. Random House, 1972.
A sprawling literary novel, joint winner of the 1973 National Book Award for fiction, about mythological characters and the power and telling of myths. It is structured in three parts: the *Dunyazadiade*, a variation on the tale of Scheherazade; the *Perseid*, which follows Perseus after the events in the legend; and the *Bellerophoniad*, which examines the role of the hero as artist. Intelligent, complex and a notable examination of the nature of myth and creation.

4A-20. Giles Goat-Boy or, The Revised New Syllabus. Doubleday, 1966.
A sprawling, multi-layered modernist allegory. In a future world called the University, where man and technology enjoy a complex relationship, a boy is reared with goats and grows up through education, initiation and transcendence to martyrdom. A demanding discourse on the nature of heroism filtered through a full array of self-conscious literary devices, it is an erudite monument and a fantasy landmark.

Barthelme, Donald, 1931–1989.
ABOUT: CA, SMFL, SFE, ESF

4A-21. The Dead Father. Farrar, Straus, 1975.
An elliptical absurdist fable of a journey from city to countryside where the body

of a giant, not-yet-dead father figure is being taken to its ultimate resting place. Through bizarre encounters, rituals of enigma and an apocryphal text, "A Manual for Sons" (reproduced in full, together with illustrations, as the characters read it), Barthelme offers a unique, surrealist and comic nihilist mini-saga.

Beagle, Peter S., 1939– .
ABOUT: WW, SFW, CA, SMFL, SFE, MF, SFFL, RG, ESF, FL, HF

4A-22. A Fine and Private Place. Viking, 1960.
A reflective ghost story which delicately touches upon greater concerns like the meaning of life and the permanence of love, written when the author was only nineteen. Set in a cemetery, the tale, both sentimental and skillfully humorous, unfolds serenely, with a diverse cast of realistic and colorful characters both human and ghostly, toward a carefully modulated climax. A minor masterpiece. Also annotated as [H4-25].

4A-23. The Folk of the Air. Ballantine, 1987.
Beagle's return to fantasy, after an eighteen-year hiatus, brings back Farrell, the hero of his story "Lila the Werewolf." A wanderer, he returns to Avicenna, California, and becomes involved with the League of Archaic Pleasures (Beagle's version of the Society for Creative Anachronism), magic and a twilight zone where time and space are telescoped. Thinly plotted but humorous and enjoyable.

*4A-24. The Last Unicorn. Viking, 1968.
The last unicorn travels the land in search of its vanished kin. Along the way it encounters both purity and wickedness. A strong quest novel from a different viewpoint. Both a serious tale and a gentle parody of the conventions of the quest romance, *The Last Unicorn* succeeds on both fronts. Strong symbolism abounds, but the book remains a delightfully light-hearted read. Was clumsily adapted into an animated feature by Saul Bass (1982).

Bear, Greg(ory Dale), 1951– .
ABOUT: CA, NE, TCSF

4A-25. The Infinity Concerto. Berkley, 1984; **The Serpent Mage.** Berkley, 1986.
A tough kid from modern Los Angeles ventures into a parallel world of magic, after an elderly Hollywood composer leaves him the key to a mysterious building. Bear's imagined world, full of much beauty and cruelty, owes much to Coleridge's Xanadu and offers a refreshing reinterpretation of old themes.

Behm, Marc, 1925– .
4A-26. The Ice Maiden. Zomba, 1983.
A light-hearted contemporary romp about a set of New York vampires struggling with the rising cost of living. Led by an eerily beautiful woman, they find that the logical crime is to steal from a Mafia casino. A unique fantasy outing by a film screenwriter famed for his classic psychological mystery, *The Eye of the Beholder*.

Bellairs, John, 1938– .
About: CA, SMFL, SFFL, FL

4A-27. The Face in the Frost. Macmillan, 1969.
A sinister battle between opposing wizards, with a detective-like investigation into the whereabouts and identity of the foe. Leavened by frequent humor, this is a strong compendium of fantasy themes and magic in all its sundry manifestations, with many a dark corner unveiled to scary effect. Also annotated as [4B-17].

Bemmann, Hans (Germany), 1922– .

4A-28. The Stone and the Flute. Viking, 1986. Tr. by Anthea Bell of *Stein und Flöte*, 1983.
A massive European fantasy in the Anglo-Saxon tradition of *Lord of the Rings* [3-340]. Rich in texture with many intertwining threads of plot and narrative inventiveness but a sparing use of supernatural elements. The theme at the heart of the novel is the misuse of power, but the emphasis is on the moral growth of Listener, the hero, rather than on mere adventure.

Berger, Thomas, 1924– .
About: CA, NE, SMFL, SFE, SFFL

4A-29. Arthur Rex. Delacorte, 1978.
A grown-up retelling of the legend of King Arthur, in which both sex and magic take a bawdily entertaining part. Embellishing rather than altering the Malory canon, Berger breathes new human qualities into the known figures of myth, with rounded characterizations of Guinevere and Mordred standing out. A witty and stylish version of the Camelot legend.

4A-30. Being Invisible. Little, Brown, 1987.
Having cleverly subverted the western (*Little Big Man*) and redrawn the Arthurian genre (*Arthur Rex*), Berger here succeeds in invigorating the well-worn theme of the everyman who becomes invisible. Fred Wagner writes advertising copy for mail-order catalogs and, one day, while facing himself in a full-length mirror, makes a passing wish. A deliberately low-key novel dissects with warmth and affection the human impact of wish fulfillment in contemporary society. Unlike H. F. Saint's *Memoirs of an Invisible Man*, published the same year to greater commercial success, Berger's version posits no rational or pseudo-scientific explanations for the invisibility phenomenon.

Bernanos, Michel (France), 1924–1964.
About: SMFL

4A-31. The Other Side of the Mountain. Houghton Mifflin, 1968. Tr. of *La Montagne morte de la vie*, 1967.
A rare example of French fantasy by the short-lived son of renowned Catholic author Georges Bernanos. Two stranded sailors find themselves adrift in a strange world dominated by an eerie mountain, which they eventually attempt to climb.

A surreal vision of life beyond death. Compare Niven and Pournelle's *Inferno* [4A-197], which relies less on symbolism and is more obvious. Also annotated as [H4-30].

[For other works of this author, see the companion guide to horror.]

Bisson, Terry.

4A-32. Talking Man. Arbor House, 1986.
Delightful small-scale American fantasy with a pronounced touch of country-and-western backroads exuberance. Wry supernatural happenings in a dusty Kentucky junkyard where the creator of the world has taken refuge with his teenage daughter. Wonderful use of magic as an aspect of everyday life makes this endearing novel stand out with a voice, locale and feel all its own.

Blaylock, James, 1950– .
ABOUT: CA, MF

4A-33. The Digging Leviathan. Ace, 1984.
A gentle, baroque cross between a Southern California *Tristram Shandy* and a far-fetched scientific romance in the Edgar Rice Burroughs Barsoom vein. A bunch of romantic eccentrics seek to reach a subterranean world with the assistance of a complex mechanical mole, while rivals take a strange sea route in the same direction. An affectionate romp full of dreams and much keenly observed humanity.

4A-34. The Elfin Ship. Ace, 1982.
A delightfully improbable world of faerie where elves turn out to be great lovers of fine cheese, magical airships abound, and glorious adventure is afoot. Gently subverting many genre clichés—mad goblins, evil dwarves, a cloak of invisibility, magic coins and a watch that stops time—this early Blaylock novel presents a magical world with consummate skill and affection. The concluding books in this trilogy include *The Disappearing Dwarf* (1983) and *The Stone Giant* (1989).

4A-35. Homunculus. Ace, 1986.
A tangle of mildly sinister misadventures in Victorian London,with shades of Dickens, Sax Rohmer and Rider Haggard. Blaylock assembles a fantastic motley crew of humorous characters involved in a picaresque and unlikely tale of zombies, fish, preachers, messiahs and malevolent hunchbacked geniuses. A joyful romp. Compare fellow Californian Tim Powers's own version of nineteenth-century London, *The Anubis Gates* [4A-207].

4A-36. The Land of Dreams. Arbor House, 1988.
Set in the world of the World Fantasy Award story winner "Paper Dragons," *The Land of Dreams* takes place in Northern California as the twelve-year solstice comes to a coastal town. An evil carnival run by a sinister gentleman capable of turning into a crow is the focus of attention for three local orphans. A magic phantasmagoria. Compare Bradbury's *Something Wicked This Way Comes* [4A-45].

4A-37. The Last Coin. Ziesing, 1988.
An endlessly funny fantasy about the nature of reality in Blaylock's customary laid back style and manner. This one involves pigs bearing silver spoons, and men named for money in quest of a fabulous coin. With hints of Illuminati-type conspirators, dissertations on breakfast cereals and wonders aplenty, this is one of the author's most complex and ingenious pastoral fantasies and a great pleasure to read, even when Blaylock indulges in overelaborate whimsy.

Blish, James, 1921–1975.
    ABOUT: F, CA, TCA, NE, SMFL, SFE, MF, SFFL, TCSF, ESF, FL, HF

*4A-38. Black Easter. Doubleday, 1968; **The Day after Judgment.** Doubleday, 1971.
Black Easter and *The Day after Judgment* form the fantasy segment of Blish's After Such Knowledge sequence, which also encompasses science fiction (*A Case of Conscience*, 1958) and a historical novel (*Doctor Mirabilis*, 1964). A fantasia on the problem of evil, the two novels confront apocalyptic fears and the subtle relationship between science, magic and religion in the shadow of the nuclear threat and chronicle the inevitable build-up to Armageddon. A striking and sensitive achievement by any standards, the novels employ allegory, blank verse, parody and many distancing elements of style to raise the specter of the unnamable as few works of fiction have managed before or since. A unique fantasy landmark. Compare the treatment of the coming of Armageddon and the Devil in C. S. Lewis's *That Hideous Strength* (1945).

Borges, Jorge Luis (Argentina), 1899–1986.
    ABOUT: CA, NE, SMFL, SFE, RG, TCSF, PE, ESF

4A-39. The Book of Imaginary Beings. Dutton, 1969. Tr. by Norman Thomas di Giovanni of *El libro de los seres imaginarios*, 1967.
A much expanded version of Borges's *Handbook of Fantastic Zoology* (*Manual de zoología fantástica*, 1957). A fabulous modern bestiary of curious creatures ordered in short, alphabetically arranged entries. Some derive from legends and myths, while others are total fabulations. Borges's dazzling talent is such that the uninformed casual reader is often incapable of telling one group from the other.

4A-40. Doctor Brodie's Report. Dutton, 1972. Tr. by Norman Thomas di Giovanni of *El informe de Brodie*, 1970.
A thin collection regrouping short stories written by Borges between 1966 and 1970, this was his last published collection of tales. Laconic and mysterious vignettes that include "The Intruder," "The Duel," the title story and eight others.

4A-41. Labyrinths. New Directions, 1964. Various translators.
The definitive collection of Borges material in English, using material from *Ficciones* (1956), *El aleph* (1957), *Discusión* (1957), *Otras inquisiciones* (1960) and *El hacedor* (1960). The collection includes twenty-three stories including the

classic "Tlön, Uqbar, Orbis Tertius," about a new world where external objects are whatever each person wants; "Pierre Menard," about the man who rewrote parts of *Don Quixote* word for word as well as "The Circular Ruins," "The Library of Babel," "The Garden of Forking Paths," "The Lottery in Babylon" and many other subtle fables full of wonderful intelligence, a wealth of invention and tight, almost mathematical style. The volume also features ten essays and seven parables. *Ficciones* is also annotated as [3-43].

4A-42. A Universal History of Infamy. Dutton, 1972. Tr. by Norman Thomas di Giovanni of *Historia universal de la infamia*, 1954.
The first of Borges's volumes of short stories, originally written for an Argentinian newspaper in the 1930s. A chronicle of the lives of famous villains like Billy the Kid and the Tichborne Claimant and of little-known rascals, peppered with challenging and delightful apocrypha. The volume also includes his first story, "The Street Corner Man," and other short tales.

Boyett, Steven R.

4A-43. The Architect of Sleep. Ace, 1986.
While exploring underground caves, a young student comes across a subterranean world of intelligent raccoons. The first volume of a projected series, the novel presents a sharply delineated, almost medieval civilization, where the nonanthropomorphic creatures communicate with sign language and display complex political systems. A strong contrast to the customary woolly-eyed animal sagas so frequent in contemporary fantasy.

Bradbury, Ray, 1920– .
ABOUT: WW, GSF, SFW, CA, TCA, NE, SMFL, SFE, MF, SFFL, RG, TCSF, PE, ESF, HF

4A-44. Dandelion Wine. Doubleday, 1957.
A bucolic evocation of Bradbury's youth through rose-colored glasses. Though not strictly fantastic, this poetic blend of nostalgia and ever-so-slightly macabre happenings defines the author's view of the past as a country of the bizarre and the wonderful, and is central to Bradbury's fantasy world.

4A-45. Something Wicked This Way Comes. Simon & Schuster, 1962.
The carnival comes to a sleepy, peaceful, provincial American town and with it come quirky forces of evil and magic. An often macabre tale of an adolescent's rite of passage, this is Bradbury's most accomplished fantasy novel, full of colorful characters and images, and beautifully modulated fear. The novel was filmed in 1979 by Jack Clayton, with Jason Robards, to mixed effect.

*4A-46. The Stories of Ray Bradbury. Knopf, 1980.
A definitive 884-page collection of Bradbury's best short fiction in both the SF and fantasy fields. Includes selections from *The Illustrated Man* (1951), *The Martian Chronicles* (1950), *The Machineries of Joy* (1964), *The October Country* (1955), *I Sing the Body Electric* (1969) and other collections. Bradbury has always arguably produced his best, most evocative work in short form, and these stories

range from his gentle, bucolic Illinois nostalgia to his boisterous Irish drinking-bar fantasies, horror and even crime. Also features six previously uncollected stories. A perfect introduction to the work of fantasy's most noted stylist. Also annotated as [H4-52].

[For other works of this author, see the companion guide to horror.]

Bradley, Marion Zimmer, 1930– .
ABOUT: CA, TCA, NE, SMFL, SFE, SFFL, RG, TCSF, ESF, HF

4A-47. Darkover series (*The Sword of Aldones*, Ace, 1962; *The Planet Savers*, Ace, 1962; *The Bloody Sun*, Ace, 1964; *Star of Danger*, Ace, 1965; *Winds of Darkover*, Ace, 1970; *The World Wreckers*, Ace, 1971; *Darkover Landfall*, DAW, 1972; *The Spell Sword*, DAW, 1974; *The Heritage of Hastur*, DAW, 1975; *The Shattered Chain*, DAW, 1976; *The Forbidden Tower*, DAW, 1977; *Stormqueen*, DAW, 1978; *Two to Conquer*, DAW, 1980; *Sharra's Exile*, DAW, 1981; *Hawkmistress!*, DAW, 1982; *Sword of Chaos*, DAW, 1982; *Thendara House*, DAW, 1983; *City of Sorcery*, DAW, 1984; The Heirs of Hammerfell, DAW, 1989).
Another massive, and continuing, series that straddles both the fantasy and SF genres, the Darkover novels take place on a four-mooned colonial planet settled by Terra and then forgotten. Plots of the earlier novels follow classic heroic fantasy lines under the joyful influence of Abraham Merritt, C. L. Moore and Leigh Brackett, with warrior castes in conflict, psychic powers and feudal societies in torment. Later books, from *The Heritage of Hastur* onward, benefit from more mature characterization, speculations on the nature of male/female intimacy and a deepening of fantastic elements through new conflicts as Darkover is rediscovered by the Terran Empire. A large fandom has evolved surrounding the Darkover books, and Bradley has also edited several anthologies of Darkover stories penned by herself and others.

4A-48. The Mists of Avalon. Knopf, 1982.
A long Arthurian novel in which Bradley adopts a feminist stance, with the narrative developing through the eyes of women central to the plot. An all-encompassing vision of the conflict between Christian and pagan worlds, exploring anthropology, religion and metaphysics, this is historical writing on a grand scale, with all the magic conviction and resonance of ballad and ancient lore. Wonderful, living portraits of Igraine, Viviane, Guinevere and Morgan Le Fay toughen up the worn stories of the standard Arthurian canon and make this quite an experience.

Brin, David, 1950– .
ABOUT: CA, NE, TCSF

4A-49. The Practice Effect. Bantam, 1984.
Light-hearted fantasy from a practitioner of hard science fiction in a frivolous mood reminiscent of Piers Anthony or L. Sprague de Camp. A contemporary

scientist is shifted into the customary parallel world of magic, where the quirky "practice effect," an unusual twist on the laws of physics, operates to amusing effect. Escapist but entertaining.

Broderick, Damien (Australia), 1944– .
ABOUT: CA, NE, TCSF, ESF

4A-50. The Dreaming Dragons. Norstrilia Press, 1980.
An aboriginal Australian scientist warns of a dreadful secret in a strange outcropping of rock. Combining psychology with metaphysical transcendence, this is a challenging parable of nuclear dangers through a fantasy prism.

Brooks, Terry, 1944– .
ABOUT: CA, SMFL, RG, FL

4A-51. Shannara trilogy (*The Sword of Shannara*, Ballantine, 1977; *The Elfstones of Shannara*, Ballantine, 1983; *The Wishsong of Shannara*, Ballantine, 1985).
One of the most commercially successful Tolkien retreads, Brooks's saga substitutes a magic sword for the eponymous ring and elves for hobbits, but retains all the essential tragi-comic elements of the classical quest as race against time to avert the coming of evil. Fast-moving, smooth but derivative piece of entertainment.

Brown, Mary (U.K.).

4A-52. The Unlikely Ones. Century, 1986.
A long but endearing quest novel featuring a crow, a toad, a goldfish, a cat, a unicorn, a decrepit knight and a young girl. The unconventional, twee-defying characterization, vital to the plot and search, introduces highly adult, realistic, even sensual relationships into the fray to good effect. A clever sweep of the broom through an overexploited area of fantasy writing.

Brunner, John (U.K.), 1934– .
ABOUT: CA, NE, SMFL, SFE, SFFL, TCSF, ESF, FL

4A-53. The Traveler in Black. Ace, 1971.
A rare incursion into fantasy by the prolific science fiction author. *The Traveler in Black* reworks four stories initially published in magazines (a fifth story was added for *The Compleat Traveler in Black*, 1985). The Traveler, a godlike creation, strives to combat Chaos and return a sense of order to the Universe. Compare Moorcock's Elric and Eternal Champion tales [4A-183, 185], where mortal humans are the instruments of change in the struggle between good and evil.

Brust, Steven K., 1955–   .
ABOUT: CA

4A-54. Vlad Taltos series (*Jhereg*, Ace, 1983; *Yendi*, Ace, 1984; *Teckla*, Ace, 1986; *Taltos*, Ace, 1988).
Mayhem and mystery in the Dragaeran Empire, where two races coexist with much discomfort: witchcraft-practicing humans, the Easterners; and elitist sorcerers, the Dragaerans. Taltos, a petty thief and crime lord, manipulates both sides to his own advantage in a series of lightweight but entertaining adventures of the fantastic.

Burgess, Anthony (U.K.), 1917–   .
ABOUT: CA, NE, SFE, SFFL, TCSF, ESF

4A-55. Beard's Roman Women. Hutchinson, 1977.
A slight but haunting novel of love and ghosts by an acclaimed mainstream writer. A middle-aged author mourning for his dead wife discovers mysterious traces of her in the photos he takes of Rome. A sentimental tale of loss and lust, as dead wife and present mistress crisscross paths in a surreal manner. A neglected little masterpiece.

4A-56. The Eve of Saint Venus. Sidgwick & Jackson, 1964.
Novella based on the tale in Burton's *Anatomy of Melancholy* about a young man who slips a ring onto the finger of a statue of Venus and brings her to life. Compares interestingly with the similarly inspired "Venus of Ille" by Mérimée [H2-66] and *The Tinted Venus* by Anstey [2-7]. Burgess's comedy is far more sophisticated than Anstey's, and Venus gets a more sympathetic hearing here than in either of the nineteenth-century examples. (BS)

Calvino, Italo (Italy), 1923–1985.
ABOUT: CA, NE, SMFL, SFE, TCSF, ESF

4A-57. Our Ancestors. Harcourt, 1980.
A trilogy of Calvino's more dream-like short novels: *The Cloven Viscount* (1957), *The Baron in the Trees* (1957) and *The Non-Existent Knight* (1957). Humorous allegories using fantasy motives to slyly reflect on world affairs, these *contes philosophiques* in the Voltaire tradition, now read out of their contemporary context, are little gems of fantastic storytelling, funny, moral and gently picaresque. Also annotated as [3-74].

Card, Orson Scott, 1951–   .
ABOUT: CA, NE, TCSF

*4A-58. Tales of Alvin Maker series (*Seventh Son*, Tor, 1987; *Red Prophet*, Tor, 1988).
Set in a nineteenth-century America where history has taken a divergent path and magic reigns, Card's still ongoing series focuses on Native Americans and frontier

folk. The author's dark vision carries over from his SF titles and works well in a fantasy context full of legends, dreams and sorrows, despite the hackneyed, formulaic rite-of-passage plots.

Carey, Peter (Australia), 1943– .
ABOUT: CA

4A-59. Illywhacker. Faber & Faber, 1985.
A sprawling picaresque feat of magic realism by the young Australian author whose next novel, *Oscar and Lucinda* (1988), won the Booker Prize. Herbert Badgery, a roguish con man with an almost Methuselah-like span of years but also an inveterate liar and fabulist, chronicles his past deeds against the background of Australian history from the late 1880s to the present day. An invigorating example of imagination set loose and wild.

Carroll, Jonathan, 1949– .
ABOUT: CA, H, MF, PE

4A-60. Bones of the Moon. Century, 1987.
A delicate excursion into Carroll's own land of dreams, occupying an uneasy place between fantasy and horror. A contemporary woman is haunted by realms of childhood fantasy. The contrast between her nightmares and her daily life is keenly etched and effectively delineates the emotional impact of the carefully drawn and evocative prose.

*4A-61. The Land of Laughs. Viking, 1980.
A couple of researchers investigate the life of an enigmatic author of children's books for a proposed biography. In his curiously ethereal home town, they encounter his mysterious if welcoming daughter and, as they reconstitute the pieces of his life, slowly move into a new realm of fantasy, intimately connected with his books, until their ventures reach a chilling end. An effective modern fable and an impressive debut for Carroll, an American author resident in Austria, who stands apart from most contemporary fantasy trends and strands.

4A-62. Sleeping in Flame. Century, 1988.
A tale in which reality and fantasy merge in convolutions of magic and suspense. Walter Esterling is rescued as a baby from garbage cans in an Atlanta back alley. Later, now a successful screenwriter in Vienna, he becomes increasingly aware of his paranormal powers, which threaten to engulf him, his wife and child. A perfectly modulated modern fantasy.

Carter, Angela (U.K.), 1940– .
ABOUT: CA, WW, F, SMFL, SFE, MF, SFFL, TCSF, ESF

4A-63. The Bloody Chamber and Other Stories. Gollancz, 1979.
A collection of elegant fables exploring female sexual identity through fantasy narratives that owe much to fairy tales and legends. Stylish, often quite erotic and daring genre subversions by a leading British author.

4A-64. The Infernal Desire Machines of Dr. Hoffman. Hart-Davis, 1972.
A heady blend of surrealism, passion and adventure, and a modern fantasy of epic proportions. The picaresque tale of the war against the sinister Doctor Hoffman who wishes to demolish all the structures of reason and reality (an initial alternate title in the U.S. was *The War of Dreams*). An erotic and dream-like achievement.

4A-65. Nights at the Circus. Chatto & Windus, 1984.
A truculent and expansive tale with a strong Dickensian flavor, *Nights at the Circus* follows the life and amorous exploits of Fevvers, the "Cockney Venus," a giant circus woman with authentic wings. Flamboyant and picaresque, a witty novel on the borderlines of traditional fantasy.

4A-66. The Passion of New Eve. Gollancz, 1977.
A wild feminist futurist fantasy in which an innocent Englishman travels to a war-torn America where, after a series of nightmarish and bizarre avatars, he is surgically transformed into a woman, and becomes a new pagan goddess. A marvelously cruel and imaginative fable about sexual identity and the American landscape.

Chapman, Vera (U.K.), 1898– .
ABOUT: CA, SMFL, RG, FL

4A-67. Three Damosels trilogy (*The Green Knight*, Collings, 1975; *King Arthur's Daughter*, Collings, 1976; *The King's Damosel*, Collings, 1976).
Yet another drawn-out retelling of the life and times of King Arthur, but from a feminist perspective. The radicalization of the material of romance is subtly effected, and the myth is inventively revitalized from the margins of the main events and thus given new strength and insights.

Charnas, Suzy McKee, 1939– .
ABOUT: CA, NE, SFE, SFFL, TCSF, PE

4A-68. Dorothea Dreams. Arbor House, 1986.
A gently modulated supernatural tale of ghosts, haunting dreams of the French Revolution and artists set in present-day Albuquerque. A quiet, understated novel which works well despite constantly hovering on the borders of fantasy.

[For other works of this author, see the companion guide to horror.]

Cherryh, C(arolyn) J(anice), 1942– .
ABOUT: NE, SFE, RG, TCSF, FL

4A-69. Angel with a Sword. DAW, 1985.
The first book in Cherryh's Merovingen series, featuring adventures in an exotic city with a Venice-like thousand bridges and a strongly Dickensian atmosphere. Entertaining lightweight fantasy fare with a strong gallery of rogues and Mondragon, a glamorous hero of gently epic proportions. Cherryh's novel has been succeeded by a series of shared-world anthologies involving other writers, includ-

ing Janet Morris, Mercedes Lackey and Robert Lynn Asprin, in Merovingen intrigues (*Festival Moon, Fever Season, Troubled Waters, Smuggler's Gold*).

4A-70. Quest of Morgaine series (*Gate of Ivrel*, DAW, 1976; *Well of Shiuan*, DAW, 1978; *Fires of Azeroth*, DAW, 1979).
An accomplished quest trilogy with SF premises of gates between worlds, which Morgaine the witch has to close, with the assistance of Vanye, an outcast. Evil constantly lurks behind the corner, but Cherryh's skill rests in blending the developing relationship between the characters with fast-moving, colorful adventures.

Cohn, Nik (Ireland), 1946- .
    ABOUT: CA

4A-71. King Death. Harcourt, 1975.
Heavily ironic fable in which a contract killer who is Death personified is lionized by the media, eventually becoming a bizarre superstar—a career move which corrupts him in the same way that it has corrupted so many others. Compare Gore Vidal's *Messiah* (1954). (BS)

Constantine, Storm (U.K.).

4A-72. Books of Wraeththu series (*The Enchantments of Flesh and Spirit*, Mac-Donald, 1987; *The Bewitchments of Love and Fate*, MacDonald, 1988).
Wildly romantic, ongoing series by a new young British author. A modern punk sensibility imbues the adventures of the sexually ambiguous Wraeththu in a paint-by-numbers heroic fantasy setting redeemed by the imaginative variations Constantine weaves around her lost characters. The critical verdict is still out, but much promise has been shown in the initial two volumes.

Cook, Glen, 1944- .
    ABOUT: CA, NE, SFFL, TCSF

4A-73. Dread Empire series (*A Shadow of All Night Falling*, Berkley, 1979; *October's Baby*, Berkley, 1980; *All Darkness Met*, Berkley, 1980; *The Fire in His Hands*, Pocket, 1983; *With Mercy Towards None*, Baen, 1985; *Reap the East Wind*, Tor, 1987; *An Ill-Fate Marshalling*, Tor, 1988).
Vigorous heroic fantasy on a grand scale as rival barbarian empires fight, with sword and magic, bloody battle after bloody battle. Cook weaves elaborate political scenarios full of connivance and treachery around finely choreographed scenes of mighty armies in combat. With a gallery of full-blooded characters at odds with their destiny, this ongoing saga is both gripping and impressive. Compare Moorcock's Dorian Hawkmoon series [4A-185].

4A-74. Sweet Silver Blues. NAL, 1987; **Bitter Gold Hearts.** NAL, 1988; **Cold Copper Tears.** NAL, 1988.
Closely modeled on Raymond Chandler, an agreeable mystery fantasy series featuring tough private eye Garrett in a hard-boiled land of magic. Garrett has a

partner, the Dead Man, to help him solve the customarily convoluted tales of murder, blackmail and robbery which pepper his eventful path. Gently parodic, but the strong plotting makes these hybrid novels most enjoyable.

Coover, Robert, 1932– .
ABOUT: CA, SMFL, SFE

4A-75. The Universal Baseball Association, Inc. J. Henry Waugh, Prop. Random House, 1968.
A clever metaphor about the power of fantasy over reality, Coover's novel features J. Henry Waugh, a nebbish who devises a complicated baseball board game. The game soon becomes more real to him than the surrounding world and begins to regulate his life. A comic reflection on the humdrum rhythms of everyday life, sport and American social mores.

Crisp, Quentin (U.K.), 1908– .
ABOUT: CA

4A-76. Chog; a Gothic Fantasy. Eyre Methuen, 1979.
Misanthropic and macabre comedy in which the servants of a grotesque aristocrat hope to be remembered in his will, but find their servitude extended when he leaves everything to his dog, Fido. Fido's demands eventually become intolerable, but not until he has fathered a chimerical child on a local prostitute, which eventually brings the farce to its conclusion. The grotesquerie is appealing, though Crisp's wit is not as stiletto-sharp here as in his autobiographical writings. (BS)

Crowley, John, 1942– .
ABOUT: CA, NE, SMFL, SFE, MF, TCSF

4A-77. Aegypt. Bantam, 1987.
The first volume in a projected four-part series about the secret history of the world. Peopled with quietly idiosyncratic characters in search of truth and enlightenment, this long novel blends childhood fantasies, alchemy and astrology, and the theme of parallel Eastern mystical lands to much effect into a dense, poetic but often oblique narrative about the nature of reality. A major work in the making.

4A-78. The Deep. Doubleday, 1975.
Crowley's intriguing first novel is an enigmatic adventure quest on the borderlines of SF. A stranger with a crippled memory has to puzzle out the mystery of the strife-torn world on which he has arrived (from outerspace?). Metaphysical and at times Shakespearean, and full of layers of bizarre symbolism. Compare Wolfe's *Soldier of the Mist* [4A-273].

***4A-79. Little, Big.** Bantam, 1981.
A quiet, long pastoral tale of faerie, its interconnections with our reality, the world of fantasy, human feelings and failings, magic, love and prosaic heroism. A

now-recognized landmark of modern fantasy, Crowley's novel encompasses many worlds in its ambitious scope and triumphs on all counts, although the plot always remains simple and straightforward in its eerie evocation of the strange. A literate, touching and unassuming masterpiece. Compare Helprin's *Winter's Tale* [4A-137] and Wolfe's *Free Live Free* [4A-271].

Davidson, Avram, 1923– .
About: WW, GSF, SFW, CA, TCA, NE, SMFL, SFE, MF, SFFL, RG, TCSF, ESF, FL, HF

*4A-80. Peregrine: Primus. Walker, 1971; **Peregrine: Secundus.** Berkley, 1981.
Typical Davidson adventures in "unhistory," full of picaresque journeys in a world reminiscent of the Roman and Byzantine Empires. Prince Peregrine, exiled from his country of birth, wanders the wide world with servant and attending sorcerer, meeting myriad bizarre characters. Sterling, classical fantasy in a classical mode.

4A-81. The Phoenix and the Mirror. Doubleday, 1969; **Vergil in Averno.** Doubleday, 1987.
Adventures in an alternate first century with the author of the *Aeneid* [1-85], which form part of Davidson's projected Vergil Magus sequence. An intriguing world of never never, with glimpses of both medievalism and quasi-forgotten ancient sciences, with intricate and fast-moving plots. Vergil, part sorcerer/necromancer, part poet, stands as an attractive but ambivalent figure of modernity in a still unformed world. Erudite and witty entertainments of the first order.

4A-82. Strange Seas and Shores, Doubleday, 1971; **The Best of Avram Davidson,** ed. by Michael Kurland, Doubleday, 1979; **The Collected Fantasies of Avram Davidson,** Doubleday, 1982.
A wide-ranging introduction over three volumes (with little overlap) to the impressive imagination and stylish delights of a premier fantasist. With wit, and often humor, Davidson is one of the most protean of authors, equally at ease in all areas. Of note are "The Source of the Nile" and "The Trefoil Company." The second collection also includes a foreword by Peter S. Beagle.

de Camp, L(yon) Sprague, 1907– .
About: WW, GSF, SFW, F, CA, TCA, NE, SMFL, SFE, MF, SFFL, RG, TCSF, ESF, HF

4A-83. Novaria series (*The Goblin Tower*, Pyramid, 1968; *The Clocks of Iraz*, Pyramid, 1971; *The Fallible Fiend*, NAL, 1973; *The Unbeheaded King*, Ballantine, 1983; *The Honorable Barbarian*, Ballantine, 1989).
Thoroughly amusing heroic fantasy adventures, often on the very verge of gentle parody, following a reluctant hero struggling with the mantle of unwanted royalty, lost wives, goblins, wizards' conventions and assorted demons. Peopled with a mighty gallery of buffoon-like minor characters, de Camp's fast-moving series is an impressive achievement in humorous storytelling at its most picaresque and imaginative.

Delany, Samuel R., 1942– .
ABOUT: CA, TCA, NE, SMFL, SFE, SFFL, RG, TCSF, ESF

*4A-84. Nevèrÿon series (*Tales of Nevèrÿon*, Bantam, 1979; *Neveryóna*, Bantam, 1983; *Flight from Nevèrÿon*, Bantam, 1985; *The Bridge of Lost Desire*, Arbor House, 1988).
A cycle of stories and commentary set at the beginning of civilization, and the very antithesis of deeds of warriors à la Conan [3-182]. Delany's books are both a structuralist reconstruction of heroic fantasy and a painstakingly researched panorama of barbarian times in which attitudes, slavery, sexual relationships and historical roots are reassessed in a modernist perspective.

de Lint, Charles (Canada).

4A-85. Greenmantle. Ace, 1988.
Contemporary fantasy with an idosyncratic touch involving Mafia hitmen, small-time punks, lottery players and mysterious woods. The Canadian setting blends with classical folklore elements to good effect, and the focus on strong characters is an added plus.

Dickinson, Peter (U.K.), 1927– .
ABOUT: CA, NE, SMFL, SFE, SFFL, RG, TCSF, ESF, HF

4A-86. The Blue Hawk. Gollancz, 1976.
Although published as a young adult novel (it won the *Guardian*'s award for best children's book of the year), *The Blue Hawk* does not read as such. An elliptical historical story with biblical accents, it is set in an imaginary ancient kingdom fraught with dreaded rituals. Tron, a young boy, saves a blue hawk he has befriended from a sacrificial ceremony, thus unleashing uncontrollable forces as the gods withdraw their favors from the realm and the king dies. A complex but rewarding tale of conflict and growing, with decidedly adult overtones. Also annotated as [4B-37].

Dickson, Gordon R. 1923– .
ABOUT: CA, TCA, NE, SMFL, SFE, MF, SFFL, RG, TCSF, ESF, FL

4A-87. The Dragon and the George. Ballantine, 1976.
A gently humorous tale of an English professor transported to a parallel world not unlike medieval England, where magic dominates. Here his consciousness is placed in a dragon's body and he strives to rescue his fiancée. Strong on action and irony, a lighthearted variation on epic traditions of chivalry and the quest for eternal justice.

Disch, Thomas M., 1940– .
ABOUT: F, CA, TCA, NE, SMFL, SFE, MF, SFFL, TCSF, PE

4A-88. The Businessman. A Tale of Terror. Harper, 1984.
The protean Disch, whose every book appears to come from a different mold altogether, here tackles the supernatural in a wry and knowing way, all his own.

His comic and macabre tale of multiple hauntings eschews the staple ingredients of copy-book horror and takes on an abnormal logic of nightmarish proportion, satirizing the American midwest mentality quite savagely, if always with tongue planted firmly in cheek. A quirky, wicked little masterpiece. Also annotated as [H4-98].

*4A-89. On Wings of Song. St. Martin's, 1979.
An impressive *bildungsroman* of a future when flight can be attained by virtue of the purity of one's singing. A biting attack on the puritanical, repressive elements in American society, with a baroque backdrop of castrati opera singers in a decadent New York of tomorrow, Disch's novel stands alone in the contemporary fantasy landscape as an ambiguous, bitter but spiritual work of great power.

[For other works of this author, see the companion guide to horror.]

Donaldson, Stephen R., 1947– .
ABOUT: CA, SFW, SMFL, MF, RG, FL

*4A-90. Chronicles of Thomas Covenant the Unbeliever (*Lord Foul's Bane*; *The Illearth War*; *The Power That Preserves*; all Holt, Rinehart & Winston, 1977. The SF Book Club edition of the first title preceded the trade hardcover.); **Second Chronicles of Thomas Covenant** (*The Wounded Land*, Ballantine, 1980; *The One Tree*, Ballantine, 1982; *White Gold Wielder*, Ballantine, 1983).
Physically massive quest and redemption sagas in the firmly established Tolkien mold, wherein Thomas Covenant, a leper, is magically transported from the bleakness of his present-day situation in our world to the Land, a magical realm whose survival is closely linked to his myriad adventures and warped personality. Darkly metaphysical, the Covenant Chronicles are a stunning achievement from the pen of a then-beginning writer, despite gaping structural and stylistic flaws and turgid overwriting. Rewarded with enormous commercial success, the Donaldson novels are, however imperfect, a landmark in contemporary high fantasy, and should be applauded for the unheroic nature of their true-to-life fallible characters, a far cry from Tolkien's jolly hobbits.

4A-91. Mordant's Need series (*The Mirror of Her Dreams*, Ballantine, 1986; *A Man Rides Through*, Ballantine, 1987).
A naive and fallible girl from Chicago is unwittingly transported into a beleaguered fantasy land. Donaldson's familiar plotline is sharpened by the relative smaller size of his second epic saga, wherein the alien kingdom of Mordant's complex politics and Machiavellian court are finely etched, in contrast with the anti-heroine's recurring doubts and obsession with mirrors, which takes on a new significance in her new magical environment. Less wish fulfillment and more maturity on display than in the author's Covenant tales.

du Maurier, Daphne (U.K.), 1907–1989.
ABOUT: GSF, CA, SMFL, SFE, SFFL, PE, ESF

4A-92. The House on the Strand. Gollancz, 1969.
Through the use of an experimental drug, a young London publisher is transported in time six hundred years back to rugged Cornwall. Here he can only

observe the goings-on, because contact with natives of the time jolts him back to reality. With well-etched adult characterization, this uncommon novel of a man's downfall questions the nature of fantasy. Compare Matheson's *Bid Time Return* [4A-177] and Jack Finney's *Time and Again* [4A-105], both more sentimental time travel romances. Also annotated as [H4-102].

[**For other works of this author, see the companion guide to horror.**]

Eddings, David, 1931– .
ABOUT: CA

4A-93. Belgariad series (*Pawn of Prophecy*, Ballantine, 1982; *Queen of Sorcery*, Ballantine, 1982; *Magician's Gambit*, Ballantine, 1983; *Castle of Wizardry*, Ballantine, 1984; *Enchanter's End Game*, Ballantine, 1984); **Malloreon series** (*Guardians of the West*, Ballantine, 1987; *King of the Murgos*, Ballantine, 1988; *Demon Lord of Karanda*, Ballantine, 1988; *The Sorcerers of Dorshiva*, Ballantine, 1989).
Epic high fantasy in the Tolkien tradition (the Malloreon sequence is ongoing). Set against a history of seven thousand years of the struggles of gods, kings and men in barbarian lands, the heroic protagonists battle with sorcerers and prophecy. Derivative but popular series.

Eisenstein, Phyllis, 1946– .
ABOUT: CA, NE, SMFL, MF, RG, TCSF

4A-94. Sorcerer's Son. Ballantine, 1979.
Despite being faithful to most of the more hackneyed heroic fantasy tropes (feudal societies, chivalry, sorceresses, magic and mighty castles galore), Eisenstein's novel succeeds by remaining stylish, literate and genuinely romantic at heart. Cray, offspring of a gentle sorceress and a demon, becomes a knight errant in search of his destiny, unleashing events he often has little control over. After a long gap, two sequels were scheduled for 1989.

Elkin, Stanley L(awrence), 1930– .
ABOUT: CA

*4A-95. The Living End. Dutton, 1979.
An extraordinary tragicomic journey through Heaven and Hell and the moral desert of the American midwest as a wine merchant, his killer and other blessed innocents are transported to a ferocious version of the hereafter. Sharply satirical and with a striking portrait of God in all his might and anger, this is literate, evocative fantasy at Elkin's best. Compare Hales's *Chariot of Fire* [4A-127] and Disch's *The Businessman* [4A-88].

Ellison, Harlan, 1934– .
ABOUT: GSF, SFW, CA, TCA, NE, H, SMFL, SFE, SFFL, RG, TCSF, PE, ESF

4A-96. The Essential Ellison. Nemo Press, 1987.
A massive, over 1,000 page compendium regrouping much of Ellison's best material (fiction as well as much nonfiction), although many further gems can

still be found in the better individual collections (worth nothing are *Deathbird Stories*, Harper, 1975; *Strange Wine*, Harper, 1978; *Shatterday*, Houghton Mifflin, 1980; *Stalking the Nightmare*, Phantasia, 1982, and *Angry Candy*, Houghton Mifflin, 1988). Ever a master fantasist with an uncanny feel for genre-straddling concepts of great originality crisscrossing science fiction, fantasy, horror and mystery writing, Ellison is flamboyant, goes for the gut and more often than not succeeds in hitting all the right nerves. The best fantasy stories among the many selections here include "The Deathbird," "Jeffty Is Five," "Strange Wine," "Alive and Well and on a Friendless Voyage," "Shattered Like a Glass Goblin" and "One Life Furnished in Early Poverty." A sterling sampling. Also annotated as [H4-103].

[For other works of this author, see the companion guide to horror.]

Ende, Michael (Germany), 1950– .
ABOUT: CA

4A-97. Momo. Doubleday, 1981. Previously published as *The Grey Gentlemen*. Burke, 1974. Tr. by J. Maxwell Brownjohn of *Momo*, 1973.
Part suspense novel, part modern allegory from the author of *The Neverending Story*, though less obviously meant for children. This is an unusual fantasy in which Momo, a ragamuffin, flees from the grey men, mysterious time thieves who are taking over the world. A bizarre mad-hatter of a professor and his prescient tortoise come to her help on the very edge of time. A challenging good-versus-evil clash with touches of fairy tale and surrealism.

Ericsson, Steve.

4A-98. Days between Stations. Simon & Schuster, 1985.
A young couple, stripped of memory and emotion, embark on a sensual odyssey through a desolate future landscape in an attempt to reconstruct their pasts. Part love story, part post-apocalyptic tableau, part metaphysical detective story, this debut novel defies categorization, and is reminiscent of Ballard at his most entropic.

Farmer, Philip José, 1918– .
ABOUT: CA, TCA, NE, SMFL, SFE, MF, SFFL, RG, TCSF, ESF

4A-99. A Feast Unknown. Essex House, 1969.
A strikingly erotic (some even say pornographic) African romp by one of fantasy and science fiction's most daring breakers of taboos. In a world controlled by a secret group of immortals who hold the secret of the elixir of life, Lord Grandrith and Doc Caliban, two superheroes openly inspired by Tarzan and Doc Savage, struggle for supremacy and knowledge. A crude parable about violence and sexuality, but also gripping pulp reading with Dionysian power.

*4A-100. World of Tiers series (*The Maker of Universes*, Ace, 1965; *The Gates of Creation*, Ace, 1966; *A Private Cosmos*, Ace, 1968; *Behind the Walls of Terra*, Ace, 1970; *The Lavalite World*, Ace, 1977).
An exuberant set of fabulous adventures involving Robert Wolff, a teacher who is

transported to a parallel world and finds glory, love and his former Lordly status, and Kickaha, an Indian trickster supreme, in a group of pocket universes modeled on Babylonian ziggurats. Splendid fantasies, full of color and action, where men are strong and heroic and women are shapely and beautiful. Compare Burroughs's Martian novels [3-61].

Feist, Raymond.

4A-101. Riftwar saga (*Magician*, Doubleday, 1982; *Silverthorn*, Doubleday, 1984; *Darkness at Sethanon*, Doubleday, 1986; *Prince of Blood*. Doubleday, 1989).
Good-humored, vigorous fantasy saga with strong elements of romance. Succeeds in entertaining despite or because of an abundance of genre clichés: illegitimate royalty in exile, human and supernatural warriors, beautiful princesses, pirates, and mad kings, elves, dwarves and dragons. This rich broth with further hints of past Chaos Wars and Dragon Lords is never quite to be taken seriously. Enjoyable schlock epic.

Findley, Timothy (Canada), 1930– .
ABOUT: CA

4A-102. Not Wanted on the Voyage. Delacorte, 1985.
A retelling of the story of Noah and the Ark in a starkly humorous mood. Even more fantastic than its biblical origins, with mythological creatures, angels and swordsmen galore inhabiting an ironic world of wonders. A rare, highly successful foray into fantasy by a well-regarded mainstream practitioner.

Finney, Charles G(randison), 1905–1984.
ABOUT: WW, GSF, SFW, F, CA, SMFL, SFE, SFFL, RG, PE, ESF, HF

4A-103. The Ghosts of Manacle. Pyramid, 1964.
Eight short stories make up Finney's only collection. An effective blend of fantasy, gentle horror and uncanny tales, including some tales with a Wild West cowboy locale, a distinctly underutilized fantasy setting.

4A-104. The Magician Out of Manchuria in **The Unholy City** [3-138]. Pyramid, 1968.
Lustful blend of heroic fantasy and comedy in an early twentieth-century Chinese setting. A lighthearted romp with amusingly sketched characters—a sex-starved queen; a Falstaffian, greedy and selfish magician; his ineffective disciple—all embroiled in jolly japes; this is escapist fantasy at its best. Contrast the Chinese locale in Barry Hughart's *Bridge of Birds* [4A-142].

Finney, Jack (pseud. of Walter Braden Finney), 1911– .
ABOUT: GSF, CA, TCA, NE, SMFL, SFE, MF, TCSF, ESF, HF

*4A-105. Time and Again. Simon & Schuster, 1970.
A modern classic of romantic fantasy. A contemporary time traveler journeys back

to the New York of 1882. A loving portrayal of times past and the spirit of place unfolds as the protagonist finds, loses and seeks love beyond the barrier of time. True fantasy despite the external science fiction trappings. Contrast Matheson's *Bid Time Return* [4A-177] and Tim Powers's *The Anubis Gates* [4A-207].

[For other works of this author, see the companion guide to horror.]

Ford, John M., 1957–   .
ABOUT: NE

4A-106. The Dragon Waiting. Simon & Schuster, 1983.
A surprise but worthy winner of the World Fantasy Award, this early novel by a young American author who has not truly fulfilled his early promise is a powerful tale of an alternative world where the Roman Empire still reigns. The incursion of a particularly chilling form of evil is the pretext for an invigorating yarn, which succeeds in improvising by weaving intelligent new variations on well-worn fantasy themes.

Foster, Alan Dean, 1946–   .
ABOUT: NE, SFE, SFFL, TCSF

4A-107. Spellsinger series (*Spellsinger*, Phantasia Press, 1983; *The Hour of the Gate*, Phantasia Press, 1984; *The Day of the Dissonance*, Phantasia Press, 1984; *The Moment of the Magician*, Phantasia Press, 1984; *The Path of the Perambulator*, Phantasia Press, 1985; *The Time of the Transference*, Warner, 1987).
Formula heroic fantasy with a parade of comical villains and all-too-fallible heroes. Lighthearted romp through the clichés and a great popular success.

Fowles, John (U.K.), 1926–   .
ABOUT: CA, MF, ESF

4A-108. The Magus. Cape, 1966.
Fowles's second novel, following *The Collector*, has since attained lofty cult status. The whole book, with its loving, lyrical descriptions of the luxuriance of the Greek islands, is bathed in a hypnotic phantasmagoric atmosphere. This mood lingers on, even after the rational explanations brought to bear at the conclusion of the novel. But though its spell of fantasy is denied, the novel belongs to the genre through its clever accretion of layers of disbelief, ghostly and godly apparitions, magical feel and pagan apparel. A seminal example of fantasy atmospherics. Also annotated as [H4-117].

Frayn, Michael (U.K.), 1933–   .
ABOUT: SFE, MF, SFFL, TCSF

4A-109. Sweet Dreams. Collins, 1973.
A gently humorous tale of life after death, where the hereafter turns out to be both very British and middle class. The hero, following his death in an automobile crash, soon tires of Heaven's beatitudes and rewards and settles for a steady career

as a designer for an advertising agency and eventually meets God. A joyful satire. Compare Niven and Pournelle's *Inferno* [4A-197] and Stanley Elkin's *The Living End* [4A-95].

Gallico, Paul, 1897–1976.
ABOUT: CA, SFE, SFFL, RG, ESF, HF

4A-110. The Man Who Was Magic. Heinemann, 1967.
Sentimental fantasy whose young heroine lives in a city of conjurors, where the trickery behind apparent magic is common knowledge. Into this disenchanted world comes a youth whose real magic is perceived as a threat by the citizens but as a marvelous promise by the heroine. Gallico's sentimentality is more extreme than Robert Nathan's (see [3-262–3-266 and 4A-194–4A-195]) but this "fable of innocence" is the only one of his novels where it tempts him into outright fantasy. Of similar interest is the short story "The Lost Hour" in *Confessions of a Story-Teller* (1961). (BS)

García Márquez, Gabriel (Colombia), 1928–   .
ABOUT: CA, PE

4A-111. One Hundred Years of Solitude. Harper, 1970. Tr. of *Cien años de soledad*, 1967.
A band of adventurers establish a new village in the South American jungle. The history of the village and its people, followed over an entire century, is full of tales of wonder and suffering. One of the accepted masterpieces of Latin American magical realism, this important novel blends reality and the surreal in an effortless blend.

Gardner, John, 1933–1982.
ABOUT: CA, H, SMFL, SFE, MF, FL, HF

4A-112. Grendel. Knopf, 1971.
A melancholy retelling of the *Beowulf* epic as seen through the eyes of the bitter monster Grendel. Contrasting the savage but sane attitude of the monster, whose first-person narrative shapes the story, with the mercurial unpredictability of humankind, Gardner achieves a genuine sense of pathos and poetry.

[For other works of this author, see the companion guide to horror.]

Garrett, Randall, 1927–1987.
ABOUT: SMFL, SFE, RG, TCSF, ESF, HF

4A-113. Lord Darcy series (*Too Many Magicians*, Doubleday, 1967; *Murder and Magic*, Ace, 1979; *Lord Darcy Investigates*, Ace, 1981).
A minor classic of the parallel worlds genre where magic works and is considered as a science, the Lord Darcy volumes (the initial novel, and two collections of stories) take a leaf from Rex Stout's lighthearted Nero Wolfe detective stories. Lord Darcy is a sleuth for the government, brought in to elucidate and confront curious cases for which neither rational nor supernatural explanations are imme-

diately available. The blending of fantasy, SF and detective genres works well and makes these yarns most entertaining divertimenti. Michael Kurland has offered a sequel (*Ten Little Wizards*, 1988).

Gary, Romain (France), 1914–1980.
ABOUT: CA, SFE, ESF

4A-114. The Dance of Genghis Cohn. NAL, 1968.
A former SS officer now working as a police detective is possessed and tormented by the dybbuk of a Jewish comedian for whose death (among many others) he was responsible more than twenty years before. A tragicomic allegory about the haunting of modern Germany by its terrible past; a fine example of modern Jewish fantasy. Compare those works of Bernard Malamud and Isaac Bashevis Singer which tend toward the grotesque and fantastic. (BS)

Gaskell, Jane (U.K.), 1941– .
ABOUT: WW, GSF, F, CA, SMFL, SFE, SFFL, RG, ESF, HF

4A-115. Atlan saga (*The Serpent*, Hodder & Stoughton, 1963; *Atlan*, Hodder & Stoughton, 1965; *The City*, Hodder & Stoughton, 1966; *Some Summer Lands*, Hodder & Stoughton, 1977).
A sprawling popular romance series set in old-time Atlantis, full of sex, human-animal couplings, chases galore, mad scientists and a whole farrago of clichés. Mostly published while the author was still young, and self-consciously reprised a decade later, the series is a colorful mixture of purple prose, deliberate archaisms and nonstop episodic "perils of Pauline" as Princess Cija confronts her wild fate. An entertaining and energetic romp, it compares favorably with John Norman's sexist Gor series [4A-199], and is often a forerunner of Tanith Lee's barbarian worlds of wonder.

[For other works of this author, see the companion guide to horror.]

Godwin, Parke.

4A-116. Firelord. Doubleday, 1980; **Beloved Exile.** Doubleday, 1984; **The Last Rainbow.** Bantam, 1985.
A powerful triptych on Roman Britain and the following era, concentrating in turn on the interrelationship among people, place and myth, with a true-to-life version of Arthur and Camelot dominating the opening volume. A delicate portrait of Guinevere makes up the middle segment, while in the closing novel, a challenging blend of pagan myth and Christian thought evokes the story of St. Patrick's coming of age and revelation amid the barbaric splendor of Celtic Britain.

Goldman, William, 1931– .
ABOUT: CA, SMFL, FL

4A-117. The Princess Bride. Harcourt, 1973.
An affectionate parody of fairy tales, swashbuckling yarns and traditional fantasy clichés framed as a story within a story. Always knowing and full of intended

anachronisms, this Ruritanian romance works equally well for adults and children, and was cleverly filmed by Rob Reiner (1987).

[For other works of this author, see the companion guide to horror.]

Goldstein, Lisa, 1953– .
ABOUT: CA, MF

4A-118. The Dream Years. Bantam, 1985.
A reverse time travel romance as a young member of the surrealist group of the 1920s moves ahead in time to embark on a love affair with a contemporary woman, Solange, involved in the May 1968 student uprising in Paris. A genuinely innovative setting for a fantasy novel of much power and imagination, with a rewarding blend of ideas and imagery.

*4A-119. The Red Magician. Pocket, 1982.
An innovative first novel, which won the National Book Award, based on Central European folklore, an area little explored by modern writers (with the exception of Isaac Bashevis Singer). Although at times the parallels to the Holocaust are somewhat obvious, this vigorous and stylish tale of the battle between a good magician and an evil wizard over the soul of a Jewish village is a wonderful addition to the fantasy landscape.

Grass, Günter (Germany), 1927– .
ABOUT: CA, SMFL

4A-120. The Tin Drum. Pantheon, 1962. Tr. by Ralph Manheim of *Die Blechtrommel*, 1959.
A sprawling masterpiece of contemporary literature in which Oskar, a child, wills himself to stay small and not grow in protest to the iniquities and suffering in the world that surrounds him. A Chaucerian parable that follows Danzig and Germany through World War II and beyond, *The Tin Drum* uses a diversity of narrative techniques to explode the traditional framework of the novel and attain a suprarealistic dimension which has many affinities with fantasy.

Gray, Alasdair (U.K.), 1934– .
ABOUT: CA, MF

4A-121. Lanark: A Life in Four Parts. Canongate, 1981.
Gray's first novel is a true Scottish epic, both in scope and ambition. Beginning in a realistic mode that follows the life of a Glasgow artist until his demise, the book then liberally dips into the fantastic with a superb exploration of the afterworld. An erotic and highly personal variation on the *Divine Comedy*, Gray's sprawling book gleefully borrows from many literary sources, but the fantastic cities of his imagination created on the other side long remain in the reader's memory.

4A-122. 1982 Janine. Cape, 1984.
Psychological fantasy from a maverick Scottish author, with a distracting pen-

chant for weird typography (he also designs his books). A voyage through the brain of a middle-aged alcoholic engineer in which obsession, social and political meanderings, fantasy and a whole gamut of sharp emotions blend and clash to destructive effect. A unique example of literature with metaphysical Joycean overtones.

Greenland, Colin (U.K.), 1954– .
ABOUT: CA

4A-123. Daybreak on a Different Mountain. Allen & Unwin, 1984; **The Hour of the Thin Ox.** Allen & Unwin, 1986.
Conflict in a post-imperial society, with magical elements gently downplayed. Strong emphasis on characterization and emotional conflicts in a mutedly mysterious world with puzzling wars raging in the background. Oblique but entertaining early efforts by a promising young British author.

Gregorian, Joyce Ballou, 1946– .
ABOUT: CA, FL

4A-124. The Broken Citadel. Atheneum, 1975.
A sprawling romp through an assortment of Middle Eastern mythologies, developed through the relationship among three characters, an eleven-year-old Massachusetts girl, Leron, Prince of Tredana, and Semirimia, an immortal-like Assyrian queen. Exotic and gripping storytelling on a large canvas, followed by two sequels, *Castledown* (1977) and *The Great Wheel* (1987).

Grimwood, Ken.
ABOUT: MF

*4A-125. Replay. Arbor House, 1987.
A man dies, only to live again and again. This enables him to change his life and relationships and make different decisions at crucial stages. A complex plot surrounds a familiar wish fulfillment daydream, and results in a surprisingly fluid, commercial and accomplished novel, reminiscent of Jack Finney and Richard Matheson in their time travel fantasies. 1988 World Fantasy Award.

Grubb, Davis, 1919–1980.
ABOUT: WW, GSF, CA, SFFL, PE, ESF

4A-126. Ancient Lights. Viking, 1982.
A picaresque tale of a battle between light and darkness set in rural West Virginia, from the author of the celebrated *Night of the Hunter* [H4-130]. A bawdy blend of the Rabelaisian and the Gnostic, the novel chronicles at sprawling length the bizarre rise of a messianic figure and is never less than intriguing. Compare some of Lafferty's similarly unclassifiable novels (see [4A-156–4A-157]).

[For other works of this author, see the companion guide to horror.]

Hales, E(dward) E(lton) Y(oung) (U.K.), 1908– .
ABOUT: FL

4A-127. Chariot of Fire. Hodder & Stoughton, 1977.
A stylish and witty voyage through Hell, after the protagonist and his girlfriend drown while in Venice. The parody of Dante sets a middle-aged British bureaucrat loose in the Second Circle of Hell, encountering many famous and infamous characters from history and soon unwittingly becoming a key figure in the reorganization of the rail link betwween Hell, Limbo and Heaven. Compare Stanley Elkin's *The Living End* [4A-95].

Hambly, Barbara.

4A-128. Darwath trilogy (*The Time of the Dark*, Ballantine, 1982; *The Armies of Midnight*, Ballantine, 1983; *The Walls of Air*, Ballantine, 1983).
Standard trilogy in the Tolkien mold, with some clever variations brought to bear on the quest motif and the good-versus-evil conflict, involving a California history student and a biker/painter. Compare the larger moral dimension of Stephen Donaldson's Covenant saga [4A-90].

4A-129. The Ladies of Mandrigyn. Ballantine, 1984.
Conflict in a medieval world of sundered kingdoms, mercenaries, magicians and amazons. Strong emphasis on the uneasy relationship between mercenary captain Sun Wolf and his female second-in-command Starhawk provides the book with a distinct touch of romance revisited by feminism, in stark contrast to the garish environment through which the characters move.

4A-130. The Silent Tower. Ballantine, 1986; **The Silicon Mage.** Ballantine, 1988.
A fantasy world and present-day California intersect, bringing a modern woman face to face with magic. The combination of computer lore and myth strikes an original note in this deftly plotted series, with a notable Industrial Revolution background with touches of Georgette Heyer's vision of Regency England.

[For other works of this author, see the companion guide to horror.]

Hancock, Niel.
ABOUT: RG, FL

4A-131. Atalantan Earth series: Circle of Light (*Greyfax Grimwald*; *Faragon Fairingay*; *Calix Stay*; *Squaring the Circle*; all Popular Library, 1977); The Wilderness of Four (*Across the Far Mountain*; *The Plains of the Sea*; *On the Boundaries of Bleakness*; *The Road to the Middle Islands*; all Popular Library, 1982).
Gentle, lightweight if overlong ersatz *Lord of the Rings* series. This time, the main character of the quest set in Atalantan Earth days is Broco, an ill-humored dwarf accompanied by an otter and a bear. Fabulous wizards battle against the coming of darkness while a complex and originally thought-out cosmology pervades the series, taking the reader through many fascinating landscapes, even venturing beyond death. One of the better Tolkien-inspired sagas.

Harris, MacDonald (pseud. of **Donald Heiney**), 1921– .
ABOUT: CA

4A-132. The Little People. Morrow, 1985.
An American academic on sabbatical in England comes across a race of small survivors from the realm of Faerie in a remote wood. Once he befriends them, his life begins changing, for better and worse. Compare Robert Holdstock's more animist version of the same theme in *Mythago Wood* [4A-139].

Harrison, M(ichael) John (U.K.), 1945– .
ABOUT: F, CA, SMFL, SFE, MF, SFFL, TCSF

***4A-133. Viriconium series** (*The Pastel City*, NEL, 1971; *A Storm of Wings*, Doubleday, 1980; *In Viriconium*, Gollancz, 1982; *Viriconium Nights*, Gollancz, 1985; last two collected as *Viriconium*, Unwin Hyman, 1988).
Each of the Viriconium books by M. John Harrison can be read independently of the others. Viriconium, a city of marvels, is also very much a city of the mind and entropy. The first two novels owe much to Peake and Jack Vance, presenting a motley bunch of both heroic and cowardly characters involved in ambiguous quests and adventures, and are a triumph of style over content. *In Viriconium* sees Harrison's archetypal city in a bleak, autumnal mood, reflecting the anomie of contemporary sensibilities, while *Viriconium Nights* is a collection of elliptical short stories.

Hazel, Paul, 1944– .
ABOUT: CA

4A-134. Finnbranch series (*Yearwood*, Little, Brown, 1980; *Undersea*, Little, Brown, 1982; *Winterking*, Little, Brown, 1984).
Remarkably realistic trilogy set in the twilight days of the Celtic Bronze Age, moving to modern-day America in the final volume. A strong treatment of myth and its relationship to nature, with literate nods to Arthurian legend and religious symbolism, Hazel's dark vision is a disturbingly powerful one, combining historical bleakness and fantasy to convincing effect.

Heinlein, Robert A(nson), 1907–1988.
ABOUT: GSF, CA, TCA, NE, SMFL, SFE, MF, SFFL, RG, TCSF, ESF, HF

4A-135. Glory Road. Putnam, 1963.
A vigorous and bawdy outing in which Heinlein sought to recapture the charms and fancies of his earlier *Unknown* fantasies. A right-wing, libertarian soldier of fortune, grown tired of the foibles of his contemporary world, answers an advertisement for adventures of the sword-and-sorcery type in a parallel world of (often) wish fulfillment, which he enters through a pentacle of power. Always exciting and full of strong-thighed men and pneumatic women, a classic entertainment which was unfortunately to become a model for an endless school of morally dubious cardboard fighting fantasies over the following decades.

4A-136. The Unpleasant Profession of Jonathan Hoag. Gnome Press, 1959.
Initially a long novella in 1942 in *Unknown Worlds*, *Jonathan Hoag* demonstrates how light-hearted and gently frivolous Heinlein could be in his halcyon
days. A couple of private detectives, married and New York-based like Nick and
Nora Charles in *The Thin Man*, which must have served as inspiration, are called
on to investigate a mysterious case. This soon dips straight into a sinister realm of
supernatural conspiracies. A tense and witty masterpiece.

[For other works of this author, see the companion guide to horror.]

Helprin, Mark, 1947–   .
ABOUT: CA, MF

4A-137. Winter's Tale. Harcourt, 1983.
A sprawling fantasy of New York as the city of infinite dreams. An impressive
bildungsroman of picaresque size and scope, Helprin's novel is a rare example of
American magical realism, a paean to the hustle and bustle of a Dickensian city,
where poverty and wonder coexist under the earnest gaze of a flying white horse.
Seen through the often naïve eyes of Peter Lake, foundling, thief and supreme
mechanic, the city races toward apocalypse carrying its cast of hundreds with deft
assurance. A modern fairy tale that turns into a powerful and haunting vision.

Hoban, Russell, 1925–   .
ABOUT: CA, NE, SFFL, TCSF, HF

4A-138.   Pilgermann. Cape, 1983.
A narrative of marvels and mystery as Pilgermann, an eleventh-century European
Jew who becomes a visionary wanderer, surveys the events of the First Crusade.
Through the device of an all-seeing character speaking from the present, Hoban
confronts the roots of Judaism and religious experience. A unique, deeply metaphysical novel in which the fantastic is implicitly accepted as an integral part of
everyday life.

Holdstock, Robert (U.K.), 1948–   .
ABOUT: CA, NE, H, SFE, MF, TCSF

***4A-139. Mythago Wood.** Gollancz, 1984.
A winner of the World Fantasy Award, Holdstock's most accomplished novel is a
powerful examination of the persistence of myths and the power of the unconscious. Time and space are suspended in a part of a Herefordshire forest where
figures born of myth wield magical powers. A sentimental but evocative love story
motivates the narrator's discovery of the wood. Compare Belgian writer Jean
Ray's *Malpertuis* (1943), which features a house inhabited by gods of the ancient
Greek pantheon. A sequel, *Lavondyss*, which continues in a similar evocative
vein, appeared in late 1988.

Holt, Tom (U.K.).
ABOUT: MF

4A-140. Expecting Someone Taller. Macmillan, 1987.
A humorous modern fantasy in which an unremarkable but down-to-earth every-day man accidentally inherits the Ring of the Nibelungs. Along with it soon come magic powers, riches galore and untold trouble in the person of mischievous gods and warriors from the Wagnerian pantheon. A gentle modern parody of the Germanic legends which inspired the composer, with a jaunty mixture of comic and cosmic.

Horwood, William (U.K.), 1944– .
ABOUT: SMFL

4A-141. Duncton Wood. Hamlyn, 1980; **Duncton Quest.** Century Hutchinson, 1988.
An impressive animal fantasy with a sharply drawn portrait of a secret world of sentient moles facing forces of evil spreading across their land. A complex allegorical content and religious undertones add much depth to the customary quest motif. The realistic English countryside setting and Horwood's resistance to anthropomorphy (unlike Adams's human-like rabbits of *Watership Down* [4B-1]) provide the saga with color and pathos. A third volume, *Duncton Found*, was published in 1989.

Hughart, Barry.
*****4A-142. Bridge of Birds.** St. Martin's, 1984.
A novel of an ancient China that never was, *Bridge of Birds* draws upon Chinese folklore (with a nod toward Judge Dee, the creation of mystery writer Robert Van Gulik) to exotic and picaresque effect. Number Ten Ox, a brawny village lad, embarks upon a quest with wily Master Li Kao, which will bring them face to face with a gallery of delightfully drawn villains, deities, ghosts and dangerous women. A first-rate, innovative fantasy adventure, which shared the World Fantasy Award. Hughart followed up with a further volume of adventures for his two characters, with *The Story of the Stone* (Doubleday, 1988).

Irwin, Robert (U.K.), 1946– .
ABOUT: CA

4A-143. The Limits of Vision. Viking, 1986.
Surreal comedy in which a London housewife's daily routine of cleaning is transformed into a heroic fantasy of unending war against Mucor, the demon of filth, in which she is aided by imaginary visitors eclectically borrowed from the wide world of literature and philosophy. Her husband seems to be planning to have her certified before he runs off with another woman, but all is not yet lost! Clever, sharply satirical and very funny. (BS)

Jacobs, Harvey, 1930– .
ABOUT: CA, SFE, SFFL

4A-144. The Egg of the Glak. Harper, 1969.
The only collection of stories by a little-known and unprolific minor master of the genre. From the bizarre title story to tales of deep-sea monsters, Jacobs spins a magic web, walking the tightrope between New York-based realism and the most fantastic notions. An author to be rediscovered.

Jeter, K. W., 1950– .
ABOUT: NE, TCSF

4A-145. Infernal Devices. St. Martin's, 1987.
A "steam punk" Victorian fantasy of great charm. An engaging mystery story involving clockmakers, automata and men like fish, Jeter's brew of Victoriana askew creates a strong mood of place and time, with intruding horror elements at times reminiscent of Lovecraft. Compare the Victorian fantasies of Tim Powers and James Blaylock.

Kavan, Anna (pseud. of **Helen Woods**) (U.K.), 1901–1968.
ABOUT: CA, SFE, SFFL, TCSF, ESF

4A-146. Eagles' Nest. Peter Owen, 1957.
Bleak fantasy by the author of the drug-influenced SF of *Ice*. The destitute narrator sets off on an absurd journey to the rock fortress of Eagles' Nest and finds himself in a searing hot alien landscape. Full of hallucinatory visions, this is one of the finest examples of Anna Kavan's power to explore the nocturnal worlds of our dreams. Compare Iain Banks's *The Bridge* [4A-17].

Kay, Guy Gavriel (Canada), 1954– .
ABOUT: MF

*4A-147. Fionavar Tapestry (*The Summer Tree*, McClelland & Stewart, 1984; *The Wandering Fire*, Arbor House, 1986; *The Darkest Road*, Arbor House, 1986).
Five Canadian university students are transported to a land of faerie by a magician. Here they must confront the inevitable forces of evil, exemplified by the dark god, Rakoth Maugrim. An inventive heroic fantasy trilogy openly modeled on Tolkien (Kay collaborated with Christopher Tolkien on the editing of the posthumous *Silmarillion* [4A-251]). With a rich blend of romance, suspense and sorcery, which incorporates Arthurian elements to good effect, the trilogy stands out among its myriad rivals through the naturalness of the young protagonists and the intelligent plotting that never fears to move sideways from its role model. A clever variation on a classic fantasy pattern, and an object lesson to trilogy writers on how to innovate within a pattern of tradition.

Kelly, James Patrick, dates unknown and **John Kessel,** 1950– .
ABOUT: NE

4A-148. Freedom Beach. Bluejay, 1985.
A man awakens in a weird surreal resort, where statues talk and guests are forbidden to write anything. Possibly a vision of hell, this is a Kafkaesque vision, inspired by the cult television program *The Prisoner,* which tackles the eternal theme of the interface between dream and reality and is puzzling and inventive throughout.

Kerr, Katherine.

4A-149. Daggerspell. Doubleday, 1986; **Darkspell.** Doubleday, 1987.
Robust fantasy epic (with a third volume in the Deverry saga still to come) with Celtic myths and legends used to strong effect. The heroics are gently down-played and the characters display a pleasant level-headedness in contrast to the more usual invincible cardboard cutouts familiar to the modern trilogy genre. Dual plot on two levels of time moves slowly, but this is still an impressive beginning for a new writer in the traditional mold.

King, Stephen, 1947– .
ABOUT: WW, SFW, CA, NE, SFE, SFFL, RG, PE, FF

4A-150. Dark Tower series (*The Gunslinger,* Donald M. Grant, 1982; *The Drawing of the Three,* Donald M. Grant, 1987).
The first two volumes in, according to King, a projected sequence of six or seven books. The Dark Tower unusually combines elements of the spaghetti western with sword and sorcery. Roland, the eponymous gunslinger with echoes of chivalrous knights, pursues the Dark Man across a bleak landscape of horrors. Following his foe's death at the end of the first volume, he continues his quest for the mysterious Dark Tower. Partly inspired by the Robert Browning poem, a striking saga with strong mythical power. Also annotated as [H4-164].

4A-151. The Eyes of the Dragon. Philtrum Press, 1984.
Written by King as a gift to his children and meant to be read aloud before bedtime, *The Eyes of the Dragon* is an entertaining if unassuming romp through classic fantasy territory. The charm of magic, a beautiful kingdom with a sympathetic royal family, an evil magician and the obligatory struggle between good and evil are all dutifully present, but orchestrated with craft and attention.

in collaboration with **Peter Straub,** 1943– .

*4A-152. The Talisman. Viking, 1984.
Two of the field's biggest commercial talents combine for a sprawling quest epic set in a modern-day America which is paralleled by the Territories, a somber world where magic has replaced technology. The youthful protagonist owes clear inspiration to Twain's Huckleberry Finn and Tom Sawyer, and a strong streak of nostalgic Americana pervades the book. Inventive and cinematic and miles away

from both authors' customary horror excesses and galleries of grotesques. Also annotated as [H4-178].

[For other works of this author, see the companion guide to horror.]

Kotzwinkle, William, 1938– .
ABOUT: CA, SFE, MF, TCSF

4A-153. Fata Morgana. Knopf, 1977.
A glittering European-based quest fantasy which begins as a mock "opéra comique" detective story with touches of melodrama. Witty and erotic misadventures abound as nineteenth-century sleuth Paul Picard follows the trail of a sinister magician and his alluring but mysterious wife through Germany, Hungary and Transylvania. An invigorating romp and game of mirrors fantasy. Contrast Angela Carter's denser *Nights at the Circus* [4A-65].

Kress, Nancy.

4A-154. The Golden Grove. Bluejay, 1984.
Grim but potent historical fantasy featuring the expert weaver Arachne who, for challenging the deities, is transformed into a spider. Kress reworks the myth and sharply darkens the mood, with a strong emphasis on the Greek island locale, the totem-like Spider Stone and intelligent characterization.

Kurtz, Katherine, 1944– .
ABOUT: WW, CA, NE, SMFL, SFFL, RG, FL

4A-155. Chronicles of Deryni (*Deryni Rising*, Ballantine, 1970; *Deryni Checkmate*, Ballantine, 1972; *High Deryni*, Ballantine, 1973).
Commercially influenced by Tolkien's elevation to cult status, the Deryni tales were among the first of many heroic fantasy trilogies from young American authors in the 1970s. The series blends a heady broth of medieval Celtic myths with an alternative world of standard genre mold, where a race with magical powers strives to fight off the domineering church and forces of obscurantism. Derivative but enjoyable, the series proved popular, and Kurtz followed the initial trilogy with two further trios of prequels: the Legends of Camber of Culdi series (*Camber of Culdi*, Ballantine, 1976; *Saint Camber*, Ballantine, 1978; *Camber the Heretic*, Ballantine, 1981) and the Histories of King Kelson series (*The Bishop's Heir*, Ballantine, 1984; *The King's Justice*, Ballantine, 1985; *The Quest for Saint Camber*, Ballantine, 1986) and a collection of stories, *The Deryni Archives* (Ballantine, 1986). The Heirs of Saint Camber series began in 1989 with *The Harrowing of Gwynedd*.

Lafferty, R(aphael) A(loysius), 1914– .
ABOUT: SFW, CA, TCA, NE, SMFL, SFE, MF, SFFL, RG, TCSF, ESF

4A-156. The Devil Is Dead. Avon, 1971.
Finnegan, a Neanderthal sailor and artist, fights a secret war against the devil to determine who will control the world. A raffishly picaresque tale, full of alco-

holic vigor and absurdity and typical of the effusive Lafferty's skewed perception of the world as a stage. A never less than enjoyable if far from straightforward narrative.

*4A-157. Fourth Mansions. Ace, 1969.
Catholic allegory, madcap conspiracy yarn or just a tall tale? *Fourth Mansions* is all the aforementioned and more, a typical breathless romp through an unrecognizable version of the modern world, with entire brigades of larger-than-life characters festooning the colorful scene thick and fast, as yet another secret history of the world is unveiled for the reader's puzzlement and delight. Or is it? Archetypal if undefinable and unmistakable Lafferty opus of smiles and question marks.

Laubenthal, Sanders Anne, 1943–   .
ABOUT: CA, SFFL, FL, HF

4A-158. Excalibur. Ballantine, 1973.
An original addition to the classic Arthurian canon, inspired by an ancient legend of the Welsh discovering America. Here, Madoc, a descendant of Arthur, has brought the grail to Alabama for another epic confrontation between good and evil. A much-admired extrapolation which instills new breath into the traditional myth.

Lee, Tanith (U.K.), 1947–   .
ABOUT: SFW, CA, NE, SMFL, SFE, RG, TCSF, FL, HF

4A-159. Birthgrave Trilogy (*The Birthgrave*, DAW, 1975; *Vazkor, Son of Vazkor*, DAW, 1978; *Quest for the White Witch*, DAW, 1978).
Tanith Lee's first, sprawling novel for the adult market, *The Birthgrave* is a widescreen heroic fantasy which owes much to the Conan barbarian novel template [3-182] and to the naive traditions of comics and Hollywood epics. Its strong female protagonist, who awakens at the outset inside a volcano, fully grown but amnesiac, benefits from awesome special powers and liberally uses her sexuality throughout her epic quest for self-knowledge. The search which her son, Vazkor, undertakes in the sequels parallels her incident-filled journeys. A vigorous feminist sword-and-sorcery saga which, despite its inconsistencies in logic and florid overwriting, has been a major influence in weaning the genre away from Conan-type penis-fixated heroics.

4A-160. Dreams of Dark and Light. Arkham House, 1986.
A massive collection regrouping the best of Tanith Lee's short fiction. Both science fiction and fantasy are equally represented. Included are stories related to her Flat Earth series, and stunning variations on fairy tale themes and other fantasy/horror tropes. An excellent introduction to the work of one of contemporary fantasy's most protean practitioners.

4A-161. Flat Earth series (*Night's Master*, DAW, 1978; *Death's Master*, DAW, 1979; *Delusion's Master*, DAW, 1981; *Delirium's Mistress*, DAW, 1986; *Night's Sorceries*, DAW, 1987).
In a much distant past, when the Earth is still flat, Demons, the Lords of

Darkness, still influence and control the destinies of all creatures, be they dead or alive. A powerfully etched fantasy series full of strong emotions, pathos, and love lost, regained and damned, which follows the growing pains of the immortals. First-class storytelling full of cruelty, eroticism and much power. Possibly Lee's major achievement.

4A-162. Volkhavaar. DAW, 1977.
An elegant tale of conflict between a teenage slave girl and an evil sorcerer over the object of her affection, this novel, short by Lee's standards, is a near-perfect example of the good-versus-evil trope in high fantasy. A moral and symbolic reenactment of a classical myth.

Le Guin, Ursula K., 1929– .
ABOUT: SFW, F, CA, TCA, NE, SMFL, SFE, MF, SFFL, RG, TCSF, ESF, FL, HF

4A-163. Orsinian Tales. Harper, 1976.
A formidable collection of deceptive fables set in an apocryphal country of vaguely Eastern European flavor. The naturalistic setting allows Le Guin to tackle important themes—the need for love, human liberty, persecution—in an elegantly oblique manner. Only the setting belongs to fantasy.

4A-164. The Wind's Twelve Quarters. Harper, 1975.
A sterling collection of Le Guin's best short fiction, including her first story, "April in Paris," and two Earthsea-based stories, "The Word of Unbinding" and "The Rule of Names." Illuminating introductions map the stories' origins and the inspiration behind the "psychomyths" (parables or allegories of the mind). Also contains SF material. Later stories appear in *The Compass Rose* (Harper, 1982) and *Buffalo Gals and Other Animal Presences* (Capra Press, 1987).

Leiber, Fritz, 1910– .
ABOUT: WW, GSF, SFW, F, CA, TCA, NE, H, SMFL, SFE, MF, SFFL, RG, TCSF, PE, ESF, FL, HF

*4A-165. Fafhrd and the Gray Mouser series (*Swords in the Mist*, Ace, 1968; *Swords Against Wizardry*, Ace, 1968; *The Swords of Lankhmar*, Ace, 1968; *Swords Against Deviltry*, Ace, 1970; *Swords Against Death*, Ace, 1970; *Swords and Ice Magic*, Ace, 1977; *Rime Isle*, Whispers Press, 1977; *Heroes and Horrors*, Whispers Press, 1978; *The Knight and Knave of Swords*, Morrow, 1988).
Exemplary sword-and-sorcery stories (and a loosely constructed novel, expanded from earlier material, *The Swords of Lankhmar*) which span Leiber's writing career from 1937 onward. He began collecting the material and ordering the stories in chronological order in the late 1960s. Fafhrd and the Gray Mouser are the epitome of barbarian adventurers crisscrossing the ancient world of Nehwon, jousting, thieving, loving, not necessarily winning but always surviving the worst possible calamities. Alternating from deeply reflective to humorous moods, their tales are bawdy, baroque, strongly erotic, full of derring-do, grotesquerie and irony and rank among the very best of sword and sorcery. The writing creates many sharply drawn characters, at large in a chaotic world of deities and rogues

galore, and is sprinkled with wit. Superlative adventure fiction. *The Knight and Knave of Swords* incorporates a complete novel, *The Mouser Goes Below*, and shorter fictions to complete the series.

[For other works of this author, see the companion guide to horror.]

Lessing, Doris (U.K.), 1919– .
ABOUT: CA, NE, SFE, SFFL, TCSF

4A-166. The Fifth Child. Cape, 1988.
A brilliant and concise tale of the effect of an evil changeling's birth and life, and the influence it has on his family. A quiet yarn of dark foreboding and economy by a leading contemporary author with a strong feel for the fantastic.

Leven, Jeremy, 1941– .
ABOUT: CA

4A-167. Satan. Knopf, 1982.
A guilt-stricken Jewish psychiatrist who is trying (ineffectually) to oppose certain dehumanizing trends in modern psychotherapeutic practice discovers Satan reincarnate as a mechanical intelligence. Satan demands to be psychoanalyzed and brought to a proper understanding of his own nature—a heroic task to which the hero eventually (and surprisingly) proves equal. A brilliant study of the problem of evil; a *tour de force* of philosophical fiction. (BS)

Lindholm, Megan.

4A-168. Wizard of the Pigeons. Ace, 1986.
A sharply unconventional fantasy with a contemporary setting. Down and outs and other assorted marginals live by the rules of magic in present-day Seattle, and participate in the struggle between Light and Darkness. A refreshing cast of characters and neatly drawn atmospherics make the book genuinely original, despite the familiar theme.

Lupoff, Richard A(llen), 1935– .
ABOUT: CA, NE, SMFL, SFE, SFFL, TCSF, ESF, FL

4A-169. Sword of the Demon. Harper, 1977.
A stylish, inventive fantasy based on Japanese Buddhist mythology. Kishimo moves from naked awakening through corporeal womanhood to the state of goddess, while struggling with other adverse deities. An original journey toward enlightenment utilizing myths and legends seldom mined elsewhere in modern fantasy.

Lynn, Elizabeth A., 1946– .
ABOUT: NE, SMFL, RG, TCSF

4A-170. Chronicles of Tornor (*Watchtower*, Berkley, 1979; *The Dancers of Arun*, Berkley, 1979; *The Northern Girl*, Berkley, 1980).
A historical trilogy depicting the evolution of medieval society, the Chronicles of

Tornor offer little in the way of fantastic elements, outside some minor instances of telepathy and telekinesis, but stand out for their well-rounded characterization of both heroes and villains. The series is also notable in featuring a post-feminist society where women are effectively equal in a subtle, matter-of-fact sort of way, and homosexuality is common. An interesting departure from the quest mode of most contemporary fantasy. *Watchtower* won the World Fantasy Award in 1980.

MacAvoy, R(oberta) A(nn), 1949– .
ABOUT: CA, MF

4A-171. The Book of Kells. Bantam, 1985.
Two contemporary protagonists open a time gate between twentieth-century Dublin and tenth-century Ireland through tracing the inscriptions on a carved Celtic cross. This is a pretext for an impressive historical reconstruction of the troubled siege of Christianity by Vikings with sundry appearances by goddesses, legendary warriors and nascent myths.

4A-172. Tea with the Black Dragon. Bantam, 1983.
A gentle supernatural mystery and the author's first published novel. A contemporary fantasy involving a San Francisco musician's search for her missing daughter, with the cheerful assistance of Mayland Young, an ageless scholarly Oriental reminiscent of a benevolent Fu-Manchu who claims to have begun life as a dragon. The two ill-assorted, bumbling characters reappear in *Twisting the Rope* (1986).

4A-173. Trio for Lute series (*Damiano*, Bantam, 1984; *Damiano's Lute*, Bantam, 1984; *Raphael*, Bantam, 1984).
This trilogy set in Renaissance Italy follows the adventures of a young witch and musician, whose friend and spiritual advisor is the Archangel Gabriel. His growth and rite of passage emerges through ongoing battles against the devil. Fine period detail and considered use of humor leaven the customary good-versus-evil struggle into a rich tapestry of landscapes and vivid characterization.

MacDonald, John D., 1916–1986.
ABOUT: CA, TCA, NE, SFE, MF, SFFL, RG, TCSF, ESF

*4A-174. The Girl, the Gold Watch and Everything. Fawcett, 1962.
Sadly, this was crime writer John D. MacDonald's only foray into fantasy. *The Girl, the Gold Watch and Everything* is a wonderfully buoyant and gripping fantasy mystery. Gentle schlemiel Kirby Winter, whose job until the death of his uncle Omar was to studiously give Omar's money away, is now pursued by crooks, beautiful women and tax authorities anxious to discover the secret of the old man's seemingly unlimited wealth. Alas, all Kirby has inherited is a gold watch. An amusing combination of thriller, sex comedy and downright fantasy which never lets up.

Marti-Ibanez, Felix (Cuba), 1912(?)–1972.
ABOUT: WW, CA, FL

4A-175. All the Wonders We Seek. Clarkson Potter, 1963.
"Thirteen tales of suspense and prodigy" by a leading Cuban author. The Latin American settings impart a strong touch of magical realism and gentle exoticism, although the themes of the stories cover the whole gamut of traditional fantasy. Strong imagery abounds.

Mason, David, 1924–1974.
ABOUT: SMFL, SFE, SFFL

4A-176. The Sorcerer's Skull. Lancer, 1970.
An elegant fantasy quest yarn with all the classical elements dutifully present, but also featuring some inventive new twists, including a sorcerer's plans to spread the blight of vampirism through the world. A promising novel by an author whose career was unfortunately cut short soon after it was written.

Matheson, Richard, 1926– .
ABOUT: WW, GSF, SFW, CA, TCA, NE, SMFL, SFE, SFFL, RG, TCSF, PE, ESF, HF

4A-177. Bid Time Return. Viking, 1975.
A splendid romantic fantasy from an author whose superlative storytelling skills have for several decades mostly been lost to Hollywood screenwriting. A contemporary man falls in love with the photograph of a nineteenth-century actress and wills himself back into the past to meet and woo her. Full of much bittersweet yearning, this assured novel confidently treads a sentimental tightrope without ever falling into precious mawkishness. Compare Jack Finney's time travel romances [4A-105]. Matheson scripted the film version directed by Jeannot Szwarc in 1980, which featured Christopher Reeve and Jane Seymour.

4A-178. What Dreams May Come. Putnam, 1978.
A touching tale of existence beyond death, *What Dreams May Come* relates the story of a man whose personality survives after his violent death. After attempting to console his devastated wife, he adjusts himself to his new environment and condition in the hereafter, known as Summerland, before setting off to rescue the soul of his wife from the Limbo to which her suicide has consigned her. Highly sentimental and based on actual research by the author (the book includes a bibliography of books about survival after death), this romantic drama takes on darker hues than his *Bid Time Return* or Jack Finney's love across time fantasies.

[For other works of this author, see the companion guide to horror.]

McCaffrey, Anne, 1926– .
ABOUT: CA, TCA, NE, SFE, SFFL, RG, TCSF, ESF

4A-179. Dragon series (*Dragonflight*, Ballantine, 1968; *Dragonquest*, Ballantine, 1971; *The White Dragon*, Ballantine, 1978; *Dragonsdawn*, Ballantine, 1988; *The Renegades of Pern*. Ballantine, 1989).
Even though the author insists it is SF, the Dragon series also takes pride of place

in the fantasy commercial pantheon. On a long-lost colony of Earth, humans and dragons live in harmony and telepathic contact. The medieval atmosphere and magical dragons owe much to the fantasy mainstream. A parallel series with the same background exists for the young adult market (*Dragonsong*, 1976; *Dragonsinger*, 1977; *Dragondrums*, 1979, all Atheneum), from which McCaffrey is also spinning off adult novels.

Millhiser, Marlys, 1938– .
ABOUT: CA, SMFL, SFFL

4A-180. The Mirror. Putnam, 1978.
A contemporary woman is transported back into the past, while her grandmother takes her place in the present. Forced to live each other's lives, the women's attitudes illuminate the condition of women and marriage in the past and present. A challenging feminist fantasy. Compare with Jack Finney and Richard Matheson's time travel romances ([4A-105] and [4A-177]), all seen from a male perspective. Also annotated as [H4-237].

Moorcock, Michael (U.K.), 1939– .
ABOUT: WW, SFW, F, CA, NE, SMFL, SFE, MF, SFFL, RG, TCSF, ESF, HF

4A-181. Chronicles of Corum and Count Brass (*The Knight of the Swords*, Mayflower, 1971; *The Queen of the Swords*, Mayflower, 1971; *The King of the Swords*, Berkley, 1971; *The Bull and the Spear*, Allison & Busby, 1973; *The Oak and the Ram*, Allison & Busby, 1973; *The Sword and the Stallion*, Berkley, 1974). Considered the most polished of Moorcock's fantasy series. Last patrician survivor of a fabled race, the Vadhagh, overtaken by teeming, vulgarian humanity, Corum is another classic Moorcock character in exile, up against the insidious Lords of Chaos. Colorful, peopled with gods of all shapes and sizes and varying powers, Corum's world is a barbaric battleground of solitary quests and travails. A detached sense of melancholy pervades these fast-moving adventure books, giving a strong moral emptiness to the struggles of the protagonists.

4A-182. Dancers at the End of Time series (*An Alien Heat*, McGibbon & Kee, 1972; *The Hollow Lands*, Harper, 1974; *The End of All Songs*, Harper, 1976; *Legends from the End of Time*, Harper, 1976; *The Transformation of Miss Mavis Ming*, W. H. Allen, 1977).
Romantic and effete immortals trade love, ennui and theatrical posturing in their out-of-bounds eyrie. A detached but haunting series featuring familiar fantasy landscapes revisited by the destructive, pernicious influence of entropy. The *fin-de-siècle* atmosphere borrows much from nineteenth-century affectations, with a nod toward Dickens, Shaw and Firbank, as the eponymous Moorcockian time-traveling protagonists search for love and a sense of humanity. An oddly moving, dream-like sequence deserving of reappraisal.

4A-183. Elric saga (*The Stealer of Souls*, Herbert Jenkins, 1963; *Stormbringer*, Neville Spearman, 1965; *The Singing Citadel*, Mayflower, 1970; *The Sleeping*

Sorceress aka *The Vanishing Tower*, NEL, 1971; *Elric of Melniboné* aka *The Dreaming City*, Hutchinson, 1972; *The Jade Man's Eyes*, Unicorn, 1972; *The Sailor on the Seas of Fate*, Quartet, 1976; *The Weird of the White Wolf*, DAW, 1977; *The Bane of the Black Sword*, DAW, 1977; *The Fortress of the Pearl*, Gollancz, 1989). With his drawn-out saga of Elric, the albino swordsman, Moorcock single-handedly redefined the heroic fantasy genre peopled by muscular warriors created by Robert Howard with Conan [3-182]. Elric of Melniboné, a helpless, feeling pawn of forces he cannot control, has his life torn asunder despite jousting triumphs, as an almighty battle rages in the Multiverse between Law and Chaos. His relationship with his blood-sucking sentient sword, Stormbringer, is full of ambiguity and pathos, and he often cannot help bringing grief and destruction to his loved ones as he wanders a colorfully drawn barbarian world in upheaval. A romantic creation who caught the imagination of many, Elric was the first prototype of a new kind of heroic but fallible hero. Much of the Elric saga was rewritten and reorganized in the mid-1970s into some form of chronological order, and earlier titles were cannibalized into different formats.

*4A-184. Gloriana, or the Unfulfill'd Queen. Allison & Busby, 1978.
Moorcock's bittersweet variation on *The Faerie Queene* [1-79] is a remarkable achievement that transcends most of his more commercially popular heroic fantasy sagas. In a parallel and apocryphal Albion, the virgin, pipe-smoking Queen Gloriana reigns, encumbered by her aching body senses in a vast Gothic palace with shades of Peake's Gormenghast. The romantic but somewhat villain-ous Captain Quire becomes the instrument of her undoing and ultimate pleasure. An evocative, tender and haunting novel which ranks among the best examples of contemporary fantasy with a classical, historical background.

4A-185. History of the Runestaff (*The Jewel in the Skull*, 1967; *Sorcerer's Amulet* aka *The Mad God's Amulet*, 1968; *The Sword of the Dawn*, 1968; *The Secret of the Runestaff*, 1969; *Count Brass*, 1973; *The Champion of Garathorn*, 1973; *Quest for Tanelorn*, 1975; all Mayflower).
In a far future Europe, where Great Britain has become the seat of all evil, Dorian Hawkmoon survives the genocide of his people and family and is taken prisoner. Fitted with a magic jewel embedded in his skull, he escapes and takes refuge with Count Brass, ruler of Kamarg. He and the count's daughter, Yisselda, fall in love as they struggle against the forces of darkness. The mighty battle between good and evil has never been bloodier in the Moorcock canon, but here, short pastoral moments of rest and love punctuate the ever-raging clashes of swords and mon-strous armies. First-class sword and sorcery on an epic scale, with no flagging of the imagination. The final volume, *Quest for Tanelorn*, unsatisfyingly attempts to unify and wrap up the Law-versus-Chaos struggle present in all Moorcock's fantasy series, and Hawkmoon is joined in the struggle by the author's other heroes, Elric, Corum and Erekosë, the Eternal Champion (from *The Eternal Champion*, 1970, and *Phoenix in Obsidian*, 1970, both Mayflower).

*4A-186. The War Hound and the World's Pain. Timescape, 1981.
Later Moorcock fantasy in a decidedly bleak mood. Ulrich von Bek, a German mercenary of the Thirty Years War, makes a deal with an ambivalent version of the devil to restore his soul. In search of the Grail, he crisscrosses a world full of

dark despair and doom. With war raging both in Heaven and on Earth, Moorcock's somber viewpoint gives this autumnal quest fantasy a strongly personal underpinning, resulting in a gripping book. Two later novels follow the fate of the von Bek family: *The Brothel in Rosenstrasse* (1982), a mildly erotic Mittel-Europa parallel history, and the weaker *The City in the Autumn Stars* (1986).

Moore, Brian (Canada), 1921– .
ABOUT: CA, SMFL, SFE, MF, SFFL

4A-187. Cold Heaven. Farrar, Straus, 1983.
A moving tale about the thin line between life and death from an acclaimed mainstream novelist. A woman whose husband has died following a motorboat accident, which she had supernatural premonitions of, finds that he refuses to rest in peace. More than a ghost story, this is a quietly effective and sparingly crafted novel of partly religious speculation, echoed in French director Alain Resnais's later film *L'Amour à Mort*.

4A-188. The Great Victorian Collection. Farrar, Straus, 1975.
An ironic tale of the mysterious appearance in a California parking lot of a wondrous collection of Victorian artifacts and bric-a-brac, and how this miraculous manifestation affects the life of the protagonist, a professor of history, and the disbelieving world at large. An elegant and imaginative *tour de force* and a parable on art and dreams, *The Great Victorian Collection* stands comfortably apart from most contemporary fantasy.

Morris, Jan (U.K.), 1926– .
ABOUT: CA

4A-189. Last Letters from Hav. Viking, 1985.
A travel book with a difference by one of the travel genre's most acclaimed practitioners. Hav is an imaginary Levantine peninsula and city with elements of Turkey, Russia and Greece. Morris chronicles a six-month stay there and offers a perfect lesson in impressionistic world-building with subtle touches of color, pseudo-history, religion, politics and exoticism. An engrossing, witty fantasy travelog though parts are apocryphal.

Mujica Láinez, Manuel (Argentina), 1910–1984.
ABOUT: CA

4A-190. The Wandering Unicorn. Lester & Orpen Dennys, 1982. Tr. by Mary Fitton of *El unicornio*, 1965.
Praised by Borges as "a glowing dream set in the past," *The Wandering Unicorn* is an enthralling medieval romance based on the ancient legend of Melusine, the immortal outcast, half woman, half serpent, and her love for a mortal knight whom she pursues across twelfth-century Europe to a climax in front of the Holy City besieged by Saladin and his hordes. Interesting use of fantasy archetypes from a South American perspective which proves less heroic, and more realistic, than the Anglo-Saxon perspective customary in the Tolkien canon.

Munn, H(arold) Warner, 1903–1982.
About: WW, GSF, CA, SMFL, SFE, SFFL, RG, PE, ESF, HF

4A-191. Merlin's Ring. Ballantine, 1974; **Merlin's Godson.** Ballantine, 1976.
A vast saga ranging from the collapse of Atlantis to the European Middle Ages,
Merlin's Ring comprises the earlier *King of the World's Edge* (1967; published in
Weird Tales, 1939) and its sequel, *The Ship from Atlantis* (1967). It features
Romans in America with other races besides Indians and their later adventures in
the Dread Sargasso Sea. An entertaining blend of the Haggard lost race novel and
the fantasy quest, it was followed after a long hiatus by *Merlin's Godson*. This
proves a longer, picaresque and more ambitious work, synthesizing myth and
history, climaxing with the advent of Joan of Arc. An underappreciated achievement which begs reassessment. Also annotated as [3-259].

[For other works of this author, see the companion guide to horror.]

Murphy, Pat

4A-192. The Falling Woman. Tor, 1986.
Highly evocative tale featuring a woman archaeologist with the psychic power to
see past residents of her present-day location. Searching Mayan ruins, these
ghostly apparitions begin communicating with her. A sharp sense of place, finely
etched characterization and much empathy for the disorders of human relationships elevate a standard plot to a higher plateau of quality. Winner of the Nebula
Award, normally given to a work of science fiction.

Myers, John Myers, 1906–1988.
About: GSF, CA, SMFL, MF, SFFL, ESF, HF

4A-193. The Moon's Fire-Eating Daughter. Donning, 1981.
A sequel of sorts to the author's earlier *Silverlock* [3-261], in which a timid
geography professor is abducted by Venus and transported to a realm of fantasy,
where he faces various farcical misadventures. Full of self-conscious literary
references, puns, wordplay and overwrought style, this is an unusual example of
light fantasy.

Nathan, Robert, 1894–1985.
About: GSF, SFW, CA, SMFL, SFE, SFFL, RG, ESF, HF

4A-194. The Devil with Love. Knopf, 1963.
The hero, desperate to possess the woman he loves, calls upon the devil for
assistance; Lucifer, who is having doubts about competing with God for souls
rather than hearts, sends the archdemon Samael to help out and to figure out
where love should figure in his own calculations and endeavors. The thoughtful
and melancholy Lucifer is carried forward from *The Innocent Eve* [3-263]; Nathan continued his ironic rehabilitation of the fallen angels in *Heaven and Hell
and the Megas Factor* (1975), where emissaries of God and Satan learn to love one

another when they must combine forces to save mankind from the destructive possibilities inherent in modern technology. (BS)

4A-195. So Love Returns. Knopf, 1958.
A widowed writer is rewarded for his grace under the pressure of grief by a visitation from a magical girl who briefly reilluminates his life with love. One of Nathan's many sentimental erotic fantasies; the theme (which echoes his early success, *Portrait of Jennie* [3-265]) recurs frequently in his later work. *Mia* (1970) is the most straightforward reprise, though it also follows *The Wilderness-Stone* (1960) in placing a more mature woman in parallel with the magical young girl. *The Elixir* (1971) enlivens the theme by placing it in a pleasantly humorous context which borrows eclectically from English mythology—a late fascination of Nathan's which also shows to good effect in the delicate and effective historical fantasy *The Fair* (1968). (BS)

Niven, Larry, 1938– .
ABOUT: CA, TCA, NE, SMFL, SFE, SFFL, RG, TCSF, ESF, HF

4A-196. The Magic Goes Away. Ace, 1978; **The Magic May Return.** Ace, 1981; **More Magic.** Berkley, 1984.
Niven's novel, which constitutes the first volume in this series of sorts, is an ambivalent tale of a world where magic is on the wane. A group of motley magicians embark on the obligatory quest to seek out the last god capable of retrieving the situation. The results are unexpectedly bleak. The subsequent volumes, assembled by Niven, return to the world of his creation when magic was still in abundance, and include stories by Fred Saberhagen, Dean Ing, Steven Barnes, Poul Anderson, Mildred Downey Broxon and others, some of which intelligently challenge Niven's initial premise.

in collaboration with **Jerry Pournelle,** 1933– .

4A-197. Inferno. Pocket Books, 1976.
Following his death at a drunken science fiction convention, the protagonist lands in Hell. Both parody and homage to Dante's vision of the hereunder, Niven and Pournelle's vision is dark and ironic, and shows a distinctly misanthropic view of humanity in its gallery of grotesques, cowards and psychopaths. Great fun all the same. Compare Elkin's *The Living End* [4A-95].

Nooteboom, Cees (Netherlands), 1933– .
ABOUT: CA

4A-198. In the Dutch Mountains. Viking, 1987. Tr. by Adrienne Dixon of *Uitgeverij de Arbeiderspes,* 1984.
A Spanish Inspector of Roads in the province of Zaragoza is writing a history of the Netherlands, which stretch from Amsterdam to the highest peaks and passes of Europe. To the southern part of the country come two young show people chased by an evil Snow Queen. As the narrator's story is invaded by irreality, he ponders the relationships between art, history and life in this blend of modernist fable, in the Calvino mood, and fairy tale.

Norman, John (pseud. of **John Frederick Lange, Jr.**), 1931– .
ABOUT: CA, NE, SMFL, SFE, SFFL, RG, TCSF, ESF

4A-199. Gor series (*Tarnsman of Gor*, 1966; *Outlaw of Gor*, 1967; *Priest-Kings of Gor*, 1968; *Nomads of Gor*, 1969; *Assassin of Gor*, 1970; *Raiders of Gor*, 1971; *Captive of Gor*, 1972; all Ballantine; *Hunters of Gor*, 1974; *Marauders of Gor*, 1975; *Tribesmen of Gor*, 1976; *Slave Girl of Gor*, 1977; *Beasts of Gor*, 1978; *Explorers of Gor*, 1979; *Fighting Slave of Gor*, 1980; *Rogue of Gor*, 1981; *Guardsman of Gor*, 1981; *Savages of Gor*, 1982; *Blood Brothers of Gor*, 1983; *Kajira of Gor*, 1983; *Players of Gor*, 1984; *Mercenaries of Gor*, 1985; *Dancer of Gor*, 1985; *Renegade of Gor*, 1986; *Vagabonds of Gor*, 1987, all DAW).
Tarl Cabot, a contemporary New England college professor, is kidnapped and brought to Gor, a planet located on the opposite side of the sun in the same orbit as Earth. In this savage, barbarous world of conflict, he becomes a mighty warrior in a society where the survival of the fittest reigns. Initially a slavish imitation of the scientific romances of Edgar Rice Burroughs, the highly popular Gor novels became around the mid-1970s both highly repetitive and a philosophical vehicle for the author's tendentious views on the slavery and bondage of women, seen as an inferior species. Sadly, the prurient results have not halted the success of the series.

Norton, Andre (Alice Mary), 1912– .
ABOUT: WW, SFW, CA, TCA, NE, SMFL, SFE, MF, SFFL, RG, TCSF, ESF, FL, HF

*4A-200. Witch World series (*Witch World*, Ace, 1963; *Web of the Witch World*, Ace, 1964; *Year of the Unicorn*, Ace, 1965; *Three Against the Witch World*, Ace, 1965; *Warlock of the Witch World*, Ace, 1967; *Sorceress of the Witch World*, Ace, 1968; *Spell of the Witch World*, DAW, 1972; *The Crystal Gryphon*, Atheneum, 1972; *The Jargoon Pard*, Atheneum, 1974; *The Trey of Swords*, Grosset & Dunlap, 1977; *Zarathor's Bane*, Ace, 1978; *Lore of the Witch World*, DAW, 1980; *Gryphon in Glory*, Atheneum, 1981; *Ware Hawk*, Atheneum, 1983; *Gryphon's Eyrie* (with A. C. Crispin), St. Martin's, 1985).
A highly popular and seemingly everlasting fantasy series, with strong feminist pointers, the Witch World books are set in a mysterious matriarchal parallel world, Estcarp, where sorcery and a coven of good witches reign. Much inspired by folklore from England and the Celts, the plots are serviceable sword-and-sorcery yarns and adventures which seldom dig deep between the outset of a given task and the customary happy end. This makes them ideal escapist reading for young adults. Compare Marion Zimmer Bradley's Darkover series [4A-47] or Anne McCaffrey's Dragon series [4A-179].

Nye, Robert (U.K.), 1939– .
ABOUT: CA, SMFL, ESF

4A-201. Merlin. Hamish Hamilton, 1978; **Faust.** Hamish Hamilton, 1980.
Two of a trio of contemporary novels (the other, *Falstaff*, 1976, contains no elements of fantasy) retelling classic stories through a modern perspective. The

treatments of both Merlin and Faust are imbued with a strong touch of eroticism and picaresque bravado and bawdiness. Self-consciously literary but innovative reevaluations of classic themes.

O'Brien, Flann (pseud. of Brian O'Nolan) (Ireland), 1911–1966.
ABOUT: CA, SMFL, SFE, MF, SFFL, ESF

4A-202. The Third Policeman. McGibbon and Kee, 1967.
The final, posthumously published novel by the great Irish comic writer is a surrealistic romp through a grisly, unsettling but always hilarious version of the afterlife as private hell. Two policemen hound the nameless narrator, a thief, murderer and would-be philosopher. Supremely absurd and devilishly unique fantasy. Compare with the similarly picaresque tales of R. A. Lafferty [4A-156–4A-157].

Panshin, Alexei, 1940- , and Cory Panshin, 1947- .
ABOUT: CA, TCA, NE, SFE, SFFL, TCSF, ESF

4A-203. Earth Magic. Ace, 1978.
Intriguing example of heroic fantasy which follows the exploits of the son of Black Morca, a barbaric warrior chief and tyrant. Exploring visions of reality against magic, balancing rationality and passion, the novel explores the authors' preoccupation with the roots of literary romance in a literate portrayal of the Earth goddess myth.

Phelps, Gilbert (U.K.), 1915- .
ABOUT: CA, SFFL, ESF

4A-204. The Winter People. Bodley Head, 1963.
Lost race story—arguably the last significant example of the species—which features an Andean people whose remarkable cultural and biological adaptations allow them to survive in extreme circumstances; but perhaps they are an illusion of their finder, to be interpreted as an allegory of the psyche. Similar in structure to Martens's *Death Rocks the Cradle* [H3-143] and in theme to Coblentz's *When the Birds Fly South* [3-81]. (B.S.)

Pierce, Meredith Ann, 1958- .
ABOUT: CA, PE

4A-205. The Darkangel. Little, Brown, 1982; **A Gathering of Gargoyles.** Little, Brown, 1984.
The first two volumes in the projected trilogy of Aeriel and the Darkangel. Set on a deliberately anachronistic moon, where vampires, maidens, witches and beasts live alongside denizens with diversely colored skins, these Gothic, breathless adventures display a fresh, assured imagination. Stylized but oddly effective, these novels were initially intended for a young adult audience, but are worthy of serious adult attention. Also annotated as [4B-134].

Polikarpus, Viido, and Tappan King.

4A-206. Down Town. Arbor House, 1985.
A young child separated from his mother in the rush hour crowd discovers a fantastic subterranean domain. Hailed there as a champion, he seeks to destroy the existing tyranny that reigns supreme. Peopled with extraordinary characters and a genuine sense of wonder, this superior, bewitching fantasy appeals to all ages.

Powers, Tim, 1952– .
ABOUT: F, NE, H, MF, TCSF

*4A-207. The Anubis Gates. Ace, 1983.
Winner of the first Philip K. Dick Memorial Award, this splendid time travel yarn soon dips into sheer grotesque fantasy. An American academic is plunged head first into a manic, sprawling nineteenth-century London, where the action involves him with Coleridge, Lord Byron, gypsy sorcerers, beggars and monsters of colorful ilk. A cunning, relentless mix of horror and humor and a perfect, exuberant example of modern fantasy.

4A-208. The Drawing of the Dark. Ballantine, 1979.
Picaresque tale of swordsmanship and supernatural derring-do in this early novel by Tim Powers. Sixteenth-century Vienna is threatened by a Turkish invasion, while a dreadful and magical brew is fermenting in an ancient vat beneath a local inn, a process which has continued for thirty-five centuries. Witty and exciting, an overlooked novel.

4A-209. On Stranger Tides. Ace, 1987.
Adventures with pirates in the Caribbean, with sinister voodoo, the search for a fountain of immortality and a romantic love element. A swashbuckling version of Hollywood's classic sea epics with a marked difference. Wonderfully broad characterization and endless supernatural incidents pepper this rite-of-passage story of a gentle British puppeteer's transformation into a feared pirate leader. A most likable oddity in today's flood of formulaic fantasies.

Pratchett, Terry (U.K.).
ABOUT: F, TCSF

4A-210. Discworld novels (*The Colour of Magic*, Colin Smythe, 1983; *The Light Fantastic*, Colin Smythe, 1986; *Equal Rites*, Gollancz, 1987; *Mort*, Gollancz, 1987; *Sorcery*, Gollancz, 1988; *Wyrd Sisters*, Gollancz, 1988; *Pyramids*, Golloncz, 1989).
Tolkien meets Douglas Adams, or fantasy with a strong comic twist, in this continuing and often hilarious saga of a world which defies all the laws of logic and probability. Skewers many a fantasy archetype with glee and gentle wit, while mistreating many of the conventions of the genre which too many formula authors take ever so seriously. A whiff of fresh, debunking air which is already, ironically, acquiring cult status.

Pratt, Fletcher, 1897–1956.
ABOUT: WW, GSF, SFW, F, CA, NE, SMFL, SFE, MF, SFFL, RG, TCSF, ESF, FL, HF

4A-211. The Blue Star. Ballantine, 1969.
Set against an original quasi-eighteenth-century Ruritanian background where gunpowder has not been invented and magic occurs, this slight novel (published in shorter form in 1952) of intrigue, chase and adventure is notable for its imaginative setting, quite different from the familiar settings of so many formulaic fantasy yarns. Naïve and unheroic lovers are pitted against repressive and revolutionary forces while they hold the Blue Star, which enables its bearer to read the thoughts of others. Also annotated as [3-305].

Pynchon, Thomas, 1937– .
ABOUT: CA, NE, SFE, MF, TCSF

4A-212. The Crying of Lot 49. Lippincott, 1966.
A short novel by the enigmatic leading post-modernist American author, which, in the guise of an increasingly absurd quest by protagonist Oedipa Maas, uncovers Pynchon's customary gigantic web of global conspiracies. The images (rock groups, Nazi psychoanalysts, drugs) essentially belong to the 1960s, but the search for the secret history of the world, paralleled in Pynchon's two other major books, *V* (1963) and *Gravity's Rainbow* (1973), was to become a vital fantasy fixture in later works by John Crowley and R. A. Lafferty.

4A-213. Gravity's Rainbow. Viking, 1973.
Sprawling post-modernist novel set on a bizarre sideline of World War II, where a character's erections attract German flying bombs and rockets. Bizarre confluence of entropic consideration and picaresque relationships. Borderline fantasy, but a major literary achievement by the enigmatic author of *V* (1963).

Reamy, Tom, 1935–1977.
ABOUT: CA, SFE, TCSF

*4A-214. Blind Voices. Putnam, 1978.
A magical, gaudy traveling show comes to visit a sleepy Kansas town in the late 1920s. Intimations of evil and powerful sorcery blend to evocative effect with Reamy's finely textured recreation of Depression-era America. Compare Charles G. Finney's *Magician Out of Manchuria* [4A-104] and Bradbury's *Something Wicked This Way Comes* [4A-45].

Reaves, J. Michael.
ABOUT: TCSF

4A-215. Darkworld Detective. Bantam, 1982.
An original blending of genres, involving Kamus of Kadizar, a hard-boiled private investigator in a heroic fantasy setting on an alien planet where magic works. Features four gently tongue-in-cheek cases: "The Big Spell," "The Mal-

tese Vulcan," "Murder on the Galactic Express" and "The Man with the Golden Raygun," all acknowledging their origins, including the search for a powerful talisman named the Black Mask! Compare with Glen Cook's *Sweet Silver Blues* and its sequels [4A-74].

4A-216. The Shattered World. Timescape, 1984.
An epic quest for redemption in a world where magic rules. A master thief becomes a pawn in a war between two factions of sorcerers; cursed by demonic spells and occasionally changed into a bear, he flees on a quest inextricably bound up with the fate of the world. With flying dragons, vampires and a whole zoology of arcane monsters, this is a colorful yarn on a grand, wondrous scale.

Redgrove, Peter (U.K.), 1932– .
   ABOUT: CA

4A-217. The Sleep of the Great Hypnotist. Routledge & Kegan Paul, 1979.
A machine which enhances the natural power of hypnotism to bring about miraculous cures is used by its inventor to impose upon his daughter an obligation to discover a way of resurrecting his intelligence after death. Her eventual success is suitably ironic. Redgrove's intense interest in psychology and the paranormal is reflected in increasingly bizarre fashion in his subsequent novels *The Beekeepers* (1980) and *The Facilitators; or, Mister Hole-in-the-Day* (1982), which similarly feature remarkable research projects and grotesque attempts to exercise power in defiance of the natural order. Stylistically avant-garde, enlivened by some very striking imagery—as one would expect from a poet of some note. (BS)

Roessner, Michaela.

4A-218. Walkabout Woman. Bantam, 1988.
Rooted in the concept of the Dreamtime of Australian aborigines, this first novel by a young American writer succeeds on all counts as a genuinely innovative fantasy. Strongly linking its characters to the landscapes they live in, Roessner displays a strong sense of myth. Compare with Patricia Wrightson's Australian trilogy for young adults [4B-158].

Roth, Philip, 1933– .
   ABOUT: CA, SMFL, SFE, SFFL

4A-219. The Breast. Holt, Rinehart, 1972.
Ironical, self-consciously Kafkaesque novella in which a professor of literature awakens metamorphosed into a giant breast. A metaphorical fable of the absurd which represents Roth's only incursion into fantasy.

Rucker, Rudy, 1946– .
   ABOUT: CA, NE, MF, TCSF

4A-220. White Light. Virgin, 1980.
A dazzling mathematics-inspired fantasy and the first of Rucker's novels to be published in book form. An enjoyable gonzo out-of-body journey through a

madcap universe modeled on recollections of after-death experiences. A **mathematics** lecturer not unlike the author meets Donald Duck, Jesus, the devil, Einstein and others in a variety of madcap but logical settings such as the infinite hotel and library as he searches for the answer to Cantor's continuum problem. Both flippant and clever, a rare example of science fantasy from a master prankster.

Rushdie, Salman (India), 1947– .
ABOUT: CA, SMFL, SFE, MF

4A-221. Grimus. Gollancz, 1975.
The first novel by the now-established mainstream novelist is a magical realist fabulation, with outstanding touches of whimsy. The picaresque tale of a Red Indian innocent at large in a rather absurd world moves deftly between philosophy and metaphysics without ever truly settling for any unified or dominant mood, but the results are always entertaining.

Russ, Joanna, 1937– .
ABOUT: CA, TCA, NE, SFE, SFFL, RG, TCSF, ESF

4A-222. The Adventures of Alyx. Pocket Books, 1983 (an earlier version, *Alyx*, with four novelettes featuring the heroine and Russ's SF novel *Picnic on Paradise*, appeared from Gregg Press in 1976).
Set in ancient Phoenicia, the adventures of Alyx, an adventuress of fortune, owe much to the male tenets of heroic fantasy, while vigorously subverting its traditions by proto-feminist attitudes and a strong female character and swordswoman. Compare Fritz Leiber's Grey Mouser yarns [4A-165].

Ryman, Geoff (Canada)
ABOUT: MF

4A-223. The Unconquered Country. Allen & Unwin, 1986.
A deserving winner of the World Fantasy Award in novella form following its magazine publication (in *Interzone*, 1984), this strong parable about the tragic events that shattered Cambodia under the Khmer Rouge was Ryman's first published work of fiction. A British-based Canadian writer, he tells of a harsh world in chaos, in which the speculative elements serve to highlight the sometimes barbaric propensities of twentieth-century warfare and oppression.

4A-224. The Warrior Who Carried Life. Allen & Unwin, 1983.
A pacifist fable in a heroic fantasy setting which, stylishly written and plotted, always keeps one step ahead of the reader, through imaginative subversion of classic tropes such as the liberating talisman and the voyage to the land of the dead, and through a powerful empathy for the well-drawn characters.

Saberhagen, Fred, 1930– .
ABOUT: CA, NE, SMFL, SFE, SFFL, RG, TCSF, PE, ESF

4A-225. Empire of the East. Ace, 1979.
A sweeping post-holocaust fantasy epic, initially published as separate volumes:

The Broken Lands (1968), *The Black Mountains* (1971) and *Changeling Earth* (1973). Text revised for omnibus reprint. Science is here a liberating force which can be transmuted into magic, freeing Earth from the Dark Forces. Flat characterization is rescued by quirky technology (valkyrie robots, technological djinn) and spirited nonstop adventure and battles between good and evil. Saberhagen has used the same setting, although with less satisfactory results, in a series of sequels: *The First Book of Lost Swords* (1983); *The Second Book of Lost Swords* (1983) and *The Third Book of Lost Swords* (1986), *The Fourth Book of Lost Swords* (1989); *The Fifth Book of Lost Swords* (1989); all Tor. The first three were collected as *The Lost Swords* (SFBC/Nelson Doubleday, 1988).

[For other works of this author, see the companion guide to horror.]

Saxton, Josephine (U.K.), 1935– .
ABOUT: CA, SFE, SFFL, TCSF

4A-226. The Travails of Jane Saint. Virgin, 1980.
A feminist quest fantasy with much humor and genre subversion. A surreal world of talking dogs, wacky philosophers and alchemists peppers the onward journey to salvation of the eponymous heroine. An idiosyncratic, ironic dream fantasy with serious, topical underpinnings.

Scarborough, Elizabeth Ann, 1947– .
ABOUT: CA

4A-227. Songs from the Seashell Archives (*Song of Sorcery*, Bantam, 1982; *The Unicorn Creed*, Bantam, 1983; *Bronwyn's Bane*, Bantam, 1983; *The Christening Quest*, Bantam, 1985).
Light-hearted and often mischievous adventures in the enchanted realm of Argonia. A motley collection of princess, witch cousin and suitor (a handsome gypsy) embark on quests, battles and magic-wielding in a world of sea serpents, evil wizards, mercenary mages, swan princesses and other assorted wonders. A successful blend of humor and traditional fantasy of great entertainment value.

Scliar, Moacyr (Brazil), 1937– .

4A-228. The Centaur in the Garden. Ballantine, 1985. Tr. by Margaret A. Neves of *O centauro no jardin*, 1960.
A Jewish centaur is born in Brazil to a family of Russian immigrants to South America. A comic parable about growing up Jewish in Latin America, the novel encompasses the centaur's falling in love, marriage, and romance with another creature. A remarkable creation of gentle philosophical disposition.

Shea, Michael, 1946– .
ABOUT: CA, SFE, MF

4A-229. Nifft the Lean. DAW, 1982.
Openly using the colorful locale of Jack Vance's *The Dying Earth* [3-345], these

four imaginative adventures of Nifft, a clever, professional thief, are masterpieces of the grotesque. A vivid evocation of the netherworld, with teeming beasts and goddesses of all ilk and hue at play, the book splendidly conveys a nightmarish intensity and imagery. *A Quest for Simbilis* (DAW, 1974) offers similar adventures.

4A-230. Polyphemus. Arkham House, 1987.
Shea's first collection of stories, all reprinted from *The Magazine of Fantasy and Science Fiction*, shows him at ease in all fantastical domains, ranging from sheer horror to pure fantasy and whimsy. Many of the stories evoke other writers like Lovecraft, Clark Ashton Smith, Leiber or Vance, and Shea's personal voice does not always come through strongly in all its protean manifestations. Introduction by Algis Budrys.

[For other works of this author, see the companion guide to horror.]

Silverberg, Robert, 1935– .
ABOUT: CA, TCA, NE, SFE, SFFL, RG, TCSF, ESF

4A-231. Gilgamesh the King. Arbor House, 1984.
A splendid historical fantasy and fable about death, desire and power. Silverberg fleshes out the myth of Gilgamesh with vigor and much color. Seen through the eyes of the hero, these brooding adventures reach satisfying levels of humanity and wonder. The epic deeds of the warrior king are interspersed with ambivalent manifestations of magic, which serve only to deepen the alien feel of the novel's historicity.

*4A-232. Majipoor Trilogy (*Lord Valentine's Castle*, Harper, 1980; *Majipoor Chronicles*, Arbor House, 1982; *Valentine Pontifex*, Arbor House, 1983).
Epic fantasy on a grand scale which marked Silverberg's return to writing after a long interval. Although little new ground is broken, the Majipoor books, colorful in the extreme, bawdy, picaresque and chock full of the most incredible adventures, are a perfect example of knowing, professional modern fantasy, borrowing classic themes of legend and chivalry, and seamlessly blending them into the detailed minutiae of the elaborate world-building experiences of SF, here applied to the creation of a complex, Byzantine-like planetary society. Compare Jack Vance.

[For other works of this author, see the companion guide to horror.]

Simak, Clifford D., 1904–1988.
ABOUT: CA, TCA, NE, SMFL, SFE, SFFL, RG, TCSF, ESF, FL, HF

4A-233. Enchanted Pilgrimage. Putnam, 1975.
An enjoyable tale of three parallel universes where a medieval setting survives to this day as alien Caretakers, goblins and gnomes seek to reunite magic and technology in all realms. A clever blending of genres with Simak's customary touch of pastoral humanism.

4A-234. The Fellowship of the Talisman. Ballantine, 1978.
A rare fantasy outing by a master of science fiction. Set in the present in an

alternative world where England remains medieval and Catholic, it follows the perils of a journey across dangerous wastelands of a religious manuscript coveted by forces of evil. An interesting quest variation with Arthurian overtones and a dash of Tolkien among the hardy bunch of heroes.

Sinclair, Andrew (U.K.), 1935– .
ABOUT: CA, MF, SFFL, ESF

4A-235. Gog. Weidenfeld & Nicolson, 1967; **Magog.** Weidenfeld & Nicolson, 1972; **King Ludd.** Weidenfeld & Nicolson, 1988.
A large metafictional piece of mythology about Albion by a British mainstream author. Sprawling contemporary romance through which run threads of English history and legend: Robin Hood, Boadicea, William Blake and others. Strongly allegorical and embedded in contemporary British politics, the trilogy scales imaginative heights in between shallow self-referential and repetitive patches, but remains a major achievement.

Spinrad, Norman, 1940– .
ABOUT: CA, TCA, NE, SFE, SFFL, TCSF, ESF

4A-236. The Iron Dream. Avon, 1972.
An alternative worlds novel structured as a pure clichéd sword-and-sorcery epic written by Adolf Hitler himself, *The Iron Dream* is a crude, didactic attempt equating the genre to brawny fascist impulses. Much of the irony is second degree, and might be lost on the standard youthful genre-gobbler.

Springer, Nancy, 1948– .
ABOUT: CA, RG

4A-237. Chronicles of Isle (*The White Hart*, 1979; *The Silver Sun*, 1980 [revised from *The Book of Suns*, 1977]; *The Sable Moon*, 1981; *The Black Beast*, 1982; *The Golden Swan*, 1983, all Pocket Books).
Intricately textured adult fairy tale series. With brave deeds, wondrous beasts, treasures and conflict, Springer weaves originality from standard images from long ago.

Stanton, Mary.

4A-238. The Heavenly Horse from the Outermost West. Baen, 1988.
An assured talking animal fable in which a mare, obsessed by humankind, follows her path to destiny. The equine fantasy world is well realized and follows familiar good-versus-evil patterns, with clever touches in the introduction of a distinct theology with a heaven and hell in which horses of diverse breeds live and compete at deity level.

Stasheff, Christopher, 1944– .
ABOUT: CA, NE, SFE, RG, TCSF

4A-239. Warlock series (*The Warlock in Spite of Himself*, 1969; *King Kobold*, 1971, revised as *King Kobold Revived*, 1984; *The Warlock Unlocked*, 1982; *Escape Velocity*, 1983; *The Warlock Enraged*, 1984; *The Warlock Wandering*, 1985; *The Warlock Is Missing*, 1986; *The Warlock Heretical*, 1987; *The Warlock's Companion*, 1988; all Ace).

An entertaining blend of SF and sword and sorcery, this popular series follows the fortunes of Rod Gallowglass, an Earthman, and his goofy robot, Fess, on the planet Gramarye, where magic works. The successive novels have never recaptured the verve of the first two installments in the curious duo's adventures, but all provide light-hearted fun encompassing time travel, elves, wizards and the whole gamut of genre paraphernalia familiar to all readers. Undemanding fun.

Stewart, Mary (U.K.), 1916– .
ABOUT: CA, SMFL, SFFL, RG, FL, HF

*4A-240. Life of Merlin series (*The Crystal Cave*, Hodder & Stoughton, 1970; *The Hollow Hills*, Hodder & Stoughton, 1973; *The Last Enchantment*, Hodder & Stoughton, 1979; *The Wicked Day*, Morrow, 1983).

A major, melancholy series retelling the eternal legend of Merlin and Arthur. A richly woven tapestry peopled by princes, soldiers and magicians, charged with the spirits of older mythologies, Stewart's romantic vision of days, friendships and treacheries past, as seen through the eyes of Arthur, blends historical touches with magic and stands as one of the few genuine Arthurian classics.

Sturgeon, Theodore, 1918–1985.
ABOUT: WW, GSF, SFW, CA, TCA, NE, SFE, SFFL, RG, TCSF, PE, ESF

4A-241. Godbody. Donald J. Fine, 1986.
A posthumously published novel on which Sturgeon had been working for almost two decades, *Godbody* is deceptively all surface gloss. A charismatic Christ-like figure mysteriously appears in a small American town. His effect on both men and women inspires both love and fright. A short, strongly erotic novel of empathy which still feels unfinished but through which evident traces of Sturgeon's talent and preoccupations shine.

[For other works of this author, see the companion guide to horror.]

Süskind, Patrick (Germany).
ABOUT: CA

*4A-242. Perfume. Hamish Hamilton, 1986. Tr. by John E. Woods of *Das Parfum*, 1985.
Winner of the 1987 World Fantasy Award, a striking German novel set in revolutionary France. Jean-Baptiste Grenouille, the cool monster of a protago-

nist, has an extraordinary sense of smell, but lacks all personal odor himself. **His obsessive** quest for the ultimate essence drives him to murder. A vigorous tale of exotic horror, which was a major worldwide best-seller. Also annotated as [H4-293].

Swann, Thomas Burnett, 1928–1976.
ABOUT: WW, SFW, CA, SMFL, SFE, MF, SFFL, RG, ESF, FL

4A-243. Day of the Minotaur. Ace, 1966.
Historical fantasy set in ancient Crete. An ill-assorted trio of two children and a giant minotaur venture into the Country of the Beasts, a forest inhabited by fabled creatures: blue monkeys, dryads, centaurs. Gently bucolic, but with an overall somber tone shadowing the adventures, a tale of conflict between humanity and unfallen beasts. Two prequels featuring some of the characters were written and published later, to constitute a trilogy of sorts: *The Forest of Forever* (1971) and *Cry Silver Bells* (1977).

4A-244. Lady of the Bees. Ace, 1976.
An unusual retelling of the legend of Romulus and Remus, the founders of Rome. Reared by a wolf and Mellonia, a tree-dryad who shares the narrative with a faun, the twins fulfill their historic but tragic destiny in a bucolic setting of idyllic qualities. Mellonia also appears in *Green Phoenix* (DAW, 1972), an earlier novel by Swann, about her youth and the days of Troy.

Tarr, Judith, 1955– .
ABOUT: CA

4A-245. Hound and the Falcon trilogy (*The Isle of Glass*, Bluejay, 1985; *The Golden Horn*, Bluejay, 1985; *The Hounds of God*, Bluejay, 1986).
Elf-born Alfred lives in twelfth-century England where he grows up a devoted monk. But his beauty, healing powers and ability to read others' minds set him apart from the rest and he is soon drawn toward the temporal world and pitted against its savagery. Moving from the court of Richard Lionheart to the Siege of Constantinople, Tarr's trilogy offers a great display of history and theology, and despite the inevitable quest element, stands resolutely aside from the more customary modern fantasy trilogy patterns.

Tennant, Emma (U.K.), 1937– .
ABOUT: CA, SFE, MF, TCSF

4A-246. Hotel de Dream. Gollancz, 1976.
In a rundown British hotel, the dreams of its failed inhabitants escape and begin interacting with each other, and even start to have an effect on the outside world. A clever variation on the personal fantasy world dear to a writer like Philip K. Dick, deceptively treated with suitable English reserve in the guise of a mainstream novel of manners.

Tepper, Sheri S.

4A-247. Marianne, the Magus and the Manticore. Ace, 1985; **Marianne, the Madame and the Momentary Gods.** Ace, 1988.
Marianne, born in luxury in a tiny imaginary nation nestled between Turkey and Iran, moves to America as a student. Here she is obliged to call on her native magic when terrible foes appear on the scene. The irruption of myth and fabled creatures into contemporary society offers great scope for a series of soulful adventures.

Thacker, Eric (U.K.), 1923– , and Anthony Earnshaw (U.K.), 1924– .
ABOUT: CA

4A-248. Musrum. Cape, 1968.
Magnificently bizarre avant-garde fable heavily illustrated by Earnshaw, which tells of the quasi-mythical hero Musrum's various fantastic adventures, including his epic campaign agains the Weedking. The patchwork of ideas and themes is somewhat chaotic, as might be expected given the story's lightly encrypted celebration of the hallucinatory qualities of agaric mushrooms. It has obvious affinities with the works of Alfred Jarry, especially *Faustroll* (1911), but its uniqueness in English literature is compromised only by the work with which the two authors followed it, *Wintersol* (1971)—which offers further details of the "musroid world" in the context of a very odd Christmas fantasy. *Wintersol* also features one of the two best dedications in the history of fantasy literature (see [3-170] for the other). (BS)

Thomas, D(onald) M(ichael) (U.K.), 1935– .
ABOUT: CA, SMFL, TCSF

***4A-249. The White Hotel.** Gollancz, 1981.
A book of dreams, sex and violence and much controversy. Lisa Erdman, an opera singer and patient of Freud, has odd precognitions of a confused, painful future, as she moves through the turmoil of Europe between the wars, is killed in the Babi-Yar massacre and later emerges into a sunny, ambiguous version of the afterlife. Part case study of a deranged woman affected by her sexuality and pronounced eroticism, and part poem and hallucination, *The White Hotel* is a unique novel which questions not only the nature of reality and the senses but also the fabric of fantasy as wish fulfillment.

Thurber, James, 1894–1961.
ABOUT: SFW, CA, SMFL, RG, ESF, FL, HF

4A-250. The Wonderful O. Simon & Schuster, 1957.
A pirate who loathes the letter O is brought by a supposed treasure map to the island of Ooroo. Disappointed in his quest for riches, he sets out to abolish the hated letter from the island's affairs, but there are four words which the islanders will not surrender (three of them are hope, love and valor). A neat and elegant fable, every bit as delightful as Thurber's earlier exercises in the same vein [3-336–3-337]. (BS)

Tolkien, J(ohn) R(onald) R(euel), 1892–1973.
ABOUT: WW, GSF, SFW, F, CA, SMFL, SFE, MF, SFFL, RG, TCSF, ESF, FL, HF

*4A-251. The Silmarillion. Allen & Unwin, 1977.
Reconstructed by his son Christopher, this is the major work of mythology that Tolkien held in higher esteem than *The Lord of the Rings* [3-340]. A painstaking history of the elves, which traces the legacy of evil introduced by Morgoth into Middle-earth, *The Silmarillion* ranges from the creation of the Universe to the advent of faerie, and remains incomplete; its final part, planned to map the epic of Numenor, was never finished by Tolkien. A monument of high fantasy, a major work of apocryphal scholarship and a necessary foundation stone for all Tolkien studies.

4A-252. Unfinished Tales. Allen & Unwin, 1980.
A collection of narratives ranging in time from the Elder Days of Middle-earth to the end of the War of the Ring. Both supplement and apocrypha to the main Tolkien canon, it is strictly for those fascinated by his world, its languages, its legends, its politics and its kings. For scholars principally.

Treece, Henry (U.K.), 1912–1966.
ABOUT: CA, SMFL, SFFL

4A-253. The Green Man. Bodley Head, 1966.
A late period, dark and pessimistic fantasy set in the sixth century, *The Green Man* evokes the violent world of Beowulf and Arthur the hunter. Binding together the many myths touched upon in Treece's earlier historical novels, and contributing an ambiguous form of existential angst to the stuff of legends, bloody battles, revenge and deceit, Treece's final book caps an impressive oeuvre in somber hues.

Updike, John, 1932– .
ABOUT: CA, SMFL, MF, SFFL, ESF

4A-254. The Centaur. Knopf, 1963.
A schoolmaster is also Chiron, the centaur. Through the prism of myth, Updike evokes the gods of the ancient Greek pantheon among his familiar landscape of a small American town, which here provides a perfect foil for the inner fantasy world of the protagonists, a middle-aged man and his son, Peter or Prometheus, a teenager on uneasy emotional terrain. The determined reliance on myth turns this tale of 1947 in leafy Pennsylvania into a distinct, subtle moral fantasy.

4A-255. The Witches of Eastwick. Knopf, 1984.
A sharp intrusion of the fantastic into Updike's familiar landscapes of suburban America. Three women with growing supernatural powers come under the influence of Darryl Van Horne, a satanic figure of Falstaffian stature drawn with broad strokes. An invigorating modern fable from a major contemporary author. Filmed by George Miller in 1986, with Jack Nicholson, Cher, Michelle Pfeiffer and Susan Sarandon.

[For other works of this author, see the companion guide to horror.]

Vance, Jack, 1916– .
ABOUT: WW, GSF, SFW, F, CA, TCA, NE, SMFL, SFE, MF, SFFL, RG, TCSF, ESF, FL

4A-256. The Eyes of the Overworld. Ace, 1966.
A return to the wondrous world of *The Dying Earth* [3-345], but with a new, humorous dimension introduced by chief protagonist Cugel, a wily thief whose greed is all too often his nemesis, even on the brink of victory. Lacks the background poignancy of the earlier work, but is always entertaining. Various sequels exist: *Cugel's Saga* (Simon & Schuster, 1983), *Rhialto the Marvelous* (Underwood-Miller, 1984) and Michael Shea's *A Quest for Simbilis* (DAW, 1974), also featuring Cugel.

4A-257. Lyonesse: Suldrun's Garden. Berkley, 1983; **Lyonesse II: The Green Pearl.** Underwood-Miller, 1985. **Lyonnesse III: Madouc.** Underwood-Miller, 1989.
Celtic fantasy trilogy on a large, somewhat impressionistic scale (the second volume is more a collection of tales). Quests, bravery, chivalry, minor touches of magic and warring kings in dynastic conflict form an oblique background to a tapestry of strongly delineated relationships. Resourceful female characters are in marked contrast to Vance's other books.

Van Lustbader, Eric
ABOUT: SFE, RG

4A-258. Sunset Warrior series (*The Sunset Warrior*, Doubleday, 1977; *Shallows of Night*, Doubleday, 1978; *Dai-San*, Doubleday, 1978; *Beneath an Opal Moon*, Doubleday, 1980).
Vivid sword and sorcery with strong tinges of Oriental mythology, from a writer who has since moved on to best-sellerdom with his more conventional thrillers. In a China of thousands of years ago, portrayed in great detail, a tale of quests and battles unfolds, combining a well-realized, basically alien society with a clearly defined conflict and swashbuckling action.

Vercors (pseud. of **Jean Bruller**) (France), 1902– .
ABOUT: CA, NE, SMFL, SFE, TCSF, ESF

4A-259. Sylva. Putnam, 1962. Tr. by Rita Barisse of *Sylva*, 1961.
A fox turns into a beautiful woman. She is taken in by a nobleman whose mistress is a drug addict. Gradually, Sylva the fox loses her feral habits and learns human values, while the other woman descends into madness. A fable of humanization and dehumanization, drawn with a rather thick brush. Compare with David Garnett's *Lady into Fox* [3-152].

Vian, Boris (France), 1920–1959.
ABOUT: CA, NE, SFE

*4A-260. Heartsnatcher. Rapp & Whiting, 1968. Tr. by Stanley Chapman of *L'Arrache-coeur*, 1953.
A somber and poetic minor masterpiece of the absurd by France's erstwhile

surrealist and jazz lover. A psychiatrist is isolated in a primitive village by the coast where animals are almost human and vice versa. A striking, poignant view of a world and a landscape askew.

Walton, Evangeline, 1907– .
> ABOUT: WW, GSF, CA, SMFL, RG, PE, ESF, FL, HF

4A-261. Books of the Welsh Mabinogion (*The Virgin and the Swine*, Willett, Clark, 1936, retitled *The Island of the Mighty*, Ballantine, 1970; *The Children of Llyr*, Ballantine, 1971; *The Song of Rhiannon*, Ballantine, 1972; *Prince of Annwn*, Ballantine, 1974).
Vigorous retelling and expansion of the classic Welsh Celtic myths [1-47] into a series of cohesive novels (not published in the order in which they should be read). Walton's achievement is to emphasize the magic and the mystery in the myths while adhering to the social implications and heroic clash of cultures that pervade the legends. First volume also annotated as [3-356].

Wangerin, Walter, Jr., 1944– .
> ABOUT: CA, SMFL

4A-262. The Book of the Dun Cow. Harper, 1978; **The Book of Sorrow.** Harper, 1985.
Effective talking animal fantasies exploring Christian themes, with a nod toward Chaucer's Nun's Priest, which is acknowledged as a source. Set in the fictional world of the medieval beast fable before the coming of Man, these tales burst with energy and deeply moral concerns. Animal "Keepers" fight the "Wyrm," the source of evil in the Universe, whom God has imprisoned under the face of the world. The preaching of a vigorous Christian message does not hold Wangerin's zestful tales down. Also annotated as [4B-149].

Warner, Sylvia Townsend (U.K.), 1893–1978.
> ABOUT: GSF, CA, SMFL, SFFL, RG, ESF, FL

4A-263. Kingdoms of Elfin. Viking, 1977.
A cohesive collection of sixteen fairy stories, most of which had initially appeared in *The New Yorker*. Codifying with great wit and precision the life-styles and social structures of fairy land, many of the tales involve interaction with humanity, with often sad and cruel consequences. A wonderful bunch of stories, in no way fey, and a considerable fabulistic achievement.

Watson, Ian (U.K.), 1943– .
> ABOUT: CA, NE, SMFL, SFE, SFFL, TCSF

4A-264. The Gardens of Delight. Gollancz, 1980.
Borderline fantasy by one of Britain's most intellectual science fiction authors. A starship seeking a lost colony comes upon an alien world in the very image of the Hieronymus Bosch triptych representing Hell, Paradise and the Garden of

Earthly Delights. A metaphysical and esoteric alchemical quest with layers of symbols and allegories and a rewarding read.

Wellman, Manly Wade, 1903–1986.
ABOUT: WW, GSF, SFW, CA, NE, SMFL, SFE, SFFL, RG, TCSF, PE, ESF

4A-265. Silver John series (*Who Fears the Devil?*, Arkham House, 1963; *Worse Things Waiting*, 1973; *The Old Gods Waken*, Doubleday, 1979; *After Dark*, Doubleday, 1980; *The Lost and the Lurking*, Doubleday, 1981; *The Hanging Stones*, Doubleday, 1982; *The Voice of the Mountain*, Doubleday, 1984; *The Valley So Low*, 1987; *John the Balladeer*, 1988).

The tales of John the balladeer and his silver-stringed guitar. Initially short stories published in *The Magazine of Fantasy and Science Fiction* and collected in the first volume of the series, and then followed by novels, the Silver John tales introduce fascinating elements of native American folklore to the fantasy mainstream with great assurance, as many Ozark and Appalachian legends are unearthed and vividly brought to life as John's travels continue down American backroads. Traditional but enjoyable yarns.

[For other works of this author, see the companion guide to horror.]

White, T(erence) H(anbury) (U.K.), 1906–1964.
ABOUT: WW, GSF, SFW, F, CA, SMFL, SFE, MF, RG, ESF, FL, HF

4A-266. The Once and Future King. Collins, 1958.

Although the first three novels, *The Sword in the Stone* (1938), *The Witch in the Wood* (1939) and *The Ill-Made Knight* (1940), were published earlier, the complete *The Once and Future King* saw publication only two decades later with *The Witch in the Wood*, retitled *The Queen of Air and Darkness*, and the first appearance of the final novel in the cycle, *The Candle in the Wind*. It has now become the standard retelling of the Arthurian canon, having inspired a stage musical and movies and spawned countless imitations, variations and alternative sagas involving Arthur, Merlin, Guinevere, Lancelot and other archetypal characters. At times deliberately anachronistic and colloquial, but always moving, humorous and highly visual, *The Once and Future King* still stands as a definitive Arthurian monument. An entertaining postscript to it, *The Book of Merlyn*, was published posthumously in 1977. Also annotated as [3-370].

Wibberley, Leonard (pseud. of Patrick O'Connor) (U.K.), 1915–1983.
ABOUT: CA, SFE, SFFL, TCSF, ESF, HF

4A-267. The Quest of Excalibur. Putnam, 1959.

An amiable farce in which King Arthur is transported to a future, contemporary England where he has to contend, in succession, with the vagaries of British bureaucracy at its worst, the puzzling automobile and a gently ineffective monarchy. A lighthearted satire with enjoyable moments.

Willard, Nancy, 1936–   .
ABOUT: CA, HF

4A-268. Things Invisible to See. Knopf, 1985.
A quietly pastoral fantasy set in America in the 1930s. The genteel atmosphere and relationships unwittingly parallel the actions of the Lords of the Universe in a metaphysical tale in which reality and fantasy lead a peaceful, if edgy, coexistence. Compare Mark Helprin's *Winter's Tale* [4A-137] and John Crowley's *Little, Big* [4A-79] and *Aegypt* [4A-77]. Also annotated as [4B-156]

Willis, Connie, 1945–   .
ABOUT: CA, NE, TCSF

4A-269. Lincoln's Dreams. Bantam, 1987.
This touching novel of a woman's unwanted psychic link with the horrors of the past, in this case the American Civil War, won the John W. Campbell Memorial Award. An emotional odyssey of dream-time with no rational explanations which might tip it into SF, it packs a powerful punch. Contrast Jack Finney's and Richard Matheson's mental time travel romances [4A-105, 4A-177].

Wolfe, Gene, 1931–   .
ABOUT: CA, TCA, NE, SMFL, SFE, MF, SFFL, RG, TCSF

*4A-270. Book of the New Sun (*The Shadow of the Torturer*, Timescape, 1980; *The Claw of the Conciliator*, Timescape, 1981; *The Sword of the Lictor*, Timescape, 1982; *The Citadel of the Autarch*, Timescape, 1982; *The Urth of the New Sun*, Tor, 1987).
Seldom has a work straddled both the fields of fantasy and science fiction so well that it can confidently be claimed for both genres by respected critics. A wondrous and unimaginably remote future has seen the Earth undergo both societal and geological changes, but the general atmosphere, sometimes reminiscent of Vance's *The Dying Earth* [3-345], distinctly belongs to the fantasy genre despite the SF trappings, which include space flight, time travel, genetic engineering, robots and other classic tropes. Severian, an apprentice torturer, strays from his chosen path and, following a series of picaresque adventures, unveils the reality of the universe he inhabits. From torturer to ruler, he becomes the herald of the age of the New Sun. A striking fictional achievement which ranks high among the best imaginative as well as stylistic achievements of mature, modern fantasy writing.

4A-271. Free Live Free. Ziesing, 1984.
An assorted bunch of weird, wonderful and lovable characters converge on an old condemned house which soon has to make place for a modern freeway. Delightful, picaresque characterization and subtle supernatural touches cleverly blend for a low-key but stunningly effective semi-pastoral mysterious fantasy.

4A-272. Peace. Harper, 1975.
A deceptively simple "Book of the Dead," as the (presumably) deceased narrator tells of his life, his past, friends and pastoral surroundings in a form of quiet

celebration. As understated tale within a tale unfolds, a vibrant, living tapestry of life emerges, woven full of humanity and humility.

4A-273. Soldier of the Mist. Gollancz, Tor, 1986.
The first volume in an ongoing historical fantasy sequence involving Latro, a Greek soldier in 497 BC who has suffered a head wound and has lost the ability to remember more than a day at a time. His travels, related in the obligatory diary, follow an elusive route through a beautifully evoked landscape and time, with curious, often unexplained supernatural elements and puzzling events woven into the narrative. Despite future tomes still to come, already an impressive feat of fantasy telling.

Yarbro, Chelsea Quinn, 1942– .
ABOUT: CA, NE, SFE, MF, SFFL, RG, TCSF, PE

4A-274. Ariosto. Pocket Books, 1980.
An alternative Renaissance romance, *Ariosto* features as its main character the author of the epic poem *Orlando Furioso* [1-4], itself a classic feat of fantasy. The novel features two parallel strands, the first a fantasy world conjured by Ariosto's imagination where North America is under enlightened Italian rule, while the realistic plot is set in a utopian version of Florence with Ariosto no longer heroic but fat and middle-aged. Both worlds converge toward a brief but sad epilogue. A splendid historical background drawn with meticulous care underlines this unusual novel about various dreams of utopia.

[For other works of this author, see the companion guide to horror.]

Yolen, Jane, 1939– .
ABOUT: CA, SFE, SFFL, RG, FL, HF

4A-275. Tales of Wonder. Schocken, 1983.
Thirty stories initially published in *The Magazine of Fantasy and Science Fiction* and various collections marketed as children's books. Immaculate storytelling of tales of diverse provenance—fairy tales, myths, Arthurian stories—which all demonstrate the art of one of America's best (but often underrated) fantasists.

Zelazny, Roger, 1937–
ABOUT: WW, SFW, CA, TCA, NE, SMFL, SFE, MF, SFFL, RG, TCSF, ESF, FL, HF

*4A-276. Amber series (*Nine Princes in Amber*, Doubleday, 1970; *The Guns of Avalon*, Doubleday, 1972; *Sign of the Unicorn*, Doubleday, 1975; *The Hand of Oberon*, Doubleday, 1976; *The Courts of Chaos*, Doubleday, 1978; *Trumps of Doom*, Arbor House, 1985; *Blood of Amber*, Arbor House, 1986; *Sign of Chaos*, Arbor House, 1987).
Zelazny's most commercially popular fantasy series, the ongoing Amber novels initially ended after five volumes with *The Courts of Chaos*. The author returned to it after a seven-year break. An accomplished quest narrative parallels the

psychological growth and evolution of Corwin, a prince of Amber banished to our Earth, which is revealed as a shadow version of reality as he struggles to balance form and chaos throughout his adventures and save his native world and kingdom. Imaginative use is made of Arthurian elements, Grail archetypes and Tarot imagery, providing a powerful philosophical undertone to basically fast-moving formulaic travails particularly strong on characterization. The second group of Amber novels, beginning with *Trumps of Doom*, follow a similar pattern, with Merlin searching for Corwin's whereabouts, but lack the wild imagination of earlier books in the series.

4A-277. Changeling Saga (*Changeling*, Ace, 1980; *Madwand*, Phantasia, 1981). Exiled to Earth from his parallel world where magic reigns, changeling Pol Detson is at the center of a fiercely contested battle between good and evil which influences the fate of both worlds. Through struggle and often painful rites of passage, a tenuous equilibrium is reached, which has to be saved again in *Madwand*, the better of the two novels in the series. Journeyman efforts from Zelazny's talented fabulist pen are redeemed by strong plotting and nicely unexpected twists.

4A-278. Creatures of Light and Darkness. Doubleday, 1969. With its powerful gods of the Egyptian pantheon transposed into space, this is Zelazny's most potent manipulation of myths. Heroic conflicts abound among the new masters of space and matter. Sometimes experimental in its use of verse, verse techniques and short scenes, this ambitious novel is often short on plot and still divides Zelazny fans and critics.

4A-279. Dilvish of Dilvar series (*The Changing Land*, Ballantine, 1981; *Dilvish, the Damned*, Ballantine, 1982). Banished to Hell, the warrior Dilvish escapes and with the assistance of his devilish companion Black returns to the land of the living to seek revenge on his foe, the sorcerer Jelerak. This he accomplishes after many delays and episodic encounters with assorted magical fiends. The tone is often reminiscent of Moorcock's early Elric stories [4A-183]. The stories collected in *Dilvish, the Damned*, although published in book form after the novel *The Changing Land*, were mostly written (for magazines) before and precede the novel in chronology.

4A-280. Jack of Shadows. Walker, 1971. Both a parable about the nature of reality and a quest for redemption, this terse, almost too-fast-moving novel, follows the exploits of Shadowjack, the master thief, as he attempts to control the opposing worlds of Darkside and Dayside, on an Earth that does not rotate. Through triumph, adversity and several deaths, Jack finally becomes one with his errant soul in the midst of Chaos. A sometimes humorous tale of light and darkness in conflict, characteristic of Zelazny at his most exuberant.

Zeldin, Theodore (U.K.)

4A-281. Happiness. Collins, 1988. A dense first novel with a heavy didactic slant from an eminent historian and Oxford don. Sumdy obtains a tourist visa to Paradise and, like a modern Candide, accompanied by a dog called Jolly and a cockroach called Forgetmenot, casts an innocent eye on the places she visits on the way and the often bizarre characters she meets. Her absurd journey conveys a multi-layered view of world institutions which sees the history of humankind as primarily a search for happiness. A difficult but ironic philosophical allegory with much to offer the persevering reader.

Anthologies

4A-282. Amazons! and **Amazons II.** Ed. by Jessica A. Salmonson. DAW, 1979, 1982.

Two original anthologies featuring heroic women at sword and play. The earlier volume, which won the World Fantasy Award, contains thirteen pieces by authors like C. J. Cherryh, Joanna Russ, Janet Fox, Andre Norton, Tanith Lee and Elizabeth Lynn, with a reading list by the editor and Susan Wood. The 1982 volume is uneven and often resorts to formula heroine clichés.

4A-283. Arabesques. Ed. by Susan Shwartz. Avon, 1988.

An ingenious collection of new stories to the Arabian Nights canon, including original material by Gene Wolfe, Tanith Lee, Larry Niven, Jane Yolen, Andre Norton, Nancy Springer and Harry Turteldove among others. An exotic bazaar of high fantasy. Compare with Piers Anthony's *Hasan* [4A-9].

*4A-284. Black Water: An Anthology of Fantastic Literature. Ed. by Alberto Manguel. Lester & Orpen Dennys, 1983. U.S. subtitle: *The Book of Fantastic Literature.* Clarkson Potter, 1984.

A massive anthology of the fantastic (as opposed to fantasy), unique both in size (seventy-two stories, 967 pages) and scope, collecting important classic fantastic material from many languages, while eschewing most contemporaries. The collection principally draws on the literary mainstream, thus demonstrating the extent to which fantastic expression is an accepted mainstream tradition. Features, among many others, Italo Calvino, Graham Greene, Borges, D. H. Lawrence, Nabokov, Herman Hesse, Marguerite Yourcenar, Henry James, Kipling, Pushkin and Julio Cortázar. The few modern authors selected are Le Guin, Bradbury, Cynthia Ozick, Joanne Greenberg, Alex Comfort, Mandiargues, Brian Moore and Francis King. An impressive accumulation of disturbing tales, many translated by the editor, who also provides headnotes to each and biographical notes for each author. A more recent, equally eclectic anthology is *The Book of Fantasy*, ed. by Jorge Luis Borges, Silvina Ocampo and Adolfo Bioy Casares (Viking, 1988). First published in Argentina in 1940, twice revised, and now in English, this volume collects almost eighty pieces, stories, story fragments and anecdotes, from the seventeenth to the twentieth century. Latin American contributors are prominent, but the selection is balanced and varied.

4A-285. Dark Imagining: A Collection of Gothic Fantasy. Ed. by Robert H. Boyer and Kenneth J. Zahorski. Dell, 1978.

Sixteen selections of darker fantasy from George MacDonald, Merritt, Clark

Ashton Smith, Leiber, Anderson, Le Guin, Conan Doyle, Rider Haggard, Algernon Blackwood, Bradbury, Lovecraft, Beagle and others. Skirts the thin line between fantasy and horror and convincingly demonstrates how tenuous categorizations are. Good introduction and general headnotes.

4A-286. Dragons of Light. Ace, 1980; **Dragons of Darkness.** Ace, 1981. Ed. by Orson Scott Card.
Two superior anthologies of original dragon stories and poems, many of which breathe new life into a previously tired and predictable fantasy staple. Features material by Zelazny, George Martin, Michael Bishop, Greg Bear, Jessica Salmonson, Jane Yolen and many others. The initial editions were also illustrated.

4A-287. Elsewhere. Ed. by Terri Windling and Mark Arnold. Ace, 1981, 1982, 1984.
Three ground-breaking anthologies of high fantasy, featuring material by a refreshing assortment of talents from far afield: Robin McKinley, Tanith Lee, Patricia McKillip, Amos Tutuola, Yeats, García Márquez, Graves, Kotzwinkle, Le Guin, Russ, Leiber, Yolen, Blaylock, Angela Carter, etc. Good blend of original and reprint material of high literary quality. The first volume won the World Fantasy Award for best anthology.

4A-288. Faery! Ed. by Terri Windling. Ace, 1985.
Reprints and original stories, drawing on fairy tales and myth. Twenty stories and several poems blend gracefully for a representative sampling of tales of Celtic, Chinese, South American and European inspiration. Includes material by Angela Carter, Jane Yolen, William Wu, Keith Taylor, Patricia McKillip and others.

4A-289. The Fantastic Imagination: An Anthology of High Fantasy. Ed. by Robert H. Boyer and Kenneth J. Zahorski. Avon, 1977, 1978.
Two collections mapping high fantasy, with material spanning 1811 to 1977, and incorporating European, British and American masters of the art. Each volume includes sixteen selections and a useful introduction with suitable historical perspective. Authors featured include Dunsany, George MacDonald, Cabell, Tolkien, C. S. Lewis, Beagle, Le Guin, Vera Chapman, Evangeline Walton, Kenneth Morris, Selma Lagerlöf, C. L. Moore, Joan Aiken and many others. An invaluable survey of literary fantasy with biographical and bibliographical notes to each selection. More eclectic than Boyer and Zahorski is *Fantastic Worlds: Myths, Tales, and Stories* (Oxford, 1979), edited with commentary by Eric S. Rabkin. More than fifty short works are included, from classical to contemporary literature: myth, fairy tales, fantasy, horror and science fiction. Useful but dated annotated bibliography. Well suited to classroom use.

4A-290. Fantasy Hall of Fame. Ed. by Robert Silverberg and Martin H. Greenberg. Arbor House, 1983.
A massive anthology, with all twenty-two selections resulting from a poll taken at the World Fantasy Convention, covering the wide spectrum of fantasy from Poe to 1973. Mostly well-known stories from Fritz Leiber, Ursula K. Le Guin, Abraham Merritt, Theodore Sturgeon, L. Sprague de Camp and many others.

4A-291. First World Fantasy Awards. Ed. by Gahan Wilson. Doubleday, 1977; **The World Fantasy Awards, Vol. 2.** Ed. by Fritz Leiber and Stuart David Schiff. Doubleday, 1980.
Selections of World Fantasy Award winners and nominees, and a choice that naturally makes itself. Outstanding material, including many modern classics, by Aickman, Wellman, Bloch, Leiber, Davidson, Bradbury, Russell Kirk, Hugh Cave, Ramsey Campbell and many others. An excellent introduction to the best of the genre. Some stories date from the 1930s and 1940s, but most are from the 1970s. The second volume lists the World Fantasy Awards, 1973–76. Also annotated as [H4-362].

4A-292. Flashing Swords. Ed. by Lin Carter. Dell, 1973, 1974, 1976, 1977, 1981. Five volumes of original sword-and-sorcery fantasy by Leiber, Vance, Poul Anderson, Norton, Kurtz, Moorcock and others, including two stories by the editor himself.

4A-293. Imaginary Lands. Ed. by Robin McKinley. Ace, 1985.
One of the best anthologies of all original material of the 1980s. Includes stories by James Blaylock ("Paper Dragons," a World Fantasy Award winner), Robert Westall, Peter Dickinson, Jane Yolen, P. C. Hodgell, Patricia McKillip, Michael de Larrabeiti, Joan D. Vinge and the editor. Maintains an overall high standard with a satisfying blend of moods and styles. Also annotated as [4B-169].

4A-294. Invitation to Camelot. Ed. by Parke Godwin. Ace, 1988.
While Arthurian novels abound, usually at trilogy length, short stories are few and infrequent. This anthology succeeds in bringing myriad new angles to the subject and legend, with twelve original stories by Tanith Lee, John M. Ford, Chelsea Quinn Yarbro, Elizabeth Ann Scarborough, Morgan Llywelyn and others.

4A-295. Lands of Never. Allen & Unwin, 1983; **Beyond Lands of Never.** Allen & Unwin, 1984. Both ed. by Maxim Jakubowski.
Showcase anthologies for Unwin's Unicorn fantasy imprint collecting new material by mostly British-based authors, with occasional contributions from the U.S. Notable stories are Tanith Lee's "Draco, Draco," selected by several best-of-year anthologies, and Brian Aldiss's first Helliconia short story, "The Girl Who Sang." Paul Ableman, William Horwood and Jane Gaskell are represented by their first short stories in a decade, while material by Robert Silverberg, Joy Chant, Chris Evans, Ian Watson, Angela Carter, Steve Rasnic Tem, John Grant, J. G. Ballard, Garry Kilworth, Rob Chilson, Robert Holdstock, David Langford, Rachel Pollack, Jessica Amanda Salmonson and the editor completes the selection.

4A-296. Liavek (*Liavek*, Ace, 1985; *The Players of Luck*, Ace, 1986; *Wizard's Row*, Ace, 1987; *Spells of Binding*, Ace, 1988). Ed. by Will Shetterly and Emma Bull.
A shared-world fantasy series put together by a group of Minneapolis writers. The setting is classic fantasy, with fewer sword-and-sorcery elements than the Thieve's World series [4A-301] and more overt use of magic. Principal contributors include Gene Wolfe, Jane Yolen, Steven Brust, Patricia Wrede, Nancy Kress, Barry Long-

year, Megan Lindholm, John M. Ford, Alan Moore, Kara Dalkey, Charles de Lint and Greg Frost.

4A-297. Masterpieces of Fantasy and Enchantment. Ed. by David Hartwell. St. Martin's, 1988.
A challenging compendium of fantasy tales from a wide spectrum, not always featuring the necessarily obvious stories by certain writers. Combines stories by Dickens, Walpole and Nathaniel Hawthorne with works by contemporary practitioners like Le Guin, Moorcock, Lynn, Russ, Delany, Dick, Davidson and many others. A solid historical survey of the genre.

4A-298. Moonsinger's Friends. Ed. by Susan Shwartz. Bluejay, 1985.
A collection of new stories in honor of Andre Norton, grouping stories by Marion Zimmer Bradley (a Lythande story), C. J. Cherryh, Judith Tarr, Joan D. Vinge, Tanith Lee, Poul Anderson, Anne McCaffrey and others. A fair sampling of contemporary fantasy in tribute to a grand lady of the genre.

*4A-299. New Worlds of Fantasy. Ace, 1967, 1970, 1971; **Year's Finest Fantasy.** Berkley, 1978, 1979; **Fantasy Annual 3, 4 & 5.** Pocket, 1981, 1981, 1982. All ed. by Terry Carr.
Carr's first series of anthologies regrouped outstanding contemporary reprint material and reached a very high standard. The second series (which changed titles when it moved publishers in midstream) restricted its scope to stories published during the previous calendar year. However, Carr's taste and assured editorial touch ensured that the material he selected was genuinely the best of the year, thus guaranteeing a similar level of quality and fewer slip-ups. Taken overall, the Carr anthologies offer the best fantasy short fiction of their time. Compare the weaker annual edited by Carter and Saha [4A-305]. For library holdings of these titles, see chapter 11.

4A-300. The Phoenix Tree: An Anthology of Myth Fantasy. Ed. by Robert H. Boyer and Kenneth J. Zahorski. Avon, 1980.
A collection of myth-based fantasies displaying the same taste for erudition and historical research evidenced by the editors' other anthologies [4A-285, 4A-289]. Includes stories or novel excerpts by Dunsany, Disraeli, Lovecraft, Richard Adams, Borges and others.

4A-301. Thieve's World (*Thieve's World*, 1979; *Tales from the Vulgar Unicorn*, 1980; *Shadows of Sanctuary*, 1981; *Storm Season*, 1982; *The Face of Chaos*, 1983; *Wings of Omen*, 1984; *The Dead of Winter*, 1985; *Soul of the City*, 1986; *Blood Ties*, 1986; *Aftermath*, 1987; *Uneasy Alliances*, 1988; *Thieve's World 12: Stealer's Day*, 1989, all Ace). Ed. by Robert Lynn Asprin and Lynn Abbey (from vol. 6).
The first and most popular of the shared-world concept of anthologies, presenting a series of tightly woven short stories in which various authors continue a basic storyline with set characters within a pre-set structure. The locale of Thieve's World is a semi-medieval, barbaric sword-and-sorcery world not unlike that inhabited by Leiber's Grey Mouser, and the books are entertaining if light-weight. Main authors to have contributed to the series, in addition to the editors, are Marion Zimmer Bradley, John Brunner, Joe Haldeman, Andrew Offutt, Philip José Farmer, A. E. van Vogt, C. J. Cherryh, Janet Morris (who also wrote a

novel, *Beyond Sanctuary*, Baen, 1985, in the series), Robin Bailey, Diane Duane and Poul Anderson. Compare with another shared-world series created by Janet Morris regrouping famous characters in Hell, *Heroes in Hell* (Baen, 1986) and *Rebels in Hell* (Baen, 1986).

4A-302. Top Fantasy. Ed. by Josh Pachter. Dent, 1985.
Twenty-four authors select and introduce a story of their own that they consider their favorite or their best. Some idiosyncratic and interesting choices, but an excellent level of quality throughout. Features material by Ballard, Michael Bishop, Bloch, Bradbury, Marion Zimmer Bradley, Ramsey Campbell, Disch, Tanith Lee, Le Guin, McCaffrey, Silverberg, Gene Wolfe and others.

4A-303. Unicorns!; Magicats!; Faery!; Bestiary!; Mermaids!; Sorcerers!; Demons!; Dogtales! Ed. by Gardner Dozois and Jack Dann. Ace, 1982–88.
A continuing series of thematic reprint anthologies, regrouping some of the best stories devoted to particular subjects dear to the fantasy genre. Excellent choices, featuring not only accepted classics but also forgotten and underrated stories. Even though all the field's big names are represented, an effort is also made to highlight nongenre authors who have occasionally ventured into fantasy. Each volume also provides a valuable recommended reading list. The best of the compendium fantasy reprints. Compare the more uneven *Asimov's Magical Worlds of Fantasy*, ed. by Asimov (Greenberg & Waugh, Signet 1983 to 1988), volumes so far on *Wizards, Witches, Cosmic Knights, Magical Wishes, Spells, Giants* and *Mythical Beasts*.

*4A-304. The Year's Best Fantasy and Horror. Ed. by Ellen Datlow and Terri Windling. St. Martin's, 1988.
The most recent in the "best of" anthology stakes, but the opening effort by the two editors (Datlow concentrates on horror while Windling selects the fantasy) is proof enough of excellent judgment: this volume includes both World Fantasy Award winners, Le Guin's "Buffalo Gals" and Jonathan Carroll's "Friend's Best Man." A large and entertaining selection in both areas genuinely reflects the high standards of contemporary writing and, publishers allowing, this series should become the indispensable adjunct to the year's literary production, as was Terry Carr's [4A-299].

4A-305. The Year's Best Fantasy Stories. Ed. by Lin Carter (vols. 1–6) and Arthur W. Saha (vols. 7–14). DAW, 1975–88.
The longest-running "best of" fantasy series of anthologies, but not always the most reliable. Terry Carr provided a more representative selection of the year's best [4A-299]. With Lin Carter in the editorial chair, the emphasis was too often on blustery sword-and-sorcery material and even previously unpublished material, creditably taken from small magazines, but the level of choices was too idiosyncratic. Saha's touch is less assured, debatable but also somewhat pedestrian, as is witnessed by checking the selections against the World Fantasy Award winners and nominees and the anthologies' low batting average of consensus choices. This annual now suffers by comparison with the new annual edited by Datlow and Windling [4A-304]. Vol. 14, 1988, was the last. For library holdings of this title, see chapter 11.

4B

Modern Fantasy for Young Adults, 1950–88

Francis J. Molson and Susan G. Miles

Young adult fantasy—the most recent of fantasy subgenres to enjoy critical acceptance—is best understood in relation to the emergence of young adult literature and the prior origin and development of children's literature, in particular children's fantasy. The major reason for the current preference for "young adult" is that, as it conveniently functions as an umbrella term for anything and everything teens read, it also lends dignity and respect to that reading material. Further, the age of the putative reader implied by "young adult" is by no means settled; for instance, "fourteen and over," "twelve and up," "thirteen to eighteen" and "tenth to twelfth grade" have all at one time or another been proposed. Disagreement over the range of age or reading level "young adult" implies, it should be noted, is not unimportant, for there is greater psychological and emotional disparity between, say, an eleven-year-old preteen and a fifteen-year-old teen than between an adult of twenty-one and one of twenty-five. Still, whether "young adult" is the most appropriate term or what is the correct age or grade level of the putative readership of YA literature is not the point; what is, is why YA literature exists today. Even if we adopt the least flattering explanation, i.e., YA literature is merely another way of exploiting a segment of the population that is too self-conscious and too liberal with its money, the fact remains that narratives are being written, published and reviewed, and made available to those in passage between childhood and adulthood, whatever the actual boundary years may be.

In their survey of the reading material adolescents had access to over the years, Donelson and Nilsen [4B-177] rightly emphasize the heavily didactic intent of much of the literature recommended for or made accessible to young readers in the eighteenth and early nineteenth centuries. Moreover, most publishers and authors must have believed this intent was best realized in a primarily mimetic format, since it was one of the most often used. This didactic intent and its preferred format undoubtedly impeded the development of literary fantasy but obviously did not stop it, for by the middle of the nineteenth century, what is clearly children's fantasy can be distinguished. Two important developments contributed to the formation of the new subgenre. The first was the revival of the fairy tale as a genre valid in itself as well as one suitable for children—a revival directly attributable to the impact of the Brothers Grimm and Andersen's tales. The second was the publication in 1865 and 1872 respectively of the hugely imaginative *Alice's Adventures in Wonderland* [2-23] and *Through the Looking Glass* [2-23], which testified then, and still do, not only to the validity and staying power of fantasy but also to the many positive uses of "wasting time," in particular, assisting in the creation of fantasy.

Not only did the Grimm and Andersen tales, along with the other literary fairy tales that began to appear at this time, delight readers of every age, they also fostered in them a taste for similar reading fare. One manifestation of this taste was the Victorian and Edwardian predilection for book-long literary fairy tales, some of which are still popular with young readers: George MacDonald's *At the Back of the North Wind* (1871) [2-114], *The Princess and the Goblin* (1872) [2-114] and *The Princess and Curdie* (1883); the two Alice books; E. Nesbit's the Psammead trilogy—*Five Children and It* (1902) [3-269], *The Phoenix and the Carpet* (1904) [3-269] and *The Story of the Amulet* (1906) [3-269]—and *The Enchanted Castle* (1907) [3-268]; J. M. Barrie's *Peter Pan in Kensington Gardens* (first version, 1906) [3-18] and the early Baum Oz stories [3-20]. In addition to their specifically fantastic elements, most of these narratives feature young protagonists who, placed in at least minimally realistic social contexts and struggling to gain control of the circumstances swirling around them, do achieve some successes and, hence, to a degree take charge of their own lives. These features surely proved attractive to many young readers, particularly those twelve and over, and are those, it should be noted, that are characteristic of today's YA literature. In short, ever since the emergence of the subgenre in the mid-nineteenth century, older youth, like their younger brothers and sisters, have read and enjoyed children's fantasy. To the question "What did preteens and teens read before what is called YA fantasy originated?" then there are two answers. The first is, as we have just observed, whatever children's fantasy they found appealing. The second involves an early instance of a phenomenon that is very familiar today, i.e., whatever adult fantasy they could get their hands on to read and end up liking. Accordingly, older youth might very well have enjoyed, just like their elders, whatever fantasy was being produced by writers like Irving, Poe, Dickens, Stoker, M. R. James, Stockton, Cabell, Dunsany, Haggard and Kenneth Morris.

Designating 1950 as the year to begin an overview of YA fantasy is somewhat arbitrary given what we have just said about the children's and adult fantasy available to adolescents prior to that year. Moreover, selecting 1950 eliminates a number of titles that otherwise clearly would qualify as young adult. J. R. R. Tolkien's *The Hobbit* (1938) [3-339], A. de Saint Exupéry's *The Little Prince* (1943) [3-316] and T. H. White's *The Sword in the Stone* (1938) [3-370] immediately come to mind. Other, perhaps less recognized titles are Elizabeth Goudge's

The Little White Horse (1946), Walter De la Mare's *Collected Stories* (1945) [3-110], T. H. White's *Mistress Masham's Repose* (1946) [3-369], Padraic Colum's *The Boy Apprenticed to an Enchanter* (1920) and Allison Uttley's *A Traveler in Time* (1940). On the other hand, it is relatively easy to defend the appropriateness of choosing 1950 for, as Donelson and Nilsen indicate, during the 1950s not only was YA literature securely established but it also expanded in subject matter and improved in quality. This phenomenon did not mean, incidentally, that each type of YA literature matured at the same pace; and fantasy, it must be admitted, was one genre that lagged. Still, in the 1950s there did appear a number of titles that have come to be considered superior instances of YA fantasy: Philippa Pearce's *Tom's Midnight Garden* (1958) [4B-129], C. S. Lewis's Narnian Chronicles [4B-101], Katharine Briggs' *Hobberdy Dick* (1955) [4B-20], Arthur Calder-Marshall's *The Fair to Middling* (1959) [4B-22], Eleanor Farjeon's *The Silver Curlew* (1953) [4B-43] and Elizabeth Pope's *The Sherwood Ring* (1958) [4B-138].

In spite of some solid achievements in the 1950s, real growth in YA fantasy had to await three developments. The first and perhaps most important was the acceptance by parents, teachers, librarians and reviewers of the candor YA literature increasingly manifested as it depicted many of the central concerns of adolescence—generational and parental conflict, self-doubts, anxiety over physical changes, career indecision, dating and sex. Once the battle for honesty and virtually unrestricted subject matter was won, YA writers could turn their attention to new directions and emphases, e.g., exploring the advantages of using fantasy to dramatize other central topics, such as coming of age. The second development was the acceptance of science fiction as a valid subgenre of children's and YA literature. Crucial to this acceptance was the pioneering work in the 1950s of Robert Heinlein and Andre Norton whose so-called juveniles, it should be noted, often are masterly blends of YA and science fiction topics. Also significant was the decision of the John C. Winston Company to inaugurate its science fiction series for young readers; its success—twenty-six titles by an array of authors before the end of the decade—testified to the viability of children's and YA science fiction. Thus, by the end of the 1950s not only was science fiction established as an alternative to realism for attracting, challenging and entertaining young readers; its flourishing also helped to ready the latter to accept other alternatives, like fantasy. The third development was the extensive presence of science fiction and fantasy in comics and films—media very popular with teenagers. Witness the superheroes already celebrated in the comic book—Superman, Captain Marvel, Captain America and Batman; witness the many monster movies with their varied assortment of invading aliens, werewolves, mutant insects, zombies and other horrific creatures. The proliferation of science fiction and fantasy in the popular media dispelled, it would appear, all doubt about the viability of special markets designed to take advantage of whatever appealed to adolescents. One consequence is that publishers increasingly became receptive to YA fantasy of various kinds.

In the 1960s YA fantasy came of age as types already in evidence increased in numbers and new types appeared. High fantasy, for instance, was well represented: the five volumes of Lloyd Alexander's Prydain chronicles [4B-8]; the five volumes in Susan Cooper's Dark Is Rising sequence [4B-28]; Ursula Le Guin's Earthsea trilogy [4B-98]; Alan Garner's Weirdstone sequence [4B-53]. Indicative of the critical esteem the relatively new subgenre was already garnering is that individual titles from three of these sequences were awarded either the Newbery Medal for the outstanding children's book of the year—Alexander's *The High King* [4B-8] and Cooper's *The Grey King* [4B-28]—or the National Book Award—Le Guin's *The Farthest Shore* [4B-98]. Also well represented were retellings of traditional tales or adaptations from myth: Garner's *Elidor* [4B-50] and *The Owl Service* [4B-51], again Le Guin's Earthsea trilogy, Nicholas Gray's *The Seventh Swan* [4B-60], William Mayne's *Earthfasts* [4B-114], John Gordon's *The Giant under the Snow* [4B-55], Rosemary Harris's *The Moon in the Cloud* [4B-68], Mary Steele's *The Journey Outside* [4B-146] and Joan North's *The Cloud Forest* [4B-122]. Mixed fantasy continued to be popular, especially that in the tradition of E. Nesbit with its emphasis on intelligent, resourceful protagonists and a refusal to patronize the readers, e.g., Penelope Farmer's *The Summer Birds* [4B-45] and its two sequels, and John Aiken's *The Wolves of Willoughby Chase* [4B-5] and its sequels. During the decade writers for the YA audience were already willing to take chances and experiment. For example, in *The Mouse and His Child* [4B-71], Russell Hoban brilliantly interweaves the plot possibilities of the conventional toy-transformation story, the traditional family story and an extraordinarily rich, allusive and witty style to explore in new and daring ways the dictum that stories for youth should have happy endings. In his tour de force, *The Phantom Tollbooth* [4B-88], a most worthy descendant of Lewis Carroll and the linguistic inventiveness of the Alice books, Norton Juster delights any reader, young or old, who enjoys verbal nonsense. And in *The Face in the Frost* [4B-17], a book that deserves much wider recognition than it has received, John Bellairs deliciously combines magic, history, atmosphere and large amounts of humor.

Today, YA fantasy encompasses virtually all types of fantasy and YA topics. Ghost story and horror, for instance, can be found in the work of Lois Duncan and Vivien Alcock. Virginia Hamilton, an author highly honored for her distinctively wrought portraits of black experience, blends the latter and the ghost story in *Sweet Whispers, Brother Rush* [4B-65]. But perhaps it is Margaret Mahy who has been most effective in melding the ghost story and YA topics, in particular the challenge of effectively sustaining family life under adverse circumstances. Time-slip fantasy, for another instance, has been successfully employed to incorporate historical material presumably of interest to teens—e.g., the New York jazz scene in T. Ernesto Bethancourt's *Tune in Yesterday* [4B-18]; early working conditions for children in Jill Paton Walsh's *A Chance Child* [4B-128] or David Wiseman's *Jeremy Visick* [4B-157]; the Holocaust in Jane Yolen's *The Devil's Arithmetic* [4B-163]; and the willingness of organized religion in an ancient kingdom to manipulate its adherents for its own political ends in Peter Dickinson's *The Blue Hawk* [4B-37]. The talking animal story, perhaps the oldest of fantasy types, continues to prove its versatility. In *Watership Down* [4B-1] Richard Adams not only plausibly renders rabbit consciousness and its life, but also brilliantly suggests a rabbit mythology. Walter Wangerin, Jr. pours new life into the medieval beast fable of Chaunticleer as he speculates in *The Book of the Dun Cow* [4B-149] about the ongoing struggle of good and evil. Clare Bell incorporates the most recent insights into animal behavior as she narrates her engrossing story, *Ratha's Creature* [4B-16], about the wildcat who becomes exile, leader and then savior of her feline tribe. And Robin Hawdon transforms the social organization and life of the nondescript ant into a metaphor for contemporary politics in *A Rustle in the Grass* [4B-70]. Humor, as might be expected, is definitely present, as exemplified by Richard Peck in his amusing stories about Alexander Armsworth and Blossom Culp, *The Ghost Belonged to Me* [4B-131] and its several sequels, and by Allen Andrews in *The Pig Plantagenet* [4B-13] with its witty and unexpected adaptation of the mock epic to narrate the exploits of a "heroic" pig. As a final instance of the scope of YA fantasy today, the school story has very successfully been assimilated: in Gillian Cross's *The Dark Behind the Curtain* [4B-32], the ghost of a London mass murderer not only haunts the cast of a school dramatization of the killer's life but also augments the tension among the members; in *Through the Hidden Door* [4B-150], a lost race story, Rosemary Wells depicts the brutality and venality of school officials with a frankness that rivals Robert Cormier's.

Several observations concerning contemporary YA fantasy remain. Not surprisingly, one is the presence of strong female protagonists who range from the ice cold, beautiful Sybel in Patricia McKillip's *The Forgotten Beasts of Eld* [4B-116], whose treatment of her lover Coren is the mirror image of the conventional male lover's use of his beloved, to the unconventional but likable and genuinely heroic Harry Crew of Robin McKinley's high fantasy, *The Blue Sword* [4B-118], and fourteen-year-old Tina in Suzy Charnas's breezily written *The Bronze King* [4B-26], who not only almost falls in love with a man much older than herself but also defeats the Kraken invading New York City. A second observation is that, just when observers might be tempted to think that YA fantasy can do nothing but duplicate past successes, original stories appear. For instance, demonstrating what still can be done with the Nesbitian device of using magic to bring about unintended results, in *The Castle of Bone* [4B-44] Penelope Farmer has items placed inside a magical cupboard returned to their original or pristine form with sometimes unexpected and terrifying consequences, as when Penn becomes a baby and his friends don't know what to do. Or, for another instance, Meredith Pierce in *The Darkangel* [4B-134] pours into the old wineskin of vampire stories the new wine of her Darkangels or vampyres, situating them in a strikingly original world on the moon they seek to control.

A third and final observation is that YA fantasy flourishes today because it satisfies two genuine needs of the audience it is designed to reach. The first is aesthetic. YA fantasy at its best is very effective storytelling, providing believable characters, stimulating description, original setting and distinctive writing. No wonder, then, that a number of YA fantasy novels have received critical honors like the Newbery Medal or the National Book Award or the Carnegie Medal or the Guardian Award, or been designated ALA Notable Book of the Year. The second need is psychological. It is true that detractors of YA fantasy dismiss the genre as escapist, trivial or obvious and, as such, deserving of critical scorn. Admittedly, some YA literature, including fantasy when it is merely formulaic, can be downright silly, e.g., when it suggests that suffering from acne or fretting about what is fashionable is really important, or even seriously misleading—especially when it implies that youth can approach its problems, to adapt Ursula Le Guin's description of the phenomenon, as math problems are approached: i.e., the definitive answers or solutions may be found in the back of some textbook of life. But youth do need and deserve assistance as they confront the central concerns of adolescence. YA fantasy, like most YA literature, speaks to those in passage from childhood to adulthood, and readers can take comfort in learning that they are not the only ones who feel lonely, unwanted or even unloved; or who believe that they really cannot get along with parents or siblings; or who are convinced that they are misfits. A kind of storybook guidance, YA fantasy provides imaginative and vicarious opportunities to identify and empathize; to try out different roles or assume new faces; or to pursue different options or to take off in new directions. As an especially effective medium of dramatizing the journey of self-discovery or coming of age, YA fantasy assists in revealing to adolescents that they are not immortal, that evil exists both within and outside, that they are capable of great evil as well as great good, and that they must make choices or render judgments if they are to grow into authentic adulthood. In other words, YA fantasy offers, precisely because it is young adult and fantastic, an escape that is genuinely bibliotherapeutic, that is, positive, supportive and worthwhile.

Bibliography

Cross-references to works of fantasy appealing to younger readers (some younger than young adults) published prior to 1950 and annotated in other chapters are included here for the convenience of users. Many works nominally written for adults are equally suitable for young adults. Several hundred are listed in Lynn [4B-182], which should be consulted for further guidance.

Adams, Richard (U.K.), 1920– .
ABOUT: CA, SMFL, MF, SFFL, RG, PE, FL, HF

*4B-1. Watership Down. Rex Collings, 1972 (14–18).
Searching for a safe place to establish a new warren, three rabbits, Hazel, Bigwig and Fiver, go through a series of adventures which instruct them in the values and practices that ensure peace and security in the warren, toughen them for the leadership roles and provide additional rabbits, especially females, necessary for stability. This fascinating reconstruction of rabbit life, consciousness and mythology is also a penetrating look at politics and military tactics. Winner of the 1973 Carnegie Medal, the 1973 Guardian Award for Children's Fiction and the 1977 California Reading Association's Young Reader Medal. Compare to *A Rustle in the Grass* [4B-70].

Aiken, Joan (U.K.), 1924– .
ABOUT: WW, CA, SFFL, RG, FL, HF

4B-2. The Far Forests: Tales of Romance, Fantasy and Suspense. Viking, 1977 (13+).
This volume features fifteen sophisticated, surreal stories by a master author which are bound to delight and amuse. Stories include "Lodging for the Night," "Postman's Knock," "As Gay as Cheese," "Furry Night," "Five Green Moons," "Sultan's Splash," "The Far Forests," "The Story about Caruso," "The Rented

Swan," "Safe and Soundproof," "Cricket," "Our Feathered Friends," "The Man Who Had Seen the Rope Trick," "The Cold Flame," "A Taxi to Solitude."

4B-3. The Shadow Guests. Cape, 1980 (13+).
Bewildered and hurt by his mother and brother's mysterious disappearance in Australia, Cosmo Curtoys returns to England and school and to live with his cousin Eunice Doom; on the property he is visited by the ghosts of several ancestors, learns about a family curse and accepts the necessity of growing up and dying. A school-family-curse ghost story with effective ambience and interesting characters and plot. Contrast *Sweet Whispers, Brother Rush* [4B-65].

4B-4. A Whisper in the Night. Gollancz, 1982 (13+).
A collection of thirteen short stories each having a surprising, eerie or ironic twist at the end. Stories included are "Lob's Girl," "Miss Spitfire," "Finders Keepers," "The Windowbox Waltz," "The Swan Child," "Merminster," "Mrs. Chatterbox," "Two Races," "Old Filliken," "Snow Horse," "The Hunchback of Brook Green," "Homer's Whistle," and "The Lost Specimen." These are evocative, imaginative tales.

4B-5. The Wolves of Willoughby Chase. Cape, 1962, (10–12).
After Bonnie's parents leave on a trip, she and her cousin Sylvia are severely harassed by the new, evil governess, and are forced to flee and embark, befriended by the resourceful Simon, on a series of adventures which culminate in the overthrow of the governess and her minions and the return of happiness. Borderline fantasy, the story is a quickly moving, lighthearted yarn in the style of a Victorian novel. First in a series which includes *Black Hearts in Battersea* (1964), *Nightbirds on Nantucket* (1966), *The Cuckoo Tree* (1971), *The Stolen Lake* (1981), *The Whispering Mountain* (1968), which won the 1969 Guardian Award for Children's Fiction, and *Dido and Pa* (1986).

Alcock, Vivien (U.K.), 1924– .
ABOUT: CA

4B-6. The Haunting of Cassie Palmer. Methuen, 1980 (10–12).
Cassie, the seventh child of a seventh child, is unwilling to use the psychic powers her mother insists she has. On a dare she conjures up Deveril, finding herself haunted and in trouble because of the spirit. Engagingly written, this amusing story moves quickly with the requisite number of scary passages. Compare *The Haunting* [4B-109].

4B-7. The Stonewalkers. Methuen, 1981 (11+).
All the statues near the moor inexplicably come alive and threaten the lives of Poppy, Emma and Rob who are saved when, just as unexpectedly, a rock slide entombs the statues. Compact, tautly written, nightmarish story also dramatizes troubled mother-daughter relationship.

Alexander, Lloyd, 1924– .
ABOUT: WW, CA, SMFL, SFFL, RG, ESF, FL, HF

***4B-8. The Book of Three.** Holt, 1964 (11–15).
Anxious to become a hero and assigned the task of Assistant Pig-Keeper, young

Taran flubs and unexpectedly becomes embroiled in conflict between the Horned King, leader of the evil Arawn, and Gwydion, champion of the good people in Prydain. Enticing and original retelling of elements from the *Mabinogion* [1-47] also features attractive characters, humor, deft style and a completely believable Secondary World. The first volume in the five-part Chronicles of Prydain, which has become a contemporary classic of heroic fantasy for youth, is followed by *The Black Cauldron* (1965), which was a 1966 Newbery Honor Book; *The Castle of Llyr* (1966); *Taran Wanderer* (1967); and *The High King* (1968), which won the 1969 Newbery Medal. Contrast *The Ash Staff* [4B-47].

*4B-9. The Marvelous Misadventures of Sebastian. Dutton, 1970 (10–12).
Sebastian is forced to flee for his life, embarking, along with a white cat and a princess in disguise, on a series of unexpected, sometimes zany and other times perilous adventures which culminate in the overthrow of the evil regent, Grinssorg; a career as a composer for the young man; and his marriage with Princess Isabel. Characteristic Alexander: quick-moving and captivating narrative, much humor, attractive characters and a convincing Secondary World. 1971 National Book Award winner.

4B-10. Westmark. Dutton, 1981 (11–15).
Young, naive Theo, swept into the political upheaval brought about when the evil Cabrarus plots to have himself declared heir to the throne of Westmark, is forced to take sides and shed some of his innocence. He makes new friends, including Mickle, who turns out to be the presumably dead young princess, and helps restore Mickle to her parents and peace to the kingdom. Winner of the 1982 American Book Award. Sequels are *The Kestrel* (1982) and *The Beggar Queen* (1983). The trilogy, set in a mythical land, is picaresque adventure, peopled with diverse and surprisingly subtle characters and featuring many plot twists.

Ames, Mildred 1919- .
ABOUT: CA

4B-11. The Silver Link, the Silken Tie. Scribner, 1984 (13+).
This otherwise realistic problem story of two psychologically troubled teens, Felice and Tim, who sense a common link involving psi powers and become close friends, is fantasy only because of the psi powers described and the narrative frame that presupposes a secret conspiracy to subvert the nation's youth. Out-of-the-ordinary protagonists, sensitive handling of young love and topical subject matter are highlights. Compare *Stranger with My Face* [4B-40].

Andersen, Hans Christian. Stories for the Household [2-4]

Anderson, Margaret (U.K.), 1931- .
ABOUT: CA

4B-12. In the Keep of Time. Knopf, 1977 (10+).
Set in Scotland and focusing on an ancient tower, this time shift novel concerns four youngsters swept into the swirl of fourteenth-century wars between the Scots

and invading English and then into a twenty-first century which rejects modern technology. Above-average story because of its surprising plot switches. Sequels in the Time Trilogy are *In the Circle of Time* (1979) and *The Mists of Time* (1984). Compare *Beadbonny Ash* [4B-46].

Andrews, Allen (U.K.), 1913– .
    ABOUT: CA

4B-13. The Pig Plantagenet. Hutchinson, 1980 (12+).
The plan to exterminate the forest animals is foiled by the swift pig, Plantagenet, who not only warns his compatriots but also leads them out of ambush and into safety. Mock epic and yet somehow elegant, densely allusive in wit and humor, and rich in droll and heroic characterization, the story favorably compares with *Watership Down* [4B-1] and should appeal to all ages. *Castle Crespin* (1982) is a sequel. Contrast *The Book of the Dun Cow* [4B-149].

Andrews, J. S. (U.K.), 1934– .
    ABOUT: CA, SFFL, HF

4B-14. The Bell of Nendrum. Bodley Head, 1969. U.S. title: *The Green Hill of Nendrum* (1970) (13+).
When the twentieth-century teenager Nial goes on a weekend excursion in his new boat, he finds himself transported back to the tenth century after a storm. He becomes involved in the adventures of the people in a monastery as they are threatened by a Viking attack, until an accident returns him to his own time. Using time slip, this is an exciting story with interesting characters and an evocative setting. Contrast *The Wind Eye* [4B-154].

Babbitt, Natalie, 1932– .
    ABOUT: CA, FL, HF

4B-15. Tuck Everlasting. Farrar, Straus, 1975 (10–12).
Winnie Foster accidentally discovers that the Tucks, a family passing through that she grows fond of, have acquired the secret to immortality, and is herself offered the secret. A brief, beautifully crafted and fable-like story provides both young and old readers insight into the rival claims of change and stasis. Winner of the 1975 Christopher Book Award and the 1978 International Board on Books for Young People (IBBY) Honor List. Compare *The Summer Birds* [4B-45].

Barrie, J. M. Peter Pan [3-18]

Baum, L. Frank. The Wonderful Wizard of Oz [3-20]

Bell, Clare, 1952– .

4B-16. Ratha's Creature. Atheneum, 1983 (14–16).
After Ratha is banished because of the independence shown as she learns to control fire, the wildcat is forced to live among enemies; eventually her courage

and resourcefulness are necessary to the clan's survival. Distinctive story, brilliant in concept and execution, maintains suspense and excitement until the end. The Clan Ground series also includes *Clan Ground* (1984). Contrast *The Cats of Seroster* [4B-152].

Bellairs, John, 1938- .
ABOUT: CA, SMFL, SFFL, RG, FL, HF

4B-17. The Face in the Frost. Macmillan, 1969 (14+).
Prospero and Roger Bacon combine forces to defeat—only after sometimes hilarious, sometimes scary adventures—the evil wizard Melichus, who is attempting to control "a country whose name doesn't matter." Witty, richly allusive, fresh and charming writing enlivens this always entertaining one-of-a-kind narrative.

Bethancourt, T. Ernesto, 1932- .
ABOUT: CA

4B-18. Tune in Yesterday. Holiday House, 1978 (14–16).
Via a Gate to the Past in the local cemetery, Richie and Matty travel to the New York City of 1942, hear a number of jazz artists, date and stumble upon a Nazi plot to bomb the *Normandie*. Quick-moving, adventurous time travel story entertainingly recreates the 1940s, especially the jazz scene. The sequel is *The Tomorrow Connection* (1984). Compare *Hangin' Out with Cici or My Mother Was Never a Kid* [4B-127].

Bond, Nancy, 1945- .
ABOUT: CA, SMFL, FL

***4B-19. A String in the Harp**. Atheneum, 1976 (11–15).
While forced to live in Wales, Peter finds an ancient tuning key that may have belonged to the legendary bard Taliesen. As a result, Peter not only is pulled back into the latter's time and involved in his life and destiny but is also able to rebuild his own personal life, especially his relationship with his father. A longish tale, the story skillfully and sympathetically blends high fantasy, Welsh mythology, and typical YA concerns of family and parental conflicts. 1977 Newbery Honor Book and winner of the 1977 International Reading Association Children's Book Award. Contrast *Shadows on the Wall* [4B-121]; compare *A Game of Dark* [4B-115].

Briggs, K(atharine) M(ary) (U.K.), 1898–1980.
ABOUT: CA, RG

4B-20. Hobberdy Dick. Eyre & Spottiswoode, 1955 (11–14).
When an unloving city-bred Puritan family moves into an old country manor in the mid-seventeenth century, its resident hobgoblin, Hobberdy Dick, takes it upon himself to wrangle a brighter, happier future for the household. Steeped in descriptions of the old ways of the English countryside, the story has charming elements of a romantic fairy tale. Compare *The Perilous Gard* [4B-137].

4B-21. Kate Crackernuts. Kestrel, 1979 (12–14).
In this retelling of the old English fairy tale, set in wartime Scotland in the seventeenth century, Katherine's father marries Kate's mother, who becomes jealous of the fairer, younger Katherine. When she uses black magic against her, Katherine and Kate escape for protection, later to be reunited with their loving father. Incorporating traditions and politics of the time, as well as a Scottish dialect, this is a difficult but engrossing tale of truth triumphant over evil.

Calder-Marshall, Arthur (U.K.), 1908– .
About: CA, SMFL, SFFL, ESF

4B-22. The Fair to Middling. Hart-Davis, 1959 (12–14).
Several youths and their teachers at the Winterbottome School for the handicapped, who attend the local fair, undergo extraordinary experiences which have miraculous or significant effects upon them; but what actually occurs or why is uncertain. A verbally rich and evocative rendition of the theme that we must first accept what we are if happiness is to be ours.

Cameron, Eleanor (Canada), 1912– .
About: CA, SFFL, ESF, HF

4B-23. Beyond Silence. Dutton, 1980 (13–16).
Vacationing in Scotland to get over his older brother's death, Andrew Cames hears and sees the voices and bodies of a cousin with the same name and of Deidre, who had lived two generations earlier, and is drawn into their affairs. Timeslip narrative combines realistic and sympathetic insight into guilt and grief over a sibling's death and fascinating study of the possible ways time can be experienced and understood. Contrast *Beadbonny Ash* [4B-46].

4B-24. The Court of the Stone Children. Dutton, 1973 (11–16).
After outcast schoolgirl Nina befriends a woman who runs a French museum in contemporary San Francisco, she also befriends a nineteenth-century ghost of a young girl who seeks Nina's assistance in solving her soldier father's murder under Napoleon and thereby clearing his reputation; the deed is acomplished and Nina pursues her dream of becoming a curator. This 1974 National Book Award winner is a sustaining mystery with realistic characters which deftly incorporates the ghostly otherworld.

Carroll, Lewis. Alice's Adventures in Wonderland and Through the Looking Glass [2-23]

Chant, Joy (U.K.), 1945– .
About: CA, SMFL, MF, SFFL, RG, FL, HF

4B-25. Red Moon and Black Mountain. Allen & Unwin, 1970 (13–16).
Oliver, Perry and Nick Powell are transported to Vandarei, where Oliver becomes the great hero Li'vanh and defeats the hellish Fendarl; his siblings also play important roles in the struggle against Fendarl and his armies. The sword-and-

sorcery formula is enlivened by originality in setting and characters and the theme of coming of age, and set in the context of a struggle between good and evil. The prequel to this title is *The Grey Mane of Morning* (1977) and the sequel is *When Voiha Wakes* (1983). Contrast *The Weirdstone of Brisingamen* [4B-53].

Charnas, Suzy McKee, 1939- .
ABOUT: CA, NE, SFE, SFFL, TCSF, PE

4B-26. The Bronze King. Houghton Mifflin, 1985 (11+).
Puzzled by explosions under her feet and the mysterious disappearance of objects, including the statue of King Jagiello in Central Park, Tina, aided by the old wizardly fiddler, Paava, and a young violinist, Joel, struggles to save New York from the evil Kraken. Low fantasy successfully blends light-dark conflict, believable daughter-mother tensions, offbeat characterizations, realistic setting and often humorous commentary. Sequel is *The Silver Glove* (1988).

[For other works of this author, see the companion guide to horror.]

Chetwin, Grace (U.K.).
ABOUT: CA

4B-27. Gom on Windy Mountain. Lothrop, 1986 (12–14).
After a series of both lighthearted and serious adventures, in which young Gom realizes he is truly the son of his father, the village woodcutter, and his mother, Wife, the powerful wizard, the young wizard-to-be sets out to find his mother and his heritage. Vivid setting and humorous and insightful characterization strengthen the quick-moving story. This is a prequel to the Tales of Gom trilogy, consisting of *The Riddle and the Rune* (1987), *Crystal Stair* (1988) and *Starstone* (1989). Sharply contrast *A Wizard of Earthsea* [4B-98].

Collodi, Carlo. The Story of a Puppet; or, The Adventures of Pinocchio
[2-29]

Cooper, Susan (U.K.), 1935- .
ABOUT: CA, SMFL, SFE, SFFL, RG, ESF, FL, HF

***4B-28. Over Sea, Under Stone**. Cape, 1965 (10–13).
Simon, Jane and Barney, on holiday in Cornwall, King Arthur's land of the west, come upon an old map and, assisted by Great-Uncle Merriman, set out to find the hidden treasure, which is actually the Holy Grail sought after by both the Dark and the Light. In the first volume, the Dark Is Rising series begins quietly and remains relatively straightforward adventure; in subsequent volumes, the series turns complex, often allegorical-symbolic, and is even at times heavy going; the cast of characters widens; and the stakes have universal implications. Other volumes are *The Dark Is Rising* (1973), 1973 Boston Globe-Horn Book Award and 1974 Newbery Honor Book; *Greenwitch* (1973); *The Grey King* (1974), 1976 Newbery Medal Award; and *Silver on the Tree* (1977). Contrast *The Lion, the Witch and the Wardrobe* [4B-101].

4B-29. Seaward. Atheneum, 1983 (13+).
Mysteriously entering the world of death ruled by the Lady Taranis but protected by her brother, Lugan, the lord of life, West and Cally must journey to the sea, where they will decide which destiny is theirs. A somewhat complicated and obscure fantasy, imbued with Welsh mythology, the story deepens upon slow and careful reading. Contrast *The Beginning Place* [4B-97].

Corbett, W. J. (U.K.), 1938- .
ABOUT: CA

4B-30. The Song of Pentecost. Methuen, 1982 (11+).
The Harvest Mice, led by Pentecost, contract with Snake to guide them to their new home at Lickey Hills; on their journey they find new friends and survive every danger. Very interesting story with offbeat characters, ample wit, at times lyrical style and philosophic musings should appeal to all kinds of readers. Akin to Hoban's *The Mouse and His Child* [4B-71] with its mixture of violence, characters and musings, yet warmer and more celebratory of life than the latter. Winner of the 1982 Whitbread Prize. Compare to *Redwall* [4B-79].

Cresswell, Helen (U.K.), 1934- .
ABOUT: CA, SFFL, HF

4B-31. The Night Watchmen. Faber, 1969 (10–12).
While convalescing, Henry meets two men who refer to themselves as "night watchmen," and the boy assists Josh and Caleb to evade their "green-eyed" enemies and catch their mysterious night train. Ostensibly simple story masks sensitive characterization and ghostly atmosphere. Contrast *The Old Powder Line* [4B-125].

Cross, Gillian (U.K.), 1945- .
ABOUT: CA

4B-32. The Dark behind the Curtain. Oxford, 1984 (14+).
Taking part in a school play, Colin Jackus and Ann Ridley are shocked to learn that the evil Sweeney Todd the cast is recreating is also calling back past unknown forces that both suffered from and inflicted great pain. Unusual plot, insightful commentary on school problems and effective evocation of mood make for superior YA storytelling. Compare *Through the Hidden Door* [4B-150].

Curry, Jane Louise, 1932- .
ABOUT: CA, SFFL, ESF, HF

4B-33. The Daybreakers. Harcourt, 1970 (10–12).
When Callie and her school friends from Apple Lock accidentally find themselves back in ancient Abaloc, they discover that they are responsible for the future of their town and the safety of one small child. In the sequel, *The Birdstones* (1977), set the following year, the children make up an imaginary schoolmate and are surprised when she turns out to be a child in hiding from Abaloc, whose presence

causes great danger. Sensitively told, marked by remarkably realistic characterization and dialogue as well as an evocative setting, the story uses time shift and elements of mystery. Recipient of 1971 Notable Book of the Southern Council on Literature for Children and Young People Awards.

4B-34. Poor Tom's Ghost. Atheneum, 1977 (12–15).
The Nicholas family, who are involved in theater, inherit the ancestral home. They soon become aware that they also inherited its unsettling past, when they hear voices which lead to an old dead Shakespearean actor relative whose character is melding with Mr. Nicholas and causing many difficulties and possibly a tragedy, which is averted by his young son. An enticing story which uses a device similar to that in Dunlop's *Clementina* [4B-41], in which the past is relived through a new generation of characters. Winner of the 1978 Ohioana Book Award.

4B-35. The Wolves of Aam. Atheneum, 1981 (13–15).
Runner, the fastest of all the Tiddi, aided by two friends and two wolves, searches for his stolen dreamstone, hoping to learn if it is the famous skystone Mirelidar. In the sequel, *The Shadow Dancers* (1983), Lek, the conjuror, is wrongfully accused of stealing the stone and he sets out on a dangerous mission to seek another stone with similar powers. Full of danger, this series of high fantasy builds to suspense.

Davies, Andrew (U.K.), 1936– .
ABOUT: CA

4B-36. Conrad's War. Blackie, 1978 (11+).
Virtually obsessed with war and its paraphernalia, Conrad experiences "leaks" of time which carry him back to World War II, where his "play" turns into real fighting and he slowly learns some of the truth about actual war. Wild imagination, economically pointed style, vivid, sympathetic characterization and skilled plotting, especially of time shifts, mark this entertaining story.

de la Mare, Walter. Broomsticks and Other Tales [3-110]; The Three Mulla-Mulgars [3-111]

Dickinson, Peter (U.K.), 1927– .
ABOUT: CA, NE, SMFL, SFE, SFFL, RG, TCSF, ESF, HF

4B-37. The Blue Hawk. Gollancz, 1976 (13+).
Believing he has been inspired to alter the rituals by Gdu, the god whose priest he will someday become, and banished into the desert to train the blue hawk, Tron is recruited by the pharaoh to aid his plan to overthrow the power of the corrupt priests. The story effectively blends brilliant recreation of an ancient kingdom and its myths and rituals, unusual but credible style and characterization, and realistic nature description. Winner of the 1977 Guardian Award. Contrast *Divide and Rule* [4B-112]. Also annotated as [4A-86].

Downer, Ann, 1960– .

4B-38. The Spellkey. Atheneum, 1987 (14–16).
Catlin, an outcast otherworld girl, and Badger, an ordinary stableboy, by chance thrown together and sentenced together, discover their enforced journey becomes one of questioning, self-discovery and love. A quest story with an unusually twisting plot, sardonic commentary, interesting characters and an offbeat love story. Compare *Giftwish* [4B-113].

Duncan, Lois, 1934– .
    About: CA, SFFL

4B-39. Locked in Time. Little, Brown, 1985 (13+).
When she meets her father's new bride, the beautiful Lisette, and Lisette's children, motherless Nore Robbins immediately senses something is wrong at Shadow Grove; soon she discovers that Lisette considers her a threat to the family's long-kept secret of perennial youth and must be eliminated. Atmosphere and suspense, coupled to a modicum of romance, add up to effective writing.

4B-40. Stranger with My Face. Little, Brown, 1981 (13+).
Seventeen-year-old Laurie Stratton learns not only that in the neighborhood a look-alike has suddenly appeared—the evil Lia, who turns out to be a hitherto unknown twin sister—but that both girls are Navajo and can practice astral projection. An engrossing mystery and thriller that deftly and plausibly mingles reality and the supernatural. Compare *The Silver Link, the Silken Tie* [4B-11].

Dunlop, Eileen (U.K.), 1938– .
    About: CA

4B-41. Clementina. Oxford, 1985 (13+).
Several youths on holiday in Scotland slowly uncover the reason behind the uncanny occurrences and behavior involving some of the group members when they learn that they are linked to similar people, places and events long ago and may be acting out the same sequence of events which led to tragedy years before. Good characterization of various teen behaviors. Compare *Poor Tom's Ghost* [4B-34].

4B-42. The House on the Hill. Oxford, 1987 (10+).
Philip, an unwilling guest in his great-aunt's old mansion, and Susan, his cousin and also a house guest, sense a ghostly presence, whose nature and purpose they set out to discover, in the process solving a mystery involving Aunt Jane. Interesting plot, atmospheric setting and plausible and winning portrait of old-young relationship characterize the ghost story. Compare *The Griffin Legacy* [4B-91].

Farjeon, Eleanor (U.K.), 1881–1965.
    About: CA, SFFL, ESF, HF

4B-43. The Silver Curlew. Oxford, 1953 (9-12).
In an expanded variation of Rumpelstiltskin, Doll and Poll Codling have to find a way to outwit the Black Imp who demands Doll's baby as the price for helping

her spin twelve skeins of flax and win the king's hand. Otherwise conventional fairy tale boasts humor, distinctive dialogue and enough mature insight into human nature to interest the older reader. Contrast *Beauty* [4B-119]. See also *Martin Pippin in the Apple-Orchard* [3-132]; *The Soul of Kol Nikon* [3-133].

Farmer, Penelope (U.K.), 1939- .
ABOUT: CA, SFFL, ESF, HF

*4B-44. A Castle of Bone. Atheneum, 1972 (11-14).
Accidentally discovering that an old cupboard transforms objects placed into it into an earlier state—in particular their friend, Penn, who is changed into a very small boy—Hugh, along with two other youths, must enter, through the cupboard, into a world he has constantly dreamed about so that Penn will regain his real age. Highly original plot and provocative variations on fairy tale motifs are features of this brilliantly conceived and written novel.

4B-45. The Summer Birds. Chatto & Windus, 1962 (11-13).
After a strange, bird-like boy suddenly appears in the neighborhood and magically teaches all of Miss Hallibutt's class to fly, only the passionate intervention of Charlotte prevents the youths from accepting the boy's invitation to go with him and "fly forever." A charming, poignant yet magical story with much sensitivity and insight into youth's anxiety over growing up. Sequels in the Emma series include *Emma in Winter* (1966) and *Charlotte Sometimes* (1969). Compare *Tuck Everlasting* [4B-15].

Finlay, Winifred (U.K.), 1910- .
ABOUT: CA

4B-46. Beadbonny Ash. Harrap, 1973 (12-14).
Depressed by the accidental death of her father and feeling unloved and rejected by her mother, Bridie finds so much relief in sixth-century Scottish history that she is physically drawn into that past, where she becomes involved in political intrigue and mysterious religious rites. YA subject matter and concerns are transported into the past, where they are cleverly and effectively transformed in a vivid setting and atmosphere. Contrast *Beyond Silence* [4B-23]; compare *In the Keep of Time* [4B-12].

Fisher, Paul R., 1960- .
4B-47. The Ash Staff. Atheneum, 1979 (12-15).
Upon the death of their teacher and guardian, Rhawn, his six wards, led by the eldest, Moleander or Mole, journey to the safety of King Gion and his court, where young Mole is drawn into the struggle against the evil Ammar to subjugate Pesten and where he demonstrates qualities of leadership and heroism. The first of a trilogy which begins as a routine, almost matter-of-fact coming-of-age/good-evil struggle story, but which, as the characters age, becomes denser and richer in characterization, atmosphere and theme. The Ash Staff series includes *The Hawks of Fellheath* (1980), *The Princess and the Thorn* (1980) and *Mont Cant Gold* (1984). Contrast *The Book of Three* [4B-8].

Fouqué, Baron Friedrich de la Motte. Undine [2-59]

Furlong, Monica (U.K.), 1930– .
ABOUT: CA

4B-48. Wise Child. Gollancz, 1987 (11+).
After abandonment by her parents, one of whom is a beautiful "bad" witch, nine-year-old Wise Child is "auctioned off" to the village and "bought" by the local doran or "good" witch. She then undergoes training, becoming eventually a doran. Entertaining and informative narrative effectively combines relatively matter-of-fact tone and richly detailed recreation of training requisite to become a witch. Compare *The Daymaker* [4B-64].

Garfield, Leon (U.K.), 1921– .
ABOUT: CA, SFFL

4B-49. The Ghost Downstairs. Longman, 1972 (13–15).
When lonely and envious Mr. Fast, a court clerk, unwittingly strikes a deal with the devil for 100 pounds in exchange for seven years off the end of his life, he unwisely thinks he has fooled the devil by giving him the years off the front end of his life. This slim volume with its stylized characterization and eerie black-and-white illustrations effectively portrays the shady transaction and its consequences.

Garner, Alan (U.K.), 1934– .
ABOUT: SFW, F, CA, SMFL, SFE, MF, RG, ESF, FL, HF

4B-50. Elidor. Collins, 1965 (12–14).
When four children are transported into Elidor, given four treasures to guard and then returned to their house, they become the object of invading spearmen and are actively caught up in the struggle to save Elidor. Stimulating, well-written narrative contains still fresh handling of transition between primary and secondary worlds and latter's bizarre effects upon the former. Contrast *The Night Rider* [4B-76].

*4B-51. The Owl Service. Collins, 1967 (12–14).
Roger, his stepsister Alison, and Gwyn, son of their father's housekeeper, discover that their bickering and, more importantly, class differences and misunderstandings become the occasion of a reenactment of an ancient Celtic legend of infidelity, violence and death. Seemingly conventional teen story slowly becomes suspenseful, ominous and haunting: convincing evidence of the potency of old legend and myth. Winner of both the Carnegie Medal and the Guardian Award in 1968. Compare *The Wild Hunt of Hagworthy* [4B-105].

4B-52. Red Shift. Collins, 1973 (14+).
Although set in different time periods, three stories of love and its resiliency, or lack of it, in the face of social differences and political difficulty unfold concurrently and are joined not only by the impact one distinctive place can have on people but also by the community of suffering. Brilliantly imaginative in concept and articulation, the narrative is told primarily through dialogue and through abrupt time shifts; hence it is at times difficult to follow.

4B-53. The Weirdstone of Brisingamen. Collins, 1960. U.S. title: *The Weirdstone* (1961) (12–14).
To triumph over the evil Nastrond, the wizard Cadellin and the dwarf Fenodyree accept into their company Colin and Susan as the carriers of the Firefrost or the Weirdstone, the sustainer of High Magic. Otherwise formulaic good/evil conflict narrative is enriched by extensive allusions to Nordic-British legend and effective interplay between the placid surface and ominous undercurrents. The sequel is *The Moon of Gomrath* (1963). Contrast *Red Moon and Black Mountain* [4B-25].

Gordon, John (U.K.), 1925– .
    ABOUT: CA, SFFL, HF

4B-54. The Edge of the World. Hardy, 1983 (11+).
Shortly after Kit and Tekker see a frightening horse's head–like creature, they are thrust into a red desert and on a quest to preserve Kit's brother's life by rescuing the long-lost Stella, hidden away by Ma Grist, her evil sister-witch. The slow pace and plot jerks are more than offset by eerie atmosphere and the strange, distinctive Secondary World.

4B-55. The Giant Under the Snow. Hutchinson, 1968 (11–13).
Three teens assist in the final defeat of the Warlord, who attempts to reestablish his evil rule by using the gigantic Green Man, who mysteriously awakens after a centuries-long sleep. Setting and characterization, in particular the zest the teens show while flying like birds, highlight otherwise formulaic ethical fantasy.

4B-56. The House on the Brink. Hutchinson, 1970 (14+).
The mystery of an eerie black log emerging from the river and terrifying a woman living nearby is solved by Dick and his friend Helen. Effective blending of mood, situation, description and young love makes for a successful narrative.

Goudge, Elizabeth (U.K.), 1900–1984.
    ABOUT: CA, SFFL, RG, ESF, HF

4B-57. Linnets and Valerians. Brockhampton Press, 1964 (11–13).
After running away from their strict grandmother's home where they have been sent while their soldier father is in Egypt, the four plucky Linnet children stumble upon and then live with their elderly bachelor vicar uncle, who educates them and helps solve the mysterious disappearance of members of the Valerian family. Incorporating elements of voodooism and the appearance of magical animals, this is an engaging tale of the victory of good over evil.

Grahame, Kenneth. The Wind in the Willows [3-157]

Gray, Nicholas (U.K.), 1921–1981.
    ABOUT: CA, SFFL, ESF, FL, HF

4B-58. Grimbold's Other World. Faber, 1963 (11–13).
Muffler, a foundling, befriends Grimbold, a black cat, and shares with him the world of daylight and the world of night and magic where he helps those in need,

including a young boy who was stolen from the daylight world. The story intertwines poetry and music in a charming fashion.

4B-59. Mainly in Moonlight: Ten Stories of Sorcery and the Supernatural. Faber, 1965 (10–12).

These contemporary variations of fairy and other traditional tales are filled with wit and humor and depend for their success upon the reader's ability to enjoy the similarities and differences between them and the older story types, especially in tone. Titles include "The Sorcerer's Apprentices," "A Message in a Bottle," "According to Tradition," "The Silver Ship," "The Lady's Quest," "The Man Who Sold Magic," and "The Thunder Cat."

4B-60. The Seventh Swan. Dobson, 1962 (12–14).

The only one of seven brothers still cruelly affected by an evil spell that turned them into swans, Alasdair becomes the object of a plan by his sister, Agnes; a young woman in love with him, Finella; and the bard Hudart to get him to reject despondency and build on what remains of his human nature. Retelling of the well-known tale incorporates other legends for atmosphere and setting, as well as elements of romance. Contrast *Tom Ass: Or, the Second Gift* [4B-93].

Grimm, Jakob and Wilhelm. German Popular Stories [2-71]

Gripe, Maria (Sweden), 1923– .
ABOUT: CA, HF

4B-61. The Glassblower's Children. Delacorte, 1973. Tr. by Sheila La Farge of *Glasblasarns Barn*, 1964 (10–13).

When his plan to amuse his despondent wife by kidnapping and presenting her with two small children fails, the Lord of All Wishes Town hires a sinister governess for the children and they all remain in her terrifying captivity until her sister, a good witch named Flutter Mildweather, rights the situation and returns the children to their overjoyed parents. This charming tale of good and evil is further supported by drawings which capture the mood of the story.

4B-62. In the Time of the Bells. Delacorte, 1976. Tr. by Sheila La Farge of *Klockornas Tid*, 1965 (12–15).

Young King Arvid is in a predicament: he is lonely, withdrawn, slow to learn his royal duties and is newly assigned a whipping boy, Helge, and a bride-to-be, Elisie, whom he does not love. The predicament is resolved unexpectedly as Arvid finds peace and happiness. Although somewhat talky, the story is rich in atmosphere and medieval lore, and is sensitively told. Contrast *The Half-Brothers* [4B-92].

Grosser, Morton, 1931– .
ABOUT: CA, HF

4B-63. The Snake Horn. Atheneum, 1973 (11–13).

When Danny receives a Tartold, an ancient serpent horn, as a gift, he is not aware of its mystical powers. As a musician in a musical family, Danny is curious about the instrument and eventually fashions a way to make it produce sound; in so doing, he also produces one of its previous owners from the seventeenth century. The story concerns itself with the attempts to get "Tony" back to his original time and how Danny's family will survive economically. The inclusion of timely music slang makes the story read awkwardly at times. Compare *Keeping Time* [4B-141].

Halam, Ann (U.K.), 1952- .
ABOUT: CA

4B-64. The Daymaker. Orchard Books, 1987 (11+).
Daughter of a covener, Zanne realizes she too has covener talents, attends Covenant school at Hillin and sets out on a quest to tap into the power of a mysterious "daymaker" in order to become a full-fledged covener. Formulaic coming-of-age story becomes interesting and fresh through a mystery involving the identity of the daymaker and the nature of coveners. Compare *Wise Child* [4B-48]; contrast *The Devil's Door-bell* [4B-73].

Hamilton, Virginia, 1936- .
ABOUT: CA

4B-65. Sweet Whispers, Brother Rush. Philomel, 1982 (11+).
Visited by the ghost of her uncle, Brother, who communicates to her the truth about his death and those of his brothers, Tree begins to accept her retarded brother Dab's death as well as forgive her mother for the way she was forced to raise her two children. In this 1983 Newbery Honor Book, the author's distinctive skill in dramatizing uncommon dimensions of ordinary black life is further strengthened by an unusual ghost story. Contrast *The Shadow Guests* [4B-3].

Hamley, Dennis (U.K.), 1935- .
ABOUT: CA, HF

4B-66. Pageants of Despair. Deutsch, 1974 (13–16).
During a train ride to the city where he will be staying while his seriously injured mother is in the hospital, Peter meets Gilbert, who transports him back to the time of the Middle Ages where they are involved in the literal acting out of the mystery plays. Very interesting, informative portrayal of the miracle plays of the Middle Ages.

Harris, Geraldine (U.K.), 1951- .
ABOUT: CA

4B-67. Prince of the Godborn. Greenwillow, 1982 (12+).
In the first volume of the Seven Citadels series, Prince Kerish-lo-Taan, deciding to rescue the legendary savior who is supposed to prevent the destruction of the Empire of Galkis, sets out on the quest, along with his half-brother Forollkin, to obtain the seven golden keys necessary for the rescue. The long and complex fantasy abounds with interesting, believable characters, political intrigue and a richly textured Secondary World, Zindar. Sequels in the series are *The Children of the Wind* (1982), *The Dead Kingdom* (1983) and *The Seventh Gate* (1983). Compare *Nightpool* [4B-120]; contrast *A Princess of the Chameln* [4B-155].

Harris, Rosemary (U.K.), 1923– .
   ABOUT: CA, SFFL, HF

*4B-68. The Moon in the Cloud. Faber, 1968 (12–15).
As Noah prepares for the Flood, his son Ham falsely engages Reuben, an animal trainer, to go to Egypt to gather two special cats in exchange for passage on the Ark. Reuben encounters several adventures before he returns with the animals and learns that due to the death of Ham and his wife, he and his wife, Thamar, will be allowed on the Ark after all. This winner of the 1969 Carnegie Medal was followed by the sequel *Shadow on the Sun* (1970), in which Reuben and Thamar leave the Ark and start a new life; the final volume in the trilogy, *The Bright and Morning Star* (1972), has them seeking a cure for their deaf son. Strong characterization, sophisticated humor and an interesting Egyptian setting are the strong points of this biblically based tale.

4B-69. The Seal-Singing. Faber, 1971 (13–16).
For centuries seals have been herded on the beaches of Carrigona, protected, legend has it, by St. Culzean. When they are threatened, Cat, Toby and Miranda, affected by Lucy, their long-dead ancestor, manage to save the seals and lay to rest Lucy's spirit. Attractive characters and setting, seal lore and effective atmosphere mark this offbeat fantasy. Compare *A Stranger Came Ashore* [4B-74].

Hawdon, Robin (U.K.).

4B-70. A Rustle in the Grass. Dodd, Mead, 1985 (12–14).
Under the pressure of preparing a defense against a more warlike colony of red ants, the smaller ant colony, of which Dreamer, a young leader-to-be, is a member, changes its hierarchical form of governance and triumphs, although at great cost in life and homes. Worthy of favorable comparison to *Watership Down* [4B-1] in its plausible re-creation of animal politics, battle tactics and faith systems.

Hoban, Russell, 1925– .
   ABOUT: CA, NE, SFFL, TCSF, HF

*4B-71. The Mouse and His Child. Harper, 1967 (10+).
The wind-up mouse and its child, bereft of a home, are forced into a series of sometimes harrowing, sometimes pointless and often bizarre adventures before they emerge triumphant, part of a family and self-winding. Hoban blends in unique fashion offbeat characters and plot, philosophic commentary and an extraordinarily rich style to create a heartwarming and satisfying family story, as well as a brilliant, distinctive fantasy. Compare *The Song of Pentecost* [4B-30].

Hodgell, P(atricia) C(hristine), 1951– .
   ABOUT: CA

4B-72. God Stalk. Atheneum, 1982 (13+).
In this Victorian-like space fantasy, Jame sets out to find her twin brother, Tori, after her home is destroyed. On her journey, Jame discovers that she has odd powers which intermittently save her or put her and those around her in great

danger. Appendices, character lists and maps aid the reader in following the complicated storyline. The search for Tori continues in the sequel, *Dark of the Moon* (1985).

Horowitz, Anthony, 1955– .

4B-73. The Devil's Door-bell. Hardy, 1983 (13+).
Coming to stay at Helibore Hall, Martin Hopkins is caught up in evil rites, centered around an abandoned nuclear power plant, which he escapes from by dint of his psychic powers and the aid of a journalist friend. Although contemporary in style and values, the story effectively blends in an aura of ancient rites and evil. Sequels are *The Night of the Scorpion* (1985) and *The Silver Citadel* (1986). Contrast *The Daymaker* [4B-64].

Hunter, Mollie (U.K.), 1922– .
ABOUT: CA, SFFL, HF

4B-74. A Stranger Came Ashore. Harper, 1975 (11+).
Urged by his dying grandfather, Old Da, to fear Finn Learson, the dashing stranger who came ashore one stormy night, Robbie learns that Finn is the Great Silkie and plots with the local wizard, Yarl Corbie, to outwit the seal in disguise. Skillful retelling of legend and old magic is imbued with haunting atmosphere and authentic local color. Compare *The Seal-Singing* [4B-69].

Hurmence, Belinda.

4B-75. A Girl Called Boy. Ticknor & Fields, 1982 (11–14).
In this dream fantasy, Blanche Overtha Yancey (Boy for short), who disdains her slave heritage, is transported from the present to the 1850s to be caught up in the realities of slave life; she returns to her own time with a renewed sense of her past and herself. The use of a fantasy to inform readers about life in another time/place is reminiscent of Paton Walsh's *A Chance Child* [4B-128] and Yolen's *The Devil's Arithmetic* [4B-163].

Ingelow, Jean. Mopsa the Fairy [2-91]

Ingram, Tom (U.K.), 1924– .
ABOUT: CA, HF

4B-76. The Night Rider. Bradbury, 1975 (11–14).
The lingering effects of a spell, centuries ago cast into a gold bracelet, draw Laura into the consciousness of Merta and into a blood feud whereby the young woman's life is threatened in both the past and present. Effective mingling of time-slip fantasy and YA story of uncertain teens suspicious of a new stepfather. Compare *The Cloud Forest* [4B-122]; contrast *Elidor* [4B-50].

Ipcar, Dahlov, 1917– .
ABOUT: CA, SFFL, RG, HF

4B-77. A Dark Horn Blowing. Viking, 1978 (13–16).
Although married to another, Nora, kidnapped by the Erl King to take care of his infant son, Eelie, learns to love her charge, who in turn comes to love his foster mother deeply and successfully plots to thwart his father's will and restore Nora to her husband and son. In spite of an irksome shifting point of view, the narrative, because of the presence of folklore and mythology elements, is still an enticing story of enchantment.

4B-78. Queen of Spells. Viking, 1973 (12–15).
Cherishing Tom Linn's promise that he will return in seven days, looking forward to that return, but gradually realizing that he is trapped in Faerie, Janet, in order to free her lover, must combat a series of spells. This novel-length version of the old ballad "Tam Lin" is an entertaining, sometimes very eerie love story.

Jacques, Brian (U.K.), 1920– .

4B-79. Redwall. Hutchinson, 1986 (10+).
Matthias, an eager young mouse in the peaceful community of Redwall Abbey, learns through clues left by an ancient warrior that he is the chosen leader and, by finding the elder's sword and thereby claiming his rightful place, leads the mice to victory over the evil Cluny. Billed as the middle volume of a trilogy about the Redwall mice, this is followed by *Mossflower* (1988). Compare *The Song of Pentecost* [4B-30].

James, M. R. The Five Jars [3-192]

Jones, Diana Wynne (U.K.), 1934– .
ABOUT: CA, RG, HF

4B-80. Archer's Goon. Greenwillow, 1984 (13+).
When Howard Syke's father, a writer, fails to deliver his required quarterly 2,000 words, a huge, oversized goon is sent to take up residence at his house as motivation, and Howard learns several interesting facts about his family and its relationship with the seven wizards who rule the town. An involving, humorous story with complex interrelationships among the Syke family members and the various differently personified wizards.

4B-81. Cart and Cwidder. Macmillan, 1975 (12–15).
In the first volume of the projected five-title Dalemark Sequence, Clennen the Singer is killed, and his three children inherit his magical instrument, the cwidder, which becomes an important part of the war between South and North Dalemark. Other titles in the sequence include the prequel *The Spellcoats* (1979), which covers the prehistory of Dalemark in which young Tanaqui discovers that she holds the key to conquering the evil Kankredin, and the sequel *Drowned Ammet* (1977), in which Mitt, of Holand, is exiled to the Holy Islands for questioning the rulers of his country and learns the truth and meaning behind the

Sea Festival rituals of drowning two dummys of traditional figures, Poor Old Ammet and his wife, Libby Beer. Sharing the same general setting, but not characters, these examples of early Jones are more serious and stilted than her more recent works.

4B-82. A Charmed Life. Macmillan, 1977 (11-15).
The Charmed Life series takes place in Chrestomanci's world, in which Italy is still divided into several small states, each with its own duke and capital city, and magic and old-fashioned ways are the norm. Gwendolen and Cat Chant are taken away from their familiar supernatural neighborhood to Chrestomanci's Castle to live with relatives where they counter Chrestomanci's magical powers with their own. This first title won the 1978 Guardian Award. In the sequel, *The Magicians of Caprona* (1980), which takes place in another part of Chrestomanci's world, it is the younger generation of two ever-battling magician families, the Montantas and the Petrocchis, who discover the words to a tune which will save their city, Caprona. The prequel, *The Lives of Christopher Chant* (1988), is the story of the childhood of Chrestomanci, which details how he became the great head magician. *Witch Week* (1982) also takes place in Chrestomanci's world, and there are short stories about Chrestomanci in *Warlock at the Wheel* (1985) and in *Dragons and Dreams* (1986), ed. by Jane Yolen.

4B-83. Howl's Moving Castle. Greenwillow, 1986 (13+).
Cursed by a witch to inhabit an old woman's body, young Sophie finds herself in the household of the feared Wizard Howl, who is reported to prowl the countryside in search of young women whose life he sucks from them and who is ultimately cursed himself. Light fantasy involving humorous characterization, bizarre plot turns and a happy ending.

4B-84. Ogre Downstairs. Macmillan, 1974 (12-14).
In this contemporary "blended" family setting Jack ("Ogre") gives his constantly battling son and stepson identical chemistry sets, which leads first to more competition, then to cooperation between the two boys and their other siblings as they encounter the magic and problems involved. Using typical, believable family characters and dialogue, the story intertwines everyday reality with doses of magic and fantasy to cause problems and solutions.

4B-85. The Power of Three. Macmillan, 1977 (12-14).
On the Moor, the uneasy relationship among Giants (humans) and Dorig and Lyman (the last fairy folk) heats up into armed struggle because of curses and abuses of magic, and is resolved finally by several youths from the three peoples who stake their lives on mutual trust and friendship. Overcoming a slow start, the story becomes an entertaining and informative commingling of insights into family and tribal relations and fairy lore. Contrast *An Older Kind of Magic* [4B-161].

4B-86. A Tale of Time City. Greenwillow, 1987 (13+).
After eleven-year-old Vivien is kidnapped at a train station while being evacuated from London in 1939 to escape the bombing, she finds herself with two young boys in Time City, a place outside of time and space, where they attempt to help counter the city's seemingly inevitable demise. Much excitement and unexpected plot turns.

4B-87. Warlock at the Wheel and Other Stories. Macmillan, 1984 (13+).
This entertaining collection of Jones's short stories features far-out situations and
characters, including Chrestomanci, a character from her Charmed Life series
[4B-82]. Other stories included are "The Plague of Peacocks," "The Fluffy Pink
Toadstool," "Auntie Bea's Day Out," "Carruthers," "No One," "Dragon Reserve, Home Eight" and "The Sage of Theare." A lighthearted sampling of
Jones's talent.

Juster, Norton, 1929– .
　　ABOUT: SFFL, ESF, HF

*4B-88. The Phantom Tollbooth. Epstein and Carroll, 1961 (11+).
Using a mysterious and magical tollbooth and car, Milo travels to Dictionopolis
where he is asked to embark on a quest, along with Tock the Watchdog, to Castle
in the Air to help restore Rhyme and Reason to their rightful place in the
kingdom of Wisdom. Brilliant, clever and witty one-of-a-kind narrative should
appeal to any reader who glories in verbal jokes and is looking for a contemporary book that is similar to the Alice narratives. The 1971 winner of the George G.
Stone Center for Children's Books Recognition of Merit Award.

Kelleher, Victor (U.K.), 1939– .

4B-89. Master of the Grove. Kestrel, 1982 (14+).
Lame Derin, accompanied by the witch Marna, embarks on a long, arduous
journey to the Grove, ostensibly to save his father. This journey becomes one of
self-discovery and vocation, and culminates in the defeat of the evil Master, Krob.
Slow-moving story of initiation is balanced nicely by its ethical seriousness,
convincing Secondary World and inventive variations on the journey motif.
Winner of the Australian Children's Book of the Year Award 1983. Contrast *The
Journey Outside* [4B-146].

Kennedy, Richard, 1932– .
　　ABOUT: CA

4B-90. Richard Kennedy: Collected Stories. Harper, 1987 (6–12).
In these stories, most of which first appeared in earlier forms, Kennedy exhibits
considerable skill in essaying a number of traditional forms—fairy tale, tall tale,
ghost story, narrative poetry—while incorporating contemporary subject matter
and tone. Included are: "The Porcelain Man" (1976), "The Parrot and the Thief"
(1974), "The Blue Stone" (1976), "Crazy in Love" (1980), "Inside My Feet" (1979)
and eleven other stories.

Kingsley, Charles. The Water-Babies [2-98]

Kipling, Rudyard. The Jungle Book [2-100]; **Just So Stories** [3-202];
　　Puck of Pook's Hill [3-203]

Klaveness, Jan O'Donnell.

4B-91. The Griffin Legacy. Macmillan, 1983 (11–15).
Temporarily living with her grandmother and great aunt in the ancestral home, Amy becomes aware of ghostly presences which prevail upon her to attempt to regain a lost legacy and to solve a 200-year-old mystery—a task Amy accomplishes with the help of two new friends and her relatives. Suspenseful, atmospheric and well written, the story also features strong plotting and attractive characters. Compare *The House on the Hill* [4B-42]; contrast *The Sherwood Ring* [4B-138].

Lang, Andrew. The Gold of Fairnilee [2-102].

Lawrence, Ann (U.K.), 1942– .
Aʙᴏᴜᴛ: CA, HF

4B-92. The Half-Brothers. Walck, 1973, (11–14).
In the fairy tale country of Evernia four half-brother princes vie for the hand of a beautiful duchess who is wise enough to choose the prince who allows her to be herself. In classic fairy tale fashion there are obstacles to overcome and hardships to endure before the happy ending. A delightful story with heartwarming qualities. Contrast *In the Time of the Bells* [4B-62].

4B-93. Tom Ass: Or, the Second Gift. Macmillan, 1972 (10–13).
Tom is "cursed" and transformed into a donkey. In his new form, and accompanied by a young maiden who befriends him, Tom sets out to seek his fortune, learning that indeed he had been an "Ass" and determining to "reform" himself. Pleasant, sometimes witty tale in beast fable format shows that traditional forms can still entertain. Contrast *The Seventh Swan* [4B-60].

Lawrence, Louise (U.K.), 1943– .
Aʙᴏᴜᴛ: CA, SFE, SFFL

4B-94. The Wyndcliffe. Collins, 1974 (14+).
Young, unhappy Anna Hennessy, drawn to the spirit of John Hollis, who wants her to share his love and special world at Wyndcliffe, must be saved by the frantic efforts of her brother and sister. Intensity of mood, bizarre situation and ghostly elements offset conventional romance format. Sequel is *Sing and Scatter Daisies* (1977).

Lawson, John.
Aʙᴏᴜᴛ: HF

4B-95. The Spring Rider. Crowell, 1968 (11–14).
One day soldiers, officers and President Lincoln return, as local legend insists, to the scene of a Civil War battle and involve Jacob and his sister, Gray, in this reenactment of the battle and its aftermath. Richly evocative in style and dreamlike mood, the story is poignant and stimulating legend-re-creation. The 1968 Boston Globe–Horn Book Award winner.

Lear, Edward. The Book of Nonsense [2-104]

Lee, Tanith (U.K.), 1947– .
ABOUT: SFW, CA, NE, SMFL, SFE, RG, TCSF, FL, HF

4B-96. The Castle of Dark. Macmillan, 1978 (14+).
Answering a relentless call and arriving at the Castle of Dark, Lir rescues Lilune from two old witches, precipitating the young woman's journey into self-discovery as well as the discovery of what freedom and love really entail. Wonderfully moody and evocative narrative not only hovers between high fantasy and horror but is also an unconventional love story. Compare *The Forgotten Beasts of Eld* [4B-116].

Le Guin, Ursula K., 1929– .
ABOUT: SFW, F, CA, TCA, NE, SMFL, SFE, MF, SFFL, RG, TCSF, ESF, FL, HF

4B-97. The Beginning Place. Harper, 1980 (13+).
Irena and Hugh use the land of Tembreabrezi, the former for running away, the latter to begin anew; although intended to be sacrificial victims, the couple together triumph over the "dragon" and, hence, their fears. This deliberate attempt to combine heroic fantasy features and YA concerns works, at times brilliantly, because of style, the brooding atmosphere and the distinctive Secondary World. Contrast *Seaward* [4B-29].

*4B-98. A Wizard of Earthsea. Parnassus Press, 1968 (11+).
Predicted to become a great Archmage, proud and willful Ged attends the School for Wizards on Roke where, goaded by an older student, he calls back Elfarran from the dead and thereby looses the Shadow, which first haunts him and then is hunted by him. This first part of the Earthsea trilogy, winner of the 1969 National Book Award, 1969 Boston Globe–Horn Book Award and the 1979 Lewis Carroll Shelf Award, has become a classic presentation of both coming of age and light-dark conflict because of its almost perfect blend of atmosphere, style, setting and theme. In the sequel, *The Tombs of Atuan* (1971), which was a 1972 Newbery Honor Book, Ged, attempting to retrieve a long-lost ring, is captured by Arha, and the two must cooperate to save each other. The third volume, *The Farthest Shore* (1972), a 1973 National Book Award winner, depicts Ged, now an old mage, in his quest to restore death to its rightful place in the Balance. Sharply contrast *Gom on Windy Mountain* [4B-27].

LeVert, John, 1946– .
ABOUT: CA

4B-99. The Flight of the Cassowary. Atlantic Monthly Press, 1986 (13+).
Entranced with animals and how certain people take after certain animals, teenager Paul begins to respond to those around him as an animal. His growing ability to think and then become an animal causes him much grief, and eventually his parents send him to a therapist. Flying home after walking out on a

therapy session, when he has the chance to fly anywhere, Paul reconsiders his life and decisions and chooses to fly home to be with his family. Compare *Stag Boy* [4B-140].

Levin, Betty, 1927- .
ABOUT: HF

4B-100. The Keeping Room. Greenwillow, 1981 (13+).
While working on a high school social studies assignment, Hal researches an old local farm and inexplicably becomes directly involved with its present as well as its past. With a believable plot and realistic characters, this story gracefully blends information and people from different time periods. Compare *The House in Norham Gardens* [4B-103].

Lewis, C(live) S(taples) (U.K.), 1898–1963.
ABOUT: GSF, CA, NE, SMFL, SFE, MF, SFFL, RG, TCSF, ESF, FL, HF

*4B-101. The Lion, the Witch and the Wardrobe. Geoffrey Bles, 1950 (10+).
Peter, Susan, Edmund and Lucy walk into a magical land, Narnia, and become involved in the plan of Aslan, the noble lion, and others to release Narnia from the spell of the evil White Witch. The first in the seven Chronicles of Narnia not only introduces readers to one of the most famous and convincing Secondary Worlds but sets the prevailing tone of earnest behavior and didactic intention, usually focused on children who are called to perform heroic deeds to ensure the ultimate triumph of Good. Lewis indicates that the best order in which to read the series is *The Magician's Nephew* (1955), *The Lion, the Witch and the Wardrobe* (1950), *The Horse and His Boy* (1954), *Prince Caspian* (1951), *Voyage of the Dawn Treader* (1952), *The Silver Chair* (1953) and *The Last Battle* (1956), which won the 1957 Carnegie Medal. Contrast *Over Sea, under Stone* [4B-28].

Lively, Penelope (U.K.), 1933- .
ABOUT: CA, SFFL, HF

4B-102. The Driftway. Heinemann, 1972 (11–13).
Resenting his new stepmother and running away with his younger sister, Paul finds himself on the driftway, the old highway where "messages" from the past intrude upon his self-centered consciousness and convince him that his troubles are neither unique nor critical. Relatively short narrative is packed with sensitive insights, evocative atmosphere and fine writing.

*4B-103. The House in Norham Gardens. Heinemann, 1974 (13+).
Living with her elderly great-aunts in their old Victorian house, Clare finds her dreams and waking thoughts haunted by New Guinea aborigines asking the return of a painted shield which presents the natives' history that Clare's great-grandfather had brought back to England. Richly moody, atmospheric narrative is a sensitively written study of the sustaining effect the past can have on youth. Compare *The Keeping Room* [4B-100].

4B-104. The Voyage of QV66. Heinemann, 1978 (12–14).
When tremendous flooding forces the exodus of People from earth, a group of animals set out on a quest to settle the identity of one of the group who resembles People and has fur. Atypical lively story neatly balances swift plot, plenty of humor and wit, beast fable and didactic intent. Compare *The Song of Pentecost* [4B-30].

4B-105. The Wild Hunt of Hagworthy. Heinemann, 1971. U.S. title: *The Wild Hunt of the Ghost Hounds* (1972) (11–14).
Staying for the holidays with her Aunt Mable in Hagworthy, Lucy and her new friend, Kester, sense that the village Dance, ostensibly a device to lure tourists, masks an old Celtic hunting ritual that can be dangerous. Quickly moving re-creation of myth builds plausibly to suspenseful and tantalizing conclusion. Compare *The Owl Service* [4B-51].

Lunn, Janet, 1928– .
ABOUT: CA

4B-106. The Root Cellar. Lester and Orpen Dennys, 1981 (13+).
Alone, loveless and "dumped off" at the home of Canadian relatives, Rose Larkin slips into the 1860s and, encountering relatives, purpose and emotional support, emerges ready to accept her new family. Story incorporates YA elements, time slip and sensitive depiction of Civil War years. Contrast *Playing Beatie Bow* [4B-124].

MacDonald, George. [various titles] [2-114–2-117]

MacDonald, Reby, 1930– .

4B-107. The Ghosts of Austwick Manor. Atheneum, 1982 (11–13).
When their older brother, Don MacDonald, inherits from Great Britain a Tudor-style dollhouse complete with dressed figures, his sisters, Hillary and Heather, find not only that they can enter the dollhouse and become caught up in the past lives of the inhabitants, but also that an ancient curse on the MacDonald family may be the downfall of their brother if they do not intervene. The very readable, likable story has realistic characters and dialogue, as well as a building suspense-laden plot.

Mahy, Margaret (New Zealand), 1936– .
ABOUT: CA

*4B-108. The Changeover. Dent, 1984 (13+).
Knowing that the cause of her little brother's illness is preternatural and that she can tap into her own as yet unrealized supernatural powers, Laura, abetted by Sorry Carlisle and his witch relatives, saves Jacko and defeats the evil Carmody Braque. Most interesting blend of witch lore, teenage romance and family elements also features distinctive style, unusual characters and a suspenseful plot. Winner of the 1985 Carnegie Medal.

*4B-109. The Haunting. Atheneum, 1982 (11–15).
Eight-year-old Barney, just over talking with imaginary friends and beginning to

receive supernatural images and messages, fears not only that he is the magician the Palmer family has at least one of each generation, but that his pregnant stepmother will lose her baby. Insightful and sympathetic portrait of a family is also a suspenseful ghost story with unexpected but satisfying ending. The 1982 Carnegie Medal Winner. Compare *The Haunting of Cassie Palmer* [4B-6].

4B-110. The Tricksters. Dent, 1986 (15+).
Coming together for the Christmas holidays at their seaside home, the Hamilton family and their friends are visited by four mysterious guests who may or may not be related to the previous owner and some of whom bear a striking resemblance to characters in a novel being written by one of the Hamilton children. Impressive narrative of haunting and the relationship between art and life is also marked by complex characterization and distinctive style.

Mark, Jan (U.K.), 1943- .
ABOUT: CA

4B-111. Aquarius. Kestrel, 1984 (13+).
Viner finds water in a land suffering from a drought which has not ended despite the Rain King's dancing and, hence, attains power. He surprisingly allies himself with the king and plots to save him from death. The original story has distinctive characters, an impressive setting and interesting political and sociological commentary.

4B-112. Divide and Rule. Kestrel, 1979 (14+).
This story chronicles the terror and frustration of Hanno, a sarcastic, irreligious youth, during the year after he becomes the unwilling chosen one in the annual religious lottery which determines the group's Shepherd, the ceremonial link between the god and the people. Rich in ritual and the questioning of religion, as well as murder and intrigue, this makes for an exciting book. Contrast *The Blue Hawk* [4B-37].

Martin, Graham (U.K.), 1932- .
ABOUT: CA

4B-113. Giftwish. Allen & Unwin, 1978 (11-13).
Tricked into thinking that he is a designated hero, Ewan sets out on a quest during which he initially learns he is to be a victim. Then, showing unexpected resourcefulness and courage, wielding the magic sword Giftwish and aided by newfound friends, he becomes an authentic hero as he defeats the Necromancer. This is an imaginatively conceived and competently articulated heroic fantasy with an unusually large amount of wit and humor. The sequel is *Catchfire* (1982). Compare *The Spellkey* [4B-38].

Masefield, John. The Midnight Folk [3-237]

Mayne, William (U.K.), 1928- .
ABOUT: CA, SMFL, SFE, SFFL, RG, ESF, FL, HF

*4B-114. Earthfasts. Hamish Hamilton, 1966 (11-14).
Keith and David's meeting with Nellie Jack John as he exits from an under-

ground passage 200 years after he entered begins a series of adventures, precipitated by the drummer boy's taking of the candle watching over the sleeping King Arthur and his army, and culminating in the death of David. Brilliant narrative features time slip, Arthurian and other legendary material, an impressive setting, tight plotting and distinctive writing.

4B-115. A Game of Dark. Dutton, 1971 (12–15).
Unhappy Donald Jackson feels ignored, unloved and undervalued by his bitter, sickly, invalid father and his constantly busy, preoccupied mother. From time to time he unexplainably lapses into a more exciting and friendly atmosphere as a page, then squire, to a lord in medieval times helping a village threatened by a huge predator-worm. Later he must determine for himself in which place to live. Marked by distinct characterization of a variety of persons, this story sensitively depicts the isolation of adolescence and the difficulty of choosing one's life path. Compare *A String in the Harp* [4B-19].

McKillip, Patricia, 1948– .
ABOUT: SFW, CA, SMFL, SFE, MF, SFFL, RG, FL, HF

***4B-116. The Forgotten Beasts of Eld**. Atheneum, 1974 (11+).
Into the kingdom of magical beasts ruled by the ice-cold, beautiful Sybel, the daughter of a wizard, comes the spectrum of human emotions in the form of a baby boy, Tamlorn, and the handsome prince, Coren. Sybel must choose between the power of magic and that of human emotions. The brilliant, wondrously imaginative and evocatively atmospheric plot also incorporates a moving and untraditional love story. Winner of the 1975 World Fantasy Award for Best Novel. Compare *The Castle of Dark* [4B-96].

4B-117. The Riddle-Master of Hed. Atheneum, 1976 (12–18).
In the first volume of the Riddle of the Stars, mild-mannered Morgon seeks to claim his bride, Raederle, after out-guessing a trapped wizard, but becomes sidetracked into seeking out the High One to learn the meaning of the three stars on his forehead, his harp and his sword. In the sequel, *Heir of Sea and Fire* (1977), Raederle searches for Morgon, and in the final volume, *Harpist in the Wind* (1979), they are together as Morgon battles to become the High One. An intriguing, engaging story with a marvelous range of characters and settings.

McKinley, Robin, 1952– .
ABOUT: CA, RG

***4B-118. The Blue Sword**. Greenwillow, 1982 (13+).
Kidnapped by Corlath, King of the Hillfolk, Harry Crewe, Homelander orphan, undergoes training leading to her becoming a King's Rider. She learns in the process that she is heir to the Blue Sword and a descendant of the Lady Aerin, legendary hero of Damar; expressing unprecedented "kelar," she becomes the new hero of the land. The original and distinctive story features attractive characters, a finely realized setting, believable romance and strong writing. A 1983 Newbery Honor Book. The prequel to this title is *The Hero and the Crown* (1985), winner of the 1986 Newbery Medal. Compare *Jackaroo* [4B-148].

*4B-119. Beauty—A Retelling of the Story of Beauty and the Beast. Harper, 1978 (11–15).
McKinley's first novel is the retelling of the Beauty and the Beast fairy tale in which a young girl goes to live at the Castle of the Beast in expiation of her father's misdeed and eventually falls in love with the Beast despite his appearance. A beautifully warm, full-bodied version of the classic which champions the value of inner beauty. Contrast *The Silver Curlew* [4B-43].

Milne, A. A. Winnie-the-Pooh [3-249]

Molesworth, Mrs. The Cuckoo Clock [2-123]

Morris, Kenneth. The Secret Mountain and Other Tales [3-255]

Murphy, Shirley Rousseau, 1928–
ABOUT: CA

4B-120. Nightpool. Harper, 1985 (13+).
Young Tebriel, near death but healed by a clan of talking otters, must respond to a summons to fight the Dark as well as discover his heritage as Prince of Tirror and ally of the singing dragons. The quickly moving story entertainingly combines coming of age, dark-light conflict, a distinctive Secondary World and unusual characterization. The sequels are *The Ivory Lyre* (1987) and *The Dragonbards* (1988). Compare *Prince of the Godborn* [4B-67].

Naylor, Phyllis Reynolds, 1933–
ABOUT: CA

4B-121. Shadows on the Wall. Atheneum, 1980 (12–15).
The dread that Dan Roberts feels while visiting some of the Roman ruins of York intensifies into experiences of the interpenetrating of the Roman past and present, as well as fear that he and his father suffer from a fatal disease. A rare look at gypsy life and interesting local color, along with time shift elements, enliven a realistic story of family anxiety over inherited disease. The other titles in The York Trilogy are *Faces in the Water* (1981) and *Footprints at the Window* (1981). Contrast *A String in the Harp* [4B-19].

Nesbit, E. The Enchanted Castle [3-268]; **Five Children and It** [3-269]

North, Joan (U.K.), 1920– .
ABOUT: CA, SFFL, HF

4B-122. The Cloud Forest. Hart-Davis, 1965 (11–14).
Lonely and unhappy Andrew Badger, who dreams a lot, is befriended by unconventional Ronnie Peters, and the two discover a ring which is instrumental in

solving the mystery of Andrew's birth and defeating the satanic plot of Sir Andrew Annerle. In spite of formulaic plot of good versus evil, the story succeeds because of the interesting and attractive protagonists. Compare *The Night Rider* [4B-76].

Norton, Andre (Alice Mary), 1912- .
ABOUT: WW, SFW, CA, TCA, NE, SMFL, SFE, MF, SFFL, RG, TCSF, ESF, FL, HF

4B-123. The Crystal Gryphon. Atheneum, 1972 (12–15).
Hooved and amber-eyed Kerovan, heir to Ulm and the Old Ones, along with Josian, his childhood betrothed, must defend Ulm against invasion from across the sea and sedition within. Characteristic Norton: swiftly paced action, deft style, stimulating setting and requisite heroic struggle and quest. Compare her Witch World series [4A-200].

Park, Ruth (New Zealand), 1942- .
ABOUT: CA

4B-124. Playing Beatie Bow. Nelson, 1980 (11–15).
Emotionally upset with her parents and drawn to the past, Abigail Kirk cannot return to her time until she—the Stranger as her mentor, Mrs. Tallisker, thinks of her, believing she must provide some essential service—saves members of her benefactor's family from a fire that ravages their home. Timeslip story features strong plot, convincing portrait of the poor in Victorian Australia and engaging mystery. Winner of the 1981 Best Australian Children's Book citation and the 1982 Boston Globe–Horn Book Award. Contrast *The Root Cellar* [4B-106].

Parker, Richard (U.K.), 1915- .
ABOUT: CA, SFE, ESF, HF

4B-125. The Old Powder Line. Gollancz, 1971 (11–14).
When Brian and Wendy discover a secret train station from which a train myste- riously transports them back to their own past, they enlist the aid of an elderly invalid friend and endanger all their lives. This story effectively melds the distinc- tion between this world and the other by having the present-day characters as observer/participants in their own pasts; interesting use of a train as the "vehicle" of transportation. Contrast *The Night Watchmen* [4B-31].

4B-126. A Time to Choose. Hutchinson, 1973 (12–15).
Stephen and Mary experience several strange occurrences before they realize that they are concurrently living two different lives in two different worlds and must choose one in which to live. The unfamiliar life of the other world is realistically juxtaposed with the normal, everyday 1970s family/school life of the two through the consistency of characterization.

Pascal, Francine, 1938– .
ABOUT: CA

4B-127. Hangin' Out with Cici or My Mother Was Never a Kid. Viking, 1977 (13–15).
Inexplicably transported back to 1944, Victoria, convinced her mother does not understand her, is befriended by the free-spirited Cici who, it is gradually revealed, is Victoria's mother as a teenager. A humorous, well-plotted story sensitive to the language and problems of contemporary teens. Compare *Tune in Yesterday* [4B-18].

Paton Walsh, Jill (U.K.), 1939– .
ABOUT: CA

4B-128. A Chance Child. Farrar, Straus, 1978 (13+).
After escaping from his neglectful home, Creep travels down a waterway which takes him back to the Industrial Revolution, where he befriends some workers and views the wretched working and living conditions of children prior to the enactment of child labor laws. Meanwhile, the only person who cares about him, his brother, Christopher, searches for Creep; he discovers Creep's trek across the century and reads Creep's account of life at the previous time in the Parliamentary Papers. Using the timeslip device, this story attempts to inform readers of conditions in another time. Compare *Jeremy Visick* [4B-157], *A Girl Called Boy* [4B-75] and *The Devil's Arithmetic* [4B-163].

Pearce, Philippa (U.K.), 1920– .
ABOUT: CA, SFE, SFFL, HF

***4B-129. Tom's Midnight Garden.** Oxford, 1958 (11–13).
Forced to stay with his relatives, with whom he is lonely and miserable, Tom Long, hearing a grandfather clock strike thirteen, investigates and enters a garden where he discovers a young girl, Hatty. Becoming friends, they share adventures during which Tom realizes both are alive but aging at different rates. Well-crafted, classic time shift story is enriched by sensitive characterization, evocative mood and mystery. Winner of the 1959 Carnegie Medal.

4B-130. Who's Afraid? And Other Strange Stories. Viking Kestrel, 1986 (10–12).
Collection of stories hovers between examples of ghostly tale and horror, and does best when illustrating that children too can do evil and like it, as in "A Christmas Pudding Improves with Keeping," "Samantha and the Ghost," "A Prince in Another Place," "Black Eyes," "Mr. Hurrel's Tallboy," "The Hirn," "The Yellow Ball" and others. Vintage Pearce: sensitive, economically written and effectively atmospheric.

Peck, Richard, 1934– .
ABOUT: CA

4B-131. The Ghost Belonged to Me. Viking, 1975 (11+).
When Alexander encounters the "Unseen," as Blossom Culp warns that he will,

he befriends the ghostly Inez Dumaine and becomes both hero and celebrity—modestly! A good-natured, funny and colloquially subtle ghost story that young readers immediately like is also a satisfying mystery. Alexander and Blossom's further adventures are found in *Ghosts I Have Been* (1977), *The Dreadful Future of Blossom Culp* (1983) and *Blossom Culp and the Sleep of Death* (1986).

Perrault, Charles. Fairy Tales [1-60]

Peyton, K. M. (U.K.), 1929- .
ABOUT: CA

4B-132. A Pattern of Roses. Oxford, 1972 (13-15).
As Tim Ingram fights for independence from his wealthy parents' expectations, he discovers the drawings of a dead young artist whose initials he shares; as he learns more about him and eventually encounters him, Tim becomes clearer about his own direction. The parallel stories of the two young men make for an interesting contrast. Contrast *Marianne Dreams* [4B-147].

Phillips, Ann, 1930- .

4B-133. The Oak King and the Ash Queen. Oxford, 1984 (13+).
Dan and Diana Sturgess, summoned to witness the ritual death of the summer trees, discover that the winter trees are plotting to overthrow the balance between the two groups, and become instrumental in restoring the balance. Otherwise formulaic fantasy of light versus dark is more than redeemed by informative and original plot.

Pierce, Meredith Ann, 1958- .
ABOUT: CA, PE

*4B-134. The Darkangel. Little, Brown, 1982 (13+).
Forced by the vampire to become handmaiden to his thirteen wives or wraiths, Aeriel finds herself both drawn to and repelled by her handsome, majestic, but evil master, and must choose between killing him or helping him find his fourteenth wife. Brilliantly conceived and articulated narrative is original in plot, characterization and setting as well as richly evocative of traditional myth and familiar legend: an outstanding example of Tolkien's "pot of story." In book 2 of the proposed Darkangel Trilogy, *A Gathering of Gargoyles* (1984), Aeriel seeks to gather "steeds" for her husband's brothers so they can war against the white witch. Also annotated as [4A-205].

4B-135. The Woman Who Loved Reindeer. Atlantic Monthly Press, 1985 (11+).
The golden infant boy which Caribou has forced upon her looks and behaves oddly. As he grows into manhood, not only does she discover he is a Trangl, a golden stag, with whom she falls in love, but he helps her guide her people to a new, safe country. Brilliant, offbeat fantasy combines varied setting and mores, magical atmosphere and revitalization of myth and legend.

Poole, Josephine (U.K.), 1933– .
ABOUT: CA, SFFL, HF

4B-136. The Visitor, a Story of Suspense. Harper, 1972 (13+).
The new tutor, hired while Harry is recuperating from an illness, receives immediate favor from everyone except Harry, who discovers he is the evil force behind
the town's turning against his future brother-in-law's revitalization of an ancient
mill. Utilizing elements of the supernatural, including rites and voodooism, this
story is marked by the juxtaposition of a sense of normalcy and a sense of the
bizarre.

Pope, Elizabeth, 1917– .
ABOUT: CA, HF

4B-137. The Perilous Gard. Houghton Mifflin, 1974 (12+).
In 1558 young Kate is exiled to an old castle, Perilous Gard, and discovers that the
castle secretly houses the last stronghold of the legendary Fairy Folk. She encounters the customs, magic and danger of the Druidic people when she becomes their
prisoner, and must decipher the signs to gain her freedom. This 1975 Newbery
Honor Book captures and combines the delightful essence of fairy tales as well as
a sound depiction of Tudor England. Compare *Hobberdy Dick* [4B-20].

4B-138. The Sherwood Ring. Houghton Mifflin, 1958 (13+).
Following the death of her family, Peggy arrives at her family's ancestral home,
where she soon meets the ghost of an ancestor and finds herself wrapped up in her
own romantic adventures as well as those of her ghostly relatives. Through the
time travel device, aspects of life during the period of the American Revolution
are brought to life as well as the parallel love stories. Compare *The Griffin
Legacy* [4B-91].

Preussler, Otfried (Germany), 1923– .
ABOUT: CA

4B-139. The Satanic Mill. Abelard-Schuman, 1972. Tr. by Anthea Bell of *Krabat*,
1971 (11–15).
Krabat, a fourteen-year-old beggar, becomes an apprentice at a flour mill, which
he discovers is really an evil magician's haven. Through the power of love and
kindness rather than the black magic he learns, he ultimately saves the remaining
apprentices from the magician-imposed fate of death. A very readable translation
of this tension-filled story, which utilizes strong characterization, a realistic
setting and evocative moods. Winner of the 1972 German Children's Book Prize.

Pyle, Howard. Twilight-Land [2-139]

Rayner, William (U.K.), 1929– .
ABOUT: CA, FL, HF

4B-140. Stag Boy. Collins, 1972 (13–16).
The power of an ancient antlered helmet enables Jim to identify increasingly

with a black stag until the teen can hardly separate himself from the animal. Hunters kill the stag, releasing Jim from his thralldom. Skillful blending of myth, nature description, coming of age and hunting is flawed by celebration of a macho ideal. Compare *The Flight of the Cassowary* [4B-99].

Rodowsky, Colby, 1932– .
ABOUT: CA

4B-141. Keeping Time. Farrar, Straus, 1983 (11+).
When his sister leaves his modern-day street musician family for a more traditional life-style, Drew suffers from her absence. During the family's performance of "Greensleeves," he travels back to Elizabethan London, where he meets another young musician, who teaches him to deal with his problems. This is a sensitive story of a young boy finding himself and his values. Compare the offbeat musician life of this family with Grosser's *The Snake Horn* [4B-63].

Saint Exupéry, Antoine de. The Little Prince [3-316]

Sleator, William, 1945– .
ABOUT: CA, SFFL

4B-142. Fingers. Atheneum, 1983 (13+).
To reinvigorate his brother's concert career, Sam reluctantly agrees to compose pieces that are ostensibly the long-lost work of the legendary gypsy pianist Laszlo Magyar. However, the brothers learn the music is not original but actually is Magyar's. This breezily written and intriguing story is both mystery and ghost story.

Smith, L(isa) J.
4B-143. The Night of the Solstice. Macmillan, 1987 (11+).
Three sisters and their brother are called upon to save the contemporary world from destruction by rescuing a sorceress held captive in another world. Working in a constricted timeframe, they travel back and forth between the two worlds through the mirror passageways, causing and encountering danger and crises before a climactic conclusion. Very believable characters add to this multifaceted hard-to-put-down first novel in which the siblings learn to believe in themselves.

Smith, Stephanie A.
*****4B-144. Snow-Eyes.** Atheneum, 1985 (11+).
After her father's death, Amarra, called Snow-Eyes, is taken from her home by her long-absent mother to become an unwilling servitor to the goddess Trost who hears and sometimes grants people's wishes. This haunting first novel is a powerful tale about becoming one's own person.

Stableford, Brian (U.K.), 1948– .
ABOUT: CA, NE, SFE, SFFL, TCSF

4B-145. The Last Days of the Edge of the World. Hutchinson, 1978 (13+).
The marriage between Prince Damian and Helen, daughter of the wizard Sirion Hilversu, cannot take place until the engaged pair accomplish three impossible tasks. This witty variation on many fairy tale motifs and situations should prove charming and stimulating to many readers. Compare *The Magic Three of Solatia* [4B-165].

Steele, Mary Q., 1922– .
ABOUT: CA, SFFL, ESF

4B-146. The Journey Outside. Viking, 1969 (9–15).
Delar breaks away from his Raft people, who travel around and around underground in the dark in order to discover why his people behave as they do and whether there is a better way to live. A haunting, original story with an especially effective description of encountering sunlight and aboveground, and insights into human motives, the story is fantasy and allegory. A Newbery Honor Book, 1972. Contrast *Master of the Grove* [4B-89].

Stephens, James. The Crock of Gold [3-332]

Storr, Catherine (U.K.), 1913– .
ABOUT: CA, SFE

4B-147. Marianne Dreams. Faber, 1958. U.S. title: *The Magic Drawing Pencil*, 1960 (10–12).
During her long recuperation from an undisclosed illness, Marianne intermittently draws and then dreams her drawings. In these dreams she is a character who interacts with an invalid character she has created. Through the struggles in her dreams/drawings, Marianne and the other character gain strength and mend quickly in their real lives. A charming story with distinctive characterization. Contrast *A Pattern of Roses* [4B-132].

Thurber, James. The Thirteen Clocks [3-336]; **The White Deer** [3-337]; **The Wonderful O** [4A-250]

Tolkien, J. R. R. The Hobbit [3-339]; **The Lord of the Rings** [3-340]

Travers, P. L. Mary Poppins [3-341]

Voigt, Cynthia, 1942– .
ABOUT: CA

4B-148. Jackaroo. Atheneum, 1985 (11+).
On the basis of insights into herself and society brought about because she was

marooned with a Lordling and discovered the costume of the legendary outlaw-hero Jackaroo, sensible and industrious Gwen opts for a new life of independence, risk-taking and caring for the lower classes. Longish narrative, set long ago in a faraway place, is redeemed by fresh characterization and surprising plot development. Compare *The Blue Sword* [4B-118].

Walsh, Jill Paton *see* Paton Walsh, Jill

Wangerin, Walter, Jr., 1944– .
ABOUT: CA, SMFL

4B-149. The Book of the Dun Cow. Harper, 1978 (13–15).
John Wesley accepts his destiny to challenge to the death Wyrm, embodiment of evil, and his chief henchman, Cockatrice. Wesley, his wife and his allies, the Dog, Mundo Cani, and the Weasel, kill the invaders and save the land. This richly allegorical and highly stylized beast fable concerning the struggle between good and evil brilliantly weaves its way between its medieval colors and contemporary applications. Winner of the 1980 Religious Book Award and 1981 American Book Award. The sequel, *The Book of Sorrows* (1985), continues the struggle between Wyrm and Chauntecleer to its tragic but triumphant conclusion. Contrast *The Pig Plantagenet* [4B-13]. Also annotated as [4A-262].

Wells, Rosemary, 1943– .
ABOUT: CA

4B-150. Through the Hidden Door. Dial, 1987 (11+).
A virtual outcast in his school, Barney Pennimen is befriended by a younger boy, the secretive Snowy Cobb, and the two explore an underground city apparently peopled by a lilliputian race from 100,000 years ago. Suspenseful, provocative, hard-hitting narrative combines Cormier-like probe into boys' private school and fascinating lost race motif. Compare *The Dark Behind the Curtain* [4B-32].

Westall, Robert (U.K.), 1929– .
ABOUT: CA, RG

4B-151. Break of Dark. Greenwillow, 1982 (13–15).
Authentic ghostly and horrific short fiction appears in a contemporary setting, complete with an alien hitchhiker, "Hitchhiker"; a World War II British bomber haunted by dead German pilots, "Blackham's Wimpey"; and vampires, "St. Austin Friars." A good horror read: relatively original topics; clever, plausible plot; effective atmosphere.

4B-152. The Cats of Seroster. Macmillan, 1984 (13+).
Possessed by more than just having a magic knife, tricked into performing a dangerous mission which unexpectedly expands into an attempt to recapture an entire city and assisted by powerful, telepathic cats, Cam learns that he himself is the mysterious war leader Seroster. Powerful, fascinating story of a reluctant, unlikely protagonist pushed into heroism. Contrast *Ratha's Creature* [4B-16].

4B-153. The Haunting of Chas McGill and Other Stories. Macmillan, 1983 (13+).
In addition to the title story, in which young Chas discovers the ghost of a World War I deserter, this horror collection also includes "Almost a Ghost Story," "The Vacancy," "The Night Out," "The Creatures in the House," "Sea Coal," "The Dracula Tour" and "A Walk on the Wild Side." While dealing with a variety of seemingly real subjects and events, the stories are spooky and chilling.

*4B-154. The Wind Eye. Macmillan, 1976 (13–15).
Vacationing at their recently inherited house, Mond's Heugh, on the Northumbrian coast, the troubled Studdard family experiences first increased tensions and then relief and comfort as they go sailing in a Viking-like boat, cross over into several pasts and meet the legendary St. Cuthbert. Provocative timeslip fantasy dramatizes its YA topic of family strife along with limning remarkable, nonhagiographic portrait of reputed saint. Contrast *The Bell of Nendrum* [4B-14].

White, T. H. Mistress Masham's Repose [3-369]; The Sword in the Stone [3-370]

Wilde, Oscar. The Happy Prince and Other Tales [2-157]

Wilder, Cherry (New Zealand), 1930– .
ABOUT: CA, SFE, TCSF

4B-155. A Princess of the Chameln. Atheneum, 1984 (14+).
Aidris is forced into exile after her parents are assassinated and her land invaded by the Mel' Nir. She flees for her life, undergoes training as a soldier, or kedran, and eventually is restored to her rightful throne. This is a book for readers who enjoy massively detailed, medieval-like Secondary Worlds with elements of young love and sorcery interwoven. Volume 1 of the Rulers of Hylor, it was followed by *Yorath the Wolf* (1984) and *The Summer's King* (1986). Contrast *Prince of the Godborn* [4B-67].

Willard, Nancy, 1936– .
ABOUT: CA, HF

4B-156. Things Invisible to See. Knopf, 1984 (14+).
In this combination war story, love story, baseball story and fantasy, teenaged Clare Bishop is partially paralyzed when she is struck by a stray baseball hit by Ben Harkissian. Ben's guilt prompts him to become friendly with the invalid girl; as their relationship develops, they learn to rely on each other's skills and abilities including Clare's out-of-body experiences and Ben's ability in baseball and dealing with the devil. Unique families, an ancestress and ghosts of former baseball stars help to make this a memorable book. Also annotated as [4A-268].

Wiseman, David (U.K.), 1916– .
ABOUT: CA

4B-157. Jeremy Visick. Houghton Mifflin, 1981 (11+).
Puzzlement over the fate of a twelve-year-old miner in an 1852 mining explosion

turns to keen empathy and then, intensifying, draws Matthew Clemens into the past to unearth the secret of Jeremy. Requisite technical exposition does not seriously undercut the story's sensitive characterization and evocative description. Compare *A Chance Child* [4B-128].

Wrightson, Patricia (Australia), 1921– .
ABOUT: CA, SFFL, ESF, FL, HF

*4B-158. The Ice Is Coming. Hutchinson, 1977 (11–14).
Wirrun, a young Aboriginal man, decides, since no one else seems to notice or care, that he must stop the Ninya, ancient ice creatures, in their attempt to capture the Nargun, the age-old fire monster, and to upset the balance between good and evil. Original, inventive and witty story demonstrates convincingly that formula fantasy can still be exciting and distinctive. Winner of the 1978 Australian Children's Book of the Year Award. This Australian trilogy also includes *The Dark Bright Water* (1978) and *Journey behind the Wind* (1981).

4B-159. A Little Fear. Hutchinson, 1983 (11–15).
Not wanting to be sent to a nursing home, Mrs. Tucker retreats to a cottage left to her by her brother, only to discover that she must contend with a Njimbin, a gnome, as they battle each other with magic and treachery for the right to live there. This small book with two strongly portrayed, determined characters is a story of continual one-upsmanship and won the 1984 Boston Globe–Horn Book Award.

4B-160. The Nargun and the Stars. Hutchinson, 1973 (10–13).
Invited to live with his cousins, Edie and Charlie Waters, on their mountain sheep-run, Simon Brent not only grows to like them and their life-style but also helps them chase away the Nargun, the ancient Earth spirit, which threatens their home. Distinctive setting and characterization, along with supple colloquial language, enrich the attractive portrait of Australian folk beliefs and legends.

4B-161. An Older Kind of Magic. Hutchinson, 1972 (10–13).
Rupert and Selina Potter and their friend Benny organize to save the neighboring public garden from the development plans of Sir Mortimer Wyvern, and gradually realize that they are being assisted by the magic of an assortment of indigenous water and earth spirits. A lighthearted tone, attractive characters, especially the various spirits, and local color add up to an entertaining story. Contrast *The Power of Three* [4B-85].

Yep, Laurence, 1948– .
ABOUT: CA, NE, SFE, SFFL, TCSF

4B-162. Dragon of the Lost Sea. Harper, 1982 (13+).
Shimmer, a dragon princess who can take on other forms, including human, is befriended by a young boy in her quest to recapture her clan's home from the witch Civet, and thereby regain her rightful place in the kingdom. Long mistrustful of humans, Shimmer regains respect through her relationship with Thorn as they track down Civet. In the sequel, *Dragon Steel* (1985), Shimmer imprisons Civet, but she and Thorn face the evil High King before she can free her clan. These stories,

told in the first person by Shimmer, utilize sensitive characterization and impressive settings and tell a compelling tale. Contrast *Dragon's Blood* [4B-164].

Yolen, Jane, 1939– .
ABOUT: CA, SFE, SFFL, RG, FL, HF

4B-163. The Devil's Arithmetic. Viking Kestrel, 1988 (12–14).
Hannah, resentful as well as ignorant of her Jewish heritage, is transported back to a Jewish village in Nazi-occupied Poland and is sent to a concentration camp. Except for the time travel device, the story is a realistic portrait both of Jewish village life and of the Holocaust and what it signifies. Compare *A Girl Called Boy* [4B-75].

4B-164. Dragon's Blood. Delacorte, 1982 (13+).
In order to earn the price of his freedom, Jakkin must first steal a baby dragon and secretly train it to become a fighter. Very interesting and stimulating story derives much of its success from the original supposition concerning the proper training of dragons. The other titles in the Dragon Sequence are *Heart's Blood* (1984) and *A Sending of Dragons* (1987). Contrast *Dragon of the Lost Sea* [4B-162].

4B-165. The Magic Three of Solatia. Crowell, 1974 (11–12).
In three interrelated stories set in Solatia, Sianna, her father, Sian, and her son Lahn explore the implications of using magic, in particular the three magic buttons given by the sea witch, Dread Mary, as they fend off the evil wizard Blaggard. In these contemporary fairy tales, Yolen evokes the allure of folk fairy tales through an adroit blend of old motifs and new applications. Compare *The Last Days of the Edge of the World* [4B-145].

Anthologies

4B-166. Fantasy Tales. Ed. by Barbara Ireson. Faber, 1977. U.S. title: *The April Witch and Other Strange Tales*, 1978 (13–15).
This collection of short stories, most of them reprints, includes "Of Polymuf Stock" by John Christopher, "Obstinate Uncle Otis" by Robert Arthur, "The Tower" by Marghanita Laski, "The Cork Elephant" by Ian Serraillier, "The Inner Room" by Robert Aickman, "The Never-Ending Penny" by Bernard Wolfe, "The New Sun" by J. S. Fletcher, "The Star Beast" by Nicholas Stuart Gray, "The Man Who Could Work Miracles" by H. G. Wells, "The April Witch" by Ray Bradbury, "Strange Fish" by Leon Garfield, "The Riddle" by Walter de la Mare, "The Tube That Stuck" by Claire Creswell and "The Bottle Imp" by R. L. Stevenson.

4B-167. Ghost After Ghost. Ed. by Aidan Chambers. Kestrel, 1982 (13–15).
These short stories featuring young people as ghosts or haunted by ghosts were written specifically for this anthology and include "If She Bends, She Breaks" by John Gordon, "Absalom, Absalom" by Jan Mark, "Such a Sweet Little Girl" by Lance Salway, "Sam and the Sea" by George Mackay Brown, "Christmas in the Rectory" by Catherine Storr, "His Loving Sister" by Philippa Pearce, "Dead Ghosts" by R. Chetwynd-Hayes, "Old Filliken" by Joan Aiken and "The Haunt-

ing of Chas McGill" by Robert Westall. Illustrated with one black-and-white drawing per story, this anthology is similar in approach to Asimov's anthology, *Young Ghosts* [4B-175].

4B-168. Haunting Tales. Ed. by Barbara Ireson. Faber, 1973 (12–15).
These nineteen ghost stories, mostly reprints, include "Huw" by Geoffrey Palmer and Noel Lloyd, "Hans and His Master" by Sorche Nic Leodhas, "The Haunted Trailer" by Robert Arthur, "The Magic Shop" by H. G. Wells, "John Charrington's Wedding" by E. Nesbit, "The Ghostly Earl" by R. Chetwynd-Hayes, "Through the Veil" by Sir Arthur Conan Doyle, "The Doll's Ghost" by F. Marion Crawford, "A Long Day without Water" by Joan Aiken, "The Demon King" by J. B. Priestley, "Faithful Jenny Dove" by Eleanor Farjeon, "The Twilight Road" by H. F. Brinsmead, "Fiddler, Play Fast, Play Faster" by Ruth Sawyer, "Uncle Einar" by Ray Bradbury, "The Ghost Ship" by Richard Middleton, "Jimmy Takes Vanishing Lessons" by Walter R. Brooks, "The Crossways" by L. P. Hartley and "Master Ghost and I" by Barbara Softly.

4B-169. Imaginary Lands. Ed. by Robin McKinley. Ace, 1985 (13+).
This anthology of stories centering around places and happenings includes selections written specifically for this book. The stories included are "Paper Dragons" by James Blaylock, "The Old Woman and the Storm" by Patricia McKillip, "The Big Rock Candy Mountain" by Robert Westall, "Flight" by Peter Dickinson, "Evian Steel" by Jane Yolen, "Stranger Blood" by P. C. Hodgell, "The Curse of Igamor" by Michael de Larrabeiti, "Tam Lin" by Joan Vinge and "The Stone Fey" by Robin McKinley. Typographically a very appealing book, this is an intense, sophisticated collection. Winner of the 1986 World Fantasy Convention Award for anthology/collection. Also annotated as [4A-293].

4B-170. Ready or Not. Ed. by Joan Kahn. Greenwillow, 1987 (13+).
This collection of fourteen reprinted horror stories, originally published 1946–82, has been carefully selected to appeal and entice the imagination and to make a reader's hair stand on end. Selections in this anthology include Hayes Wilson's "Please, No Strawberries," Irwin Shaw's "Peter Two," Ruth Rendell's "The Vinegar Mother," Stanley Ellin's "Robert," F. Marion Crawford's "The Doll's Ghost," Mary Norton's "Paul's Tale," Alice Rudowski's "If Big Brother Says So," Joyce Cary's "A Private Ghost," Ray Bradbury's "The Playground," Margot Arnold's "The Girl in the Mirror," Barbara Williamson's "The Thing Waiting Outside," Jane Speed's "Fair's Fair," H. R. F. Keating's "A Hell of a Story" and Roald Dahl's "The Wish."

4B-171. The Restless Ghost. Ed. by Susan Dickinson. Collins, 1970 (13+).
Nineteen ghost stories from the nineteenth and twentieth centuries, divided into two categories, are included here. Encounters contains "The Restless Ghost" by Leon Garfield, "A Pair of Hands" by Sir Arthur Quiller-Couch, "Feet Foremost" by L. P. Hartley, "The Bus Conductor" by E. F. Benson, "August Heat" by W. F. Harvey, "Coincidence" by A. J. Alan, "School for the Unspeakable" by Manley Wade Wellman and "Ghost Riders of the Sioux" by Kenneth Ulyatt; included in Experience are "Feel Free" by Alan Garner, "Minuke" by Nigel Kneale, "The Witch's Bone" by William Croft Dickinson, "Lucky's Grove" by H. R. Wakefield, "The Moon Bog" by H. P. Lovecraft, "The White Cat of Drumgunniol" by

J. S. Le Fanu, "The Bottle Imp" by R. L. Stevenson, "The Red Room" by H. G. Wells, "The Haunted Doll's House" by M. R. James, "His Own Number" by William Croft Dickinson and "The Apple of Trouble" by Joan Aiken.

4B-172. Shades of Dark. Ed. by Aidan Chambers. Hardy, 1984 (13+).
Includes "The Champions" by Vivien Alcock, "The Gnomon" by Jan Mark, "Left in the Dark" by John Gordon, "Mandy Kiss Mommy" by Lance Salway, "A Kind of Swan Song" by Helen Cresswell, "Ivor" by George McKay Brown, "The Devil's Laughter" by Jan Needle and "His Coy Mistress" by Jean Stubbs. Represents light fiction dealing with ghosts, the supernatural and mild horror. A slim volume which serves as a delightful composite of the genre.

4B-173. Supernatural Stories. Ed. by Jean Russell. Orchard Books, 1987 (10–13). This anthology is composed of selections from two earlier British titles. Stories reprinted from *The Magnet Book of Strange Tales* (1980) are "The Whistling Boy" by John Gordon, "Mr. Hornet and Nellie Maggs" by Alison Morgan, "The Demon Kite" by Farrukh Dhondy and "Just a Guess" by Dick King-Smith. Stories reprinted from *The Magnet Book of Sinister Stories* (1982) are "The Dollmaker" and "Billy's Hand" by Adele Geras, "Miss Hooting's Legacy" by Joan Aiken, "Black Dog" by Joan Phipson, "Spring-Heeled Jack" by Gwen Grant, "The Book of the Black Arts" by Patricia Miles, "The Parrot" by Vivien Alcock, "The Boy's Story" by Catherine Storr and "Welcome Yule" by Jan Mark. This volume is marked by eerie, sinister, strange stories in which a little girl is concocted from doll parts, a pill causes a happy day, a book that grants wishes and causes grief is sold by the devil, and two robots try to give eternal youth to an old woman.

4B-174. Werewolves: A Collection of Original Stories. Ed. by Jane Yolen. Harper, 1988 (12–14).
Ranging from pseudo-medieval recountings of legends (Ru Emerson's "The Werewolf's Gift" and Harry Turtledove's "Not All Wolves") to futuristic experiments in possession (Mary Whittington's "Wolfskin" and Jane Yolen's "Green Messiah"), from vaguely Central European settings (Katharine Eliska Kimbriel's "Night Calls" and Susan Shwartz's "The Wolf's Flock") to contemporary settings (Debra Doyle and J. D. Macdonald's "Bad Blood" and Sherwood Smith's "Monster Mash"), the stories show that the werewolf phenomenon or, to be more precise, the credulity to accept werewolves, has been constant through the centuries.

4B-175. Young Ghosts. Ed. by Isaac Asimov. Harper, 1985 (13+).
These twelve stories each involve a youthful ghost as a major character. The stories included are "Lost Hearts" by M. R. James, "On the Brighton Road" by Richard Middleton, "Poor Little Saturday" by Madeleine L'Engle, "The Lake" by Ray Bradbury, "A Pair of Hands" by Sir Arthur Quiller-Couch, "Old Haunts" by Richard Matheson, "An Uncommon Sort of Spectre" by Edward Page Mitchell, "The House of the Nightmare" by Edward Lucas White, "The Shadowy Third" by Ellen Glasgow, "The Twilight Road" by H. F. Brinmead, "The Voices of El Dorado" by Howard Goldsmith and "The Changing of the Guard" by Rod Serling. This is an eerie, evocative collection of stories.

Secondary Sources

Annotated here are general works dealing with children's/YA fantasy. Books dealing with individual authors are not annotated, but are cited in Lynn [4B-182].

4B-176. Cott, Jonathan. **Pipers at the Gates of Dawn: The Wisdom of Children's Literature**. Random House, 1983.
Featuring individual chapters on Dr. Seuss, Maurice Sendak, William Steig, Astrid Lindgren, Chinua Achebe, P. L. Travers and Iona and Peter Opie, this volume shares the author's reflections about and encounters with these industrious, influential personalities in children's literature. Citing intimate examples, as well as actual dialogue, each chapter sensitively reveals the person and the situations behind the creative works.

4B-177. Donelson, Kenneth L., and Alleen Pace Nilsen. **Literature for Today's Young Adults**. 3rd ed. Scott, Foresman, 1989.
That the standard textbook devoted to YA literature is now into a third edition attests to its value as introduction to, overview of and discussion of all facets of what is increasingly being considered an autonomous body of literature and one that anyone teaching junior and senior high English must be familiar with. Especially relevant is chapter 6, "Fantasy, Science Fiction, and Utopias: Of Wondrous Worlds."

4B-178. Gose, Elliott. **Mere Creatures: A Study of Modern Fantasy Tales for Children**. Univ. of Toronto, 1988.
Concentrating on ten well-known animal tales, Gose argues not only for their merit as entertainment in the best sense of that word but also for their value as projections whereby readers can reflect upon a variety of psychological concerns that they cannot or prefer not to express directly in human terms. The result is ten provocative and insightful essays.

4B-179. Kies, Cosette. **Supernatural Fiction for Teens**. Libraries Unlimited, 1978.
Containing annotations of 500 selected paperbacks, indicating appropriate age levels, this source is arranged alphabetically by author with title and subject indexes, as well as appendixes which list series and movie tie-ins and offer a directory of publishers. This slim volume helps librarians and teens locate and evaluate titles.

4B-180. Lewis, Naomi (U.K.). **Fantasy Books for Children**. New ed. National Book League, 1977.
Providing annotations to over 185 British children's fantasy titles, Lewis has compiled a selective bibliography arranged by author. The fifty-five-page volume also includes an introductory essay citing a short history as well as insights concerning the value of fantasy.

4B-181. Lochhead, Marion (U.K.). **The Renaissance of Wonder in Children's Literature**. Canongate, 1977. U.S. title: *Renaissance of Wonder: The Fantasy Worlds of J. R. R. Tolkien, C. S. Lewis, George MacDonald, E. Nesbit and Others*. Harper, 1980.
Tracing the development of children's fantasy from its origin in the second half of the nineteenth century to the present, Lochhead sees George MacDonald as the

most influential author of the genre and regards C. S. Lewis and J. R. R. Tolkien as his descendants and equals. Other writers are also mentioned, but only in passing. Also annotated as [7-34].

4B-182. Lynn, Ruth Nadelman. **Fantasy Literature for Children and Young Adults: An Annotated Bibliography**. 3rd ed. Bowker, 1989.

Annotated bibliography of 3,300 children's and YA fantasies (generally excluding SF and horror but including science fantasy and some supernatural), with 750 YA titles new to this edition. Most plot summaries are one sentence. Citations from twenty-four recommending sources are the basis for selection, with O (outstanding) and R (recommended) symbols used for the best books. Books are grouped in ten broad thematic categories, with many cross-references. Much enlarged secondary bibliography includes more than 600 authors as well as chapters on teaching resources, history and criticism, and reference and bibliography. Indexes by author/illustrator, title and subject/series. A 25% sample of annotated entries showed 38% of the books were R (recommended by three or four sources), and 4%+ were judged O (outstanding, recommended by five or more sources). Books labeled YA (grades 7–12) totaled 800 and included most of the books of this chapter and many from chapters 2, 3 and 4A.

4B-183. Pflieger, Pat. **A Reference Guide to Modern Fantasy for Children**. Greenwood, 1984.

An introduction to the work of thirty-six nineteenth- and twentieth-century British and American authors of children's and YA fantasy, the volume presents in dictionary format information about the authors, their books and their characters, places and magical objects. The "dictionary" is especially useful to anyone wanting to refresh his or her memory of books previously read.

4B-184. Yolen, Jane. **Touch Magic: Fantasy, Faerie and Folklore in the Literature of Childhood**. Philomel, 1981.

This collection of essays, some of which originally appeared in other publications in slightly different form, is a testament to the impact and importance of fantasy and folklore on children, customs and culture. A sensitively and beautifully written account of the psychological aspects of this literature.

5

Fantasy and Horror Fiction and Libraries

Neil Barron

▬

antasy and horror fiction has been regularly published since at least the eighteenth century, and most major writers have written some "fantastic" fiction. As chapters 6–9 indicate, it is only in recent years that fantastic fiction and film have been the subject of sustained scholarship. By contrast, science fiction's creation and publication were at least partially dependent on the development of science and technology. Although science fiction was also published fairly widely in general periodicals from the nineteenth century on, beginning in the mid-1920s the shorter fiction tended to move into the American pulp magazines, beginning with *Amazing* in 1926. This also happened, but to a much lesser degree, to fantasy and horror fiction, as chapter 11 indicates. *Weird Tales* [11–20] began in 1923 and is—for older readers at least—easily the best known of the pulps which emphasized fantastic fiction, mostly with supernatural/horror themes but occasionally SF themes as well, especially in the earlier years.

Almost every trade publisher has issued an occasional work of fantasy or horror fiction, but it was only relatively recently that such fiction became a distinct form of category fiction, like SF, mysteries, westerns or romances. Fantasy and sometimes horror are usually shelved with SF in chain bookstores, particularly mass-market paperbacks. With the notable exception of Arkham House, which was founded in 1938 to preserve and publicize the work of H. P. Lovecraft, few publishers have specialized in fantasy and horror fiction. The specialty publishers active in the decade following World War II, which failed as the major trade publishers entered the field, usually emphasized science fiction. (A brief summary of specialty SF publishers is provided by Robert Weinberg in his chapter in Hall's *Science/Fiction Collections* [6-37].) Only in the 1980s have publishers specialized in fantasy or horror fiction. Tables 5-1, 5-2 and 5-3 list the principal U.S. and British general and specialty publishers of fantasy and horror fiction and the related secondary literature.

The most detailed and accurate statistics for U.S. and U.K. fantastic fiction publishing are compiled by *Locus* [11-40], which provides an annual summary in each February issue and in its annual hardbound bibliographies [6-6]. Clear distinctions between science fiction, fantasy and horror fiction are sometimes difficult to make, but the figures in table 5-4 provide a reasonably accurate summary and show the relative magnitude of each type of fiction. Figures refer to books published or distributed in the U.S. and exclude British and other foreign books not distributed in the U.S. Thus the figures shown understate total publication of English-language fantastic fiction.

For all types of fantastic fiction, reprints and reissues have totaled about 40% to 47% of all titles in the 1980s. For hardcover books, the figure is about 20%. For mass-market paperbacks, the most common format, the figure has varied from about 50% to 60%. There are a large number of mass-market originals, which libraries that systematically acquire fantasy and horror fiction should acquire in prebound format and catalog like any other book. The public library practice of dumping paperbacks on spinner racks or shelves with no cataloging to make users aware of their existence is not a satisfactory policy for any library desiring to provide anything more than a quickly expendable popular fiction collection. Prebinding mass-market copies adds about $3-4 to their original modest wholesale cost ($2-3) and results in a volume likely to outlast most trade hardcovers.

Currently roughly 300 original works of fantasy in English—novels, collections and anthologies—are published in the U.S. and U.K. each year. The figure for horror is about 200, a figure which has grown rapidly in the 1980s. Because of the large number of books published, particularly in recent years, contributors to this guide were asked to be extremely selective and to choose only the best or better works for consideration by libraries and interested readers.

Table 5-1. Principal U.S. General Publishers of Fantasy and Horror Fiction

Publishers or imprints in boldface issue the largest number of titles. Paperback publishers are primarily mass market, but those which issue occasional trade paperbacks are marked by an asterisk.

Paperbacks	*Hardcover*	*Secondary Literature*
*Academy Chicago	**Ace/Putnam**	Advent: Publishers
Ace	**Arbor House**	Borgo Press
Archway	Argo *see* Atheneum	Bowling Green State
Avon	Arkham House	Univ. Popular Press
Baen	**Atheneum**	Crossroad/Continuum
*Ballantine/Del Rey	**Ballantine/Del Rey**	Gale Research
Bantam/Spectra	**Bantam/Spectra**	Garland Publishing
Bart Books	Congdon & Weed	Greenwood Press
Berkley	Crown	G. K. Hall
Carroll & Graf	**DAW**	Indiana Univ. Press

Table 5-1. (continued)

Charter
Critic's Choice
DAW
*Delacorte
Dell
Del Rey *see* Ballantine
*Donning/Starblaze
Fawcett
*Harvest
Jove
Leisure
Pageant
Paperjacks
Pinnacle
*Plume
Pocket Books
Popular Library/
   Questar
Questar *see* Popular
   Library
Signet/NAL
Spectra *see* Bantam
Starblaze *see* Donning
TOR
Warner
Worldwide Library
Zebra

Delacorte
Del Rey *see* Ballantine
Donning
Doubleday/Foundation
E. P. Dutton
Easton Press
Farrar
Donald Fine
Foundation *see*
   Doubleday
Greenwillow
Harcourt
Harper & Row
Houghton Mifflin
Maclay & Associates
Macmillan
Millennium *see* Walker
William Morrow
New American Library
Poseidon Press
Putnam
St. Martin's
SF Book Club
Simon & Schuster
Spectra *see* Bantam
Tor
Viking Penguin
Walker/Millennium
Warner
Franklin Watts

Kent State Univ. Press
Locus Press
McFarland & Co.
Meckler
Oxford Univ. Press
Scarecrow Press
Scribner's
Serconia Press
Southern Illinois Univ.
   Press
Starmont House
Twayne
UMI Research Press

Table 5-2. **Principal U.K. General Publishers of Fantasy and Horror Fiction**

See note to table 5-1. My thanks to Mike Ashley for much of the information in this table.

Paperbacks
*Abacus
Arrow
Bantam
Beaver
*Black Swan
*Chatto & Windus

Hardcover
W. H. Allen
Bantam Press
Jonathan Cape
Cassell
Century Hutchinson
Chatto & Windus

Secondary Literature
See table 5-3 under
   Dragon's World and
   Ferret Fantasy

Table 5-2. (continued)

Corgi	Collins
Coronet	**Equation**
*Equation	**Gollancz**
Fontana	**Grafton**
Futura/Orbit	**Headline**
Grafton	**Hodder & Stoughton**
Headline	Michael Joseph
Kestrel	**William Kimber**
Magnet	**MacDonald Futura**
New English Library	Macmillan
Orbit	**Methuen**
Pan	Piatkus
*Penguin	Robinson Publishing
*Picador	Robson Books
Piccolo	**Severn House**
Puffin	Simon & Schuster
Robinson	**Unwin Hyman**
Sphere	Viking
*Titan	Virago
Unwin Paperbacks	Women's Press
VGSF (Gollancz)	
Virago	
Women's Press	

Table 5-3. Specialty U.S. and U.K. Publishers of Fantasy and Horror Fiction and Related Criticism

These publishers specialize in fantastic fiction, primarily fantasy and horror but sometimes science fiction as well (publishers specializing almost exclusively in SF are omitted; see list in chapter 7 of my *Anatomy of Wonder*, 1987). These publishers typically issue no more than one or two titles per year, often less. A limited, signed, numbered, often slipcased edition is marketed to collectors, and a trade edition to a slightly larger market. Total print runs rarely exceed 2,000 copies. Co-publishing with nonspecialty trade publishers has occasionally occurred.

Advent: Publishers, Box A3228, Chicago, IL 60690. History and criticism, emphasizing SF

Arkham House, Box 546, Sauk City, WI 53583. Mostly supernatural fiction; Lovecraft's principal publisher

Axolotl Press, c/o Pulphouse, Box 1227, Eugene, OR 97440

Cheap St., Rt. 2, Box 293, New Castle, VA 24127. Original fiction handset in very fine quality editions

Corroboree Press, 2729 Bloomington Ave. S, Minneapolis, MN 55407. Emphasizes work of R. A. Lafferty

Dark Harvest, Box 941, Arlington Heights, IL 60006. Mostly horror fiction

Table 5-3. (continued)

Dragon's World/Paper Tiger, 19 Hereford Square, London SW7 4TS. Mostly illustrated books, heavily fantasy and SF

Chris Drumm, Box 445, Polk City, IA 50226. Pamphlet author bibliographies plus original pamphlet short stories

Ferret Fantasy, 27 Beechcroft Rd., Upper Tooting, London SW17 7BX. Bibliographies by George Locke of fantastic literature

Footsteps Press, Box 75, Round Top, NY 12473

W. Paul Ganley/Weirdbook Press, Box 149, Buffalo, NY 14226

Donald M. Grant, Box 187, Hampton Falls, NH 03844. Long established, emphasizing reprints from the pulps

Hypatia Press, 86501 Central Rd., Eugene, OR 97402. Prints *SFRA Newsletter*

Kerosina Publications, 27 Hampton Rd., Worcester Park, Surrey KT4 8EU, U.K.

Kinnell Pubs. Ltd., 43 Kingsfield Ave., N. Harrow, Middlesex HA2 6AO, UK

Land of Enchantment, Box 5360, Plymouth, MI 48170

Locus Press, Box 13305, Oakland, CA 94661. Bibliographies

Lord John Press, 19073, Los Alimos St., Northridge, CA 91326

Maclay & Associates, Box 16253, Baltimore, MD 21210

Morrigan Publications, 5 Mythop Ave., Lytham St. Annes, Lancashire FY8 4HZ, U.K.

Necronomicon Press, 101 Lockwood St., West Warwick, RI 02893. Lovecraft and related writers

Nemo Press, 1205 Harney St., Omaha, NE 68102. Ellison books

NESFA Press, Box G, MIT Branch PO, Cambridge, MA 02139. Indexes plus books by convention guests of honor

Outland Publishers, Box 1104, Englewood Cliffs, NJ 07632

Owlswick Press, Box 8243, Philadelphia, PA 19101

Phantasia Press, 5536 Crispin Way, West Bloomfield, MI 48033 Both fantasy and SF

Philtrum Press, Box 1186, Bangor, ME 04401. Stephen King material

Pulphouse Publishing, Box 1227, Eugene, OR 97440

Scream/Press, Box 481146, Los Angeles, CA 90048. Horror fiction

Serconia Press, Box 1786, Seattle, WA 98111. Essay collections

Soft Books, 89 Marion St., Toronto M6R 1E6, Canada

Space & Time Press, 138 W. 70th St., #4B, New York, NY 10023

SteelDragon Press, Box 7253, Powderhorn Sta., Minneapolis, MN 55407

Strange Co., Box 864, Madison, WI 53701. Mostly horror fiction

2AM Publications, Box 6754, Rockford, IL 61125-1754

Ultramarine Pub. Co., Box 303, Hastings-on-Hudson, NY 10706

Underwood-Miller, 708 Westover Dr., Lancaster, PA 17601. Fiction and occasional nonfiction, originally emphasizing work of Jack Vance

United Mythologies Press, Box 390, Station A, Weston, Ontario M9N 3N1, Canada. Lafferty booklets

Ursus Imprints, 5539 Jackson, Dept. 0, Kansas City, MO 64130. Illustration

Weird Tales Library, Box 13418, Philadelphia, PA 19101

Whispers Press, 70 Highland Ave., Binghamton, NY 13905. Horror fiction, notably in the irregular serial *Whispers* [11-21]

Xanadu, 5 Uplands Rd, London N8 9NN. Criticism

Mark V. Ziesing, Box 76, Shingletown, CA 96088

Table 5-4. Original Fantastic Fiction Published/Distributed in U.S.

1988 [volumes]	Category	1988	1987	1986	1985	1984	1983
				[percent]			
317	SF novels	26.7	29.0	34.7	31.6	32.4	32.4
264	Fantasy novels	22.2	24.9	23.9	30.2	25.3	22.0
182	Horror novels	15.3	9.4	7.2	1.4	2.8	3.5
98	Anthologies	8.3	9.4	8.5	8.1	9.3	9.2
77	Collections	6.5	7.4	7.9	6.1	8.8	7.0
64	Novelizations	5.4	7.0	2.6	4.9	4.9	6.4
134	Nonfiction	11.3	9.7	11.6	13.0	13.6	11.3
19	Omnibus	1.6	2.4	2.6	2.5	1.8	3.1
31	Miscellaneous	2.6	0.7	0.9	2.2	1.1	5.1

Source: *Locus*, February 1989

Reviewing and Selection

All reviewing media are necessarily very selective in choosing to review a small fraction of the more than 30,000 original books published each year in the U.S., of which perhaps 15% is fiction, 3%+ is fantastic fiction, and 1.5% fantasy or horror fiction. Original mass-market paperbacks are, like their pulp predecessors, heavily formulaic and are usually designated category fiction—the principal categories being science fiction (with fantasy usually included), horror fiction (sometimes included with SF and fantasy), westerns, mystery/detective, romances, men's adventure and a miscellany of smaller categories.

Space limitations and a natural desire to review the more "significant" books mean that little category fiction is reviewed in the general or library-oriented media. Table 5-5 shows the principal review media for fantasy and horror fiction, in hardcover and paperback. The general media review mostly hardcovers, especially books not designated category fiction by their publishers. The specialty journals, published by and for fans, review both formats. Of the specialty magazines, only *Locus* provides prepublication reviews with any consistency. This is important since mass-market paperbacks have shelf lives not much longer than those of monthly magazines, although wholesalers and specialty dealers can provide such paperbacks for some months after publication. *Library Journal* reviews most fantasy under the heading science fiction; horror fiction is reviewed much more selectively. *Science Fiction Chronicle*, which, like *Locus* [11-40], devotes space to fantasy and horror fiction and film, prints more reviews than any other specialty magazine, many of them of SF. All are written by one reviewer, who consistently devotes about 100 words to every book, good or bad. His lack of selectivity is combined with a frequent failure to identify rubbish as such. *Locus* includes detailed monthly listings of U.S. and British books received, hardcovers and paperbacks, original and reprints, with brief notes for most. A knowledgeable librarian or other reader can often use these listings for selection.

Table 5-5. Fantasy and Horror Fiction Reviewing

Magazine	Issues/Year	Est. No. of Fantasy/ Horror Books (including nonfiction) Reviewed Annually
General/Library		
Booklist	26	60
Choice	11	20
Horn Book	4	8
Kirkus	24	20
Kliatt YA Paperback Guide	8	25
Library Journal	26	45
Publishers Weekly	52	125
VOYA (Voice of Youth Advocates)	4	25
Specialty		
American Fantasy	4	90
Isaac Asimov's SF Magazine	13	25
British Fantasy Society Newsletter	4	150
Ghosts and Scholars	1	10
Gothic	1	5
The Horror Show	4	36
Locus	12	150
Lovecraft Studies	2	5
Magazine of Fantasy & SF	12	50
Science Fiction Chronicle	12	200–250
Studies in Weird Fiction	1	4
Weird Tales	4	40*

*projected figure, based on first two issues
Source: information from Hal Hall and Mike Ashley

Acquisitions

Standard library wholesalers are probably the best source for in-print trade and mass-market editions. Specialty press books are better ordered directly from the publisher (see table 5-3) or from dealers specializing in fantastic literature. Two of the more reliable and long established are:

Robert and Phyllis Weinberg Books, 1515 Oxford Drive, Oak Forest, IL 60452. A monthly catalog lists new and forthcoming books and fanzines, SF, fantasy and horror, domestic and some imports. Strong on paperbacks and the specialty presses.

L. W. Currey, Elizabethtown, NY 12933. Generally regarded as the foremost antiquarian dealer specializing in fantastic literature, he carries new original hardcover and selective paperback fiction and much nonfiction as well, including the many short-discount titles often purchased by libraries. His frequent catalogs of both in- and out-of-print materials are valuable and authoritative.

The classified and display ads in *Locus* list many dealers, as do those in the annual fantasy and SF issues of *AB Bookman's Weekly*, published each October since 1983 and distributed at the World Fantasy Conventions. The many conventions listed in each issue of *Locus* usually have dealer exhibits. Specialty retail bookstores are found in many metropolitan areas.

The selection criteria for this guide exclude rarity, scarcity or collectibility. But fantasy and horror fiction is avidly collected by fans, as science fiction has been collected for many years. There have been several price guides published in recent years, most of them not merely valueless but frequently very misleading. Few discuss the points necessary to identify first editions or issues (for this, see Currey [6-2]). The crucial importance of condition is often ignored, even though a merely very good copy might command half the price of a fine copy. And in a rapidly changing market, even a reliable guide would date quickly. The most reliable guides remain the catalogs of established and reliable dealers like Currey.

Cataloging

Cataloging and classification of fantasy and horror fiction vary widely. Hardcover books are usually cataloged and typically shelved with science fiction, since relatively few librarians are concerned with making distinctions among different types of fantastic literature. Academic libraries commonly use the Library of Congress classification system and classify either in the **PS** (American) or **PR** (British) literature classes or sometimes in the catchall **PZ** fiction classes. The revised guide by Burgess [6-35] provides a thorough, current explanation of LC policies of classification and subject indexing of fantastic literature, film and art.

6

General
Reference
Works

Neil Barron

Almost every reference book discussed here was published in the past decade, one measure of the growing interest in fantasy and horror literature. Many of these books are also annotated in chapter 8 of my *Anatomy of Wonder* (3rd ed., 1987). The annotations have been revised to stress their usefulness to the reader of fantasy and horror fiction. See also chapters 9, 10 and 11 for discussion of specialized reference books. Not annotated here are more general library reference works, notably *Contemporary Authors*, one of the works to which reference is made in the fiction chapters (see preface). Several H. W. Wilson publications, such as the *Fiction Catalog, Junior High School Catalog* and others, are of some value in selecting fantasy and horror fiction.

Bibliographies and Indexes

6-1. Bleiler, Everett F. **The Checklist of Science-Fiction and Supernatural Fiction**. Firebell Books, 1978.
Few knowledgeable readers doubt Bleiler's preeminence in the field of fantastic fiction scholarship, for which he was belatedly recognized by the Science Fiction Research Association's Pilgrim award. *The Checklist of Fantastic Literature* (1948) was the standard for many years. This carefully revised edition adds about 1,150 titles, drops about 600 borderline books, corrects entries and adds an index by ninety-two thematic/subject matter categories, thoroughly explained in a twelve-page chapter. First editions of about 5,000 English-language works of fantastic fiction, including translations, from 1800 to 1948 are listed by author with a title index. Entries include author, including cross-references from pseudo-

nyms, title, place of publication, publisher, year, pagination and subject code(s). The introduction and afterword explain the ground rules more fully. Bleiler says approximately one thousand of his listings are improperly omitted from Reginald [6-3], as does Currey [6-2], the only one of the three to include points of interest to the collector. An essential work for the collector and bibliographer.

6-2. Currey, L. W., comp. **Science Fiction and Fantasy Authors: A Bibliography of First Printings of Their Fiction and Selected Nonfiction**. G. K. Hall, 1979 (now available only from the compiler; see chapter 5).

A comprehensive and authoritative listing of more than 6,200 printings and editions of works published through June 1977 by 215 authors, from Wells to contemporary writers. Nonfantastic books by the authors are also listed, along with significant reference material published through mid-1979. This is the principal bibliography listing the points necessary to identify first editions or printings. Currey is continuing this bibliography in the form of interim author bibliographies in the *The New York Review of Science Fiction* (1988–   ). A work emphasizing scarce works published in the nineteenth and early twentieth centuries, with fuller notes, is George Locke's *A Spectrum of Fantasy* (Ferret Fantasy, 1980).

6-3. Reginald, R. **Science Fiction and Fantasy Literature: A Checklist, 1700–1974, with Contemporary Science Fiction Authors II**. 2 vols. Gale Research, 1979.

This work lists 15,884 books published in English from 1700 through 1974, excluding drama, verse and most children's books. Volume 2 is a biographical directory of 1,443 modern SF and fantasy authors, replacing the author's *Stella Nova* (1970). Books listed were examined and, if necessary, read to determine if they fell within the work's relatively elastic limits. More than 4,000 titles were rejected as unsuitable (see comment in Bleiler [6-1]). Biographical information was compiled from questionnaires from the authors or their estates whenever possible. The bibliographic entries are cross-referenced to the biographies. A series index by series title occupies thirty-four pages (largely superseded by Cottrill et al. [6-8]). Dated and very incomplete awards index. Title index. A supplement covering the 1975–86 period is in preparation, and will list more than 10,000 titles (this in little more than a decade), corrections and additions to earlier listings, and revisions and additions to the biographies. For large libraries. Compare Bleiler [6-1] and Currey [6-2].

*6-4. Tuck, Donald H(enry) (Australia). **The Encyclopedia of Science Fiction and Fantasy through 1968**. Advent, vol. 1, 1974; vol. 2, 1978; vol. 3, 1983.

Although increasingly dated, this is still a major bibliography, an outgrowth of the compiler's earlier works. The first two volumes include a who's who and works, listing contents of collections and anthologies, and frequently those of original magazine sources as well; fifty-two-page book title index. Volume 3 provides magazine checklists, extensive paperback information, pseudonyms, series and other information. Descriptive, sometimes evaluative comment accompanies all book listings. Although quite different from Bleiler [6-1], whose historical scope is wider, it represented a major advance in bibliographic control over fantastic literature, and credit is due its publisher for issuing it and keeping it in print.

6-5. Schlobin, Roger C. **The Literature of Fantasy: A Comprehensive Annotated Bibliography of Modern Fantasy**. Garland, 1979.
The nominal scope of this book is 1858 through mid-1979, although a few earlier titles are listed. The coverage is "restricted to adult fantasy and juvenile fantasy with strong adult appeal . . . primarily limited to prose works originally published in book form in the English language." A few foreign authors who have "conspicuously contributed to the Anglo-American literary tradition" are included, such as Calvino, Hoffmann and Singer. Horror literature is excluded "unless it contains material that would be of particular interest to the fantasy reader," which leaves a wide opening. The entries include a plot summary, but there is relatively little evaluation except that implied by the book's inclusion. Complete contents of 244 collections and 101 anthologies are listed, supplementing Contento [6-7]. Of the 800 authors of about 1,000 novels and collections, approximately a fifth have a bibliography cited. Series are annotated as a unit. Thorough author and title indexes. Moderately useful as a descriptive bibliography, but of little value as a critical guide for readers or libraries. Compare the far superior guide by Waggoner [6-34].

*6-6. Brown, Charles N., and William G. Contento, comps. **Science Fiction in Print: 1985**. Locus Press, 1986; **Science Fiction, Fantasy, & Horror: 1984, 1986, 1987, 1988**. Locus Press, 1987, 1988, 1989.
Locus [11-40] is the closest thing to a journal of record that English-language fantastic fiction has. These clothbound 8½×11-inch volumes cumulate and revise the Books Received listings in each issue, including both originals and reprints. The author list includes complete contents of collections, anthologies and fiction magazine issues, with pagination shown, and with original sources of publication if reprinted. A subject list divides the books into a variety of categories. Title index. The volume covering 1985 appeared first, followed by 1986, 1987, 1988 and 1988. The 1984 retrospective volume fills the gap between Contento [6-7] and the 1989 volume. Each successive volume has increased in size and thoroughness and introduced improvements in general layout. Surveys of the year and *Locus* reader poll results supplement the bibliography/indexes. An important, current bibliography.

*6-7. Contento, William G. **Index to Science Fiction Anthologies and Collections**. G. K. Hall, 1978; **Index to Science Fiction Anthologies and Collections 1977–1983**. G. K. Hall, 1984.
The first volume, which indexes 12,000 English-language stories by 2,500 authors in more than 1,900 anthologies and collections published through June 1977, is largely limited to SF. The supplement indexes about 8,550 short stories, 348 introductions, 506 poems and 22 plays. Some pre-1978 books and some weird, horror and suspense books are indexed. Although future supplements may appear, the indexing is continued in Brown and Contento [6-6]. Mike Ashley is working on an index to about 1,100 anthologies (no collections) of fantasy/supernatural short fiction. Schlobin [6-5] indexes 244 collections and 101 anthologies containing 3,610 stories. Bleiler [6-19] indexes 1,775 books, novels and collections, totaling about 7,200 individual stories, and provides the most detailed index.

6-8. Cottrill, Tim; Martin H. Greenberg; and Charles G. Waugh. **Science Fiction and Fantasy Series and Sequels: A Bibliography, Volume 1: Books**. Garland, 1986.

Building on works such as Reginald [6-3] and Tuck [6-4], this lists about 1,160 series and 6,600 books, mostly published from 1900 to 1985, by which time series had become extremely common, especially in mass-market paperbacks. Author, title, year, publisher and sequence in series are shown, with series and book title indexes. The series index in chapter 13 was built on this bibliography. Useful for larger libraries and specialty booksellers. Volume 2, which may never appear, is to be devoted to short fiction in series.

6-9. Hall, H. W. **Science Fiction Book Review Index, 1923-1973**. Gale Research, 1975; **Science Fiction Book Review Index, 1974-1979**. Gale Research, 1981; **Science Fiction and Fantasy Book Review Index, 1980-1984**. Gale Research, 1985.

Preceding Hall's companion secondary bibliography [6-10] were his valuable book review indexes, three cumulations of which have been published to date. The 1980-84 volume includes 16,000 author and subject citations to more than 4,700 books and articles, whose inclusion added considerably to the volume's cost and which were later included in the reference index. Hall publishes annual supplements (3608 Meadow Oaks Lane, Bryan, TX 77802), which are likely to be cumulated. Standard library book review indexes do not index the many specialty magazines Hall includes, and such reviews are often the only critical commentary available. For large libraries.

6-10. Hall, H. W. **Science Fiction and Fantasy Reference Index, 1878-1985**. 2 vols. Gale Research, 1987.

This is the most comprehensive single bibliography of the secondary literature devoted to SF and fantasy, including horror. About 19,000 books, articles, theses, interviews and audio-visual items are indexed by author (16,000 citations in vol. 1) and subject (27,000 citations in vol. 2). Approximately 1,400 entries are for non-English-language items. The emphasis is on SF, but fantasy and horror are not neglected. Most entries are from the post-1945 period, and probably 75% from the last two decades. Hall estimates that he has indexed only 50-60% of the material within his scope. Principal omissions are hundreds of fugitive fanzines, newspapers and out-of-the-way sources. (Some of the index's limitations are discussed in the review by Robert Philmus, *Science-Fiction Studies*, 15 [November 1988], 383-4.) A good starting point for the serious reader, but the set's high price will limit it to large libraries. Compare Tymn and Schlobin [6-11], which includes a number of citations not in Hall. Annual hardcover supplements to this set are compiled by Hall and issued by Borgo Press. Volume 7, 1988, was the first and covers 1986 publications. Annuals covering 1988 and later publications will be included in Brown and Contento [6-6].

6-11. Tymn, Marshall B., and Roger C. Schlobin, eds. **The Year's Scholarship in Science Fiction and Fantasy: 1972-1975**. Kent State, 1979.

This begins where Thomas Clareson's *Science Fiction Criticism* (Kent State, 1972) ended. Coverage is limited to American and British journals, selected fanzines, books and doctoral and master's theses. Supplements cover 1976-79 (1983), and 1980, 1981 and 1982 annuals, with 1983-88 bibliographies in

Extrapolation, an academic quarterly devoted to SF, and 1989 and later bibliographies in the *Journal of the Fantastic in the Arts* [11-39]. The pre-journal listings are briefly annotated. Heavily overlaps Hall [6-10], but there are enough unique entries to make consultation of both necessary.

Gothic Literature

*6-12. Frank, Frederick S. **Guide to the Gothic: An Annotated Bibliography of Criticism**. Scarecrow, 1984.
Frank is one of the foremost scholars of the Gothic, whose literature is vast. He focuses on nineteenth- and twentieth-century authors in the 2,508 numbered citations (38 of them for earlier guides), each usefully annotated, mostly descriptively, occasionally critically. Although he emphasizes the classic Gothic period, he treats late nineteenth-century and twentieth-century authors as well. A very useful starting point, continued in his 1988 bibliography [6-13]. Also annotated as [H7-81].

6-13. Frank, Frederick S. **Gothic Fiction: A Master List of Twentieth Century Criticism and Research**. Meckler, 1988.
This unannotated bibliography cites 2,491 articles, dissertations and books, most of them published in the last twenty years. Academic interest is strong—almost one-fourth of the entries are dissertations. The citations are grouped into thirteen categories, with the four chapters devoted to English Gothic fiction containing 1,497 citations. American Gothic citations total 600, including contemporary authors such as King. Other chapters survey European Gothics, werewolves and vampires and books about Gothic (horror) films. Index of critics and of authors and artists. The listing is current but necessarily selective, since entire books have been devoted to some of the subject authors, from Walpole and Shelley to Lovecraft and King. This newest listing adds about 200 citations to the 1984 work. Gothic specialists will want both books, but most libraries will find the annotated guide sufficient. Also annotated as [H7-83].

*6-14. Frank, Frederick S. **The First Gothics: A Critical Guide to the English Gothic Novel**. Garland, 1987.
From the 4,500 to 5,000 Gothic novels and chapbooks published between 1764 and 1820 Frank has selected 500 which meet several criteria: contemporary availability, artistic uniqueness or historical importance or popularity, and value in showing the development of Gothic fiction. Entries are by author with first edition shown, modern reprints (if any), type of Gothic, secondary sources and a 100 to 500 word critical synopsis. Appendixes include a useful glossary of Gothic terms, a selected bibliography of criticism and a chronology. Indexes by author, title and critic. Fourteen reproductions of engravings and woodcuts add a period feel. Titles annotated in the horror volume of this set are keyed to the fuller discussions in *The First Gothics* (see preface). Frank's chapter in Tymn [6-33] annotated 422 novels. A valuable guide for the serious student and larger library.

6-15. McNutt, Dan J. **The Eighteenth-Century Gothic Novel: An Annotated Bibliography of Criticism and Selected Texts**. Garland, 1975.
A useful guide, albeit growing dated, to the huge literature of the Gothic. Chapters include bibliographies and research guides; literary, psychological,

social and scientific backgrounds; general and specific studies; and chapters on such authors as Horace Walpole, Clara Reeve and Charlotte Smith. The approximately 1,000 entries are succinctly annotated. Compare the more current Frank bibliographies [6-12–6-13] and the more recent bibliographic guide by Fisher [H7-81].

6-16. Radcliffe, Elsa J. **Gothic Novels of the Twentieth Century: An Annotated Bibliography**. Scarecrow, 1979.
Only about one-fourth of the nearly 2,000 titles in this checklist are annotated. Many titles are fantasy, SF or straight mysteries, and others are doubtful as Gothics. Biographical data are often dated, and unreliable secondary sources were often used to compile bibliographic data. Many suitable titles were omitted. Used cautiously, this can be of use to the more knowledgeable reader exploring this relatively unmapped region of Gothic fiction.

6-17. Tracy, Anne B. **The Gothic Novel, 1790–1830: Plot Summaries and Index to Motifs**. Univ. Press of Kentucky, 1981.
Plot summaries of 208 works, motif index, index of characters, title index. Apparently derived from a 1974 doctoral thesis. Less useful and less knowledgeable than Frank's much more comprehensive chapter in Tymn [6-33] or his *The First Gothics* [6-14].

Biocritical Works

6-18. Ashley, Mike. **Who's Who in Horror and Fantasy Fiction**. Elm Tree Press, 1977.
Approximately 400 authors are briefly profiled, from Antoine Galland (1646–1715), translator of the *Arabian Nights* [1-23] to writers who had achieved moderate prominence by the 1970s, such as Stephen King. The entries range from a short paragraph to a bit more than a page and blend biographical details with descriptive and evaluative comments about key novels, collections and individual stories. Pseudonyms and cross-references are included. Supplementing the 171 pages of biocritical entries are a chronology (*Gilgamesh* to 1977), keyed to the main entries, a title index to key novels and stories, a selective listing with partial contents of weird fiction anthologies, brief profiles of U.S. and British pulp magazines (greatly expanded in the authoritative volume co-edited by Tymn [11-54], a few awards and a bibliography. One of the earlier such works, anticipated by the more comprehensive Tuck [6-4] and followed by the recent work by Sullivan [6-31].

*6-19. Bleiler, Everett F. **The Guide to Supernatural Fiction**. Kent State, 1983.
This comprehensive guide (732 8½x11-inch pages) represents more than twenty-five years of reading and reflection. In a sense it is an expansion of his checklist [6-1], excluding science fiction, the subject of a forthcoming companion guide. The subtitle reads "A full description of 1,775 books from 1750 to 1960, including ghost stories, weird fiction, stories of supernatural horror, fantasy, Gothic novels, occult fiction, and similar literature." The 1960 date includes stories published by that year in magazines but later in books. Novels and short fiction total about

7,200 individual stories. An individual story is described and evaluated, often acerbically, only once, although cited each time it appears. Arrangement is by author, then chronologically. Biographical notes precede the numbered entries. In addition to the author and book story title indexes is a fifty-three-page motif index to what Bleiler prefers to call contranatural (rather than supernatural) fiction. This could be very valuable to librarians seeking to identify a half-remembered tale, or to anyone wishing to explore an evolving theme. A major reference work to which references are made for fiction authors (see preface).

*6-20. Bleiler, Everett F., ed. **Supernatural Fiction Writers: Fantasy and Horror**. 2 vols. Scribner, 1985.
A major reference work which provides a comprehensive overview of the works of 148 authors, from Apuleius (AD second century) to Arthurian romances to today's writers. The expertise of sixty-one contributors has been carefully edited to provide clear, balanced essays including biography, description and evaluation of major works, and an assessment of the author's historical position. The essays are arranged roughly chronologically or by nationality (American, French, British, German), and each contains a selective primary and secondary bibliography. Many essays treat writers rarely or never discussed in such detail. Coverage is limited to selected Western literatures, excluding Italian, Spanish, Russian and Asian. Its scope is still wide and it is an essential contribution to its subject. Thoroughly indexed. Cross-referenced in this guide (see preface).

6-21. Cawthorn, James, and Michael Moorcock (U.K.). **Fantasy: The 100 Best Books**. Xanadu; Carroll & Graf, 1988.

6-22. Jones, Stephen, and Kim Newman. (U.K.), eds. **Horror: 100 Best Books**. Xanadu; Carroll & Graf, 1988.

6-23. Pringle, David (U.K.). **Modern Fantasy: The Hundred Best Novels, an English-Language Selection, 1946–1987**. Grafton, 1988; Peter Bedrick, 1989.
The "100 best" series began in 1985 with Pringle's excellent volume on post-World War II SF. The quality is sustained in the fantasy guide, most of whose works were also selected for evaluation in this guide. Only twenty-four of Pringle's choices are discussed in Cawthorn's equivalent years. The two-page essays average 600–700 words in Pringle, sometimes reaching 800–1,000 words in the other volumes. Most essays include plot summary and varying amounts of bio-critical comment, with Pringle including quotations to suggest the novel's tone and the author's skill with language. Cawthorn, who wrote most of the entries, has selected from a much larger historical sample than Pringle, and the average quality of his selections may be judged better. Most of his selections are evaluated in this guide. The three guides largely exclude translated works, although Jones has four. Most young adult works are excluded save for a few by key authors like Le Guin and Garner. The essays in Jones are interesting, even when one's interest is in the critic as much as the work. The horror volume evaluations were written by 100 individual authors, almost all currently active writers. All critics are profiled, each entry has a headnote, a list of recommended books beyond the basic 100 is provided, but there is no author or title index. Within their self-imposed limitations, of which the most serious is a bias toward books of the last forty

years, these are useful guides which many libraries should acquire. All three are cross-referenced to the fiction authors in this guide (see preface). Pringle is also annotated as [F7-46].

*6-24. Magill, Frank N., ed. **Survey of Modern Fantasy Literature**. 5 vols. Salem Press, 1983.
This is a companion to the 1979 set devoted to SF. It contains about 500 essays on books by 341 authors of fantasy and horror literature. Lesser titles receive about 1,000 words, most titles about 2,000, with series, trilogies and major works 3,000–10,000. Each essay has a bibliography. Volume 5 contains nineteen topical essays (theories of fantasy, witchcraft, nineteenth-century religious fantasy, fantasy games as folk literature, etc.), a chronology from 1764 to 1981, an annotated bibliography of secondary book-length literature, a list of anthologies and a detailed index. Cross-referenced to the fiction authors in this guide (see preface). A major reference work whose price will limit it to the largest libraries.

6-25. Cowart, David, and Thomas L. Wymer, eds. **Twentieth-Century American Science-Fiction Writers**. 2 vols. Gale Research, 1981. Dictionary of Literary Biography, vol. 8.
Of the ninety biocritical essays about authors who began writing after 1900 and before 1970, a number also write fantasy, such as Anthony, Bradbury, Bradley, Burroughs, de Camp, Disch, Ellison, Farmer, Jack Finney, Kuttner, Lafferty, Le Guin, Leiber, Matheson, C. L. Moore, Norton, Saberhagen, Silverberg, Sturgeon, Vance, Williamson and Zelazny. The emphasis of each three- to sixteen-page essay is on the SF, but there is brief discussion of fantasy writings. Compare the much more comprehensive compilation by Smith [6-30]. Cross-referenced to the fiction authors in this guide (see preface).

6-26. Gunn, James, ed. **The New Encyclopedia of Science Fiction**. Viking, 1988.

6-27. Nicholls, Peter (U.K.), general ed. **The Science Fiction Encyclopedia**. Doubleday, 1979. U.K. title: *The Encyclopedia of Science Fiction*. Granada, 1979.
These encyclopedias have hundreds of author entries (Nicholls has 3.5 times as many, about 1,800), and many of these authors write fantasy and sometimes horror fiction as well as SF. The Nicholls volume has 1.7 times the text of Gunn, more entries in almost every category, and equivalent entries are more detailed, as well as being more evaluative rather than simply descriptive. Gunn has almost as many film entries as Nicholls, a grotesque imbalance given Gunn's length. Gunn's greatest merit is its currency, and the inclusion of a number of significant contemporary authors. It is attractively designed on good paper and should be acquired by most libraries, but it isn't the pioneering work Nicholls was, nor is its scope or critical rigor equal to that of its Hugo-winning predecessor. Both are cross-referenced to the fiction author entries (see preface).

6-28. Rosenberg, Betty. **Genreflecting: A Guide to Reading Interests in Genre Fiction**. 2d ed. Libraries Unlimited, 1986.
Chapter 1 gives an overview of genre fiction and libraries' responsibilities in reader advisory services. The remaining six chapters survey westerns, thrillers, romances, SF, fantasy and horror. The genre chapters list books under Themes and Types, then by topic—anthologies, bibliographies, encyclopedias, history

and criticism, background, awards, etc. Many of the nonfiction books are descriptively, sometimes critically annotated, but often too briefly to judge their relative merit. Some weak books receive extraordinarily long listings, e.g., J. B. Post's *An Atlas of Fantasy* (see [6-39]). Indexes to genre authors, to genre themes and to secondary materials. The revised edition emphasizes books available in hardcover. A very uneven guide with many gaps.

6-29. Searles, Baird; Beth Meacham; and Michael Franklin. **A Reader's Guide to Fantasy**. Avon, 1982.
Three former staff members of New York's The Science Fiction Shop prepared two guides, one to SF, one to fantasy, designed for buyers or browsers at the shop and for any interested reader. The author profiles, from Richard Adams to Roger Zelazny, occupy 145 of the 216 pages. The emphasis is mostly on fantasy rather than horror fiction, but King, Stoker and a few other primarily horror writers are included. Readers who like more of the same will find useful the twenty-two-page series listing, as well as the division of books into six broad thematic categories. A best books list and a list of winners of three awards conclude the book. An original paperback, now out of print, it was useful for several years, although it includes far too many minor authors, lacks critical rigor and is growing increasingly dated.

6-30. Smith, Curtis C., ed. **Twentieth-Century Science-Fiction Writers**. 2d ed. St. James Press, 1986.
A number of the 614 SF writers profiled here also write fantasy, and this compilation is therefore cross-referenced to this guide (see preface). A supplement profiles five "major fantasy writers"—Dunsany, Eddison, Morris, Peake and Tolkien. Coverage of authors specializing in YA fiction is weak. The bibliographies must be used with caution; inaccuracies and errors are common. A valuable biocritical guide to SF writers but, like Cowart and Wymer [6-25] and the two encyclopedias [6-26, 6-27], marginal for fantasy.

***6-31**. Sullivan, Jack, ed. **The Penguin Encyclopedia of Horror and the Supernatural**. Viking, 1986.
This is the first such encyclopedia, a measure of the increasingly widespread popularity of the literature of fear, supernatural or psychological. Sullivan, who has capably written about ghost stories and related topics, and his sixty-five contributors have provided a comprehensive, readable, accurate survey, enlivened by 300 black-and-white illustrations. The 600 signed entries cover approximately 405 individuals (writers, artists/illustrators, actors, directors, composers, etc.), about 150 films and fifty-four thematic entries, such as books into film, *femme fatale*, horror and science fiction, mad doctors, opera, possession, the supernatural and writers of today (this last entry mentions many dozens of writers in addition to those who are subjects of the individual entries). Abundant cross-references enhance reference use.

6-32. Tymn, Marshall B.; Kenneth J. Zahorski; and Robert H. Boyer. **Fantasy Literature: A Core Collection and Reference Guide**. Bowker, 1979.
Boyer and Zahorski explain the rationale for their selections in a thirty-six-page chapter. They favor "high" fantasy, the creation of self-contained Secondary Worlds in which the dominant emotions for the reader are awe and wonder, and

the style is "elevated." Various subdivisions are examined, such as myth and fairy tale fantasy, Gothic fantasy (low and high), science fantasy, and sword-and-sorcery/heroic fantasy. The core collection consists of 208 novels and collections, 1858–1978, and sixteen anthologies, many of them original paperbacks published since 1960. The annotations vary from a short paragraph to about one page and mix plot summary (often excessive) with generally favorable evaluation (this core collection is by definition recommended). The restrictive selection criteria used by Boyer and Zahorski were explicitly rejected for these guides, although many of their selections will also be found here, and cross-references to this guide are made in the fiction author entries (see preface). The chapters by Tymn are badly dated. Articles as well as books are briefly annotated. Organizations, awards and library collections are described briefly.

6-33. Tymn, Marshall B., ed. **Horror Literature: A Core Collection and Reference Guide**. Bowker, 1981.

Four chapters, from Gothic works to 1980, survey almost 1,100 novels, collections and anthologies. Robert Weinberg surveys the horror pulps, 1933–40, excluding *Weird Tales* [11-20], the best and best known of such pulps. Supernatural verse in English is analyzed in detail, in a thirty-five-page introduction preceding sixty-four annotations. Other chapters survey author studies, reference works, criticism, with lists of periodicals, societies, awards and library collections. Core collection checklist selected by contributors only; no outside readers were used.

This guide, patterned after my *Anatomy of Wonder*, lacked careful editorial guidance and thus critical rigor and balance. There are seventeen Blackwood collections, heavily overlapping, all starred as core titles. The anthology annotations merely list contents and lack any critical comment. The chapter on Gothic fiction, 173 pages, 422 annotations, is almost twice the length of the chapter on the modern masters (1920–80), 94 pages, 310 annotations, a gross imbalance which ill serves readers and libraries. The guide you are reading and its companion were partly designed to avoid the deficiencies of this and of *Fantasy Literature* [6-32].

*6-34. Waggoner, Diana. **The Hills of Faraway: A Guide to Fantasy**. Atheneum, 1978.

Although only a decade old, one of the earliest relatively comprehensive studies of fantasy, adult and children's, generally excluding horror. Her touchstones are Tolkien's long essay, "On Fairy-Stories" (see [F7-62]), and Northrop Frye's influential *Anatomy of Criticism* (1957), which provide her theoretical framework and vocabulary, outlined in chapter 1. Chapter 2 discusses "eight major trends or strains" in fantasy: mythopoeic, heroic, adventurous, ironic, comic, nostalgic, sentimental and horrific, with many examples cited. A different arrangement is later presented in which subgenres of fantasy are outlined and in which all books later annotated are discussed. The 178-page bibliographic guide is arranged by author, with each of the 996 entries numbered and used in the various indexes. Citations to secondary literature about many authors follow the fiction annotations. Indexes to names, terms, illustrators and titles.

Adult and nominally children's fantasy is included, with most picture books excluded. The annotations are vigorously and clearly written, often acerbic, and effectively blend plot summary and intelligent evaluation. There are some bibliographic inaccuracies and omissions, but these are more than offset by the work's scope, clarity and forceful writing. A first-rate guide, far better than Schlobin [6-5] and Tymn et al [6-32].

Other Works

6-35. Burgess, Michael. **A Guide to Science Fiction and Fantasy in the Library of Congress Classification Scheme**. 2d ed., rev. & exp. Borgo Press, 1988.
Burgess, whose bibliographic alter ego is R. Reginald [6-3], is a cataloger. This second edition is considerably revised from the 1984 first edition, notably in the ninety-two-page list of authors (almost twice as many) and literature class numbers, when assigned (about 40% lack such numbers, mostly authors who have written only original paperbacks, which LC only infrequently catalogs). Also revised is the list of SF and fantasy/horror subject headings, the classification schedules (not only literature but art, film, etc.) with an alphabetical index to the class numbers. The introductions to each chapter note the inconsistencies which have developed over the years. Companion volumes to mystery/detective and western fiction are also available. Mostly of interest to a few catalogers and to those using large LC-classed collections of fantastic literature.

6-36. Collins, Robert A., and Robert Latham, eds. **Science Fiction & Fantasy Book Review Annual 1988**. Meckler, 1988.
When Meckler folded *Fantasy Review* [11-32] they decided to continue with an annual, reprinting most of the reviews in the *SFRA Newsletter* (see chapter 13) along with many previously unpublished reviews. The first annual includes reviews of 441 books of adult fiction, 33 YA titles, and 73 nonfiction works, almost all originals. Also included is a profile of Orson Scott Card and critical surveys of SF, fantasy, horror and nonfiction. Title index. Too many poor books were reviewed, many of them original paperbacks which were out of print by the time this annual appeared. Future volumes may have a different mix more useful to libraries. Compare the bibliographic surveys issued by *Locus* [6-6].

6-37. Hall, H. W., ed. **Science/Fiction Collections: Fantasy, Supernatural and Weird Tales**. Haworth Press, 1983.
Hall was the guest editor of this issue of *Special Collections* (vol. 2, no. 1/2), available separately as an overpriced hardcover. Chapters are devoted to seven public collections (see chapter 12, whose pertinent entries are cross-referenced to these descriptions), two large private collections, a short history of SF specialty publishers, a dated essay on the bibliographic control of fantastic literature, an essay on the cataloging and classification of SF and a dated list of specialty dealers. Most valuable for the detailed descriptions of the public collections. Libraries receiving the journal will have received this on subscription; others can safely ignore.

6-38. Inge, M. Thomas, ed. **Handbook of American Popular Literature**. Greenwood, 1988.
This spinoff from Inge's *Handbook of American Popular Culture* (3 vols., 1979–81, second ed., 1989) includes revisions of ten chapters in the earlier work plus five new essays. Each chapter includes a brief introduction, historical outline, discus-

sion of key reference works, a description of major library collections, a critical and descriptive survey of the principal historical and critical works, and a bibliography of books, articles, indexes and key periodicals. Roger Schlobin's chapter on fantasy literature excludes horror, which is also largely ignored in Kay Mussell's chapter on Gothic novels, an oversight which should be corrected in a future edition. The survey is broad, current, often fascinating, although it's peripheral to the study of fantasy and horror fiction.

6-39. Manguel, Alberto, and Gianni Guadalupi. **The Dictionary of Imaginary Places**. Macmillan, 1980. Rev. ed., Harvest/Harcourt, 1987.
Some of the approximately 1,250 entries in this dictionary compiled by two European scholars will be familiar—Oz, Shangri-La, Narnia—but more will not. The alphabetical entries range from a short paragraph to almost three large three-column pages (Peake's Gormenghast, for example). Many cross-references link entries, and the author, title and year of the source book are cited at the end of each entry. Illustrations by Graham Greenfield and excellent maps and charts complement the text, which is clearly and interestingly written. There is a relatively heavy emphasis on traditional European literature, and many works are esoteric indeed. Most SF is excluded, since works set on other planets are excluded. Lovecraft's sinister towns are here, but no locales from Dunsany or Clark Ashton Smith, which may have been judged too unearthly. The expanded edition, a trade paperback, adds fourteen pages and several dozen entries. Index by author, title and locale. An interesting, inevitably incomplete compilation which rewards casual browsing. Vastly superior to the only comparable work, J. B. Post's *An Atlas of Fantasy* (1973; rev. ed., 1979).

*6-40. Wolfe, Gary K. **Critical Terms for Science Fiction and Fantasy: A Glossary and Guide to Scholarship**. Greenwood, 1986.
Academics from various disciplines entered the critical ranks of fantastic literature beginning in the 1950s, bringing their special vocabularies and backgrounds. A valuable introduction traces the historical development of fantasy and SF critical discourse. Approximately three-fourths of this book is devoted to a glossary of almost 500 terms and concepts, ranging from brief definitions to short essays, keyed to a secondary bibliography and to authors of cited fiction. Most of the specialized terms used by this guide's contributors are included. Clear and concise and a most welcome and long overdue work that all libraries should consider.

7

History
and
Criticism

Gary K. Wolfe

—

The evolution of modern fantasy criticism is, in a sense, a garden of forking paths, and one which closely resembles the evolution of the genre itself. Although speculations about the role of the fantastic in literature were common enough during the Romantic period, especially in England and Germany, fantasy itself did not emerge as a definable genre until the nineteenth century. When the novel of domestic realism became such a dominant force in fiction, a means of clearly separating this mode from the fantastic writing that flourished at the same time seemed not only convenient but also necessary. But despite occasional essays by George MacDonald, William Morris, Oscar Wilde and others, fantasy for the most part was treated by critics and reviewers as an anomaly. Fiction, like technology, was incorporated into the Victorian ideal of Progress, and fantastic fiction often seemed a throwback to an earlier era of fairy tales and myths. An anonymous essay in *The Westminster Review* in 1853 (titled, appropriately, "The Progress of Fiction as an Art") argued that "a scientific, and somewhat sceptical age, has no longer the power of believing in the marvels which delighted our ruder ancestors." The fantastic, when it was mentioned at all, was usually mentioned in the context of children's literature. This situation obtained during much of the late nineteenth and early twentieth centuries.

The major exception to this trend could be found in essays by practicing authors. George MacDonald's 1893 essay "The Fantastic Imagination" disputed the notion that fantasy was only for children, and served as a kind of defense of his own very important contributions to the genre. G. K. Chesterton, in his 1908 volume *Orthodoxy*, included a chapter entitled "The Ethics of Elfland," which argued for the moral and ethical significance of the fantastic. E. M. Forster's influential *Aspects of the Novel* (1927) elevated fantasy (and what he called "prophecy") to the status of a major fictional technique or mode, an idea which has since been echoed by modern critics such as Eric S. Rabkin and Kathryn Hume. And in what might be regarded as the first conscious attempt at generating a critical dialogue on the fantastic, the Oxford group which came to be known as the "Inklings" collectively produced a considerable number of essays and theoretical manifestos during the 1930s and 1940s. Charles Williams, C. S. Lewis and J. R. R. Tolkien all wrote provocatively about the uses of fantasy, illustrating their theories with their own popular and enduring fiction. The most famous of the essays they produced—Tolkien's "On Fairy-Stories"—remains today one of the most widely cited critical texts in the field. Both that essay and Lewis's shorter but almost equally significant "On Stories" appeared in the 1947 Oxford University Press volume *Essays Presented to Charles Williams*.

With the Inklings, the first of our forking paths begins to diverge; fantasy is finally treated on its own terms, and not merely as an offshoot of the dominant mode of realism. Ironically, it was also Lewis, by his occasional mentions of science fiction, who helped establish the conditions for the next fork in the road. Science fiction, long treated as a branch of fantasy (not only by Lewis but by such later structuralist critics as Tzvetan Todorov), would eventually gain such popularity among academics that the study of fantasy would almost be subsumed by it. Not until the mid-1970s, with the publication of C. N. Manlove's *Modern Fantasy: Five Studies* [7-39], Eric S. Rabkin's *The Fantastic in Literature* [7-47] and W. R. Irwin's *The Game of the Impossible* [7-24], would the criticism of science fiction and fantasy again begin to take different directions, and not until the 1980s would the criticism of horror and supernatural fiction diverge again from fantasy scholarship to partially rejoin the long tradition of studies of Gothic and supernatural fiction.

It is likely that none of these developments would have taken place had it not been for a general change in the academic climate, and in critical attitudes toward the fantastic. Part of this may be ascribed to the immense popularity of Tolkien's *Lord of the Rings* trilogy [3-340] during the 1960s, but other factors may be of almost equal importance. One is the increased use of fantastic elements in the work of such "mainstream" authors as Thomas Pynchon, John Barth, Robert Coover, Vladimir Nabokov and Doris Lessing. Another is the popularity of the related genre of science fiction, and the occasional elevation of a "science fiction writer" such as Kurt Vonnegut to the ranks of the mainstream. Popular culture in general experienced a growth in respectability during this time, making fantasy a more academically "safe" arena for scholarship than it had previously been; this growing respectability may have in turn been due to the newer critical methodologies of structuralism, post-structuralism, Marxism and feminism—all of which tended to shift the focus of critical thought from established canons of masterworks to audiences and cultural matrices. Finally, there emerged a limited but valuable dialogue—both in fantasy and science fiction studies—between the populist "fan" press, which had vigorously debated the merits of various kinds of fantastic writing for decades, and the academic community.

Today, then, the scholar of fantasy can consult texts ranging from Lin Carter's cheerful "this-is-what-you-ought-to-read-next" guidebook *Imaginary Worlds* [7-10] to Christine Brooke-Rose's dense and highly theoretical *A Rhetoric of the Unreal* [7-8], from the broadly interdisciplinary collections of essays from the International Conference on the Fantastic in the Arts (see chapter 13) to detailed studies of individual authors such as Fritz Leiber or Ursula K. Le Guin. One can explore fantasy as a basic mode of narrative available to all authors (in Rabkin's *The Fantastic in Literature* [7-47] or Hume's *Fantasy and Mimesis* [7-23]) or as a distinct subgenre with clear outlines (as in de Camp's *Literary Swordsmen and Sorcerers* [7-17]). Most important, the student of fantasy must be willing to acknowledge the potential value of all such texts, and recognize that the fan's memoir may well contain information available nowhere else, or that the theorist's obscurantist prose may provide valuable new ways of looking at a text.

Fantasy scholarship today, as the cliché goes, is in a state of flux. While some will argue that fantasy and science fiction, or fantasy and horror fiction, are diametrical opposites, others will maintain that all such literature descends from the same imaginative and psychological sources. While some will argue that fantasy is notable primarily as a technique "discovered" by postmodernist writers, others will claim that the genre *is* the mainstream, and that realistic or descriptive fiction is only an aberration of the last century or two (see the introduction to chapter 1). There is no agreed-upon canon of fantasy works to discuss, and no agreed-upon definition of what fantasy is, exactly (although it seems likely that most critics hold in mind a kind of "benchmark" text, such as Tolkien's *Lord of the Rings*, against which to measure other works). In other words, fantasy criticism is no more easily located than is fantasy itself, and this is in part what makes it such a challenging and dynamic field in which to work.

Bibliography

7-1. Apter, T. E. **Fantasy Literature: An Approach to Reality**. Indiana Univ. Press, 1982.
Essentially an extended critique of traditional psychoanalytical notions of the function of fantasy, Apter's study attempts to show that authors use fantasy to extend and elucidate psychological realities, rather than to disguise them. She illustrates this with often persuasive and insightful readings of works by Conrad, Hawthorne, Poe, Hoffmann, Stevenson, Kafka, Nabokov and Borges.

*7-2. Attebery, Brian. **The Fantasy Tradition in American Literature: From Irving to Le Guin**. Indiana Univ. Press, 1980.
This unusually comprehensive and well-written study represents the first major attempt to locate fantasy in the American literary tradition. Following an introduction which provides a useful overview of fantasy theory, Attebery surveys the role of fantasy in American folk tradition; the romances of Washington Irving, Nathaniel Hawthorne and Herman Melville; and the works of Edgar Allan Poe, Mark Twain, L. Frank Baum, Edgar Rice Burroughs, James Branch Cabell, H. P. Lovecraft, Ray Bradbury and others. His coverage includes children's literature

and authors little discussed in the context of fantasy, such as Edward Eager and James Thurber. Finally, a chapter on the resurgence of fantasy after Tolkien discusses contemporary authors such as Roger Zelazny, Peter Beagle and especially Ursula K. Le Guin. The chapters on Baum and his followers are especially strong, and the study as a whole is something of a landmark, strongly recommended.

7-3. Bettelheim, Bruno. **The Uses of Enchantment: The Meaning and Importance of Fairy Tales**. Knopf, 1976.
Bettelheim received the National Book Award for this psychoanalytical account of the functions of fairy tales in the development of the child's moral consciousness. Although the work generated renewed interest in fantasy and folklore among educators and psychologists, some scholars in the field have criticized it for oversimplification and moralizing. Bettelheim's argument—that fairy tales symbolically address childhood anxieties and provide attractive models for healthy psychological development—had never before been made in such clinical detail and with such close readings of individual works. It nevertheless can occasionally be misleading to readers unfamiliar with the social and economic conditions surrounding the evolution of such tales. Compare Max Lüthi, *Once Upon a Time* [7-36].

7-4. Boyer, Robert H., and Kenneth J. Zahorski, eds. **Fantasists on Fantasy: A Collection of Critical Reflections by Eighteen Masters of the Art**. Ballantine, 1984.
A useful collection of twenty-two pieces on fantasy by authors ranging from George MacDonald and G. K. Chesterton to Michael Moorcock and Susan Cooper. Predictably, the focus of most of the essays is on method rather than critical theory, and the selection is weighted toward contemporary authors, but the volume is indispensable as the first historical anthology of fantasy criticism. Introductions to each piece by the editors succinctly place each essay in the context of the author's overall body of work.

7-5. Briggs, K(atharine) M(ary) (U.K.). **The Anatomy of Puck: An Examination of Fairy Beliefs among Shakespeare's Contemporaries and Successors**. Routledge and Kegan Paul, 1959.
The first of Briggs's erudite studies of the folklore of the supernatural in literature focuses on the Elizabethan and Jacobean periods, and includes discussions not only of fairies, but also of hobgoblins, devils, ghosts, mermaids, monsters and "spiritual creatures." Although Briggs does not specifically focus on fantasy as a literary form, her book is an invaluable resource for both scholars and would-be fantasists, with appendixes covering varieties of fairies, spells and charms, contemporary accounts of fairy experiences, and fairy tales.

7-6. Briggs, K(atharine) M(ary) (U.K.). **The Fairies in Tradition and Literature**. Routledge and Kegan Paul, 1967.
In this continuation of *The Anatomy of Puck*, Briggs extends her discussion of fairy lore in literature into the twentieth century. As in the earlier volume, the focus is more on expressions of regional folklore than on literary technique, but Briggs touches upon a large number of all-but-forgotten fantasy texts, and her scholarship is impeccable.

7-7. Briggs, K(atharine) M(ary) (U.K.). **Pale Hecate's Team: An Examination of the Beliefs on Witchcraft and Magic among Shakespeare's Contemporaries and His Immediate Successors**. Routledge and Kegan Paul, 1962.
This companion volume to *The Anatomy of Puck* explores the folklore of witchcraft, devils, imps and magicians in the literature of the Elizabethan and Jacobean periods. For students of later fantasy and supernatural fiction, the volume is especially valuable as a historical resource, and includes Briggs's usual assortment of fascinating appendixes of spells, terminology and folktales.

7-8. Brooke-Rose, Christine (U.K.). **A Rhetoric of the Unreal: Studies in Narrative and Structure, Especially of the Fantastic**. Cambridge, 1981.
The author of this densely written theoretical study is a critic and novelist whose interests range from post-structuralist models of encoding and intertextuality to a writer's concern with strategy and rhetoric. Although some will find her style here almost unreadable, Brooke-Rose does bring to bear on fantastic literature a wide spectrum of contemporary critical theory, and her book is extremely useful in that regard. Her choice of illustrative texts is somewhat eccentric, and her familiarity with genre literature somewhat limited, but discussions of such authors as Henry James, Washington Irving and Joseph McElroy are frequently illuminating.

7-9. Carpenter, Humphrey (U.K.). **The Inklings**. Allen & Unwin, 1978.
Carpenter followed up his earlier successful biography of J. R. R. Tolkien [8-85] with this more generalized study of the remarkable group of Oxford fantasists which included not only Tolkien, but also C. S. Lewis, Charles Williams and occasionally others such as John Wain and Nevill Coghill. This collective biography remains the definitive account of this group, and Carpenter's usual skill at combining exhaustive research with compelling narration makes this one of the most useful studies of fantasy writers in their intellectual and moral contexts.

7-10. Carter, Lin. **Imaginary Worlds: The Art of Fantasy**. Ballantine, 1973.
A pioneering, if flawed, popular study of the history of genre fantasy, rather heavily focusing on authors featured in the Ballantine Adult Fantasy series, which was in its fifth year when this study appeared. Carter's style is chatty and given to dramatic overgeneralizations, but it does capture the appeal of fantasy to the general reader, and provides a useful guide to the works of "classic fantasy" which characterized the revival of interest in the genre in the late 1960s. With notes, bibliographies and an index.

7-11. Cawelti, John. **Adventure, Mystery, and Romance: Formula Stories as Art and Popular Culture**. Univ. of Chicago Press, 1976.
Although Cawelti does not address genre fantasy as such—his focus is on the detective story, the hard-boiled novel, the western and what he calls the "social melodrama"—this classic study of popular formula narratives is of considerable interest because of its opening chapters, delineating the concept of "formula" as it relates both to literary form and to cultural expression. His important distinction between "moral" and "physical" fantasy deserves greater attention than it has received.

7-12. Chanady, Amaryll Beatrice. **Magic Realism and the Fantastic: Resolved versus Unresolved Antinomy.** Garland, 1985.
Arguing that magic realism and the fantastic are distinct modes of writing (rather than true genres) differentiated by the manner in which they present the supernatural/natural "antinomy," Chanady proceeds to explore this distinction largely in terms of reader-response theory. Despite some of the denseness characteristic of revised doctoral dissertations, this study is one of the few serious attempts to discuss the rather vaguely defined "magic realism" movement in the context of literary theories of the fantastic.

7-13. Clark, Beverly Lyon. **Reflections of Fantasy: The Mirror Worlds of Carroll, Nabokov, and Pynchon.** Peter Lang, 1986.
Defining "mirror-world fantasy" as narratives in which a fully realized nonrealistic world is juxtaposed to a realistic one, Clark focuses on Carroll's *Alice* books [2-23], Nabokov's *Pale Fire* and *Ada* and Pynchon's *The Crying of Lot 49* [4A-212]. Although there are some useful insights on the rhetoric of fantasy in general, the most interesting parts of the book are a discussion of Nabokov's Russian translation of Carroll and one of the few analyses of Nabokov's *Ada* as a major work of fantasy.

7-14. Collings, Michael R., ed. **Reflections on the Fantastic: Selected Essays from the Fourth International Conference on the Fantastic in the Arts.** Greenwood, 1986.
Relatively slim by the standards of the ICFA proceedings volumes, this collection nevertheless contains a perceptive essay by Brian Attebery on fantasy as an anti-utopian mode as well as author studies of Peter Beagle, Alain Robbe-Grillet, Felix Labisse, Amado Nervo and José Maria Merino (five other essays deal with science fiction, and one with "Swiss animal satire"). Like some other volumes in this series, the collection suffers from diffuseness, but offers discussions of comparative literature which are all too rare in more focused studies. (See 7-15 for general note on this series.)

7-15. Collins, Robert A., and Howard D. Pearce, eds. **The Scope of the Fantastic. Vol. 1: Theory, Technique, Major Authors; Vol. 2: Culture, Biography, Themes, Children's Literature.** Greenwood, 1985.
In 1980, Florida Atlantic University hosted the first of a series of broadly interdisciplinary conferences on the general theme of "the fantastic," and in 1985 Greenwood Press began publishing selections of papers from the annual conferences. What makes for an invigorating conference may seem less focused in book form, however, and this has been a continuing problem with the Greenwood volumes. These first two volumes, including nearly sixty essays, remain among the strongest in the series, perhaps in part because the search for definitions recurs in so many of the essays. The sections on theory and technique (which might well include the excellent overall introduction by Eric Rabkin) reveal an ongoing debate over Todorov's *The Fantastic* [7-61] and other theoretical texts; the other sections, while less clearly focused, include significant essays by Jack Zipes, Roger Schlobin, Charles Elkins, Casey Fredericks and others.

7-16. Coyle, William, ed. **Aspects of Fantasy: Selected Essays from the Second International Conference on the Fantastic.** Greenwood, 1986.
Twenty-five short essays, many of them apparently almost unchanged from

papers delivered at the 1981 ICFA conference, cover the usual wide range of topics for this series. Roger Schlobin's essay on the fool, Rosemary Jackson's on the double and Karen Schaafsma's on the hero are of general interest, while a number of author studies feature interesting observations. Among the latter are Robert Collins on Thomas Burnett Swann, James Hodge on Tolkien's calendar in *The Hobbit*, Steven Taylor on Fernando Arrabal and Lewis Carroll, William Coyle on Mark Twain and Raymond Thompson on Le Guin.

7-17. de Camp, L. Sprague. **Literary Swordsmen and Sorcerers: The Makers of Heroic Fantasy**. Arkham House, 1976.
A series of largely biographical essays on authors whose careers began before 1940 and who are largely responsible for the development of what de Camp prefers to call "heroic fantasy" rather than "sword and sorcery." Despite what would seem a rather narrow focus on this subgenre, de Camp includes chapters on J. R. R. Tolkien, T. H. White, Clark Ashton Smith and H. P. Lovecraft as well as William Morris, Lord Dunsany, E. R. Eddison, Robert E. Howard and Fletcher Pratt (the cutoff date of 1940 eliminates other important writers such as Fritz Leiber). Written in the somewhat intoxicated tone of much "in-house" criticism, the study is of more value as history than as criticism. Compare Lin Carter's *Imaginary Worlds* [7-10]. Also annotated as [8-118].

7-18. Duffy, Maureen (U.K.). **The Erotic World of Faery**. Hodder & Stoughton, 1972.
A well-researched but occasionally overpsychoanalytical history of the psychosexual aspects of "faery" in literature. By "faery," Duffy means not only fairy tales, but literature which suggests or implies the alternative universe of the fairy tale. Thus her discussion includes medieval poems, Shakespeare and modern science fiction and fantasy, but there are few extended analyses of individual works, and relatively little focus on the aesthetics or immediate historical contexts of such works.

7-19. Elgin, Don D. **The Comedy of the Fantastic: Ecological Perspectives on the Fantasy Novel**. Greenwood, 1985.
A rather unusual study of five fantasy and science fiction writers in terms of Joseph Meeker's concept of "literary ecology" (*The Comedy of Survival: Studies in Literary Ecology*, 1974). "Literary ecology" refers to the ways in which literature expresses and/or promotes a particular vision of the natural environment, and Elgin argues that fantasy, by virtue of its habit of inventing environments along with characters, can be especially revealing in this regard. The authors he discusses are J. R. R. Tolkien, C. S. Lewis, Charles Williams, Joy Chant and—rather anomalously—Frank Herbert. A specialized study, even though it contains some useful insights.

7-20. Forster, E. M. (U.K.). **Aspects of the Novel**. Harcourt, 1927.
Forster's classic study of what would now be called the poetics of the novel contains two chapters, entitled "Fantasy" and "Prophecy," which are of particular interest to modern students of the fantastic. He describes a "fantastic-prophetical axis" of literature which is characterized by a "sense of mythology," and further distinguishes between the "prophetic" tone of fiction, which merely implies the presence of supernatural forces, and the "fantastic" tone, which may make such forces manifest. His examples of the latter include Dostoyevsky and

Melville, although he also touches upon more directly fantastic authors such as William Beckford and Walter de la Mare.

7-21. Fredericks, Casey. **The Future of Eternity: Mythologies of Science Fiction and Fantasy**. Indiana Univ. Press, 1982.

Although Fredericks characterizes this intelligent and clearly written volume as "a comprehensive essay on science fiction and myth," his comments on the mythological function of narrative have wide applicability to fantastic literature, and the book's centerpiece is a long essay entitled "In Defense of Heroic Fantasy." Drawing both on literary and cultural theory and on a wide familiarity with what might be called the "in-house" criticism of the genre, he makes an excellent case for the value and sophistication of fantasies by Poul Anderson, L. Sprague de Camp, John Gardner, Fritz Leiber and others.

7-22. Hokenson, Jan, and Howard Pearce, eds. **Forms of the Fantastic: Selected Essays from the Third International Conference on the Fantastic in Literature and Film**. Greenwood, 1986.

The third of the ICFA volumes (see [7-15]), like the others in this series, both reflects the rich variety of the conference it represents and raises questions about the limits of interdisciplinary approaches. The editors go to great lengths to impose order on these twenty-six essays on art, music, film, theater and literature, and the result is a confusing array of subheadings that include such global categories as "Theoretical Approaches to the Fantastic" and such arcane ones as "Linguistic Archaism and Invention." While many of the essays are better suited for more specialized audiences, two essays on magic may be of general interest, and others on Shakespeare and Coover contain useful insights.

*****7-23**. Hume, Kathryn. **Fantasy and Mimesis: Responses to Reality in Western Literature**. Methuen, 1984.

Hume's thesis—that fantasy is a mode of literature which has become disenfranchised as a result of the ascendancy of mimesis as an evaluative aesthetic principle—covers considerably broader ground than genre fantasy, and partly for this reason it represents an extremely important approach to the study of the fantastic in literature. Her historical and critical arguments are insightful and persuasive, as are her occasional comments on individual works and authors. Hume seems most fascinated by the emergence of the fantastic mode in postmodern literature, and is most comfortable discussing authors such as John Barth, Jorge Luis Borges, Italo Calvino and Thomas Pynchon. An important study, highly recommended.

*****7-24**. Irwin, W. R. **The Game of the Impossible: A Rhetoric of Fantasy**. Univ. of Illinois Press, 1976.

One of the earliest important works which defined the emergence of fantasy scholarship in the 1970s and 1980s, Irwin's book borrows techniques of rhetorical analysis from Wayne Booth (*The Rhetoric of Fiction*, 1961) and the theory of play developed by Johan Huizinga (*Homo Ludens: A Study of the Play Element in Culture*, 1939) to construct an argument that fantasy literature invites the reader to "conspire" with the author in the game of creating impossible worlds. An important and influential contribution to the literary theory of fantasy.

*7-25. Jackson, Rosemary (U.K.). **Fantasy: The Literature of Subversion**. Methuen, 1981.
In this very important and intelligent study, Jackson begins with what amounts to a psychoanalytic critique and an extension of ideas presented in Todorov's *The Fantastic* [7-61] and proceeds to an often brilliant discussion of the role of desire and subversion in fantastic works. Arguing that the basic mode of fantasy is the oxymoron, she uses works by Dickens, Dostoyevsky, Stevenson, Mary Shelley, de Sade and Pynchon to demonstrate that the fantastic tends to subvert the "real" of the dominant culture by insisting on the presence of "a silenced imaginary other." A major study by a critic well versed in the literature as well as in critical and psychoanalytic theory. Also annotated as [H7-72].

7-26. Kerr, Howard. **Mediums and Spirit-Rappers and Roaring Radicals: Spiritualism in American Literature, 1850–1900**. Univ. of Illinois Press, 1972.
An unusual and entertaining account of the influence of the spiritualist movement on American literature of the late nineteenth century, focusing especially on works by Edward Bellamy, William Dean Howells, Henry James and Mark Twain. While Kerr provides little discussion of fantasy as such, his well-researched account provides a useful context for certain fantastic elements in the fiction of this period. Also annotated as [H7-38].

7-27. Kroeber, Karl. **Romantic Fantasy and Science Fiction**. Yale Univ. Press, 1988.
Kroeber sees much modern fantasy and science fiction as deriving from Romantic literature, and his opening chapters provide an often brilliant (though occasionally careless in details) discussion of the differences between the two genres, using *Frankenstein* and *The Time Machine* as starting points. He then focuses on Romantic fantasy as expressed primarily in the literary ballads of Coleridge and Keats, and concludes with a chapter on fantasy in postmodern fiction, with discussions of Heinrich von Kleist and Gabriel García Márquez. Although Kroeber only occasionally discusses major works of genre fantasy, his argument that fantasy is "a magnified development of oxymoron" is a persuasive one, and his linking of fantastic narrative to Romantic poetry is suggestive.

7-28. Le Guin, Ursula K. **The Language of the Night: Essays on Fantasy and Science Fiction**, ed. Susan Wood. Putnam, 1979.
Le Guin's nonfiction is characterized by the same wit and grace as her fiction, and next to Tolkien, she may be the most widely quoted of all writer-critics in the field. The twenty-four pieces assembled here are mostly very short essays written as introductions, speeches or contributions to fanzines and academic journals. Of particular interest, apart from the autobiographical sketches and introductions to her own works, are "Why Are Americans Afraid of Dragons?," "Dreams Must Explain Themselves," "The Child and the Shadow" and "From Elfland to Poughkeepsie," the latter of which is one of the most important essays to date on the role of style in fantasy. A bibliography of Le Guin's work through late 1978 is included. A revised edition was issued in 1989 by Women's Press, London.

7-29. Lem, Stanislaw (Poland). **Microworlds: Writings on Science Fiction and Fantasy**, ed. Franz Rottensteiner. Harcourt, 1985.
This collection of ten essays selected from more than a decade of critical writing by the famous Polish writer focuses heavily on science fiction, although two of

the essays are of considerable importance to the student of fantasy. "Todorov's Fantastic Theory of Literature" is an effective argument for the failure of structuralist criticism in dealing with the fantastic, and a brief personal response to the fiction of Jorge Luis Borges provides an insightful account, from a writer's point of view, of that author's fictional strategies.

7-30. Lewis, C. S. (U.K.). **An Experiment in Criticism**. Cambridge, 1961.
Lewis's influential little book is not only an effective argument against traditional evaluative criticism and a precursor of later "reader-response" theories, but also provides useful defenses of fantasy and myth as valid modes of fiction. His chapters on myth, fantasy and "realisms" are especially illuminating.

7-31. Lewis, C. S. (U.K.). **Of Other Worlds: Essays and Stories**, ed. Walter Hooper. Geoffrey Bles, 1966.
This first posthumous collection of Lewis's critical writings and fiction is now largely superseded by *On Stories and Other Essays on Literature* [7-32], which reprints all of the essays included here, and by *The Dark Tower and Other Stories* (1977), which reprints all the short fiction.

***7-32**. Lewis, C. S. (U.K.). **On Stories and Other Essays on Literature**. Harcourt, 1982.
Nineteen essays plus a transcript of a radio discussion make up what is now the standard collection of Lewis criticism related to fantasy, although serious students will also want to consult the author's comments in such "mainstream" studies as *The Allegory of Love* (1936). "On Stories," "On Science Fiction" and "On Criticism" are the most important essays in the book, which also includes four pieces on writing for children and individual essays on Charles Williams, E. R. Eddison, J. R. R. Tolkien, Dorothy L. Sayers, H. Rider Haggard and George Orwell. Indispensable for students of Lewis and his circle, *On Stories* is marked by a degree of wit and a breadth of knowledge which make it valuable to all students of the fantastic.

7-33. Little, Edmund (U.K.). **The Fantasts: Studies in J. R. R. Tolkien, Lewis Carroll, Mervyn Peake, Nicolai Gogol, and Kenneth Grahame**. Avebury, 1984.
A generally intelligent study of the various ways "other worlds" may be presented in fiction, with chapters on Tolkien's *The Lord of the Rings* [3-340], the first two volumes of Peake's Gormenghast series [3-285], Gogol's *Dead Souls*, Carroll's Alice books [2-23] and Grahame's *The Wind in the Willows* [3-157]. Little introduces the intriguing concept of "Tertiary Worlds" (on the theory that a realistic setting which provides a starting point for fantasies is itself a version of Tolkien's "Secondary World"), and argues persuasively that Gogol's *Dead Souls* can be read as a fantastic rather than a realistic work.

7-34. Lochhead, Marion (U.K.). **The Renaissance of Wonder in Children's Literature**. Canongate, 1977. U.S. title: *Renaissance of Wonder*, Harper, 1980.
A brief historical survey of the resurgence of the fantastic in the British Isles from George MacDonald and his followers, through later Victorian and Edwardian writers, to C. S. Lewis, J. R. R. Tolkien and more recent authors including Susan Cooper, Alan Garner, Joan Aiken and others. Although the focus is ostensibly on children's literature, many of the works discussed are adult fantasies. While the

work breaks little new ground, it is a useful overview of what is emerging as the standard outline of British fantasy history, and Lochhead serves a useful purpose in demonstrating the role of children's writing in this history. Also annotated as [4B-181].

7-35. Lüthi, Max (Switzerland). **The Fairytale as Art Form and Portrait of Man.** Indiana Univ. Press, 1984. Tr. by Jon Erickson of *Das Volksmärchen als Dichtung: Ästhetik und Anthropologie*, 1975.

The second of Lüthi's studies of traditional fairy tales to be translated, this volume is somewhat more technical than *Once Upon a Time*, treating fairy tales from the dual perspective of aesthetics and anthropology. Lüthi provides a highly informed examination of the role of beauty and evil in these stories, and offers detailed analyses of the linearity and dynamism of the narratives, as well as of such characteristic techniques as repetition, economy of language and "constellations" of motifs. The volume is certainly among the most valuable academic analyses of fairy tales, and is relatively free of ideological axe-grinding. Compare the analyses of Zipes [7-66, 7-67].

7-36. Lüthi, Max (Switzerland). **Once Upon a Time: On the Nature of Fairy Tales** Ungar, 1970. Introduction and notes by Francis Lee Utley. Tr. by Lee Chadeayne and Paul Gottwald of *Es war einmal . . . vom Wesen des Volksmärchens*, 1962.

This semipopular analysis of the basic themes and techniques of fairy tales by a noted Swiss folklorist introduced European scholarship of the fairy tale to English-speaking audiences and was an important precursor of Bettelheim's *The Uses of Enchantment* [7-3], although this volume is considerably less psychoanalytic in outlook. After distinguishing fairy tales from such related forms as the *sage* and saint's legend, Lüthi argues that the traditional tale provides models of growth and maturation, and supports this with extended discussions of Rapunzel, Cinderella and other tales.

7-37. McHale, Brian (U.K.). **Postmodernist Fiction.** Methuen, 1987.

McHale characterizes "postmodernist" fiction as "ontological" (as opposed to the "epistemological" nature of modernist fiction), and thereby concerned with the construction of fictional worlds. He then surveys a number of techniques characteristic of this fiction, including fantasy, self-referentiality and linguistic experimentation. While the authors he is most concerned with—Samuel Beckett, Thomas Pynchon, Vladimir Nabokov, Alain Robbe-Grillet, Carlos Fuentes and Robert Coover—are not purely writers of fantasy, many of McHale's observations, such as his discussion of the invented "zone" of fiction—are highly relevant to the study of fantasy as a genre. See also Lance Olsen's *Ellipse of Uncertainty: An Introduction to Postmodern Fantasy* [7-42].

7-38. Manlove, C. N. (U.K.). **The Impulse of Fantasy Literature.** Kent State Univ. Press, 1983.

In his second study of selected fantasy authors (following *Modern Fantasy: Five Studies* [7-39]), Manlove seeks to uncover the controlling impulse behind fantasy narratives, which he takes to be delight in the creation of new worlds and a celebration of identity. He devotes a chapter each to Charles Williams, Ursula Le Guin, E. Nesbit, George MacDonald, T. H. White and Mervyn Peake, and then discusses William Morris, Lord Dunsany, E. R. Eddison and Peter Beagle under the rather opprobrious label of "anaemic fantasy." As in his earlier work, Manlove combines close, intelligent readings of specific works with a sometimes testy tone of impatience with authors who seem to lack high moral purpose.

*7-39. Manlove, C. N. (U.K.). **Modern Fantasy: Five Studies.** Cambridge Univ. Press, 1975.

In a brief introduction, Manlove posits a rather detailed and provocative definition of fantasy as a literary genre. He then proceeds to examine a number of specific works—Charles Kingsley's *The Water Babies* [2-98], George MacDonald's fairy tales [2-114-2-117], C. S. Lewis's *Perelandra* [3-214], J. R. R. Tolkien's *The Lord of the Rings* [3-340] and Mervyn Peake's *Titus Groan* trilogy [3-285]—largely in terms of how well they fulfill or illuminate this definition. Needless to say, some of the works fail, and at times Manlove's approach seems rather reductive and inflexible. His insights into the individual works, however, are often very persuasive, and his scholarship is uniformly excellent.

7-40. Moorcock, Michael (U.K.). **Wizardry and Wild Romance: A Study of Epic Fantasy.** Gollancz, 1987.

More a reflective essay than a critical study, this book collects Moorcock's thoughts from over two decades of writing and writing about fantasy. The largest portion of it is the text for an unpublished 1977 volume to have been called *Heroic Dreams*, and despite some updating and revision, parts of the volume seem somewhat dated in their references. Nevertheless, Moorcock's insight, wit and wide reading make this an invaluable volume; of particular interest are the chapters entitled "Wit and Humour" and "Epic Pooh," the latter of which is an impassioned (and probably to many, heretical) attack on the conservatism of fantasists such as Tolkien, Milne and Richard Adams.

7-41. Morse, Donald E., ed. **The Fantastic in World Literature and the Arts: Selected Essays from the Fifth International Conference on the Fantastic in the Arts.** Greenwood, 1988.

There is evidence that Morse has been somewhat more selective and rigorous than some other editors of ICFA conference volumes (see [7-15]), and the result is one of the more rewarding and readable collections in this series. The sixteen essays focus almost entirely on individual works or artists, and the comparative literature aspect of the book is especially strong; coverage includes not only British and American works, but also works from Sweden, Argentina, Peru, Mexico, France and Canada.

7-42. Olsen, Lance. **Ellipse of Uncertainty: An Introduction to Postmodern Fantasy.** Greenwood, 1987.

Arguing that "contemporary fantasy may be thought of as the literary equivalent of deconstructionism," Olsen briefly explores (but does not fully pin down) the meanings of both postmodernism and fantasy, and then discusses the work of eight writers—Franz Kafka, Jorge Luis Borges, Alain Robbe-Grillet, Samuel Beckett, Carlos Fuentes, Thomas Pynchon, Gabriel García Márquez and J. M. Coetzee—whom he sees as undermining accepted notions of language and experience. Although he makes little reference to popular fantasy, and provides a weak concluding chapter that does not fully explore the implications of this study in terms of literary theory, his readings of these individual authors contain some useful insights. Compare with Brian McHale's *Postmodernist Fiction* [7-37].

7-43. Palumbo, Donald, ed. **Erotic Universe: Sexuality and Fantastic Literature.** Greenwood, 1986.
While the bulk of these fifteen essays concern science fiction, Palumbo's introductory essay makes a compelling case for the relationship between fantasy and sex on the grounds that both impulses help to ease anxieties about death. Other essays of particular interest to fantasy scholars include William M. Schuyler, Jr.'s discussion of the philosophy of sexuality and Ann Morris's "The Dialectic of Sex and Death in Fantasy," which addresses the fantastic elements in authors as diverse as Katherine Anne Porter, Robert Coover and John Irving.

7-44. Palumbo, Donald, ed. **The Spectrum of the Fantastic: Selected Essays from the Sixth International Conference on the Fantastic in the Arts.** Greenwood, 1988.
Palumbo's brief introductory essay on the 1984 ICFA conference is the most cheerful account to date of the event that gives rise to this series of volumes (see [7-15]), and he has arranged the essays into simple categories of poetry, art, mainstream fiction, science fiction, fantasy, comparative literature, the media and pedagogy. This makes the volume easier to consult than some others in the series, but does not solve the usual problem of diffuseness. None of the essays is broadly theoretical, although interesting theoretical concepts emerge from the pieces by Peter Malekin, Carole Gerster, Sharon Russell and Donald E. Morse.

*7-45. Prickett, Stephen (U.K.). **Victorian Fantasy.** Indiana Univ. Press, 1979.
Prickett's amiably written study is of particular value as a literary history of how modern fantasy—including the word "fantasy" itself—evolved during the Victorian period. After tracing the growth of a kind of fantasy aesthetic from the Gothic writers through the Romantic and early Victorian periods, Prickett examines those elements in Victorian history—such as Lyell's geology and the growth of an underground sexual aesthetic—which further encouraged fantastic speculation. Finally, he discusses the nonsense of Edward Lear and Lewis Carroll, the allegorical fictions of Charles Kingsley and George MacDonald and the imaginary worlds of Rudyard Kipling and E. Nesbit. A valuable resource as well as a critical text; for an interesting contrasting history of fantasy in American literature, see Brian Attebery's *The Fantasy Tradition in American Literature* [7-2].

7-46. Pringle, David (U.K.). **Modern Fantasy: The Hundred Best Novels, an English-Language Selection, 1946–1987.** Grafton, 1988. Peter Bedrick, 1989.
Pringle's follow-up to his earlier *Science Fiction: The 100 Best Novels* (Xanadu, 1985) seems, like the earlier volume, to be a deliberately provocative collection of brief descriptive essays on what Pringle argues are the definitive canon of recent fantasy. Despite its "handbook" format, this is a work of criticism more than of reference. While Pringle's discussions of commonly accepted masterpieces such as J. R. R. Tolkien's *Lord of the Rings* [3-340] add little to the critical literature on these works, his less well-known selections often call attention to worthwhile, often near-forgotten novels. The essays themselves are uniformly graceful and concise. Also annotated as [6-23].

*7-47. Rabkin, Eric S. **The Fantastic in Literature.** Princeton Univ. Press, 1976.
This influential and widely quoted study, in some ways an implicit critique of Todorov's *The Fantastic* [7-61], attempts to provide an interdisciplinary rationale for a broad range of literature characterized by "the fantastic," which Rabkin

argues is a "basic mode of human knowing" opposed to reality. Clearly influenced by earlier structuralist critics, Rabkin touches upon a wide range of works in what is essentially a theoretical essay, rather than a work of applied criticism. His most influential single concept is probably the "spectrum of the fantastic," along which he arrays works ranging from detective fiction and science fiction to "pure" fantasy. Rabkin illustrated his theories with a companion anthology, *Fantastic Worlds* (see [4A-289]).

7-48. Rottensteiner, Franz (Austria). **The Fantasy Book: An Illustrated History from Dracula to Tolkien**. Collier, 1978.
A companion volume to the author's *The Science Fiction Book* (1975), this heavily illustrated popular account of European fantasy and horror fiction contains no extended analyses of particular works or authors, but serves as a useful general introduction to these genres and includes a number of critical insights which belie its "picture-book" format. Rottensteiner is the leading Austrian critic of science fiction and fantasy. Also annotated as [H7-11] and [10-30].

7-49. Sale, Roger. **Fairy Tales and After: From Snow White to E. B. White**. Harvard Univ. Press, 1978.
Sale's attempt to bring sophisticated methods of literary analysis and literary history to the realm of children's literature results in a highly readable and perceptive analysis of works ranging from folk and literary fairy tales to Lewis Carroll, Beatrix Potter, Kenneth Grahame, Rudyard Kipling, L. Frank Baum, Walter Brooks and E. B. White. While his focus is not avowedly on the specifically fantastic elements in these books, Sale cannot avoid discussions of fantasy and its psychological significance to both adult and younger readers. A useful study of a tradition of fantastic literature too often slighted in more ambitious studies of fantasy.

7-50. Sammons, Martha C. **A Better Country: The Worlds of Religious Fantasy and Science Fiction**. Greenwood, 1988.
The title is somewhat misleading, since the author focuses exclusively on Christian fantasy and science fiction, and even defines "religious fantasy" as "a work that integrates aspects of Christianity with elements of fantasy." She further emphasizes the evangelical nature of such fiction, concluding that a similarity to the Gospels "gives this genre its legitimacy and true purpose." Despite the narrowness of perspective, the work contains solid scholarship and discusses, in addition to Tolkien and Lewis, a number of lesser-known writers, including authors of young adult fiction. A notable and unexplained omission is Charles Williams.

7-51. Schlobin, Roger C., ed. **The Aesthetics of Fantasy Literature and Art**. Univ. of Notre Dame Press, 1982.
This was the first collection of original essays on fantasy aesthetics, consisting of twelve essays and two bibliographies (fiction and criticism). The first six essays, by well-known critics in the field, concern theory and definition; two essays touch upon fantasy art; and the remainder focus on specific types of fantasy such as utopias, lost race fiction, Arthurian fantasy and heroic fantasy. Especially interesting are George P. Landow's interdisciplinary discussion of fantasy literature and art, Robert Crossley's discussion of what he calls the "applied fantasy" of

utopian fiction and Francis J. Molson's survey of children's fantasy. Also annotated as [10-32].

7-52. Scholes, Robert. **Fabulation and Metafiction**. Univ. of Illinois Press, 1979. An expanded and updated version of Scholes's 1967 *The Fabulators*, this study champions a number of writers whom Scholes sees as characterizing a postrealist literary movement characterized by self-consciousness, fantasy, delight in design and invention, and a degree of didacticism. "Metafiction" is characterized as fabulation marked by experimental narrative techniques. Authors discussed at length include Jorge Luis Borges, John Barth, Robert Coover, John Hawkes and Kurt Vonnegut and there are frequent references to writers of fantasy and science fiction. Despite its occasional cheerleading tone, this is the first major study to identify what has since become known as postmodern fiction; compare Brian McHale's *Postmodernist Fiction* [7-37].

7-53. Shinn, Thelma J. **Worlds Within Women: Myth and Mythmaking in Fantastic Literature by Women**. Greenwood, 1986.
Although avowedly not a feminist work, this study nevertheless establishes some important linkages between feminist theory and women authors of science fiction and fantasy. Shinn's longest and most important chapter, on traditional myths retold, contains illuminating discussions of works by Evangeline Walton, Marion Zimmer Bradley, Doris Lessing and others. The remaining chapters focus more on science fiction than fantasy. In general, Shinn's mastery of the literature is stronger than her familiarity with myth theory, making the work far more significant as a study of women writers than as an argument for fantastic literature as myth. Compare with Charlotte Spivack's *Merlin's Daughters: Contemporary Women Writers of Fantasy* [7-56].

7-54. Slusser, George E.; Eric S. Rabkin; and Robert Scholes, eds. **Bridges to Fantasy**. Southern Illinois Univ. Press, 1982.
This collection of thirteen essays from the 1980 Eaton Conference on Science Fiction and Fantasy includes Harold Bloom's interesting attempt to derive a theory of fantasy largely from David Lindsay's *A Voyage to Arcturus* [3-221], as well as provocative pieces by Larry McCaffery, David Clayton, Roger Sale and Robert A. Collins. Often heavily academic in tone, the essays nevertheless are characterized by sound scholarship and methodology. Individual essays treat works by Julio Cortázar, Mark Twain, Gabriel García Marquez, Ray Bradbury and Stanislaw Lem.

7-55. Slusser, George E., and Eric S. Rabkin, eds. **Intersections: Fantasy and Science Fiction**. Southern Illinois Univ. Press, 1987.
The seventh Eaton Conference on Science Fiction and Fantasy, held in 1985, focused on the relations of science fiction and fantasy, and these seventeen essays clearly reflect this focus. The first section of essays, "Discriminations," includes a number of attempts to delineate the differences between genres; a second part, "Gestations," explores historical and evolutionary questions; a third, "Fields," addresses deliberate permutations of the genres. This is an intelligent and unusually unified collection, with especially interesting essays by Robert Scholes, Roger Zelazny, Samuel R. Delany, Kathleen Spencer, George E. Slusser, Brian Attebery and Kathryn Hume.

7-56. Spivack, Charlotte. **Merlin's Daughters: Contemporary Women Writers of Fantasy**. Greenwood, 1987.
Spivack argues that women fantasy writers characteristically favor certain narrative techniques that have begun to evolve into an identifiable tradition: the use of female protagonists, the frequent appearance of matriarchal societies, circular rather than linear plots and feminine viewpoints on "conventionally masculine subjects." She explores this thesis in essays on ten modern writers: Andre Norton, Susan Cooper, Ursula K. Le Guin, Evangeline Walton, Katherine Kurtz, Mary Stewart, Patricia McKillip, Vera Chapman, Gillian Bradshaw and Marion Zimmer Bradley. While her essays sometimes lean heavily toward plot summary, the volume as a whole is an extremely useful introductory guide to the work of these writers, many of whom have received inadequate critical attention.

7-57. Starr, Nathan Comfort. **King Arthur Today: The Arthurian Legend in English and American Literature, 1901–1953**. Univ. of Florida Press, 1954.
In tracing the development of Arthurian literature after Tennyson, Starr analyzes works by Edwin Arlington Robinson, Charles Williams, T. H. White, C. S. Lewis, John Cowper Powys, Ernest Rhys, Arthur Machen, Arthur Symons and others. Individual chapters treat the increasing emphasis on psychological and historical detail, parody and satire, and modern versions of Tristan and Iseult, Merlin and the Grail. Especially valuable are discussions of now seldom-read poems and plays, and extensive primary and secondary bibliographies. For an updating of this study, see Thompson's *The Return from Avalon* [7-59].

7-58. Swinfen, Ann (U.K.). **In Defence of Fantasy: A Study of the Genre in English and American Literature since 1945**. Routledge and Kegan Paul, 1984.
As the title implies, this is a broad-ranging argument for the literary value of much recent fantasy, which the author says is defined by the "marvellous": "anything outside the normal space-time continuum of the everyday world." After excluding science fiction from discussion, Swinfen arranges her study according to a not always consistent taxonomy, including such overlapping categories as "time fantasy," "animal fantasy" and "religious fantasy." Although her "defense" adds little new to fantasy theory, Swinfen offers compelling discussions of authors including Lloyd Alexander, Ursula K. Le Guin and Mary Norton, in addition to the compulsory Tolkien and Lewis.

7-59. Thompson, Raymond H. **The Return from Avalon: A Study of the Arthurian Legend in Modern Fiction**. Greenwood, 1985.
Thompson updates Starr's *King Arthur Today* [7-57] with discussions of works through 1983 and brief analyses of what he views as the more important texts. The study usefully categorizes books as retellings, realistic versions (including modern settings), historical fiction, science fiction and science fantasy, and fantasy (further subdivided into mythopoeic, heroic, ironic and "low"). An appendix lists variant spellings of names, and a bibliography includes over 200 novels and stories. Thompson's detailed research and meticulous scholarship make this an indispensable volume for those interested in Arthurian fantasy. A more general and very useful study is *The Arthurian Encyclopedia* ed. by Norris J. Lacy (Garland, 1986).

7-60. Timmerman, John H. **Other Worlds: The Fantasy Genre**. Bowling Green Univ. Popular Press, 1983.
This brief overview of popular fantasy uses a rather narrow range of primary and secondary sources to argue, not surprisingly, that fantasy functions much like myth. Though often guilty of oversimplification, particularly in regard to the relationship of fantasy to such allied genres as science fiction, Timmerman does offer a reasonable introduction to the genre's more familiar elements.

*7-61. Todorov, Tzvetan. **The Fantastic: A Structural Approach to a Literary Genre**. Case Western Reserve Univ. Press, 1973; Cornell Univ. Press, 1975. Tr. by Richard Howard of *Introduction à la littérature fantastique*, 1970.
Todorov's seminal study—the first consistent modern attempt to identify the fantastic as a genre—has been almost as significant as a stimulus for further criticism and refutation as it is in its own right. Todorov's controversial hypothesis—that the "fantastic" is defined by that hesitation the reader experiences before a work is resolved into either "the uncanny" or "the marvellous"—seems to define a literary genre of such narrow scope as to be almost useless as a critical tool. In fact, he is partly criticizing genre theory and partly trying to shift focus from content analysis to analysis of the act of reading. The work contains illuminating discussions of examples ranging from Gérard de Nerval and E. T. A. Hoffmann to Gothic novels and detective stories. Also annotated as [H7-76].

*7-62. Tolkien, J. R. R. **Tree and Leaf**. Allen & Unwin, 1964.
This slim volume includes Tolkien's story "Leaf by Niggle" together with the final version of his profoundly influential essay "On Fairy-Stories," originally presented as a lecture at the University of St. Andrews in 1938 and subsequently published in 1947. Tolkien's immense popularity, as well as his clarity of thought, have made the essay the single most important statement on the moral and essentially Christian nature of his fantasy and, indirectly, of all fantasy in the Tolkien tradition. The famous four-part rationale of the function of fantasy—fantasy, recovery, escape and consolation—makes up the core of the essay, and it has arguably influenced later fantasy writers as well as later critics.

7-63. Wilson, Colin (U.K.). **The Strength to Dream: Literature and the Imagination**. Gollancz, 1961.
Wilson's wide-ranging discussion of the various uses of the imagination in modern literature is characterized by the same provocative insights and idiosyncratic reading as his earlier *The Outsider* (1956). Arguing that "freedom, evolution, and religion" are the essential characteristics of the modern imagination, he examines not only such mainstream writers as Oscar Wilde, D. H. Lawrence, Samuel Beckett and William Faulkner, but also H. P. Lovecraft, H. G. Wells, E. T. A. Hoffmann, J. R. R. Tolkien (in what is one of the earliest essays on this author) and M. R. James. Although sometimes given to global overgeneralizations, Wilson nevertheless deserves credit as one of the first critics to discuss writers of fantasy in the context of broader literary and cultural traditions. Also annotated as [H7-79].

7-64. Yoke, Carl B., and Donald M. Hassler, eds. **Death and the Serpent: Immortality in Science Fiction and Fantasy**. Greenwood, 1985.
Twenty essays explore a wide variety of fictional variations on the themes of

immortality and death in fantastic literature. While most of the essays focus on science fiction works, several are of particular value to the study of fantasy, such as Michael Collings's discussion of Lewis and Donaldson, Raymond H. Thompson's account of modern versions of Merlin, Robert Crossley's comparison of elves in Tolkien and Sylvia Townsend Warner, Samuel Vasbinder's discussion of vampires and other immortals in horror fiction and Helmut Pesch's essay on E. R. Eddison.

*7-65. Ziolkowski, Theodore. **Disenchanted Images: A Literary Iconology**. Princeton, 1977.

This erudite and often brilliant study of the uses of magical imagery argues that such images may function as themes, motifs or symbols, but that they characteristically undergo a historical process of "disenchantment" as they recur in literature. Discussing in detail the literary history of the animated statue, the haunted portrait and the magic mirror, Ziolkowski convincingly demonstrates how such images begin as accepted magic, later become rationalized or internalized and finally become subject to deliberate inversions. Although the focus might seem narrow, the range of texts and breadth of literary history covered make this one of the most valuable studies of fantastic imagery.

7-66. Zipes, Jack. **Breaking the Magic Spell: Radical Theories of Folk and Fairy Tales**. Univ. of Texas Press, 1979.

Zipes's essentially Marxist reading of fairy tales and fantasy provides one of the most insightful sociohistorical accounts of both folk and literary fantasy. Arguing that the original liberating function of the folk fairy tale subsequently was undermined by the mediation of commodity production, Zipes is perhaps at his strongest when discussing the Brothers Grimm and other German fantasists such as Tieck, Novalis and Hoffmann. He concludes with an important and persuasive critique of Bruno Bettelheim's *The Uses of Enchantment* [7-3].

7-67. Zipes, Jack. **Fairy Tales and the Art of Subversion: The Classical Genre for Children and the Process of Civilization**. Wildman Press, 1983.

Zipes contends that literary fairy tales are too often discussed in ignorance of their social and historical function, and here attempts to demonstrate that they have historically reflected—or on occasion subverted—bourgeois attitudes toward the socialization of children. His discussion includes Charles Perrault, the Brothers Grimm (whose revisions of their source materials are insightfully analyzed), Hans Christian Andersen, George MacDonald, Oscar Wilde and L. Frank Baum. Two particularly interesting final chapters explore fairy tale discourse in Weimar and Nazi Germany and postwar movements to create more liberating tales for children. A valuable and revealing study of an aspect of fantastic literature which is too seldom addressed.

8

Author Studies

Richard C. West

This chapter evaluates book-length treatments in English of authors who have published a substantial body of work that is considered by readers and critics to be fantasy. It is therefore limited to those fantasists who have had at least one book written about them. Inevitably, then, many outstanding authors could not be included. When Lord Dunsany has elicited a number of books about his dramas but none about the fantasy tales that many consider his best work (*Pathways to Elfland* by Darrell Schweitzer, Owlswick Press, 1989, was published too late to annotate), when there are no extended critiques of major fantasy writers such as E. R. Eddison, it is small wonder that there is a dearth of books about scores of individual authors. The most recent and useful evaluations of these authors will be found in the biocritical reference books discussed in chapter 6. See the cross-references following each author's name in the fiction chapters.

This critical neglect is reflected in many of the annotations that follow, since many outstanding authors have had little written about them. Yet, with some writers there has been the opposite problem, and I have been forced to be extremely selective in order to keep the checklist short. I have, for example, ignored books on Lewis Carroll as mathematician or photographer, on C. S. Lewis as literary critic or Christian apologist, on William Morris as socialist or printer or poet, and concentrated on critical studies dealing with the fantasy writing of all authors. Where possible, I have cited bibliographies of other criticism. The major criterion in all cases has been the quality of the scholarship and criticism in illuminating the primary literature.

Note that much of what is discussed here and in chapter 7 is of fairly recent date, since it is only within the last twenty years or so that fantasy (though it is as old as literature) has become sufficiently critically respectable to enable books about it to be published. When Borges wrote a preface to Adolfo Bioy Casares's novel *La invención de Morel* in 1940, defending a fiction that followed the order and the logic of magic rather than of the chaotic "real" world of science and nature, he was very isolated in arguing for a radical departure from the prevalent fashion of mimetic realism. But subsequently "magic realism" became common in South American literature, postmodernism also became chic, and critics took notice. At the same time, the popular success of Tolkien's work inspired the reprinting of older fantasy, new books by new authors and much critical debate. Some of the result is discussed in this chapter.

A few publishers have issued series of author studies, which have some common features that should be borne in mind when one of the individual volumes is cited:

Borgo Press has issued the **Milford Series: Popular Writers of Today** since 1977. Most of these short monographs (sixty-four pages for most earlier studies, longer for a few later volumes) are devoted to SF or fantasy authors, including Bradbury, Ellison, Howard, Le Guin, Lindsay, Morris, Pynchon, Tolkien and Vance. They tend to be more analytical than the **Starmont** guides and do not follow a fixed format.

The **G. K. Hall** bibliographies are divided into sections on primary and secondary works, with appropriate subsections. An unusual feature is that all sections are arranged by year of publication, but there are indexes by title and author. The earlier ones (such as the one by Sanders on Roger Zelazny [8-116]) give the year only at the beginning of each year's listings; later ones correct this fault by citing the year also at the top of each page.

The **Starmont** guides to fantasy and SF authors are introductory surveys that are intended to be short (usually not much more than 100 pages). The standard format is first to provide a chronology of the author's life, a canon of the primary works, a biographical chapter, a number of chapters discussing major works, two selective annotated bibliographies of primary and secondary works and an index. It is a worthwhile but uneven series; some volumes are as good as can be expected in an introductory survey, but in others, description and plot summaries replace needed critical analyses. The length of individual volumes has little relationship to the importance of the writer.

The **Twayne** and **Ungar** introductory surveys are longer. They are similar in format, each featuring a chronology, biography, chapters on major works and a bibliography. The Twayne series is an extensive one, and is devoted not only to American authors (TUSAS) and British authors (TEAS) but also to writers from many countries. The Twayne monographs usually reflect a critical consensus rather than a strongly argued individual view and are good starting points.

Anthony, Piers

8-1. Anthony, Piers. **Bio of an Ogre: The Autobiography of Piers Anthony to Age 50.** Ace, 1988.

8-2. Collings, Michael R. **Piers Anthony.** Starmont, 1983.
Anthony (1934–   ) has written both SF and fantasy, although he is now probably

better known for the latter, especially for his many series (see [4A-10] and [4A-11] for discussion of two series). The ninety-six-page Starmont guide is unavoidably dated because of Anthony's prolific output, but is still a useful introduction to the major earlier works, showing how events in his life and his personal beliefs are reflected in his fiction, especially in the theme of maturation. His strong beliefs surface with a vengeance in his autobiography, divided into five decade-long chronicles. Although he provides useful information about many of his writings, he gives such undue emphasis to his alleged mistreatment by publishers, editors and others that he is likely to irritate all but his most fervent partisans. (This pugnacious temperament often appears in interviews, such as the one by Platt [8-120], though Anthony can be generous.) No index.

Beagle, Peter S.

*8-3. Zahorski, Kenneth J. **Peter Beagle**. Starmont, 1988.
Beagle (1939–   ) has published relatively little fiction, but it has been regarded by most critics, including Zahorski, as of high quality (Manlove [7-38] dissents from the prevailing view). The 124-page Starmont guide devotes a chapter each to *A Fine and Private Place* [4A-22], *The Last Unicorn* [4A-24] and *Folk of the Air* [4A-23]. Zahorski also has good critiques of the short fiction and Beagle's wide-ranging nonfiction, and a very interesting section on Beagle's mostly unproduced screenplays. Comprehensive annotated bibliography of secondary literature. Beagle and Harlan Ellison were the subjects of a special issue of *Journal of the Fantastic in the Arts*, vol. 1, no. 3, 1988 [11-39].

Borges, Jorge Luis

8-4. Barrenechea, Ana Maria. **Borges the Labyrinth Maker**. New York Univ. Press, 1965. Ed. and tr. by Robert Lima of **La expression de la irrealidad en la obra de Jorge Luis Borges**, 1957.

8-5. Bell-Villada, Gene H. **Borges and His Fiction: A Guide to His Mind and Art**. Univ. of North Carolina Press, 1981.

8-6. Bloom, Harold, ed. **Jorge Luis Borges**. Chelsea House, 1986.

*8-7. Foster, David William. **Jorge Luis Borges: An Annotated Primary and Secondary Bibliography**. Garland, 1984.

8-8. McMurray, George R. **Jorge Luis Borges**. Ungar, 1980.

*8-9. Rodríguez Monegal, Emir. **Jorge Luis Borges: A Literary Biography**. Dutton, 1978.

8-10. Stabb, Martin S. **Jorge Luis Borges**. Twayne, 1970.

8-11. Wheelock, Carter. **The Mythmaker: A Study of Motif and Symbol in the Short Stories of Jorge Luis Borges**. Univ. of Texas Press, 1969.
There is a vast amount written about Borges (1899–1986) in English alone.

Consult Foster for a comprehensive guide to books and articles in all languages. This volume has an excellent introduction by Martin S. Stabb tracing the history of critical reaction to Borges. Foster also provides a complete list of Borges's works, including English translations.

There are a number of good, general studies of Borges's work, such as the early one by Stabb or the one by McMurray, or the collection of essays edited by Bloom. Bell-Villada's overview is noteworthy because of its relatively recent date and because it devotes separate chapters to the short stories which comprise most of Borges's fantasy.

Much criticism of Borges touches on the fantastical character of many of his stories, and two books are of particular interest in this regard. Barrenechea's is one of the earliest book-length studies of Borges in any language, and remains a classic. This is a detailed treatment, not only of the image of the labyrinth, but also of the "expression of irreality" in the poetry, stories and essays. The themes considered are those of infinity and cyclical time, chaos and cosmos, pantheism and personality, and philosophical idealism. The book's main weakness is in neglecting Borges's humor and irony. That is not as true of Wheelock's major study, which examines how the fiction, in which reality is mythically dissolved and reformulated, is for Borges a vehicle to reveal meaning. The monumental work by Rodríguez Monegal is the standard biography.

Bradbury, Ray

8-12. Greenberg, Martin Harry, and Joseph D. Olander, eds. **Ray Bradbury**. Taplinger, 1980.

8-13. Johnson, Wayne L. **Ray Bradbury**. Ungar, 1980.

8-14. Mogen, David. **Ray Bradbury**. Twayne, 1986.

8-15. Nolan, William F. **The Ray Bradbury Companion: A Life and Career History, Photolog, and Comprehensive Checklist of Writing, with Facsimiles from Ray Bradbury's Unpublished and Uncollected Work in All Media**. Gale, 1975.

8-16. Slusser, George Edgar. **The Bradbury Chronicles**. Borgo Press, 1977.
Bradbury (1920–   ) continues to have a prolific and diverse artistic career, but he is best known for his science fiction and fantasy. His frequent lapses in scientific plausibility and occasional sentimentality are balanced by his emotional power and skill in vivid detail and striking metaphor. He did not attract much academic criticism until the last several years, but the Greenberg and Olander anthology has a number of good critical articles on such themes as religion, technology and myth. Slusser's monograph was one of the first extended critiques in English, and in spite of its brevity (sixty-three pages) is a good treatment of major themes. Johnson and Mogen each provide useful overviews, with good biographical and bibliographical information; Mogen has an especially valuable chapter analyzing Bradbury's style. The beautifully illustrated volume by Nolan was not intended as a complete or formal bibliography, but it remains a very helpful source.

Cabell, James Branch

8-17. Davis, Joe Lee. **James Branch Cabell**. Twayne, 1962.

8-18. Duke, Maurice. **James Branch Cabell: A Reference Guide**. G. K. Hall, 1979.

8-19. Inge, M. Thomas, and Edgar E. MacDonald, eds. **James Branch Cabell: Centennial Essays**. Louisiana State Univ. Press, 1983.

***8-20.** Tarrant, Desmond. **James Branch Cabell: The Dream and the Reality**. Univ. of Oklahoma Press, 1967.

8-21. Wells, Arvin. **Jesting Moses: A Study in Cabellian Comedy**. Univ. of Florida Press, 1962.
Cabell (1879–1958) enjoyed an enormous literary reputation in the 1920s but was later eclipsed, though he has never lacked for defenders and had two journals devoted to his work, *The Cabellian* and *Kalki*. Duke's comprehensive bibliography has a good introduction surveying the history of Cabell's critical reception. The first extended studies were the books by Davis (an excellent overview) and Wells (a detailed critique of Cabell's characteristic irony). Wells focuses on the mammoth series that Cabell called the "Biography of the Life of Manuel" [3-63–3-72]. Tarrant provides a detailed and balanced discussion of Cabell's thought and art. The Inge and MacDonald anthology has much biographical and bibliographical information as well as literary critiques; the essay by Leslie A. Fiedler is especially noteworthy.

Calvino, Italo

8-22. Carter, Albert Howard, III. **Italo Calvino: Metamorphoses of Fantasy**. UMI Research Press, 1986.
The language, images, ideas and very great diversity of Calvino (1923–1985) are effectively and clearly explored in Carter's study, which has a chapter on the author's life and work, but focuses on his fantasy and its relationships with science, abstraction, sign, myth, reading and death in major works. Quotations are given in English translation, and there is a useful annotated bibliography. Index.

Carroll, Lewis

8-23. Guiliano, Edward. **Lewis Carroll: An Annotated International Bibliography 1960–77**. Univ. Press of Virginia, 1980.

8-24. Kelly, Richard. **Lewis Carroll**. Twayne, 1977.

***8-25.** Phillips, Robert, ed. **Aspects of Alice: Lewis Carroll's Dreamchild as Seen through the Critics' Looking-Glasses 1865-1971**. Gollancz, 1972.
The writings of Charles Lutwidge Dodgson (1832–1898) have been the subject of a great deal of commentary, and Guiliano's comprehensive bibliography includes both primary and secondary works. The Phillips anthology has an excellent and wide-ranging selection of biographical pieces as well as commentary on the Alice

books as Victorian and children's literature, as parody and satire, and from Freudian, Jungian, mythic and philosophical perspectives. No index. Kelly provides a good overview, and devotes a chapter to *Alice* [2-23].

Collier, John

8-26. Richardson, Betty. **John Collier**. Twayne, 1983.
Collier (1901–1980) has never lacked admirers, but this is the only book-length study of the man and his works. He is best known for his witty short fictions [3-83], which have similarities with those of Saki, but Richardson also intelligently discusses *His Monkey Wife* [3-84], his post-Holocaust novel, *Tom's A-Cold*, and *Defy the Foul Fiend*. A much better than average volume in this series.

de Camp, L. Sprague

8-27. Laughlin, Charlotte, and Daniel J. H. Levack, comps. **de Camp: An L. Sprague de Camp Bibliography**. Underwood/Miller, 1983.
de Camp (1907–   ) has been a prolific author, from a book on inventions in 1937 to today, as suggested by the 822 entries, many of them annotated, for books, articles and other pieces. Many magazine and book covers are reproduced. de Camp's fondness for fantasy is evident in his Harold Shea tales written in collaboration with Fletcher Pratt [3-106] and in his works derived from Robert E. Howard.

Brothers Grimm

8-28. The Brothers Grimm and Folktale, ed. by James M. McGlathery with Larry W. Danielson, Ruth E. Lorbe and Selma K. Richardson. Univ. of Illinois Press, 1988.

*8-29. Zipes, Jack. **The Brothers Grimm: From Enchanted Forests to the Modern World**. Routledge, 1988.
Jakob (1785–1863) and Wilhelm Grimm (1786–1859) have an enduring place in literary history with their retellings of *Märchen*, but their work has lately come in for much reassessment in the light of changes they introduced in their sources. The anthology has academic essays from numerous perspectives, including a chapter on the psychosocial background from Zipes's book. Zipes provides a thorough study in what is likely to remain a standard work. Both volumes have extensive, unannotated bibliographies. Other works by Zipes are annotated as [7-66] and [7-67].

Haggard, H. Rider

8-30. Etherington, Norman. **Rider Haggard**. Twayne, 1984.

8-31. Vogelsberger, Hartwig A. **"King Romance": Rider Haggard's Achievement**. Universität Salzburg, 1984.

8-32. Whatmore, D. E. **H. Rider Haggard: A Bibliography**. Meckler, 1987.
Sir Henry Rider Haggard (1856–1925) is well remembered as a writer of adventure

stories, particularly those set in a mysterious Africa (see especially those featuring his series characters, Allan Quatermain and Ayesha), though he also wrote novels inspired by Old Norse sagas and at least one work of science fiction, *When the World Shook*. He has been much criticized for his superficiality, imperialism, racism and lapses in literary style, but much admired for his vigorous imagination.

Whatmore's book is primarily a descriptive bibliography of first and other noteworthy editions of Haggard's principal works of fiction and nonfiction. Among its many other useful sections is an annotated checklist of books and articles about Haggard and his work. The arrangement throughout is by year of publication, but the subject index includes individual authors and titles.

Vogelsberger's entry in the Salzburg Studies in English Literature is called a "Romantic Reassessment" and treats major works at length (*She* [2-74] receives a chapter to itself). The focus is on the romances, but their relationship with Haggard's extensive agricultural writings is also considered, and he deals also with film versions and with contemporary and later critical reactions. His defense of Haggard's literary greatness is perhaps overly enthusiastic. Etherington also focuses on the romances, but provides a more balanced account of the good and the bad in Haggard's style, politics and legacy to later writers. His annotated bibliography of secondary sources is very good.

Howard, Robert E.

8-33. Cerasini, Mark A., and Charles Hoffman. **Robert E. Howard**. Starmont, 1987.

8-34. de Camp, L. Sprague; Catherine Crook de Camp; and Jane Whittington Griffin. **Dark Valley Destiny: The Life of Robert E. Howard**. Bluejay, 1983.

8-35. Ellis, Novalyne Price. **One Who Walked Alone: Robert E. Howard, the Final Years**. Donald M. Grant, 1986.

8-36. Herron, Don, ed. **The Dark Barbarian: The Writings of Robert E. Howard, A Critical Anthology**. Greenwood, 1984.

8-37. Lord, Glenn, ed. **The Last Celt: A Bio-Bibliography of Robert Ervin Howard**. Donald M. Grant, 1976.
Howard (1906–1936) is best known as the creator of Conan [3-182] and other works of sword and sorcery. His work shows the stylistic defects of much pulp fiction but is highly imaginative. Most of the writing about Howard is by aficionados rather than academics, as in the articles covering a broad spectrum of his oeuvre in the anthology edited by Herron. These tend to be enthusiastic but are not altogether uncritical; Fritz Leiber's appreciation of "Howard's Fantasy" is especially valuable. The Starmont guide has a balanced assessment of Howard's achievement and is a good overview. Lord provides several short autobiographical pieces by Howard, as well as a number of memoirs (including one by H. P. Lovecraft) and biographical essays. The major part of this volume, however, is a descriptive bibliography of Howard's publications. The full biography by the de Camps and Griffin should be supplemented by Ellis's detailed treatment of the author's latter days and suicide.

Le Guin, Ursula K.

*8-38. Bittner, James W. **Approaches to the Fiction of Ursula K. Le Guin**. UMI Research Press, 1984.

8-39. Bucknall, Barbara J. **Ursula K. Le Guin**. Ungar, 1981.

8-40. Cogell, Elizabeth C. **Ursula K. Le Guin: A Primary and Secondary Bibliography**. G. K. Hall, 1983.

8-41. De Bolt, Joe. **Ursula K. Le Guin: Voyager to Inner Lands and to Outer Space**. Kennikat, 1979.

8-42. Olander, Joseph D., and Martin Harry Greenberg, eds. **Ursula K. Le Guin**. Taplinger, 1979.

8-43. Selinger, Bernard. **Le Guin and Identity in Contemporary Fiction**. UMI Research Press, 1988.

8-44. Slusser, George Edgar. **The Farthest Shores of Ursula K. Le Guin**. Borgo Press, 1979.

8-45. Spivack, Charlotte. **Ursula K. Le Guin**. Twayne, 1984.
Le Guin (1929–   ) is unusual not only in having won widespread critical recognition for the high quality of her work, but also for being so subsumed into the mainstream tradition that she has had to insist that she has not abandoned SF or fantasy. In the latter category she is best known for her Earthsea trilogy [4B-98], and all of the studies cited above include discussions of one or more of these books. It has been difficult to keep this checklist reasonably short, and I have had to exclude items that deal almost exclusively with the author's science fiction.

Cogell's excellent bibliography is thorough to its date, but Le Guin continues to publish and she has been anything but critically neglected, so it needs to be supplemented. Bucknall and Spivack each provide good introductions and overviews, with Spivack surveying more, such as Le Guin's poetry. Bucknall has a good chapter on features common in Le Guin's work: the outer and inner journey; love, friendship, fidelity and betrayal; hatred of oppression and love of freedom; romanticism and realism. Spivack is excellent on Taoist, Jungian and anthropological influences. Both include biographical material. De Bolt contributes a fine short biography to his anthology, which deals mostly with SF but has a useful survey of Le Guin criticism by Bittner and three essays focusing on oral, ethical and humane elements in the Earthsea trilogy. Olander and Greenberg include essays on the psychological journey, the shadow motif and patterns of integration in the trilogy.

Slusser's sixty-page monograph (the only book listed that does not have an index) focuses on moral themes in Le Guin's SF and fantasy, including problems of individual responsibility, folly, evil and the search for selfhood. Selinger takes a largely psychoanalytic approach and most of his book treats SF, but there is a chapter on *A Wizard of Earthsea*. Bittner's study, originally his doctoral dissertation, is perhaps the best single book on Le Guin, giving broad consideration to her oeuvre and in particular the major theme of "marriage" (shorthand for complementarity between what seem to be opposites or dualisms but are really part of a whole).

Lewis, C. S.

8-46. Christopher, Joe R. **C. S. Lewis**. Twayne, 1987.

8-47. Christopher, Joe R., and Joan K. Ostling. **C. S. Lewis: An Annotated Checklist of Writings about Him and His Works**. Kent State Univ. Press, 1973.

8-48. Ford, Paul F. **Companion to Narnia**. Harper, 1980.

***8-49.** Sayer, George (U.K.). **Jack: C. S. Lewis and His Times**. Harper, 1988.

***8-50.** Schakel, Peter J. **Reading with the Heart: The Way into Narnia**. Eerdmans, 1979.

8-51. Schakel, Peter J. **Reason and Imagination in C. S. Lewis: A Study of Till We Have Faces**. Eerdmans, 1984.

Clive Staples Lewis (1898–1963) was a prolific author in many fields and is particularly well known as a Christian philosopher. He was a major critic (see discussion in chapter 7) as well as a writer of SF. His chief fantasy works are the Chronicles of Narnia [4B-101] and his version of the myth of Cupid and Psyche, *Till We Have Faces* [3-216].

An immense amount has been written about all aspects of Lewis and his varied writings. The dated bibliography by Christopher and Ostling is thorough and has excellent annotations, but it should be supplemented by the selected bibliographies in the other studies cited. Christopher's annotated checklist in his Twayne guide is particularly useful, and this volume is also a good overview of Lewis's oeuvre. Christopher also provides an ongoing "Inklings Bibliography" (which also lists work on MacDonald, Tolkien, Williams and others) in almost every issue of *Mythlore* [11-43] since vol. 3, no. 4, whole no. 12 (June 1976).

Schakel's is perhaps the best single book on the Narnia series, with detailed discussions of each of the seven books, and an awareness of the Christian background that does not lose sight of the text in order to preach a homily (a fault in much other criticism of Lewis). His bibliography will lead to other good critiques of Narnia. Ford's encyclopedic treatment is an excellent gloss on the text. Schakel also provides the best extended treatment of *Till We Have Faces*; half of this book is biographical, setting that novel in the context of Lewis's career.

There are a number of good biographies. Sayer, as the most recent, is able to make use of letters and memoirs that earlier biographers could not, as well as of his own reminiscences. His is also the most balanced treatment of its subject; others tend to be either too adulatory or too negative.

Lindsay, David

8-52. Pick, J. B.; Colin Wilson; and E. H. Visiak (all U.K.). **The Strange Genius of David Lindsay: An Appreciation**. John Baker, 1970.

8-53. Sellin, Bernard (France). **The Life and Works of David Lindsay**. Tr. by Kenneth Gunnell. Cambridge Univ. Press, 1981.

8-54. Wilson, Colin (U.K.). **The Haunted Man: The Strange Genius of David Lindsay**. Borgo Press, 1979.

8-55. Wolfe, Gary K. **David Lindsay.** Starmont, 1982.
Lindsay (1878–1945) never found a large audience for his novels of complex, abstruse and rigorous philosophy, but his admirers tend to be devoted and include many distinguished writers and critics (e.g., Loren Eiseley, C. S. Lewis, Harold Bloom). Sellin's is the only full, scholarly biography, and includes extended criticism; this was originally a doctoral thesis at the Sorbonne. The three essays in the Pick volume contain valuable memoirs, but only a little criticism. Wilson provides detailed critical commentary, particularly on *A Voyage to Arcturus* [3-221]. Wolfe gives an excellent overview, and a valuable annotated bibliography of what little criticism is available.

McCaffrey, Anne

8-56. Arbur, Rosemarie. **Leigh Brackett, Marion Zimmer Bradley, Anne McCaffrey: A Primary and Secondary Bibliography.** G. K. Hall, 1982.

8-57. Brizzi, Mary T. **Anne McCaffrey.** Starmont, 1986.

8-58. Fonstad, Karen Wynn. **The Atlas of Pern.** Ballantine, 1984.

8-59. Wood, Robin. **The People of Pern.** Donning, 1988.
McCaffrey (1926–   ) is best known for her series about the Dragonriders of Pern [4A-179], which is SF with the feel of fantasy. The geography of Pern is the subject of Fonstad's book. McCaffrey wrote the introduction and text accompanying the many attractive drawings and paintings by Wood (also annotated as [10-130]). Arbur's annotated list of primary and secondary works is valuable, and her introduction and commentary note McCaffrey's relations with other writers and the strong emotion that underlies her work. The only extended study is the fine overview by Brizzi, which has much on the Pern series and discusses all the major novels.

MacDonald, George

*8-60. Hein, Rolland. **The Harmony Within: The Spiritual Vision of George MacDonald.** Christian Univ. Press, 1982.

8-61. Raeper, William (U.K.). **George MacDonald.** Lion, 1987.

8-62. Reis, Richard H. **George MacDonald.** Twayne, 1972.

8-63. Robb, David S. **George MacDonald** (U.K.). Scottish Academic Press, 1987.

8-64. Wolff, Robert Lee. **The Golden Key: A Study of the Fiction of George MacDonald.** Yale Univ. Press, 1961.
MacDonald (1824–1905) was an eminent Victorian in his own day, but was rescued from neglect when C. S. Lewis championed him as a Christian thinker and mythmaker (while faulting him for his tendency toward prolix sermonizing in his fiction) whose fantasy is far superior to his more realistic novels. Robb admits that this has become the standard view, but argues also in favor of MacDonald's nonfantasy; his book is especially useful for placing the author in the Scottish literary tradition. Wolff's was the first book-length study and has astute scholarship on sources and influences, but is relentlessly Freudian in its

approach and is more interested in the putative psychological disposition of the author than in literary values. An antidote to this is the helpful general introduction by Reis. The best study is by Hein, who concentrates on the major fantasy novels and short fairy tales, and closely examines how MacDonald's theological convictions shaped the symbolic terrain of his imaginative prose. Raeper's massive, well-researched biography includes commentary on the fantasy; index.

Merritt, A.

8-65. Foust, Ronald. **A. Merritt**. Starmont, 1989.

8-66. Moskowitz, Sam. **A. Merritt: Reflections in the Moon Pool: A Biography**. Oswald Train, 1985.
Abraham Merritt (1884–1943) has not elicited much critical study. Moskowitz's book is primarily a biography, but also includes some autobiographical pieces by Merritt and some unpublished poems, stories and fragments, as well as a selection of letters from and to Merritt. Index. The Starmont guide by Foust was not available in time to be evaluated here.

Morris, William

8-67. Aho, Gary L. **William Morris: A Reference Guide**. G. K. Hall, 1985.

8-68. Kirchhoff, Frederick K. **William Morris**. Twayne, 1979.

8-69. Mathews, Richard. **Worlds Beyond the World: The Fantastic Vision of William Morris**. Borgo Press, 1978.

8-70. Silver, Carole. **The Romance of William Morris**. Ohio Univ. Press, 1982.

8-71. Silver, Carole, and Joseph R. Dunlap, eds. **Studies in the Late Romances of William Morris**. Papers Presented at the Annual Meeting of the Modern Language Association, December, 1975. William Morris Society, 1976.
There has been an enormous amount written about the achievements of Morris (1834–1896) in many fields, and Aho's annotated bibliography covers this. The other books focus on his prose romances, an outgrowth of his medievalism that was highly influential on later fantasy. Silver's excellent book traces romance motifs and conventions in Morris's work, considered chronologically; index. The MLA anthology concentrates on works dating from 1888–97, and discusses motifs, themes, myth, ritual, the erotic and the pastoral. Mathews provides a good survey in short compass (sixty-four pages) of all the romances, both paraphrasing and analyzing. Kirchhoff's overview focuses on Morris's literary development (rather than on all of his multi-faceted career); he devotes one chapter to the late prose romances.

Myers, John Myers

8-72. Lerner, Fred, ed. **A Silverlock Companion**. Niekas Publications (RFD 2, Box 63, Center Harbor, NH 03226), 1988.
Myers (1906–1988) is primarily known for his fiction and historical writings about the American West. He did not consider any of his work to be fantasy, but

Silverlock [3-261] and *The Moon's Fire-Eating Daughter* [4A-193] qualify by most definitions. This short (fifty-two pages) but invaluable booklet is mostly devoted to explications of the literary, mythological and other allusions in *Silverlock*, but it also contains a bibliography of Myers's entire body of writing, appreciations of all his work, biographical sketches, some previously unpublished poems and many quotations from letters from Myers.

Peake, Mervyn

8-73. Batchelor, John (U.K.). **Mervyn Peake: A Biographical and Critical Exploration**. Duckworth, 1974.

8-74. Gilmore, Maeve (U.K.). **A World Away: A Memoir of Mervyn Peake**. Gollancz, 1970.

8-75. Smith, Gordon (U.K.). **Mervyn Peake: A Personal Memoir**. Gollancz, 1984.

8-76. Watney, John (U.K.). **Mervyn Peake**. Michael Joseph, 1976.
Peake (1911–1968) was a distinguished painter and poet as well as an author, and hallmarks of his fiction are visual detail, sensitivity to nuances of language, humor and affection for the grotesque. The memoirs by his wife (Gilmore) and his friend (Smith) are valuable for their personal perspectives, and Watney offers a well-researched and written biography although he provides little in the way of criticism. The best extended critique in book form is by Batchelor, though much of this volume is devoted to biography also. Batchelor has a useful checklist of the small body of criticism that is available. Manlove devotes a chapter to Peake in two of his books [7-38, 7-39].

Pynchon, Thomas

8-77. Fowler, Douglas. **A Reader's Guide to Gravity's Rainbow**. Ardis Publishers, 1980.

*8-78. Hume, Kathryn. **Pynchon's Mythography: An Approach to Gravity's Rainbow**. Southern Illinois Univ. Press, 1987.

8-79. Scotto, Robert M. **Three Contemporary Novelists: An Annotated Bibliography of Works by and about John Hawkes, Joseph Heller, and Thomas Pynchon**. Garland, 1977.

8-80. Walsh, Thomas P., and Cameron Northouse. **John Barth, Jerzy Kosinski, and Thomas Pynchon: A Reference Guide**. G. K. Hall, 1977.

8-81. Weisenburger, Steven. **Gravity's Rainbow: Sources and Contexts for Pynchon's Novel**. Univ. of Georgia Press, 1988.
Pynchon (1937–) is difficult to classify, as evidenced by the way he is grouped with different authors by Scotto and by Walsh and Northouse. There is little to choose between these two bibliographies, for both are good and cover much the same period, and need to be supplemented in later sources. There have been several books and anthologies on *Gravity's Rainbow* [4A-213] alone. Fowler's and Weisenburger's guides can each be used in conjunction with the text, which they

explicate by scene, page or even line. Hume's is the best single study, finding meaning and pattern and some traditional techniques and structures that underlie Pynchon's more apparent preoccupation with chaos and unknowability and deconstructive techniques. Published too late to be annotated was *Thomas Pynchon: A Bibliography of Primary and Secondary Materials* (Dalkey Archive, 1989), compiled by Clifford Mead.

Rohmer, Sax

8-82. Van Ash, Cay, and Elizabeth Sax Rohmer. **Master of Villainy: A Biography of Sax Rohmer**. Edited, with Foreword, Notes and Bibliography, by Robert E. Briney. Bowling Green Univ. Popular Press, 1972.
This rambling but very readable book recounts in detail the life and professional career of the man christened Arthur Henry Ward (he changed his name to Arthur Sarsfield Ward early in his life, and adopted his celebrated pseudonym fairly early in his career), with some critical commentary on his work. Much attention is given throughout to the Dr. Fu Manchu series [H3-167], including Rohmer's account of the underworld figure in Limehouse who was the germ of this anti-hero, and background details of the novels (which often have elements of fantasy, SF and horror). Briney provides contextual notes and a bibliography of Rohmer's prolific writings. Index. This book tends to overrate Rohmer as a master of English prose style, and underrate his dependence on melodrama and the social changes that have dated his stories. But it is a good assessment of his achievement as a storyteller and craftsman.

Shiel, M. P.

8-83. Morse, A. Reynolds, ed. **Shiel in Diverse Hands: A Collection of Essays**. Morse Foundation, 1983.
Matthew Phipps Shiel (1865–1947) has been well served by this collection of essays by twenty-nine authors, written from 1924 through 1983, and gathered here with commentary on each by the editor. The iconoclastic Shiel has been attacked for his alleged racism and incipient Nazism among other philosophical faults, and some of these defenses have an air of protesting too much. But they do provide diverse viewpoints on the range of his work; Brian Stableford's essay on "The Politics of Evolution" is a particularly noteworthy overview of Shiel's themes. Reprints of Shiel's own essays "On Reading" and "On Writing" are included.

Swann, Thomas Burnett

8-84. Collins, Robert A. **Thomas Burnett Swann: A Brief Critical Biography and Annotated Bibliography**. Florida Atlantic Univ., College of Humanities, 1979.
Swann (1928–1976) is known as a stylist of delicacy and beauty, who drew more from classical sources than the more recent European sources typical of many fantasy writers. This thirty-page booklet is the only detailed study and provides quotations from Swann and from critics, along with an annotated bibliography and selections from book reviews.

Tolkien, J. R. R.

*8-85. Carpenter, Humphrey (U.K.). **Tolkien: A Biography**. Allen & Unwin, 1977.

8-86. Crabbe, Katharyn F. **J. R. R. Tolkien**. Ungar, 1981; rev. ed. 1988.

8-87. Evans, Robley. **J. R. R. Tolkien**. Warner, 1972.

8-88. Flieger, Verlyn. **Splintered Light: Logos and Language in Tolkien's World**. Eerdmans, 1983.

8-89. Foster, Robert. **The Complete Guide to Middle-earth**. Ballantine, 1978.

8-90. Helms, Randel. **Tolkien's World**. Houghton Mifflin, 1974.

8-91. Isaacs, Neil D., and Rose A. Zimbardo, eds. **Tolkien and the Critics**. Notre Dame, 1968.

8-92. Johnson, Judith A. **J. R. R. Tolkien: Six Decades of Criticism**. Greenwood, 1986.

8-93. Jonsson, Ake (Sweden). **En Tolkienbibliografi 1911–1980**. Hogskolan i Boras, 1983.

*8-94. Kocher, Paul H. **Master of Middle-earth: The Fiction of J. R. R. Tolkien**. Houghton Mifflin, 1972.

8-95. Lobdell, Jared. **England and Always: Tolkien's World of the Rings**. Eerdmans, 1981.

8-96. Lobdell, Jared, ed. **A Tolkien Compass**. Open Court, 1975.

8-97. O'Neill, Timothy R. **The Individuated Hobbit: Jung, Tolkien and the Archetypes of Middle-earth**. Houghton Mifflin, 1979.

8-98. Rogers, Deborah and Ivor. **J. R. R. Tolkien**. Twayne, 1980.

*8-99. Shippey, T. A. (U.K.). **The Road to Middle-earth**. Houghton Mifflin, 1983.

*8-100. West, Richard C. **Tolkien Criticism: An Annotated Checklist**. Kent State Univ. Press, 1970; rev. ed., 1981.
Tolkien (1892–1973) is by common (though not universal) consensus at the forefront of the field of fantasy, both as theorist and as practitioner, one who has been both "inside myth" and "inside language." As such he had been attracting a great deal of serious criticism even before his work gained widespread popularity in the 1960s, and he still does. With this plethora it has been very difficult, even by excluding the many short monographs, to keep a checklist of the best material within reasonable limits.

It is therefore imperative to cite bibliographies. I am understandably partial to my own, but the reviewers have also been appreciative of it when comparing it with the others available. I cite primary works chronologically, and secondary criticism alphabetically by author (although a considerable amount of thematic searching is possible by treating the first words of titles in the title index as a key word, and then following the extensive cross-references in the annotations). The first edition notes outstanding items, and since everyone has complained about the absence of this feature subsequently, I will certainly restore it in future editions. Johnson has later information and cites some (but far from all) of the "fanzine" material. Jonsson is in Swedish as well as English and is not annotated, but he cites extensively from fanzines, is especially good on European articles and has supplements in annual issues of the Swedish fanzine, *Arda*. See also the ongoing "Inklings Bibliography" by J. R. Christopher cited above [8-46] in the discussion of C. S. Lewis criticism (beginning in 1989, Wayne Hammond will be responsible for the Tolkien section of this).

Foster's is the best of the guides to Tolkien's invented world, but it is "complete" only through the publication of *The Silmarillion* (1977; [4A-251]) for the happy reason that Christopher Tolkien continues to publish, with exemplary scholarship, manuscripts left by his father.

There are a number of useful introductory surveys of Tolkien's work. I am fond of the Twayne study by the Rogerses, which I find delightfully written and insightful. Others may prefer the more straightforward book by Evans, or the more academic one by Crabbe. The revised edition of Crabbe is useful for a new chapter treating the fiction published posthumously through 1986 (the only extended discussion of this to date), but otherwise it is little changed from the 1981 edition; the bibliography was not updated.

Of the many collections of essays, Isaacs and Zimbardo provided almost the first one and still perhaps the best, although it deals almost exclusively with only one work, *The Lord of the Rings* [3-340]. It reprints some of the most valuable essays then available, including critiques by W. H. Auden, M. Z. Bradley (though this was severely shortened) and C. S. Lewis. (A later anthology by the same editors, *Tolkien: New Critical Perspectives*, from the Univ. Press of Kentucky in 1981, is also worthwhile but is not as outstanding.) Lobdell is another excellent collection. This includes Tolkien's guide for translators of his work, and among the best essays are Bonniejean Christensen on the text of *The Hobbit* [3-339], David Miller on narrative patterns in *Fellowship of the Ring* and Deborah Rogers on the everyday and the heroic in Tolkien. I contributed an essay on interlace structure in *The Lord of the Rings*.

Two books in particular stand out among the many written on Tolkien. Kocher's was the first full-length critical work and considered all the fiction published through 1972. It remains a standard for its well-written, balanced insightful discussions. Shippey's is a brilliant critique, especially valuable for its philological study.

Very honorable mention should also be made of Flieger (who applies Owen Barfield's theories of language to Tolkien), Helms (who makes up for some weak Freudian readings with many insights into structure and aesthetics) and Lobdell (with his provocative comparisons to Edwardian adventure fiction).

Of the several biographies available, the best is Carpenter's well-written and researched volume.

Vance, Jack

8-101. Levack, Daniel, and Tim Underwood. **Fantasms: A Bibliography of the Literature of Jack Vance.** Underwood/Miller, 1978.

8-102. Rawlins, Jack. **Demon Prince: The Dissonant Worlds of Jack Vance.** Borgo Press, 1986.

8-103. Underwood, Tim, and Chuck Miller, eds. **Jack Vance.** Taplinger, 1980. Vance (1916–　) is a prolific author of sophisticated and sardonic fantasy and SF. The Taplinger anthology mixes essays by fellow writers in the field, knowledgeable fans and academics. Of particular interest are Robert Silverberg on the two "Dying Earth" books then available [3-345; 4A-256] and Richard Tiedman on Vance as stylist. This volume also includes Marshall Tymn's fine checklist of the Vance canon, but this is not annotated, and for that one should consult Levack and Underwood. They also list both magazine and book publication and discuss the textual differences between the two, and provide a complete list of Vance's works, including translations of Vance into other languages. Rawlins gives an excellent overview, an interview with Vance and a selective bibliography of criticism.

White, T. H.

8-104. Crane, John K. **T. H. White.** Twayne, 1974.

*8-105. Warner, Sylvia Townsend (U.K.). **T. H. White: A Biography.** Cape, 1967. The critical neglect of an author of the quality and stature of White (1906–1964) is more than usually unjust. The well-researched and written biography by Warner is likely to remain the standard for some time to come. She quotes liberally from unpublished letters, diaries and manuscripts, and gives especially full treatment to the 1930s–40s. She includes critical evaluation in her treatment. Index. Crane provides an excellent overview, and his selected bibliography of the criticism available has short annotations and is very useful.

Williams, Charles

*8-106. Cavaliero, Glen. **Charles Williams: Poet of Theology.** Eerdmans, 1983.

8-107. Glenn, Lois. **Charles W. S. Williams: A Checklist.** Kent State Univ. Press, 1975.

*8-108. Hadfield, Alice Mary. **Charles Williams: An Exploration of His Life and Work.** Oxford, 1983.

8-109. Howard, Thomas. **The Novels of Charles Williams.** Oxford Univ. Press, 1983.

8-110. Shideler, Mary McDermott. **The Theology of Romantic Love: A Study in the Writings of Charles Williams.** Eerdmans, 1962.

8-111. Sibley, Agnes. **Charles Williams.** Twayne, 1982.

8-112. Spencer, Kathleen. **Charles Williams.** Starmont, 1986.
Williams (1886–1945) has never achieved wide popularity, but his work has been much admired by critics as sensitive but as disparate as C. S. Lewis and T. S. Eliot. He is noted for his "theological thrillers," novels in which only a thin and fragile veil divides the supernatural from the mundane. Glenn's annotated bibli-

ography is badly out of date (she lists only two book-length studies, for example), but it is excellent up to its date and there has been nothing to replace it. See also Christopher's "Inklings Bibliography" mentioned above [8-46] in the discussion on C. S. Lewis; beginning in 1989, Pat Hargis will prepare the Williams section of this. Hadfield's focus is on biography, and she gives a very detailed treatment. Sibley and Spencer provide good overviews, and their selective bibliographies are useful supplements to Glenn. Sibley's book has sections on the plays, the novels and the poetry, but she sees Williams's oeuvre as visionary literature and not fantasy, and her focus is on underlying ideas such as coinherence, mysticism and evil existing only as a corruption of good. Spencer is better on the fantastic character of the novels, and it is to these that most of her critique is devoted. Spencer is also unusual in seeing Williams only as an interesting minor writer; most of these books are by devotees.

Shideler's pioneering study remains a classic for its treatment of Williams's esoteric ideas, particularly his theory of romantic love as leading to love of the world and of God. Howard provides a close reading of each of the novels. Cavaliero also has good critiques of the novels, but he considers the entire oeuvre, and his is arguably the best single critical study of Williams.

Wolfe, Gene

8-113. Gordon, Joan. **Gene Wolfe**. Starmont, 1986.
Wolfe (1931–) is particularly known for the Book of the New Sun [4A-270]. He has not been widely written about, and Gordon's checklist of secondary literature consists mostly of reviews and interviews. Her introductory study divides Wolfe's work into "entertainments" and serious fiction in either a psychological or sociological vein, and gives good discussions of his major works.

Zelazny, Roger

8-114. Krulik, Theodore. **Roger Zelazny**. Ungar, 1986.

8-115. Levack, Daniel J. H., comp. **Amber Dreams: A Roger Zelazny Bibliography**. Underwood/Miller, 1983.

8-116. Sanders, Joseph L. **Roger Zelazny: A Primary and Secondary Bibliography**. G. K. Hall, 1980.

8-117. Yoke, Carl B. **Roger Zelazny**. Starmont, 1979.
Zelazny (1937–) is known for SF and fantasy that uses myth in sophisticated ways, as in *Lord of Light* and the Amber series [4A-276]. Sanders, in addition to providing an annotated bibliography that is thorough to its date, has an introduction giving a biographical sketch and an excellent essay on Zelazny's themes, prose style and use of myth. Where Sanders includes both primary and secondary works, Levack has only the former. His book is still a useful supplement to Sanders, partly for its illustrations taken from covers and dust jackets, but primarily for lengthy comments by Zelazny on each work. Yoke and Krulik both provide fine overviews and critiques of individual, major works.

COLLECTIVE BIOGRAPHIES

8-118. de Camp, L. Sprague. **Literary Swordsmen and Sorcerers: The Makers of Heroic Fantasy**. Arkham House, 1976.

8-119. Elliot, Jeffrey M. **Fantasy Voices 1: Interviews with American Fantasy Writers**. Borgo Press, 1982.

8-120. Platt, Charles. **Dream Makers: Science Fiction and Fantasy Writers at Work**. rev. ed. Ungar, 1987.

These collections provide valuable information about many major authors of fantasy about whom there has otherwise been little or nothing written. De Camp's short, readable biographies (of Lord Dunsany, E. R. Eddison, R. E. Howard, H. P. Lovecraft, William Morris, Fletcher Pratt, Clark Ashton Smith, Tolkien and T. H. White) include only a little incidental criticism, but he has selective bibliographies and an index. De Camp is also annotated as [7-17]. Elliot prefaces each of his four interviews with a brief biographical sketch, and he is good at drawing out each author's primary concerns. His interview with Wellman is particularly useful for the background of the series about John the balladeer [4A-265]. The other profiles are of horror writer Hugh B. Cave, Katherine Kurtz, with the emphasis on her Deryni series [4A-155], and John Norman on his Gor series [4A-199]. Platt is a very skillful interviewer who conducts candid and cogent dialogues, preferably in the subject's own workplace to capture this ambience, and he is ready to express his thoughts if he disagrees with his subjects. Valuable addenda are the bibliographical notes he appends to each article, discussing the major works of that author. The collection has twenty-five interviews (selected from fifty-six interviews in two earlier volumes, and reprinted unchanged for the most part except for one-paragraph updates), including chapters on fantasy writers Piers Anthony, Ray Bradbury, Fritz Leiber, Michael Moorcock and Theodore Sturgeon. Platt concentrates on SF, which he considers a more rational genre than fantasy.

9

Fantasy on Film and Television

Michael Klossner

▬

antasy films (fantastic films which are neither horror nor science fiction) include a very wide variety of works, from art films to children's fantasies (often animated) and from Hollywood ghost comedies to films based on the *Arabian Nights* or classical mythology. The most successful fantasy films (Table 9-1) have been the Indiana Jones movies, Walt Disney's animated fairy tale features and comedies such as *Big* (1988) and *Who Framed Roger Rabbit* (1988).

Fantasies have never been a commercially reliable film product. Hollywood's first expensive fantasy, *The Thief of Bagdad* (1924), was a notorious flop which convinced studios that American audiences were too pragmatic to appreciate fantasy. There has never been a fantasy film boom like the horror boom of the 1930s, the SF boom of the 1950s or the tremendous output of both SF and horror films which followed *Star Wars* (1977) and *Halloween* (1978). Even most important fantasy films have failed to inspire fantastic sequels, series or trends. *King Kong* (1933) was followed by jungle pictures, *The Thief of Bagdad* (1940) by Oriental swashbucklers and *Ulysses* (1955) by spear-and-sandal epics; in each case, the successive films retained the colorful settings of the original film but jettisoned most or all fantastic elements. The only successful fantasy series have been the marginal fantasy Tarzan and Indiana Jones movies. Even the celebrated fantasy specialist Ray Harryhausen made only three *Arabian Nights* films and two based on Greek mythology. In 1981 several lavish sword-and-sorcery films (*Conan the Barbarian, Excalibur, Clash of the Titans, Dragonslayer*) were released, but the public soon tired of the trend.

Table 9-1. Top Fantasy Rental Films

Title, Year	$ (thousands)
Raiders of the Lost Ark, 1981	115,598
Indiana Jones and the Temple of Doom, 1984	109,000
Who Framed Roger Rabbit, 1988	78,000
Snow White and the Seven Dwarfs, 1937	61,752
Big, 1988	50,800
Heaven Can Wait, 1978	49,400
Mary Poppins, 1964	45,000
Cinderella, 1949	41,087
The Golden Child, 1986	39,723
The Jungle Book, 1967	39,500
King Kong, 1976	36,915
Splash, 1984	34,103
Scrooged, 1988	33,000
Pinocchio, 1940	32,957
The Muppet Movie, 1979	32,000
Oh, God, 1977	31,500
Song of the South, 1946	29,228
Fantasia, 1940	28,660
Willow, 1988	27,835
Popeye, 1980	24,568
Peter Pan, 1953	24,532
The Dark Crystal, 1982	23,883
Greystoke: The Legend of Tarzan, 1984	23,200
The Love Bug, 1969	23,150
Sleeping Beauty, 1959	21,998
Conan the Barbarian, 1981	21,729
Time Bandits, 1981	20,533
Pete's Dragon, 1977	18,400
Pee Wee's Big Adventure, 1985	18,100
Mannequin, 1987	18,000
Harry and the Hendersons, 1987	17,680
Tommy, 1975	17,793
Clash of the Titans, 1981	17,450
Excalibur, 1981	17,100
Herbie Rides Again, 1974	17,000
The Land before Time, 1988	17,000
The Great Muppet Caper, 1981	16,652
Live and Let Die, 1973	15,925
Tarzan the Ape Man, 1981	15,896
Like Father, Like Son, 1987	15,000
Modern Problems, 1981	14,800
Conan the Destroyer, 1984	14,292
Lord of the Rings, 1978	14,122
Camelot, 1967	14,000
Herbie Goes to Monte Carlo, 1977	14,000

Table 9-1. (continued)

The Muppets Take Manhattan, 1984	13,000
The Princess Bride, 1987	13,000
Santa Claus, 1985	13,000
The Shaggy Dog, 1959	12,317
The Wiz, 1978	12,264

Source: *Variety*, January 11, 1989. The figures are rentals paid to the studios, not box-office receipts, for the U.S. and Canada only, not adjusted for inflation.

In spite of discouraging commercial prospects, dozens of exceptional fantasy films have been made (Table 9-2). In the filmography of Nicholls's *World of Fantastic Films* [9-11], four critics rate 700 important horror, fantasy and science fiction films on an equal footing. Of the 136 films which received the three highest ratings (4, 4.5 or 5), 57 were horror, 46 fantasy and 33 SF. (The count of excellent fantasy films would have been higher if Nicholls had not excluded animated films, which have recently received serious critical attention. The most detailed guide to the popular Walt Disney films is John Grant's excessively enthusiastic *Encyclopedia of Walt Disney's Animated Characters* [1987]. Richard Schickel's *The Disney Version* [1968] presents a sour, highbrow view of Disney. Leonard Maltin's *The Disney Films* [2d ed., 1984] is the most balanced account. Maltin's *Of Mice and Magic: A History of American Animated Cartoons* [rev. ed., 1987] and *The American Animated Cartoon: A Critical Anthology*, edited by Danny and Gerald Peary [1980], cover cartoons by Disney's American rivals, while John Halas's *Masters of Animation* [1987] is international in scope.)

Table 9-2. Best and Most Significant Fantasy Films and Television Programs

1923–24 Die Nibelungen (2-part film) (4)
1924 The Thief of Bagdad
1926 Faust (4.5)
1927 The Adventures of Prince Achmed (anim.)
1930 L'Age d'or (4)
1933 King Kong (5)
1933 Zero de conduit (4.5)
1934 Babes in Toyland
1934 Tarzan and His Mate
1935 A Midsummer Night's Dream
1936 The Green Pastures
1937 Lost Horizon (4)
1937 Snow White and the Seven Dwarfs (anim.)

1939 The Wizard of Oz (4)
1940 Fantasia (anim.)
1940 Pinocchio (anim.)
1940 The Thief of Bagdad (4)
1941 The Devil and Daniel Webster
1942 I Married a Witch (4)
1942 Les Visiteurs du soir
1943 The Adventures of Baron Münchausen (4)
1943 Heaven Can Wait (4)
1944 Curse of the Cat People (4.5)
1945 Blithe Spirit
1946 Beauty and the Beast (5)
1946 It's a Wonderful Life
1946 Stairway to Heaven
1947 Miracle on 34th Street

Table 9-2. (continued)

1948 The Red Shoes (4)
1950 Harvey
1950 Orpheus (4.5)
1950 Pandora and the Flying Dutchman (4)
1951 Alice in Wonderland (anim.)
1951 A Christmas Carol
1952 Monkey Business (4)
1953 The 5,000 Fingers of Dr. T (4)
1953 Ugetsu (5)
1955 Ulysses
1957 The Seventh Seal (4)
1957 Throne of Blood
1958 The Face (4.5)
1958 The Seventh Voyage of Sinbad
1959 Darby O'Gill and the Little People
1959 A Midsummer Night's Dream (anim.)
1960 Virgin Spring (4)
1961 Last Year at Marienbad (4.5)
1962 The Exterminating Angel (4.5)
1963 Jason and the Argonauts
1963 The Nutty Professor (4)
1964 Mary Poppins
1965 Juliet of the Spirits (4)
1966 One Million Years B.C.
1967 Weekend (4)
1968 Finian's Rainbow (4)
1968 Hour of the Wolf (5)
1969 Fellini Satyricon
1970 Gas-s-s-s (4)
1971 The Pied Piper
1972 The Amazing Mr. Blunden (4)
1972 The Discreet Charm of the Bourgeoisie (5)

1972 Everything You Always Wanted to Know about Sex—But Were Afraid to Ask (4)
1973 Charlotte's Web (anim.)
1973 High Plains Drifter (4)
1974 Celine and Julie Go Boating (4.5)
1974 Monty Python and the Holy Grail
1974 The Phantom of Liberty (4.5)
1975 Picnic at Hanging Rock (4)
1976 Duelle (4)
1977 The Hobbit (anim. TV film)
1977 The Last Wave (4)
1977 Providence (4.5)
1977 Three Women (4)
1978 Empire of Passion (4.5)
1978 Percival le Gallois (4)
1978 Watership Down (anim.)
1979 The Lion, the Witch and the Wardrobe (anim. TV film)
1979 Monty Python's Life of Brian (4)
1980 Popeye (4.5)
1981 Quest for Fire
1981 Raiders of the Lost Ark (4.5)
1982 Fanny and Alexander (5)
1982 Parsifal (4)
1983 Zelig (4)
1984 The Company of Wolves
1985 Dreamchild
1985 The Purple Rose of Cairo
1985 Return to Oz
1988 Big

(anim.): animated
Titles followed by (4), (4.5) and (5) received those ratings (averaging ratings by four critics) in Nicholls [9-11]; other titles were selected by Michael Klossner.

The diffuse nature of fantasy films is probably the reason that far fewer books have been written about them than about horror or SF films. Boundaries between genres are frequently artificial and murky; fantastic films of different types often appeal to the same audiences. Readers interested in the books in this chapter should consult the film and television chapters in *Anatomy of Wonder: A Critical Guide to Science Fiction* (3d ed., 1987) and *Horror Literature: A Reader's Guide* (1990), both edited by Neil Barron.

Reference Works

9-1. Halliwell, Leslie (U.K.). **Halliwell's Film and Video Guide**. 6th ed. Scribner, 1987.

Halliwell's views are often old-fashioned, but his *Guide* is the most sophisticated of three popular, one-volume, annotated guides to most English-language and selected foreign films. Most of the 16,000 entries include date, length, color or black-and-white, credits (production company, producer, director, actors, writer, literary source, photographer, composer and art director), a rating from zero to four, a brief synopsis and critique, and any alternative titles or important awards. Halliwell's rivals, Leonard Maltin's *TV Movies and Video Guide* and Steven H. Scheuer's *Movies on TV* (both annuals), include less information and generally more lenient ratings.

9-2. Nash, Jay Robert, and Stanley Ralph Ross, eds. **The Motion Picture Guide**. 12 vols. Cinebooks, dist. Bowker, 1985–87.

9-3. Variety Film Reviews. 16 vols. Garland, 1983.

Each of these two expensive sets covers almost all English-language films and many silent and foreign films. Nash provides credits (including actors and the names of characters portrayed), descriptions and criticism for about 35,000 sound films and 3,500 silents, and credits only for 2,000 minor sound films and 10,000 silents. The main set covers films through 1984; annual supplements for 1985, 1986, 1987 and 1988 releases have appeared to date. The *Variety* set has credits, descriptions and criticism of over 40,000 films from 1907 to 1980, with biennial updates for 1981–82, 1983–84, 1985–86 and 1987–88 so far. Nash's annotations are new and reflect up-to-date attitudes, while the reprinted *Variety* reviews, contemporary with the films, are often quaint. The Nash set is several hundred dollars cheaper, includes 10,000 more films and is more consistent in format and treatment, but *Variety*'s reviews are generally shrewder, wittier and more erudite. *Variety* is written by and for hard-headed film industry professionals; the Nash set is typical of film buff criticism. Since neither set is indexed by genre, students of fantastic films must use them in conjuction with the specialized reference works annotated below. (Many of the approximately 1,000 reviews reprinted in *Variety's Complete Science Fiction Reviews* [1985], ed. by Donald Willis and covering 1907 to 1984, are borderline fantasy or horror.)

9-4. Scheuer, Steven H., ed. **The Complete Guide to Videocassette Movies**. Holt, 1987.

Fantasy films for both adults and children are among the mainstays of the videocassette rental market. With over 5,000 entries, Scheuer's *Guide* is the best and most complete of many guides to films on video, although some of the unsigned, one-paragraph reviews are supercilious about acceptable popular films. Entries are in alphabetical order by title and include date, running time, country, MPAA rating, director, cast, a genre symbol and a rating of from one to four. A genre index identifies SF and horror titles, but fantasy films are scattered under several categories including drama, adventure, children's, comedy and foreign films. The 11-inch paperback is not designed for heavy use and should be prebound.

9-5. Lee, Walt. **Reference Guide to Fantastic Films: Science Fiction, Fantasy and Horror**. 3 vols. Chelsea-Lee, 1972–74.
Many well-spent years of fan scholarship lie behind this remarkable compilation. About 15,000 films are arranged by title in three sturdy 11-inch paperbacks. Many entries are incomplete; complete entries include date, country, length, credits (including casts but not names of characters), a brief nonevaluative note describing the film's fantastic elements (not a complete synopsis) and references to information (not necessarily reviews) found in hundreds of sources listed in the bibliography. About 5,000 more films are listed briefly as "exclusions" (films which appear to have fantastic elements but do not) and "problems" (for which sufficient information could not be found). The approximately 150 illustrations are mainly unfamiliar and interesting. This is by far the most complete filmography of fantastic films made before the 1970s. Lee's great achievement is that, by including absolutely everything, from films of Shakespeare's ghost plays to children's fairy tale films, from early trick movies to Hindu mythological films, he makes clear the vast influence of the fantastic on world cinema.

9-6. Lentz, Harris M., III **Science Fiction, Horror and Fantasy Film and Television Credits**. 2 vols. McFarland, 1983.
Lentz lists credits in genre films and TV programs for more than 10,000 actors, directors, producers, writers, cinematographers, special effects and makeup artists and composers of film scores. Birth and death dates are given in many but not all entries. Entries for actors include the names of characters portrayed. Volume 2 is arranged by title of film and TV series. For each film title only the director and actors are listed; it is necessary to look in other works to find who performed other functions on a film. Lentz provides the most complete information anywhere on fantastic TV series, including title, actors, character names and broadcast dates for each episode. This very complete work has been updated by a 1989 supplement, current through 1987.

9-7. Weldon, Michael. **The Psychotronic Encyclopedia of Film**. Ballantine, 1983.
Weldon includes art films and expensive productions and ranges from the 1930s to the 1980s, but B-movies of the 1950s and 1960s are his first love. Many of the over 3,000 films listed are nonfantastic exploitation movies, such as juvenile delinquent and prison films. Except in the cases of the very good and the very bad, Weldon describes but does not evaluate most films, recognizing that B-movie fans are attracted by plot elements and stars, not by conventional dramatic and cinematic values. He has something interesting to say about almost every film. As a fan critic, Weldon is superior to John Stanley, whose *Revenge of the Creature Features Movie Guide* (3d ed., 1987) has more films (almost 4,000) but less wit. Joe Bob Briggs's *Joe Bob Goes to the Drive-In* (1987) humorously describes several dozen exploitation films of the early 1980s, about half of them horror or sword-and-sorcery titles, throwing light on the psychology and simple needs of B-movie

fans. For a much more analytical study of such films, see Danny Peary's *Cult Movies* (1981), *Cult Movies 2* (1983) and *Cult Movies 3* (1988).

9-8. Willis, Donald. **Horror and Science Fiction Films**. Scarecrow, vol. I, 1972; vol. II, 1982; vol. III, 1984.
Despite his title, Willis includes fantasy films which are neither SF nor horror. Entries include the usual information (year, country, length, production company, credits, cast, variant titles) as well as citations to reviews and sources of more complete information. Volume I has about 4,000 films; Volume II, about 2,350; Volume III, 760, but many entries in Volumes II and III are critical commentaries for films listed briefly in a previous volume. As the number of films in each volume has decreased, the length of Willis's commentaries has increased. His Volume I is comparable to but much less complete than Lee's *Reference Guide* [9-5]. Willis's critical annotations are of respectable quality, but less authoritative than those in Nicholls [9-11].

Periodicals

*9-9. Cinefantastique. ISSN 0145-6032. 1970– . 5 issues a year. Frederick S. Clarke, ed. Box 270, Oak Park, IL 60303. Circ.: 20,000.

9-10. Starlog. ISSN 0191-4626. 1976– . Monthly. David McDonnell, ed. Starlog Group, 475 Park Ave., New York, NY 10016. Circ.: 350,000.
Cinefantastique is the highest-quality English-language magazine on fantastic cinema, covering horror, fantasy and SF films and TV. Issues range from sixty to ninety pages, with in-depth articles and excellent illustrations. Short pieces profile forthcoming releases. Current films and TV programs are reviewed with independence and sophistication. *Cinefantastique*'s irreverence has led to a prolonged feud with the Lucas-Spielberg empire, which has hampered the magazine's ability to cover many major productions in depth. *Starlog* is best known as a popular science fiction film magazine, but it also covers all fantastic films and TV except for horror films, which are the subject of its sister publication, *Fangoria*. Issues are usually about seventy-five pages, with informative but uncritical articles. *Starlog* maintains friendly relations with studios by not reviewing current films. Both *Cinefantastique* and *Starlog* carry major articles on historically important films from past decades; *Starlog* often discusses old TV series. *Starlog* frequently interviews filmmakers, including actors; *Cinefantastique* interviews film workers but usually eschews actors, an unjustified and snobbish policy. *Cinefantastique* is essential for students of fantastic films; *Starlog*, with its abundance of facts and paucity of analysis, is useful for large collections. Comments on forthcoming films appear regularly in *Locus* [11-40] and *Science Fiction Chronicle* [11-40]. Gahan Wilson's lively reviews in *Twilight Zone* [11-15] are worthwhile, but Harlan Ellison's rambling pieces in *Magazine of Fantasy and Science Fiction* [11-13], collected in *Harlan Ellison's Watching* (1989), are more often harangues about the iniquities of Hollywood than critiques of specific films. Two annuals, *International Index to Film Periodicals* and *Film Literature Index*, index articles and reviews in film magazines. *Film*

Review Index (2 vols., 1986, 1987), edited by Patricia King Hanson and Stephen L. Hanson, indexes both reviews in periodicals and discussions in hundreds of books of over 7,000 significant films from the silents to 1985. Lee [9-5] and Willis [9-8] provide citations to periodical literature.

Critical Studies

*9-11. Nicholls, Peter (U.K.). **The World of Fantastic Films: An Illustrated Survey**. Dodd, Mead, 1984. U.K. title: **Fantastic Cinema**. Ebury, 1984.
Nicholls's survey of fantastic films of all kinds—horror, fantasy and SF—has an exceptional critical text, illustrations carefully selected to represent many periods and types of films, and reference information. The latter is found in a filmography of 700 titles; each entry includes country, date, length, color or black-and-white, production company, principal credits and cast and a rating based on the average of four critics' opinions. 400 films are annotated briefly in the filmography; the other 300 are discussed at greater length in the well-organized text. In a field where many books omit important films or delve deeply into trivia, Nicholls includes almost all significant films and none of interest only to completists. He can be faulted only for omitting animated films and for rushing through several decades; 44 pages cover films from the 1890s to 1967, while 120 are devoted to works from 1968 to 1983. Coverage of foreign films is strong. Nicholls helps to redefine the limits of fantastic cinema by including art films by such directors as Bergman, Fellini, Truffaut and Allen. *The World of Fantastic Films* is the best one-volume critical work covering all kinds of fantastic cinema.

9-12. Searles, Baird. **Films of Science Fiction and Fantasy**. Abrams, 1988.
Searles covers only 282 films and provides less filmographic information than Nicholls [9-11]. His discussions are more often descriptive than critical. Although he includes some marginal fantasy films and animated films not in Nicholls, he omits several important titles. The many illustrations, rather than the text, are the main asset of Searles's work.

More limited in focus is Kenneth Von Gunden's *Flights of Fancy: The Great Fantasy Films* (McFarland, 1989). Each of the fifteen chapters includes a lengthy synopsis, a production history and commonplace criticism of a film judged representative of a distinct subgenre of fantasy. The films differ widely in date, quality and type. Von Gunden lists other films associated with each of the subgenres but fails to analyze in any depth the characteristics of each type, the distinctions between them and what, if anything, links them. *Flights of Fancy* illustrates the problems inherent in studying a large body of disparate works.

Specialized Studies

9-13. Essoe, Gabe. **Tarzan of the Movies**. Citadel Press, 1968.
From 1918 to 1968 eight silent films, thirty-two sound films and a TV series were made featuring Edgar Rice Burroughs's Tarzan. Essoe believes that the best of the films were the few which closely followed Burroughs's novels. Like Burroughs, he prefers Tarzan to be articulate, not tongue-tied. The author says more about

Hollywood deal-making and the production of the films than about the films themselves and the reasons for their long-standing popularity. He ignores the racism inherent in the Tarzan cycle. *Tarzan of the Movies* is clumsily written but enthusiastic and full of information, with hundreds of illustrations (some inadequately captioned) including some marvelous old posters.

9-14. Goldner, Orville, and George E. Turner. **The Making of King Kong**. A. S. Barnes, 1975.

Goldner worked as a technician on *King Kong* (1933). His account of the production of the classic is detailed, enthusiastic and almost reverential. Most illustrations are of the filmmakers at work, not stills from the film. *The Making of King Kong* is a more valuable study of the development of the stop-motion animation technique than Harryhausen's *Film Fantasy Scrapbook* [9-16]. The essays in *The Girl in the Hairy Paw* (1976), ed. by Ronald Gottesman and Harry Geduld, vary widely in quality. Several pieces describe the film's production in less detail than Goldner; others discuss *King Kong*'s folkloric, literary and cinematic antecedents and the controversy over the authorship of the screenplay. *Kong* fiction and parodies and a great variety of *Kong*-inspired art are included. An important essay on *Kong* by Noel Carroll is found in *Planks of Reason* (1984), a collection of essays on horror films edited by Barry Keith Grant. Goldner is the first choice.

9-15. Harmetz, Aljean. **The Making of The Wizard of Oz: Movie Magic and Studio Power in the Prime of MGM—and the Miracle of Production #1060.** Knopf, 1977.

The Wizard of Oz (1939) was made by four directors, ten screenwriters and nine composers and lyricists in the heyday of Hollywood for the most powerful studio in the world. MGM had its share of drunkards and neurotics in high places, but it employed hundreds of workers who were fanatically devoted to quality; Harmetz interviewed many of them. Her careful, justly cynical account demolishes old legends, refurbishes some tarnished reputations and is one of the best books about the making of a film.

9-16. Harryhausen, Ray. **Film Fantasy Scrapbook**. 3d ed. A. S. Barnes, 1981.

For twenty years before the era of *Star Wars*, Harryhausen was the most famous special effects artist in films. His stop-motion animation technique is now outdated, but his best films still have charm. He recalls the development of stop-motion by Willis O'Brien (*King Kong*), his own early work in low-budget SF films, and his popular fantasy films, most of which are based on Greek mythology or the *Arabian Nights*. The *Scrapbook* is disappointingly superficial and defensive, with poorly reproduced stills. Compare Goldner [9-14].

9-17. Hickman, Gail Morgan. **The Films of George Pal**. A. S. Barnes, 1977.

Pal and Ray Harryhausen [9-16] are the two best-known filmmakers specializing in fantasy and SF but not horror. Hickman's discussion of Pal's early innovative Puppetoon shorts and the fourteen feature films he produced or directed is fannish and only mildly critical. She tends to exonerate Pal and blame screenwriters and studio executives for whatever faults she finds in the films. Her book is useful mainly for its biographical information on Pal and for the many illustrations. *The Fantasy Film Worlds of George Pal* (1983), a ninety-minute documentary film directed by Arnold Leibovit and available on videocassette, is similarly informative but uncritical and includes the most spectacular scenes from Pal's movies.

9-18. Kinnard, Roy. **Beasts and Behemoths: Prehistoric Creatures in the Movies.** Scarecrow, 1988.
Kinnard is a well-informed guide to the low-budget American films of the 1950s about dinosaurs rampaging through the modern world. He gives only brief attention to several prehistoric caveman-versus-dinosaur fantasies; these are covered more fully, but uncritically, in a heavily illustrated section of Donald Glut's *Dinosaur Scrapbook* (1980).

9-19. Larson, Randall D. **Musique Fantastique: A Survey of Film Music in the Fantastic Cinema.** Scarecrow, 1985.
Larson discusses the scores of hundreds of fantasy, horror and SF films from the 1930s to the 1980s, with special chapters on TV scoring, electronic music, classical music, British, Japanese and other foreign films, and on four major composers; there are over 200 pages of filmography and discography and many quotations from composers and critics. An enormous amount of information is gathered, but Larson's criticism is suspect; he is favorable about the large majority of the scores, in keeping with his enthusiastic conclusion that "music has always seemed to be at its best in fantastic films."

9-20. Slusser, George, and Eric S. Rabkin, eds. **Shadows of the Magic Lamp: Fantasy and Science Fiction in Film.** Southern Illinois Univ. Press, 1985.
Of fourteen essays, six concern fantasy films. Three of these are highly theoretical and clogged with the jargon of academic literary and film criticism. Of the three accessible pieces, one on *Monty Python and the Holy Grail* is simplistic. Two have substance, but deal with films—*Excalibur, The Little Prince*—of modest importance.

Table 9-3. Fantasy Films and Their Literary Sources

Anthology films, short films and made-for-TV films and miniseries are excluded, as are films based on mythology, fairy tales, folklore and the *Arabian Nights.* Arrangement is by film title. Titles of literary works are given only if different from the film title. Titles of novels are in italics, titles of shorter fiction in quotes. Consult the author index for entry numbers of annotated novels.

Film title, Year(s)	Author, Title (if different)
The Adventures of Baron Münchausen, 1943, 1988	Raspe, Rudolph Eric
Alice in Wonderland, 1933, 1951, 1972	Carroll, Lewis
All of Me, 1984	Davis, Ed. *Me Too*
The Amazing Mr. Blunden, 1972	Barber, Antonia. *The Ghosts*
At the Earth's Core, 1976	Burroughs, Edgar Rice
Atlantis, the Lost Continent, 1961	Hargreaves, Gerald. *Atalanta, a Story of Atlantis* (play)
The Beastmaster, 1982	Norton, Andre
Beauty and the Beast, 1946	de Beaumont, Mme. Le Prince. "La Belle et la bête"

Table 9-3. (continued)

The Bed Sitting Room, 1969	Milligan, Spike, and John Antrobus (play)
Bedknobs and Broomsticks, 1971	Norton, Mary. *Bedknob and Broomstick*
Bell, Book and Candle, 1958	van Druten, John (play)
The Black Cauldron, 1985	Alexander, Lloyd. Prydain series
Blithe Spirit, 1945	Coward, Noël (play)
The Blue Bird, 1940, 1976	Maeterlinck, Maurice (play)
The Canterville Ghost, 1944	Wilde, Oscar
Charlotte's Web, 1973	White, E. B.
Chitty Chitty Bang Bang, 1968	Fleming, Ian
A Christmas Carol, 1951	Dickens, Charles
Conan the Barbarian, 1981	Howard, Robert E. Conan series
A Connecticut Yankee in King Arthur's Court, 1921, 1931, 1949	Twain, Mark
Damn Yankees, 1958	Wallop, Douglas. *The Year the Yankees Lost the Pennant*
Darby O'Gill and the Little People, 1959	Kavanagh, J. T. Darby O'Gill stories
The Devil and Daniel Webster, 1941	Benét, Stephen Vincent
Doctor Dolittle, 1967	Lofting, Hugh. Dolittle series
Dreamchild, 1985	Carroll, Lewis. *Alice in Wonderland*
Escape to Witch Mountain, 1975	Key, Alexander
Excalibur, 1981	Malory, Thomas. *Morte d'Arthur*
The Exterminating Angel, 1962	Bergamín, José. *Los náufragos de la calle de la providencia* (play)
Fellini Satyricon, 1970	Petronius. *Satyricon*
Finian's Rainbow, 1968	Harburg, E. Y., Burton Lane (play)
Freaky Friday, 1977	Rodgers, Mary
The Ghost and Mrs. Muir, 1947	Dick, R. A.
The Gnome-Mobile, 1967	Sinclair, Upton. *The Gnomobile*
Gor, 1987	Norman, John. *Tarnsman of Gor*
Greystoke: The Legend of Tarzan, 1984	Burroughs, Edgar Rice. *Tarzan of the Apes*
Gulliver's Travels, 1939	Swift, Jonathan
Harvey, 1950	Chase, Mary (play)
Heaven Can Wait, 1943	Bus-Feketé, Lazlo. *Birthday* (play)
Heaven Can Wait, 1978	Segall, Harry (play)
Here Comes Mr. Jordan, 1941	Segall, Harry. *Heaven Can Wait* (play)
I Married a Witch, 1942	Smith, Thorne. *The Passionate Witch*
It's A Wonderful Life, 1946	Stern, Philip Van Doren. "The Greatest Gift"
The Jungle Book, 1942, 1967	Kipling, Rudyard
The Land That Time Forgot, 1975	Burroughs, Edgar Rice
The Last Unicorn, 1982	Beagle, Peter S.
The Little Prince, 1974	Saint Exupéry, Antoine

Table 9-3. (continued)

Live and Let Die, 1973	Fleming, Ian
Lord of the Rings, 1978	Tolkien, J. R. R.
Lost Horizon, 1937, 1973	Hilton, James
Malpertuis, 1972	Ray, Jean
The Man Who Could Work Miracles, 1937	Wells, H. G.
Mary Poppins, 1964	Travers, P. L. *Mary Poppins* stories
Maxie, 1985	Finney, Jack. *Marion's Wall*
Miracle in Milan, 1951	Zavattini, Cesare. *Toto il Buono*
Miracle on 34th Street, 1947	Davies, Valentine
The Never-Ending Story, 1984	Ende, Michael
Oh, God! 1977	Corman, Avery
The People That Time Forgot, 1977	Burroughs, Edgar Rice
Peter Pan, 1924, 1953	Barrie, J. M.
Picnic at Hanging Rock, 1975	Lindsay, Joan
Pinocchio, 1940	Collodi, Carlo
Portrait of Jennie, 1948	Nathan, Robert
The Princess Bride, 1987	Goldman, William
Red Sonja, 1985	Howard, Robert E. based on *Red Sonja* comics by Roy Thomas
Return to Oz, 1985	Baum, L. Frank. *Land of Oz* and *Ozma of Oz*
The Saragossa Manuscript, 1965	Potocki, Jan
Scrooge, 1970	Dickens, Charles. *A Christmas Carol*
The Secret of NIMH, 1982	O'Brien, Robert C. *Mrs. Frisby and the Rats of NIMH*
Seven Faces of Dr. Lao, 1964	Finney, Charles G. *The Circus of Dr. Lao*
She 1935, 1965	Haggard, H. Rider
The Shout, 1979	Graves, Robert
Slaughterhouse-Five, 1972	Vonnegut, Kurt
Somewhere in Time, 1980	Matheson, Richard. *Bid Time Return*
The Sword in the Stone, 1963	White, T. H.
Tarzan the Ape Man, 1932, 1981	Burroughs, Edgar Rice. Tarzan series.
The Three Worlds of Gulliver, 1960	Swift, Jonathan. *Gulliver's Travels*
The Tin Drum, 1979	Grass, Günter
Topper, 1937	Smith, Thorne
Ugetsu, 1953	Ueda, Akinari. 2 stories
The Water Babies, 1978	Kingsley, Charles
Watership Down, 1978	Adams, Richard
Who Framed Roger Rabbit, 1988	Wolf, Gary. *Who Censored Roger Rabbit?*
The Wiz, 1978	Baum, L. Frank. *The Wizard of Oz*
The Wizard of Oz, 1939	Baum, L. Frank

10

Fantastic Art and Illustration

Walter Albert

Diana Waggoner, in her note on fantasy illustration in *The Hills of Faraway* [6-34], claims that "fantasy art and fantasy illustration are not the same thing. . . . Fantasy art is untroubled by considerations of internal logic [while] fantasy illustration is, or should be, the servant of literary fantasy and should conform to the same rules of logic and order that a narrative does" (p. 70). She also sees fantasy illustration as deriving from two principal sources, pulp magazines and children's books. Yet, curiously, she includes among fantasy artists Randolph Caldecott, Arthur Rackham and Kate Greenaway—all of them illustrators of children's books—and implicitly excludes them from fantasy illustration, as she defines it.

If Waggoner has some difficulty in establishing precise boundaries to distinguish fantasy art from fantasy illustration, it may be because fantasy in art has been a problematic area for critics. While the fantastic has often been associated with religious and mythological subjects, it is only in the twentieth century that a major artistic movement has made the "marvelous" a key tenet of its aesthetics. Surrealism, with its belief in the inherent creative energy of dreams and the unconscious, began as a revolution in avant-garde aesthetics but has, ironically, become a part of the establishment it intended to alter. Surrealist fantasy is so prevalent in modern advertising and, more recently, music videos, as well as in fantasy illustration that it may almost be considered an accepted "norm." Surrealism, then, has accomplished its goal of altering human consciousness even if it appears to be at the expense of the domestication of the movement.

However, if the post-World War I phenomenon of Surrealism is a major influence on contemporary fantasy illustration, the roots of fantasy illustration lie in the nineteenth century. Victoria's utilitarian society was entertained by a variety of leisure arts, many of them deriving from a fascination with fairy pictures and fairy tales—often derived from German or Oriental sources—accompanied by an obsession with the occult and the supernatural. The Victorians seemed to delight in the playful, inventive forms of an art that surprised and enchanted as they turned away from the restraints of realism and naturalism.

This flourishing of fantasy art as an infatuation with the nonutilitarian is evident in the "first generation" illustrators who consistently exploited fantasy motifs. Richard Doyle's *In Fairyland* (1870), the illustrations by the gifted Arthur Boyd Houghton for the Dalziel Brothers edition of the *Arabian Nights* (1867), and the children's books designed and illustrated by Kate Greenaway, Walter Crane and Randolph Caldecott were enormously popular. They drew on diverse traditions: the fairy tale, Oriental tales and German Romantic myths and legends. The Mother Goose rhymes were still popular and the penny dreadfuls—ancestors of the American dime novel and pulp magazines—were decorated with horrific, crude line drawings.

While popular illustration mined the twilight world of faerie fantasy, more disturbing fantasies, reflections of a darker sensibility, could be seen in France in the work of French Symbolist artists, including the jewel-adorned, highly ornate oils of Gustave Moreau and the nightmarish black-and-white lithographic series by Odilon Redon. In England this new spirit was echoed in the work of the Decadent writers and artists and in publications like *The Yellow Book*. The erotic fantasies of Aubrey Beardsley, characterized, like the work of Redon, by a highly personal use of the possibilities of line and chiaroscuro, gave expression to the spirit of an age and defined an aesthetic attitude and style.

In the 1890s, in England, France and America, a generation of artists, drawing on the French Symbolists and English Decadents, revolutionized poster and magazine design. Art Nouveau, which also introduced innovations in furniture and fabric design, could not only be identified on the magazine covers and interior illustrations and advertising layouts but would also coincide with an age of book illustration and design.

Internationally, this was the period of the ascendance of British fantasy illustrator Arthur Rackham. Rackham's vision of the world of faerie, in contrast to the Victorian idyllic pastoral, was often dark. His illustrations for Grimm, Irving's *Rip Van Winkle* and Barrie's *Peter Pan in Kensington Gardens* [F3-18] still convey something of the cozy, familial Victorian view, but there is often a sullen undercurrent that threatens that world, and it is this darker side that can be seen in the nightmarish flight of Snow White from the huntsman in Disney's *Snow White and the Seven Dwarfs*, where the forest background is clearly inspired by Rackham's early work.

Other illustrators of note were the Beardsley-influenced Harry Clarke (illustrator of Goethe's *Faust* and of Poe), the Oriental fantasist Edmund Dulac and Kay Nielsen, creator of highly sylized, allegorical theatrical vignettes, as well as the less well-known Danish artist Gustav Tenggren, who was later to make significant contributions to Disney's *Snow White* and *Pinocchio*. In addition, Nielsen's contribution to the Walpurgis-night episode of *Fantasia* is well known, and this continuity with the work of the European illustrators in American animation art is worthy of note.

If the lavish signed, limited editions of British illustrated books found a significant audience in this country, the age of British illustrators had a counterpart in great American illustrators, whose work was widely used in both magazines and books. While fantasy was not as important an element in their work as it was in the work of the British illustrators, the period from the early 1880s to the early years of World War I is often referred to as the Golden Age of American Illustration. Howard Pyle dominated much of this period, influential both as a practicing illustrator and teacher, while the illustrated book of the post-World War I period was dominated by N. C. Wyeth and his students, as well as by the enormously popular Maxfield Parrish. Wyeth is best known for his contributions to the Scribner Classics series with their predominance of adventure rather than fantasy titles. Wyeth's original work is ill served in the books by the much-reduced reproductions, but there is no question of the importance of the influence of his romantically heroic style in this period. In his later years Wyeth was to become increasingly unhappy with his designation as an illustrator rather than an artist, a distinction that has always plagued the practitioners of popular art. And Wyeth's unhappy final years are echoed in the fate of one of the most gifted illustrators of this period, W. W. Denslow, today most readily identified as the illustrator of L. Frank Baum's first Oz book, *The Wonderful Wizard of Oz* [F3-20].

Denslow's career would not parallel the successful later career of Baum, but his illustrations for such books as *Father Goose: His Book, The Pearl and the Pumpkin, The Jewelled Toad* and a series of classic children's fairy stories constitutes an impressive body of work focusing on fantasy literature. Denslow was, however, only one of a group of gifted contemporaries, which included Palmer Cox (creator of the "Brownies"), Peter Newell and, in newspaper comic strips and film animation, the prodigiously talented Winsor McCay. Many of these artists also published in the long-lived *St. Nicholas Magazine*, which was a showcase of black-and-white artwork for children's literature.

Fantasy art continued to flourish in the children's book field, but another kind of popular fantasy art would make its mark in the American pulp magazine where fantasy writing was to reach a wide audience. The most important of the magazines for fantasy literature, and one noted in the 1930s for the quality of its cover art and interior drawings, was *Weird Tales* [11-20], whose first issue was dated March 1923. This issue featured "Ooze," an "extraordinary novelette" by Anthony M. Rud, and sported a horrific cover illustration for the story, as an octopus-like creature with inappropriately mild eyes encircles a damsel-in-distress while a pop-eyed man threatens the creature with a knife and gun. The artwork was similar to the blunt, tawdry cover art of the nineteenth-century dime novel. Matters improved somewhat in 1927 when the magazine's editorial office was moved to Chicago and a local artist, C. C. Senf, began doing covers. Interestingly, Senf's work bears a strong resemblance to that of Gino Starace, illustrator of the popular French *feuilleton* series, Fantômas, but, as was the case with Starace, Senf's work, although more skillful than that of the other cover artists of the magazine's early years, tended more toward the grotesque than the fantastic.

Hugh Rankin brought an Art Deco style to the covers, and his strong sense of design and color may have resulted in the most attractive cover art to be seen on pulp magazines in the late 1920s. However, the 1930s were the most notable decade for fantasy cover art, dominated by the work of Margaret Brundage and, later in the decade, the influential Virgil Finlay, whose magazine work set the standard by which pulp magazine fantasy illustration was judged for at least a decade.

Readers of pulp magazines of the 1930s and 1940s remember with particular fondness Finlay's illustrations of the work of American fantasist A. Merritt, in *Fantastic Novels* and *Famous Fantastic Mysteries* [11-4]. Also, Finlay was as gifted at interior black-and-white drawings as he was at cover illustrations, and his work gained acceptance so quickly that in many of the late 1930s issues of *Weird Tales*—whose interior work had not previously been of the quality of its covers—all or most of the interior illustrations were by Finlay.

In addition to Finlay (and his contemporaries on *FFM* and *FN*, Hannes Bok and Lawrence), the witty, accomplished line drawings of Edd Cartier in *Unknown* [11-18], the fantasy companion to Street and Smith's hard science fiction magazine, *Astounding Science Fiction*, attracted the attention of readers while the fantastic exploits of heroes like Doc Savage and The Shadow were celebrated on covers by talented illustrators like Walter Baumhofer and Jerome Rozen. The stylized, boldly colored covers of scores of pulps showed a skill in color and line that was superior to much of the prose style inside the magazine and, indeed, probably drew attention away from the slick magazines whose idealized American scenes have often dated in ways that the pulp art has not. One of the features of paperback publishing of the 1980s has been the resurgence of the pulp-style magazine cover, reflecting both the nostalgic rediscovery of popular art of the 1930s and a writing style celebrated in the reissue of pulp fiction. (Paperback cover art is the subject of two useful books. Thomas L. Bonn's *Under Cover: An Illustrated History of American Mass Market Paperbacks* [Penguin, 1982] provides intelligent commentary and hundreds of reproductions in color and black and white. Somewhat similar is Piet Schreuders's *Paperbacks, U.S.A.: A Graphic History* [Blue Dolphin Enterprises, 1981].)

The massive paper drives of World War II were responsible for the destruction of thousands of issues of pulp magazines, but the great days of the pulps had passed, and in the wake of the paper drives and with the increasing popularity of a new medium for fantasy fiction, the paperback, the vast numbers of pulp magazines on the stands shrank dramatically. By the mid-1950s they were replaced by the digest magazines that were to provide a much reduced market for fiction. The best artists of the 1930s and early 1940s had left the field or had greatly reduced their contributions to it. Virgil Finlay's work in the 1950s for *Astrology Magazine* was as fine as much of his earlier work, but he no longer dominated the field. Indeed, no fantasy artist comparable to Finlay in stylistic recognizability and popularity was to surface until Frank Frazetta established himself as the most influential fantasy artist of the 1960s, in the wake of a revival of the work of Edgar Rice Burroughs, published in paperback by Ace Books.

For a time, Frazetta and his stylistic look-alikes dominated paperback cover art. In the 1970s Frazetta's by-now classic status was confirmed by a series of trade art books [10-81, 10-82], published by Ballantine Books, that also presaged the development of a market for fantasy art that shows no signs of diminishing today.

Although a number of small presses had published hardback editions of fantasy and science fiction in the 1950s, with dust jackets featuring the work of prominent artists of the period, this phenomenon was to be greatly outdistanced by the proliferation of small press editions in the 1970s and 1980s. Pulp writer

Robert E. Howard was one of the first to be celebrated in this fashion, with the limited editions published by Don Grant distinguished for a time by the use of artists of the quality of Jeff Jones, George Barr and Alicia Austin, but Grant was less successful in choosing artists of comparable quality for later publications. However, by this time (the mid-1970s) a number of other small presses (see chapter 5) were turning out signed, limited and trade editions of works featuring original artwork, as well as portfolios of illustrations, although relatively few contemporary illustrators have had entire books devoted to their work.

Virgil Finlay's work was once again available, in books published by Don Grant and Gerry de la Ree, a collector and now inactive publisher, but a new style was emerging and a new, post-Frazetta generation of artists. The style was dominated—in contrast to the heroic romanticism of Frazetta in which one could see the influence of Wyeth and his generation—by a hyperrealism based on the work of Surrealist artists like Dalí and Magritte. The work of the Brothers Hildebrandt for a series of annual calendars based on the Tolkien cycle was typical of the new style which, in the 1980s, has been continued by the very popular illustrator Michael Whelan.

It is too early to characterize definitively the work of this generation, but the artists are technically proficient and given to pristine, emotionally restrained, even cold treatments of fantasy subjects. On the other hand, there has also emerged a new generation of artists drawing on artists of the classic age (like Clarke, Rackham, Charles Robinson, Dulac) who are reinterpreting works illustrated by those artists. Many of these artists who have more recently come to fantasy book illustration are comic book artists, and among the most prominent—and gifted—are Michael Kaluta, Berni Wrightson, Barry Windsor-Smith and Charles Vess, whose illustrations for Shakespeare's *Midsummer Night's Dream* (Donning, 1988) are almost a textbook example of stylistic influences at work in an artist who has yet to develop in his book illustrations an individual, distinctive style. (Comic strip and comic book illustration are excluded from consideration in this critical survey, as is the so-called graphic novel, which has become moderately popular in recent years. For guidance in this area, see Inge's chapter on comic books in his *Handbook of American Popular Literature* [6-38].) Also of note, in the generation of the very popular, somewhat arid Michael Whelan, is the highly ornate work of Don Maitz, in whom the distinctive work of Edmund Dulac is fused with a more contemporary style.

Thus, the 1980s would appear to be a period of great technical competence as well as of the rediscovery of the illustrators of earlier generations in an apparent attempt to forge a new style for the age. It is a period of great diversity with artists working in animated film, music videos, paperback and hardcover book illustrations, and exhibiting original works that are bought by an avid generation of new collectors willing to pay prices for popular art that fall short of the astronomical figures of mainstream and avant-garde artists yet are symptomatic of an escalating market. It is a market that, like most new and many old markets, is susceptible to trends and fashions not always wedded to work of unusual quality, but it is a phenomenon of great vitality and even greater potential.

The adjective in the chapter title includes both fantasy and horror illustration and art. Although the emphasis in this chapter has been on fantasy, illustration or art designed to provoke fear, terror or unease is not absent. See especially entries [10-9], [10-12] and the work of Doré, some of Finlay and Giger. The work of many contemporary horror illustrators, such as J. K. Potter, has not yet been collected in books.

Bibliography

The author wishes to express his appreciation for the assistance of Robert E. Briney and Neil Barron in compiling this bibliography. Their contributions are identified as (REB) and (NB).

Unlike volumes reproducing the works of "fine" artists, relatively few of the books annotated show medium, size of original or present location. Most original illustrations for pulp magazines were discarded (see Weinberg, [10-35], for the unhappy details).

General and Multi-Subject Entries

*10-1. Best, James J. **American Popular Illustration: A Reference Guide.** Greenwood, 1984.
After a brief historical overview of the subject, the chapters focus on such topics as history and aesthetics, illustrators and illustrated works, and social and artistic contexts. Bibliographic citations for the books he discusses are given at the end of each chapter. Best is particularly good on the period up to 1920. His primary interest is in illustrative material published in the slick magazines and in books; dime novel, pulp and paperback illustration receive only cursory treatment. This undoubtedly reflects the relative paucity of secondary material on popular art of the post-1920 period and the richness of material on the "great age" of popular illustration, 1880–1920. Index of names and some subjects. Regrettably lacks illustrations.

10-2. Blashfield, Jean, ed. **The Art of Dragon Magazine.** TSR, 1988.
Includes all of the cover art from the first ten years of *Dragon* Magazine, plus color and black-and-white interior artwork, by sixty-six artists, including Larry Elmore, Clyde Caldwell, Jeff Easley and Dean Morrissey. There are a couple of covers each by Tim Hildebrandt and Carl Lundgren, plus single contributions from George Barr and Boris Vallejo. (REB)

10-3. Canham, Stephen. "**What Manner of Beast? Illustrations of 'Beauty and the Beast.'**" In *Image & Maker: An Annual Dedicated to the Consideration of Book Publication*, pp. 13–25. Green Tiger, 1984.
The last of the Green Tiger Press publications dedicated to classic illustrations for children's books, and what was intended to be the first of a series of annual publications. Canham, in his beautifully illustrated essay, discusses the ways artists have depicted the beast—and his Beauty—in the classic fairy tale.

10-4. Cochran, Russ, ed. **The Edgar Rice Burroughs Library of Illustration.** 3 vols. Cochran, 1976, 1977, 1984.
Volume 1 is dedicated to J. Allen St. John and is an impressive tribute to the artist

many consider to be the quintessential Burroughs illustrator. In Volume 2, much of which is devoted to comic strip art by Hal Foster and John Coleman Burroughs, there is also cover and interior art for the books by St. John, and by Studley and John Coleman Burroughs. Volume 3 includes comic strip and comic book art by Burne Hogarth, Russ Manning, Rex Maxon and Jesse Marsh as well as book and paperback art by St. John, Schoonover, Reed Crandall, Roy Krenkel and Frank Frazetta. There is also a perfectly dreadful illustration by Mahlon Blaine for the Canaveral Press edition of *Pellucidar*. Whatever one may think of Blaine's other work, his pairing with Burroughs was most unfortunate. Volume 3 also includes interviews with Roy Krenkel and Frazetta. This was clearly a labor of love for publisher Cochran, and the production meets very high standards.

10-5. Comini, Alessandra. **The Fantastic Art of Vienna**. Ballantine, 1978.
Twenty-five-page essay, plus fifty-nine plates (forty of them in color) and twenty-six additional illustrations. Artists range from the early sixteenth century to the mid-twentieth: Albrecht Altdorfer, Alfred Kubin, Klimt, Kokoschka, Egon Schiele, Arnold Schönberg, Friedrich Hundertwasser, etc. Grim, satirical, often self-mocking works, with an occasional flash of color or beauty. (REB)

10-6. Dean, Martyn. **The Guide to Fantasy Art Techniques**. Text by Chris Evans. Paper Tiger & Arco, 1984.
Interviews between Dean and the following artists: Jim Burns, Ian Miller, Patrick Woodroffe, Philip Castle, Syd Mead, Chris Foss, Martin Bower and Boris Vallejo. Fantasy is used rather broadly since some of the artists (Mead, Foss, Bower) work in a medium closer to science fiction hardware art. Sketches as well as examples of finished work. The artists talk about influences on their work, techniques, working habits and ways they research their illustrations.

10-7. Dean, Martyn and Roger. **The Flights of Icarus**. Paper Tiger & A & W Visual Library, 1977.
A verse cycle by Donald Lehmkuhl is used as the excuse for displaying more than 120 paintings by thirty-two British and U.S. artists, including Jim Burns, Roger Dean, Jim FitzPatrick, Jeff Jones, Michael W. Kaluta, Alan Lee, Ian Miller, Patrick Woodroffe and Berni Wrightson. Brief biographical and career notes on each artist. (REB)

10-8. de la Ree, Gerry, ed. **The Art of the Fantastic**. Gerry de la Ree, 1978.
Brief general introduction, with notes on the artists included, plus a short discussion of Lynd Ward's illustrations for the *Haunted Omnibus*, fifty-four of which are included in this compilation. Other artists included are Hannes Bok (11), Virgil Finlay (7), Lawrence (5), Frank R. Paul (7), Stephen E. Fabian (12), Edd Cartier (3), Ed Emsh, Tim Kirk, Frank Kelly Freas, Mahlon Blaine, Roy Krenkel, Frank Utpatel, Ronald Clyne, Clark Ashton Smith, Harry Clarke, Roy Hunt and such uncommon artists as G. Watson David (for *Tanglewood Tales* and John Ruskin's "The King of the Golden River") and J. R. Weguelin (for Haggard's *Montezuma's Daughter*). Thirty-three artists are represented, some by illustrations not previously published (including seven by Lynd Ward). All illustrations are reproduced from originals in the editor's collection. (REB)

10-9. Durie, Alison (U.K.). **Weird Tales**. Jupiter Books, 1979.
An anthology of cover art for this popular pulp magazine. A few of the plates are in color, but most of the reproductions are in black and white or monochromatic tints. The earliest color examples are for 1933 (J. Allen St. John and Margaret Brundage). The reproduction is particularly damaging to the covers of Hugh Rankin and C. C. Senf, most of whose work was done in the 1920s. In spite of this defect, the book is a generous sampling of the cover art of this important and influential magazine.

10-10. Edwards, Malcolm, and Robert Holdstock (U.K.). **Realms of Fantasy**. Doubleday & Dragon's World, 1983.
A successor to *Alien Landscapes* (1979), which emphasized SF worlds, this survey explores ten fictional fantasy worlds, such as Middle-earth, Le Guin's Earthsea, Peake's Gormenghast and Gene Wolfe's Urth. Approximately seventy illustrations by various British hands, forty in color. A later, similar work by the same authors is *Lost Realms* (1984). Compare the somewhat different dictionary by Manguel and Guadalupi [6-39]. (NB)

10-11. Gaunt, William, ed. **Painters of Fantasy: From Hieronymus Bosch to Salvador Dali**. Phaidon, 1974.
The short introduction is superficial and the high point is a statement that "[the fantastic] has appealed to the sense of wonder in every age. . . ." Of interest for the 104 reproductions.

10-12. Haining, Peter. **Terror! A History of Horror Illustrations from the Pulp Magazines**. Souvenir Press & A & W Visual Library, 1976. Reprinted as *The Art of Horror Stories*. Chartwell Books, 1986.
Examples of illustrations for pulp fiction, broadly defined as Gothic/penny dreadful/dime novel/pulp fiction. Several color plates, but most of the reproductions are in black and white. Captions for the illustrations contain some information on the illustrators; short chapter introductions. Fine for browsing and for a noncritical introduction to pulp illustrations, most of which have some fantasy elements.

10-13. Hammacher, Abraham Marie. **Phantoms of the Imagination: Fantasy in Art & Literature from Blake to Dali**. Abrams, 1981.
Hammacher attempts a study of the fantastic in eighteenth- through twentieth-century art, with chapters on Blake, Fuseli, the Gothic, French Symbolism and Surrealism, to which almost a third of the book is devoted.

*10-14. Johnson, Diana L. **Fantastic Illustration and Design in Britain, 1850–1930**. Museum of Art, Rhode Island School of Design, 1979. Also published as *Bulletin of Rhode Island School of Design Museum Notes*, 65:5 (April 1979).
This handsome 239-page exhibition catalog includes examples of work by artists of the great period of book and magazine illustration in England. There are substantial notes on the artists and the works exhibited, an extensive bibliography of secondary sources and two fine essays, a title essay by Johnson, and George P. Landow's "And the World Became Strange: Realms of Literary Fantasy," which includes commentary on British and American horror fiction and which was reprinted in Schlobin [F7-51].

10-15. Jones, Bruce, and Armand Eisen, eds. **Sorcerers: A Collection of Fantasy Art.** Ariel/Ballantine, 1978.
A collection of color and black-and-white work by eleven fantasy artists: Tim Conrad, Alex Nino, Steve Hickman, Michael Hague, Kenneth Smith, Brad Johannsen, Bruce Jones, Jack Kirby, George Barr, Jim Steranko and Michael Whelan. Photo and brief statement by each contributor. (REB)

10-16. Kirchoff, Mary, ed. **The Art of the Dragon Lance Saga.** TSR, 1987.
Preliminary drawings, black-and-white and color art for the Dragon Lance Saga fantasy game. A world and its inhabitants are depicted by Larry Elmore, Clyde Caldwell, Denis Beauvais, Dave Sutherland, Tom Yeates, Diana Magnuson, Keith Parkinson, Jeff Butler and Jeff Easley. Parkinson's color illustrations and Elmore's ink drawings occasionally rise above the prevailing mediocrity.

10-17. Larkin, David, ed. **Fantastic Art.** Ballantine, 1973.
Forty color illustrations by artists of the fifteenth to the twentieth century, including Bosch, Pieter Brueghel (the Younger), Turner, Richard Dadd, Gustave Moreau, Odilon Redon, Max Ernst and Ivan Albright. The introduction provides brief career biographies.

10-18. Larkin, David, ed. **The Fantastic Kingdom: A Collection of Illustrations from the Golden Days of Storytelling.** Ballantine, 1974.
Color plates of illustrations of Jessie Willcox Smith, Howard Pyle, Arthur Rackham, Charles Robinson, Maxfield Parrish, W. Heath Robinson, Jean de Bosschère, Edmund Dulac, E. J. Detmold, Paul Bransom, Kay Nielsen, Harry Clarke, Dorothy P. Lathrop and the "elusive" T. Mackenzie. Larkin gives short biographies of the artists.

10-19. Larkin, David, ed. **Once Upon a Time: Some Contemporary Illustrators of Fantasy.** Peacock Press/Bantam, 1976.
Anthology of works by a group of British illustrators, with short biographies. Includes Frank Bellamy, Pauline Ellison (with a stunning fold-out illustration for Le Guin's Earthsea trilogy), Chris McEwan, Tony Meeuwissen, Nicola Bayley, Peter Le Vasseur, Alan Lee, Reg Cartwright, Ian Miller, James Marsh, Peter Barrett, Owen Wood, Ken Laidlaw and Brian Froud.

10-20. Meyer, Susan E. **America's Great Illustrators.** Abrams, 1978.
Includes, among others, Howard Pyle, N. C. Wyeth and Maxfield Parrish. Biocritical essays with numerous examples of the artists' work. One of the essential reference works for the Golden Age of American illustration.

*10-21. Meyer, Susan E. **A Treasury of the Great Children's Book Illustrators.** Abrams, 1983.
Short but substantial essays, copiously illustrated, on Lear, Tenniel, Crane, Caldecott, Kate Greenaway, Beatrix Potter, E. H. Shepherd, Rackham, Dulac, Nielsen, Pyle, Wyeth and Denslow. Bibliography and index.

10-22. Page, Michael, and Robert Ingpen (U.K.). **Encyclopedia of Things That Never Were.** Dragon's World, 1985; Viking, 1987.
Page wrote the text of this book exploring myths, legends and other fantastic and supernatural topics. Chapters deal with broad topics, such as things of the night,

with entries alphabetical within each chapter, with a master index. Ingpen's color illustrations—for which he won the 1986 Hans Christian Andersen Award—are imaginative and plentiful. (NB)

10-23. Palumbo, Donald, ed. **Eros in the Mind's Eye: Sexuality and the Fantastic in Art and Film**. Greenwood, 1986.
About half the eighteen original essays in this collection claim to deal with sexuality and the fantastic but they often—particularly in the early essays on medieval and Renaissance artists—have only slight fantasy content. Two essays are of particular interest: Sylvie Pantalacci's "Surrealistic Female Monsters" and Gwendolyn Layne's "Subliminal Seduction in Fantasy Illustration." However, Layne's "Mum's the Word: Sexuality in Victorian Fantasy Illustration (and Beyond)" (pp. 59–74) is disappointing and leans heavily on unsupported quotations from Brigid Peppin's *Fantasy* [10-24] for a cursory overview of this seminal period for modern illustration. And the substantial use of female nudes in Rackham's post-1916 work does not support Layne's statement that his work was "pure of [sexual] content." Sarah Clemens's essay, "And Now, This Brief Commercial Message: Sex Sells Fantasy!," is also of interest. Illustrations chosen are almost exclusively of color works and the darkish reproduction—along with the absence of color—obscures the detail to which the reader is referred. Still, given the lack of serious discussion of modern fantasy illustration, the best things here are of some importance.

10-24. Peppin, Brigid (U.K.). **Fantasy: The Golden Age of Fantastic Illustration**. Watson-Guptill, 1975.
On fantasy illustration in England in the Victorian and Edwardian periods (1860–1920), historically rather than critically oriented. Less probing than Johnson [10-14] but with more color-plate examples of artists' work.

*10-25. Peppin, Brigid (U.K.), and Lucy Micklethwait (U.K.), eds. **Book Illustrators of the Twentieth Century**. Arco, 1984.
More than 800 British illustrators working in the twentieth century are covered in this encyclopedia. The biographical entries contain a selected list of book and periodical illustrations, as well as a short bibliography of secondary sources. There are also several hundred well-chosen black-and-white illustrations. A major reference text that complements Simon Houfe's *Dictionary of British Book Illustrators and Caricaturists 1800–1914* (Antique Collectors' Club, 1978).

10-26. Petaja, Emil, comp. and ed. **The Hannes Bok Memorial Showcase of Fantasy Art**. SISU Publishers, 1974.
Examples of early twentieth-century magazine illustrations, as well as of work by a score of modern illustrators, mostly in black and white, but with color plates of illustrations by Alicia Austin, George Barr, Jack Gaughan and Tim Kirk. The artists also profile themselves and their work.

10-27. Petersen, Sandy; Tom Sullivan; and Lynn Willis, eds. **Petersen's Field Guide to Cthulhu Monsters**. Chaosium, 1988.
Dictionary entries on twenty-seven "terrors of the hyper-geometrical realms," drawn from the writings of H. P. Lovecraft and featuring color and black-and-

white illustrations by Tom Sullivan. A sense of fun lurks in the pages of this book, published by a firm well known in the fantasy game market.

10-28. Poltarnees, Welleran. **All Mirrors Are Magic Mirrors: Reflections on Pictures Found in Children's Books**. Green Tiger, 1972.
The Green Tiger Press Rackham calendars of the 1970s are notable for the splendor of the reproductions and are among the handsomest examples of the recent calendar revival, while the Press's annual apointment books are copiously illustrated with black-and-white and color children's book illustrations by nineteenth- and twentieth-century book illustrators. Poltarnees's observations on what he sees in illustrations are evidence of a first-rate critical eye. Highly recommended. The author's pseudonym is derived from Dunsany's fictions.

10-29. Robertson, Bruce (U.K.). **Fantasy Art**. North Light Books, 1988.
Numerous examples from fine art, illustrations for books and magazines, and advertising graphics dramatically highlight Robertson's text. Much of the book is a practical guide to techniques for creating fantasy art.

10-30. Rottensteiner, Franz (Austria). **The Fantasy Book: An Illustrated History from Dracula to Tolkien**. Collier, 1978.
A superficial study of fantasy in literature. Although the 202 illustrations, 40 in color, are not always identified by artist, they constitute something of an anthology of fantasy illustration, with many examples of pulp and paperback cover artwork, including European work seldom seen in North America. Also annotated as [H7-11] and [F7-48].

10-31. Sackmann, Eckart. **Great Masters of Fantasy Art**. Berlin: Taco, 1986. Tr. by Hugh Beyer.
Collection of forty-four paintings by sixteen fantasy artists. Apart from two European artists (Oliviero Berni and Vincente Segrelles), the artists are American and British: Frazetta, Boris Vallejo, Rowena, Greg Hildebrandt, Carl Lundgren, Freas, Corben, Barclay Shaw, Rodney Matthews, Paul Lehr, Richard Hescox, Tim White, Michael Whelan and Don Maitz. General introduction, plus photo and short article on each contributor. (REB)

10-32. Schlobin, Roger O., ed. **The Aesthetics of Fantasy Literature and Art**. Univ. of Notre Dame Press, 1982.
The first of the two articles on fantasy illustration in this collection of essays, by Landow, was originally published in Johnson [10-14]. Terry Reece Hackford's "Fantastic Visions: British Illustration of the *Arabian Nights*," is an original, detailed comparative study of illustrations by four illustrators (Arthur Boyd Houghton, J. D. Batten, H. J. Ford and Edmund Dulac) for editions of the *Arabian Nights*. Hackford points out that all four artists "share a reliance upon the pictorial conventions associated with realism" but develop "distinctive means" for "manipulating, intensifying or departing" from those conventions. The illustrations are well chosen, although the black-and-white reproduction of the Dulac color originals inevitably betrays the points the author is trying to make. Also annotated as [7-51].

10-33. The Studio: Jeffrey Jones, Michael Kaluta, Barry Windsor-Smith and Berni Wrightson. Dragon's Dream, 1979.
The four artists are interviewed in their Manhattan loft studio where they talk about their careers and their *fin-de-siècle* roots. The interviews are illustrated with photographs of the artists and examples of their recent work. Grimmer Graphics has announced publication of *The Michael Wm. Kaluta Treasury*, which will feature more recent work by the artist.

10-34. Summers, Ian, ed. **Tomorrow and Beyond: Masterpieces of Science Fiction Art**. Workman, 1978.
The former art director of Ballantine has assembled over 300 color reproductions from sixty-seven illustrators, primarily American. Much of the work depicted appeared on mass-market paperback covers of the 1970s, as well as on LP jackets, in articles and the like. No biographical information on the illustrators is provided nor are medium and size of original shown. Yet the survey is a broad one and is valuable for larger collections devoted to contemporary book illustration. (NB)

*10-35. Weinberg, Robert. **A Biographical Dictionary of Science Fiction and Fantasy Artists**. Greenwood, 1988. Don Grant, 1978.
In addition to the more than 250 entries, there are an introduction providing a historical overview, an essay on the collecting of original art, a list of major awards for science fiction/fantasy artists, a bibliography and an index. Each of the entries is a mini-essay with biographical and critical information and a bibliography of the artist's work. The bibliographies are in themselves a major feature of the book since they show appearances in magazines and hardback and paperback artwork. Entries are based where possible on information supplied by the artists. Inevitably, there will be complaints about omissions (the prolific Michael Hague is one notable omission), but this is a major addition to the short list of references on genre artists.

10-36. Weinberg, Robert. **The Weird Tales Story**. Fax, 1977.
See especially chapters 6 ("Cover Art") and 7 ("Interior Art") for numerous examples of the artwork accompanied by a running commentary by Weinberg on the art and artists. A frustrating aspect of the book is the lack of an index and the separation of the reproductions from the appropriate commentary. Durie [10-9], with its more numerous and larger-format reproductions, is a valuable complement to this volume. Also annotated as [11-55] and [H7-45].

10-37. Weis, Margaret, ed. **The Art of the Dungeons & Dragons Fantasy Game**. TSR 1985.
Color and black-and-white art by fifteen artists, principally Clyde Caldwell, Jeff Easley and Larry Elmore. A few items are reprinted from *Amazing Stories*, including a George Barr cover. Lots of dash and color, with little subtlety except in two quiet paintings by Dean Morrissey. (REB)

Individual Artists

Achilleos, Chris (Cyprus), 1947– .

10-38. Achilleos, Chris. **Beauty and the Beast**. Dragon's World, 1978.

10-39. Achilleos, Chris. **Medusa.** Dragon's World, 1988.

10-40. Achilleos, Chris. **Sirens.** Dragon's World, 1986.
These three volumes provide a comprehensive survey of Achilleos's work in advertising and for paperbacks, film posters and even (in *Medusa*) for tattoo designs. In *Medusa*, some of the artist's work is traced from concept through sketches to the finished version. His style, with its heroic, dramatic figures, seems particularly well suited to movie posters. As with other artists of his generation, the influence of Frazetta is obvious, but the figures lack that artist's romantic dash; in their warrior armor, both men and women seem more inclined to set forth to battle than to dally in amorous interludes.

Artzybasheff, Boris (U.S.S.R.), 1899–1965

10-41. Artzybasheff, Boris. **As I See.** Dodd, Mead, 1954.
The only collection of this artist's book and magazine illustrations (including those for Finney's *The Circus of Dr. Lao* [F3-137]) and his editorial depictions of the machines of industry and war, all reproduced in superb gravure printing. Artist's commentary, in an oblique and philosophical style, reveals general social attitudes, but no specific commentary on the drawings. (REB)

Austin, Alicia, 1942– .

10-42. Austin, Alicia. **Alicia Austin's Age of Dreams.** Introduction by George Barr; Afterword by Austin. Don Grant, 1978.
An anthology of her color and line work, printed on fine stock and elegantly produced. Austin's hieratic, sumptuously robed figures and the decorative nature of her design recall the English Decadents, particularly Aubrey Beardsley and Harry Clarke.

Barr, George, 1937– .

10-43. Barr, George. **Upon the Winds of Yesterday and Other Explorations: The Paintings of George Barr.** Don Grant, 1976.
Numerous examples of Barr's color and black-and-white artwork. Barr works in several styles, ranging from a cockeyed whimsy to neoromantic treatments of mythological subjects. Thus, there is not the impression—so common with many contemporary fantasy artists—of a single style imposed upon every project.

Beardsley, Aubrey (U.K.), 1872–1898.

*10-44. Reade, Brian (U.K.). **Aubrey Beardsley.** Studio Vista, Macmillan, 1967.
Beardsley's decorative, frank treatment of subjects his contemporaries found obscene revolutionized the concept of line drawing. Reade's book is considered by many critics to be the definitive study of his work. See also Brigid Brophy's *Black and White: A Portrait of Aubrey Beardsley* (Cape, 1968).

Blaine, Mahlon, 1894–1970.

10-45. Legman, G. **The Art of Mahlon Blaine.** Peregrine Books, 1982.
Introduction by artist Robert Arrington, "The Art of Mahlon Blaine" by G. Legman, "A Mahlon Blaine Bibliography" compiled by Roland Trenary and over eighty pages of Blaine drawings and paintings, including four pages in color. Much of Blaine's work was strongly influenced by Beardsley in both style and content. His subjects range from fantastic erotica (the 1929 portfolio *Venus Sardonica* and work for Olympia Press) to Apache and Hopi Indian legends. His elaborately detailed and macabre drawings for Burke's *Limehouse Nights*, Ewers's *The Sorcerer's Apprentice* and *Alraune*, Beckford's *Vathek* and Flaubert's *Salammbô* constitute his best work. (REB)

Bok, Hannes, 1914–1964

10-46. Bok, Hannes. **Beauty and the Beasts: The Art of Hannes Bok.** Gerry de la Ree, 1978.

10-47. Brooks, C. W. **The Revised Hannes Bok Checklist.** T-K Graphics, 1974.

10-48. de la Ree, Gerry, ed. **Bok.** Gerry de la Ree, 1974.

10-49. de la Ree, Gerry, and Gene Nigra, eds. **A Hannes Bok Sketchbook.** Gerry de la Ree, 1976.

10-50. Petaja, Emil. **And Flights of Angels: The Life and Legend of Hannes Bok.** Bokanalia Memorial Foundation, 1968.
Bok was largely self-taught and developed a style heavily influenced by the work of Maxfield Parrish. His precise and polished drawings and paintings feature age-softened landscapes, preternaturally limber human figures and monsters both grotesque and comic. In the science fiction magazine world of the 1940s, Bok's work was equaled only by that of Virgil Finlay [10-70–10-77] and Edd Cartier [10-53] for stylistic distinctiveness. In the 1950s, unlike Finlay, whose principal market continued to be magazines, Bok illustrated dust jackets for the new small press market and did some of his finest work in this field. The major work devoted to his art (*Beauty and the Beasts*) unfortunately contains none of his color illustrations, but does provide a generous sampling of his work for the science fiction and fantasy pulps. The *Sketchbook* contains work dating back to his high-school days, while the Petaja biography and de la Ree *Bok* include essays by artist and writer contemporaries, which offer multiple perspectives on his career. (REB/WA)

Booth, Franklin, 1874–1948.

10-51. Booth, Franklin. **The Art of Franklin Booth.** Nostalgia Press, 1976.
Reprint of a 1925 tribute to Booth, with an introduction by Meredith Nicholson, an appreciation by Earnest Elmo Calkins and sixty plates: scenes from classical antiquity, dream images, fantastic architecture, biblical scenes, etc. Booth was one of the finest pen-and-ink craftsmen of the early twentieth century, his fine-lined work often looking like steel engraving. His most characteristic drawings

convey an impression of vastness: small foreground figures dominated by huge vaulted ceilings, impossibly tall buildings, looming walls or cliffs. (REB)

Burns, Jim (U.K.), 1948– .

10-52. Burns, Jim. **Lightship.** Text by Chris Evans. Dragon's World, 1985.
125 color and 9 black-and-white illustrations, including preliminary studies and alternative versions. Book jackets and paperback covers for many works by Robert Silverberg, C. L. Moore, Frank Herbert, Philip José Farmer, etc.; space scenes, futuristic vehicles, alien landscapes, imaginary beasts. (REB)

Cartier, Edd, 1914– .

10-53. Cartier, Edd. **Edd Cartier: The Known and the Unknown.** Ed. by Dean Cartier. Gerry de la Ree, 1977.
Cartier withdrew from science fiction/fantasy illustration in the 1950s; this book is an anthology of his work. Examples are drawn from his illustrations for *Unknown* and for *Astounding Science Fiction,* and for fantasy calendars for the years 1949 and 1950. Cartier's precise, humorous but wry drawings have not aged and are among the most distinctive, accomplished work for pulp magazines of the era. And, as Cartier's son Dean notes in his dedication, Cartier's gnomes are a particular delight.

Cherry, David A., 1949– .

10-54. Cherry, David A. **Imagination: The Art & Technique of David A. Cherry.** Donning, 1987.
Forty-one paintings, most done for book jackets and paperback covers, with individual commentary on each painting, covering both subject and technique, plus a general preface by the artist and a biographical afterword. The inclusion of much journeyman work dilutes the impact of the more accomplished paintings. (REB)

Clarke, Harry (U.K.), 1889–1931.

*10-55. Bowe, Nicola Gordon (U.K.). **Harry Clarke: His Graphic Art.** The Dolmen Press, 1983. Distributed in North America by H. Keith Burns, Los Angeles. Clarke's illustrations for *Faust* are thought to be his finest work, but it is his drawings for Poe's *Tales of Mystery and Imagination* that are his most popular, with numerous reprints since their first publication in 1919. Bowe's fine biocritical study is illustrated by numerous black-and-white reproductions (Clarke's most distinctive medium), including a number of drawings published here for the first time.

Coll, Joseph Clement, 1881–1921.

*10-56. Coll, Joseph Clement. **The Magic Pen of Joseph Clement Coll.** Ed. by Walt Reed. Don Grant, 1970.
Pen-and-ink illustrations from books and magazine serials by A. Conan Doyle,

Sax Rohmer, Talbot Mundy, Edgar Wallace and others, including some preliminary studies and unfinished drawings. Text includes a short article, "How Coll Worked," by the compiler. Much of Coll's early work appeared in the pages of the *Associated Sunday Magazine* from 1903 to 1913 and is largely forgotten, but his work for *Collier's Weekly Magazine* from 1911 to his death is more accessible. In addition, his influence can be seen clearly in the work of the talented but almost completely forgotten *Blue Book* artist of the 1930s and 1940s, John Richard Flanagan (1895–1964). Coll was in the tradition of Howard Pyle [10-110] and thus links "mainstream" popular art (books and the slick magazines) with newspaper supplements and the pulps. This collection is a significant contribution to the history of modern American illustration. (REB/WA)

Corben, Richard, 1940– .

10-57. Bharucha, Fershid. **Richard Corben: Flights into Fantasy.** Thumb Tack Books, 1981.
Paintings, drawings and comic strips from all stages of Corben's career, from underground comics to book jackets and paperback covers. Extensive commentary by Bharucha, including photos and biographical information, plus comments by several of Corben's fellow illustrators (Eisner, Wrightson, Moebius, etc.). (REB)

Crane, Walter (U.K.), 1845–1915.

*10-58. Spencer, Isobel (U.K.). **Walter Crane.** Studio Vista, Macmillan, 1975.
Spencer shows how Crane continued the "transformation of narrative illustration begun by the pre-Raphaelites." Crane belonged to the generation immediately preceding that of Rackham [10-111–10-113], and it is clear that Rackham was greatly indebted to him. Crane's work appeared in *St. Nicholas*, and meetings with Denslow [10-60] and Pyle [10-110] during a visit to America confirm a crucial link between the British and American Arts & Crafts movements.

Dean, Roger (U.K.), 1944– .

10-59. Dean, Roger. **Views.** Text by Dominy Hamilton and Carla Capalbo in association with Roger Dean. Dragon's Dream, 1975.
Paintings, record jackets, posters and other commercial art, characterized by the artist's distinctive combination of the ethereal and the grotesque; biographical and career summary, with notes on sources and techniques. Dean's work on jazz and rock record jackets and on related posters and stage designs left its mark on a generation of consumers, as well as on other artists. *Magnetic Storm* (Paper Tiger, 1984) illustrates the varied work of Roger and his brother, Martyn, in architecture, film TV, album covers, posters and video games. (REB/NB)

Denslow, W. W., 1856–1915.

*10-60. Greene, Douglas G., and Michael Patrick Hearn. **W. W. Denslow.** Central Michigan Univ.: Clarke Historical Library, 1976.
The authors note that Denslow was "the first American to create picture books in

the aesthetic tradition of Walter Crane, Kate Greenaway, and Randolph Caldecott." An ironic commentary on the career of this great popular illustrator who is now remembered only as the illustrator of *The Wonderful Wizard of Oz* [F3-20]. Some of the best scholarship on American popular literature is written by Baum enthusiasts, and the Baum Society magazine, *The Baum Bugle* [11-26], contains much illustrated material as well as articles on illustration. This splendid biography, with a comprehensive bibliography of Denslow's work, is in that tradition for its scholarship, although it is regrettable that this plainly produced, sparsely illustrated book could not have been published in a format more suitable for the creator of the modern American picture book.

Detmold, Charles Maurice (U.K.), 1883–1908, and Edward Julius Detmold (U.K.), 1883–1957.

10-61. Larkin, David. **The Fantastic Creatures of Edward Julius Detmold.** Scribner, 1976.
Fantastic is used rather loosely here since the Detmolds' bestiary consists of uncommonly detailed and imaginatively designed portraits of animals and insects. However, there is no question about the fantastic elements in Edward's illustrations for the *Arabian Nights,* and several of the color plates for this edition rank among the finest fantastic illustrations of the modern period.

Dillon, Leo, and Diane Dillon, both 1933– .

10-62. Dillon, Leo and Diane. **The Art of Leo and Diane Dillon.** Ed. by Byron Preiss. Ballantine, 1981.
Numerous color plates, examples of the Dillons' work for various media: album covers, paperbacks, magazines. Impressive work in a variety of styles, drawing on artistic sources from Renaissance oils to expressionist woodcuts, but not always fantastic in content. As Harlan Ellison points out in his preface, the Dillons are perfectionists who may not be appreciated by editors facing imminent deadlines but are greatly respected by their peers for their skill and graphic imagination. With a long critical introduction by Preiss.

Donahey, William, 1883–1970.

10-63. Cahn, Joseph M. **The Teenie Weenies Book: The Life and Art of William Donahey.** Green Tiger, 1986.
Donahey was a Cleveland artist whose comic strip, the *Teenie Weenies,* was a national success for more than fifty years and spawned a number of book editions. Of special interest is a chapter by Welleran Poltarnees on the graphic ancestors of Donahey's little people and on the phenomenon of the fascination many people have with the "miniature." As is customary with Green Tiger Press books, the choice of color and black-and-white illustrations is superb, with color work that should put more prestigious publishers to shame.

Doré, Gustave (France), 1832–1883.

*10-64. Gosling, Nigel. **Gustave Doré**. Praeger, 1973.

The well-written, informative text by Gosling is accompanied by an impressive gallery of drawings by Doré, arranged by subject (satire, adventure, horror, etc.). His magnificent, awesome illustrations for Dante are represented, as well as some wonderful drawings for Perrault's *Contes* that must have given nightmares to generations of children. One can understand, on seeing an illustration for *Paradise Lost* of a winged Satan plummeting in a starlit sky toward a clouded globe, why Dunsany thought of Doré for his stories of gods and men, and it is a measure of Sime's success [10-122–10-123] that he captures some of Doré's grandeur without imitating him.

Doyle, Richard (U.K.), 1824–1883.

*10-65. Engen, Rodney (U.K.) **Richard Doyle**. Catalpa Press, 1983.
Uncle of Arthur Conan Doyle and best known for the color illustrations for *In Fairyland* (1870) and the posthumously published *Jack the Giant-Killer*, Doyle was on the staff of *Punch*. Numerous examples of fantasy black-and-white illustrations but very little of the fine color work. The Victorians loved books about fairies and Doyle's unsentimental work is among the finest examples of fairy art.

Dulac, Edmund (France/U.K.), 1882–1953.

*10-66. White, Colin. **Edmund Dulac**. Scribner, 1976.
Dulac and Rackham were contemporaries whose lavish signed, limited editions were—and still are—much prized by collectors. Dulac's work was influenced by Persian miniatures and even his illustrations for Andersen have a distinctly Oriental cast. His illustrations for the *Arabian Nights* have set a standard by which all other renderings are judged. Colin White's sensible biography is flawed only by inferior color reproductions (181 reproductions in all, 39 in color) and a bibliography that lists only first editions and does not always succeed in describing the first trade issues in such a way that they can be readily distinguished from the numerous successive printings. White does not disparage Dulac's later work, and his discussion is always nicely judged in its handling of biographical and artistic detail. A more recent, less ambitious book that provides a good introduction to Dulac's art is the Peacock Press/Bantam Books *Edmund Dulac*, edited by David Larkin, with an introduction by Brian Sanders, and forty color plates.

Escher, M(aurits) C(ornelis) (Netherlands), 1898–1972.

10-67. Escher, M. C. **The World of M. C. Escher**. Ed. by J. L. Locher. Abrams, 1971.
In addition to the 300 reproductions, eight in color, there are five essays on Escher's work, plus a bibliography and list of exhibitions of the artist's work. Much of his work is based on mathematics and geometry, and much of it is overly didactic in intent. But even in the geometric prints there are fantastic beasts and

monsters, and one of the most pervasive themes in his work is the transformation of one kind of life into another, one of the most basic fantasy concepts. (REB)

Fabian, Stephen E., 1930– .

10-68. Fabian, Stephen E. **Fantasy by Fabian: The Art of Stephen E. Fabian**. Ed. by Gerry de la Ree. Gerry de la Ree, 1978.

10-69. Fabian, Stephen E. **More Fantasy by Fabian: The Art of Stephen E. Fabian**. Ed. by Gerry de la Ree. Gerry de la Ree, 1979.
Fabian is a prolific magazine and book illustrator of science fiction and fantasy, strongly influenced by Virgil Finlay. The two de la Ree books include work originally published by de la Ree as well as illustrations done for books and magazines. At least half a dozen portfolios of Fabian's work have been published, including *Fabian in Color* (Starmont, 1980), which contains eight color plates and includes a separate eight-page booklet of the artist's "comments and reflections" on the paintings. (WA/REB)

Finlay, Virgil, 1914–1971.

10-70. de la Ree, Gerry, ed. **Virgil Finlay Remembered**. Gerry de la Ree, 1981.

10-71. Finlay, Virgil. **The Book of Virgil Finlay**. Ed. by Gerry de la Ree. Gerry de la Ree, 1975.

10-72. Finlay, Virgil. **Finlay's Lost Drawings**. Ed. by Gerry de la Ree. Gerry de la Ree, 1975.

10-73. Finlay, Virgil. **The Second/Third/Fourth/Fifth/Sixth Books of Virgil Finlay**. Ed. by Gerry de la Ree. Gerry de la Ree, 1975, 1978, 1979, 1979, 1980.

*****10-74**. Finlay, Virgil. **Virgil Finlay**. Ed. by Don Grant. Don Grant, 1971. Introduction by Sam Moskowitz; checklist of Finlay's work compiled by Gerry de la Ree.

10-75. Finlay, Virgil. **Virgil Finlay: An Astrology Sketchbook**. Ed. by Don Grant. Don Grant, 1975.

10-76. Finlay, Virgil. **Virgil Finlay in The American Weekly**. Nova, 1977.

10-77. Finlay, Virgil. **Virgil Finlay: 1914–1971**. Ed. by Gerry de la Ree. Gerry de la Ree, 1971.
In the 1970s there were an unprecedented number of books devoted to Virgil Finlay, who began his extensive career as a magazine illustrator in *Weird Tales* in the mid-1930s. Farnsworth Wright, the legendary editor of the magazine, was so taken with Finlay's work that he published, in 1935, an illustrated edition of Shakespeare's *Midsummer Night's Dream*, which was to initiate a series of inexpensive popular editions of the classics. The intended series was a failure, but Finlay's reputation as the finest of American pulp illustrators was unchallenged for at least a decade. After his return from military service in World War II, Finlay continued to work in the declining pulp market, still meticulous about detail and still the master of pen-and-ink drawing. Several portfolios of Finlay's work for

the pulps were published as early as the late 1940s, but it was not until 1971, and after his death, that there would be an outpouring of tributes to his work, celebrating the black-and-white work (except for four color plates in the first Don Grant publication). Throughout the decade the tributes continued to appear, most often under the imprint of Gerry de la Ree, an enterprising collector of popular art. Frazetta and his successors may currently be more honored, but when the definitive history of the artists of the pulp years is written, Virgil Finlay will be seen as the professional who raised standards and created a model of excellence that honors him and the field.

FitzPatrick, Jim (Ireland), 1948– .

10-78. FitzPatrick, Jim. **The Book of Conquests**. Paper Tiger, 1978.

10-79. FitzPatrick, Jim. **Érinsaga. The Mythological Paintings of Jim FitzPatrick**. De Danann Press, 1985.

10-80. FitzPatrick, Jim. **The Silver Arm**. Paper Tiger, 1981.
FitzPatrick's subject, in both text and artwork, is the legendary history of pre-Celtic and Celtic Ireland. His intricately detailed drawings, paintings and decorations form a unique body of work, incorporating and building upon traditional Irish motifs. *Érinsaga* contains an illustrated retrospective of the artist's work, plus detailed commentary on the more than 100 drawings and paintings included. The printing quality in the Paper Tiger books does not do complete justice to the artwork, but the fine detail and glowing colors are faithfully reproduced in several portfolios and in a 1986 *Érin-saga* wall calendar published in West Germany. (REB)

Frazetta, Frank, 1928– .

*10-81. Frazetta, Frank. **The Fantastic Art of Frank Frazetta**. Scribner, 1975.

10-82. Frazetta, Frank. **Frank Frazetta, Book One–Book Five**. Ed. by Betty Ballantine. Peacock Press, 1977, 1978, 1980, 1985.
Undoubtedly the most influential of contemporary fantasy book illustrators. After a two-decade career as a comic book and magazine artist, Frazetta did a series of covers for Ace reprints of Edgar Rice Burroughs that established him as the finest Burroughs illustrator since J. Allen St. John. This series was so successful that Frazetta embarked on a new career as a creator of paperback covers. The collections of his artwork marked a new phase in the acceptance of his work and of modern fantasy illustration as an art form. Elements of his distinctive style can be seen in the work of illustrators such as Boris Vallejo, Rowena and Michael Whelan, and it is probably safe to say that no single illustrator has influenced the field since the 1960s in the way that he has.

Freas, Frank Kelly, 1922– .

10-83. Freas, Frank Kelly. **The Art of Science Fiction**. Donning, 1977.

10-84. Freas, Frank Kelly. **The Astounding Fifties: A Portfolio of Illustrations**. Freas, 1971.

10-85. Freas, Frank Kelly. **A Separate Star**. Greenswamp, 1984.
The Astounding Fifties, the second Freas portfolio (the first was issued by Advent in 1957), is devoted to interior illustrations for *Astounding Science Fiction*, 1953–59. In the introduction Freas mentions that he illustrated over 160 stories in *Astounding* during this period, and that the eighty-four drawings included here represent "both some of the best and some of the worst of my work." (REB)

Freas, winner of ten Hugos, is probably the best known of all science fiction illustrators since the early 1950s. People are the center of his art, in contrast to the hardware emphasis of other illustrators. His anecdotal text in *The Art of Science Fiction* clearly explains the development of each illustration. The self-published *A Separate Star* collects more recent work, from preliminary sketches to finished work. His commentary might be useful to aspiring illustrators. (NB)

Froud, Brian (U.K.), 1948– .

10-86. Froud, Brian. **The Land of Froud**. Ed. by David Larkin. Introduction by Brian Sanders. Peacock Press/Ballantine, 1974.

10-87. Froud, Brian. **The World of the Dark Crystal**. Knopf, 1982.
Froud is best known for his gnomic book illustrations for *Fairies* and his designs for the 1983 Jim Henson/Frank Oz film *The Dark Crystal*, but his art—as the examples in this collection show—is markedly influenced by British illustrators like W. Heath and Charles Robinson, Dulac, S. H. Sime and, especially, Arthur Rackham.

Gallardo, Gervasio (Spain), 1934– .

10-88. Gallardo, Gervasio. **The Fantastic World of Gervasio Gallardo**. Peacock Press/Bantam, 1976.
Born in Spain in 1934, Gallardo has worked in Europe and the U.S. His commercial and fine art shows his debt to Surrealism, especially Magritte, but has a more playful quality. He did many covers for Ballantine's Adult Fantasy paperback series in the 1970s. This ninety-six-page paperback collects reproductions of many of these book covers as well as his other work in a variety of media. (NB)

Giger, H. R. (Switzerland), 1940– .

10-89. Giger, H. R. **H. R. Giger's Necronomicon**. Big O, 1978.

10-90. Giger, H. R. **H. R. Giger's Necronomicon 2**. Editions C, 1985.
Giger is a Swiss artist and illustrator who achieved prominence with his set designs for the 1979 film *Alien*, for which he and others won an Academy Award for visual effects. The autobiographical account in the 1978 volume reveals a preoccupation with death, the fantastic and the morbid, evident in all his work. He strikingly juxtaposes or blends the human figure with mechanical structures to create biomechanoid images of great power, in which a decadent eroticism is

prevalent. The 1985 collection is more of the same, unsettling and visceral in its impact. Giger is one of the more important artists working in nongenre fantastic art, and libraries with large art collections should consider one of his oversized collections. (NB)

Gorey, Edward, 1925- .

*10-91. Gorey, Edward. **Amphigorey**. Putnam, 1972.

10-92. Gorey, Edward. **Amphigorey Also**. Congdon & Weed, 1983.

10-93. Gorey, Edward. **Amphigorey Too**. Putnam, 1975.
Many of Gorey's early books, small volumes long out of print, are included in these three collections. Gorey has created a neo-Victorian world in books which he both writes and illustrates. His witty, menacing line drawings bring to deliciously chilling life the texts of books that are graced by titles such as *The Doubtful Guest, The Gashlycrumb Tinies* and *The Deranged Cousins*. Gorey has also edited and illustrated collections of ghost stories and designed the sets and costumes for a notable modern stage production of *Dracula*, starring Frank Langella. These stage designs have been preserved in *Dracula: A Toy Theater* (Scribner, 1979). (WA/REB)

Hildebrandt, Tim and Greg, both 1939- .

10-94. Hildebrandt, Greg. **From Tolkien to Oz: The Art of Greg Hildebrandt**. Ed. by William McGuire. Unicorn Publishing House, 1985.

10-95. Hildebrandt, Tim and Greg. **The Art of the Brothers Hildebrandt**. Ed. by Ian Summers. Ballantine, 1979.

10-96. Hildebrandt, Tim and Greg. **The Brothers Hildebrandt**. Catalog of an exhibition of their work at the Maryland Funnybook Festival, 1978.
The Hildebrandt brothers speak of an early enthusiasm for Johnny Gruelle and for Pyle, Wyeth and Parrish, later wedded to an interest in Surrealists like Dalí and Magritte. Their characteristic lighting effects are based on photos, but used only as references. Recently the two artists have worked separately, with Greg illustrating fantasy classics such as *Dracula* and *The Wizard of Oz* while Tim has returned to the illustration of children's books. The exhibition catalog includes— in addition to sketches and preliminary drawings, finished color work and photographs—an interview with the artists. (WA/REB)

Jones, Jeffrey (U.K.), 1944- .

10-97. Jones, Jeffrey. **Yesterday's Lily**. Dragon's Dream, 1980.
Biographical sketch, interview with Jones, critical essay by Irma Kurtz and more than sixty pages of color paintings and black-and-white artwork by Jones. Not only SF and fantasy book covers, but western paintings and some very impressive portraits and delicate pencil drawings. (REB)

Jones, Peter (U.K.), 1951– .

10-98. Jones, Peter. **Solar Wind**. Perigee/Paper Tiger, 1980.
Ninety-five paintings, mostly for paperback and book covers. Biographical sketch, notes on technique, some commentary on subject matter. The first half of the book consists of fantasy paintings, principally sword and sorcery, in which the influences of Frazetta and Jeff Jones are clearly evident. Even amid the spaceships and futuristic war machines in the remainder of the book, Frazetta-ish figures are prominent participants. The paintings give the impression of barely arrested motion; there is scarcely a static composition in the lot. (REB)

Kirk, Tim, 1947– .

10-99. Beahm, George, ed. **Kirk's Works: An Index of the Art of Tim Kirk**. Heresy Press, 1980.
The major portion of this book is an index of Kirk's work, accompanied by numerous examples. Only the wraparound cover illustration is in color; all of the interior reproductions are in black and white. However, much of Kirk's best work is in the witty interiors he has done for magazines and books, and this essential text gives a broad picture of his talents. Kirk's illustrations of Dunsany are as attractive as those of Sime, who has surely been a major influence on him.

Krenkel, Roy G., 1918–1983.

10-100. Krenkel, Roy G. **Cities and Scenes from the Ancient World**. Owlswick Press, 1974.
Krenkel's illustrations for L. Sprague de Camp's *Great Cities of the Ancient World* (Doubleday, 1974), together with many additional drawings and a color frontispiece. Preface by Sanford Zane Meschkow and introductory essay by Krenkel. Many of these drawings show Krenkel's debt to Franklin Booth [10-51], to whom the book is dedicated. (REB)

Lawson, Robert, 1892–1957.

10-101. Lawson, Robert. **Robert Lawson, Illustrator: A Selection of His Characteristic Illustrations**. Ed. by Helen L. Jones. Little, Brown, 1971.
Includes an index of titles and a checklist of books illustrated by Lawson. Jones was his editor at Little, Brown and she includes comments from the artist's correspondence on his work. His first published work was fantasy and shows the influence of both Arthur Rackham and Charles Robinson, as well as Hugh Lofting and Dorothy Lathrop. A delightful sense of humor helped make Lawson one of the finest, and least dated, illustrators of children's books of his period.

Maitz, Don, 1953– .

10-102. Maitz, Don. **First Maitz: Selected Works by Don Maitz**. Ursus Imprints, 1988.
This collection of Maitz's work consists largely of paperback cover art, not

surprising for an artist who has painted over 150 covers since his professional debut in 1975. Ron Walotsky comments that Maitz's style has the "feeling and look of the old master illustrators like Arthur Rackham or N. C. Wyeth." To that short list, one could also add Edmund Dulac, Maxfield Parrish, Sulamith Wülfing and Frank Frazetta. This is not to disparage Maitz, who is a very accomplished illustrator, but the accompanying text is not very enlightening except when Maitz talks about his working methods.

Mathews, Rodney (U.K.), 1945- .

10-103. Mathews, Rodney. **In Search of Forever**. Paper Tiger, 1985.
Mathews early developed an interest in nature and still prefers drawing animals—often very fantastic animals—to people. Some of his work has a playful quality. It has been featured in several calendars and on many posters, and has illustrated many works of Michael Moorcock. He uses various media—ink, ink and gouache, and watercolor—for his books, LP jackets and posters, logos and alphabets. The text by Mathews and Nigel Suckling provides interesting details about Mathews's work, which heavily favors the fantastic, with typical science fiction icons uncommon. (NB)

Morrill, Rowena *see* Rowena

Mugnaini, Joseph A., 1912- .

10-104. Mugnaini, Joseph A. **Joseph Mugnaini: Drawings and Graphics**. Scarecrow, 1982.
Italian born, U.S. educated, Mugnaini is best known to fantasy readers for his book jackets and interiors for several of Ray Bradbury's books. He works in various media, and many samples of his work are included, some of them from his many Limited Editions Club books. This collection's major weakness is the absence of any color reproductions, but it is otherwise strongly recommended. (NB)

Nielsen, Kay, 1886-1957.

*10-105. Nielsen, Kay. **Kay Nielsen**. Ed. by David Larkin. Introduction by Keith Nicholson. Peacock Press/Bantam, 1975.
Nielsen, a Danish expatriate who settled first in London and later in California, was younger than Dulac and Rackham, his great contemporaries, but his illustrations of classic fairy tales are in no way inferior to theirs, and two of his books, *In Powder and Crinoline* (1913) and *East of the Sun and West of the Moon* (1914), are among the finest of the Golden Age of British illustration. Some of the perversity of Beardsley and Clarke is evident in his elegant aristocrats, but there are also an innocence and naiveté that contrast strangely with the Decadent strain. In the absence of a major study on Nielsen, the Bantam trade paperback is a good introduction to his work. It should, however, be supplemented by *The Unknown Kay Nielsen* (Peacock Press/Bantam, 1977), introduced by a moving tribute by

Hildegarde Flanner, who knew the Nielsens in California, and, especially, by another fine Green Tiger Press tribute, Welleran Poltarnees's *Kay Nielsen: An Appreciation* (1976). Here, the color reproductions approach the quality of the original publications and the drawings, printed on heavy tinted stock, are particularly well served.

Parrish, Maxfield, 1870–1966.

*10-106. Ludwig, Coy. **Maxfield Parrish**. Watson-Guptill, 1973.
Much of Parrish's work is not fantasy, but some of his best-known work is, including illustrations for Kenneth Grahame's *Dream Days* and *The Golden Age*, and the *Arabian Nights*. In addition, Parrish's techniques presage those of later illustrators, and his use of color has been widely imitated.

Peake, Mervyn (U.K.), 1911–1968.

10-107. Gilmore, Maeve, and Shelagh Johnson. **Mervyn Peake: Writings and Drawings**. Academy Editions and St. Martin's, 1974.
Not a formal biography, but a retrospective account of Peake's life and career as author, poet, playwright and illustrator. The 200 illustrations include twelve color plates. Bibliography of books by and about Peake, list of books he illustrated (including Lewis Carroll, Grimm, Coleridge and Robert Louis Stevenson) and a list of his principal exhibitions. (REB)

Pitz, Henry C., 1895–1976.

10-108. Likos, Patricia. **Henry C. Pitz 1895–1976: The Art of the Book**. Brandywine River Museum, 1988.
Catalog of a 1988 exhibition. Henry Pitz is well known to students of modern illustration for his many books on Howard Pyle and his successors. What has been lost sight of is the illustrative work of Pitz, himself an artist, and his crucial role in the history of the illustrated book in America. This catalog attempts to correct some of this, and the well-chosen examples of his work show his skill at fantastic illustration. His line drawings are particularly fine, and the examples of his work from the 1920s and 1930s show him maintaining a high standard of pictorial design in the manner of the Brandywine school, with some elements of Nielsen and Rackham.

Powers, Richard, 1921– .

10-109. Powers, Richard. **Spacetimewarp**. Nelson Doubleday, 1983.
This portfolio of sixteen loose plates, thirteen of them book covers, was a premium of the Science Fiction Book Club. Powers was one of the most prolific illustrators of paperback covers and hardcover jackets in the 1950s and 1960s. Robert Weinberg [10-35] considers him to be, with Finlay and Frazetta, one of the major influences on the field and to have "changed the perception of science fiction from space opera to real literature." Powers's background was in "fine" art at a time when science fiction and fantasy illustrators typically had begun

their career in the pulps. His images tend toward the abstract/surrealistic, unlike the hard-edged photographic realism favored by many science fiction illustrators. (NB)

Pyle, Howard, 1853–1911.

*10-110. Pitz, Henry C. **Howard Pyle: Writer, Illustrator, Founder of the Brandy-wine School**. Clarkson N. Potter, 1975.
Pyle wielded enormous influence as an illustrator and as a teacher and he may be said to have founded the modern American illustrative style, with his influence extending to N. C. Wyeth and his students. Pitz's study is a model of its kind, by a practicing illustrator who understood Pyle's art and aims. A bibliography of Pyle's work for books and magazines is included.

Rackham, Arthur, 1867–1939.

*10-111. Gittings, Fred. **Arthur Rackham**. Macmillan, 1975.

10-112. Hudson, Derek. **Arthur Rackham: His Life and Work**. Scribner, 1960.

10-113. Latimore, Sarah Briggs, and Grace Clark Haskell. **Arthur Rackham: A Bibliography**. San Marco Bookstore (Jacksonville, FL), 1987 (first published London, 1936).
Rackham was, for many people, the finest illustrator of his generation and his vision of the classic world of Andersen, Grimm and Barrie the definitive visualization of that world. His influence extends to the present generation of fantasy illustrators (Froud, Hildebrandt, Maitz, among many) and a number of books are still in print, albeit in pale copies of their original splendor. Hudson's biography is painstaking and uninspired, and he finds himself unable to respond to much of the later work. However, the first edition was lavishly produced with tipped-in color plates, heavy stock for the text paper, and illustrated endpapers. Gittings's study was more economically produced, but its strengths are an abundance of wonderful line drawings, a more balanced evaluation of Rackham's career and a reasonable attempt at recording magazine appearances. Both Hudson and Gittings describe only the limited and first trade editions of the books illustrated by Rackham, and there are no comments on the quality of the reproduction of the color originals, which does vary, particularly between the American and British editions. The Lattimore/Haskell bibliography includes books published only through 1935, but the descriptions are more detailed than in either Hudson or Gittings.

Robinson, Charles (U.K.), 1870–1937.

10-114. de Freitas, Leo. **Charles Robinson**. Academy Editions, St. Martin's, 1976.
Charles Robinson is not as generally admired as his brother, W. Heath Robinson, but his fantasy line drawings and color illustrations are among the most charming of the period and, perhaps, among the most influential for contemporary fantasy artists. The illustrations for his *Bee: The Princess of the Dwarfs* (1912) are strikingly modern and would not look out of place on a 1980s fantasy paperback

cover. See especially the work of Craig Russell and Michael W. Kaluta, both of whom appear to be familiar with Robinson's work. De Freitas provides a critical introduction and numerous examples of Robinson's work in color and black and white.

Robinson, W. Heath (U.K.), 1872-1944.

10-115. Beare, Geoffrey. **The Illustrations of W. Heath Robinson.** Werner Shaw, 1983.

10-116. Robinson, W. Heath. **The Fantastic Paintings of Charles & William Heath Robinson.** Ed. by David Larkin. Peacock Press/Bantam, 1976.
W. Heath Robinson was noted for his versatility; after early successes as the illustrator of Poe, Shakespeare and De la Mare, he became noted for his comic drawings in which he satirized the contraptions of the machine age. Charles seems never to have lost a certain Romantic lyricism that turned, in W. Heath's later work, to humor. The biography by Beare includes an excellent bibliography. There are, however, only three examples of Robinson's color illustrations and, for this reason, the Peacock Press collection is a useful supplement.

Rowena (Rowena Morrill), 1944- .

10-117. Morrill, Rowena. **The Fantastic Art of Rowena.** Introduction by Boris Vallejo; Foreword by Theodore Sturgeon. Pocket Books, 1983.
Photo and biographical sketch of the artist. "Description of painting technique," illustrated with progressive stages of one of the plates. Twenty-six plates with individual commentary by the artist. The most immediately noticeable feature of almost any Rowena painting is the incredible satiny texture of flesh and clothing. She confesses to "a real weakness" for this effect, and no one does it better. Many of her paintings feature muscular males or lush females, sometimes caught in static and seemingly uncomfortable poses. In quite a different vein is her fine portrait of the young hero of Theodore Sturgeon's *The Dreaming Jewels.* (REB)

Salomoni, Tito (Italy), 1928- .

10-118. Salomoni, Tito. **The Surrealistic World of Tito Salomoni.** Prestige Art Galleries (Skokie, IL), 1984.
Salomoni has done cover work for a number of paperback publishers and magazines, and his work has been published extensively in this country and abroad. Most of the illustrations appear to be nonillustrative work, and Salomoni appends comments to a number of them. An accomplished artist in the Surrealist tradition with Chirico, Escher, Magritte and Dalí evoked as influences in the short preface.

Schomburg, Alex, 1905- .

10-119. Gustafson, Jon. **Chroma: The Art of Alex Schomburg.** Father Tree Press, 1986.
Introductions and appreciations by Harlan Ellison, Stan Lee, Frank Kelly Freas,

Vincent Di Fate, Brian Aldiss, George Barr. Extensive biographical and critical commentary by Gustafson, with interpolated comments by Schomburg. More than eighty reproductions of science fiction magazine and book covers, comic book covers and fine art, plus a generous sampling of black-and-white work; the non–science fiction material ranges from advertising work in the 1920s to landscapes and architectural renderings. Individual commentary on most of the pieces reproduced. (REB)

Segrelles, Vicente (Spain), 1940– .

10-120. Segrelles, Vicente. **The Art of Segrelles**. NBM, 1987.
After an early career alternating between advertising and illustration, Segrelles left advertising in 1970 to concentrate on paperback cover artwork in England and the United States. In 1980, he began the series of *Mercenary* graphic novels, which is published in fourteen countries. The twenty-nine color plates include several double-page spreads. The illustrations are primarily fantastic and romantic-historical in subject. Segrelles is particularly effective in the creation of fantastic beasts and monsters. The cover illustration, with its evocative melancholy background, is representative of his best work.

Sendak, Maurice, 1928– .

*10-121. Lanes, Selma G. **The Art of Maurice Sendak**. Abradale/Abrams, 1980.
Sendak, the most popular and honored children's book artist of this generation, is the subject of this detailed study. His illustrations are grounded in the work of the great nineteenth-century illustrators such as Crane and Caldecott, as well as the early twentieth-century American comic strip artist Winsor McCay. His illustrations also show his affection for the movies, but the diverse influences have been integrated into a highly accomplished style in which the fantastic is as appealing to adults as to children. A recently published book of essays by Sendak on illustrators and illustration (*Caldecott & Co.*, Farrar, Straus, 1988) is an ideal complement to Lanes's detailed study, whose numerous color examples of Sendak's color and black-and-white work enhance the pleasure of a well-written text.

Sime, S(idney) H(erbert) (U.K.), 1867–1941.

10-122. Heneage, Simon, and Henry Ford. **Sidney Sime: Master of the Mysterious**. Thames & Hudson, 1980.

10-123. Skeeters, Paul W. **Sidney H. Sime: Master of Fantasy**. Ward Ritchie, 1978.
Sime is now known principally as the illustrator of many of Dunsany's collections of fantastic tales, but his early work is of almost as much interest. His fantastic creatures may have influenced Dr. Seuss, and his satirical drawings are as fine as the work of the great French nineteenth-century magazine illustrators. Sime worked largely in black and white, but the drawings have much of the richness and range one normally associates with color. Sime is well served in both these books, and although many of the Dunsany illustrations appear in both works, Sime was so prolific in his earlier years that many striking examples of his

work are not duplicated. Skeeters also includes some rare examples of Sime's color work, including some delicious monochrome illustrations from Sime's *From An Ultima Dim Thule* and *Beasts That Might Have Been*.

Vallejo, Boris (Peru), 1941– .

10-124. Vallejo, Boris. **The Fantastic Art of Boris Vallejo**. Ballantine, 1978.

10-125. Vallejo, Boris. **Fantasy Art Techniques**. Dragon's Dream, 1985.

10-126. Vallejo, Boris. **Mirage**. Ballantine, 1982.
Peruvian-born Boris, as he signs his paintings, is one of the more popular illustrators (a three-time Hugo nominee), especially in the field of heroic fantasy/sword and sorcery. His first collection includes forty color plates, along with early paintings, pen-and-ink drawings and cartoons. *Mirage* assembles eleven black-and-white drawings with commentary by Boris, and twenty-nine color plates with bad poetry by his wife, Doris, on the facing page. The techniques volume, while nominally aimed at would-be art students, collects many examples of Vallejo's work, preliminary sketches, Polaroid photos of models, and finished paintings. Boris was, for a time, the most successful emulator of Frazetta's heroic style, although he quite outdid the master in creating steatopygian females. (NB)

Whelan, Michael, 1950– .

10-127. Whelan, Michael. **Michael Whelan's Works of Wonder**. Ballantine, 1987.

10-128. Whelan, Michael. **Wonderworks: Science Fiction and Fantasy Art**. Ed. by Polly and Frank Kelly Freas. Donning, 1979.
Whelan is one of the most accomplished of today's illustrators, and these two retrospective collections reproduce both working sketches and the finished art, usually much larger than the American paperback covers it adorned. In the Ballantine collection, there is extensive commentary by the artist on the individual works and on his painting technique. Hugo Award winner, 1988. (NB/REB)

White, Tim (U.K.), 1952– .

10-129. White, Tim. **The Science Fiction and Fantasy World of Tim White**. New English Library, 1981; Paper Tiger, 1988.
Most of the examples of White's work—he is an artist who has worked in a number of media—are of his paperback cover art. The earliest examples, from 1973, are of science fiction hardware, gleaming ships against the backgrounds of deep space or settled in peaceful fields. Increasingly, fantasy creatures invade his futuristic settings, but human figures, only intermittently seen, are distant from the viewer, too small for detail to register, turned away or moving away from the foreground or, in the occasional startling closeup, offering up an untroubled profile, as pure of emotion as the ships and fantastic creatures. The illustrations were commissioned for English publications, and his work deserves to be better known in this country.

Wood, Robin

10-130. Wood, Robin. **The People of Pern**. Donning, 1988.
A gallery of color portraits for Anne McCaffrey's Dragon series [F4A-179]. Wood is best known for her drawings of children and animals in fantasy settings. McCaffrey wrote the introduction and accompanying text. Also annotated as [8-59].

Woodroffe, Patrick (U.K.), 1940– .

10-131. Woodroffe, Patrick. **A Closer Look: The Art Techniques of Patrick Woodroffe**. Dragon's Dream & Harmony Books, 1986.
An indispensable complement/supplement to *Mythopoeikon*. Woodroffe discusses his techniques in a variety of mediums. There is a fine sequence of drawings for "The Hunting of the Snark," and in addition to numerous color reproductions, there are many examples of his black-and-white pen work. The Dalí influence is less evident but the influence of the crowded canvases of Bosch is, if anything, more pervasive than in his earlier work.

10-132. Woodroffe, Patrick. **Hallelujah Anyway**. Dragon's World, 1984.
This is a collection of illustrated lyrics, billed as an "exploration of the border between reality and imagination." Most of the illustrations are tomographs, which blend painting with photographs of backgrounds and of intricate cut-outs and models built by the artist. (REB)

10-133. Woodroffe, Patrick. **Mythopoeikon: Fantasies, Monsters, Daydreams**. Dragon's World, 1976.
A kaleidoscopic collection of Woodroffe's work, with a running commentary by the artist. Woodroffe speaks of his early infatuation with Dalí, the Flemish and Dutch "primitives" and Hieronymus Bosch. A number of his early pen-and-ink drawings are included, and this work is as virtuosic as his color paintings. His work is all fantastic in treatment—even when the subject, like Dashiell Hammett, is not fantastic—and his paperback cover illustrations for reprints of A. Merritt's novels are particularly successful. Woodroffe is a self-taught artist of great versatility.

10-134. Woodroffe, Patrick. **The Second Earth: The Pentateuch Re-Told**. Dragon's World, 1987.
A "very much enlarged" edition of *The Pentateuch of the Cosmogony* (Dragon's World, 1979). The paintings, drawings, calligraphy and text are integrated into a seamless whole, portraying the birth, life-cycle and apocalyptic fate of a manlike race on another planet, as revealed by five books of alien scripture found on a derelict spacecraft in the twenty-fourth century. Artwork from the original edition has been extensively rearranged and sometimes reduced or cropped (not always to its advantage), with much new material added. (REB)

Wrightson, Berni, 1948– .

10-135. Wrightson, Berni. **A Look Back**. Ed. by Christopher Zavisa. Land of Enchantment, 1979.
Wrightson created *Swamp Thing* for DC Comics and some distinctive horror

adaptations and original stories for Warren Publications, but has also done posters, book illustrations (for *Frankenstein* and Stephen King's *Silver Bullet*) and, with Michael Kaluta, greatly influenced younger artists. His gallery of grotesques is unmistakable and this elaborate tribute was well deserved. The text includes comments by the artist on his work.

11

Fantasy and Horror Magazines

Mike Ashley

Fantasy and Horror have formed a part of the magazine scene for as long as magazines have featured fiction. As magazines began to take shape in the seventeenth and eighteenth centuries, they were predominantly political broadsheets with little to distinguish a magazine from a newspaper or a political tract. When fiction appeared, it was often of a political or satirical nature, though one exception was *The Adventurer* (1752–54), edited by John Hawkesworth, which contained, in addition to its essays and political sermonizing, a number of the editor's own stories, many in the then current vogue for Oriental fiction, mostly fantasy.

The earliest regular publication to devote itself to the weird and wonderful was an Irish periodical, *The Marvellous Magazine* (1822). It ran for only thirteen weekly issues but featured much that was, in its own words, "spicy, sensational, curious, strange, eccentric, extraordinary, surprising, supernatural, comical and whimsical." It ran many abridgments of Gothic novels and stories along with retellings of legends and folklore. These were to become standard fare in many popular magazines, but few let them dominate the contents. One early exception was *The Romancist and Novelist's Library* (1839–42), edited by William Hazlitt the Younger. Collecting Gothic and Romantic stories and novellas, it was originally issued as a weekly magazine, but after two years Hazlitt converted it to a part-work collection issued serially. At that time it was common for forthcoming novels to be issued as serial part-works before being bound as the final volume. The same thing happened to Hazlitt's magazine and collection, and there is little to distinguish between the bound volumes of a magazine and an anthology (a situation that has recurred in recent years).

By the nineteenth century magazines were published in profusion throughout Europe and America and those featuring fiction regularly carried fantasy and horror. *Bentley's Magazine* (1837–68), for instance, carried Richard Barham's popular *Ingoldsby Legends* as well as reprints of Poe's stories. *The Dublin University Magazine* (1833–77) carried many of J. Sheridan Le Fanu's ghost stories and, during his period as editor (1861–70), heavily emphasized the supernatural. One of the best known, longest-lived and most influential of the Victorian magazines was *Blackwood's* (1817–1980), published in Scotland, which featured many ghost stories including the best known of them all, "The Haunted and the Haunters" by Lord Bulwer Lytton (1859). Selections of weird stories have been assembled as *Strange Tales from Blackwood* (1950) and *Ghost Tales from Blackwood* (1969). *Blackwood's* and other leading Victorian magazines and reviews are indexed in *The Wellesley Index to Victorian Periodicals, 1824–1900*, edited by Walter E. Houghton (4 vols., 1966); American magazines are indexed in *Poole's Index to Periodical Literature, 1802–1906* (6 vols., 1882–1908).

An often overlooked publishing feature of the last century was the Christmas Annual and Giftbook. The most influential of the early ones was *The Keepsake* (1828–57), edited by Frederick Reynolds, which published most of the supernatural stories by Mary W. Shelley and Sir Walter Scott. Charles Dickens, who added impetus to the vogue for ghost stories at Christmas, frequently published special Christmas issues of his own magazines, *Household Words* (1850–59) and *All The Year Round* (1859–95), and by the latter half of the century these special issues and annuals had become a significant source for supernatural stories. For instance, Fisher Unwin's annual for 1886, *The Witching Hour*, edited by Henry Norman, contained all supernatural stories. Routledge's Christmas annual for 1877 featured Mrs. Riddell's novel *The Haunted River* [H2-83]; in fact, Mrs. Riddell's stories became a regular Christmas feature for the annuals. These volumes have not been adequately indexed or assessed.

The heyday of the popular periodical began in 1891 with the publication of *The Strand Magazine* (1891–1950; see *Index to the "Strand Magazine"* by Geraldine Beare, 1982). This, and such imitators as *The Idler* (1892–1911), *Pall Mall* (1893–1937), *Pearson's* (1896–1939) and *The Royal* (1898–1939), regularly carried supernatural stories. *The Novel Magazine* (1905–37) developed its use of weird fiction as a marketing feature, publishing at least one "uncanny story" each issue from 1913 to 1921. Several of these were later collected in book form (see omnibus *Ghost Stories and Other Queer Tales* [1931]). Sam Moskowitz has surveyed this period in the introduction to his anthology *Science Fiction by Gaslight* (1968), but his emphasis is necessarily on SF and the full import of horror and fantasy fiction in these magazines has yet to be documented adequately.

The same is true for the United States, where magazines like *Harper's* (1850–) and *Atlantic Monthly* (1871–) regularly carried weird fiction. This is still true today, more so in the United States, where fiction has remained a stronger feature of magazines than in Britain. Popular periodicals like *The Saturday Evening Post* and *Playboy* became strong markets for stories of the bizarre and grotesque. (For representative anthologies see *Shapes That Haunt the Dark* [1907], edited by William Dean Howells and Henry Mills Alden from *Harper's*; *The Saturday Evening Post Fantasy Stories* [1951], edited by Barthold Fles; and *The Playboy Book of Horror and the Supernatural* [1967] and other selections anonymously edited by Ray Russell.)

The development of fantastic fiction in nineteenth-century American magazines has been chronicled by Sam Moskowitz in his introduction to *The Crystal Man* (1973) by Edward Page Mitchell and in *Science Fiction in Old San Francisco: Vol. 1, History of the Movement from 1854 to 1890* (1980). He has also surveyed its development in the pulp magazines of the first decades of this century in his anthology *Under the Moons of Mars* (1970). It was through the pulp magazines, pioneered by Frank A. Munsey's *Argosy* (1882–), that the true specialist fiction magazine evolved.

The Specialist Publications

Despite the false reputation given *The Black Cat* (1895–1923), which was a general magazine with a penchant for the offbeat story, the first specialist weird fiction magazine was not American or English but German. *Der Orchideengarten* (1919–21) selected material from a wide variety of European authors and was beautifully illustrated and decorated. In America *The Thrill Book* (1919) verged on being a fantasy magazine, but gave too great an emphasis to adventure fiction. The first regular English-language fantasy magazine was *Weird Tales* [11-20]. It has also proved the most durable, for although it ceased publication in 1954 it has had four subsequent revivals. *Weird Tales* was never a major financial success but was sufficiently popular to encourage imitators, of which *Strange Tales* [11-17] was the best. Other lesser magazines from this period were *Ghost Stories* (1926–31), *Tales of Magic and Mystery* (1927–28) and *Mind Magic* (1931), which catered more to the gullible believer than the fantasy fan.

It was not until *Unknown* [11-18] that a new slant was brought to fantasy and horror fiction in the pioneering hands of editor John W. Campbell, Jr. The legacy of *Unknown* was later inherited by *Beyond* [11-2] and *The Magazine of Fantasy and Science Fiction* [11-13], which, through a series of highly capable editors, has become the leading fantasy publication available today.

In the heyday of the pulps, during the 1920s and 1930s, there were many specialist magazines of borderline fantasy/horror interest. There were the weird menace pulps such as *Terror Tales* (1934–41) and *Horror Stories* (1935–41), where the menace was usually directed by madmen and maniacs rather than the supernatural. Their history is well documented in Robert K. Jones's *The Shudder Pulps* [11-53]. There were also the character/hero-villain pulps, of which *Doc Savage* (1933–49) and *The Shadow* (1931–49) are the best known. These often included fantastic or supernatural episodes, although the only title character to have exclusively supernatural powers was featured in *Doctor Death* (1935). There are a growing number of specialist books about the pulps, and the hero pulps in particular, the best of which is the four-volume series *Yesterday's Faces* by Robert Sampson (1983–87). More general, though personalized, pulp histories are available in *The Fiction Factory* (1955) by Quentin Reynolds about the firm of Street & Smith, *Pulpwood Editor* (1937) by pulp editor and publisher Harold Hersey and *The Pulp Jungle* (1967) by prolific writer Frank Gruber. A useful basic overview of the pulps is Ron Goulart's *Cheap Thrills: An Informal History of the Pulp Magazines* (1972), which includes coverage of the hero, terror and weird fiction titles. Tony Goodstone's *The Pulps: 50 Years of American Pop Culture* (1970) is a good sampler of pulp fiction with a chapter on supernatural fiction and a colorful selection of covers. Another representative selection will be found in Peter Haining's *The Fantastic Pulps* (1975). Bill Blackbeard's chapter "Pulps and Dime Novels" in Inge's *Handbook of American Popular Literature* [6-38] provides a useful, current overview of pulp magazines of all types.

Today only a limited number of professional fantasy and horror magazines survive, the best of the new ones being *Rod Serling's "The Twilight Zone" Magazine* [11-15], which ceased publication as this guide was being written. There has been a trend toward serial anthologies such as the *Shadows* [H4-359] series, but the greatest growth in magazine fantasy and horror fiction has been in the small press field. There has always been a healthy amateur press field, pioneered and promoted by H. P. Lovecraft among others. The first specialist fantasy small press magazine, *The Recluse* (1927), came from within the Lovecraft circle of epistolarians. The specialist fantasy amateur magazines (or "fanzines") came into their own in the 1930s allied to the burgeoning SF fan field. The leading fan magazines of the day, *The Fantasy Fan* [11-31] and *The Phantagraph* (1935–46), have their more sophisticated counterparts today in *Whispers* [11-21], *Weirdbook* [11-19], *The Horror Show* [11-10], *Fantasy Book* [11-7], *Shayol* (1977–85), *Argonaut* (1972–) and *Eldritch Tales* [11-3]. Even the recently revived *Weird Tales* is an outgrowth of the small press movement. Jessica Amanda Salmonson's anthology series, *Tales by Moonlight* (1983 and 1988), has presented stories by small press writers, the second volume specifically selecting the best from small press magazines.

The small press field is also noted for its critical and academic magazines which study, review and analyze fantasy fiction. Many of these are dedicated to the works of a particular author, most significantly H. P. Lovecraft (see *The Acolyte* [11-22], *Crypt of Cthulhu* [11-27], *Lovecraft Studies* [11-41] and *Nyctalops* [11-45]), but also covering such diverse authors as L. Frank Baum (*The Baum Bugle* [11-26]), Edgar Rice Burroughs (*Erbania* [11-29]), F. Marion Crawford (*The Romantist* [11-48]), Robert E. Howard (*Amra* [11-24], *The Howard Collector* [11-38] and the recent *Cromlech* [1985–]), M. R. James (*Ghosts & Scholars* [11-35]), Mervyn Peake (*Peake Studies* [11-46]), Edgar Allan Poe (*Poe Studies* [11-47]), Clark Ashton Smith (*Nyctalops* [11-45] and the new *Klarkash-Ton* [1988–]), and J. R. R. Tolkien (*Mythlore* [11-43] and *Niekas* [11-44]). These magazines usually feature the author as a pivot around which is balanced a view of that author's influence on weird or fantasy fiction and a study of associational aspects. More general studies of the field are less common but include *American Fantasy* [11-23], *Dark Horizons* [11-28] and *Horrorstruck* [11-37] plus the new *Midnight Graffiti* (1988–).

The fan field also provides the medium for spreading news, information and reviews. The leading news magazine is *Locus* [11-40], which emphasizes SF but also provides good coverage of the fantasy and horror fields. Other specialist news magazines include *American Fantasy* [11-23], which is too irregular to be topical, *Mystery Scene* [11-42], which has rather divided loyalties, and the defunct *Fantasy Review* [11-32], which until its recent demise was the best in a limited field. There are also many magazines devoted to the pulp field; the best of the current titles are *Echoes* (1982–) and *The Pulp Collector* (1985–), while former titles of note were *The Pulp Era* (1959–76) and *Xenophile* (1974–78).

Studies and Indexes

The first source of reference for study of all of the fiction titles included in this section is *Science Fiction, Fantasy, and Weird Fiction Magazines* [11-54] by Marshall B. Tymn and Mike Ashley, which is the only complete work on these specialist magazines. Few other detailed studies of the field have been written, although Robert Weinberg's *The Weird Tales Story* [11-55] is an affectionate memoir of this leading title.

The primary index to all weird fiction and fantasy magazines is *Monthly Terrors* [11-68] by Frank H. Parnell and Mike Ashley, which indexes all titles to the end of 1983. All other indexes are either related directly to the SF field (such as Day [11-60] and Metcalf [11-64]) or the pulp field in general. *The Pulp Magazine Index* (1989) by Leonard Robbins indexes 198 titles by issue, author, artist, title and character, but covers only a few magazines of fantasy interest. The index overlaps to a degree a larger-scale series, started by the late Michael L. Cook and assisted by Stephen T. Miller, to index all pulps. Volume 1 covers *Mystery, Detective, and Espionage Fiction, 1915–1974* (1988), Volume 2, *Adventure, War and Sports Fiction* (forthcoming) and Volume 3, *Science Fiction, Fantasy, and Weird Fiction Magazines* (forthcoming). The best index to all current titles is the annual *Science Fiction, Fantasy, & Horror*, compiled by Charles N. Brown and William G. Contento [6-6], which covers all publications, including magazines, from 1984 to date. Considerable scholarly work has been carried out on modern writers of horror and fantasy as well as those who wrote primarily for the pulps, but little bibliographic work has been done on the weird and fantastic in the popular magazines, especially in Britain, which is almost virgin territory for the dedicated bibliophile.

Bibliography

Magazines Featuring Fiction

Annotated below are selected past and current magazines featuring horror and fantasy fiction. Publication addresses are given for current magazines only but subscription details are omitted due to frequency of changes. Information is current as of January 1989. Abbreviations for awards: HN, HW = Hugo nominee, winner; WFA = World Fantasy Award (see chapter 13).

Holdings information for selected magazines was obtained by Randall Scott, who compiled chapter 12. To conserve space, the holding library is designated by a number corresponding to the item number of the library in chapter 12. The letter in parentheses following the library number denotes A (all), M (most) or S (some). In a few instances holdings are on microfilm or microfiche, and these are designated mf after the letter. "All" denotes a complete run, and a current subscription if the magazine is currently published. "Most" denotes ownership of at least half and, in many cases, almost all issues published. "Some" denotes that fewer than half the published issues were held, or that the library simply designated its holdings as "incomplete."

*11-1. Avon Fantasy Reader. 1947–52 (18 issues). Irregular. Donald A. Wollheim, ed. Avon Books, New York. Indexed in Day, Metcalf, Parnell, Strauss.
Although designed as a regular anthology series, *AFR* has become closely identified as a magazine. It concentrated on reprinting fiction selected widely from the pulps, especially *Weird Tales* [11-20], and from classic literature. Authors most represented include William Hope Hodgson, Robert E. Howard, Ray Bradbury and Lord Dunsany. Essential for its key selection of primary material. *AFR* had a companion *Avon Science Fiction Reader* (1951–52), which also published fantasy. Two representative anthologies were edited by George Ernsberger as *Avon Fantasy Reader* and *2nd Avon Fantasy Reader* (both 1968). Compare *Magazine of Horror* [11-14].
Holdings: 1 (A), 2 (A), 4 (A), 6 (A), 9 (M), 11 (A), 12 (A), 14 (A), 16 (A), 17 (A), 19 (A), 21 (A), 23 (A), 27 (A), 35 (A), 36 (A), 38 (S), 39 (A), 40 (S), 42 (S)

11-2. Beyond Fantasy Fiction. 1953–55 (10 issues). Bi-monthly. Horace L. Gold, ed. Galaxy Publishing, New York. Indexed in Metcalf, Strauss, Parnell.
A literary fantasy magazine that published more classic stories than are generally remembered despite the turn of the tide against fantasy in the 1950s. The best stories are more in the vein of science fantasy, with Gold treating *Beyond* as a fantasy companion to the SF magazine *Galaxy*, much as John W. Campbell had created *Unknown* [11-18] as a fantasy equivalent to *Astounding SF*. Authors include Robert Sheckley, Theodore Sturgeon and Damon Knight, with the best-known story being "The Wall around the World" by Theodore Cogswell. Selective anthology, *Beyond* (1963), published anonymously. Compare *Unknown* and *The Magazine of Fantasy and Science Fiction* [11-13].
Holdings: 1 (A), 2 (A), 4 (A), 6 (A), 9 (M), 11 (A), 12 (S), 13 (M), 14 (A), 15 (A), 16 (A), 17 (M), 19 (A), 21 (A), 23 (A), 27 (A), 28 (A), 35 (S), 36 (A), 38 (M), 39 (A), 41 (A), 42 (S)

11-3. Eldritch Tales. No ISSN. 1975– . Quarterly. Crispin Burnham, ed. 1051 Wellington Rd., Lawrence, KS 66044. Circulation: 1,000. Indexed in Parnell.
Subtitled "A Magazine in the Weird Tales Tradition," *ET* (titled *The Dark Messenger Reader* for issue #1) has until recently concentrated more on the Lovecraftian influence rather than the true *Weird Tales* tradition of the off-beat and bizarre. It has matured gradually and is now one of the more regular and reliable small press magazines. In addition to fiction and verse each issue carries news and reviews (film and book). Compare *Weirdbook* [11-19].
Holdings: 23 (M), 26 (M), 28 (S)

11-4. Famous Fantastic Mysteries. 1939–53 (81 issues). Monthly/Quarterly/Bi-monthly. Mary Gnaedinger, ed. Frank A. Munsey Co./Popular Publications, New York. Indexed in Day, Metcalf, Parnell, Strauss.
A pulp magazine highly prized today for its artwork by Virgil Finlay and Lawrence Stevens. Initially reprinted lead novels and stories from the early Munsey pulp magazines, selecting scientific romances or fantastic adventures (especially lost race) but including many weird fantasies. Later reprints were selected from book sources generally unavailable in the U.S. at the time. Authors selected included A. Merritt, William Hope Hodgson, Philip M. Fisher and Francis Stevens. Companion titles *Fantastic Novels* (1940–41, 1948–51) and *A. Merritt's Fan-*

tasy Magazine (1949–50) had same policy. Compare *Avon Fantasy Reader* [11-1]. Holdings: 1 (M), 2 (A), 6 (A), 9 (M), 11 (M), 12 (A), 13 (S), 14 (A), 16 (A), 17 (M), 19 (A), 21 (A), 23 (A), 26 (S), 27 (A), 28 (S), 29 (S), 35 (A), 36 (A), 38 (S), 39 (A), 41 (A), 42 (S)

11-5. Fantastic. 1952–80 (208 issues). Monthly/Bi-monthly. Now merged with *Amazing SF Stories* (ISSN 0279-1706), Patrick L. Price, ed. Box 110, Lake Geneva, WI 53147. Indexed in Boyajian, Metcalf, NESFA, Parnell, Strauss.

A digest magazine, uneven in quality, which for much of its life published formula SF and later reprinted lesser material. It had three major periods, however. First from 1952 to 1954, under editor Howard Browne, who endeavored to produce a literary magazine with quality fantasy by Ray Bradbury, Fritz Leiber, Theodore Sturgeon and Richard Matheson and new and reprinted fiction by such establishment names as E. M. Forster, Raymond Chandler and Stephen Vincent Benét. From 1960 to 1965, Cele Goldsmith Lalli encouraged new and innovative fantasy. Under her, new writers like Roger Zelazny, Piers Anthony and Thomas M. Disch emerged, and established writers like Fritz Leiber and Edmond Hamilton reemerged. *Fantastic* did much to lay the foundations for a revival of interest in fantasy, especially sword and sorcery, in the mid-1960s. From 1970 to 1978, under Ted White, *Fantastic* became a major source for sword and sorcery and also a vehicle for supernatural and innovative fiction by writers like Barry Malzberg, Jack Dann, Gordon Eklund and Avram Davidson. *Fantastic* was a HN in 1963 and 1972 and White was HN as best editor from 1974 to 1977. Had a short-lived fantasy companion, *Dream World* (1957), which printed "wish-fulfillment" stories. Selective anthologies are *The Best from Fantastic* (1970), edited by Ted White, and *Fantastic Stories: Tales of the Weird and Wondrous* (1987), edited by Martin H. Greenberg and Patrick L. Price.

Holdings: 1 (S), 2 (A), 4 (M-mf), 6 (A), 9 (S), 11 (S), 12 (S), 13 (S), 14 (A), 15 (A), 16 (A), 17 (M), 18 (S), 19 (A), 21 (A), 23 (M), 27 (A), 28 (S), 29 (S), 35 (M), 36 (M), 38 (A), 39 (A), 42 (S)

11-6. Fantastic Adventures. 1939–53 (129 issues). Monthly/Bi-monthly. Raymond A. Palmer, Howard Browne, eds. Ziff-Davis, Chicago. Indexed in Day, Gallagher, Metcalf, Strauss.

Pulp magazine which initially provided formula sensational adventure stories, mostly SF/lost race, aimed at the younger reader. During the war years it shifted to humorous lighthearted fantasies by Nelson S. Bond, Robert Bloch and David Wright O'Brien. After World War II, and especially under Browne, it improved in quality and became an important source for weird fantasies by Theodore Sturgeon, Fritz Leiber, Walter M. Miller, Jr., William Tenn and L. Sprague de Camp. It was later merged with *Fantastic* [11-5]. See *Guide* by Gallagher [11-52].

Holdings: 2 (A), 4 (A-mf), 6 (A), 9 (A), 11 (A), 12 (S), 13 (S), 14 (A), 15 (A), 16 (S), 17 (M), 19 (A), 21 (A), 23 (S), 27 (A), 28 (S), 29 (A), 35 (A), 36 (A), 37 (A-mf), 38 (M), 39 (A), 40 (S-mf), 41 (S), 42 (S)

11-7. Fantasy Book. ISSN 0277-0717. 1981–   . Quarterly. Dennis Mallonee, ed. Heroic Publishing, 6433 California Ave., Long Beach, CA 90805. Circulation: 5,000. Indexed in Boyajian, Brown, Parnell.

Small press magazine, attractively illustrated, with the emphasis on high fantasy though also including humorous and dark fantasy. Each issue contains ten to twelve stories, the occasional classic reprint, two or three poems and a serial. The magazine suspended publication in 1987 due to publishing commitments but was to be relaunched in 1989 with the same policy and format but with the addition of interior full-color graphic story material. Its format has been closely imitated by the new *Marion Zimmer Bradley's Fantasy Magazine* (1988– , ISSN 0897-9286, quarterly, PO Box 72, Berkeley, CA 94701).
Holdings: 1 (S), 2 (A), 4 (S), 6 (A), 13 (S), 15 (A), 16 (S), 17 (A), 27 (A), 28 (S), 38 (S), 39 (A), 41 (S)

11-8. Fantasy Fiction. 1953 (4 issues). Bi-monthly. Lester del Rey, ed. Future Publications, New York. Indexed in Metcalf, Parnell, Strauss.
High-quality digest magazine, short-lived only due to the whims of the publisher. Maturely edited by Lester del Rey, it carried a mixture of dark fantasy and humor, successfully blending the twin traditions of *Weird Tales* [11-20] and *Unknown* [11-18]. Leading contributors were Robert Sheckley, L. Sprague de Camp, Poul Anderson and Philip K. Dick, with collectible covers by Hannes Bok. Compare *Beyond* [11-2].
Holdings: 1 (A), 4 (A), 6 (A), 9 (M), 11 (M), 13 (A), 14 (A), 17 (A), 19 (A), 21 (A), 23 (A), 27 (A), 35 (A), 36 (A), 39 (A)

11-9. Fantasy Tales. No ISSN. 1977– . Semi-annual. David A. Sutton and Stephen Jones, eds. Robinson Publishing, 11 Shepherd House, Shepherd Street, London W1Y 7LD. Circulation: 10,000. Indexed in Brown, Parnell.
Small press publication issued in emulation of *Weird Tales* [11-20]. Despite the title it concentrates on weird fiction, featuring both new and established writers from Britain and America. In 1988 *FT* received a professional boost when publication was taken over by a national British publisher with distribution on a "paperback magazine" basis. Quarterly publication and U.S. distribution are goals in 1990. Issues contain eight to ten stories plus verse and editorial features. Anthology, *The Best from Fantasy Tales* (1988), edited by Jones and Sutton. *FT* was a WFA nominee in 1981, 1982, 1983 and 1987 and winner in 1984.
Holdings: 27 (M), 35 (S), 39 (A), 41 (S)

11-10. The Horror Show. ISSN 0748-2914. 1982– . Quarterly. David B. Silva, ed. Phantasm Press, 14848 Misty Springs Lane, Oak Run, CA 96069. Circulation: 44,000.
A large-format small press magazine concentrating on horror and terror stories by the new generation of writers in the wake of Stephen King. A mature and professional approach by editor/publisher Silva has made it one of the leading small press publications. Each issue includes eight to ten stories, an interview, book and film reviews and a variety of other features. A few special issues have concentrated on Dean R. Koontz, Steve Rasnic Tem, J. K. Potter, Robert McCammon and Dennis Etchison. A representative anthology, *Best of the Horror Show* (1987), edited by Silva, and including an index to the first nineteen issues, was published by another small press which publishes *2 AM* (1986– , ISSN 0886-8743, quarterly, PO Box 6754, Rockford, IL 61125), a magazine of similar content though of lesser quality in production. *THS* was nominated for WFA in 1986

and 1987 and was co-winner in 1988. The editor announced in summer 1989 that publication would cease by year's end.
Holdings: 27 (S)

11-11. Interzone. No ISSN. 1982–   . Bi-monthly. David Pringle, ed. 124 Osborne Rd., Brighton BN1 6LU, England. Circulation: 15,000. Indexed in Boyajian, Brown.
A small press magazine that has steadily grown in stature since its early experimental issues and now has national distribution. *IZ* owes much of its initial inspiration to the Michael Moorcock issues of *New Worlds*, though there is a greater emphasis on surreal, dark and technophobic fantasy and SF. *IZ* has developed several new writers including Scott Bradfield and Alex Stewart. In addition to the fiction, each issue carries news, perceptive reviews and interviews and the occasional illustrated feature. Selective annual anthologies have appeared from three different publishers in 1985, 1987 and 1988, edited by John Clute, Simon Ounsley and David Pringle. *IZ* was a HN in 1986, 1987 and 1988.
Holdings: 4 (S), 15 (A), 27 (S), 28 (S), 38 (A), 39 (A), 41 (A), 42 (S)

*11-12. Isaac Asimov's Science Fiction Magazine. ISSN 0162-2188. 1977–   . 13 issues per year. Gardner Dozois, ed. Davis Publications, 380 Lexington Ave., New York, NY 10017. Circulation: 82,000. Indexed in Boyajian, Brown, NESFA; self-indexed at end of each annual volume.
Although marketed as a science fiction magazine, in recent years *IAsfM* has published the whole range of fantastic fiction including light and dark fantasy but avoiding straight sword and sorcery. *IAsfM* is a particularly good source for a new treatment of the *Unknown*-style fantasy, a policy developed by initial editor George Scithers, who also enjoyed the occasional light, humorous spoof. Stories from *IAsfM* have been regularly nominated for and won awards. Scithers was HW for best editor in 1978 and 1980 and later editor Shawna McCarthy was HW in 1984. The magazine also runs book reviews and other nonfiction features. There have been many derivative anthologies but only *Isaac Asimov's Fantasy* (1985), edited by Shawna McCarthy, is wholly fantasy.
Holdings: 2 (M), 4 (A), 5 (A), 6 (A), 13 (M), 14 (S), 15 (A), 16 (S), 17 (M), 21 (S), 23 (A), 27 (A), 28 (S), 29 (M), 35 (S), 38 (A), 39 (A), 41 (A), 42 (S)

*11-13. The Magazine of Fantasy and Science Fiction. ISSN 0024-984X. 1949–   . Monthly. Edward L. Ferman, ed. Mercury Press, Box 56, Cornwall, CT 06753. Circulation: 60,000. Indexed in Boyajian, Brown, Day, Metcalf, NESFA and Strauss; self-indexed at end of each six-issue volume.
The premier magazine featuring fantasy and weird fiction, which has retained a consistent quality of literary and mature fiction over a succession of editors. It was founded by Anthony Boucher and J. Francis McComas with the intention of being wholly fantasy-based, following the success of *Avon Fantasy Reader* [11-1]. SF has always been a strong feature but has seldom dominated the fantasy content. Each issue carries a selection of long and short stories, a book review column by Algis Budrys, a media column by Harlan Ellison and a science column by Isaac Asimov. *F&SF* is unique in its lack of interior art, aside from a few cartoons. More stories from *F&SF* have been nominated for and won awards than from any other fantasy magazine. *F&SF* was a HN for every year from 1957 to 1971

and a HW eight times. Ferman has likewise been HN as best editor for every year from 1972 and HW three times. Ferman also won the WFA for Professional Achievement in 1979. There have been many anthologies selecting from *F&SF* including twenty-four annual selections and three major retrospectives. Three especially useful volumes are *The Eureka Years* (1982), edited by Annette Mc-Comas, which looks at the magazine's formative years, and the two omnibuses, *The Best Fantasy Stories from Fantasy and Science Fiction* (1985), edited by Edward L. Ferman, and *The Best Horror Stories from Fantasy & Science Fiction* (1988), edited by Edward Ferman and Anne Jordan.

Holdings: 1 (S), 2 (A), 3 (M), 4 (A), 5 (M), 6 (A), 9 (M), 11 (M), 12 (A), 13 (M), 14 (A), 15 (A), 16 (M), 17 (A), 18 (S), 19 (A), 21 (A), 23 (A), 27 (A), 28 (M), 29 (M), 35 (M), 36 (M), 37 (A), 38 (A), 39 (A), 41 (M), 42 (S)

11-14. Magazine of Horror. 1963–71 (36 issues). Bi-monthly/Quarterly. Robert A. W. Lowndes, ed. Health Knowledge, New York. Indexed in Cook, Metcalf, NESFA, Parnell, Strauss.

Primarily a reprint magazine selecting fiction from the pulps, especially *Weird Tales* [11-20] and *Strange Tales* [11-17], and from earlier as well as scarcer sources. Printed both old and new stories by David H. Keller and Robert E. Howard and featured many new stories in the traditional style. *MoH* had three fantasy companions: *Weird Terror Tales* (1969–70) and *Bizarre Fantasy Tales* (1970–71) were almost identical in policy, and *Startling Mystery Stories* (1966–71) featured weird mysteries. Compare *Avon Fantasy Reader* [11-1].

Holdings: 4 (S), 13 (S), 14 (M), 21 (M), 23 (A), 27 (A), 28 (S), 35 (M), 36 (A), 38 (M), 39 (M)

*11-15. Rod Serling's "The Twilight Zone" Magazine. ISSN 0279-6090. 1981–1989. Bi-monthly. Tappan King, ed. Montcalm Publishing, New York. Indexed in Boyajian, Brown, Parnell.

A large-format ninety-six-page magazine inspired by Rod Serling's innovative television series, in keeping with which *TZ* usually published offbeat stories of odd things happening to everyday people. Each issue carried seven or eight stories plus a number of illustrated media features, book, film and video reviews and news. Liberally illustrated, the magazine offered a good range of fiction from traditional to experimental. Ceased publication with June 1989 issue. A digest reprint of stories from *TZ*, *Night Cry* (1984), became a regular quarterly companion magazine which, though it lasted only eleven issues, carried a strong selection of horror stories beyond the normal pale of *TZ*.

Holdings: 1 (M), 2 (M), 3 (M), 4 (M), 5 (A), 15 (M), 17 (A), 19 (A), 27 (S), 28 (S), 38 (A), 39 (M), 41 (S)

11-16. Science Fantasy. 1950–67 (93 issues). Bi-monthly. John Carnell, Kyril Bonfiglioli, eds. Nova Publications/Roberts & Vinter, London. Indexed in Metcalf, NESFA, Parnell, Strauss.

Originally a digest-sized SF companion to *New Worlds*, edited by Walter Gillings, *SF* developed its own distinct character under Carnell during the mid-1950s and early 1960s. Each issue featured a lead novella, often by John Brunner or Kenneth Bulmer, and five or six short stories. *SF* was one of the few magazines to feature fantasy in the 1950s and is noted for publishing the early historical fantasies by Thomas Burnett Swann and the Elric stories by Michael Moorcock. From 1964 to 1966 new editor Bonfiglioli dramatically changed the character of the magazine, now in pocketbook format, and introduced author Keith Roberts. Retitled *Impulse* from 1966 to 1967, and primarily edited by Roberts, it featured his "Pavane" series. *SF* was HN in 1962 and 1964.

Holdings: 1 (S), 4 (A), 11 (M), 14 (A), 15 (M), 16 (S), 17 (M), 19 (A), 21 (S), 23 (M), 27 (A), 28 (S), 35 (A), 36 (A), 38 (S), 39 (A), 41 (M). *Impulse*: 16 (S), 17 (A), 21 (A), 23 (A), 35 (A), 38 (A), 39 (A), 41 (A), 42 (S)

11-17. Strange Tales. 1931–33 (7 issues). Bi-monthly. Harry Bates, ed. Clayton Magazines, New York. Indexed in Cockcroft, Cook/Miller, Parnell.

The only serious rival pulp magazine to *Weird Tales* [11-20], and although short-lived it had an immediate impact. Although written by many of *WT*'s regular authors the stories were stronger in action, more formula-based and less offbeat and thus more digestible by the majority of readers. Issues of *ST* are now highly prized by collectors. Most of the stories were reprinted in *Magazine of Horror* [11-14] and its companions and in the facsimile anthology *Strange Tales* (1976) from Odyssey Publications.

Holdings: 1 (A), 4 (S), 14 (A), 23 (A), 27 (A), 36 (A)

*11-18. Unknown (later **Unknown Worlds**). 1939–43 (39 issues). Monthly/Bi-monthly. John W. Campbell, Jr., ed. Street & Smith, New York. Indexed in Day, Hoffman, Metzger, Parnell.

The most innovative of the fantasy pulps presenting a more mature and logical face to weird fiction than earlier titles. Editor Campbell asked authors to project a rational sequence of events from a "what-if?" fantasy situation, thereby turning the supernatural into a quasi-science. *Unknown* carried a strong selection of short fiction but is best remembered for its lead novels, which included work by Eric Frank Russell, L. Ron Hubbard, L. Sprague de Camp, Jack Williamson, Robert A. Heinlein, Fritz Leiber and Cleve Cartmill. *Unknown* had a long-running British reprint edition (1939–49). Campbell assembled a pulp sampler, *From Unknown Worlds* (1948), prior to a planned but aborted revival of the magazine. Likewise, Stanley Schmidt (editor of *Analog* [formerly *Astounding SF*], the former companion to *Unknown*) has also recently edited a selective anthology, *Unknown* (1988), prior to a possible revival. Other representative anthologies include *The Unknown* (1963) and *The Unknown Five* (1964), both edited by D. R. Bensen [F3-28], and *Hell Hath Fury* (1963), edited by George Hay.

Holdings: 1 (M), 2 (A), 4 (A), 6 (A), 9 (M), 11 (A), 14 (A), 15 (A), 16 (A), 17 (M), 18 (A), 21 (A), 23 (A), 27 (A), 35 (A), 36 (A), 38 (M), 39 (A), 41 (S), 42 (S)

11-19. Weirdbook. ISSN 8755-7452. 1968–   . Irregular. W. Paul Ganley, ed. Box 149, Amherst Branch, Buffalo, NY 14226. Circulation: 1,000. Indexed in Boyajian, Brown, Parnell.

A small press magazine that over the twenty years of its twenty-three issues has maintained a standard of enjoyable diversity. It is less sophisticated than other leading small press titles, being produced solely as a hobby, and the fiction is not always of a high quality—though it has improved in recent years—but it does provide a healthy selection of offbeat stories much in the tradition of *Weird Tales*

[11-20]. Recent issues have presented longer stories with an increasing bias toward fantasy over horror. *Weirdbook* is very much a "fan's" magazine. It was nominated for the WFA in 1979, 1982, 1983, 1985 and 1986 and won in 1987. Ganley publishes an irregular companion magazine, *Weirdbook Encores* (formerly *Eerie Country* [1976-   ]).
Holdings: 4 (S), 14 (A), 23 (S), 26 (S), 39 (A)

*11-20. Weird Tales. ISSN 0898-5073. 1923-   . Quarterly. Darrell Schweitzer, John Betancourt, George H. Scithers, eds. Terminus Publishing, PO Box 13418, Philadelphia, PA 19101. Circulation: 10,000. Indexed in Cockcroft, Jaffery, Parnell.

In its first incarnation, 1923-54, *WT* was the leading pulp magazine of horror and fantasy, though its heyday was 1929-40, under editor Farnsworth Wright. *WT* was subtitled "the Unique Magazine," a soubriquet well earned through its publication of many offbeat stories for which there was no other market. *WT* is best remembered as the primary market for H. P. Lovecraft's fiction (the Cthulhu mythos began to take shape in its pages) and Robert E. Howard's fantasies (including the Conan stories, which gave birth to the sword-and-sorcery subgenre), but in addition *WT* was a leading market for many fantasy authors including Clark Ashton Smith, Edmond Hamilton, August Derleth, Seabury Quinn, Frank Owen, Henry Kuttner, Manly Wade Wellman, Robert Bloch and Ray Bradbury, many of whom made their first or early sales to the magazine. It has seen four revivals (in 1973, 1981, 1985 and 1988) of which the latest is the most faithful to the magazine's original intent. It contains seven to eight stories of fantasy and horror, up to ten items of verse, plus nonfiction features, interviews, reviews and a good selection of interior art. *WT* has been well-mined by anthologists and a good selection of stories will be found in *The Unexpected* (1961), *The Ghoul Keepers* (1961), *Weird Tales* (1964) and *Worlds of Weird* (1965), all edited by Leo Margulies; *Weird Tales* (1976), edited by Peter Haining and reproduced in facsimile; and *Weird Tales: 32 Unearthed Terrors* (1988), edited by Stefan R. Dziemianowicz, Robert Weinberg and Martin H. Greenberg, which selects one story from each year of the magazine's original run.
Holdings: 1 (M), 3 (M), 4 (M), 5 (S), 6 (S), 11 (M), 12 (S), 13 (S), 14 (M), 15 (S), 16 (S), 17 (M), 19 (M), 21 (M), 23 (M), 24 (A), 26 (S), 27 (A), 29 (S), 35 (S), 36 (A), 37 (S), 38 (M), 39 (S), 41 (S-British edition), 42 (S)

*11-21. Whispers. No ISSN. 1973-   . Irregular. Stuart David Schiff, ed. Whispers Press, 70 Highland Ave., Binghamton, NY 13905. Circulation: 3,000. Indexed in Boyajian, Brown, Parnell.

Originally intended to follow on from *The Arkham Collector* (see under [11-25]) after Derleth's death, *Whispers* has now established itself as the leading small press magazine of weird fiction. Its publication schedule has become irregular of late, but each issue is an impressive production in digest format, 176 pages. Past issues have included special author features including Manly Wade Wellman, Ramsey Campbell and Stephen King. Most issues contain between fifteen and twenty stories, news and review features, poetry and art portfolios. A series of anthologies has evolved, also called *Whispers* [H4-361], containing both reprints from the magazine and new material. Both magazine and anthology series place an emphasis on nontraditional treatments of horror and fantasy themes. Schiff

won the WFA in the Non-Professional category in 1975, 1977, 1983 and 1985, was a HN in 1984 and 1985 and won the 1984 British Fantasy Award.
Holdings: 3 (M), 4 (A),14 (A), 15 (M), 21 (S), 23 (S), 27 (S), 28 (M), 35 (S), 38 (A), 39 (A), 41 (M)

Magazines about Fantasy and Horror

Annotated below are selected past and current magazines which provide discussion, analysis and criticism of fantasy and horror fiction. Some of the titles also include fiction but are included in this section because the fiction is secondary.

11-22. The Acolyte. 1942–46 (14 issues). Quarterly. Francis T. Laney and Duane W. Rimel, eds.
One of the most popular fanzines of the 1940s, *The Acolyte* was started by two devotees of H. P. Lovecraft and became an organ for Lovecraft discussion, though that had not been its prime purpose. It did cover a variety of topics in weird fiction and also published fiction and verse. Regular contributors included Forrest J. Ackerman, Sam Moskowitz, Fritz Leiber and Anthony Boucher. *The Acolyte* was mimeographed, with issues of thirty to thirty-two pages each. Compare *Crypt of Cthulhu* [11-27] and *Lovecraft Studies* [11-41].
Holdings: 4 (A), 12 (S), 21 (M), 23 (S), 28 (S)

11-23. American Fantasy. No ISSN. 1982– . Quarterly. Robert and Nancy Garcia, eds. PO Box 41714, Chicago, IL 60641. Circulation: 3,500. Indexed in Brown.
A slick, quality production with an emphasis on articles, interviews, news and reviews but with two or three stories per issue, all profusely and attractively illustrated and packaged. *AF* evolved from the much smaller *Chicago Fantasy Newsletter* (1979–81), which concentrated on news and reviews. The first two issues of *AF* were almost the last, but the magazine was relaunched on a firmer financial basis in 1986, though issues have still been irregular. It is the leading review magazine in the fantasy field. The Garcias were nominated for the WFA in 1983 and won in 1988.
Holdings: 12 (S), 13 (S), 27 (S), 28 (S), 38 (S), 39 (S)

11-24. Amra. No ISSN. 1956– . Irregular. George R. Heap/George Scithers, eds. Box 8243, Philadelphia, PA 19101. Circulation: 1,000. Self-indexed every tenth issue.
Originally the newsletter of the Hyborian League and dedicated to the works of Robert E. Howard, under Scithers *Amra* expanded to cover all aspects of "swordplay & sorcery." It was in its pages that the term "sword and sorcery" was coined. Regular contributors of essays, verses, fiction and reviews include Fritz Leiber, L. Sprague de Camp, Poul Anderson and Lin Carter, and the neatly multilithed magazine was noted for its illustrations by Roy Krenkel and George Barr. *Amra* is moribund, with issue #72 ready but awaiting publication. HN 1962, HW 1964, 1968. Compare *Erbania* [11-29] and *The Howard Collector* [11-38]. Collections of essays from *Amra* have been published as *The Conan Reader* (1968) and *The Spell of Conan* (1980), both edited by L. Sprague de Camp.
Holdings: 4 (S), 12 (S), 14 (S), 17 (S), 21 (M-early), 23 (S), 27 (S), 28 (M), 38 (M), 39 (M), 41 (S)

11-25. The Arkham Sampler. 1948–49 (8 issues). Quarterly. August Derleth, ed. Arkham House, Sauk City, WI. Indexed in Parnell.

A literary quarterly issued primarily as a vehicle to show the type of fiction published by Arkham House, this soon became one of the earliest scholarly publications with extensive reviews and comment on fantasy and weird fiction. Noted for its first printing of new fiction by H. Russell Wakefield and John Beynon Harris, it also reprinted lesser-known stories. There was an inevitable emphasis on the life and works of H. P. Lovecraft, which enhances the magazine's collector's value today. Derleth repeated the concept on a lesser scale with *The Arkham Collector* (1967–71), which featured fiction, verse, news and reviews. Compare *Whispers* [11-21]. The name *The Arkham Sampler* survives today in a series of chapbooks issued annually by The Strange Company, Madison, WI, with individual issues featuring fiction, verse, photographs or artwork.
Holdings: 1 (M), 3 (M), 4 (A), 5 (M), 9 (M), 11 (A), 14 (A), 15 (A), 19 (A), 21 (S), 23 (A), 27 (M), 28 (S), 29 (A), 33 (A), 35 (A), 36 (A), 38 (M), 42 (S)

11-26. The Baum Bugle. ISSN 005-6677. 1957– . Three times a year. Michael Gessel, ed. International Wizard of Oz Club, PO Box 748, Arlington, VA 22216. Circulation: 2,000.

An attractive glossy magazine, specializing in popular and scholarly articles about Oz, its creator L. Frank Baum and other authors and artists, with biographical and critical studies and first edition checklists. Research into the people and places within the Oz books appears frequently and there are features on the Oz films and other media adaptations. Fiction appears rarely and is usually by Baum. A specialist magazine with a dedicated treatment of its subject. For large libraries only or those with a specialist Baum collection.
Holdings: 3 (M), 5 (M), 11 (A), 13 (S), 16 (M), 17 (S), 23 (S), 28 (S)

Cinefantastique *See* [F9-9; H9-10] for annotation.
Holdings: 3 (M), 4 (S), 5 (A), 10 (S), 14 (S), 17 (M), 21 (S), 23 (M), 27 (M), 28 (S), 29 (S), 36 (M), 37 (S), 38 (A), 41 (S), 42 (S)

11-27. Crypt of Cthulhu. No ISSN. 1981– . Every six weeks. Robert M. Price, ed. Cryptic Publications, 216 Fernwood Ave, Upper Montclair, NJ 07043. Circulation: 550. Index to first 50 issues in issue #55.

Crypt is one of the leading current small press magazines dedicated to studying the life and works of H. P. Lovecraft in particular and the *Weird Tales* school in general. Articles vary from the studious to the humorous and cover a wide variety of themes and topics despite the apparent limitations. *Crypt* also publishes Lovecraftian fiction by or associated with the *Weird Tales* fraternity. Compare *Lovecraft Studies* [11-41] and *Nyctalops* [11-45].
Holdings: 13 (S), 23 (S)

11-28. Dark Horizons. No ISSN. 1971– . Irregular. Jon Harvey, ed. British Fantasy Society, 15 Stanley Road, Morden, Surrey, SM4 5DE, England. Circulation: 350. Indexed in Holland, Parnell.

The official journal of the British Fantasy Society (see chapter 13), *DH* has had an irregular and uneven history with its best issues under editors Stephen Jones (#9–15) and David Sutton (#23–30). Issues are predominantly nonfiction with analyses

of fantasy themes or authors' works, but usually a story and poetry are also included and occasional special fiction issues appear. The BFS also publishes a *Newsletter* and two fiction annuals, *Winter Chills* and *Mystique*.
Holdings: 38 (S), 39 (M)

11-29. Erbania. No ISSN. 1956– . Twice yearly. D. Peter Ogden, ed. 8001 Fernview Lane, Tampa, FL 33615. Circulation: 350.
The longest running of the magazines dedicated to the memory of Edgar Rice Burroughs. Contains essays on every aspect of his life and work in all media, as well as on such Burroughs-associated writers as Otis Adelbert Kline, Robert E. Howard, John Norman and Philip José Farmer. Issued in large format with from fifteen to twenty pages. Compare *Amra* [11-24].
Holdings: information not collected

11-30. Fantasiae. 1973–80. Monthly. Ian M. Slater, ed. Fantasy Association, Los Angeles, CA.
The monthly newsletter of the defunct Fantasy Association, aimed at coverage of all writers in the fantasy field, but especially those at the literary end of the spectrum, exemplified by the mythographic works of Tolkien and Lewis. Contents included news, reviews and author features with issue sizes varying between eight and twenty-four pages.
Holdings: 3 (M), 4 (A), 15 (A), 27 (A), 28 (M), 36 (A), 38 (M), 39 (A)

11-31. The Fantasy Fan. 1933–35. (18 issues). Monthly. Charles D. Hornig, ed. Elizabeth, NJ.
The first regular amateur magazine devoted to weird fiction, containing stories, news and reviews, plus nonfiction features. It is most noted for its stories by H. P. Lovecraft, Clark Ashton Smith, David H. Keller and Robert Bloch and for running the revised version of Lovecraft's essay "Supernatural Horror in Literature" (incomplete) [H8-7]. Especially useful for its interviews and behind-the-scenes news by Mort Weisinger and Julius Schwartz.
Holdings: 4 (S), 12 (S), 14 (S), 21 (S), 28 (S)

*11-32. Fantasy Review [formerly **Fantasy Newsletter**]. 1978–87 (103 issues). Monthly. Paul Allen, later Robert A. Collins, eds. Meckler Publishing, Westport, CT.
Initially a newsletter on current and forthcoming publications, *FN* rapidly expanded under both editors into an intelligent review of the fantasy field with regular columns by Fritz Leiber, Karl Wagner, Jack Chalker and Somtow Sucharitkul, plus news, interviews, critical and analytical essays and, after a merger with Neil Barron's *Science Fiction and Fantasy Book Review* in 1984, the most extensive review section of any small press magazine. It ceased publication through lack of financial support and has been converted into an annual volume [6-36]. HN, 1983, 1984, 1985, 1986, 1987. WFA nominee 1979, WFA winner 1980, 1982.
Holdings: 4 (A), 10 (M), 11 (A), 13 (S), 15 (A), 17 (A), 19 (S), 26 (A), 27 (A), 29 (S), 36 (S), 38 (A), 39 (A), 41 (S)

11-33. Fear. ISSN 0954-8017. 1988– . Monthly. John Gilbert, ed. Newsfield Ltd., PO Box 20, Ludlow, Shropshire, SY8 1D8, England. Circulation: 100,000.
A heavily illustrated, visual magazine strongly influenced by the film and televi-

sion media, reflected in its contents coverage of visual events. Early issues emphasized horror fiction, but from the third issue there was a slight increase in the coverage of fantasy fiction. Each issue carries short fiction and serializations of novels and nonfiction, and the magazine is especially strong in author interviews and profiles as well as in media news and reviews.
Holdings: information not collected

11-34. The Ghost. 1943–47 (4 issues). Annual. W. Paul Cook, ed. Driftwind Press, N. Montpelier, VT.
A noted fanzine of the 1940s which, despite its primary interest in the works of H. P. Lovecraft, published a variety of useful scholarly and reflective essays on fantasy personalities and works, including E. Hoffman Price's series "The Book of the Dead," August Derleth's "The Weird Tale in English since 1890" and bibliophilic columns by Rheinhart Kleiner and H. C. Koenig. For the specialist collector and library; issues are now rare. Compare *The Acolyte* [11-22].
Holdings: 3 (M), 21 (A)

11-35. Ghosts & Scholars. No ISSN. 1979– . Annual. Rosemary Pardoe, ed. Haunted Library, Flat 1, 36 Hamilton St., Hoole, Chester, CH2 3JQ, England. Circulation: 500. Indexed in Holland, Parnell.
A small press magazine dedicated to the ghost stories of M. R. James and his imitators. Each issue contains two or three stories, articles about James's works and studies of fellow writers. A much respected magazine, with stories selected for annual "year's best" anthologies, it has also generated its own anthology, *Ghosts & Scholars* (1987), edited by Richard Dalby and Rosemary Pardoe.
Holdings: 26 (S)

11-36. Gothic. ISSN 0193-0184. 1979–80 (first series), 1986–1988. Annual. Gary W. Crawford, ed. PO Box 80051, Baton Rouge, LA 70898. Circulation: 100. First series indexed in Parnell.
A scholarly annual devoted to studies of all aspects of Gothicism in literature with an emphasis on prose fiction. The first series included fiction and was issued in large format. The second series was in a smaller format with around forty pages, unillustrated, and included four or five critical analyses of Gothic themes and a number of detailed reviews of related books. An essential reference source for all Gothic collections that died from lack of support. Compare *Poe Studies* [11-47].
Holdings: 5 (M), 15 (S), 17 (M), 26 (A), 31 (S), 41 (S)

11-37. Horrorstruck. 1987–88 (9 issues). Bi-monthly. Paul F. Olson, ed. Carruth Bay Press, Glen Ellyn, IL.
In its short run *Horrorstruck* showed considerable promise as a leading study of horror fiction. It contained regular columns on various features of the field, interviews, analyses and reviews. The emphasis was on modern horror but classic horror was not ignored. Contributing editors included Charles de Lint, Gordon Linzner, Dean R. Koontz, Thomas F. Monteleone, William F. Nolan, J. K. Potter and Robert Weinberg.
Holdings: none reported.

11-38. The Howard Collector. 1961–73 (18 issues). Irregular. Glenn Lord, ed.
A small press magazine dedicated to the memory of Robert E. Howard. Each issue averaged thirty-six pages, was professionally printed and brought into print a wealth of items by Howard himself (almost 100) plus many items of memorabilia, essays, reviews and letters. Although Howard almost single-handedly created the sword-and-sorcery field, the magazine concentrated more on Howard's life and works and not solely on the fantasy field. A representative sample of the editor's selection of the best from the magazine was published as *The Howard Collector* (1979). Compare *Amra* [11-24].
Holdings: 4 (A), 21 (S), 23 (S), 27 (A), 35 (M), 38 (M), 39 (S)

11-39. Journal of the Fantastic in the Arts. ISSN 0897-0521. 1988– . Quarterly.
Carl B. Yoke, executive ed. Orion Publishing, 1401 N. Salina St., Syracuse, NY 13208. Circulation: 300.
Sponsored by the International Association for the Fantastic in the Arts (see chapter 13), which provides this journal as a membership benefit, this is the most recent of the academic journals devoted to its subject. The scope is broad, including fantastic literature, film, painting and the performing arts. Some articles are revised from papers presented at the IAFA's annual conference. Special issues are planned dealing with individual authors, film and other topics. The authors are mostly academics writing for other academics, which often makes for rather heavy going. Articles will be supplemented by interviews, reviews and commentary. Primarily for university libraries.
Holdings: 17 (A), 38 (A), 39 (A)

*11-40. Locus. ISSN 0047-4959. 1968– . Monthly. Charles N. Brown, ed. Locus Publications, PO Box 13305, Oakland, CA 94661. Circulation: 8,200. Indexed annually.
The "newspaper" of the SF field, *Locus* also gives wide news coverage to all developments in the fantasy and horror fields as well as extensive reviews. *Locus* presents an annual Locus Award based on readers' votes in categories including Best Fantasy Novel. The annual readers' survey shows that over 50% of the readers read both SF and fantasy. *Locus* is especially useful for its monthly listing of books and magazines received, which forms the basis for the annual *Science Fiction, Fantasy & Horror* [6-6] bibliography. *Locus* has been a HN every year since 1970 and a HW thirteen times. *Science Fiction Chronicle* (ISSN 0195-5365, 1979– , monthly, Andrew Porter, ed., Box 2730, Brooklyn, NY 11202-0056) is the field's other news magazine with considerable duplication of the major news in *Locus*. Regular columns cover fantastic films and British publications, with Frederik Pohl's irregular Pohlemic column a highlight. Each issue includes a list of next month's books by publisher. A summary of book and magazine markets is included several times yearly. There are many reviews, all by Don D'Ammassa, almost all a short paragraph long, regardless of the book's importance, and lacking much critical rigor. As in *Locus*, coverage of fantasy and horror is secondary. A second choice for libraries. Compare also *Fantasy Review* [11-32] and *Mystery Scene* [11-42].
Holdings: 1 (A), 3 (M), 4 (A), 5 (S), 12 (S), 13 (A), 14 (M), 15 (A), 17 (A), 21 (A), 23 (A), 27 (A), 28 (M), 29 (A), 36 (S), 38 (M), 39 (A), 41 (A), 42 (S)

11-41. Lovecraft Studies. No ISSN. 1979– . Twice yearly. S. T. Joshi, ed. Necronomicon Press, 101 Lockwood St., West Warwick, RI 02893. Circulation: 500.
Indexed in *Fubar* #6, Soft Books, Toronto.
A scholarly small press magazine dedicated to the study of the life and works of
H. P. Lovecraft. Unlike *Crypt of Cthulhu* [11-27], its nearest rival, *LS* is wholly
studious with detailed analyses of Lovecraft's writings. Each forty-page issue
usually contains four to six articles or bibliographies plus a selection of critical
reviews. The text is unleavened by any artwork.
Holdings: 17 (S), 26 (M), 38 (S), 39 (M)

11-42. Mystery Scene. No ISSN. 1985– . Bi-monthly. Ed Gorman, Bob Randisi,
eds. Mystery Enterprises, 3840 Clark Rd. SE, Cedar Rapids, IA 52403.
Despite the title and the fact that it also covers western fiction, *MS* devotes a large
portion of its news, reviews and interviews to horror fiction. The related fields of
horror and mystery fiction share many writers, and this magazine is a useful guide
to that common ground and helps put horror fiction into perspective with other
popular genre fiction. Compare *Fantasy Review* [11-32] and *Locus* [11-40].
Holdings: information not collected

11-43. Mythlore. ISSN 0163-8246. 1969– . Quarterly. The Mythopoeic Society,
Box 6707, Altadena, CA 91001. Circulation: 1,000. Submissions to Glen H. Good-
Knight, ed., 740 S. Hobart Blvd., Los Angeles, CA 90005.
The journal received by members of the Mythopoeic Society (see chapter 13), its
subtitle indicates its content: "a journal of J. R. R. Tolkien, C. S. Lewis, Charles
Williams and the genres of myth and fantasy studies." Articles, reviews, letters,
columns on current fantasy and Middle-earth linguistics. Intermediate between a
fanzine and an academic journal and a good choice for any library or reader with
a strong interest in the Inklings, as this trio of writers is informally known.
Holdings: 3 (M), 4 (S), 5 (M), 15 (A), 17 (S), 19 (S), 21 (M), 27 (M), 28 (S), 31 (A), 35
(S), 37 (S), 38 (A)

11-44. Niekas. No ISSN. 1962–69, 1977– . Irregular. Ed Meskys, ed. RFD 1, Box
63, Center Harbor, NH 03226. Circulation: 750.
Originally a small amateur press magazine of SF interest, *Niekas* changed considerably in 1965 with the editor's reading of *Lord of the Rings* [F3-340] and became,
for a period, the leading Tolkien-based magazine, featuring Robert Foster's
detailed glossary and guide to Middle-earth [F8-89]. *Niekas*, in its revived form, is
a highly professional-style magazine, slickly produced but retaining the fannish
touches. It still emphasizes fantasy but has broadened its coverage from Tolkien
to all areas of high/heroic fantasy and SF, including a special issue on Arthurian
fiction. HN 1966, HW 1967.
Holdings: information not collected

*11-45. Nyctalops. No ISSN. 1970– . Irregular. Harry O. Morris, ed. Silver
Scarab Press, 502 Elm St. SE, Albuquerque, NM 87102. Circulation: 500. Indexed
in Parnell. Inquire about subscriptions.
An amateur magazine originally dedicated to the memories of H. P. Lovecraft
and Clark Ashton Smith (issue #7, August 1972, is an especially important Smith
issue). While this basis remains, recent issues have expanded to cover all areas of
dark fantasy with a growing emphasis on what might be termed "decadent"

fantasy with the outré artwork of J. K. Potter and Morris himself, the surreal fiction of Thomas Ligotti and the obscure verse by Sutton Breiding and Neal Wilgus. One final issue was planned for 1989. Compare *Crypt of Cthulhu* [11-27] and *The Romantist* [11-48].
Holdings: 4 (S), 14 (S), 17 (M), 21 (A), 23 (S), 26 (S), 28 (S), 39 (S)

11-46. Peake Studies. ISSN 1013-1191. 1988– . Irregular. G. Peter Winnington, ed. Les 3 Chasseurs, 1413 Orzens, Vaud, Switzerland.
PS is a new, independent journal intended to complement and possibly even supersede the *Mervyn Peake Review* published by the Peake Society (see chapter 13), which has become primarily a newsletter in recent, irregular issues. *PS* covers the same territory as a forum for criticism and debate on all aspects of Peake's career as a novelist, artist, poet and playwright. It contains articles, reviews, news and comment.
Holdings: information not collected

11-47. Poe Studies [formerly **Poe Newsletter**]. ISSN 0032-1877. 1968– . Twice yearly. Alex Hammond, ed. Washington State Univ. Press, Pullman, WA 99164. Circulation: 550.
A scholarly journal of sixty-four pages, dedicated to the study of Poe's work and the broader issues of Gothic fiction and the influence of Poe on mystery and horror fiction. Compare *Gothic* [11-36].
Holdings: 1 (A), 3 (M), 4 (S), 5 (A), 15 (A), 19 (A), 28 (S), 29 (A), 31 (A), 35 (A)

11-48. The Romantist. 1977– . Annual. John C. Moran, Jesse F. Knight, Steve Eng, eds. F. Marion Crawford Memorial Society, Saracinesca House, 3610 Meadowbrook Ave., Nashville, TN 37205. Circulation limited to 300.
Although issued by the F. Marion Crawford Memorial Society, and thus regularly featuring aspects of his life and work, *The Romantist* explores the wider Romantic literary tradition, especially in weird and fantasy fiction and verse. The five irregular issues published to date (one double and one triple issue strive to follow the "annual" schedule) have stretched this realm to include essays about M. P. Shiel, Arthur Machen, Algernon Blackwood, H. Warner Munn, George Sterling, John Gawsworth, Clark Ashton Smith, Leslie Barringer and even Lew Wallace, as well as coverage of composer Erich Korngold and Irish singer John McCormack. Each issue is attractively printed, runs to eighty pages or more, and carries ten to twelve essays and comment, plus reviews, poetry and related features. Compare *Nyctalops* [11-45].
Holdings: 10 (A), 15 (A), 26 (A), 37 (S)

11-49. Shadow. 1968–74 (21 issues). Irregular. David A. Sutton, ed. Birmingham, England.
In its time *Shadow* was Britain's only serious magazine devoted to the study of supernatural fiction. Although early issues were poorly duplicated, the magazine contained a variety of well-researched articles on a wide range of topics. It remains one of the few magazines to have given any serious coverage to European horror writers, like Jean Ray. It is best remembered today for R. Alain Everts's primary study of the life of William Hope Hodgson.
Holdings: 16 (S), 27 (S)

11-50. Studies in Weird Fiction. No ISSN. 1986–   . Twice yearly. S. T. Joshi, ed. Necronomicon Press, 101 Lockwood Street, West Warwick, RI 02893. Circulation: 500.

A scholarly magazine, fan-based, designed to promote the criticism of fantasy, horror and supernatural fiction, after Poe. Issues to date have evaluated aspects of the works of Clark Ashton Smith, William Hope Hodgson, Arthur Machen, T. E. D. Klein and Donald Wandrei. There is a distinct bias toward classic writers and the *Weird Tales* school even though studies of modern writers are not discouraged. A moderately produced publication of around forty pages, each issue includes five or six essays and a similar number of reviews. Suitable for libraries with a large collection of weird fiction.

Holdings: 4 (S)

Serial Anthologies

This information regarding holdings of selected serial anthologies was collected by Randall Scott. The second and third titles were not annotated. Cross-references from the annotated anthologies were made to this holdings list.

The Best from Fantasy and Science Fiction, 1952– . [11-13]
Holdings: 1 (M), 3 (M), 4 (S), 9 (S), 13 (S), 17 (S), 19 (S), 23 (M), 27 (A), 28 (S), 31 (S), 35 (S), 36 (M), 37 (S), 38 (A), 39 (A), 40 (S)

The Fontana Book of Great Ghost Stories, 1964–80
Holdings: 17 (S), 23 (M), 36 (M), 39 (M)

The Fontana Book of Great Horror Stories, 1966–74
Holdings: 17 (S), 23 (M), 27 (S), 36 (A), 39 (M)

New Worlds of Fantasy, 1967– [F4A-299]
Holdings: 4 (S), 13 (S), 17 (S), 23 (M), 27 (S), 35 (S), 38 (S)

The Pan Book of Horror Stories, 1959– [H4-357]
Holdings: 4 (S), 17 (M), 19 (S), 23 (M), 36 (M), 39 (M)

Shadows, 1978–87 [H4-359]
Holdings: 4 (S), 14 (A), 17 (A), 19 (S), 23 (M), 28 (M), 38 (A), 39 (S)

Whispers, 1977– [H4-361]
Holdings: 4 (S), 9 (S), 13 (S), 14 (S), 15 (A), 17 (S), 23 (M), 28 (S), 37 (S), 38 (A), 39 (S)

The Year's Best Fantasy Stories, 1975– [F4A-305]
Holdings: 4 (S), 13 (M), 15 (S), 17 (S), 19 (S), 23 (M), 28 (S), 36 (S), 38 (A), 39 (M)

The Year's Best Horror Stories, 1971– [H4-363]
Holdings: 4 (S), 13 (S), 15 (S), 17 (S), 23 (M), 28 (S), 36 (M), 38 (A), 39 (S)

The Year's Finest Fantasy/Fantasy Annual, 1978–82 [F4A-299]
Holdings: 4 (S), 5 (S), 10 (A), 14 (S), 17 (S), 22 (M), 27 (S), 28 (S), 29 (S), 38 (A), 39 (A)

Studies

Few serious studies of fantasy and horror fiction have considered the contribution made by magazine and serial publications. Most coverage has been superficial and part of general studies of the field. The following titles are primary reference sources.

11-51. Cook, Michael L. **Mystery, Detective, and Espionage Magazines**. Greenwood, 1983.
In the same format as Tymn and Ashley's *Science Fiction, Fantasy, and Weird Fiction Magazines* [11-54] with a useful, though too brief, historical introduction by Cook, a long section on English-language magazines, an overview of foreign magazines and coverage of book clubs. There are seven appendixes listing magazines by category, key writers, a magazine chronology from 1882 to 1982, American and Canadian true detective magazines, Sherlock Holmes–related material and other periodicals of interest. Despite its title this book contains entries on many fantasy magazines (forty-seven entries overlap with Tymn/Ashley, sometimes with conflicting data) and is useful for its coverage of borderline mystery/terror/horror magazines and as a guide to the many writers who have sold to the related fields. The entries are not as comprehensive as in Tymn/Ashley but contain much data not readily available elsewhere.

11-52. Gallagher, Edward J. **The Annotated Guide to Fantastic Adventures**. Starmont, 1985.
A useful annotated story index to one of the less important fantasy titles [see 11-6]. Gives plot outlines for all 852 stories and serials in chronological order. Also has a seventeen-page historical survey useful for its grouping of stories by type and style; plus appendixes listing editorial departments, artists, story motifs and author biographies. Indexes stories by author and title.

11-53. Jones, Robert Kenneth. **The Shudder Pulps: A History of the Weird Menace Magazines of the 1930's**. FAX, 1975.
The only book-length survey and analysis of that group of magazines that emphasized sex and sadism and the mildly erotic, concentrating on unsophisticated terror with little, if any, supernatural connection. A well-written history drawing on many contemporary sources and recent interviews with the leading writers of the day. Jones shows the evolution (or degeneration) from Gothic fiction and traces the influence of the terror pulps on the associated mystery, fantasy and SF fields.

*11-54. Tymn, Marshall B., and Mike Ashley. **Science Fiction, Fantasy, and Weird Fiction Magazines**. Greenwood, 1985.
The definitive volume on fantasy magazines in all their forms. Divided into four sections plus a historical introduction by Thomas Clareson. The main section covers 279 English-language magazines, with the other sections covering 15 associational English-language anthologies, 78 academic periodicals and major fanzines and 178 non-English-language magazines. There are two appendixes covering major cover artists plus a chronology of magazines from 1882 to 1983. Entries vary in length and there is the inevitable emphasis on SF magazines

which have dominated the "fantasy" field. All significant fantasy and weird fiction magazines are covered, with each entry containing an informative and occasionally critical essay plus a bibliography and reference to index, reprint and location sources. There is also a detailed publication history. A basic reference work. Note also Cook's *Mystery, Detective, and Espionage Magazines* [11-51].

*11-55. Weinberg, Robert. **The Weird Tales Story**. FAX, 1977.

11-56. Weinberg, Robert. **WT50**. Weinberg, 1973.
The Weird Tales Story is a loving tribute to the leading weird pulp magazine [11-20] and is the only complete history of the title. This volume is valuable for its historical coverage of the magazine and its survey of the major stories and artwork, plus its personalized memoirs by some of the leading contributors. It reproduces many of the covers, though for more complete coverage see Durie's *Weird Tales* [10-9]. The book drew to some degree from Weinberg's earlier *WT50*, which was a more idiosyncratic tribute to the magazine and contains additional retrospectives and appraisals plus some fiction. Also annotated as [H7-45] and [10-36].

Indexes and Checklists

For most of their history fantasy and horror magazines have remained secondary to the science fiction field and have been indexed only when grouped with their SF companions. As a result, until the appearance of *Monthly Terrors* [11-68] no comprehensive index existed to all weird and fantasy titles. The following annotated entries cover all of the specialist indexes including those for predominantly SF titles.

*11-57. Boyajian, Jerry, and Kenneth R. Johnson. **Index to the Science Fiction Magazines**. 8 vols., 1977–84. Twaci Press, 1981–86.
Reliable and neat annual index covering contents by issue, author, title and artist with a useful appendix of "SF in Miscellaneous Magazines." Duplicates much that is in NESFA [11-67] but is easier to read. Covers many titles of fantasy interest. Two useful supplements were *Index to the Semi-Professional Fantasy Magazines 1982* and *1983*, covering lesser-known titles of fantasy interest.

*11-58. Cockcroft, T[homas] G. L. **Index to the Weird Fiction Magazines**. Originally published by the author, 2 vols.: 1. Title, 1962; 2. Author, 1964. Rev. ed., Arno Press, 1975.
Index to eight English-language magazines: *Weird Tales, Strange Tales, Strange Stories, The Thrill Book, Strange Tales* (British), *Oriental Stories, Magic Carpet Magazine* and *Golden Fleece*, the latter three of only borderline fantasy interest. Largely superseded by Parnell [11-68] but still valuable for its index by story title as well as its useful notes and appendixes. Lacks an issue-by-issue contents listing.

11-59. Cook, Michael L. **Monthly Murders: A Checklist and Chronological Listing of Fiction in the Digest-Size Mystery Magazines in the United States and England**. Greenwood, 1982.
A massive 1,167-page index concentrating on mystery magazines but with some overlap with Parnell [11-68], though generally less detailed. Indexed by issue

contents and by author but not by story title. Contains a few titles of fantasy interest not indexed by Parnell, especially *Alfred Hitchcock's Mystery Magazine*, *Doc Savage* (from 1944 only), *London Mystery Magazine*, *The Man from U.N.C.L.E. Magazine*, *Shock Mystery Tales*, *Strange* and *Web Terror Stories*. Cook also completed, just before his death, his companion index to the mystery pulp magazines: *Mystery, Detective and Espionage Fiction: A Checklist of Fiction in the U.S. Pulp Magazines, 1915–1974* (Garland, 1988), compiled with Stephen T. Miller. It indexes several magazines of fantasy interest (some also covered by Parnell) including *Ace Mystery, Book of Terror, Captain Hazzard, Captain Satan, Captain Zero, Detective Tales* (the companion to *Weird Tales*), *Dime Mystery, Doc Savage, Doctor Death, Dr. Yen Sin, Dusty Ayres and His Battle Birds, Eerie Mysteries, Eerie Stories, G-8 and His Battle Aces, Horror Stories, Jungle Stories, Mind Magic, The Mysterious Wu Fang, The Shadow, Strange Stories, Strange Tales, Tales of Magic and Mystery, Terror Tales, Uncanny Stories* and *Uncanny Tales*.

*11-60. Day, Donald B. **Index to the Science Fiction Magazines, 1926–1950**. Perri Press, 1952. Rev. ed., G. K. Hall, 1982.
Pioneering index to major SF titles, which also covers titles of fantasy interest: *Avon Fantasy Reader, Famous Fantastic Mysteries, Fantastic Novels, Fantasy Fiction, Magazine of Fantasy & Science Fiction, A. Merritt's Fantasy* and *Unknown*. Indexes by author and story title but not by issue. The revised edition includes Day's corrections but is otherwise not updated. Index continued by Metcalf [11-64] and Strauss [11-69].

11-61. Hoffman, Stuart. **An Index to Unknown and Unknown Worlds by Author and by Title**. Sirius Press, 1955.
An idiosyncratic index by author, story title and principal characters. The title index provides a sublist of locale and characters. Introduction by Robert Bloch. Preferable to Metzger [11-65].

11-62. Holland, Steve. **Fantasy Fanzine Index**. British Fantasy Society, 1987.
A neat thirty-six-page booklet indexing contents of thirty-one British small press publications running to eighty-five separate issues. Contents indexed by issue and author. Useful for monitoring growth in British fantasy publications.

11-63. Jaffery, Sheldon, and Fred Cook. **Collector's Index to Weird Tales**. Bowling Green Univ. Popular Press, 1985.
Indexes *Weird Tales* [11-20] only, so does not supersede Cockcroft [11-58] or Parnell [11-68] but does complement them as the author index lists stories in chronological rather than alphabetical order. Also indexes contents by issue and title with separate indexes to poetry and cover artists. Also annotated as [H7-45].

*11-64. Metcalf, Norm. **The Index of Science Fiction Magazines 1951–1965**. J. Ben Stark, 1968.
A continuation of Day [11-60] with additional errata on that volume. Concentrates on SF magazines but has titles of fantasy interest: *Avon Fantasy Reader, Beyond Fantasy Fiction, Bizarre Mystery, Fantastic, Fantastic Adventures, Fear!, Magazine of Fantasy & Science Fiction, Magazine of Horror* and *Science Fantasy*. Index was published in haste and contains some erroneous data on pen names but

is otherwise more readable and reliable than Strauss [11-69]. Indexes by author, story title, artist and editor, but not by issue.

11-65. Metzger, Arthur. **An Index and Short History of Unknown**. T-K Graphics, 1976.
A twenty-eight-page booklet containing a brief history of *Unknown* [11-18] followed by an index by author and by title, a note on important reprints and a list of cover artists. Has little advantage over Day [11-60], Parnell [11-68] or Hoffman [11-61].

*11-66. New England Science Fiction Association. **Index to the Science Fiction Magazines, 1966–1970**. NESFA, 1971.

*11-67. New England Science Fiction Association. **The NESFA Index: Science Fiction Magazines and Original Anthologies**. NESFA, 11 vol., 1973–84, covering 1971–72, 1973, 1974, 1975, 1976, 1977, 1978, 1979–80, 1981, 1982, 1983.
Reliable and accurate continuation of Strauss [11-69] with computer print-out format indexing by issue, author and title. The subsequent annual volumes also cover anthologies with original material. Covers both SF magazines and titles of fantasy interest. Duplicates to a large degree the work by Boyajian and Johnson [11-57]. Later years now indexed by Brown and Contento [6-6].

*11-68. Parnell, Frank H., and Mike Ashley. **Monthly Terrors: An Index to the Weird Fantasy Magazines Published in the United States and Great Britain**. Greenwood, 1985.
Indexes 1,733 issues of 168 English-language magazines containing more than 50% weird fantasy. Main indexes are by issue and author, with artist and editor indexes and appendixes on series and connected stories, honorable mentions (thirty magazines that almost qualified for entry), chronological listing of magazines and geographical listing. Has a foreword by Peter Haining plus a short historical survey by the compilers of the weird fantasy magazines from 1919 to 1983. This is the major index to all weird fiction magazines, particularly important for its coverage of small press publications and rare titles not normally included in the standard indexes. Author index contains brief biographical details plus much information on pseudonyms not available elsewhere. No title index. Note also Cockcroft [11-58].

11-69. Strauss, Irwin S. **The MIT Science Fiction Society's Index to the SF Magazines, 1951–1965**. MIT Science Fiction Society, 1965.
Covers same period as Metcalf [11-64] but is generally less reliable or accurate and is poorly printed despite its computer print-out format. Has the advantage of an issue-by-issue index in addition to the author and story title indexes. Covers more titles than Metcalf, of which *Weird Tales* and *Phantom* are of fantasy interest. Continued by NESFA [11-66].

12

Library Collections

Randall W. Scott

Producing this section on library special collections of horror and fantasy literature has been a cooperative venture involving at least fifty librarians around the world. A few collections, like those built around the works of H. P. Lovecraft or J. R. R Tolkien, can be easily and accurately described, but it has been difficult for the typical "fantasy and horror librarian" to produce precise statements about his or her collection. Most of the materials form parts of larger collections normally thought of as science fiction collections. Much of the task has therefore been to focus on hidden specialties. The procedure leaves suspicions that a slight twist of thought might have illuminated still more interesting facets of some of these collections.

The emphasis has been on research collections, and usually special, noncirculating collections with holdings that can be counted upon to remain stable. Although most public libraries collect and circulate fantasy and horror fiction, such collections are difficult for out-of-town researchers to use. The collections listed here are those most likely to be available in full at all times. Libraries whose collections, when described in published accounts or in response to questionnaires, do not seem to offer fantasy or horror materials at a level beyond that which could be expected from any research library have not been included in this listing.

The prospective library user should be aware that any national library, university library or metropolitan public library will have at least a few of the important texts and reference books in horror and fantasy. National libraries, such as the British Library and the national libraries of Canada and Australia, typically receive materials through copyright deposit arrangements, and thus do not automatically arrange them in the logical categories that result from a more intentional acquisitions program. It is always worth asking at any large nearby library before deciding to buy an expensive item, or deciding to make a voyage.

474

This directory is intended primarily to aid prospective researchers to identify possible sources of material to study. It will also serve to help prospective donors and sellers of horror and fantasy material to find suitable depositories or customers. In this way the flow of information both into and out of these libraries should be expedited.

The researcher/librarian relationship can sometimes be fragile when materials of a quasi-recreational nature are involved. It is important, therefore, that users who are traveling to any of these collections call ahead, identify themselves and make sure of the schedule of open hours. This level of seriousness will almost certainly motivate the librarian in charge to provide the best possible service.

Most of the libraries listed have said that they will provide photocopies, and some will loan materials through interlibrary loan (ILL). In every case, however, libraries will not photocopy materials if they believe that to do so would violate copyright or privacy (in the case of personal letters or papers), of if the act of photocopying would endanger fragile materials. Similar restrictions apply to ILL, of course.

One tool of potential practical value to researchers is the OCLC (Online Computer Library Center) network, which links several thousand libraries worldwide, including many of those listed here. Access to an OCLC terminal at a library anywhere (or through CompuServe) means access in some detail to the holdings records of other libraries. These holdings records are rarely complete, however, since OCLC became widely used only in the mid-1970s, and earlier cataloging is only gradually being added to the database. OCLC libraries have been identified in this directory in most cases.

In the course of putting together this directory, I compiled a union list of horror and fantasy serials (pulps, journals, magazines and serial anthologies). The libraries with the best serial collections have been designated as in the top ten (or twenty) for completeness in serial holdings. Those libraries not so designated either have significantly smaller collections or chose not to represent themselves here. Holdings of specific journals and serial anthologies are shown in chapter 11.

Private libraries routinely open to the public have been included in the main listing, but four private collections not included there should be noted. Since private collections usually have very small or inconsistent staffing, they often have little time for such activities as answering mail inquiries, and may therefore present special problems to their prospective users. The four collections are:

The Count Dracula Permanent Collection of Vampire Memorabilia. 29 Washington Square West, Penthouse North, New York, NY 10011. 212-533-5018. Maintained by the Count Dracula Fan Club and the International Frankenstein Society. Viewing by appointment.

The Los Angeles Science Fantasy Society Library. 11513 Burbank Blvd., North Hollywood, CA 91601. 818-760-9234. A club collection primarily for members' use, with 7,000 volumes and over 120 magazine titles. Public use by appointment.

The MIT Science Fiction Society Library. MIT Student Center, Room W20-473, Cambridge, MA 02139. 617-258-5126. A club collection with a long history and reputation as one of the most complete science fiction magazine collections in North America. Hours irregular, mostly evenings. Some material circulates to members, room-use only for the public.

The San Francisco Academy of Comic Art. 2850 Ulloa St., San Francisco, CA 94116. 415-681-1737. A collection of over 4.5 million newspaper comic strips; also includes horror and fantasy fiction and pulp magazines. Call for appointment.

Please send corrections or additions to this compilation to the editor (see list of contributors).

The arrangement of this directory is alphabetical by state for the United States, followed by other countries in alphabetical order.

Directory

Arizona

12-1. University of Arizona Library. Special Collections, Tucson, AZ 85721. 602-621-6423.
A science fiction collection of 18,000 volumes, with current acquisitions restricted to science fiction, rather than fantasy and horror. In spite of current policy, the extensive older holdings make this a valuable resource. The periodicals held put this collection in the top twenty for library collections of fantasy and horror serials, and they are supplemented by some microfilm. This is a noncirculating collection, and is 90% cataloged. The University of Arizona is an OCLC library, so many of its holdings can be checked remotely on the OCLC network. Photocopies are sometimes available, but materials are not released for interlibrary loan.

California

12-2. San Francisco Public Library. McComas Collection of Fantasy and Science Fiction, Civic Center, San Francisco, CA 94102. 415-558-3511.
A science fiction and fantasy collection of 2,900 volumes including approximately 760 fantasy volumes. The fantasy periodical collection is excellent, ranking in the top twenty libraries surveyed. The collection is active, adding a few volumes regularly by purchase. The materials do not circulate, either locally or through interlibrary loan.

12-3. University of California, Los Angeles. Special Collections, University Library, 405 Hilgard Avenue, Los Angeles, CA 90024. 213-825-4988.
A fantastic fiction collection of over 10,000 volumes that does not separate science fiction from fantasy. Ray Bradbury manuscripts, 1.5 linear feet, and a collection of over 400 early editions of H. Rider Haggard. An extensive magazine and pulp collection ranks this collection among the top twenty for fantasy and horror serials. The collection is cataloged, but has limited staff to answer written information requests. Limited photocopying is available, but not interlibrary loan.

12-4. University of California, Riverside. Eaton Collection, University Library, P.O. Box 5900, Riverside, CA 92517. 714-787-3233.
A science fiction collection with over 50,000 items, comprehensive enough to include something of most fantasy and horror authors. Fantasy and horror are not treated separately. Includes over 200 sound recordings, nearly 500 films, over 200 shooting scripts and over 2,000 comic books, all with something like 50% horror/fantasy content. The fantasy and horror periodical collection is one of the ten most complete. Over 60 linear feet of fanzines. Uncorrected proofs of Terry Brooks, Nancy Springer; manuscripts and letters of Colin Wilson. The collection grows by 5,000 to 10,000 items yearly, through purchases, gifts and exchanges. The collection is fully catalogued on OCLC, noncirculating, and provides photocopies and restricted interlibrary loan. An occasional newsletter is published.

Bibliography: *Dictionary Catalog of the J. Lloyd Eaton Collection*. 3 vols. Boston: G. K. Hall, 1983.

"The J. Lloyd Eaton Collection." *Special Collections* II, 1/2 (Fall–Winter 1982), 25–38.

District of Columbia

12-5. Library of Congress. Washington, DC 20540. 202-707-5000.
The nature and extent of this library's holdings of fantastic literature and related materials do not lend themselves to concise or tabular descriptions. The Library of Congress does not maintain a special collection of fantasy or horror literature, nor does it make special efforts to collect such materials. Publications received under the copyright law are added to the general collections, while foreign publications are purchased. No statistics are kept on the library's holdings or annual receipts of fantastic literature.

The Manuscript Division (phone: 202-707-5383) holds the papers of Shirley Jackson (approximately 4,400 items) and the George M. Gould collection of Lafcadio Hearn (approximately 2,700 items). It also holds letters and other manuscripts of a number of other horror or fantasy authors, but does not consider these holdings to be significant. In addition, the Manuscript Division holds collections of radio scripts and playscripts, some of which would classify as horror and suspense, but material in these collections is not retrievable by subject. Original materials in the Manuscript Division are not available on interlibrary loan but may be examined (preferably by advance appointment) in the Manuscript Reading Room.

The Rare Book and Special Collections Division (phone: 202-707-5434) collects comprehensively the works of Kingsley Amis, Donald Barthelme, Ray Bradbury, Roald Dahl, Stephen King, Robert Nathan, Joyce Carol Oates and Colin Wilson, and maintains significant holdings of the published works of Ambrose Bierce, Wilkie Collins, Walter De la Mare, Nathaniel Hawthorne, Lafcadio Hearn, Shirley Jackson, William Morris, Edgar Allan Poe and James Thurber. Custody of a Pulp Fiction Collection is divided between the Rare Book and Special Collections Division and the Serial and Government Publications Division (phone: 202-707-5467). The fantasy and horror content of the pulp and periodical collection ranks it in the top twenty of collections surveyed.

The Motion Picture, Broadcasting and Recorded Sound Division (phone: 202-707-5840) holds more than 125,000 films and television programs, and over 1,500,000 audio recordings, but neither collection is currently accessible by genre or subject. Interlibrary loan for recorded materials is not available, and copying of records is not permitted. Questions concerning access should be directed to the division.

Illinois

12-6. Northern Illinois University. Founders Library, DeKalb, IL 60115. 815-753-0255.
Over 100 volumes of horror and fantasy fiction, plus a few letters of H. P. Lovecraft, and published works of Lord Dunsany and August Derleth. Complete holdings of several fantasy magazines puts this collection in the top twenty for serial fantasy. The collection is growing by twenty volumes per year through gift and purchase, and has been a Science Fiction Writers of America depository since 1983. The collection is fully cataloged, and may be used by appointment only. Photocopies are available.

12-7. Wheaton College. Marion E. Wade Center, Buswell Memorial Library, Wheaton, IL 60187-5593. 312-260-5908.
Over 700 volumes of the fiction of C. S. Lewis, George MacDonald, J. R. R. Tolkien and Charles Williams, plus 60 critical books and 188 dissertations; 945 letters, mostly of Williams; and 199 sound recordings, many of them oral history interviews. The collection is growing through purchase and gift at a rate of about 200 items per year. The collection is 50% cataloged, and noncirculating. Unpublished material may not be photocopied.

12-8. Wheaton College. Special Collections, Buswell Memorial Library, Wheaton, IL 60187-5593. 312-260-5705.
The library holds 160 published volumes, and over 60 linear feet of manuscripts and letters, by Madeleine L'Engle. Also included are thirty-six sound recordings, six videotapes and a filmstrip. The L'Engle collection is increased regularly by gift and purchase. A collection of Lewis Carroll material totals eighty-five volumes and is not currently growing. Most published material is cataloged; all is noncirculating. Unpublished material in the L'Engle collection is available only with her written permission.

Indiana

12-9. Indiana University. Lilly Library, Bloomington, IN 47405. 812-855-2452.
The Lilly Library has no separate fantasy or horror collection, but has significant holdings in these areas. The collection holds papers of August Derleth, Robert Bloch and Fritz Leiber, and first edition collections of Derleth, H. Rider Haggard and H. P. Lovecraft. The Lilly Library houses the Elisabeth Ball and Andrew Lang fairy tale collections, and holds fantasy and horror periodicals that rank it in the top twenty of collections surveyed. These are active collections, with new materials acquired regularly through gift and purchase, and the holdings are fully cataloged on OCLC.

Iowa

12-10. University of Iowa Libraries. Special Collections Department, Iowa City, IA 52242. 319-335-5921.

The library collects film and TV scripts, plus popular fiction by Iowa authors, but does not have an estimate of the fantasy/horror content of the collection. Works by Thomas M. Disch and Edgar Allan Poe are included, plus some R. A. Lafferty manuscript material. The collection includes some fantasy magazines. The materials are cataloged on OCLC, with photocopies available but not interlibrary loan.

Kentucky

12-11. University of Louisville Library. Rare Books and Special Collections, Louisville, KY 40292. 502-588-6762.

An Edgar Rice Burroughs collection of 20,000 items, plus special collections of Ambrose Bierce, L. Frank Baum, Isak Dinesen, Lafcadio Hearn and Ursula Le Guin, and some published work by most horror and fantasy authors. A fantasy and horror pulp collection ranks among the top twenty of collections surveyed. The five author collections listed above are fully cataloged, and the Burroughs and pulp collections are partially cataloged. The collection is active, added to regularly through purchase and gifts. Materials are for room use only. Photocopies can be provided, but not interlibrary loan.

Bibliography: Goddin, Geoffrey. "Lafcadio Hearn." *Library Review* 32 (March 1982).

McWhorter, G. T. "Edgar Rice Burroughs." *Library Review* 30 (May 1980).

McWhorter, G. T. "Karen Blixen/Isak Dinesen." *Library Review* 36 (Sept. 1986).

Maryland

12-12. University of Maryland, Baltimore County. Special Collections, Albin O. Kuhn Library & Gallery, Baltimore, MD 21228. 301-455-2353.

Primarily a science fiction collection of 5,500 volumes, with a fanzine collection containing over 15,000 items. Many fantasy and horror authors are represented, with manuscripts by Roger Zelazny. The collection is growing by 300 volumes per year through purchase and gifts. The magazine collection includes more titles than most libraries ranked in the top twenty for fantasy and horror serials, but they are mostly incomplete runs. The hardcover fiction (2,500 volumes) is fully cataloged; the paperbacks (3,000 volumes) are listed only. The collection is noncirculating, with photocopies available.

Michigan

12-13. Michigan State University Library. Special Collections, East Lansing, MI 48824-1048. 517-355-3770.

Approximately 1,500 volumes of horror and fantasy fiction within a larger science fiction and fantasy collection. Special interest in Robert Bloch and A. Conan

Doyle (vertical files) and Jorge Luis Borges and Edward Gorey (published works); also includes representative published works of almost all horror and fantasy authors. The magazines held would place this collection in the top ten for fantasy and horror periodicals if they were complete runs. This collection is active, but growing only slowly through donations. MSU has been a Science Fiction Writers of America depository since 1982. All books and magazines are cataloged on OCLC, and are noncirculating. Photocopies are available, but not interlibrary loan.

New Mexico

12-14. Eastern New Mexico University. Golden Library, Jack Williamson Science Fiction Library, Portales, NM 88130. 505-562-2636.
A total of nearly 10,000 volumes of science fiction, fantasy and horror are not inventoried separately by these categories, but the collection holds published material by most fantasy and horror authors. Manuscript material of Brian W. Aldiss, Poul Anderson and Piers Anthony is held. The fantasy and horror periodical collection is one of the ten most complete. Through local recording and from the Science Fiction Oral History Association the collection has sound recordings of Anderson, Peter Beagle, Robert Bloch, Ray Bradbury, Marion Zimmer Bradley, Jack Chalker, C. J. Cherryh, Harlan Ellison, Stephen King, Katherine Kurtz, Richard Matheson, Ray Russell and Roger Zelazny. The library has been a Science Fiction Writers of America depository since 1970. The overall collection is growing at about 200 volumes per year. The collection is fully cataloged. Photocopies are available, and 30% of the fiction books circulate with one-week interlibrary loan available.

New York

12-15. New York Public Library. General Research Division, Microforms Division, Fifth Avenue and 42nd Street, New York, NY 10018. 212-930-0838.
The General Research Division has over 5,000 volumes of science fiction in closed stacks, of which an estimated 40% are fantasy and horror. Paperbacks are being filmed routinely in the Microforms Division, and currently over 2,000 are on film with a similar estimate of 40% fantasy and horror. The most unusual aspect of this library collection is its commitment to preservation through microfilming of both paperbacks and magazines. An effort is being made by the Microforms Division to acquire science fiction, fantasy and horror literature not owned on paper, and thus the Microforms Division is in the unusual position of keeping track of the General Research Division's holdings. The magazine collection as combined in film and in hard copy is a good one, ranking in the top ten of those surveyed. The collection is growing actively and is completely cataloged. The materials do not circulate, but are available for use by the general public. Photocopies are available.

The library's Pforzheimer Collection contains materials relating to Mary W. Shelley. Access to this collection is by appointment only (phone: 212-930-0740).

Bibliography: Dowd, Alice. "The Science Fiction Microfilming Project at the New York Public Library," *Microform Review* XIV, 1 (Winter 1985), 15–20.

12-16. Syracuse University. George Arents Research Library. 600 E. S. Bird Library, Syracuse, NY 13244-2010. 315-443-2697.

The Rare Books Division holds a science fiction collection of about 3,000 volumes, of which only an estimated 10% are fantasy or horror. The Manuscripts Division has manuscripts by fantasy authors Piers Anthony, Anne McCaffrey, Andre Norton and Roger Zelazny, and has a large collection of Forrest Ackerman papers. Fantasy and horror periodicals are represented by a few complete runs and some partial runs. The collection is uncataloged and noncirculating. Acquisitions by gift amount to about twenty-five volumes and 3 linear feet of manuscripts per year. Photocopies are available, but not interlibrary loan.

Bibliography: Lerner, Fred. "Syracuse University," *Special Collections* II, 1/2 (Fall–Winter 1982), 59–62.

Ohio

12-17. Bowling Green State University. Jerome Library, Popular Culture Library, Bowling Green, OH 43403. 419-372-2450.

The science fiction collection of about 10,000 volumes, plus 23 linear feet of manuscripts and letters, includes fantasy and horror, but no separate counts are available. Extensive holdings of the published works of all fantasy and horror authors are included. Manuscript material of Robert Bloch, Charles L. Grant and Carl Jacobi is held. One of the ten most complete collections of fantasy and horror periodicals. This is an active collection, growing rapidly through gift and purchase. The collection is 75% cataloged, with holdings available on OCLC. Photocopies are available, but not interlibrary loan.

The Rare Books Division of the Center for Archival Collections (phone: 419-372-2411) in the Jerome Library has an extensive Robert Aickman collection, including forty manuscripts, correspondence, etc., and Aickman's personal library of over 3,000 volumes. An extensive Ray Bradbury manuscript collection is also housed in the Rare Books Division.

12-18. Kent State University Library. Special Collections, Kent, OH 44242. 216-672-2270.

A Stephen Donaldson collection of books and manuscripts, with works of several other fantasy and horror authors, makes up a science fiction and fantasy collection of about 1,000 volumes. An exhibit in 1981, "Ohio's Contribution to Science Fiction & Fantasy," featured authors born in Ohio. The collection is active, growing by gifts and purchase, and is noncirculating. Cataloging is on OCLC.

12-19. Ohio State University Libraries. Division of Rare Books and Manuscripts, 1858 Neil Ave. Mall, Columbus, OH 43210. 614-268-5725.

A very extensive American fiction collection includes thousands of volumes of fantasy and horror, but there is no practical way to sort them and count by these categories. Under the designation "The William Charvat Collection of American Fiction," Ohio State has been working for years to assemble a complete American fiction collection up to the year 1926, and has been collecting new fiction comprehensively since 1986. The intervening years are substantially represented as well, and the goal is to fill them in where possible. A computer search of 173 fantasy and horror authors' names in the OSU computer produced about 4,400 volumes.

The library holds an especially large James Thurber collection, including 22 linear feet of Thurber's papers. The horror and fantasy periodical collection is one of the twenty most complete. The library reports a near-complete Arkham House collection. The collection is growing through gifts and purchases. Part of it is circulating through interlibrary loan. Cataloging is on OCLC. Photocopies are available.

Oklahoma

12-20. University of Tulsa. McFarlin Library. Special Collections Department, 600 S. College Ave., Tulsa, OK 74104. 918-631-2496.
Works by a handful of fantasy and horror authors are included in the science fiction collection, which is not a primary focus of the library. Books by M. P. Shiel, James Thurber and R. A. Lafferty, and some Arkham House editions of H. P. Lovecraft, are held. A large collection of Lafferty manuscripts is the most significant relevant holding. Cataloging is on OCLC, and photocopies are available.

Oregon

12-21. American Private Press Association Library. 112 E. Burnett St., Stayton, OR 97383. 503-769-6088.
A collection of over 200,000 fanzines, 1,000 books and 3,000 letters, including both science fiction and fantasy. Separate counts are not kept by genre. The collection is strongest in 1960s and 1970s fanzines, and includes extensive fantasy periodicals, one of the ten most complete fantasy periodical collections. Open to the public. An internal catalog covers all books, and 70% of the fanzines. Photocopies are available, but not interlibrary loan.

Pennsylvania

12-22. Pennsylvania State University. Pattee Library, Special Collections Department, University Park, PA 16802. 814-865-1793.
A fiction collection of 1,600 volumes. The library collects utopias, science fiction, H. P. Lovecraft, Robert E. Howard and Arkham House. Several fantasy and horror authors are included as science fiction, with manuscripts of August Derleth and Talbot Mundy. Aside from Lovecraft, utopias are the only fantasy-related material being actively purchased, though the other collections are growing through gifts. Horror and fantasy represent 20% or less of the collection. The collection is two-thirds cataloged, and some holdings are on OCLC. Photocopies are available.

12-23. Temple University Libraries. Rare Book Collection, Science Fiction & Fantasy Collection, Philadelphia, PA 19122. 215-787-8230.
Until 1984 the collection of 8,000 books and 5,000 periodical issues excluded fantasy. Since then, 10,000 new and unsorted volumes have arrived, which do include fantasy, but exact figures are unavailable. Perhaps 20% are horror or fantasy. Over 1,000 fanzines also have undetermined fantasy content. The fantasy

and horror part of the collection is growing by purchase and gift at the rate of about seventy-five volumes per year. The library has significant holdings of almost all fantasy and horror authors, with manuscripts of James Blish, Marion Zimmer Bradley, Walter De la Mare and John Cowper Powys. Gothic horror is collected outside the SF&F collection, but still in the Rare Book Collection, with strong holdings of Mervyn Peake, Monk Lewis, Horace Walpole, George MacDonald, H. P. Lovecraft and Robert E. Howard, and a complete or nearly complete Arkham House collection. The collection of fantasy and horror periodicals is one of the ten most complete. The collection is 65% cataloged, and holdings are on OCLC. Photocopies are available.

Rhode Island

12-24. Brown University. John Hay Library, Providence, RI 02912. 401-863-2146.
The definitive H. P. Lovecraft collection, with over 700 printed and over 5,000 manuscript items, half by Lovecraft himself and half by Lovecraft correspondents such as August Derleth, Frank Belknap Long, C. L. Moore, E. Hoffmann Price and Clark Ashton Smith. A separate Clark Ashton Smith collection includes over 5,000 manuscripts and 5,000 letters, and a separate John Buchan collection is maintained. A complete run of *Weird Tales* is held. Publisher collections include the complete works of Arkham House including most ephemera, and complete Donald W. Grant and Necronomicon Press collections. Psychic science, the occult, conjuring and magic are also collecting specialties. The collection is active, and cataloged. The Lovecraft collection is cataloged on the Research Libraries Information Network (RLIN).

South Carolina

12-25. University of South Carolina. Thomas Cooper Library, Special Collections, Columbia, SC 29208. 803-777-8154.
The result of an isolated purchase, this library has a complete set of Arkham House publications as of 1975, plus a collection of H. P. Lovecraft first editions. The collection is not being added to, but is being preserved as a noncirculating resource, cataloged on OCLC.

Tennessee

12-26. Bibliotheca Crawfordiana. F. Marion Crawford Memorial Society, Saracinesca House, 3610 Meadowbrook Ave., Nashville, TN 37205. 615-226-1890.
A fiction collection of about 1,225 volumes contains books by F. Marion Crawford and about thirty other mostly contemporary (late nineteenth-, early twentieth-century) horror and fantasy authors. The collection also includes 500 letters, 25 pieces of art and diverse related items, including 200 articles about Crawford. The collection holds some fantasy and horror periodicals. The collection is growing (at about forty items per year) through purchase, gifts and exchanges. The holdings may be used by appointment only. Photocopies are available, but not interlibrary loan.

Texas

12-27. Texas A&M University. Evans Library, Special Collections Division, College Station, TX 77843-5000. 409-845-1951.
A science fiction collection of 21,000 volumes, including an unknown percentage of horror and fantasy material. Includes 20 linear feet of manuscripts and letters, 115 videotapes and 15 films. Horror has not been a collecting emphasis. The collection of horror and fantasy periodicals is one of the ten most complete. This is a very active collection, adding about 2,000 volumes per year through purchase, gifts and exchanges. The books are about 70% cataloged; manuscripts are uncataloged. Photocopies are available, but not interlibrary loan.

12-28. University of Texas at Austin. Harry Ransom Humanities Research Center, Box 7219, Austin, TX 78713. 512-471-9119.
The Harry Ransom Humanities Research Center has nearly 7,000 volumes of fiction and hundreds of magazines, manuscripts and letters organized into several distinct collections of interest to the student of fantasy and/or horror: The I. R. Brussel Bibliography Collection of James Branch Cabell, the Dan Laurence Collection of Robert Nathan and the Adrian Homer Goldstone Collection of Arthur Machen. The Ellery Queen Collection has an extensive "psychic detective" section and many Bram Stoker, William Hope Hodgson and Edgar Allan Poe titles. Also available is the Dorothy Sayers Wilkie Collins Collection, Arthur Conan Doyle's Spiritualism Library, M. P. Shiel's and John Gawsworth's Realm of Redondo Collection, the George Matthew Adams Lafcadio Hearn Collection and the library and archive of T. H. White. In all, the Center holds substantial manuscripts or letters of nearly fifty fantasy authors. The publisher holdings include complete sets of Kelmscott Press, Arkham House, Carcosa, Dark Harvest and Roy Squires.

In 1982 the Center acquired the L. W. Currey Science Fiction and Fantasy Collection, essentially his bibliography collection. While primarily utopias and science fiction, it contains comprehensive fantasy holdings, both high and dark. The H. P. Lovecraft, Ray Bradbury, David H. Keller, David Lindsay and Clark Ashton Smith holdings are particularly noteworthy. Holdings are also strong in promotional, script and other materials related to fantastic film.

The periodical collection, in number of titles, is one of the most extensive. In terms of completeness it is in the top twenty of the libraries surveyed. The collection is developing along the lines of established strength through purchase and regular gifts. Most of its books are cataloged. Photocopies are available, but not interlibrary loan.

Utah

12-29. Brigham Young University. Lee Library, Provo, UT 84602. 801-378-6730.
This collection holds an estimated 4,000 volumes of fantasy and horror fiction, within a larger science fiction/fantasy collection. Some fantasy and horror magazines are held. The collection is active, adding about fifty volumes annually. It is a circulating collection except for a small percentage held in the Rare Book Collection and vault. The books are fully cataloged, and available through interlibrary loan, as are photocopies.

Virginia

12-30. University of Virginia. Alderman Library, Special Collections Department, Charlottesville, VA 22903-2498. 804-924-3025.
The Sadleir-Black Collection of Gothic Fiction contains over 1,000 titles published mainly between 1765 and 1830. Focusing on English writers and imprints, it is unique in its coverage of minor authors writing in this genre and its holdings of original and subsequent editions of their works. Along with the English editions are American, French and German editions dating from the same period. The University of Virginia Library also holds manuscript material of Ambrose Bierce, Jorge Luis Borges, Chas. Brockden Brown, James Branch Cabell (extensive), Robert W. Chambers, Nathaniel Hawthorne, Lafcadio Hearn, Jack London and Edgar Allan Poe. The collection is noncirculating and growing.

Wisconsin

12-31. Marquette University Libraries. Department of Special Collections, 1415 W. Wisconsin Ave., Milwaukee, WI 53233. 414-224-7256.
The J. R. R. Tolkien Collection includes 6.4 cubic feet of original manuscripts of *The Hobbit, Farmer Giles of Ham, The Lord of the Rings* and *Mr. Bliss*; copies of books by Tolkien; and books, periodicals, art, games and other secondary material relating to Tolkien. The manuscripts are available for use on microfilm only in the Department of Special Collections; all Tolkien holdings are noncirculating. A brochure, "JRR Tolkien Collection, an Inventory to the Manuscripts at Marquette University" (typescript, thirty-nine pages, revised 1987) is available by mail for $4.00. An estimated 500 volumes of related interest are available in the general circulating collection. The Tolkien collection is fully cataloged, and photocopies are available.

12-32. State Historical Society of Wisconsin. 816 State St., Madison, WI 53706. 608-262-3266.
The August Derleth papers include fantasy pulps (issues that include Derleth contributions) and most Arkham House books, as well as Derleth's manuscripts and personal papers. Manuscripts or letters by Steven Vincent Benét, Algernon Blackwood, Robert Bloch, Ray Bradbury, Arthur Conan Doyle, H. P. Lovecraft, Donald Wandrei and Colin Wilson are also part of the collection, which is noncirculating.

12-33. University of Wisconsin, La Crosse. Murphy Library, La Crosse, WI 54601. 608-785-8511.
The Paul W. Skeeters Collection of fantasy, science fiction and horror literature holds 1,100 volumes, primarily first editions, and an Arkham House collection of about 100 titles. Among the authors collected are Joan Aiken, Algernon Blackwood, James Branch Cabell, A. Conan Doyle, Lord Dunsany, H. Rider Haggard, Talbot Mundy, Sax Rohmer, M. P. Shiel and Bram Stoker. The collection grows by purchase of five volumes per year on the average. The books are fully cataloged on OCLC, and noncirculating. Photocopies are available, but not interlibrary loan.

Wyoming

12-34. University of Wyoming. Coe Library, Box 3924, Laramie, WY 82071. 307-766-6385.

A collection of science fiction and fantasy, including extensive manuscripts. Of note in the horror genre is the Robert Bloch collection, which consists primarily of materials from 1947 to date, and includes publications by and about Bloch, and manuscripts, fanzines, contracts, scripts, videotapes, correspondence and uncorrected proofs. This library reports its holdings in cubic feet: the overall collection takes up 275 cubic feet, to which 10–15 cubic feet per year are added through gifts. Catalogs and finding aids are available on site. The collection may be used in-house only, and interlibrary loan is not offered. Photocopies are available.

Australia

12-35. University of Queensland Library. Special Collections, St. Lucia, Queensland 4067, Australia. Phone: Brisbane 3773249.

This library holds the Donald Tuck collection of science fiction and fantasy, used to compile his *The Encyclopedia of Science Fiction and Fantasy through 1968* [6-4]. Most fantasy and horror authors are represented by published books. Most fantasy and horror primary magazines are in the collection, placing this periodical collection in the top twenty of those surveyed. The collection is actively growing through purchase of materials, and is fully cataloged. Hardcover books circulate and are available for interlibrary loan. Photocopies are available.

12-36. University of Sydney Library. Rare Books and Special Collections, Science Fiction and Fantasy Collection, Sydney, N.S.W. 2006, Australia. 02-692-4162.

Of a science fiction and fantasy collection of over 44,000 volumes, an estimated 50 to 60% are fantasy and horror. Manuscript material by Brian Aldiss, Lloyd Alexander, Harlan Ellison, H. P. Lovecraft and Clark Ashton Smith is included. The library has holdings of all fantasy and horror authors, with significant amounts (over two-thirds of their output) of at least ninety authors, plus a half-dozen each of sound recordings and filmstrips, and seven pieces of Virgil Finlay art. The collection of fantasy and horror periodicals is one of the ten most complete. There are 12,000 science fiction (including horror and fantasy) comic books of related interest. The collection grows by 250 to 300 volumes per year through purchases and donations. A Science Fiction Writers of America depository since 1980. The books are 20% fully cataloged; another 40% can be located by a title list on cards. Photocopies are available, but this is a noncirculating collection; no interlibrary loan.

Canada

12-37. Queen's University. Special Collections, Douglas Library, Kingston, Ontario, Canada K7L 5C4. 613-545-2528.

This library holds a science fiction collection of 1,600 books and 2,500 magazines, with a Gothic-fantasy orientation, and a 6-inch pile of H. P. Lovecraft manuscript material. The magazines are in Special Collections, but the novels are in the main stacks. Most fantasy and horror authors are represented. The collection is fully cataloged, but not growing. Photocopies are available, but not interlibrary loan.

12-38. Toronto Public Library. Spaced Out Library, 40 St. George Street, Toronto, Ontario, Canada M5S 2E4. 416-393-7748.
A collection of nearly 18,000 volumes of science fiction and fantasy, plus over 15,000 periodicals, for which separate fantasy and horror statistics are not maintained. The collection policy defines the Spaced Out Library as an adult research collection of science fiction and fantasy, and the curator estimates that the collection may be 50% fantasy. There is very little dark fantasy, except for writers like Stephen King and Peter Straub for whom there is a current demand. The fantasy and horror periodical collection is one of the ten most complete. The collection is actively growing through purchases and gifts, and is fully cataloged. There is a circulating library of 6,000 paperbacks in addition to the noncirculating main collection listed above. Photocopies can be supplied, but not interlibrary loan. An occasional newsletter is published.
  Bibliography: Aylward, David. "Spaced Out Library: Toronto Public Library's Spaced Out Collection," *Special Collections* II, 1/2 (Fall–Winter 1982) 63–67.

12-39. University of New Brunswick. Science Fiction and Fantasy Collection, Ward Chipman Library, Box 5050, St. John, New Brunswick, Canada E2L 4L5. 506-648-5703.
A science fiction collection of over 15,000 items, which includes fantasy materials but excludes most strictly horror or Gothic material. An extensive periodical collection includes complete runs of most fantasy fiction pulps and magazines, and is one of the ten most complete fantasy periodical collections. This is an active collection, adding regularly through gifts and purchase. The books are fully cataloged, and items that are not rare circulate locally and through interlibrary loan. Photocopies are available.

12-40. University of Winnipeg Library. 515 Portage Ave., Winnipeg, Manitoba, Canada R3B 2E9. 204-786-9805.
A science fiction collection of 2,425 volumes (plus 140 volumes of reference and critical works) includes detective, horror, weird, ghost and fantasy fiction. Of this total, 161 volumes are considered fantasy, and 45 horror. The collection includes works by nearly all horror and fantasy authors. Only a few fantasy and horror periodicals are held, with *Fantastic Adventures*, 1939–45, on microfilm. The overall collection is active, adding fifty volumes annually. The books are fully cataloged. This is a circulating collection, but with closed stacks. Interlibrary loan and photocopies are available.

England

12-41. Science Fiction Foundation. North East London Polytechnic, Longbridge Road, Dagenham, Essex, RM8 2AS, England. 01-590-7722.
A collection of fiction, manuscripts, microfilm, audio recordings and videotapes, numbering over 13,000 total items. Books by many fantasy and horror authors are

included, but are not sorted as fantasy and/or horror. The periodical collection has some holdings of most fantasy magazines, with enough complete runs to rank in the top twenty of collections surveyed. An internal catalog is available, as are photocopies.

Switzerland

12-42. Maison d'Ailleurs. Musée de l'Utopie, des Voyages Extraordinaires et de la Science-Fiction, Rue du Four 5, CH-1400 Yverdon-les-Bains. Switzerland. 024-216438.

Fantasy and horror are not counted separately in this 25,000-volume collection of science fiction, fantastic voyages and utopian novels. Fantasy and horror are ordinarily collected only when they overlap with the collection's three main areas of interest, but most fantasy authors are represented, and there is some manuscript material from H. P. Lovecraft. The collection has extensive correspondence files, and some manuscripts, sound and video recordings and artworks. The Maison holds growing collections of most fantasy magazines. The collections are 15–20% cataloged, and noncirculating (duplicates are circulated as a separate library). Photocopies are available, but not interlibrary loan (to date). The collection is active, growing by 400–450 volumes per year through gifts and purchases.

13

Core Collection, Awards, Organizations, Series

Neil Barron

Core Collection

Librarians desiring to evaluate or strengthen their collection should begin with the first-purchase recommendations in this listing, particularly those books with multiple recommendations. Readers, especially those relatively unfamiliar with fantasy or horror fiction, should probably begin with this listing, then let their developing interests guide them.

This core collection best books listing is derived from several sources:

1. First-purchase recommendations by this guide's contributors, which are denoted by an asterisk preceding the entry number in the numbered annotations and preceding the surname in this listing.

2. Books selected by these knowledgeable outside readers, whose initials follow the book titles:

DH: David Hartwell, respected editor of fantasy and SF, editor of several excellent anthologies, Ph.D. in comparative literature, Columbia University

SM: Sam Moskowitz, editor and author of many books and articles, with a special interest in the early history of SF; Pilgrim Award winner, 1981

RR: R. Reginald, best known for his authoritative bibliography of fantastic literature [6-3]; owner of Borgo Press

DW: Diana Waggoner, author of *The Hills of Faraway* [6-34], one of the best earlier surveys of fantasy

A few of their selections were not annotated in the bibliographies. Readers were not equally familiar with all annotated books, and the absence of their initials does not necessarily mean they thought the book less meritorious but simply that they were not sufficiently familiar with it to judge.

3. Three 100 best books guides by Cawthorn and Moorcock [6-21], Jones and Newman [6-22] and Pringle [6-23], designated F, H and MF, respectively.

4. The 33 titles in the *Locus* all-time best fantasy listing (see under Locus awards in this chapter), designated L.

5. The 208 novels and collections and 16 anthologies in Tymn's *Fantasy Literature* [6-32], designated FL.

All books are listed in the sequence in which they appear in this guide. Consult the indexes for entry numbers of annotated books. Titles followed by a year of publication were not annotated, although in some cases portions of their contents are included in books which are annotated. Recommendations of best films (as distinct from books about films) will be found in chapter 9.

Development of the Fantastic Tradition through 1811

*Apuleius. *The Golden Ass* (DH, SM, DW)
**The Arabian Nights' Entertainments* (DH, SM, RR, DW)
Ariosto. *Orlando Furioso* (RR, DW)
*Beckford, William. *Vathek* (DH, SM, RR, DW, F)
**Beowulf* (DH, SM, RR, DW)
Bunyan, John. *The Pilgrim's Progress* (DW)
*Dante Alighieri. *The Divine Comedy* (DH, SM, RR, DW)
**Dragons, Elves and Heroes*, ed. by Lin Carter (DH, SM, FL)
**Sir Gawain and the Green Knight* (DH, SM, RR, DW)
German Romance, ed. by Thomas Caryle (DH)
Gilgamesh Epic (RR)
Goethe, J. W. von. *Faust, Part One* (RR, DW)
**Golden Cities, Far*, ed. by Lin Carter (DH, SM, FL)
*Homer. *The Odyssey* (DH, SM, RR)
Huon of Bordeaux (DW)
Kalevala (RR, DW)
*Lewis, Matthew G. *The Monk* (DH, SM, RR, DW, F, H)
Mabinogion (RR, DW)
*Malory, Sir Thomas. *Le Morte d'Arthur* (DH, SM, RR, DW)
*Mandeville, Sir John. *The Travels of Sir John Mandeville* (DH, SM)
Marlowe, Christopher. *Dr. Faustus* (RR, H)
Milton, John. *Paradise Lost* (DW)
*Montalvo, Garcia Ordonez de. *Amadis of Gaul* (DH, SM)
*Ovid. *Metamorphoses* (DH, SM, DW)
*Perrault, Charles. *Fairy Tales* (DH, SM, DW)
*Potocki, Jan. *The Saragossa Manuscript* (DH, SM, RR)

Rabelais, François. *Gargantua and Pantagruel* (DW)
Radcliffe, Ann. *The Mysteries of Udolpho* (DW)
Raspé, Rudolf Erich. *Baron Münchhausen's Travels* (RR)
Song of Roland (RR)
Romance of the Rose (DW)
Shakespeare, William. *Macbeth* (H)
———. *A Midsummer Night's Dream* (DW)
*———. *The Tempest* (DH, SM, RR, DW)
———. *A Winter's Tale* (1623) (DW)
Spenser, Edmund. *The Faerie Queene* (DH, DW)
*Swift, Jonathan. *Gulliver's Travels* (DH, SM, RR, DW, F)
Tieck, Ludwig. *Tales from the Phantasus* (DH)
Volsunga Saga (RR)
Voltaire. *Candide* (1759) (DW)
*———. *Zadig* (DH, SM)
*Walpole, Horace. *The Castle of Otranto* (DH, SM, RR, DW, F)
———. *Hieroglyphic Tales* (1785) (DH)

The Nineteenth Century, 1812–99

Abbott, Edwin A. *Flatland* (1899) (F)
Andersen, Hans Christian. *Stories for the Household* (RR, DW)
*Anstey, F. *A Fallen Idol*
*———. *Vice Versa* (DH, SM, RR, DW)
Arnold, E. L. *Phra the Phoenician* (RR)
Bangs, J. K. *A Houseboat on the Styx* (RR)
Barham, R. H. *The Ingoldsby Legends* (DW)
*Butler, Samuel. *Erewhon/Erewhon Revisited* (DH, SM, RR)
*Carroll, Lewis. *Alice's Adventures in Wonderland/Through the Looking-Glass*
    (DH, SM, RR, DW, F, L, FL)
———. *The Hunting of the Snark* (RR)
———. *Sylvie and Bruno* (RR)
Chambers, Robert W. *The Maker of Moons* (RR)
*Chamisso, Adalbert von. *Peter Schlemihl* (DH, SM)
Clifford, Lucy. *Anyhow Stories* 1882 (DH)
Collodi, Carlo. *Pinocchio* (DW)
Cott, Jonathan, ed. *Beyond the Looking Glass* (1973) (DH, FL)
Craik, Mrs. *Avillion* (DW)
———. *The Little Lame Prince and His Travelling Cloak* (1875) (DW)
Crawford, F. Marion. *Khaled* (RR, DW)
*Dalton, James. *The Invisible Gentleman* (DH, SM)
Dawson, Emma F. *An Itinerant House and Other Stories* (1896) (SM)
*Dickens, Charles. *The Chimes* (DH, SM, RR, DW)
*———. *A Christmas Carol* (DH, SM, DW, F)
*———. *The Haunted Man* (DH, SM)
*du Maurier, George. *Peter Ibbetson* (DH, SM)
———. *Trilby* (RR)
*Fouqué, Baron de la Motte. *Undine* (DH, SM, RR, DW, FL)

*France, Anatole. *Thaïs* (DH, SM)
*———. *The Well of St. Clare* (DH, SM, RR)
*Garnett, Richard. *Twilight of the Gods* (DH, SM, F, FL)
*Gautier, Théophile. *One of Cleopatra's Nights* (DH, SM)
———. *Works* [selections] (RR)
Gogol, Nikolai. *Works* [selections] (DH)
Grimm, J. and W. *German Popular Stories* (DH, DW)
Haggard, H. Rider. *Eric Brighteyes* (RR, FL)
———. *King Solomon's Mines* (RR)
*———. *She* (DH, SM, RR, DW, F, H, FL)
———. *The World's Desire* (DW, FL)
Hauff, Wilhelm. *Tales* (RR)
*Hawthorne, Nathaniel. *Twice-Told Tales* (DH, SM, DW, RR)
Hogg, James. *The Brownie of Bodsbeck* (RR)
Housman, Laurence. *All-Fellows* (DH)
———. *The Cloak of Friendship* (DH)
———. *A Farm in Fairyland* (DH)
———. *Gods and Their Makers* (DH)
*Hudson, W. H. *A Crystal Age* (DH, SM)
Ingelow, Jean. *Mopsa the Fairy* (FL)
*Irving, Washington. *Sketch-Book* (DH, SM, RR, DW)
Jerome, J. K. *Told after Supper* (DW)
*Jerrold, Douglas. *A Man Made of Money* (DH, SM)
Keats, John. *Lamia, Isabella, The Eve of St. Agnes . . .* (DH)
Kipling, Rudyard. *Jungle Books* (RR, DW)
Lang, Andrew. *Prince Prigio and Prince Ricardo* (DW)
Lear, Edward. *The Book of Nonsense* (RR, DW)
Lloyd, John Uri. *Etidorhpa* (RR)
*Louÿs, Pierre. *Aphrodite* (DH, SM, RR)
MacDonald, George. *At the Back of the North Wind* (DW, FL)
———. *The Princess and the Goblin* (FL)
———. *The Princess and Curdie* (FL)
———. *The Gifts of the Child Christ* (1873) (FL)
*———. *Lilith* (DH, SM, RR, DW, FL)
*———. *Phantastes* (DH, SM, RR, FL)
*———. *Works of Fancy and Imagination* (DH, SM, RR)
Melville, Herman. *Moby Dick* (1851) (F)
Meredith, George. *The Shaving of Shagpat* (RR)
Mitchell, Edward Page. *The Crystal Man and Other Stories* (1973) (SM)
Morris, William. *Early Romances* (DH)
*———. *The Story of the Glittering Plain* (DH, SM, RR, F, FL)
———. *The Sundering Flood* (FL)
*———. *The Water of the Wondrous Isles* (DH, RR, FL)
———. *The Well at the World's End* (RR, SM, DW, FL)
———. *The Wood Beyond the World* (RR, DW, FL)
*Brien, Fitz-James. *Poems and Stories* (DH, SM, RR)
Oliphant, Margaret. *A Little Pilgrim in the Unseen* (DW)
Pyle, Howard. *Twilight-Land* (DW)

*Rossetti, Christina. *Goblin Market* (SM, DW)
Ruskin, John. *The King of the Golden River* (RR, DW, FL)
Ryder, Frank G., and Robert M. Browning, eds. *German Literary Fairy Tales* (1983) (DH)
*Sterling, John. *Essays and Tales* (DH, SM)
*Stockton, Frank R. *The Bee-Man of Orn* (DH, SM, RR, DW)
Sue, Eugène. *The Wandering Jew* (RR, H)
Thackeray, William M. *The Rose and the Ring* (DW)
*Twain, Mark. *A Connecticut Yankee in King Arthur's Court* (DH, SM, RR, DW)
*Wells, H. G. *The Wonderful Visit* (DH, SM)
*Wilde, Oscar. *The Happy Prince/A House of Pomegranates* (DH, SM, RR, DW)
Yeats, W. B. *Early Poems and Stories* (DW)
Zipes, Jack, ed. *Victorian Fairy Tales* (1987) (DH)

From Baum to Tolkien, 1900–56

*Anderson, Poul. *The Broken Sword* (DH, SM, RR, DW, F, MF, FL)
———. *Three Hearts and Three Lions* (DW, F, MF, FL)
*Anstey, F. *The Brass Bottle* (SM, RR, DW)
*———. *In Brief Authority* (SM)
*Arnold, Edwin Lester. *Lieut. Gullivar Jones, His Vacation* (SM)
*Baker, Frank. *Miss Hargreaves* (SM)
Barrie, J. M. *Dear Brutus* (DH)
*———. *Peter Pan* (DH, SM, DW)
Barringer, Leslie. Gerfalcon trilogy (RR, DW)
Bates, Herbert E. *Seven Tales and Alexander* (1929) (FL)
*Baum, L. Frank. *The Wonderful Wizard of Oz* (SM, RR, DW, L, FL)
Beerbohm, Max. *Zuleika Dobson* (F)
*Benét, Stephen Vincent. *Thirteen O'Clock* (DH, SM, RR)
*Benson, Stella. *Living Alone* (SM)
*Blackwood, Algernon. *The Centaur* (SM, RR)
———. *The Dance of Death and Other Tales* (1928) (FL)
*———. *The Human Chord* (SM)
Bloch, Robert. *Dragons and Nightmares* (RR)
*Borges, Jorge Luis. *Ficciones* (DH, SM, RR)
Boucher, Anthony, ed. *The Best from Fantasy and Science Fiction* (DH, DW)
———. *The Compleat Werewolf* (DW, H)
Bowen, Marjorie. *The Haunted Vintage* (DW)
Brackett, Leigh. *The Sword of Rhiannon* (1953) (F)
Bradbury, Ray. *The Martian Chronicles* (1950) (DW)
Bramah, Ernest. *The Wallet of Kai Lung* (DW)
*Bulgakov, Mikhail. *The Master and Margarita* (DH, SM, RR)
*Bullett, Gerald. *Mr. Godly Beside Himself* (SM)
*Burroughs, Edgar Rice. *A Princess of Mars* (DH, SM, RR, DW, F)
*———. *Tarzan of the Apes* (DH, SM, RR, DW, F)
*Cabell, James Branch. *The Cream of the Jest* (SM, DW, FL)
*———. *Figures of Earth* (SM, FL)

*————. *The High Place* (SM, DW)
*————. *Jurgen* (SM, RR, DW)
*————. *The Silver Stallion* (SM, RR, DW, FL)
*————. *Something about Eve* (SM, DW, H, FL)
————. *The Witch-Woman* (FL)
Chambers, Robert W. *The Slayer of Souls* (RR)
*Chesterton, G. K. *The Man Who Was Thursday* (DH, SM, RR, DW, F, H)
Coblentz, Stanton A. *When the Birds Fly South* (RR)
Coles, Manning. *Brief Candles* (DW)
————. *The Far Traveller* (1956) (DW)
*Collier, John. *Fancies and Goodnights* (DH, SM, RR, DW, FL)
————. *His Monkey Wife* (DW)
Colum, Padraic. *The Boy Apprenticed to an Enchanter* (1920) (FL)
Connelly, Marc. *The Green Pastures* (DW)
Coppard, A. E. *Adam and Eve and Pinch Me* (RR)
de Camp, L. Sprague. *The Land of Unreason* (F)
————. *Lest Darkness Fall* (1941) (DW)
————. *The Tritonian Ring* (DH, RR, DW, F)
*————, with Fletcher Pratt. *The Incomplete Enchanter* (DH, SM, RR, DW, F, MF, L)
de la Mare, Walter. *Broomsticks* (DH, DW, FL)
Dick, R. A. *The Ghost and Mrs. Muir* (DW)
Doyle, A. C. *The Lost World* (1912) (F)
Dunsany, Lord. *The Blessing of Pan* (DW)
*————. *The Charwoman's Shadow* (SM, DW, FL)
*————. *The Gods of Pegana* (DH, SM, RR, FL)
————. *The King of Elfland's Daughter* (RR, DW, F, FL)
*————. *The Sword of Welleran* (DH, SM, RR, FL)
Eddison, E. R. *Mistress of Mistresses* (DH, RR, DW)
*————. *The Worm Ouroboros* (DH, SM, RR, DW, F, L, FL)
Farjeon, Eleanor. *Martin Pippin in the Apple-Orchard* (DW)
*Finney, Charles G. *The Circus of Dr. Lao* (SM, RR, DW, F)
Forster, E. M. *The Celestial Omnibus* (RR)
France, Anatole. *Penguin Island* (DW)
*————. *The Revolt of the Angels* (SM, RR)
*Fraser, Ronald. *Flower Phantoms* (SM)
*Garnett, David. *Lady into Fox/A Man in the Zoo* (SM, RR, DW, F)
*Gilman, Charlotte Perkins. *Herland* (SM, DW, F)
Golding, William. *Pincher Martin* (1956) (MF)
*Grahame, Kenneth. *The Wind in the Willows* (DH, SM, DW)
Graves, Robert. *Seven Days in New Crete* (1949) (MF)
Hearn, Lafcadio. *Kwaidan* (RR, DW)
*Hecht, Ben. *Fantazius Mallare* (SM, RR)
Heinlein, Robert A. *Waldo and Magic, Inc.* (DH, DW)
*Hesse, Herman. *Steppenwolf* (SM, RR)
*Hilton, James. *Lost Horizon* (SM, RR, DW, F)
*Hodgson, William Hope. *The Night Land* (DH, SM, RR, F)
*Howard, Robert E. *Conan the Conqueror* (DH, SM, RR, DW, F, MF)

Hubbard, L. Ron. *Slaves of Sleep* (F)
*———. *Typewriter in the Sky*
*Hudson, W. H. *Green Mansions* (DH, SM, RR)
Hyne, C. J. Cutcliffe. *The Lost Continent* (DW)
*Irwin, Margaret. *Still She Wished for Company* (SM)
*———. *These Mortals* (SM)
*Jarry, Alfred. *The Supermale* (SM)
Kipling, Rudyard. *Just So Stories* (RR, DW)
———. *Puck of Pook's Hill* (DW)
Kuttner, Henry. *The Dark World* (RR, DW, F)
*Leiber, Fritz. *Two Sought Adventure* (DH, SM, RR, DW, F, FL)
Lewis, C. S. *Out of the Silent Planet* [trilogy] (RR, DW, FL)
———. *The Screwtape Letters* (RR, DW)
*———. *Till We Have Faces* (SM, DW, FL)
*Lindsay, David. *Devil's Tor* (SM, RR)
*———. *The Haunted Woman* (F)
*———. *A Voyage to Arcturus* (SM, RR, DW, F, H, FL)
Linklater, Eric. *God Likes Them Plain* (FL)
Lofting, Hugh. *The Voyages of Dr. Dolittle* (1922) DW)
London, Jack. *The Star Rover* (DW)
Lovecraft, H. P. *The Dream-Quest of Unknown Kadath* (RR, DW, FL)
*Machen, Arthur. *The Hill of Dreams* (FL)
Masefield, John. *The Midnight Folk* (DW)
*Merritt, A. *Dwellers in the Mirage* (SM, RR, DW, F)
*———. *The Face in the Abyss* (SM, RR, DW, FL)
———. *The Fox Woman and Other Stories* (FL)
———. *The Moon Pool* (DH)
*———. *The Ship of Ishtar* (SM, DW, F, FL)
Milne, A. A. *Winnie-the-Pooh* (RR, DW)
———. *Once on a Time* (1917) (DW)
*Mirrlees, Hope. *Lud-in-the-Mist* (DH, SM, RR, DW, FL)
*Moore, C. L. *Black God's Shadow* (DH, SM, DW, F, FL)
*Morley, Christopher. *Thunder on the Left* (SM)
Morris, Kenneth. *The Book of the Three Dragons* (FL)
———. *The Fates of the Princes of Dyved* (FL)
*———. *The Secret Mountain* (DH, SM, RR, FL)
Myers, John Myers. *Silverlock* (RR, DW, MF, L)
Nathan, Robert. *The Bishop's Wife* (RR)
*———. *Portrait of Jennie* (SM, RR)
Nesbit, E. *The Enchanted Castle* (DW)
———. *Five Children and It* (RR, DW)
Noyes, Alfred. *The Devil Takes a Holiday* (DW)
O'Neill, Joseph. *Land Under England* (1935) (F)
*Orwell, George. *Animal Farm* (RR)
Pain, Barry. *Collected Tales*, vol. 1 (1916) (FL)
*Pargeter, Edith. *By Firelight* (SM)
*Peake, Mervyn. *Titus Groan* and sequels (DH, SM, RR, DW, F, MF, L)
*Phillpotts, Eden. *Circé's Island and The Girl and the Faun* (SM)

*———. *Pan and the Twins* (SM)

*Powys, John Cowper. *A Glastonbury Romance* (SM, DW)

———. *Porius* (SM)

*Powys, T. F. *Mr. Weston's Good Wine* (SM)

*———. *The Two Thieves* (SM)

*———. *Unclay* (SM)

*Pratt, Fletcher. *The Blue Star* (DH, SM, DW)

———. *The Well of the Unicorn* (RR, F, MF, FL)

Quinn, Seabury. *Roads* (F)

*Read, Herbert. *The Green Child* (SM)

Richardson, Maurice. *The Exploits of Engelbrecht* (1946) (F)

Rolfe, Frederick W. *Hadrian VII* (RR, DW)

Saint Exupéry, Antoine de. *The Little Prince* (RR)

Shaw, G. B. *The Adventures of the Black Girl* (DW)

Smith, Thorne. *The Night Life of the Gods* (DW, F)

*———. *The Stray Lamb* (SM)

———. *Topper* (RR, DW)

*———. *Turnabout* (SM, DW, F)

*Stephens, James. *The Crock of Gold* (DH, SM)

Stevens, Francis. *The Citadel of Fear* (F)

Stockton, Frank R. *The Story Teller's Pack* (1897) (FL)

Stuart, Frank R. *Caravan for China* (1939) (F)

Thurber, James. *Fables for Our Time* (RR, DW)

*———. *The Thirteen Clocks* (DH, SM, DW, FL)

*———. *The White Deer* (DH, SM, DW)

Tolkien, J. R. R. *Farmer Giles of Ham* (1949) (FL)

*———. *The Hobbit* (DH, SM, RR, DW, L, FL)

*———. *The Lord of the Rings* (DH, SM, RR, DW, F, MF, L, FL)

Travers, P. L. *Mary Poppins* (DW)

Twain, Mark. *Captain Stormfield's Visit to Heaven* (DW)

———. *The Mysterious Stranger* (DW)

Uttley, Alison A. *A Traveller in Time* (1939) (DW)

*Vance, Jack. *The Dying Earth* (DH, SM, RR, DW, F, MF, L, FL)

van Vogt, A. E. *The Book of Ptath* (F, MF)

*Viereck, George. *My First Two Thousand Years/Salome/Invincible Adam* (SM, RR)

Visiak, E. H. *Medusa* (H)

*Wall, Mervyn. *The Unfortunate Fursey/Return of Fursey* (SM)

Walton, Evangeline. *The Virgin and the Swine* (DH, RR, DW, FL)

*Warner, Sylvia Townsend. *Lolly Willowes* (SM)

Wells, H. G. *The Man Who Could Work Miracles* (DW)

White, T. H. *The Elephant and the Kangaroo* (DW)

———. *Mistress Masham's Repose* (DW, F, FL)

*———. *The Sword in the Stone* [tetralogy] (DH, SM, MF, RR, DW, F, MF, L, FL)

*Williams, Charles. *All Hallows' Eve* (SM, RR, DW, FL)

*———. *Descent into Hell* (SM, FL)

———. *The Greater Trumps* (DW, FL)

——. *Many Dimensions* (DW, FL)
——. *Shadows of Ecstasy* (FL)
——. *War in Heaven* (DW, F, FL)
Wodehouse, P. G. *Laughing Gas* (DW)
Woolf, Virginia. *Orlando* (DH, RR)
Wright, Austin Tappan. *Islandia* (RR, DW)
*Wylie, Elinor. *The Venetian Glass Nephew*
*Wylie, Philip. *The Disappearance* (SM)

Modern Fantasy For Adults, 1957–88

Ackroyd, Peter. *Hawksmoor* (DH, F, H, MF)
Adams, Richard. *Shardik* (RR, DW)
Aldiss, Brian W. *The Malacia Tapestry* (RR)
Amis, Kingsley. *The Alteration* (1976) (F)
Anderson, Poul. *A Midsummer Tempest* (RR, FL)
——. *Three Hearts and Three Lions* (DW, F, MF, FL)
Anthony, Piers. *Hasan* (RR, DW)
——. *A Spell for Chameleon* (L, FL)
——. Xanth series (RR, DW [first 3 only])
Arnason, Eleanor. *The Sword Smith* (FL)
Ballard, J. G. *The Day of Creation* (1987) (MF)
——. *The Unlimited Dream Company* (MF)
Beagle, Peter. *A Fine and Private Place* (DW, MF, FL)
*——. *The Last Unicorn* (DH, RR, DW, MF, L, FL)
Bernanos, Michel. *The Other Side of the Mountain* (RR)
Blaylock, James. *The Digging Leviathan* (MF)
*Blish, James. *Black Easter* (DH, RR, F, MF, FL)
*——. *The Day after Judgment* (DH, RR, F, MF, FL)
Brackett, Leigh. Skaith trilogy (*The Ginger Star*, 1974; *The Hounds of Skaith*, 1974; *The Reavers of Skaith*, 1976) (DW)
Bradbury, Ray. *Dandelion Wine* (MF)
——. *Something Wicked This Way Comes* (DH, DW, L)
*——. *The Stories of Ray Bradbury* (DH, RR)
Bradley, Marion Zimmer. Darkover series (RR, DW)
Bradshaw, Gillian. *Hawk of May* (1980) and sequels (DW)
Broderick, Damien. *The Dreaming Dragons* (DW)
Brooks, Terry. *The Sword of Shannara* (FL)
Brunner, John. *The Traveler in Black* (FL)
Bull, Emma. *War for the Oaks* (1987) (DW)
Burgess, Anthony. *The Eve of St. Venus* (RR)
Burroughs, William. *Cities of the Red Night* (1981) (MF)
Calvino, Italo. *Our Ancestors* (RR)
*Card, Orson Scott. *Seventh Son, Red Prophet* (DW)
*Carroll, Jonathan. *The Land of Laughs* (DW, SM, H, MF)
Carter, Angela. *The Infernal Desire Machines of Dr. Hoffman* (RR, F, MF)
——. *Nights at the Circus* (MF)
——. *The Passion of New Eve* (MF)

Chapman, Vera. Three Damosels trilogy (RR, FL)
Cherryh, C. J. *The Dreamstone* (1983) (DW)
——. Quest of Morgaine trilogy (RR, DW, FL)
——. *The Tree of Swords and Jewels* (1983) (DW)
Crowley, John. *Aegypt* (MF)
*——. *Little, Big* (RR, DW, MF, L)
*Davidson, Avram. *Peregrine: Primus*
*——. *Peregrine: Secundus*
——. *The Phoenix and the Mirror* (DH, RR, MF, FL)
——. *Strange Seas and Shores* (DH)
de Camp, L. Sprague. Novaria series (DW)
*Delany, Samuel R. Nevèrÿon series (DH, RR)
de Lint, Charles. *Yarrow* (1986) (DW)
——. *Svaha* (1989) (DW)
Dickinson, Peter. *The Blue Hawk* (RR, DW)
Dickson, Gordon R. *The Dragon and the George* (MF, FL)
*Disch, Thomas M. *On Wings of Song* (DH)
*Donaldson, Stephen R. Thomas Convenant trilogies (DH, RR, MF, L, FL)
du Maurier, Daphne. *The House on the Strand* (RR)
Eddings, David. Belgariad series (RR, DW)
——. Mallorean series (RR)
Eisenstein, Phyllis. *Sorcerer's Son* (MF)
*Elkin, Stanley. *The Living End*
Ellison, Harlan. *Essential Ellison* (DH, RR, DW)
Farmer, Philip José. *A Feast Unknown* (MF)
*——. World of Tiers series (RR)
Finney, Charles G. *The Magician Out of Manchuria* (DH)
*Finney, Jack. *Time and Again* (RR, DW, MF)
Ford, John M. *The Dragon Waiting* (DW)
Fowles, John. *The Magus* (DH, MF)
Frayn, Michael. *Sweet Dreams* (MF)
García Márquez, Gabriel. *One Hundred Years of Solitude* (DH)
Gardner, John. *Grendel* (DH, DW, H, MF, FL)
Garrett, Randall. Lord Darcy series (RR)
Gaskell, Jane. Atlan saga (RR, DW, F)
Goldman, William. *The Princess Bride* (RR, FL)
Goldstein, Lisa. *The Dream Years* (MF)
*——. *The Red Magician* (DH)
Gray, Alasdair. *Lanark* (MF)
Gregorian, Joyce. *The Broken Citadel* (DW, FL)
*Grimwood, Ken. *Replay* (MF)
Hales, E. E. Y. *Chariot of Fire* (DW, FL)
Hambly, Barbara. *Dragonsbane* (1986) (DW)
——. *The Ladies of Mandrigyn* (DW)
——. *The Silent Tower* (DW)
Hancock, Niel. Circle of Light series (FL)
*Harrison, M. John. Viriconium series (DH, F, MF)
Heinlein, Robert A. *Glory Road* (RR, MF, L)

————. *The Unpleasant Profession of Jonathan Hoag* (DH)
Helprin, Mark. *Winter's Tale* (MF)
Hoban, Russell. *Pilgermann* (RR, DW)
*Holdstock, Robert. *Mythago Wood, Lavondyss* (DW, H, MF)
Holt, Tom. *Expecting Someone Taller* (H)
Horwood, William. *Duncton Wood, Duncton Quest* (RR)
*Hughart, Barry. *Bridge of Birds* (DW)
Jacobs, Harvey. *The Egg of the Glak* (DW)
*Kay, Guy Gavriel. Fionavar series (DH, MF)
Kennealy, Patricia. *The Copper Crown* (1985) (DW)
*King, Stephen and Peter Straub. *The Talisman* (RR)
Kotzwinkle, William. *Fata Morgana* (RR, MF)
Kress, Nancy. *The Prince of Morning Bells* (1981) (DH)
Kurtz, Katherine. *Deryni Rising* (RR, L, FL)
Kuttner, Henry. *The Mask of Circe* (1971) (FL)
*Lafferty, R. A. *Fourth Mansions* (RR, MF)
Laubenthal, S. A. *Excalibur* (DW, FL)
Lee, Tanith. Birthgrave trilogy (RR, DW)
————. *Companions on the Road* (1977) (FL)
————. *Dreams of Dark and Light* (DH, DW, FL)
————. *East of Midnight* (1978) (FL)
————. *Volkhavaar* (DW, FL)
————. *The Winter Players* (1976) (FL)
Le Guin, Ursula K. *Orsinian Tales* (RR, DW)
————. *The Wind's Twelve Quarters* (RR, FL)
*Leiber, Fritz. Fahfrd and the Grey Mouser series (DH, SM, RR, DW, F, MF, FL)
Lessing, Doris. *Briefing for a Descent into Hell* (1971) (MF)
————. *The Fifth Child* (DW)
Lindholm, Megan. *Wizard of the Pigeons* (DW)
Lupoff, Richard. *Sword of the Demon* (RR, FL)
Lynn, Elizabeth A. Chronicles of Tornor (DW)
MacAvoy, R. A. *The Book of Kells* (DW)
————. *Tea with the Black Dragon* (DW, MF)
————. Trio for Lute series (DW)
*MacDonald, John D. *The Girl, the Gold Watch and Everything* (MF)
Martí-Ibanez, Felix. *All the Wonders We Seek* (FL)
Matheson, Richard. *Bid Time Return* (RR)
McCaffrey, Anne. *Dragonflight, The White Dragon* (RR, DW, L)
Moorcock, Michael. *Stormbringer* (F, MF)
*————. *Gloriana* (DH, RR, DW, MF)
*————. *The War Hound and the World's Pain* (DH, MF)
Moore, Brian. *Cold Heaven* (MF)
————. *The Great Victorian Collection* (RR, MF)
Mujica Láinez, Manuel. *The Wandering Unicorn* (RR)
Nathan, Robert. *So Love Returns* (RR)
Niven, Larry. *The Magic Goes Away* (DW)
*Norton, Andre. Witch World series (RR, MF, L, FL)
O'Brien, Flann. *The Third Policeman* (MF)

*Powers, Tim. *The Anubis Gates* (H, MF)
——. *The Drawing of the Dark* (RR, F)
Pratchett, Terry. Discworld series (F)
Pratt, Fletcher. *The Blue Star* (RR, DW)
Priest, Christopher. *The Glamour* (1984) (MF)
Purtill, Richard. *The Mirror of Helen* (1983) (DW)
——. *The Stolen Goddess* (1980) (DW)
Pynchon, Thomas. *The Crying of Lot 49* (DH, MF)
*Reamy, Tom. *Blind Voices* (RR)
Rucker, Rudy. *White Light* (DW, MF)
Rushdie, Salman. *Grimus* (MF)
Russ, Joanna. *The Adventures of Alyx* (DH)
Ryman, Geoff. *The Unconquered Country* (MF)
Shea, Michael. *Nifft the Lean* (MF)
Sherrell, Carl. *Raum* (1977) (FL)
*Silverberg, Robert. Majipoor series (RR, DW, L)
Simak, Clifford. *Enchanted Pilgrimage* (FL)
——. *The Fellowship of the Talisman* (RR)
Sinclair, Andrew. *Gog* (MF)
Stasheff, Christopher. Warlock series (RR)
*Stewart, Mary. Life of Merlin series (RR, FL)
*Süskind, Patrick. *Perfume*
Swann, Thomas Burnett. *Day of the Minotaur* (RR, DW, MF, FL)
——. *Lady of the Bees* (DW)
——. *The Tournament of Thorns* (1976) (DW)
Tarr, Judith. The Hound and the Falcon trilogy (RR)
Tennant, Emma. *Hotel de Dream* (MF)
Tepper, Sheri S. *Marianne, the Magus and the Manticore* (DW)
——. The True Game trilogy. (*King's Blood Four*, 1983; *Necromancer Nine*, 1983; *Wizard's Eleven*, 1984) (DW)
*Thomas, D. M. *The White Hotel*
Thurber, James. *The Wonderful O* (DW)
Tolkien, J. R. R. *The Father Christmas Letters* (1976) (FL)
*——. *The Silmarillion* (RR, DW, FL)
——. *Smith of Wootton Major* (1967) (FL)
——. *Unfinished Tales* (DW)
Treece, Henry. *The Golden Strangers* (1956) (F)
——. *The Great Captains* (1956) (F)
——. *The Green Man* (RR)
Vance, Jack. *The Eyes of the Overworld* (RR, MF, FL)
Vercors. *Sylva* (RR)
*Vian, Boris. *Heartsnatcher*
Walton, Evangeline. Books of the Welsh Mabinogion (RR, DW, FL)
Warner, Sylvia Townsend. *Kingdoms of Elfin* (FL)
Wellman, Manly Wade. Silver John series (RR, DW)
White, T. H. *The Once and Future King* (DH, RR, DW, F, MF, L, FL)
Willis, Connie. *Lincoln's Dreams* (DW)
*Wolfe, Gene. Book of the New Sun series (DH, RR, DW, L)

———. *Peace* (MF)
———. *Soldier of the Mist* (DH)
Yarbro, Chelsea Quinn. *Ariosto* (DW, MF)
*Zelazny, Roger. Amber series (RR, L, FL)
———. *Creatures of Light and Darkness* (RR)
———. *Jack of Shadows* (MF, FL)

Anthologies

Black Water, ed. by Manuel (DH, RR)
Dark Imagining, ed. by Boyer and Zahorski (FL)
Discoveries in Fantasy, ed. by Lin Carter (1972) (FL)
Dreamers of Dreams, ed. by Douglas Menville and R. Reginald (1978) (FL)
The Fantastic Imagination, ed. by Boyer and Zahorski (DH, FL)
Fantasy Hall of Fame, ed. by Silverberg and Greenberg (RR)
Great Short Novels of Adult Fantasy, ed. by Lin Carter (1972/1973) (FL)
Kingdoms of Sorcery, ed. by Lin Carter (1976) (FL)
Masterpieces of Fantasy and Enchantment, ed. by Hartwell (DH)
New Worlds for Old, ed. by Lin Carter (1971) (FL)
New Worlds of Fantasy/Year's Finest Fantasy, ed. by Carr (RR)
Phantasmagoria, ed. by Jane Mobley (1977) (FL)
Year's Best Fantasy and Horror, ed. by Datlow and Windling
Year's Best Fantasy Stories, ed. by Carter and Saha (FL)
The Young Magicians, ed. by Lin Carter (1969) (FL)

Modern Fantasy for Young Adults, 1950–88

*Adams, Richard. *Watership Down* (DH, SM, RR, DW, MF, L)
Aiken, Joan. *A Harp of Fishbones and Other Stories* (1972) (FL)
———. *The Wolves of Willoughby Chase* (RR, DW)
*Alexander, Lloyd. *The Book of Three* (DH, SM, RR, FL)
*———. *The Marvelous Misadventures of Sebastian* (SM)
———. *Westmark* (DW)
Babbitt, Natalie. *Tuck Everlasting* (DW, FL)
Bellairs, John. *The Face in the Frost* (RR, DW, FL)
*Bond, Nancy. *A String in the Harp* (SM, FL)
Boston, Lucy M. The Children of Green Knowe series (1954+) (DW)
Briggs, Katharine M. *Hobberdy Dick* (DW))
Cameron, Eleanor. *The Court of the Stone Children* (RR, DW)
Chant, Joy. *The Grey Mane of Morning* (FL)
———. *Red Moon and Black Mountain* (RR, DW, MF, FL)
*Cooper, Susan. *Over Sea, Under Stone* (SM, DW [first book])
Cresswell, Helen. *The Night Watchmen* (DW)
Curry, Jane Louise. *The Wolves of Aam* (DW)
Dickinson, Peter. *The Blue Hawk* (DW)
Farjeon, Eleanor. *The Glass Slipper* (1946) (DW)
———. *The Silver Curlew* (DW)
*Farmer, Penelope. *A Castle of Bone* (SM)

———. *The Summer Birds* (DW)
Garner, Alan. *Elidor* (FL)
*———. *The Owl Service* (DH, SM, MF, FL)
———. *Red Shift* (F, FL)
———. *The Weirdstone of Brisingamen* (RR, DW, FL)
Gordon, John. *The Giant under the Snow* (DW)
Goudge, Elizabeth. *Linnets and Valerians* (DW)
Gray, Nicholas. *Grimbold's Other World* (RR, DW)
———. *Mainly in Moonlight* (DW)
Hamilton, Virginia. *Sweet Whispers, Brother Rush* (DW)
*Harris, Rosemary. *The Moon in the Cloud* (DW)
*Hoban, Russell. *The Mouse and His Child* (RR, DW)
Ipcar, Dahlov. *A Dark Horn Blowing* (DW)
———. *Queen of Spells* (DW)
Jones, Diana Wynne. *A Charmed Life* (DH, RR, DW)
———. *Eight Days of Luke* (1975) (DW)
———. *Ogre Downstairs* (DW)
———. *The Power of Three* (DW)
*Juster, Norton. *The Phantom Tollbooth* (SM, RR)
Kendall, Carol. *The Gammage Cup* (1959) (FL)
———. *The Whisper of Glocken* (1965) (FL)
Langton, Jane. *The Diamond in the Window* (1962) (FL)
Lawrence, Ann. *Tom Ass* (DW)
Lawson, John. *The Spring Rider* (DW)
*Le Guin, Ursula K. *A Wizard of Earthsea* (DH, SM, RR, DW, F, MF, L, FL)
L'Engle, Madeleine. *A Wrinkle in Time* (1962) (DW, L)
*Lewis, C. S. *The Lion, the Witch and the Wardrobe* (DH, SM, RR, DW, MF, L, FL)
Lively, Penelope. *The Driftway* (DW)
*———. *The House in Norham Gardens* (SM, DW)
———. *The Wild Hunt of Hagworthy* (RR, DW)
*Mahy, Margaret. *The Changeover* (SM)
*———. *The Haunting* (SM)
*Mayne, William. *Earthfasts* (DW, FL)
*McKillip, Patricia. *The Forgotten Beasts of Eld* (DH, SM, RR, DW, MF, L, FL)
———. *The Riddle-Master of Hed* (RR)
———. *The Throne of the Erril of Sherrill* (1973) (FL)
*McKinley, Robin. *Beauty* (DH, SM, RR)
*———. *The Blue Sword*
Nichols, Ruth. *The Marrow of the World* (1972) (FL)
O'Shea, Pat. *The Hounds of the Morrigan* (1985) (DW)
Parker, Richard. *The Old Powder Line* (DW)
Paton Walsh, Jill. *A Chance Child* (DW)
*Pearce, Philippa. *Tom's Midnight Garden* (SM)
Peyton, K. M. *A Pattern of Roses* (DW)
Picard, Barbara Leonie. *The Faun and the Woodcutter's Daughter* (1957) (DW)
*Pierce, Meredith. *The Darkangel* (SM, RR, DW)
Rayner, William. *Stag Boy* (FL)

*Smith, Stephanie. *Snow-Eyes* (DH, SM)
Snyder, Zilpha K. *The Truth about Stone Hollow* (1974) (DW)
Wangerin, Walter, Jr. *The Book of the Dun Cow* (DH, RR)
Westall, Robert. *The Cats of Seroster* (DW)
――――. *The Devil on the Road* (DW)
*――――. *The Wind Eye* (SM, DW)
*Wrightson, Patricia. *The Ice Is Coming* (SM, RR, DW)
――――. *The Nargun and the Stars* (FL)
Yep, Laurence. *Dragon of the Lost Sea* (RR)
Yolen, Jane. *Dragon's Blood* (RR)
――――. *The Magic Three of Solatia* (FL)

Anthology

Imaginary Lands, ed. by Robin McKinley (DW)

Secondary Sources

Cameron, Eleanor. *The Green and Burning Tree* (1969) (DW)
Cott, Jonathan. *Pipers at the Gates of Dawn* (DW)
Lynn, Ruth N. *Fantasy Literature for Children and Young Adults* (RR)
Pflieger, Pat. *A Reference Guide to Modern Fantasy for Children* (RR)

General Reference Books

Bleiler, Everett F. *Checklist of Science-Fiction and Supernatural Fiction* (RR)
Currey, L. W. *Science Fiction and Fantasy Authors* (RR)
Reginald, R. *Science Fiction and Fantasy Literature* (RR)
*Tuck, Donald H. *Encyclopedia of Science Fiction and Fantasy through 1968*
    (DH, SM, RR, DW)
Schlobin, Roger. *The Literature of Fantasy* (RR)
*Brown, Charles N. *Science Fiction in Print: 1985/Science Fiction, Fantasy, &*
    Horror (SM)
*Contento, William. *Index to Science Fiction Anthologies and Collections* and
    supplement (DH, SM)
*Frank, Frederick. *Guide to the Gothics*
*――――. *The First Gothics* (DH, SM)
Ashley, Mike. *Who's Who in Horror and Fantasy Fiction* (RR)
*Bleiler, Everett F. *The Guide to Supernatural Fiction* (DH, SM)
*――――. *Supernatural Fiction Writers* (DH, SM, DW)
Pringle, David. *Modern Fantasy* (RR)
*Magill, Frank N. *Survey of Modern Fantasy Literature* (DH, SM, RR)
Nicholls, Peter. *The Science Fiction Encyclopedia* (RR, DW)
Rosenberg, Betty. *Genreflecting* (DW)
*Sullivan, Jack. *The Penguin Encyclopedia of Horror and the Supernatural* (DH,
    SM)
Tymn, Marshall, et al. *Fantasy Literature* (RR, DW)
*Waggoner, Diana. *The Hills of Faraway* (SM, RR, DW)

Inge, M. Thomas. *Handbook of American Popular Literature* (DW)
*Wolfe, Gary K. *Critical Terms for Science Fiction and Fantasy*

History and Criticism

*Attebery, Brian. *The Fantasy Tradition in American Literature* (DH, SM)
Boyer, Robert H. and Kenneth J. Zahorski. *Fantasists on Fantasy* (RR, DW)
Briggs, K. M. *The Anatomy of Puck* (DW)
——. *The Fairies in Tradition and Literature* (DW)
——. *Pale Hecate's Team* (DW)
Carpenter, Humphrey. *The Inklings* (RR, DW)
Carter, Lin. *Imaginary Worlds* (SM)
de Camp, L. Sprague. *Literary Swordsmen and Sorcerers* (SM, RR, DW)
Gove, Philip Babcock. *The Imaginary Voyage in Prose Fiction* (1941) (DW)
*Hume, Kathryn. *Fantasy and Mimesis* (DH, SM)
*Irwin, W. R. *The Game of the Impossible* (SM)
*Jackson, Rosemary. *Fantasy: The Literature of Subversion* (DH, SM)
Ketterer, David. *New Worlds for Old* (1974) (DW)
Le Guin, Ursula K. *The Language of the Night* (DH, SM, RR, DW)
Lem, Stanislaw. *Microworlds* (SM)
Lewis, C. S. *An Experiment in Criticism* (DH, DW)
——. *Of Other Worlds* (SM, DW)
*——. *On Stories* (SM, DW)
*Manlove, C. N. *Modern Fantasy: Five Studies* (SM, RR)
Moorcock, Michael. *Wizardry and Wild Romance* (DW)
*Prickett, Stephen. *Victorian Fantasy* (SM)
*Rabkin, Eric S. *The Fantastic in Literature* (SM, DW)
Sale, Roger. *Fairy Tales and After* (DW)
Scholes, Robert. *Fabulation and Metafiction* (DW)
Slusser, George, et al. *Bridges to Fantasy* (DW)
*Todorov, Tzvetan. *The Fantastic* (DH, SM, RR)
*Tolkien, J. R. R. *Tree and Leaf* (DH, DW)
Wilson, Colin. *The Strength to Dream* (SM)
*Ziolkowski, Theodore. *Disenchanted Images* (SM)
Zipes, Jack. *Fairy Tales and the Art of Subversion* (DH)

Author Studies

Dunbar, Janet. *J. M. Barrie: The Man behind the Image* (1970) (DW)
*Zahorski, Kenneth J. *Peter Beagle* (DW)
*Foster, David William. *Jorge Luis Borges*
*Rodríguez Monegal, Emir. *Jorge Luis Borges*
Nolan, William F. *The Ray Bradbury Companion* (RR, DW)
*Tarrant, Desmond. *James Branch Cabell* (DW)
Clark, Anne. *Lewis Carroll: A Biography* (1970) (DW)
*Phillips, Robert, ed. *Aspects of Alice*
*Zipes, Jack. *The Brothers Grimm*
de Camp, L. Sprague, et al. *Dark Valley Destiny* (RR, DW)

Lord, Glenn, ed. *The Last Celt* (RR)
*Bittner, James W. *Approaches to the Fiction of Ursula K. Le Guin*
Ford, Paul F. *Companion to Narnia* (DW)
*Sayer, George. *Jack*
*Schakel, Peter J. *Reading with the Heart*
———. *Reason and Imagination in C. S. Lewis* (DW)
Arbur, Rosemarie. *Leigh Brackett, Marion Zimmer Bradley, Anne McCaffrey* (DW)
*Hein, Rolland. *The Harmony Within*
Wolff, Robert Lee. *The Golden Key* (DW)
Milne, Christopher. *The Enchanted Places* (1974) (DW)
Swann, Thomas Burnett. *A. A. Milne* (1971) (DW)
Mathews, Richard. *Words Beyond the World* (DW)
*Hume, Kathryn. *Pynchon's Mythography*
Collins, Robert A. *Thomas Burnett Swann* (DW)
*Carpenter, Humphrey. *J. R. R. Tolkien* (RR, DW)
Flieger, Verlyn. *Splintered Light* (DW)
Foster, Robert. *The Complete Guide to Middle-earth* (DW)
Helms, Randel. *Tolkien's World* (DW)
*Kocher, Paul H. *Master of Middle-earth* (RR, DW)
O'Neill, Timothy. *The Individuated Hobbit* (DW)
Purtill, Richard. *J. R. R. Tolkien: Myth, Morality and Religion* (1985) (DW)
*Shippey, T. A. *The Road to Middle-earth*
*West, Richard C. *Tolkien Criticism* (DW)
Wilson, Colin. *Tree by Tolkien* (1974) (DW)
*Warner, Sylvia Townsend. *T. H. White* (DW)
*Cavaliero, Glen. *Charles Williams: Poet of Theology*
*Hadfield, Alice Mary. *Charles Williams*
de Camp, L. Sprague. *Literary Swordsmen and Sorcerers* (SM, RR, DW)
Elliot, Jeffrey M. *Fantasy Voices 1*
Platt, Charles. *Dream Makers*

Fantasy on Film and TV

Lee, Walt. *Reference Guide to Fantastic Films* (RR)
Lentz, Harris M., III. *Science Fiction, Horror and Fantasy Film and Television Credits* (RR)
Briggs, Joe Bob. *Joe Bob Goes to the Drive-In* (DW)
Willis, Donald. *Horror and Science Fiction Films* (RR)
Cinefantastique
*Nicholls, Peter. *The World of Fantastic Films*
Harmetz, Aljean. *The Making of The Wizard of Oz* (DW)
Harryhausen, Ray. *Film Fantasy Scrapbook* (DW)

Fantastic Art and Illustration

*Best, James J. *American Popular Illustration*
Dean, Martyn. *The Guide to Fantasy Art Techniques* (RR)

Haining, Peter. *Terror!* (RR)
*Johnson, Diana L. *Fantastic Illustration and Design in Britain, 1850–1930* (DW)
Larkin, David, ed. *The Fantastic Kingdom* (RR, DW)
*Meyer, Susan E. *A Treasury of the Great Children's Book Illustrators* (DW)
Page, Michael, and Robert Ingpen. *Encyclopedia of Things That Never Were* (DW)
*Peppin, Brigid, and Lucy Micklethwait. *Book Illustrators of the Twentieth Century*
Petaja, Emil. *The Hannes Bok Memorial Showcase of Fantasy Art* (RR)
Rottensteiner, Franz. *The Fantasy Book* (RR, DW)
Summers, Ian. *Tomorrow and Beyond* (RR)
*Weinberg, Robert. *A Biographical Dictionary of Science Fiction and Fantasy Artists* (RR)
*Reade, Brian. *Aubrey Beardsley*
Bok, Hannes. *Beauty and the Beasts* (DW)
*Bowe, Nicola G. *Harry Clarke*
*Coll, Joseph Clement. *The Magic Pen of Joseph Clement Coll*
*Spencer, Isobel. *Walter Crane* (DW)
*Greene, Douglas G., and Michael Patrick Hearn. *W. W. Denslow* (DW)
Dillon, Leo and Diane. *The Art of Leo and Diane Dillon* (DW)
*Gosling, Nigel. *Gustave Doré*
*Engen, Rodney. *Richard Doyle*
*White, Colin. *Edmund Dulac*
*Finlay, Virgil. *Virgil Finlay*, ed. by Don Grant (DW)
———. *The [Second-Fifth] Books of Virgil Finlay* (RR)
*Frazetta, Frank. *The Fantastic Art of Frank Frazetta* (DW)
———. *Frank Frazetta, Book One–Book Five* (RR)
Freas, Frank Kelly. *The Art of Science Fiction* (RR)
———. *The Astounding Fifties* (DW)
Gallardo, Gervasio. *The Fantastic World of Gervasio Gallardo* (DW)
*Gorey, Edward. *Amphigorey* (DW)
Lawson, Robert. *Robert Lawson, Illustrator* (DW)
*Nielsen, Kay. *Kay Nielsen* (DW)
*Ludwig, Coy. *Maxfield Parrish* (RR, DW)
Gilmore, Maeve, and Shelagh Johnson. *Mervyn Peake* (DW)
*Pitz, Henry. *Howard Pyle* (DW)
*Gittings, Fred. *Arthur Rackham* (DW)
*Lanes, Selma G. *The Art of Maurice Sendak* (DW)
Skeeters, Paul W. *Sidney H. Sime* (RR)
Whelan, Michael. *Wonderworks* (RR)

Fantasy and Horror Magazines

Avon Fantasy Reader
Beyond Fantasy Fiction
Famous Fantastic Mysteries (DH, RR)
Isaac Asimov's Science Fiction Magazine
The Magazine of Fantasy and Science Fiction (RR)

Rod Serling's "The Twilight Zone" Magazine
Unknown/Unknown Worlds (RR)
Weirdbook (RR)
Weird Tales (RR)
Whispers (RR)
Amra (RR)
Arkham Collector (RR)
Fantasy Commentator (1943–   ) (SM)
Fantasy Newsletter/Review (RR)
The Golden Atom (1939–43) (SM)
Locus (RR)
Nyctalops
The Phantagraph (ca. 1935–46) (SM)
Science Fiction Chronicle (RR)
*Tymn, Marshall B., and Mike Ashley. *Science Fiction, Fantasy and Weird Fiction Magazines*
*Weinberg, Robert. *The Weird Tales Story* (RR)
*Boyajian, Jerry, and Kenneth R. Johnson. *Index to the Science Fiction Magazines, 1977–1984*
*Cockcroft, T. G. L. *Index to the Weird Fiction Magazines* (RR)
Day, Bradford M. *An Index of the Weird & Fantastica in Magazines* (1953) (SM)
*Day, Donald B. *Index to the Science Fiction Magazines, 1926–1950*
*Metcalf, Norm. *The Index of Science Fiction Magazines, 1951–1965*
*NESFA. *Index to the Science Fiction Magazines, 1966–1970*
*————. *The NESFA Index*
*Parnell, Frank H., and Mike Ashley. *Monthly Terrors* (RR)

Awards

Works of popular literature are rarely considered for prestigious awards, which is why most of the following awards are unknown outside the narrow confines of category fiction readers. The numbers voting for the awards range from a presumably knowledgeable committee to a few hundred readers, often members of an organization which sponsors the award.

The listings which follow are selective and are largely limited to fantasy and horror literature and films (and some science fiction) or to individuals associated with these fields. See also the organizations listing for additional details about selected awards. Foreign-language awards are excluded from these listings. Consult the index for entry numbers of annotated books.

The American Book Award (TABA)

Sponsored by the Association of American Publishers, the awards are given for books written by U.S. authors and published by U.S. publishers. A successor to the National Book Awards (see following), they have been presented since 1980 in various categories. Science fiction was among the original categories but was eliminated when the categories were revised.

1983   Goldstein, Lisa. *The Red Magician* (best original paperback)
1980   Pohl, Frederik. *JEM* (best hardcover science fiction)
            Wangerin, Walter, Jr. *The Book of the Dun Cow*
            L'Engle, Madeleine. *A Swiftly Tilting Planet* (best children's paperback; reprint of 1978 edition; science fiction)

Balrog Award

Named for a Tolkien creature and awarded at various local conventions but voted on by anyone who requested a ballot. Both SF and fantasy were included. Year of award shown. Categories include novel, short story, collection, anthology, poet, artist, amateur publication, professional publication, amateur and professional achievement, SF film, fantasy film, occasionally a special judges award. The award is a statuette with a balrog crouching above the base. 1985 was the last year of the award.

1985   Brin, David. *The Practice Effect* (SF novel)
            Donaldson, Stephen. *Daughter of Regals* (collection)
            E.T. and *Starman* (SF films)
            Raiders of the Lost Ark (fantasy film)
1984   Martin, George R. R. *Armageddon Rag* (novel)
            Zelazny, Roger. *Unicorn Variations* (collection)
1983   Donaldson, Stephen. *The One Tree* (novel)
            Asprin, Robert, ed. *Storm Season* (anthology)
1982   Kurtz, Katherine. *Camber the Heretic* (novel)
            Asprin, Robert, ed. *Shadows of Sanctuary* (anthology)
            Forbidden Planet (SF film, 1956)
            King Kong (fantasy film, 1933)

British Fantasy Award

Presented by the British Fantasy Society (see organizations) and called the August Derleth Award from 1972 through 1976; given to the best novel of the preceding year. Derleth co-founded Arkham House, the oldest surviving fantastic fiction specialty publisher. From 1977 to date the Derleth award has been given only to the best novel; winners in other categories receive the British Fantasy Award. A scroll was presented from 1972 through 1975, a statuette thereafter. Categories have varied over the years and currently include novel, film, short fiction, small press publication, artist and a special award to an individual. Only winners in the first two categories are shown. Year of award shown.

1988   Campbell, Ramsey. *The Hungry Moon*
            Hellraiser
1987   King, Stephen. *It*
            Aliens
1986   Klein, T. E. D. *The Ceremonies*
            A Nightmare on Elm Street
1985   Campbell, Ramsey. *Incarnate*

1984	Straub, Peter. *Floating Dragon*
	Videodrome
1983	Wolfe, Gene. *The Sword of the Lictor*
	Blade Runner
1982	King, Stephen. *Cujo*
	Raiders of the Lost Ark
1981	Campbell, Ramsey. *To Wake the Dead*
	The Empire Strikes Back
1980	Lee, Tanith. *Death's Master*
	Alien
1979	Donaldson, Stephen. *The Chronicles of Thomas Covenant the Unbeliever* (trilogy)
	Close Encounters of the Third Kind
1978	Anthony, Piers. *A Spell for Chameleon*
	Carrie
1977	Dickson, Gordon R. *The Dragon and the George*
	The Omen
1976	Moorcock, Michael. *The Hollow Lands*
	Monty Python and the Holy Grail
1975	Moorcock, Michael. *The Sword and the Stallion*
	The Exorcist
1974	Anderson, Poul. *Hrolf Kraki's Saga*
	The Legend of Hell House
1973	Moorcock, Michael. *The King of the Swords*
	Tales from the Crypt
1972	Moorcock, Michael. *Knight of the Swords*

Canadian Science Fiction and Fantasy Award

Called the Casper, this is presented at an annual Canadian national convention to English- or French-speaking Canadian writers. Trophies have varied over the years, and the number of categories has grown. Only English-language novels or individuals are shown.

1988	de Lint, Charles. *Jack the Giant Killer*
1987	Kay, Guy Gavriel. *The Wandering Fire*
1986	Merril, Judith. For lifetime editing
1985	Kernaghan, Eileen. *Songs from the Drowned Land*
1984	no award
1983	Merril, Judith. For lifetime contributions
1982	Gotlieb, Phyllis. *Judgment of Dragons* and lifetime achievement
1981	Wood, Susan. For lifetime contributions (posthumous)
1980	van Vogt, A. E. For lifetime contributions

Carnegie Medal

This is the British equivalent of the Newbery Medal (see following) and is awarded to the outstanding book for children written in English and published in the U.K. A Library Association committee selects from members' lists. Nonfiction as well as fiction is eligible. Only fantasy winners are listed.

1988	Price, Susan. *The Ghost Drum*
1985	Mahy, Margaret. *The Changeover*
1983	Mahy, Margaret. *The Haunting*
1974	Lively, Penelope. *The Ghost of Thomas Kempe*
1972	Adams, Richard. *Watership Down*
1969	Harris, Rosemary. *The Moon in the Cloud*
1968	Garner, Alan. *The Owl Service*
1963	Clarke, Pauline. *The Twelve and the Genii*
1962	Boston, Lucy Maria. *A Stranger at Green Knowe*
1959	Pearce, Philippa. *Tom's Midnight Garden*
1957	Lewis, C. S. *The Last Battle*
1956	Farjeon, Eleanor. *The Little Bookroom*
1953	Norton, Mary. *The Borrowers*
1948	de la Mare, Walter. *Collected Stories*
1946	Goudge, Elizabeth. *The Little White Horse*

Crawford Award

Named for William L. Crawford (1911–1984), who founded and edited one of the earliest semi-professional magazines (*Marvel Tales*, 1933), the award is given to the outstanding new writer of fantasy fiction. It is announced at the annual International Conference for the Fantastic in the Arts by the IAFA (see organizations).

1989	Michaela Roessner
1988	Elizabeth Marshall Thomas
1987	Judith Tarr
1986	Nancy Willard
1985	Charles de Lint

August Derleth Fantasy Award

Named for the co-founder of Arkham House, this award was presented annually by the British Fantasy Society (see above) in several categories, but since 1977 has been given only for the novel, with the BFS award given in all other categories. See under British Fantasy Society for awards.

J. Lloyd Eaton Award

Named after a San Francisco–area physician and SF collector, this is awarded to the author of the best work of criticism of SF or fantasy published two years prior to the year of the award shown below. Winners are selected by the curator of the Eaton Collection [12-4], George Slusser, and his conference co-directors. The award consists of a plaque.

1989	Alkon, Paul K. *Origins of Futuristic Fiction*
1988	Aldiss, Brian W. *Trillion Year Spree*
1987	Clareson, Thomas D. *Some Kind of Paradise*
	Stableford, Brian. *Scientific Romance in Britain*
1986	Hume, Kathryn. *Fantasy and Mimesis*
1985	Greenland, Colin. *The Entropy Exhibition*
1984	Huntington, John. *The Logic of Fantasy: H. G. Wells and Science Fiction*
1983	Rose, Mark. *Alien Encounters*
1982	Franklin, H. Bruce. *Robert A. Heinlein: America as Science Fiction*
1981	Wolfe, Gary K. *The Known and the Unknown*
1980	Brosnan, John. *Future Tense*
1979	Carter, Paul A. *The Creation of Tomorrow*

Gandalf Award

Named for a Tolkien creature like the Balrog, this is officially known as the Grand Master of Fantasy award. It was presented as part of the world SF convention (Hugo) award ceremonies for a writer's lifetime contribution to fantasy literature. Lin Carter (1930–1988) was the principal person responsible for selecting the winner and presenting the statuettes, which he personally paid for.

1981	C. L. Moore
1980	Ray Bradbury
1979	Ursula K. Le Guin
1978	Poul Anderson
1977	Andre Norton
1976	L. Sprague de Camp
1975	Fritz Leiber
1974	J. R. R. Tolkien

A special Gandalf award for book-length fantasy was given for two years:

1979	McCaffrey, Anne. *The White Dragon*
1978	Tolkien, J. R. R. *The Silmarillion*

IAFA Distinguished Scholarship Award

A panel of judges of the International Association for the Fantastic in the Arts (see organizations) presents this award at the annual ICFA meetings late each winter in Florida. A cash prize of $500 and a plaque are given the winner for total contributions to the study of fantastic literature or film.

1989	C. N. Manlove
1988	Kathryn Hume
1987	Brian Stableford
1986	Brian W. Aldiss

International Fantasy Award

Established by four British fans for a 1951 British convention and given to fiction and nonfiction judged of interest by a panel of American and British judges. Only fiction is listed.

1957	Tolkien, J. R. R. *Lord of the Rings*
1955	Pangborn, Edgar. *A Mirror for Observers*
1954	Sturgeon, Theodore. *More Than Human*
1953	Simak, Clifford D. *City*
1952	Collier, John. *Fancies and Goodnights*
1951	Stewart, George R. *Earth Abides*

Locus Award

Begun in 1971 and voted by readers. More than 1,000 people voted for the 1988 awards, many more than those voting for any other single award. Categories have varied over the years. Only best fantasy novel is listed. Year of award shown.

1989	Card, Orson Scott. *Red Prophet*
1988	Card, Orson Scott. *Seventh Son*
1987	Wolfe, Gene. *Soldier of the Mist*
1986	Zelazny, Roger. *Trumps of Doom*
1985	Heinlein, Robert. *Job: A Comedy of Justice*
1984	Bradley, Marion Zimmer. *The Mists of Avalon*
1983	Wolfe, Gene. *The Sword of the Lictor*
1982	Wolfe, Gene. *The Claw of the Conciliator*
1981	Silverberg, Robert. *Lord Valentine's Castle*
1980	McKillip, Patricia. *Harpist in the Wind*
1979	McIntyre, Vonda. *Dreamsnake*
1978	Tolkien, J. R. R. *The Silmarillion*

[Earlier awards were for SF novels only]

Approximately 600 *Locus* readers voted their all-time best fantasy novels, tabulated in the August 1987 issue. Here are the thirty-three titles in descending rank order:

Tolkien, J. R. R. *The Lord of the Rings*
Tolkien, J. R. R. *The Hobbit*
Le Guin, Ursula K. *A Wizard of Earthsea*
Wolfe, Gene. *The Shadow of the Torturer*
Beagle, Peter S. *The Last Unicorn*
White, T. H. *The Once and Future King*
Zelazny, Roger. *Nine Princes in Amber*
Donaldson, Stephen R. *The Chronicles of Thomas Covenant*
McCaffrey, Anne. *Dragonflight*
Crowley, John. *Little, Big*
Carroll, Lewis. *Alice's Adventures in Wonderland*
Peake, Mervyn. *The Gormenghast Trilogy*
McKillip, Patricia. *The Riddlemaster of Hed*

Pratt, Fletcher, and L. Sprague de Camp. *The Incomplete Enchanter*
Adams, Richard. *Watership Down*
Vance, Jack. *The Dying Earth*
Heinlein, Robert A. *Glory Road*
Anthony, Piers. *A Spell for Chameleon*
Stoker, Bram. *Dracula*
Baum, L. Frank. *The Wizard of Oz*
Myers, John Myers. *Silverlock*
Bradbury, Ray. *Something Wicked This Way Comes*
McCaffrey, Anne. *The White Dragon*
King, Stephen. *The Stand*
Silverberg, Robert. *Lord Valentine's Castle*
Lewis, C. S. The Chronicles of Narnia
King, Stephen. *The Shining*
Leiber, Fritz. *Conjure Wife*
Kurtz, Katherine. *Deryni Rising*
Eddison, E. R. *The Worm Ouroboros*
Norton, Andre. *Witch World*
King, Stephen. *Salem's Lot*
L'Engle, Madeleine. *A Wrinkle in Time*

Milford Award

Awarded by the Borgo Press its first year, this is now awarded at and by the Eaton conference each spring for lifetime contributions to the publishing and editing of SF and fantasy literature. The award consists of a plaque.

1989	Martin H. Greenberg
1988	Lloyd Arthur Eshbach
1987	H. L. Gold
1986	Harlan Ellison
1985	T. E. Dikty
1984	Edward L. Ferman
1983	Terry Carr
1982	Lester and Judy-Lynn del Rey
1981	Robert Silverberg
1980	Donald A. Wollheim

Mythopoeic Award

Chosen each year by volunteer members of the Mythopoeic Society (see organizations) and presented at the annual Mythcon. The Fantasy award is for a book-length work of fantasy in the spirit of the Inklings (Tolkien, Lewis, Williams) and published the preceding year. The Scholarship award is for a work on the Inklings published during the preceding three years. No awards were made in the years not listed.

Fantasy Award

1989	Bishop, Michael C. *Unicorn Mountain*
1988	Card, Orson Scott. *Seventh Son*
1987	Beagle, Peter. *The Folk of the Air*
1986	Hughart, Barry. *Bridge of Birds*
1985	Yolen, Jane. *Cards of Grief*
1984	Chant, Joy. *When Voiha Wakes*
1983	Kendall, Carol. *The Firelings*
1982	Crowley, John. *Little, Big*
1981	Tolkien, J. R. R. *Unfinished Tales*
1975	Anderson, Poul. *A Midsummer Tempest*
1974	Stewart, Mary. *The Hollow Hills*
1973	Walton, Evangeline. *The Song of Rhiannon*
1972	Chant, Joy. *Red Moon and Black Mountain*
1971	Stewart, Mary. *The Crystal Cave*

Scholarship Award

1989	Tolkien, Christopher. *Return of the Shadow*
1988	Christopher, Joe R. *C. S. Lewis*
1987	Purtill, Richard. *J. R. R. Tolkien: Myth, Morality and Religion*
1986	Cavaliero, Glen. *Charles Williams, Poet of Theology*
1985	Schakel, Peter J. *Reason and Imagination in C. S. Lewis*
1984	Shippey, T. A. *The Road to Middle-earth*
1983	Ford, Paul F. *Companion to Narnia*
1982	Carpenter, Humphrey. *The Inklings*
1976	West, Richard C. *Tolkien Criticism*
	Christopher, Joe R., and Joan K. Ostling. *C. S. Lewis: An Annotated Checklist*
	Glenn, Lois. *Charles W. S. Williams: A Checklist*
1974	Lindskoog, Kathryn. *C. S. Lewis, Mere Christian*
1973	Kocher, Paul H. *Master of Middle-earth*
1972	Walter Hooper
1971	C. S. Kilby, Mary McDermott Shideler

National Book Award

Begun in 1950 by U.S. book publishers, booksellers and book manufacturers, selections were made by members of the National Institute of Arts and Letters. Awards were given in a number of categories, including adult and children's fiction. Superseded by the American Book Award (see above).

1974	Cameron, Eleanor. *The Court of the Stone Children*
	Pynchon, Thomas. *Gravity's Rainbow*
1973	Le Guin, Ursula K. *The Farthest Shore*
	Barth, John. *Chimera*
1971	Alexander, Lloyd. *The Marvelous Misadventures of Sebastian*
1969	Le Guin, Ursula K. *A Wizard of Earthsea*
1964	Updike, John. *The Centaur*

John Newbery Medal

Awarded since 1922 by the Children's Literature Division of the American Library Association for the most distinguished contribution to American literature for children. The bronze medal, given at the summer ALA conference, is named for John Newbery (1713-1767), a London bookseller who first conceived the idea of publishing books especially for children.

1985	McKinley, Robin. *The Hero and the Crown*
1983	McKinley, Robin. *The Blue Sword* (honor book, not winner)
1976	Cooper, Susan. *The Grey King*
1972	O'Brien, Robert C. *Mrs. Frisby and the Rats of NIMH*
1969	Alexander, Lloyd. *The High King*
1963	L'Engle, Madeleine. *A Wrinkle in Time*
1948	DuBois, William Pene. *The Twenty-One Balloons*
1947	Bailey, Carolyn Sherwin. *Miss Hickory*
1945	Lawson, Robert. *Rabbit Hill*
1923	Lofting, Hugh. *The Voyages of Doctor Dolittle*

Pilgrim Award

Judges from the Science Fiction Research Association (see organizations) select the winner, who is given the award at the summer convention. The award, a framed certificate, is given to the individual judged to have contributed most to the study of fantastic literature or film. The award is very similar to the IAFA Distinguished Scholarship award described above. The Pilgrim is named for the book by the first recipient, *Pilgrims through Space and Time*.

1989	Ursula K. Le Guin
1988	Joanna Russ
1987	Gary K. Wolfe
1986	George E. Slusser
1985	Samuel R. Delany
1984	Everett F. Bleiler
1983	H. Bruce Franklin
1982	Neil Barron
1981	Sam Moskowitz
1980	Peter Nicholls
1979	Darko Suvin
1978	Brian W. Aldiss
1977	Thomas D. Clareson
1976	James Gunn
1975	Damon Knight
1974	I. F. Clarke
1973	Jack Williamson
1972	Julius Kagarlitski
1971	Marjorie Hope Nicolson
1970	J. O. Bailey

Mrs. Ann Radcliffe Award

Given annually for outstanding achievements in television, film and literature. The award, a scroll and a medal, is presented at a dinner held each April in Los Angeles. This is one of three awards given by the Count Dracula Society (see organizations) to honor outstanding achievement in Gothic literature and film.

1988–77	Information unavailable
1976	Leonard Wolf
1975	Arthur Lenig
1974	Thomas Tryon
1973	Devendra P. Varma
1972	Henry Eichner
1971	Ray Bradbury
1970	Fritz Leiber
1969	Robert Bloch
1968	A. E. van Vogt
1967	August Derleth
1966	Forrest J. Ackerman
1965	Ray Bradbury
1964	Russell Kirk, Donald A. Reed
1963	Forrest J. Ackerman

Saturn Award

Presented annually by the Academy of Science Fiction, Fantasy and Horror Films (see organizations) in Los Angeles. Awards are given to both films and individuals. Members vote for the best films, and committees select the acting and technical awards. Only those for best fantasy and horror films, in that order, are shown, by year of film release.

1987	*The Princess Bride*
	The Lost Boys
1986	*The Boy Who Could Fly*
	The Fly
1985	*Ladyhawke*
	Fright Night
1984	*Ghostbusters*
	Gremlins
1983	*Something Wicked This Way Comes*
	The Dead Zone
1982	*The Dark Crystal*
	Poltergeist
1981	*Raiders of the Lost Ark*
	American Werewolf in London
1980	*Somewhere in Time*
	The Howling

1979	*The Muppet Movie*
	Dracula
1978	*Heaven Can Wait*
	The Wicker Man
1977	*Oh, God*
	The Little Girl Who Lives Down the Lane
1976	*The Holes*
	Burnt Offerings
1975	*Doc Savage*
	Young Frankenstein
1973	*The Golden Voyage of Sinbad*
	The Exorcist
1972	*Blacula* [no fantasy film award first year]

Bram Stoker Award

Awarded by the 300 members of the Horror Writers of America (see organizations) for the best novel, first novel, short fiction and nonfiction work, and life achievement. The award consists of a sculpture of a Gothic castle designed by Disney artist Steve Kirk. It is analogous to the Nebula Award given by the Science Fiction Writers of America. The award was first given in 1988.

1989	Harris, Thomas. *The Silence of the Lambs* (novel)
	Wilde, Kelley. *The Suiting* (first novel)
	Charles Beaumont: Selected Stories (collection)
	Ray Bradbury, Ronald Chetwyn-Hayes (life achievement)
1988	King, Stephen. *Misery* (novel)
	McCammon, Robert. *Swan Song* (novel)
	Cantrell, Lisa. *The Manse* (first novel)
	Ellison, Harlan. *The Essential Ellison* (collection)
	Spark, Muriel. *Mary Shelley* (nonfiction)
	Fritz Leiber, Clifford Simak, Frank Belknap Long (life achievement)

Reverend Dr. Montague Summers Memorial Award

Given annually for outstanding achievement in Gothic literature. The gold trophy is presented at the Mrs. Ann Radcliffe awards dinner in Los Angeles. Summers was one of the foremost scholars of Gothic literature (see chapter 8 of the companion guide to horror).

1988–77	Information unavailable
1976	Don Glut
1975	Raymond McNally
1974	E. B. Murray
1973	Bob Clampett
1972	William Crawford
1971	Devendra P. Varma

1970	Frank H. Cunningham
1969	Donald A. Reed

Twilight Zone Dimension Awards

A one-shot given for the best book and film as judged by readers of *Rod Serling's "The Twilight Zone" Magazine* [11-15]. The award was a curved lucite slab with a light in the base.

1985	King, Stephen, and Peter Straub. *The Talisman*
	Indiana Jones and the Temple of Doom
	Ghostbusters

Horace Walpole Gold Medal

Given annually for achievements in fantasy, horror, terror or science fiction literature or film. The gold medal is presented at the Mrs. Ann Radcliffe awards dinner in Los Angeles. The award is named for the author of one of the first and best known of all Gothic novels [F1-92, H1-108].

1988–77	Information unavailable
1976	Margaret L. Carter
1975	Devendra P. Varma
1974	W. S. Lewis, Manuel Weltman
1973	Radu Florescu, Raymond McNally
1972	Christopher Lee, Rod Serling
1971	George Pal, Barbara Steele
1970	Rouben Mamoulian, Devendra P. Varma
1969	Vincent Price
1968	Donald A. Reed

World Fantasy Award

Given each fall at the World Fantasy convention and selected by a panel of judges, the award is nicknamed the Howard after Howard Phillips Lovecraft and Robert E. Howard. The statuette by Gahan Wilson is modeled approximately on Lovecraft and is none too flattering. Only winning novels, anthologies/collections and recipients of Life Achievement awards are shown, in that order.

1988	Grimwood, Ken. *Replay*
	Shepherd, Lucius. *The Jaguar Hunter*
	Cramer, Kathryn, and Peter D. Pautz, eds. *The Architecture of Fear*
	Hartwell, David G., ed. *The Dark Descent*
	Everett F. Bleiler
1987	Süskind, Patrick. *Perfume*
	Tiptree, James, Jr. *Tales of the Quintana Roo*
	Jack Finney

1986	Simmons, Dan. *Song of Kali*
	McKinley, Robin, ed. *Imaginary Lands*
	Avram Davidson
1985	Holdstock, Robert. *Mythago Wood*
	Hughart, Barry. *Bridge of Birds*
	Barker, Clive. *Books of Blood*, vols. 1–3
	Theodore Sturgeon
1984	Ford, John M. *The Dragon Waiting*
	Davies, Robertson. *High Spirits*
	Jack Vance, L. Sprague de Camp, Richard Matheson,
	E. Hoffmann Price and Donald Wandrei
1983	Shea, Michael. *Nifft the Lean*
	Grant, Charles L., ed. *Nightmare Seasons*
	Roald Dahl
1982	Crowley, John. *Little, Big*
	Windling, Terry, and Mark Arnold, eds. *Elsewhere*
	Italo Calvino
1981	Wolfe, Gene. *The Shadow of the Torturer*
	McCauley, Kirby, ed. *Dark Forces*
	C. L. Moore
1980	Lynn, Elizabeth A. *Watchtower*
	Salmonson, Jessica Amanda, ed. *Amazons!*
	Manly Wade Wellman
1979	Moorcock, Michael. *Gloriana*
	Grant, Charles L., ed. *Shadows*
	Jorge Luis Borges
1978	Leiber, Fritz. *Our Lady of Darkness*
	Cave, Hugh B. *Murgunstrumm and Others*
	Frank Belknap Long
1977	Kotzwinkle, William. *Doctor Rat*
	McCauley, Kirby, ed. *Frights*
	Ray Bradbury
1976	Matheson, Richard. *Bid Time Return*
	Davidson, Avram. *The Enquiries of Dr. Esterhazy*
	Fritz Leiber
1975	McKillip, Patricia. *The Forgotten Beasts of Eld*
	Wellman, Manly Wade. *Worse Things Waiting*
	Robert Bloch

Organizations

Just as fans of science fiction have formed clubs and other organizations in support of their hobby, so have fans of fantasy/horror fiction and film. Some organizations have relatively broad interests, such as the British Fantasy Society; others are very specialized, such as those devoted to the works of a single writer. Membership ranges from a few dozen to a few hundred, and some exist more on paper than as active, functioning organizations. Because they are staffed exclusively by volunteers, responses to queries are often slow, as I discovered. Some organizations to which I wrote may exist, but repeated queries produced no responses, and I have therefore omitted them from this listing. If an organization would like to be listed in future editions of this guide, please write the editor (see list of contributors for address). Information in this section is current as of early 1989. Listed individuals will usually forward queries to their successors if they don't respond directly.

When an organization gives an award for a book or film or to an individual, such awards are listed in the awards section. Some publications are listed in chapter 11 and are cross-referenced by entry number. The date the organization was founded is given following its name.

Academy of Science Fiction, Fantasy and Horror Films. 1972
334 W. 54th St., Los Angeles, CA 90037. Donald A. Reed, President.

Founded to give recognition to fantastic cinema. Reed claims a membership of about 3,000, many of them associated with the film industry. The Saturn Awards are given annually for outstanding achievements. Some award ceremonies have been televised over independent stations. A monthly newsletter, *Saturn*, lists the many free screenings for members and contains related news.

Association of Science Fiction & Fantasy Artists. Late 1970s.
Ms. Robin Brunner, Box 55188, Indianapolis, IN 46205.

A professional organization of about 350 members, most of them illustrators/artists or art directors. The *ASFA Quarterly* has how-to articles, convention and gallery art show reports, interviews and market news. Awards called Chesleys (after Chesley Bonestell, 1888–1986) are given each year in a variety of categories.

British Fantasy Society. 1971.
Di Wathen, 15 Stanley Rd., Morden, Surrey, SM4 5DE, U.K.

Devoted to the study of fantasy and horror literature, film and art. Publishes the *British Fantasy Society Newsletter* (1971–), quarterly; *Winter Chills* (1986–), annually; and *Dark Horizons* [11-28] and occasional booklets about or by authors. Presents the BFS and August Derleth awards (see awards).

Count Dracula Society. 1962.
Donald A. Reed, 334 W. 54th St., Los Angeles, CA 90037.

An organization whose 500 members overlap those of the Academy of Science Fiction, Fantasy and Horror Films, also run by Reed. Three awards are given at a dinner each April: Mrs. Ann Radcliffe, a scroll and a medal, for outstanding achievements in TV, film or literature; Horace Walpole Gold Medal for achievement in fantasy, horror or SF literature or film; and the Dr. Montague Summers Memorial Award, a gold trophy, for outstanding achievement in Gothic literature.

F. Marion Crawford Memorial Society. 1977.
Saracinesca House, 3610 Meadowbrook Ave., Nashville, TN 37206.

Crawford (1854–1909) was a prolific writer, but it is mostly for his horror fiction, notably "The Upper Berth," that he is best known. The society publishes an annual, *The Romantist* [11-48].

August Derleth Society. 1977.
Dr. Frank Attix, 3333 Westview Lane, Madison, WI 53713.
The August Derleth Society Newsletter is published three to four times yearly. Derleth (1909-1971) was the co-founder of Arkham House (see chapter 5) and a prolific regional writer. The society gives an annual creative writing award to the University of Wisconsin English Department. The British Fantasy Society gives the August Derleth Award each year (see awards).

Horror Writers of America. 1987.
Lisa Cantrell, Secretary, Box 655, Madison, NC 27025.
A professional organization analogous to the Science Fiction Writers of America and, like the SFWA, not limited to American writers. Affiliate members receive all publications and services, including the right to recommend works for the Bram Stoker Awards, but may not vote for awards or officers. Active members must have sold short fiction, articles or filmscripts. The society's newsletter, *Transfusions*, six issues yearly, has member news, articles, market information, etc. Annual membership directory. An annual convention is held at which the Bram Stoker Awards for superior achievement are given (see awards).

International Association for the Fantastic in the Arts. 1982.
Olena H. Saciuk, Call Box 5100, Caja 2 Universidad Interamericano, San German, PR 00753.
Similar to the Science Fiction Research Association but with a broader scope. Members receive the quarterly *IAFA Newsletter*, an annual membership directory and the *Journal of the Fantastic in the Arts* [11-39]. An annual conference is held in Florida each winter at which the William L. Crawford Award, IAFA Distinguished Scholarship Award and (irregularly) the Robert A. Collins Service Award are given. Most members are academics, but academic affiliation is not a requirement for membership.

International Wizard of Oz Club. 1957.
Box 95, Kinderhook, IL 62345.
L. Frank Baum is still one of the most popular children's authors, mostly for the Oz books, of which he wrote fourteen. *The Baum Bugle* [11-26] is for the Oz enthusiast, and the club sells many Oz-related magazines, books and other items.

C. S. Lewis Societies
Lewis has had a devoted following for many years. The New York C. S. Lewis Society was founded in 1969 and has about 525 members. Its current secretary is Mrs. John Kirkpatrick, 466 Orange St., New Haven, CT 06511. A monthly bulletin, *CSL*, contains reports of meetings, short articles, essays, reviews, letters and notices. A monthly meeting is held in New York, open to all without charge. The Southern California C. S. Lewis Society, Box 533, Pasadena, CA 91102, publishes *The Lamp-Post*, a quarterly, and holds meetings in the southern California area.

The Mythopoeic Society. 1967.
Box 6707, Altadena, CA 91001.
Founded to study and discuss fantasy and mythopoeic literature, particularly the works of the Inklings—J. R. R. Tolkien, C. S. Lewis and Charles Williams.

Publishes *Mythlore* [11-43], a quarterly; *Mythprint* (1980–), a monthly newsletter; and *The Mythic Circle* (1987–), a quarterly fiction and poetry magazine. The society sponsors the annual summer Mythopoeic conference, Mythcon, at which the Mythopoeic Awards are given, one for the best fantasy novel "in the spirit of the Inklings," the other for scholarship about the Inklings; see awards.

Although I did not receive direct replies from many Inkling-related societies, Joe R. Christopher, a scholar who is very knowledgeable in this area, supplied some information which I summarize here for anyone interested. Unrelated to the Mythopoeic Society but with similar interests is The Inner Ring: The Mythopoeic Literature Society of Australia, which publishes a quarterly, *The Ring Bearer*; write Managing Editor, *The Ring Bearer*, University of Queensland, St. Lucia, Queensland 4068, Australia.

A somewhat fan-oriented group is the American Tolkien Society, Box 373, Highland, MI 48031-0373, which publishes a quarterly journal, *Minas Tirith Evening-Star*. This is not related to the Tolkien Society of America, which merged with the Mythopoeic Society. Charles Williams enthusiasts may wish to investigate The Charles Williams Society, Richard Wallis, Treasurer, 6 Matlock Ct., Kensington Park Rd., London W11 3BS, which issues a quarterly newsletter and apparently has an American branch. The Tolkien Society appears to be located at 12 Madeley Rd., Earling, London W5 2LH. It publishes a newsletter, *Amon Hen*, a journal, *Mallorn*, and a linguistic journal. Local British clubs, called "smials," often issue their own fan publications.

The Mervyn Peake Society. 1975.
John Watney, Flat 36, 5 Elm Park Gardens, London SW10 9QQ.

Peake is best known for his remarkable Gormenghast trilogy [3-285]. A skilled artist, he illustrated many books, including a number of his own. The society publishes the *Mervyn Peake Newsletter* about three times yearly and the annual *Mervyn Peake Review* [11-46].

Science Fiction Research Association. 1970.
Thomas J. Remington, Treasurer, English Department, University of Northern Iowa, Cedar Falls, IA 50614.

The oldest organization devoted to the study and teaching of fantastic literature and film, its members include academics, editors, publishers, libraries and interested readers. The *SFRA Newsletter*, ten issues yearly, contains reviews, announcements of forthcoming books, work in progress, organization news, etc. Members also receive *Extrapolation* (quarterly) and *Science-Fiction Studies* (three issues yearly) and an annual membership directory. The Pilgrim Award for lifetime contribution to the study of fantastic literature (see awards) is presented at an annual summer conference.

Science Fiction Writers of America. 1965.
Peter D. Pautz, Box 4236, West Columbia, SC 29171.

Although the majority of the 1,035 members are probably more interested in SF than in fantasy or horror fiction, many authors write both. Like the recently founded Horror Writers of America, both affiliate and active memberships are available. Members receive the quarterly *SFWA Bulletin* (market reports, how-to articles, etc.), the bi-monthly *SFWA Forum* (for active members only; information on markets, contracts, etc.) and an annual directory, which lists the agents of the members. At the annual conventions, usually held on either the east or west coast, the Nebula Awards are presented. Because most awards are for SF, they are not listed in this guide.

Series

Listed here are series of three or more books, at least one of which is annotated in this guide. Some books require or at least benefit from a reader's knowledge of earlier books in the series. Books are therefore listed in their internal reading sequence or by year of publication if the sequence is unimportant. Included here are prequels, works "describing earlier events involving characters or settings from a previous work" (Wolfe, [6-40]). Series may be organized around a continuing character (Conan), a place (Oz, Gormenghast), a world (Middle-earth), including multiply authored shared worlds (Thieve's World), the last having become common in the late 1980s.

Following the author listing is an index by keywords in the series titles, cross-referenced to the author. Thus, Chronicles of Narnia is also listed as Narnia, Chronicles of. Series titles are sometimes not fixed; I have therefore used the "standard" title, if any, or the publisher's title. Most series are in the fantasy guide; relatively few are in the horror guide. Consult the index for entry numbers.

Aiken, Joan. Willoughby Chase
  The Wolves of Willoughby Chase,
    1962
  Black Hearts in Battersea, 1964
  Nightbirds on Nantucket, 1966
  The Stolen Lake, 1981
  The Cuckoo Tree, 1971
  The Whispering Mountain, 1968
  Dido and Pa, 1986

Alexander, Lloyd. The Chronicles of
    Prydain
  The Book of Three, 1964
  The Black Cauldron, 1965
  The Castle of Llyr, 1966
  Taran Wanderer, 1967
  The High King, 1968

Alexander, Lloyd. Westmark
  Westmark, 1981
  The Kestrel, 1982
  The Beggar Queen, 1983

Anderson, Margaret. Time trilogy
  In the Keep of Time, 1977
  In the Circle of Time, 1979
  The Mists of Time, 1984
Anderson, Poul, and Karen Anderson.

King of Ys
  Roma Mater, 1987
  Gallicenae, 1987
  Dahut, 1988
  The Dog and the Wolf, 1988

Anthony, Piers. Apprentice Adept
  Split Infinity, 1980
  Blue Adept, 1981
  Juxtaposition, 1982
  Out of Phaze, 1987
  Robot Adept, 1988
  Unicorn Point, 1989

Anthony, Piers. Incarnations of Immortality
  On a Pale Horse, 1983
  Bearing an Hourglass, 1984
  With a Tangled Skein, 1985
  Wielding a Red Sword, 1986
  Being a Green Mother, 1987
  For Love of Evil, 1988

Anthony, Piers. Xanth, Magic of
  A Spell for Chameleon, 1977
  The Source of Magic, 1979
  Castle Roogna, 1979
  Centaur Aisle, 1981

Anthony (*continued*)
  Ogre, Ogre, 1982
  Night Mare, 1982
  Dragon on a Pedestal, 1983
  Crewel Lye, 1985
  Golem in Gears, 1986
  Vale of the Vole, 1987
  Heaven Cent, 1988

Asprin, Robert Lynn. Myth
  Another Fine Myth, 1978
  Myth Conceptions, 1980
  Myth Directions, 1982
  Hit or Myth, 1983
  Myth-ing Persons, 1984
  M.Y.T.H. Inc. Link, 1986
  Little Myth Marker, 1985
  Myth-Nomers and Impervections,
    1987
  M.Y.T.H. Inc. in Action, 1989

Asprin, Robert Lynn. Thieve's World
  Thieve's World, 1979
  Tales from the Vulgar Unicorn,
    1980
  Shadows of Sanctuary, 1981
  Storm Season, 1982
  The Face of Chaos, 1983
  Wings of Omen, 1984
  The Dead of Winter, 1985
  Soul of the City, 1986
  Blood Ties, 1986
  Aftermath, 1987
  Uneasy Alliances, 1988
  Thieves World 12: Stealer's Sky,
    1989

Bangs, John Kendrick. Houseboat
  A Houseboat on the Styx, 1895
  The Pursuit of the Houseboat,
    1897
  The Enchanted Typewriter, 1899

Barrie, J. M. Peter Pan
  The Little White Bird, 1902
  Peter Pan in Kensington Gardens,
    1906
  Peter Pan, 1904 (play)

  When Wendy Grew Up, 1957
  Peter and Wendy, 1911
Barringer, Leslie. Neustrian Cycle
  Gerfalcon, 1927
  Joris of the Rock, 1928
  Shy Leopardess, 1948

Baum, L. Frank. Oz
  The Wonderful Wizard of Oz, 1900
  The [Marvelous] Land of Oz, 1904
  Ozma of Oz, 1907
  Dorothy and the Wizard of Oz,
    1908
  The Road to Oz, 1909
  The Emerald City of Oz, 1910
  The Patchwork Girl of Oz, 1913
  Tik-Tok of Oz, 1914
  The Scarecrow of Oz, 1915
  Rinkitink in Oz, 1916
  The Lost Princess of Oz, 1917
  The Tin Woodman of Oz, 1918
  The Magic of Oz, 1919
  Glinda of Oz, 1920
  (For later Oz books by other au-
    thors, see Cotrill [6-8], which
    lists all issued through 1985)

Blish, James. After Such Knowledge
  Doctor Mirabilis, 1964
  Black Easter, 1968
  The Day after Judgment, 1971
  A Case of Conscience, 1958

Bradley, Marion Zimmer. Darkover
  Darkover Landfall, 1972
  The Sword of Aldones, 1962
  The Planet Savers, 1962
  The Bloody Sun, 1964
  Star of Danger, 1965
  Winds of Darkover, 1970
  The World Wreckers, 1971
  The Spell Sword, 1974
  The Heritage of Hastur, 1975
  The Shattered Chain, 1976
  The Forbidden Tower, 1977
  Stormqueen, 1978
  *The Keeper's Price, 1980
  Two to Conquer, 1980
  Sharra's Exile, 1981

Sword of Chaos, 1982
Hawkmistress!, 1982
Thendara House, 1983
City of Sorcery, 1984
*Free Amazons of Darkover, 1985
*The Other Side of the Mirror, 1987
*Red Sun of Darkover, 1987

Bramah, Ernest. Kai Lung
The Wallet of Kai Lung, 1900
Kai Lung's Golden Hours, 1922
Kai Lung Unrolls His Mat, 1928
The Moon of Much Gladness, 1932
Kai Lung beneath the Mulberry Bush, 1940
Kai Lung: Six, 1974

Brooks, Terry. Shannara
The Sword of Shannara, 1977
The Elfstones of Shannara, 1983
The Wishsong of Shannara, 1985

Burroughs, Edgar Rice. Mars
A Princess of Mars, 1917
The Gods of Mars, 1918
The Warlord of Mars, 1919
Thuvia, Maid of Mars, 1920
The Chessmen of Mars, 1922
The Master Mind of Mars, 1922
A Fighting Man of Mars, 1928
Swords of Mars, 1936
Synthetic Men of Mars, 1940
Llana of Gathol, 1948
John Carter of Mars, 1964
Gilmour, William. *Lost on Jupiter*, 1961
Resnick, Michael D. *The Forgotten Sea of Mars*, 1965

Burroughs, Edgar Rice. Tarzan
Tarzan of the Apes, 1914
The Return of Tarzan, 1915
The Eternal Lover, 1925
The Beasts of Tarzan, 1916
The Son of Tarzan, 1917
Tarzan and the Jewels of Opar, 1918
Jungle Tales of Tarzan, 1919
Tarzan the Untamed, 1920

Tarzan the Terrible, 1921
Tarzan and the Golden Lion, 1923
Tarzan and the Ant Men, 1924
The Tarzan Twins, 1927
Tarzan, Lord of the Jungle, 1928
Tarzan and the Lost Empire, 1929
(For later volumes see Cottrill [6-8])

Cabell, James Branch. Biography of the Life of Manuel of Poictesme
Beyond Life, 1919
Figures of Earth, 1921
The Silver Stallion, 1926
Music from behind the Moon, 1926
The Way of Ecben, 1929
The White Robe, 1928
The Soul of Melicent, 1913 (rev. as *Domnei*, 1921)
Chivalry, 1909 (rev. 1921)
Jurgen, 1919
The Line of Love, 1905 (rev. 1921)
The High Place, 1923
Gallantry, 1907 (rev. 1928)
Something about Eve, 1927
The Certain Hour, 1916
The Cords of Vanity, 1909 (rev. 1920)
From the Hidden Way, 1916 (rev. 1924)
The Jewel Merchants, 1921
The Rivet in Grandfather's Neck, 1915
The Eagle's Shadow, 1904 (rev. 1923)
The Cream of the Jest, 1917
The Lineage of Lichfield, 1922
Straws and Prayer-Books, 1924

Cabell, James Branch. Smirt
Smirt, 1934
Smith, 1935
Smire, 1937

Chant, Joy. Red Moon and Black Mountain
Red Moon and Black Mountain, 1970
The Grey Mane of Morning, 1977
When Voiha Wakes, 1983

*Short fictions by Bradley and the Friends of Darkover

Chapman, Vera. Three Damosels
  The Green Knight, 1975
  King Arthur's Daughter, 1976
  The King's Damosel, 1976

Cherryh, C. J. Quest of Morgaine
  Gate of Ivrel, 1976
  Well of Shiuan, 1978
  Fires of Azeroth, 1979

Chetwin, Grace. Tales of Gom
  Gom on Windy Mountain, 1986
  The Riddle and the Rune, 1987
  Crystal Stair, 1988
  Starstone, 1989

Cook, Glen. Dread Empire
  A Shadow of All Night Falling, 1979
  October's Baby, 1980
  All Darkness Met, 1980
  The Fire in His Hands, 1983
  With Mercy Towards None, 1985
  Reap the East Wind, 1987
  An Ill-Fate Marshalling, 1988

Cook, Glen. Garrett series
  Sweet Silver Blues, 1987
  Bitter Gold Hearts, 1988
  Cold Copper Tears, 1988

Cooper, Susan. Dark Is Rising
  Over Sea, Under Stone, 1965
  The Dark Is Rising, 1973
  Greenwitch, 1973
  The Grey King, 1974
  Silver on the Tree, 1977

de Camp, L. Sprague. Novaria
  The Goblin Tower, 1968
  The Clocks of Iraz, 1971
  The Fallible Fiend, 1973
  The Unbeheaded King, 1983

de Camp, L. Sprague and Fletcher
  Pratt. Harold Shea
  The Incomplete Enchanter, 1941
  The Castle of Iron, 1950
  Wall of Serpents, 1960

Delany, Samuel R. Nevèrÿon
  Tales of Nevèrÿon, 1979

Neveryóna, 1983
Flight from Nevèrÿon, 1985
  The Bridge of Lost Desire, 1988

Donaldson, Stephen R. Chronicles of
  Thomas Covenant
  Lord Foul's Bane, 1977
  The Illearth War, 1977
  The Power that Preserves, 1977
  The Wounded Land, 1980
  The One Tree, 1982
  White Gold Wielder, 1983

Dunsany, Lord. Jorkens
  *The Travel Tales of Mr. Joseph
  Jorkens*, 1931
  Mr. Jorkens Remembers Africa,
  1934
  Jorkens Has a Large Whiskey,
  1940
  The Fourth Book of Jorkens, 1948
  *Jorkens Borrows Another Whis-
  key*, 1954

Eddings, David. Belgariad
  Pawn of Prophecy, 1982
  Queen of Sorcery, 1982
  Magician's Gambit, 1983
  Castle of Wizardry, 1984
  Enchanter's End Game, 1984

Eddings, David. Malloreon
  Guardians of the West, 1987
  King of the Murgos, 1988
  Demon Lord of Karanda, 1988
  The Sorcerers of Darshiva, 1989

Eddison, E. R. Zimiamvian
  The Mezentian Gate, 1958
  A Fish Dinner in Memison, 1941
  Mistress of Mistresses, 1935

Farmer, Penelope. Emma
  The Summer Birds, 1962
  Emma in Winter, 1966
  Charlotte Sometimes, 1969

Farmer, Philip José. World of Tiers
  The Maker of Universes, 1965
  The Gates of Creation, 1966
  A Private Cosmos, 1968

Behind the Walls of Terra, 1970
The Lavalite World, 1977

Feist, Raymond. Riftwar Saga
Magician, 1982
Silverthorn, 1984
Darkness at Sethanon, 1986
Prince of the Blood, 1989

Fisher, Paul R. Ash Staff
The Ash Staff, 1979
The Hawks of Fellheath, 1980
The Princess and the Thorn, 1980
Mont Cant Gold, 1984

Foster, Alan Dean. Spellsinger
Spellsinger, 1983
The Hour of the Gate, 1984
The Day of the Dissonance, 1984
The Moment of the Magician, 1984
The Path of the Perambulator, 1985
The Time of the Transference, 1987

Garrett, Randall. Lord Darcy
Murder and Magic, 1979
Too Many Magicians, 1967
Lord Darcy Investigates, 1981

Gaskell, Jane. Atlan saga
The Serpent, 1963
Atlan, 1965
The City, 1966
Some Summer Lands, 1977

Godwin, Parke. Camelot
Firelord, 1980
Beloved Exile, 1984
The Last Rainbow, 1986

Gregorian, Joyce Ballou. Tredana
The Broken Citadel, 1975
Castledown, 1977
The Great Wheel, 1987

Haggard, H. Rider. Allan Quatermain
Marie, 1912
Allan's Wife, 1887
Child of Storm, 1913
A Tale of Three Lions, 1887

Maiwa's Revenge, 1888
Allan the Hunter, 1898
Allan's Wife and Other Tales, 1889
The Holy Flower, 1915
Heu-Heu, 1924
She and Allan, 1920
The Treasure of the Lake, 1926
The Ivory Child, 1916
Finished, 1916
King Solomon's Mines, 1885
The Ancient Allan, 1920
Allan and the Ice-Gods, 1927
Allan Quatermain, 1887

Haggard, H. Rider. She
Wisdom's Daughter, 1923
She and Allan, 1920
She, 1886
Ayesha: The Return of She, 1905

Hambly, Barbara. Darwath
The Time of the Dark, 1982
The Walls of Air, 1983
The Armies of Midnight, 1983

Hancock, Niel. Atalantan Earth
Circle of Light
Greyfax Grimald, 1977
Faragon Fairingay, 1977
Calix Stay, 1977
Squaring the Circle, 1977
Wilderness of Four
Across the Fair Mountain, 1982
The Plains of the Sea, 1982
On the Boundaries of Bleakness, 1982
The Road to the Middle Islands, 1982
Windameir Circle
The Fires of Windameir, 1985
The Sea of Silence, 1987
A Wanderer's Return, 1988

Harris, Geraldine. Seven Citadels
Prince of the Godborn, 1982
The Children of the Wind, 1982
The Dead Kingdom, 1983
The Seventh Gate, 1983

Harris, Rosemary. Egypt series
  The Moon in the Cloud, 1968
  Shadow on the Sun, 1970
  The Bright and Morning Star, 1972

Harrison, M. John. Viriconium
  The Pastel City, 1971
  A Storm of Wings, 1980
  In Viriconium, 1982
  Viriconium Nights, 1985

Hazel, Paul. Finnbranch
  Yearwood, 1980
  Undersea, 1982
  Winterking, 1984

Horowitz, Anthony. No series name
  The Devil's Doorbell, 1983
  The Night of the Scorpion, 1985
  The Silver Citadel, 1986

Horwood, William
  Duncton Wood, 1988
  Duncton Quest, 1988
  Duncton Found, 1989

Howard, Robert E. Conan
  Howard's Conan stories have been published in at least four book versions under varying titles. Listed below is the first series only, which includes all the original stories. See Cottrill [6-8] for the various reprint series, later books by other authors, etc.
  The Coming of Conan, 1953
  Conan the Barbarian, 1954
  The Sword of Conan, 1952
  King Conan, 1953
  Conan the Conqueror, 1950
  Tales of Conan, 1955 (rewritten by L. Sprague de Camp)
  The Return of Conan, 1954 (by de Camp and Bjorn Nyberg; rev. as *Conan the Avenger*, 1968)

Jacques, Brian. Redwall
  Redwall, 1986
  Mossflower, 1988

Jones, Diana Wynne. Charmed Life
  The Lives of Christopher Chant, 1988
  A Charmed Life, 1977
  The Magicians of Caprona, 1980
  Warlock at the Wheel, 1985
  Dragons and Dreams, 1986, ed. by Jane Yolen

Jones, Diana Wynne. Dalemark
  Drowned Ammet, 1977
  Cart and Cwidder, 1975
  The Spellcoats, 1979

King, Stephen. Dark Tower
  The Gunslinger, 1982
  The Drawing of the Three, 1987

Kurtz, Katherine. Chronicles of Deryni
  Deryni Rising, 1970
  Deryni Checkmate, 1972
  High Deryni, 1973
  The Deryni Archives, 1986

Kurtz, Katherine. Histories of King Kelson
  The Bishop's Heir, 1984
  The King's Justice, 1985
  The Quest for Saint Camber, 1986

Kurtz, Katherine. Legends of Camber of Culdi
  Camber of Culdi, 1976
  Saint Camber, 1978
  Camber the Heretic, 1981

Lee, Tanith. Birthgrave
  The Birthgrave, 1975
  Vazkor, Son of Vazkor, 1978
  Quest for the White Witch, 1978

Lee, Tanith. Flat Earth
  Night's Master, 1978
  Death's Master, 1979
  Delusion's Master, 1981
  Delirium's Mistress, 1986
  Night's Sorceries, 1987

Le Guin, Ursula K. Earthsea
  A Wizard of Earthsea, 1968
  The Tombs of Atuan, 1971
  The Farthest Shore, 1972

Leiber, Fritz. Fafhrd and the Gray Mouser
Two Sought Adventure, 1957
Swords Against Deviltry, 1970
Swords Against Death, 1970 (reprints stories comprising *Two Sought Adventure*, and adds other stories)
Swords in the Mist, 1968
Swords Against Wizardry, 1968
The Swords of Lankhmar, 1968
Swords and Ice Magic, 1977
Rime Isle, 1977
Heroes and Horrors, 1978
The Knight and Knave of Swords, 1988

Lewis, C. S. Chronicles of Narnia
The Magician's Nephew, 1955
The Lion, the Witch and the Wardrobe, 1950
The Horse and His Boy, 1954
Prince Caspian, 1951
The Voyage of the Dawn Treader, 1952
The Silver Chair, 1953
The Last Battle, 1956

Lewis, C. S. Space trilogy
Out of the Silent Planet, 1938
Perelandra, 1943
That Hideous Strength, 1945

Lynn, Elizabeth A. Chronicles of Tornor
Watchtower, 1979
The Dancers of Arun, 1979
The Northern Girl, 1980

MacAvoy, R. A. Trio for Lute
Damiano, 1984
Damiano's Lute, 1984
Raphael, 1984

MacDonald, George. Faery
At the Back of the North Wind, 1871
The Princess and the Goblin, 1872
The Princess and Curdie, 1883

McCaffrey, Anne. Dragon series/Pern
Dragonflight, 1968

Dragonquest, 1971
The White Dragon, 1978
Dragonsong, 1976
Dragonsinger, 1977
Dragondrums, 1979
Moreta, Dragonlady of Pern, 1983
Nerilka's Story: A Pern Adventure, 1986
The Renegades of Pern, 1989
[The first three books are sometimes referred to as the Dragonriders of Pern series, the second three as the Harper Hall or Menolly the Singer series]

McKillip, Patricia. Riddle of the Stars
The Riddle-Master of Hed, 1976
Heir of Sea and Fire, 1977
Harpist in the Wind, 1979

Moorcock, Michael. Chronicles of Corum and Count Brass
Some of the books in Moorcock's many series have been revised as well as reprinted under different titles. Revisions are listed, but not retitlings.
The Knight of the Swords, 1971
The Queen of the Swords, 1971
The King of the Swords, 1971
The Bull and the Spear, 1973
The Oak and the Ram, 1973
The Sword and the Stallion, 1974

Moorcock, Michael. Dancers at the End of Time
An Alien Heat, 1972
The Hollow Lands, 1974
The End of All Songs, 1976
Legends from the End of Time, 1976
The Transformation of Miss Mavis Ming, 1977

Moorcock, Michael. Elric
The Stealer of Souls, 1963
Stormbringer, 1965
The Singing Citadel, 1970
The Sleeping Sorceress, 1971
The Vanishing Tower, 1971
Elric of Melniboné, 1972

Moorcock (*continued*)
  The Jade Man's Eyes, 1973
  The Sailor on the Seas of Fate, 1976
  The Weird of the White Wolf, 1977
  The Bane of the Black Sword, 1977
  Elric at the End of Time, 1985
  The Fortress of the Pearl, 1989

Moorcock, Michael. History of the Runestaff
  The Jewel in the Skull, 1967 (rev. 1977)
  Sorcerer's Amulet, 1968
  The Sword of the Dawn, 1968 (rev. 1977)
  The Secret of the Runestaff, 1969
  Count Brass, 1973
  The Champion of Garathorn, 1973
  Quest for Tanelorn, 1975

Munn, H. Warner. Merlin
  King of the World's Edge, 1966
  The Ship from Atlantis, 1967
  Merlin's Ring, 1974 (combines the first two books)
  Merlin's Godson, 1976

Murphy, Shirley Rousseau. Dragonbards
  Nightpool, 1985
  The Ivory Lyre, 1987
  The Dragonbards, 1988

Naylor, Phyllis Reynolds. York Trilogy
  Shadows on the Wall, 1980
  Faces in the Water, 1981
  Footprints at the Window, 1981

Nesbit, Edith. Five Children
  Five Children and It, 1902
  The Phoenix and the Carpet, 1904
  The Story of the Amulet, 1906

Norman, John. Gor
  Tarnsman of Gor, 1966
  Outlaw of Gor, 1967
  Priest-Kings of Gor, 1968
  Nomads of Gor, 1969
  Assassin of Gor, 1970
  Raiders of Gor, 1971
  Captive of Gor, 1972

  Hunters of Gor, 1974
  Marauders of Gor, 1975
  Tribesmen of Gor, 1976
  Slave Girl of Gor, 1977
  Beasts of Gor, 1978
  Explorers of Gor, 1979
  Fighting Slave of Gor, 1980
  Rogue of Gor, 1981
  Guardsman of Gor, 1981
  Savages of Gor, 1982
  Blood Brothers of Gor, 1983
  Kajira of Gor, 1983
  Players of Gor, 1984
  Mercenaries of Gor, 1985
  Dancer of Gor, 1985
  Renegade of Gor, 1986
  Vagabonds of Gor, 1987

Norton, Andre. Witch World
  Witch World, 1963
  Web of the Witch World, 1964
  Year of the Unicorn, 1965
  Three Against the Witch World, 1965
  Warlock of the Witch World, 1967
  Sorceress of the Witch World, 1968
  Spell of the Witch World, 1972
  The Crystal Gryphon, 1972
  The Jargoon Pard, 1974
  The Trey of Swords, 1977
  Zarsthor's Bane, 1978
  Lore of the Witch World, 1980
  Gryphon in Glory, 1981
  Ware Hawk, 1983
  Gryphon Eyrie, 1985 (with A. C. Crispin)
  Four from the Witch World, 1989 (ed. by Norton; "shared world")

Peake, Mervyn. Gormenghast
  Titus Groan, 1946
  Gormenghast, 1950
  Titus Alone, 1959

Peck, Richard. Blossom Culp
  The Ghost Belonged to Me, 1975
  Ghosts I Have Been, 1977

The Dreadful Future of Blossom Culp, 1983
Blossom Culp and the Sleep of Death, 1986

Pratchett, Terry. Discworld
The Colour of Magic, 1983
The Light Fantastic, 1986
Equal Rites, 1987
Mort, 1987
Sourcery, 1988
Wyrd Sisters, 1988
Pyramids, 1989

Saberhagen, Fred. Book of Swords
The First Book of Lost Swords, 1983
The Second Book of Lost Swords, 1983
The Third Book of Lost Swords, 1986
The Fourth Book of Lost Swords, 1989
The Fifth Book of Lost Swords, 1989

Saberhagen, Fred. Empire of the East
The Broken Lands, 1968
The Black Mountains, 1971
Changeling Earth, 1973

Scarborough, Elizabeth. Songs from the Seashell Archives/Argonia
Song of Sorcery, 1982
The Unicorn Creed, 1983
Bronwyn's Bane, 1983
The Christening Quest, 1985

Silverberg, Robert. Majipoor
Lord Valentine's Castle, 1980
Majipoor Chronicles, 1982
Valentine Pontifex, 1983

Sinclair, Andrew
Gog, 1967
Magog, 1972
King Ludd, 1988

Springer, Nancy. Chronicles of Isle
The White Hart, 1979
The Silver Sun, 1980 (rev. of *The Book of Suns*, 1977)

The Sable Moon, 1981
The Black Beast, 1982
The Golden Swan, 1983

Stasheff, Christopher. Warlock
The Warlock in Spite of Himself, 1969
King Kobold, 1971 (rev. as *King Kobold Revived*, 1984)
The Warlock Unlocked, 1982
Escape Velocity, 1983
The Warlock Enraged, 1984
The Warlock Wandering, 1985
The Warlock Is Missing, 1986
The Warlock Heretical, 1987
The Warlock's Companion, 1988

Stewart, Mary. Life of Merlin
The Crystal Cave, 1970
The Hollow Hills, 1973
The Last Enchantment, 1979
The Wicked Day, 1983

Tarr, Judith. Hound and the Falcon
The Isle of Glass, 1985
The Golden Horn, 1985
The Hounds of God, 1986

Tolkien, J. R. R. Lord of the Rings
The Fellowship of the Ring, 1954
The Two Towers, 1954
The Return of the King, 1955

Tolkien, J. R. R. Middle-earth
The Silmarillion, 1977
Unfinished Tales, 1980
The Book of Lost Tales, Part I, 1983
The Book of Lost Tales, Part II, 1984
The Lays of Beleriand, 1985
The Shaping of Middle-Earth, 1986
The Lost Road and Other Writings, 1987
The Return of the Shadow, 1988
The Treason of Isengard, 1989

Vance, Jack. Dying Earth
The Dying Earth, 1950
The Eyes of the Overworld, 1966

Vance (*continued*)
    Cugel's Saga, 1983
    Rhialto the Marvelous, 1984
    A Quest for Simbilis by Michael
    Shea, 1974

Van Lustbader, Eric. Sunset Warrior
    The Sunset Warrior, 1977
    Shallows of Night, 1978
    Dai-San, 1978
    Beneath an Opal Moon, 1980

Viereck, George S., and Paul Eldridge.
    Three Immortals
    My First 2000 Years, 1928
    Salome, 1930
    The Invincible Adam, 1932

Walton, Evangeline. Books of the
    Welsh Mabinogion
    Prince of Annwn, 1974
    The Children of Llyr, 1971
    The Song of Rhiannon, 1972
    The Virgin and the Swine, 1936
    (reprinted as *The Island of the
    Mighty*, 1970)

Wellman, Manly Wade. Silver John
    Who Fears the Devil?, 1963
    Worse Things Waiting, 1973
    The Old Gods Waken, 1979
    After Dark, 1980
    The Lost and the Lurking, 1981
    The Hanging Stones, 1982
    The Voice of the Mountain, 1984
    The Valley So Low, 1987
    John the Balladeer, 1988

White, T. H. Camelot
    The Sword in the Stone, 1938
    The Witch in the Wood, 1939

    The Ill-Made Knight, 1940
    The Once and Future King, 1958
    (includes *Sword*, rev.; *Witch*,
    rev. and retitled *The Queen of
    Air and Darkness*; *Ill-Made
    Knight*; and *The Candle in the
    Wind*)
    The Book of Merlyn, 1977

Wilder, Cherry. Rulers of Hylor
    A Princess of the Chameln, 1984
    Yorath the Wolf, 1984
    The Summer's King, 1986

Wolfe, Gene. Book of the New Sun
    The Shadow of the Torturer, 1980
    The Claw of the Conciliator, 1981
    The Sword of the Lictor, 1982
    The Citadel of the Autarch, 1982
    The Urth of the New Sun, 1987

Wrightson, Patricia. Australian trilogy
    The Ice Is Coming, 1977
    The Dark Bright Water, 1978
    Behind the Wind (U.S. title:
    Journey Behind the Wind), 1981

Yolen, Jane. Dragon sequence
    Dragon's Blood, 1982
    Heart's Blood, 1984
    A Sending of Dragons, 1987

Zelazny, Roger. Amber
    Nine Princes in Amber, 1970
    The Guns of Avalon, 1972
    Sign of the Unicorn, 1975
    The Hand of Oberon, 1976
    The Courts of Chaos, 1978
    Trumps of Doom, 1985
    Blood of Amber, 1986
    Sign of Chaos, 1987

Series Index

Australian trilogy (Wrightson)

Belgariad (Eddings)

Biography of the Life of Manuel of Poictesme (Cabell)

Birthgrave (Lee)

Blossum Culp (Peck)
Book of Swords (Saberhagen)

Book of the New Sun (Wolfe)

Books of the Welsh Mabinogion (Walton)

Camber of Culdi, Legends of (Kurtz)

Camelot (Godwin)

Camelot (White)

Charmed Life (Jones)

Chronicles of Corum and Count Brass (Moorcock)

Chronicles of Deryni (Kurtz)

Chronicles of Isle (Springer)

Chronicles of Narnia (Lewis)

Chronicles of Prydain (Alexander)

Chronicles of Thomas Covenant (Donaldson)

Chronicles of Tornor (Lynn)

Circle of Light (Hancock)
Conan (Howard)

Corum (Moorcock)

Count Brass (Moorcock)

Dalemark (Jones)

Dancers at the End of Time (Moorcock)

Dark Is Rising (Cooper)

Darkover (Bradley)

Dark Tower (King)

Darwath (Hambly))

Deryni, Chronicles of (Kurtz)

Devil Is Dead (Lafferty)

Discworld (Pratchett)

Dragonbards (Murphy)

Dragon sequence (Yolen)

Dragon series (McCaffrey)

Dread Empire (Cook)

Dying Earth (Vance)

Earthsea (Le Guin)

Elric (Moorcock)

Emma (Farmer)

Empire of the East (Saberhagen)

Faery (MacDonald)

Fafhrd and the Gray Mouser (Leiber)

Finnbranch (Hazel)

Five Children (Nesbit)

Flat Earth (Lee)

Garrett (Cook)

Gom, Tales of (Chetwin)

Gor (Norman)

Gormenghast (Peake)

Harold Shea (de Camp and Pratt)

Heirs of Saint Camber (Kurtz)

History of the Runestaff (Moorcock)

Hound and the Falcon (Tarr)

Houseboat (Bangs)

Incarnations of Immortality (Anthony)

Jorkens (Dunsany)

Kai Lung (Bramah)

King of Ys (Anderson)

Legends of Camber of Culdi (Kurtz)

Life of Merlin (Stewart)

Lord Darcy (Garrett)

Lord of the Rings (Tolkien)

Lords of Darkness (Lee)

Mabinogion, Books of the Welsh (Walton)

Magic of Xanth (Anthony)

Majipoor (Silverberg)

Mallorean (Eddings)

Manuel of Poictesme (Cabell)

Mars (Burroughs)

Merlin (Munn)

Merlin, Life of (Stewart)

Morgaine, Quest of (Cherryh)

Myth (Asprin)

Narnia, Chronicles of (Lewis)

Neustrian Cycle (Barringer)

Nevèrÿon (Delany)

Novaria (de Camp)

Oz (Baum)

Pern (McCaffrey)

Peter Pan (Barrie)

Prydain, Chronicles of (Alexander)

Quest of Morgaine (Cherryh)

Red Moon and Black Mountain (Chant)

Redwall (Jacques)

Riddle of Stars (McKillip)

Riftwar (Feist)

Rulers of Hylor (Wilder)

Runestaff (Moorcock)

Seven Citadels (Harris)

Shannara (Brooks)

She (Haggard)

Silver John (Wellman)

Smirt (Cabell)

Songs from the Seashell Archives (Scarborough)

Space trilogy (Lewis)

Spellsinger (Foster)

Sunset Warrior (Van Lustbader)

Swords, Book of (Saberhagen)

Tales of Gom (Chetwin)

Tarzan (Burroughs)

Thieve's World (Asprin)

Thomas Covenant, Chronicles of (Donaldson)

Three Damosels (Chapman)

Three Immortals (Viereck)

Tiers, World of (Farmer)

Time trilogy (Anderson)

Tornor, Chronicles of (Lynn)

Tredona (Gregorian)

Trio for Lute (MacAvoy)

Viriconium (Harris)

Warlock (Stasheff)

Westmark (Alexander)

Wilderness of Four (Hancock)

Willoughby Chase (Aiken)

Windameir Circle (Hancock)

Witch World (Norton)

World of Tiers (Farmer)

Xanth, Magic of (Anthony)

York (Naylor)

Zimiamvian (Eddison)

Author
Index

Annotations in this index are cited by entry numbers (1-26, 3-216); introductions are cited by page numbers, which are italicized and lack a hyphen. In order to make this index as useful as possible, and keep it to a reasonable length, only substantive references (defined as having some descriptive or critical comment) to authors, editors, or illustrators are included. References are to books by or about authors, editors, or illustrators, with books by the person normally cited first. Author materials mentioned in chapter 12, Library Collections, are indexed. Cross-references from real names to pseudonyms are included.

Certain types of material were not indexed: (1) references to authors with little or no substantive content, e.g., simple mentions of stories in a collection or anthology; (2) mentions of authors in the compare and contrast statements; (3) passing references to authors as subjects, such as in essay collections or in studies which treat a number of authors (such secondary literature is indexed by Hall [6-10] and Tymn and Schlobin [6-11], by Morrison in his introduction to chapter 8, and in the sources whose abbreviations follow About:, as explained in the preface); (4) translators; (5) authors of books listed only in chapter 13; (6) authors of short fiction in collections or anthologies. For the last, consult Bleiler [6-19], Contento [6-7], Schlobin [6-5], and Brown and Contento [6-6], which collectively index the contents of several thousand anthologies and collections.

Arrangement is letter by letter, ignoring spaces.

Title
Index

Titles within series are individually indexed only if the book is specifically discussed, as distinct from simply listed. Otherwise the entry is indexed by series name only. This applies mainly to chapter 4A. Film titles, titles of short fiction in collections or anthologies, and foreign language titles of translated works are not included. For contents of series see the author annotation or the series list in chapter 13. Authors/editors are shown in parentheses following the title only to distinguish between works having the same title.

Arrangement is word by word.

Theme Index

For most books annotated in the bibliographies there is a compare or contrast statement which refers to other books with similar themes, structures, narrative devices, etc. This thematic/subject index permits readers to see on a larger scale the recurrent themes in fantasy or horror fiction. It is considerably more specific and detailed than the six rough groupings in *A Reader's Guide to Fantasy* [6-29], or the classified scheme used by Waggoner [6-34], but is far less detailed than the "index of motifs and story types" in Bleiler [6-19], from which this list was partially derived. Other sources consulted include Bleiler's *Checklist* [6-1] and the Magill survey [6-24]. See also the fiction chapters introductory essays for additional discussion of selected themes.

After selected contributors had reviewed this list for its usefulness and precision, they then considered each annotated novel (collections, anthologies and nonfiction were not indexed unless they were thematically organized). If they judged a book could usefully be indexed/characterized by one to three of the following terms (not all books were so judged), they posted the entry number after the term. The following index represents their collective judgments. In this index only, item numbers are grouped by chapter and abbreviated (e.g., the citation "3-178; 4-30, 97" should be read as "3-178, 4-30, 4-97"). SA = see also.

After death experiences 1-19; 2-2, 12, 54, 80, 103, 135; 3-26, 38, 47, 83, 85, 87, 91, 113, 139, 161, 163, 179, 183, 207, 213, 217, 238, 256, 298, 317, 347, 365, 373, 374; 4A-16, 95, 125, 127, 138, 187, 197, 220, 249, 270

Alchemy 1-19; 3-108

Allegory 1-12, 73, 79; 2-45, 79, 83, 90, 98, 113, 115, 116, 122, 124, 126, 132, 137, 140, 149, 157; 3-29, 30, 34, 37, 55, 77, 78, 79, 86, 87, 91, 98, 119, 134, 135, 159, 174, 189, 221, 251, 266, 290, 298, 300, 301, 302, 303, 304, 310, 318, 344, 352, 359, 360, 363, 384, 385; 4A-78, 219; 4B-146

Alternate histories 4A-3, 42, 80, 81, 86, 105, 115, 189, 198, 236